WOMEN AND GIRLS IN THE CRIMINAL JUSTICE SYSTEM

Policy Issues and Practice Strategies

Edited by
Russ Immarigeon, M.S.W.

Civic Research Institute
4478 U.S. Route 27 • P.O. Box 585 • Kingston, NJ 08528

Printed in the United States of America

Library of Congress Cataloging in Publication Data
Women and Girls in the Criminal Justice System: Policy Issues and Practice Strategies
Russ Immarigeon, Ed.

ISBN 1-887554-52-1
Library of Congress Control Number: 2005936319

About the Editor

Russ Immarigeon, M.S.W., received his master's degree from the School of Social Welfare at the State University of New York at Stony Brook. He is the Editor of the periodicals *Women, Girls & Criminal Justice*, *Offender Programs Report* and *VOMA Connections*; Managing Editor of *Journal of Offender Monitoring*; a regular contributor to *Community Corrections Report*, *Crime Victims Report,* and *Corrections Managers' Report;* and co-editor, with Meda Chesney-Lind, of the book series *Women, Crime and Criminology.* Mr. Immarigeon is also co-author, with Meda Chesney-Lind, of *Women's Prisons: Overcrowded and Overused* (National Council on Crime & Delinquency, 1991) and co-editor, with Shadd Maruna, of *After Crime and Punishment: Pathways to Offender Reintegration* (Willan Publishing, 2004). He has contributed articles and book reviews to the major criminal justice journals, including *Contemporary Justice Review*, *Federal Probation*, *Prison Journal*, *Punishment & Society,* and *Criminal Justice.*

Introduction

Thirty years ago, according to a *Denver Post* news article, a prison reform advocate told a local audience that, in the reporter's words, "So few women belong in jails or prison, Colorado would do well to be the first state to shut down such facilities" (Bell, 1975).

In the 1970s, the situation for women and girls involved with local, state, and federal juvenile and criminal justice systems was very different than it is today. In June, 1971, for instance, President Richard M. Nixon told criminal justice, judicial, and law enforcement officials gathered in Williamsburg, Virginia, for the First National Conference on Corrections, "Locking a convict up is not enough." President Nixon reasoned that prisoners should be given "the keys of education, of rehabilitation, of useful planning, of hope" that are necessary "to open the gates to a life of freedom and dignity." The purpose of this historic conference, coming less than a handful of years after President Lyndon B. Johnson's Commission on Law Enforcement and Administration of Justice issued its important reports, was to make meaningful recommendations for prison reform.

At that conference, Edith Elisabeth Flynn, then the associate director of the National Clearinghouse for Criminal Justice Planning and Architecture and later a prominent professor of criminal justice at Northeastern University in Boston, observed that little data was available about women offenders. She stated that the most authoritative volume on women and crime had been published in 1951, 20 years earlier. Furthermore, she added, "This situation did not change with the completion of the most comprehensive study to date on the problem of crime and corrections in the United States. [President Lyndon B. Johnson's] Commission on Law Enforcement and Administration of Justice did not include a single paragraph or statistic on the female offender, nor could any such material be found in its nine supportive Task Force reports" (President's Commission on Law Enforcement and Administration of Justice, 1968, p. 113)

The 1960s and 1970s were times when incarcerated women and girls were given scant attention, the conditions of confinement for women and girls were more convenient than constitutional, and treatment intervention programs, as well as the nature of probation and parole supervision, were largely an afterthought.

Now, 30 years later, over 100,000 women are confined in federal and state prisons in the United States. No matter how you look at it, the number of women now incarcerated in the United States is an extraordinary departure from previous periods in our history. Between 1925 and 1980, women were incarcerated in state or federal prisons at a rate of approximately six to 10 per 100,000 persons in our country. Over the next 20 years, that rate grew to approximately 60 per 100,000, a six-fold increase. From 1980 to 2001, women's proportion of the overall U.S. prison population nearly doubled from 4% to 7%. In federal prisons alone, the number of incarcerated women soared ten-fold, to 10,245 over the 21-year period, 1980-2000; the number of women in local jails increased an astounding 100% to approximately 70,000. in this same time frame (see Kruttschnitt & Gartner, 2003).

For many years, sentenced women were generally ignored or neglected, locked up in male surroundings, or lost among caseloads of men. Subsequently, more attention has been given them, but their numbers are still small compared with men who are imprisoned or under correctional supervision. At the start of the 21st century, however, women offenders and prisoners have perhaps reached the tipping point where they can no longer be shunted aside, left managed—just adequately or at least silently—by staff and officials at individual facilities or offices.

In recent years, newspaper articles from across the United States have reported that women are becoming more noticeable in number within criminal justice and correctional systems. In states as diverse as Arizona, Alabama, Connecticut, Maine, Oklahoma, South Dakota, and Vermont, prison officials and state policy makers have been struggling with the prospects of too many women for too few cells.

At the same time, academics, advocates, policy makers, and practitioners in the field of corrections are broadening their acknowledgement of the importance of developing consciously designed plans, programs, and policies for women offenders. In 2003 and again in 2005, hundreds of men and women from across the country traveled to Maine and to Minnesota for national workshops on women and juvenile offenders, sponsored by the Association of Programs for Women Offenders. In 2004, more than 500 women and men attended the 11th National Roundtable on Women in Prison, which was held in Atlanta, Georgia. In 2005, the Minnesota Department of Corrections and the Association on Programs for Female Offenders convened the 11th National Workshop on Adult & Juvenile Female Offenders, which was held in Bloomington, Minnesota. Two national publications—the Civic Research Institute's practitioner-oriented newsletter, *Women, Girls & Criminal Justice*, from which articles in this volume are collected, and the academic journal, *Women & Criminal Justice*, published by The Haworth Press—are in their seventh and fifteenth years of publication respectively. In 2006, Sage Publications will start publishing *Feminist Criminology*, a quarterly journal edited by the Division on Women and Crime of the American Society of Criminology. Moreover, national organizations such as the National Institute of Corrections (www.nic.org) have websites that contain extensive resource material on women in community and institutional corrections.

Participants at these conferences, as well as readers of these resource materials, learn that gender matters, a lesson that has been described and discussed through a series of articles, reports, training sessions, and workshops sponsored by various community-based and governmental organizations over the past decade. That's the primary lesson of an emerging correctional consciousness: Men and women differ biologically, economically, politically, and socially. Whereas men and women share certain characteristics and roles, either individually or collectively, they are also clearly distinct in other respects. These differences are important, for men as well as for women, in any assessment of how criminal justice and corrections agencies can effectively manage or treat offenders in their care or prisoners under their custody or supervision.

Women, Girls & Criminal Justice, a bi-monthly, 16-page publication, first appeared in print in late 1998. In its seventh year at this writing, this periodical has become a leading publication for practitioners and policymakers across the United States who are interested in the development and impact of various programs and policies that affect women and girls. This collection gathers together many of the articles that appeared in the first four years.

In the inaugural issue of *Women, Girls & Criminal Justice*, Tracy Huling, who initially served as co-editor, and I wrote the following:

> It is acknowledged by professionals in all disciplines that working with women and girls in the criminal justice system is different than working with men and boys. Advocates, practitioners, scholars, and administrators conclude that many women and girls would be ideal candidates for community-based programs designed to address their specific needs. But there is often disagreement and uncertainty about how to implement alter-

natives. For those incarcerated, corrections professionals face many issues unique to women and girls that affect all aspects of institutional and program management. … Academic and other professional journals often fail to cross the divide between those studying the issues and those working directly with women and girls. While more has been done in recent years to address the concerns, needs, and challenges of women and girls in the criminal justice and corrections systems, much more is required, and what is done needs to be more widely disseminated and discussed (Huling & Immarigeon, 2000, p. 1)

For that first issue, we solicited articles on gender-specific programming, women imprisoned for killing their abusive spouses, the impact of federal legislation on incarcerated mothers and their children, and the design of drug treatment programs that are sensitive to the cultural and psychosocial needs of women. Subsequently, I have continued to solicit articles from academics, administrators, practitioners, researchers, and others who can address the critically important issues that still challenge those who work with women and girls in the American criminal justice system. In the early issues, especially those mirrored in this volume, too few articles were written by incarcerated or formerly incarcerated women and girls, who also have much to say about the validity, vibrancy, and, indeed, effectiveness of correctional programming. This shortcoming has been rectified in more recent issues.

The articles published here are divided into six parts, covering criminal justice policy, juvenile justice, mothers and children, risk and classification, physical and mental health care, and programs and practices. In the course of compiling these articles, first for the periodical and now for this volume, I have gained a deep sense of gratitude and respect for the work and perspectives described by the many authors who have contributed articles. By now, it is increasingly accepted that the treatment of women and girls in the criminal justice system should never again be an afterthought. Moreover, the work of these many authors suggests that this is a broad and complex field that merits more detailed attention, a task we will continue to pursue in coming years.

—Russ Immarigeon
October 15, 2005

References

Bell, C., "Close Up Prisons, Jails, for Women, Feminist Urges." *Denver Post*. (January 28, 1975, page not available).

Huling, T. & Immarigeon, R., "Editors' Welcome,"1(1) *Women, Girls & Criminal Justice* 1, 16 (2000).

Kruttschnitt, C., & Gartner, R., "Women's Imprisonment." In M. Tonry (Ed.), *Crime and Justice: A Review of Research, Vol. 30* (pp. 1-82) (University of Chicago Press, 2003).

President's Commission on Law Enforcement and Administration of Justice (1968). T*he Challenge of Crime in a Free Society* (Avon Books, 1968).

Table of Contents

Chapter 3: Penal Policies and Women Inmates in the 1990s
Candace Kruttschnitt, Ph.D. and Rosemary Gartner, Ph.D.

Chapter 4: Prisoner Reentry: Social Capital and Family Connections
Creasie Finney Hairston, Ph.D. and James Rollin, Ph.D.

Chapter 5: Sexually Abused Women in State and Local Correctional Institutions, 1980-2000
Kristine Mullendore, J.D. and Laurie Beever, J.D.

Chapter 6: The Impact of the Drug War on Women: A Comparative Analysis in Three States

Marc Mauer, M.S.W., Cathy Potler, J.D. and Richard Wolf, J.D.

Chapter 7: Exploring Alternatives to Incarceration for Minnesota's Bulging Women's Prison Population

The Minnesota Department of Corrections' Alternatives to Incarceration—Female Offenders Committee of the State Advisory Task Force on Female Offenders

Chapter 8: Prison Overcrowding in Alabama's Women's Prison: Real Solutions for Real Problems

Tim Roche

PART 2: JUVENILE JUSTICE ISSUES AND PROGRAMS

Chapter 9: Promoting Justice for Girls in an Unjust System

Francine T. Sherman, J.D.

Chapter 13: Working With Girls: The Need for Talk and the Art of Listening
Rebecca Maniglia, M.A.

Chapter 14: "Bad Girls, Bad Girls, Whatcha Gonna Do?"
Lyn Mikel Brown, Ed.D. and Meda Chesney-Lind, Ph.D.

PART 3: MOTHERS AND CHILDREN

Chapter 20: Prison Nurseries: New Beginnings and Second Chances
Kelsey Kauffman, Ed.D.

Chapter 21: Forgotten Victims: The Children of Incarcerated Mothers
Maureen Norton-Hawk, Ph.D.

Chapter 22: Mother-Child Programs: Connecting Child Welfare and Corrections Agencies
Susan Phillips, LMSW

Chapter 23: Summit House: Alternative to Prison for Mothers, Better Future for Kids
Karen V. Chapple, M.A., E. Paula Cox, Ph.D. and Jamie MacDonald-Furches, B.A.

Chapter 24: Girls and Their Babies: "Time" Together at Florida's YMCA Character House
Jennifer A. Lynch, B.S.

Chapter 25: Federal F.O.R.U.M.—Helping Federal Women Prisoners to Stay in Touch With Their Children
Ann Jaede

Chapter 26: The Alameda County MOMS Program
Kris Anderson and Julie Harmeyer

PART 4: GENDER-SPECIFIC CLASSIFICATION, RISK ASSESSMENTS, AND PROGRAMMING

Chapter 27: Can Classifying Women Offenders Give Greater Priority to Community Corrections?
Russ Immarigeon, M.S.W.

Chapter 28: Questions of Survival in Gender-Specific Projects for Women in the Criminal Justice System
Pat Carlen, Ph.D.

Chapter 29: Gender Responsive Strategies: Theory; Policy; Guiding Principles and Practices

Barbara Bloom, Ph.D., Barbara Owen, Ph.D. and Stephanie Covington, Ph.D.

Chapter 30: Involving Women Prisoners in Gender-Specific Planning for Girls
Karen A. Woods, M.S.W. and Julie Jenkins, M.A.

Chapter 31: Risk Assessment in Canadian Corrections: Some Diverse and Gendered Issues
Margaret Shaw, Ph.D. and Kelly Hannah-Moffat, Ph.D.

Chapter 32: Assessing Female Offenders: Prediction Versus Explanation
Christopher T. Lowenkamp, M.S. and Edward Latessa, Ph.D.

Chapter 33: Women Offenders and Prison Classification: A Paradox
Patricia Van Voorhis, Ph.D. and Lois Presser, Ph.D.

Chapter 34: The Women's Assessment Project

Mary Grace, M.Ed., M.S., Jenny O'Donnell, Psy.D., William Walters, Ph.D.,
Walter S. Smitson, Ph.D. and Mary Carol Melton

PART 5: DRUG TREATMENT, HEALTH CARE, AND MENTAL HEALTH SERVICES

Chapter 35: Preventing "Violations" Through Drug Treatment

Dorinda L. Welle, Ph.D. and Gregory P. Falkin, Ph.D.

Chapter 36: Maryland's Programs for Incarcerated and Community-Based Women With Mental Illness and Substance Abuse Disorders
Joan B. Gillece, Ph.D. and Betty G. Russell, Ph.D.

Chapter 37: Assessing the Needs of Women in Prison-Based Therapeutic Communities
Nena Messina, Ph.D., William Burdon, Ph.D., Michael Prendergast, Ph.D. and Meredith Patten, M.S.

Chapter 38: Women and Self-Harm in Community and Institutional Settings
Cathy Fillmore, Ph.D. and Colleen Anne Dell, Ph.D.

Chapter 39: Female Offenders and Disabilities
Lili Garfinkel

Chapter 40: Improving Access to Health Care for California's Women Prisoners
Nancy Stoller, Ph.D.

Chapter 41: Health Symptoms and the Inability to Engage in Self-Care and Self-Medication for Incarcerated Women
M. Katherine Maeve, R.N., Ph.D.

Chapter 45: Client Advocates Use First-Hand Experience to Improve Services
Marilyn Montenegro, Ph.D., L.C.S.W.

Chapter 46: Women and Community Service Orders: The Experience in Scotland
Kathryn Goodwin and Gill McIvor, Ph.D.

Chapter 47: Women in Community Corrections in Colorado

Suzanne Gonzalez Woodburn, M.A., Linda Harrison, M.A., and Kim English

Chapter 48: The John P. Craine House: A Community Residential Program for Indiana Women and Their Children

William H. Barton, Ph.D., and Cheryl Justice, M.S.W.

Chapter 49: Alternative Interventions for Women in Ohio

Mary Carol Melton, Mary Grace, M.Ed., M.S., Nancy Schmidtgoessling, Ph.D. and Walter S. Smitson, Ph.D.

Chapter 50: Day Reporting Program for Women in Pennsylvania

Joyce Dougherty, Ph.D.

Chapter 51: Changing Minds: Going to College at a Maximum-Security Prison

Michelle Fine, Ph.D., Maria Elena Torre, M.A., Kathy Boudin, M.A., Iris Bowen, M.A., Judith Clark, M.A., Donna Hylton, M.A., Migdalia Martinez, B.A., "Missy" (Anonymous Prisoner), Rosemarie A. Roberts, Ph.D., Pamela Smart, M.A., M.S. and Debora Upegui

Chapter 52: The Citizens, Victims, and Offenders Restoring Justice Project
Heather Burns, M.S.W.

Part 1

Policy Matters

The increased arrests and rise in "criminality" of women and girls over recent decades have given the appearance of credibility and legitimacy to the growing number of women and girls confined in juvenile or adult correctional facilities across the United States. In the American justice system, however, pre-sanctioning events, such as arrests or crimes, occur independently of sanctioning events, such as detention or incarceration. Accordingly, there is no inherent reason to assume that conviction leads to particular sanctions, whether they are located in community-based programs or in correctional institutions.

Criminal justice sanctions for women and girls, as with those for men and boys, are decided as part of a practice- or policy-based decision-making process on the part of various criminal justice practitioners, from probation officers to judges. In short, the decision to sentence someone to community service or to jail, for instance, is a specific decision that is made in lieu of other possible decisions. In short, sanctions do not occur magically or out of whole cloth. They are the end result of a process that is either well- or ill-informed in terms of what options are suitable for particular persons. In this context, then, the rise of women's imprisonment in recent years should be viewed as a consequence of policies established by a range of parties from local practitioners to state legislators. Sentencing options, therefore, reflect local or state policies, and so it is important to focus, first, on the policy context wherein women and girls face criminal justice decision-makers.

The eight chapters in this section cover a diverse array of issues that affect the treatment of women and girls by the criminal and juvenile justice systems of the United States. Certainly, these chapters do not address the full range of policy matters that might be considered in a comprehensive overview of such issues, but they do reflect a series of serious inquiries:

- Northeastern University prison historian Nicole Hahn Rafter, author of the important treatise, *Partial Justice: Women, Prisons and Social Control* (Transaction Books, 1990), begins with a brief examination of four past, present, and future periods of American history and the responses to women's criminality that were, or might be, characteristic of those times.

- Canadian criminologist Maeve McMahon describes and assesses at some length an important 1998 conference on women offenders and community corrections that was organized by the International Community Corrections Association, a group that has been influential in promoting a "What Works?" approach to programmatic interventions in criminal justice.

- Social scientists Candace Kruttschnitt from Minnesota and Rosemary Gartner from Canada write about the growing prison population of women in the 1990s in California and the state penal response to this emerging trend; Kruttschnitt and Gartner are authors of the recent volume, *Marking Time in the Golden State: Women's Imprisonment in California* (Cambridge University Press, 2005).

- Social workers Creasie Finney Hairston, who is Dean of the Jane Addams School of Social Work at the University of Illinois, Chicago, and James Rollins, a former Saginaw, Michigan, police chief who also teaches on the Addams faculty, examine the relationship between social capital and family relationships.

- Attorneys Kristine Mullendore and Laurie Beever, from Michigan and New Hampshire respectively, provide a valuable overview of case decisions, for the period 1980 to 2000, as they affect imprisoned women with histories of being sexually abused.

- Marc Mauer, assistant director of The Sentencing Project in Washington, D.C., and New York City-based attorney-researchers Cathy Potler and Richard Wolfe report results from a three-state study of the impact of the "drug war' on women.

- A Minnesota Department of Corrections-based report explores the possibilities in that state for the expanded use of alternatives to incarceration to control the rise of its women's prison population.

- Last, Tim Roche, currently President of New York State Youth Advocate Programs, shares his findings, gathered through research conducted at the Justice Policy institute in Washington, D.C., as part of a class action lawsuit in Alabama, that also suggest ways to rely increasingly on alternatives to incarceration.

Chapter 1

Women's Prison Reform: Past, Present, and Future

by Nicole Hahn Rafter, Ph.D.

INTRODUCTION

At least four major turning points in public policy toward women prisoners and prisons are readily identifiable. These turning points are times of radical reorientation, years in which the public rejected one set of policies and adopted a new paradigm, an entirely new approach to women's prison reform.

The first three turning points occurred in the past, specifically in 1820, 1870, and 1970. Looking at these three points of reorientation can help us understand what has been tried in the past. It can also help us understand how we got where we are today, because the results of these three major shifts are still with us. They influence the work we do today. The fourth of my turning points is the present, at the start of the 21st century.

INTRODUCTION OF PRISON REFORM INTO THE PENAL SYSTEM

The Concept of Reformation

Let me begin with 1820, an important point historically because it was when the American public adopted the fundamental policy toward crime and criminals that continues to motivate many of us today: the idea that government and private citizens can and should do something to reduce crime.

We are all familiar with the idea that with effort we can reduce crime and reform criminals. Today the idea is so widely accepted that we tend to take it for granted. However,

---

An earlier version of this chapter appeared in Women, Girls & Criminal Justice, *Vol. 1, No. 5, August/September 2000.*

before 1820, no one tried to reform criminals. Offenders were viewed as sinners, people who were evil. Because the first Americans considered criminal behavior to be a matter of choice, greed, or malice, they responded to crime with punishment, pure and simple. Many offenders were executed. Others were branded, whipped, or consigned to the stocks for public mockery. Still others were sent into exile—chased out of town or, in very serious cases, out of the colony.

The change leading up to the 1820 reforms began about 1790, soon after the Revolutionary War. The Quakers of Philadelphia, who endorsed the concept of reformation, introduced the changes. This new idea—that criminals might be reformed into good citizens—took time to mature and spread, but by about 1820 it was being implemented through the building of the first penitentiaries, our first real prisons. These were large institutions, designed not just to punish but also to encourage reformation. The penitentiaries isolated prisoners from the corrupting influences of society. They also isolated prisoners from one another by assigning them to single cells, at least at night. The emphasis in the early penitentiaries fell on penitence and repentance, ideas of reform rooted in religion. But these early penal institutions also put some hope in training. Through rigid routines, harsh discipline, and heavy labor, they tried to instill better work habits that, along with repentance, might lead criminals to mend their ways.

Women were held alongside men in these early penitentiaries. However, there were many fewer women than men—often just one or two among 100 or 200 male prisoners. Outwardly, the women were treated the same as the other convicts. But in actuality their experience of incarceration was very different. The women were more isolated from the companionship of their own kind. They had more fear of sexual assault and less privacy from the opposite sex. In addition, they tended to be neglected by the all-male staff of the penitentiaries, which felt that male criminals were more capable of reform than fallen women.

In sum, 1820 was the first major turning point in American attitudes toward prisoner reform because that was the time, roughly, when the traditional view of criminals as hopeless sinners was set aside in favor of a newer approach that tried not only to punish prisoners but also to reform them. The new approach was implemented through incarceration. Incarceration was used to punish and to reform women as well as men, although officials of the first penitentiaries were much more interested in reforming the men.

Penal Institutions as the Target of Reform

Another major turning point was the year 1870, especially in the prisons of the Northeast and Midwest. People who had previously been active in the movement to abolish slavery led a new thrust toward prison reform. The Civil War had ended, but their desire to improve society had not. Searching for a new cause, they found one in prison reform. These reformers began by investigating the condition of penitentiaries in states east of the Mississippi. Their work constituted the first real research on prisons. Their disappointed conclusion was that penitentiaries, far from reforming convicts, were schools for crime.

To remedy this situation, the reformers called a conference in Cincinnati in 1870. It drew people interested in prison reform from all over North America and even Europe. It turned out to be the first meeting of the organization known today as the American Correctional Association. Participants drew up a platform for prison reform, a comprehensive set of principles that continues, in part, to be endorsed today. According to one of their principles, prisons should reform as well as punish. According to others: We should teach prisoners to read and write, train them to hold jobs, and meet their needs for exercise and health care. The 1870 reformers also endorsed indeterminate sentencing, so that prisoners who did reform could be rewarded with early release on parole.

Another of these principles held that women should be incarcerated in separate prisons, supervised by other women, and provided with female-specific treatment programs. Earlier reformers had not conceived of varying treatment by sex, but the 1870 reformers did.

In sum, those who attended the 1870 prison congress formulated the rehabilitation philosophy that dominated U.S. prison policy for the next 100 years. And their work led to the opening of separate women's prisons—at Indianapolis, Indiana, in 1873; at Framingham, Massachusetts, in the mid-1870s; and at Bedford Hills, New York, in 1901. In the new prisons for women, other women—the professional ancestors of today's women prison superintendents—supervised inmates. Treatment was based on the "separate spheres" idea, the notion that men and women inhabit different "spheres" and are inherently "different." Women, according to this concept, are naturally more delicate and domestic than men. Thus, the best sort of reform programs for female prisoners will teach them to be obedient servants and good wives. While today we have discarded the separate spheres ideology, the idea of gender-specific treatment programs remains influential. In fact, it underlies many of the latest initiatives in female prison reform.

BACKLASH AGAINST IDEA OF REHABILITATION

The rehabilitation philosophy dominated U.S. prison philosophy in the Northeast and parts of the Midwest for a full century, but about 1970 reaction against it set in. This reaction came from both the political right and left. Conservatives objected to "coddling" criminals; they argued that we should forget rehabilitation and concentrate on punishment. This argument, of course, has radically transformed our prison systems since 1970. Meanwhile, also about 1970, liberals started objecting to coerced treatment, arguing that you can't force people to change. Liberals also objected to indeterminate sentencing that, they suspected, might be leading to longer terms for black than white people. These arguments, too, have transformed U.S. prisons, especially by encouraging a return to flat or determinate sentencing. The tide turned decisively against the idea of rehabilitating criminals.

INTRODUCTION OF SEX-EQUALITY IN PRISON PROGRAMS

At the same time the women's movement was gathering steam. Women throughout the Western world became feminists, and some of them were concerned about their "sisters" in prison. Feminists' concerns were heightened by the concurrent civil rights movement, which also raised issues about equality and justice.

In the early 1970s feminist researchers found that female prisoners were actually likely to be sentenced to longer terms of incarceration than their male counterparts convicted of the same offenses. Feminists objected to these differential sentencing laws and got them overturned. They also criticized gender-specific programs that doomed women prisoners to programs in cosmetology and typing, instead of training them for jobs that might pay adequate wages. Reformers began to demand that female prisoners be given training in auto repairs and other programs offered by men's prisons. They argued that male and female prisoners should be treated equally. This was a dramatic change from past prison policy, according to which men and women should axiomatically be treated differently. Sex-differential treatment was thrown out the prison's back door while sex-equality for prisoners came in the front.

In sum, we abandoned the goal of rehabilitation around 1970. We instituted flat sentencing, which has lead to severe prison overcrowding. We also introduced a new goal for dealing with women prisoners, that of equal treatment.

THE PRESENT: LESSONS LEARNED AND POSITIVE SIGNS

Thirty years later, at the start of the 21st century, we are still struggling with the changes in public mood and policy that began about 1970. So many currents are running together at the moment that it is difficult to discern new directions. However, one factor makes women's prison reform today different from that of any time in the past, and that is, *today we know more*. We know a lot more than ever before about the causes of crime and the effects of incarceration. We know more about prison history. We know what past reformers have tried, what has worked, and what has not worked. Finally, for the first time, we are able to scientifically identify male-female differences in the causes of crime and in the effects of imprisonment.

To be more specific, let me review five major points on which we have better information today and which, collectively, make the current situation more positive for women's prison reform than at earlier stages in history:

- We know that the switch to flat sentences is a primary cause of the recent, huge increases in our prison populations and in the immense increases in costs of imprisonment.

- We know that the enactment of severe sentences for drug offenders has seldom put the big drug dealers out of business. Instead, the drug laws have mainly netted minor offenders—those who have nothing with which to bargain for leniency. These minor offenders include large numbers of women who were merely accomplices—in some cases, unwitting accomplices.

- We know that the new drug laws have been racist in their effects—not in intent, but in effect. The petty female drug offenders these laws have sent to prison are predominantly members of racial and ethnic minorities. The drug laws have also had a disproportionately negative effect on the children of racial and ethnic minority women. When a mother goes to prison on a mandatory 10-year sentence, her children are often left completely parentless. Thus the drug laws contribute to destruction of black and Hispanic families and to the deterioration of black and Hispanic communities. They are helping to create a permanent underclass. The drug laws are criminogenic or crime causing—again, not in intent, but in effect.

- We have learned from recent research that the causes of crime are different for women and men. To be sure, both sexes are more likely to resort to crime if they are raised in impoverished families or with inconsistent parenting. However, it is now clear that women offenders are much more likely than men to have histories of sexual abuse and that these histories are somehow related to their subsequent offending. Many were molested or raped in childhood. We don't yet understand all the steps involved, but there seems to be a causal sequence that starts with childhood abuse, proceeds to substance abuse, and then involves offending. We also know that when adult women commit crimes of interpersonal violence, they are much more likely than men to be responding as victims to prior abuse. So, it is clear today, as never before, that the causes of crime differ considerably for men and women; in the women's case, it involves prior victimization.

- We know much more today than in the past about the nature of women's prisons. We know that they tend to impose male standards on female populations, that they have fewer programs than men's prisons, and that they seldom rehabilitate. We know that women have less access than men to alternatives to incarceration. We know that the goal of equal treatment is impossible, given differences in the size of male and female prisoner populations. And we know that the majority of women prisoners are doing time, not for violent crimes, but for property and public-order offenses.

Today we have reached a point of conflict and confusion in prison policy. But we have a lot more solid information than in the past about the *causes* of female crime, the *nature* of women's prisons, and the *effects* of incarceration on women.

Moreover, another hopeful sign is that the public seems ready for another major shift in prison policy. Crime rates are down and we are in a period of prosperity, which may soften the punitiveness with which we have approached prison policy for the past 30 years.

In other words, we may be on the verge of another paradigm shift, a swing back of the pendulum toward rehabilitating offenders. At least we may be ready again for rehabilitative efforts with female offenders, the law-breakers with whom, today, the public has some sympathy. Such a stance opposes the situation in 1820 when men were considered more reformable than women.

FUTURE OUTLOOK

This takes me to the year 2025 and to a vision of what reforms in women's prison policy might accomplish by that date. My vision has three parts:

- We will have fewer prisons for women. They will be small institutions, because when rehabilitation does occur behind bars, it does so in small prisons where staff can work individually with inmates. These prisons, moreover, will house mainly offenders convicted of crimes of violence. We will have stopped incarcerating most property and public-order offenders. We will even have stopped incarcerating battered women who struck back against their abusers.

- We will be making much more use of alternatives to incarceration, such as intensive probation, halfway houses, and community treatment. We will be trying to rehabilitate female offenders in these non-prison settings, not only for their own sake but also for the sake of their children and communities and ourselves as well, because prisons are criminogenic institutions.

- We will have saved vast sums by closing some prisons, and we will be able to spend some of the savings on drug treatment and other resources for women at risk. We will be rehabilitating again, picking up where the first prison reformers started about 1820, and hopefully doing the job better this time around.

About the Author

Nicole Hahn Rafter, Ph.D., teaches in the Law, Policy and Society Program at Northeastern University. She is the author of Partial Justice: Women, Prisons, and Social Control *(Transaction Books, 1990). This chapter is an edited version of a speech presented at the NIJ-sponsored National Symposium on Women Offenders held in Washington, D.C. from December 13-15, 1999.*

Chapter 2

Is Assisting Female Offenders an Art or Science?

by Maeve McMahon, Ph.D.

Note: An earlier version of this chapter appeared in Women, Girls & Criminal Justice, *Vol. 2, Nos. 2 and 3, February/March 2001 and April/May 2001. In September 1998, the International Community Corrections Association (ICCA) held its* What Works: Women and Juvenile Females in Community Corrections *conference in Arlington, Virginia. Professor McMahon was asked by ICCA to chair the conference and prepare comments on it, as well as edit the proceedings. Her full comments have been published in* Assessment to Assistance: Programs for Women in Community Corrections *(American Correctional Association and the International Community Corrections Association, 2000). This chapter is an edited excerpt.*

INTRODUCTION

> . . . the study of female criminality and its control, as well as the issue of gender in more general theories, faces constant problems of marginalization, incorporation, and tokenism. (Downes and Rock, 1998, p. 309)

In 1998, the International Community Corrections Association (ICCA) hosted a research conference on female offenders and community corrections. In doing so, ICCA was innovative in a variety of ways. First, it put the focus on female offenders—a topic that has been relatively neglected, not only within the field of criminology generally, but also within the sub-field of gender issues in criminology. Where women are concerned, a far stronger focus has been on their experiences as the *victims* of crime rather than as the *perpetrators* of it. However, ideological factors are also at work, which inhibits a focus on female offenders, particularly from feminist perspectives. As Downes and Rock (1998, p. 320) observe:

> [Some researchers] more feminist than criminological, would deflect attention away from the criminal woman. Feminist politics or grand theories urge the ending of what has just begun. Just as an earlier generation did not wish to endanger the politics of race by looking too closely at the links between blacks and crime (other than in the context of the unjust criminalization of blacks and the racism of the criminal justice system), so some feminists have argued that no good purpose can be served by exploring the criminality of women.... A feminist criminology, it has been argued, is prone to "correctionalism" and collusion with patriarchy, [and] being used as an instrument against women.

Focusing on female offenders does raise difficult dilemmas. But avoiding them is hardly the best path to their resolution.

INNOVATIVE APPROACHES AND DIVERSE PERSPECTIVES

ICCA was also innovative in bringing together speakers from diverse backgrounds and disciplinary perspectives. In particular, by bringing together speakers from psychological and sociological points of view, the stage was set for an opportunity to confront both the actions of female offenders and the reactions to them. While the interdisciplinary dialogue that ensued was not always an easy one, nor by any means comprehensive (most notably absent was the participation of any female offenders as a distinct group of participants, although individuals, such as Kim Pate from the Canadian Association of Elizabeth Fry Societies, spoke eloquently on the basis of their advocacy work with this group) the papers presented and the discussions that followed represented some important steps toward addressing issues about female offenders from more holistic perspectives. As a sociologist, I learned much from the psychological insights offered, and particularly those presented by Stephanie Covington (2000). While statements are frequently made in more sociologically oriented literature in criminology about the high percentages of female offenders who have experienced physical and sexual abuse, and who themselves engage in substance abuse and other forms of self-harm, it is rare to see a thorough documentation of these problems in the specific context of female psychological development.

As a critical criminologist, I also appreciated contributors' emphasis on the *similarities* between those women who happen to be in conflict with the law and women more generally. Many girls and women have had experiences of physical and sexual abuse, but it is those of us who are additionally disadvantaged because of poverty and racism that are most vulnerable to becoming enmeshed in the criminal justice system. As Covington concisely stated in her presentation, their crimes "are actually social issues." Taking this statement as seriously as it should be has enormous implications for how one views both the problems of female offenders and potential responses to them.

COMMUNITY-BASED PROGRAMS FOR OFFENDERS

The ICCA conference was further innovative in directing attention to the importance of utilizing community-based programs for female offenders. Yet, just as there has been a dearth of feminist research on female offenders, and just as social-psychological perspectives on the topic have been lacking, so has community corrections generally been an under-researched topic. In any given country, there tends to be far more literature available about prisons than about community alternatives. Moreover, such literature as does exist tends to be overwhelmingly focused on programs for males. Once again then, dialogue at the conference was often impeded by a lack of basic information, as well as by the absence of a history of well formulated thought on females and community correctional programs.

As conference Chair, I sometimes felt that I was witnessing a schizophrenic moment with respect to discussions of female offenders. One reason for this was the diversity of discourses and perspectives brought to the topic by participants—including psychological, sociological, managerial, journalistic, practitioner, and reformist. Another was that this conference was taking place at a specific time for both feminism and female offenders. The past few decades have seen a tremendous growth in knowledge about, and sensitivity to, gender issues. But they have also seen various forms of "backlash" against feminism. With respect to criminal justice, a growing awareness of the need for programming, including community programming, specific to women has been evident. Yet, and as Meda Chesney-Lind noted in the particular case of the United States, the 1990s also saw a fascination with a "new" violent offender and specifically with "girls, often girls of color, carrying guns, and fighting with other girls" (Chesney-Lind, 2000, p. 140). The question of whether or not violence by females is increasing remains, I think, unresolved. But at the conference there was less preoccupation with this than with the impression that we are witnessing a transition. Those individuals working for and with females in criminal justice are dissatisfied with their continuing position as an afterthought with respect to policy. They are looking for a new, more resolute, and more specifically woman-centered focus in the development of programs, and especially community-based ones. The observations which Pat Carlen and other feminist scholars have been making for decades still ring true, and even more strongly than has previously been the case.

> In view . . . of the vast feminist literature on the need for women to circumvent the demands of traditional gender controls and develop as persons in their own right, in view, too, of our increasing knowledge of the particular needs of women law-breakers and ex-prisoners (O'Dwyer, et al, 1987), there has been an astonishing dearth of supportive and rehabilitative programs fashioned specifically for female offenders. (Carlen, 1990, p. 2)

CONSENSUS ABOUT FEMALE OFFENDERS AND CORRECTIONS

Profiles of Female Offenders

One of the clear points of consensus at the conference concerned the profile of female offenders, and especially those who are imprisoned. Here, Vivien Stern's (1998, pp. 137-8) observations about female imprisonment around the world are familiar in light of materials presented at the conference:

> [T]he most remarkable fact about women in prison is how few of them there are. All over the world women make up a tiny proportion of those locked up. The proportions are truly startling. On average only one out of every twenty prisoners is a woman. Women constitute roughly 50 per cent of the population of any country, yet provide only 5 per cent of its prisoners. This is not specific to any one country or region, but is reflected all over the world. In Spain, the proportion of women is 10 per cent, in the United States over 6 per cent, in France 4 per cent, in Russia 3 per cent, and it Morocco it is 2 per cent. But nowhere in the world do women make up more than one in ten of the whole prison population.

Not only is there a general consensus that women make up a small proportion of over-all prison populations, but there is also a consensus about the kinds of women likely to end up in prison. Vivien Stern in her global profile again concisely states what was reiterated in the conference papers, Who are the women in prison? The answer to this too is similar in every country. "Women in prison are overwhelmingly poor. Many have themselves been victims of abuse, sexual or physical, sometimes from early childhood" (Stern, 1998, p. 138).

While the size of the female prison population is small compared to that of men, concerns were expressed at the conference about the rapid rate at which the imprisonment of women seems to be increasing. The most dramatic and well-documented case of this is in the United States where, as Elliott Currie (1998, p. 14) observes:

> [I]n 1970 there were slightly more than 5,600 women in state and federal prisons across the United States. By 1996 there were nearly 75,000—a thirteen fold increase. For most of the period after World War II, the female incarceration rate hovered at around 8 per 1000,000; it did not reach double digits until 1977. Today it is 51 per 100,000. Women's incarceration rates in Texas, Oklahoma, and the District of Columbia now surpass the overall rates for both sexes that prevailed nationally in the late 1960s and early 1970s. At current rates of increase, there will be more women in America's prisons in the year 2010 than there were inmates of both sexes in 1970.

Of note is that this increase proportionately outstrips that of men. As reported by Stern (1998, p. 153) where the United States male prison population tripled between 1980 and the mid-1990s, the female prison population grew sixfold during that period. Signs of growth in women's imprisonment are similarly evident in England and Wales. Where there were 1,800 women prisoners in 1987 (Carlen, 1990, p. 74), by June 1997 there were 2,624 women prisoners. Where between 1992 and 1995 alone there was a 29% increase in the imprisonment of men, the corresponding increase with respect to women was 57% (Stern, 1998, p.153). Data from other countries is less readily available. But there are the indications that dramatic increases in the incarceration of women are also taking place.

A further point that clearly emerged at the conference is that while poverty and social disadvantage, as well as histories of abuse, render women vulnerable to coming into conflict with the law, this situation is exacerbated for members of some ethnic minority groups. In the United States, the staggering rates of imprisonment of women of color gives much rise for concern. As Chesney-Lind and Bloom observed (1997, p. 51):

> ... women of color are disproportionately incarcerated in the United States. African-American women are incarcerated at a rate of seven times that of white women (143 vs. 20 per 100,000), and women of color represent more than 60 percent of the adult women in state and federal prisons nationwide (American Correctional Association, 1992). Women of color are also disproportionately represented on the death rows of this country relative to their proportion in the general population.

In the Canadian context, similar trends are evident with the situation of Aboriginal women being particularly disproportionate. Although Aboriginal people constitute less than 5% of the Canadian population, all estimates suggest that the rate at which Aboriginal women are imprisoned greatly exceeds their proportion in the population. According to Faith (1993, p. 138), for example, almost 25% of federally sentenced women in Canada are Native.

Limits of Our Information

Ironically, while the conference saw a strong consensus about the basic profile of women in prison—and particularly about their vulnerable status—there was also a strong consensus that we know embarrassingly little about them from a research perspective. In the first place, many basic facts and figures about women and corrections remain unclear. For example, Canadian participants at the conference could not readily agree on how many women there actually are in Canadian prisons. When it came to documenting the situation of women in community corrections the picture was even murkier. For, and as noted by Covington, "[r]eliable and detailed data about females in community corrections programs is not collected annually in the U.S. or in Canada." No doubt diligent digging would produce data on women in specific community programs—for example in the Canadian context on women in the federal parole system, or in individual provincial parole systems. But this vital task remains to be done, and it, in turn, is only part of the picture that needs to be compiled. Completing a community corrections profile of females in community corrections in the Canadian context would also require gathering data on probation systems, as well as on fine options, bail supervision, and miscellaneous other programs in Canada's 10 provinces, the North West Territories and Nunavut.

This dismal lack of information with respect to basic statistical data on the involvement of women in community correctional programs extends to matters of substance, or of what is actually going on within those programs. Fragments of information exist, and there are descriptive studies of individual programs. But when it comes to assessing the outcome of community programs the picture is obscure. Barbara Bloom's opening statement in her conference paper is apt: "The literature regarding gender-specific outcome evaluation is sparse and, for community corrections, almost non-existent." As Meda Chesney-Lind observed, a similar situation applies with respect to consideration and evaluation of community-based programs for girls where there is "virtually no solid, empirical research on program effectiveness."

SHARED PERSPECTIVES ON FEMALE OFFENDERS

While the conference was startlingly short on what might be described as "hard" data about women and community correctional programs, there was nonetheless a wealth of knowledge and insights shared by speakers, discussants, and participants. Moreover, people's diverse experiences (e.g. as researchers, managers, policy-makers, legal decision-makers, reformers and front-line workers), and ensuing reflections seemed to coalesce into what might be described as a set of shared principles. In a brief summary such as this, oversimplification is inevitable. Nonetheless the principles articulated can be described as follows:

- Women offenders should be defined primarily as women, rather than as offenders (with the same applying for girls). As Stephanie Covington expressed it, "Our lens should be that of women's lives."

- Correctional programs for women should be gender-sensitive, but not biologically reductionistic.

- The importance of relatedness and connectedness for women's mental and personal health needs to be recognized. This in turn suggests that top priority should be given to the use of community correctional programs, and that the use of imprisonment should be radically reduced. Imprisonment, by definition, fosters alienation and isolation from society. Community programs carry the potential for positively strengthening bonds between individual women and multiple resources in the community.

- The fact that the vast majority of female offenders have been victimized in various ways should not be allowed to inhibit recognition of the resourcefulness of female offenders, their strengths, and their capacities for survival.

- There should be a holistic definition of the situation of female offenders, and a holistic approach in the delivery of community services. In turn, this means that it is not only women's behavior but their feelings that should be addressed. A holistic approach involves giving attention to women's individual and social situations, including with respect to issues of housing, employment, education, recreation, and so on.

There was further consensus that, as people working in and around the system:

- We need to improve our ability to articulate our positions and standpoints, both in communicating among ourselves and with others.

- We need to create more opportunities for discussion between, and build more alliances among, researchers, policy-makers, reformers, practitioners, and females subject to the criminal justice system.

- We need to create public awareness about the expense, waste, and dangers of incarcerating women and girls.

- We need to become more political, and to communicate our views more effectively in the public culture—including to the media and politicians.

DILEMMAS AND CONTRADICTIONS

> . . . a competent feminist probation officer might know, on the one hand, that her client will gain advantage if it can be demonstrated that she is a good housewife and mother. On the other hand, by privileging that woman's house-wifely and mothering performances she will also be colluding in, and promoting, the stereotype of the criminal woman who is NOT a wife and mother, and thereby possibly disadvantaging single, divorced, childless and lesbian female offenders. That such dilemmas exist should not be surprising. (Carlen, 1990, p. 109)

What Is "Good" for Female Offenders?

Discussion at the conference was replete with dilemmas, ironies, and contradictions. This in turn gave rise to numerous important questions. One predicament that arose is that many people at the conference seemed to feel that they intuitively know what is "good" for female offenders. For example, statements to the effect of "I feel in my gut that we should..." were not uncommon. At the same time, participants seemed to feel a compulsion to have their ideas in some sense "proved," and typically in the language of evaluation. It was as if participants hoped that a magic wand of social science might be waved over a plethora of woman-centered and community-based programs, and the blessing to be given was that of solid proof that these programs "work" (specifically in the form of reducing recidivism). Some of the researchers who presented papers also adhered to this kind of thinking. For example, one of the researchers questioned: "We instinctively know what works. But how do we prove it?"

In effect, there was an expectation that social scientific research would provide a mantle of credibility to community-based and holistic programs for women, and ultimately by providing incontrovertible evidence that such programs reduce, and carry the potential to eliminate re-offending. In practice, however, and given the paucity of relevant studies, and the lack of such evidence, related discussions periodically ended up in a vacuum. Yet the vacuum was never acutely felt because the values which most participants shared—of caring, compassion, and empowerment—served to carry the discussion along, despite various theoretical, political, and research impasses met along the way.

Nevertheless, the line of thinking that "we know intuitively what is good and what should be done, and we want social science research to prove the benefits with respect to recidivism" raises some fundamental issues. I have no wish to throw sociological cold water on admirable reformist visions, but much of the history of the past few centuries of correctional reform, at least in North America, can be read as a series of well-intentioned movements followed by unintended, and often negative, consequences. As David Rothman (1980) has expressed it, the "conscience" of reformers becomes the "convenience" of administrators. Michel Foucault (1977) has even more trenchantly critiqued modern, and supposedly progressive, reform in the penal sphere. For him, knowledge and power are reflections of one another, and social scientific knowledge in general is synonymous with the sinister, complex, and subtle exercise of social control. In turn, Stanley Cohen (1985) has used a Foucauldian analysis in deconstructing the use of community corrections generally, and in revealing their dark side—particularly with respect to their potential of yielding "wider, stronger, and different nets of social control" exerted on offenders who most likely would never have gone to prison in the first place.

While I take issue with aspects of Foucault's and Cohen's perspectives they are also critically important in directing attention to, and stimulating reflection on, the ideological frameworks within which we are currently operating. Some of the immediate questions arising, and which were more or less explicitly alluded to at the conference include:

- What is the notion of "good" to which we adhere in discussing female offenders and community corrections?

- Are there intuitive views of what is good being expressed in discussions which are at odds with those adhered to in much of the research literatures, and particularly in those which are positivist in orientation?

- How do we reconcile the feminist ethic of caring, empathy, and empowerment articulated in discussions and in some of the papers with the mainstream criminological emphasis on "What Works?" and the use of recidivism rates as a primary indicator?

While Barbara Bloom raises some questions about research preoccupations with recidivism, this is an issue that perhaps needs to be confronted more directly and extensively. It is pertinent that journalist Sasha Nyary, a commentator at the conference, was puzzled by the research emphasis on meta-analysis involving as many studies as possible and by the key focus on recidivism. Who, she questioned, is asking for this? How often do the media, politicians, and the public focus on such studies anyway? In short, the research discourse and its preoccupations often seemed far removed from public culture ones, and even those of people actively involved in corrections.

In advancing discussion about ethics and morality in relation to female offenders and corrections, the words of Andrew Skotnicki are pertinent. In discussing correctional reform during the past few centuries he contends that our reliance on social scientific discourse constitutes a barrier to our considering more pluralist conceptions of "the good." In his words:

> [T]he meaning and justification for the criminal justice enterprise has been continually appraised in terms of a set of theoretical propositions grounded in the methodologies of the social sciences. These methodologies have been accorded a "de jure" status in channeling information into the debate over the direction of criminal justice, and in setting the linguistic parameters for the debate itself. It is my contention that the weight created by the burden of crime and its cure is simply too strong for such a foundation to bear. Fundamental questions of meaning currently rest, without significant opposition, on a "thin" conception of the "good" . . . our constant and relentless search for the right form will be seriously compromised, along with all other correctional innovations, until we incorporate a more pluralist conception of the good into our reformist methodologies. (Skotnicki, 1998, pp. 1-2)

It seems to me that the humanitarian and feminist discourses articulated at the conference represent one strategy for a broadened conception of the "good" as called for by Skotnicki. Within these discourses perhaps the most notable feature is a relentless focus on the person as, first and foremost, a human being. Where problems began to arise was in the juxtaposition of this arguably broader and deeper perspective with conventional criminological perspectives on indicators such as recidivism rates and using the latter as barometers of what is desirable. In short, the journey down a more pluralistic and humanistic route seemed to reach an impasse when the junction with positivism was encountered.

A basic question requiring further attention then is: What are the content and contours of the discourses currently being applied to female offenders—and especially in their feminist, humanitarian, and social scientific forms? How do these discourses complement, contradict, and circumvent one another? What are their points of incompatibility, and how might these be dealt with?

Holistic Approaches in Repressive Contexts

Other dilemmas that arose at the conference could give rise to similarly extended discussions. For the sake of brevity, however, I list them in bullet form:

- Many participants were aware that there is now a general tendency whereby governments have been withdrawing support for public and welfare services, and, at the same time, extending and expanding the repressive arm of the state. While it is admirable to advocate for increased program and service provision for female offenders, such advocacy needs to be done firmly within a context of broader social, economic, and political realities. This is particularly the case in the United States with its appallingly high rate of imprisoning women. If one considers, for example, the situation in New York State where there has been a mandatory minimum of 15 years for a minor drug offense, the question needs to be raised: Should one's primary efforts be directed to focusing attention on the fundamental injustice, futility, and costs of this rather than on the provision of more programs within the prison system itself? In conjunction with this, shouldn't there be greater protest about the decline of services and the need for more programs within the community?

- A related dilemma is embodied in the question: How compatible is a holistic approach and its therapeutic component with the ultimately coercive and repressive orientation of corrections? Stephanie Covington expressed this concern, shared by some of the other speakers and participants, as follows: "Many women and girls who work in the criminal justice settings struggle daily with the contradiction that a system based on power and control is antithetical to what helps women to change, grow and heal. Creating new gender-specific programs or changing an existing program can only be a partial solution. Systemic change is essential."

- Another related dilemma—which received even less attention at the conference—can be expressed in the question: Would a more holistic approach simply make the female correctional system more subtle and effective in exerting control over those who are already among the most vulnerable women in our societies? Few of the participants paid much attention to earlier literatures embodying critiques of previous forms of the rehabilitation approach. Again, while I am more than sympathetic to the reformist endeavor, it is also incumbent upon us to be mindful of historical pitfalls, including the potential linking of therapeutically oriented programs with lengthened and indeterminate sentences. The ethics of coerced treatment also need to be considered. Arguably, resolving these issues may again point feminist researchers in reductionist and abolitionist directions: women offenders' problems are, for the most part, social problems and thereby best addressed, insofar as is possible, outside of the criminal justice system.

AREAS OF DISSENT

What Defines "Success"?

Many presenters, commentators and participants at the ICCA conference in 1998 were uncomfortable with the notion of reduced recidivism as the primary signifier of "success." Overall, the importance of recidivism rates appeared to be simultaneously rejected and clung to. More direct confrontation of this issue, and more systematic explorations of alternative theoretical and methodological frameworks, should be considered as priorities.

Who Is a "Client?"

Another point of dissension revolved around the question: Who is the "client" when it comes to female corrections? For most participants it is individual female offenders. But for others, notably those oriented in more positivist and managerial directions, it was the public that seemed to be the client. At first glance one's definition of the client appears to be a relatively simple matter. It is also one often resolved at that level by making assumptions. But the consequences of these assumptions are enormous. Defining the public as the primary client of corrections can lend itself to the development of increasingly punitive penal policies. This is reflected in North America where political preoccupation (often in the absence of adequate or accurate information) with perceptions of public concern about crime is used as a rationale for intensified policing and toughening of sentencing. It would be an interesting and important research project to examine how definitions of the client are interwoven with contemporary penal policy both generally, and in the specific case of female offenders.

Is the Actuarial Approach Most Appropriate for Corrections?

The most important point of dissension, I think, was many people's dissatisfaction with the actuarial approach in corrections. At the conference, the actuarial approach was most clearly evident in a paper given by Larry Motiuk and Kelly Blanchette (2000), researchers at Correctional Services of Canada. The immediate focus of participants' concern about actuarial justice was on the current use of, and emphasis on, concepts of "risk" and "criminogenic needs." It is particularly important to address this issue given the Correctional Service of Canada's emphasis on actuarial approaches in both research and practice, as well as Canada's international influence in this respect. Indeed, as Motiuk stated in his presentation, he had just returned from a European conference on corrections, and Europeans consider Canada as the "foremost leader" with respect to matters of "risk" in corrections.

While issues of risk and actuarial justice are extremely important, they are also, at least in my experience, not always easily articulated. I frequently find myself asking, "What is wrong with risk, and, by extension, with actuarial justice?" This question can be difficult to answer. Although many feminists interested in criminal justice have expressed discomfort with the notion of risk, the content of their discomfort has not been expressed in any great detail. As Kelly Hannah-Moffat (1999, p. 75) notes, "[F]eminists have not yet analysed [sic] the concept of risk as it applies to women's penal regimes; nor have they provided a detailed critique of existing techniques for measuring risk, except to suggest that these measures do not adequately reflect the context of women's experiences and behaviors." As in the feminist literature in criminology, conference participants' concern about risk and related concepts as currently used were stated more implicitly than explicitly.

One Size Does Not Fit All. The first problem that many participants seemed to have with notions of risk, criminogenic need, and actuarial justice is that this frame of thinking permeates the correctional system more generally and is thereby primarily focused on men. The themes "one size does not fit all" and "equality does not mean sameness" were frequently repeated in making this basic observation.

I agree that the uniform application of analytical frameworks across genders can be problematic. But it is also important to question—as indeed some participants did—whether it is appropriate or helpful to apply the actuarial approach to male offenders either. Indeed one might argue that the feminist approaches promoted at the conference also have much to offer in improving correctional approaches to men.

A Misplaced Emphasis on Risk? The emphasis on "risk" in actuarial discussions of female offenders seems strange for several reasons. It is strange first because the notion of risk is—albeit more or less explicitly—in turn allied both with notions of dangerousness and likelihood of re-offending. Yet women are far less likely to engage in violently dangerous behavior than men. Further, the data presented by actuarial proponents suggest very low recidivism rates on the part of federally sentenced women in Canada. Specifically, in the recidivism study of 219 released women discussed by Motiuk and Blanchette, only one woman had her conditional release violated in connection with a new offense. This represents an offense-related recidivism rate of less than one percent! While seven other women were returned to custody owing to "technical violations" and while the follow-up period of six months was relatively short, the image of 218 of 219 released women not being convicted of new offenses is difficult to reconcile with the emphasis on risk. As Motiuk himself observed in his presentation, "[W]e're enjoying very low recidivism [by female offenders]." Further, he and Blanchette noted in a preface to their paper, "Assessment instruments for male offenders are often "borrowed" which may be contributing to over estimates of risk for female offenders." Having said this, however, they then proceed to present their research using these virtually gender-neutral instruments.

What Do "Criminogenic" and "Risks" Really Mean? Another problem with the actuarial approach in corrections is that it is often, at least in my experience, difficult to understand what is actually being said. The terms "criminogenic" and "risks" as used in the literature are cases in point. Therefore it was a bit of a relief to hear Motiuk state, in the context of the European conference he had just attended, that the concept of criminogenic needs is "hard for foreigners to understand." In essence, as Barbara Bloom noted in her presentation, the logic is that certain of an offender's needs are considered to be risk factors with respect to recidivism. In the words of Motiuk and Blanchette, "We consider need areas to be dynamic factors and a subset of an overall offender risk." In turn the correctional system's business is to focus on those representing high risks and to concentrate its efforts in that direction (Andrews et al, 1990; Gendreau, 1996; Bonta et al, 1995). Meanwhile, those considered lower-risk could be used as a "target for less intensive services [expediting] their safe and controlled release at the earliest possible moment in the sentence" (Motiuk & Blanchette, 2000, p. 237).

While this approach is logical at one level it carries some disturbing implications. The first is that, if women are recognized as low risk (and especially compared to the higher risk believed to be posed by men), following the actuarial approach would suggest that they be a low priority for receipt of services. In short, the traditional neglect of women within corrections seems to be reinforced by the actuarial approach.

Also disturbing is the view of female offenders that emerges in the actuarial literature. As Bloom (2000) wondered, "Does women's offending relate to criminogenic risks and needs, or is it a factor of the complex interconnection of race, class, gender, trauma, or both?" (p. 122). To this I would add that we also need to consider the actions of criminal justice agents and agencies. Women's actions are only part of the picture. Also important are decision-making by police, prosecutors, and others in determining who actually ends up in corrections.

A further question is: What precisely are the "criminogenic needs" with respect to female offenders? While Motiuk and Blanchette discussed many of the problems also discussed by others at the conference, I have difficulty providing specific answers based on their paper, or on the actuarial literature more generally. Rather, the concept of "needs" seems to merge with that of "risks" and, in the process, the focus shifted away from the feminist emphasis on the offender as a person, and toward a focus on potential criminal behavior. As reaffirmed by Kelly Hannah-Moffat (1999, p. 83), within the Correctional Service of Canada there is "an interesting slippage" between needs and risks to the point that, in some cases, "these two categories are indistinguishable."

A Faulty Predictor of Violent Recidivism? One example of this merging and shifting is Motiuk and Blanchette's unusually unequivocal statement that, "A history of attempted suicide was found to be a potent predictor of violent recidivism in a sample of federally sentenced women." (Blanchette and Motiuk, 1995, p. 7). When I first read this statement I had a mental image of the Governor of the women's prison in Lithuania, where I have spent some time, reading Motiuk and Blanchette's article and finding that this was one of the most clearly understandable statements in the article. I then had the image of the Governor using the statement to direct his staff to put any female prisoners who had ever attempted suicide into the most secure section of the prison, and to make sure that they stayed there until their full sentences had been served, with no possibility of early release. Of course, no such interpretation is intended by Motiuk and Blanchette, but arguably their analysis easily *lends itself* to such an interpretations.

A woman who has been, or is, suicidal is a woman with problems, and needs assistance. But putting this scenario into an actuarial, and purportedly recidivism-predicting framework diminishes the focus on her problem and shifts it into an image of her as a "high risk" candidate, and not only for recidivism, but for violent recidivism. With this focus, surely the orientation of the correctional system moves toward delaying and constraining her access to the community.

A further problem with the observation that "a history of attempted suicide was found to be a potent predictor of violent recidivism," and in Motiuk and Blanchette's attendant observations that between one-third and one-half of the federal female offender population have a history of attempt suicide, is that they are difficult to reconcile with the authors' observations elsewhere about the low recidivism rate of female offenders. Again, while not intended, the sequential observations that up to half of female offenders have attempted suicide, and attempting suicide is a potent predictor of violent recidivism among female offenders, can logically lead in the direction of linking federally sentenced women with violence and re-offending. While not wishing to dispute that some federally released women do go on to re-offend, and occasionally violently, it is the *generality* of the image that is disturbing, and arguably misleading.

Meanwhile, the data cited by Motiuk and Blanchette in presenting their case about the link between attempt suicide and recidivism are sketchy. No information is presented about the basis upon which the 81 federal female offenders studied was selected. Further, the information that 17 of these re-offended, that eight of these were for robbery, that over half of the variance in the "violent recidivism" remained unexplained, and that 20% of the 45% that was explained was attributed to "[h]aving a history of attempted suicide" seems to me to greatly dilute the authors' claim. If I am interpreting the data correctly the "most highly predictive variable" of attempted suicide explained less than 5% of the recidivism by 21% of the women studied. Meanwhile, no information is provided about the remaining 79% of the sample who did not violently re-offend (or re-offend at all?) and their histories of attempted suicide. This fragmentary picture seems a long way from the image of a "potent predictor."

Also of concern is Motiuk and Blanchette's linking of their observations about attempted suicide and violent recidivism to those on the significance of self-mutilation by women prisoners when they state, "Accordingly, other researchers found much higher rates of previous self-injury among female recidivists than non-recidivists." Again, rather than positing self-mutilation as an indicator of a woman's need for help the focus is on its being a potential predictor of re-offending.

Objective vs. Subjective Assessment Tools. Another problem with the actuarial literature produced by Canadian correctional researchers is its frequently authoritative tone. In part, this tone derives from the authors' emphasis on the scientific nature of their approach. As Motiuk and Blanchette state, the Offender Intake Assessment (OIA) process consists of "the latest generation of risks and needs assessment technology" and one that uses "objective assessment tools." The purportedly scientific nature of the approach was more clearly highlighted by their colleague Paul Gendreau (2000) in a talk preceding the conference, when he elaborated on the virtues of the "actuarial" approach, and in contrast to the more old-fashioned, and implicitly unscientific, "clinical" approach. Thus he emphasized that under the actuarial approach there is a "statistical association between prediction and outcome," and that "predictors are measured by standardized, reliable, objective measures." By contrast, the clinical approach relies more heavily on people and professionals and "the rules for collecting and interpreting information are subject to considerable personal discretion." In Gendreau's account, in terms of delivering "superior performance" the actuarial approach "is three to four times better" than the clinical one. Following his vision the argument is that computerized forms with relevant items being checked off by technocrats is far superior than, for example, having a social-scientifically trained intake officer sitting down with an offender to discuss how they might best proceed through the morass of correctional institutions and programs.

Taken to its logical extreme one can envision a future where even the need for correctionally employed technocrats is eliminated. Why shouldn't the offenders themselves sit in front of a computer and check off relevant items, perhaps attached to a lie detector that imposes mini electric shocks as necessary to minimize the potential for errors in replying?

One can imagine the appeal of this highly assertive tone to correctional policy makers and politicians. Consider, for example, the title of an article by Don Andrews (1996) that confidently states, "Criminal Recidivism is Predictable and Can Be Influenced." What are in practice very complex phenomena get transmuted into appealingly simple statements, and sometimes even into slogans.

In fairness, the complexities of understanding and predicting recidivism are not completely ignored in the literature. For example, Motiuk and Blanchette (2000) state, "Although objective classification instruments can yield significant gains both in understanding and predicting criminal behavior, *the fact remains that the amount of variance left unexplained continues to outweigh that which can be explained for a variety of correctional outcomes* (e.g., temporary absence, parole)" (p. 237, emphasis added). However, once mentioned, this crucial point is left to the side and they proceed as if their data and approach were all encompassing. Although they mention the need for a "variety of technologies" no elaboration is provided.

While the tone of the actuarial literature in corrections is often authoritative and confident, actually making sense of it can be very difficult. Consider, for example, the conference statement by Motiuk and Blanchette:

> While the OIA process was developed principally for assessing offender risks and needs upon admission to federal custody, the scope of our risks/ needs assessment and assessment process has been streamlined. In keeping with individual ratings for both "criminal risk" and "case need" levels as well as for each need area, alignment of the community version of risk/need assessment process was straightforward. This situation makes possible a systematic assessment and re-assessment process which spans admission to the end of sentence. Presently, full automation of this new community re-assessment is complete. (Motiuk & Blanchette, 2000, p. 248)

If I understand them correctly, they are saying, "Our assessment process was initially designed for offenders entering federal prisons. It is now also used during offenders' transition to the community. The data are computerized."

Understanding the literature is further complicated in that many of its claims are highly contestable. For example, it is frequently claimed that the system is "objective." The first point one can make here is that the correctional system *per se* is in no way objective. Those offenders who end up in corrections do so as a result of a long series of decision-making by individuals where subjectivity comes into play at every step of the way—including decisions by members of the public (e.g., by victims about whether or not to report), and by the police (e.g., about whether or not to lay charges, and what charges to lay), as well as by prosecutors, defense lawyers, judges, and juries. Therefore what is being studied by correctional researchers is not any objective picture of offenders, but rather a relatively small subgroup of offenders, predominantly from vulnerable groups in any given society, who have been successfully focused on, and processed by, other components of the justice system.

The claim that these newer assessment "tools" are objective is further questionable in that they currently continue to rely on the mainstay of traditional clinical approaches, namely professional judgment. As Motiuk and Blanchette said:

> An overall rating of criminal risk is the compilation of professional judgments from the results of the criminal history record and offence severity record. In addition, a review of detention criteria for the current offence(s) reflects the nature of the offence(s) and the degree of harm to the victim(s)

is taken into account. One should keep in mind that the establishment of criminal risk might also incorporate a great deal of other assessment information as well.

Given the acknowledgement that professional judgments are still key in actuarial decision-making as currently engaged in, issues arise of a disjuncture between discourse and practice. Although the actuarial discourse emphasizes notions of being scientific and objective, actual practices within the complex world of corrections may have much in common with traditionally established ones. As Hannah-Moffat (p. 75) notes, "In practice, the assessment and management of women prisoners' risk is quite subjective and fluid." Moreover, while the research publications of the Correctional Service of Canada give the impression that various classification instruments determine where an offender is sent, Hannah-Moffat (p. 78) documents that in the real world of corrections other factors come into play including perceptions of "escape risk" and *"notoriety*—likely to evoke a negative public image..." (Emphasis in original). Indeed officials of the Correctional Service of Canada have acknowledged their own departures from actuarial practice. In the words of one report quoted by Hannah-Moffat (p. 81; FSWP, 1994, p. 11):

> [Practical uses of risk technologies are not] depersonalised or concerned primarily about independent, abstract statistical categories and populations.... [W]hen actuarial tools are used, correctional officials frequently use "overrides" to adjust risk assessment scores to what they feel is most appropriate. The use of overrides means that exceptions can be made to the initial classification instrument when warranted, both to increase and decrease the security classification.

More generally, the very notion of objectivity raises deep epistemological issues that are, unfortunately, beyond the present scope. In a nutshell, my own position is that no analytical framework is ever objective, and rather represents a partial, and to some extent ideological, view of the matter at hand. Rather than claiming objectivity it is perhaps more fruitful, and truthful, to be reflexive about the frameworks we use, including the interests that they represent, and those that they undermine. Informed and transparent subjectivity is arguably preferable to detached and highly questionable objectivity.

Overall, while the assessment tools discussed by Motiuk and Blanchette, and by their colleagues, might be useful in matching individual offenders to correctional programs it is arguably a dangerous enterprise to link their use to overconfident claims about their ability to reduce recidivism. Especially given the inevitability of some recidivism occurring, and current media and public culture preoccupations—in the Canadian case particularly with respect to ex-prisoners (usually males) who re-offend—the actuarial approach with its emphasis on "risk" can easily be used in moving in a very repressive direction. At an extreme this repressive direction could lead to the totalitarian conclusion: every prisoner—male or female—is potentially a recidivist and therefore the only way to prevent recidivism is to prevent the release of all prisoners. The abolition of parole in many places in the U.S., and the thinking behind "three-strikes-and-you're-out" legislation, as well as calls for increased use of capital punishment, are contemporary steps in the direction of this dire logic.

CHALLENGES IN ASSISTING FEMALE OFFENDERS

Importance of Context

> [W]e have to change our belief system. (Dave Worth, quoted in Cayley, 1998, p. 362)

Perhaps the greatest challenge faced by those who wish to assist female offenders is to keep constant vigilance in being aware of the broader context. At any given moment in time a practitioner may be preoccupied with helping an ex-prisoner to regain custody of her children, or to recover from relapse into an addiction; a researcher may be preoccupied with tracking down an elusive piece of data; a policy-maker may be preoccupied with how to respond to a Minister's request for a "quick fix" speech in response to the latest crisis; and a prison guard may be preoccupied with evaluating the mood of those under her charge. But unless we bear in mind that crime "usually begins in circumstances of poverty, joblessness, family breakdown, sexual violence, drug addiction, and neighborhood abandonment" (Cayley, 1998, p. 357), we are vulnerable to having our work usurped and carried off in directions not of our own choosing. A particular danger is that women-centered and holistic approaches might be accepted and used only insofar as they are amenable to the actuarial approach that is ascendant in corrections.

Here, Canada represents an important case in point. For, despite having produced a resolutely woman-centered and holistic blueprint that emphatically rejected an emphasis on "risk" (TFFSW, 1990), and having established five new women's prisons, recent developments suggest that the vision has only been partially implemented, and that a preoccupation with purported risks continues to be predominant. In short, the subsuming of needs to risks proceeds apace. As Kelly Hannah-Moffat observes (1999, p. 73):

> ... the implementation of this model has been marred by exclusion, and by redefinitions of the meaning of woman-centered corrections and of the experiences and realities of the female offender (as outlined in *Creating Choices* and by feminist researchers and advocates). Some of the most significant of these changes include the definition, assessment and management of women's risk and need in the new regional prisons.

High Risk vs. High Needs Offenders

Hannah-Moffat goes on to elaborate on how multiple discourses of "need" are present in correctional settings—including therapeutic, administrative, feminist, and actuarial vocabularies. Moreover, with the actuarial slippage between "needs" and "risks," the fact that women are often defined as "high need" has, according to Hannah-Moffat, made little difference in how they are actually treated. She elaborates:

> The emergent needs-talk which informs women's correctional management does not rely on feminist interpretations of women's needs or their claims to entitlement; rather, it depends on correctional interpretations of women's needs as potential or modified risk factors that are central to the efficient management of incarcerated women. The Correctional Service of Canada's adoption of the premise that federally sentenced women are generally "high

need" and not "high risk", their claims that these prisoners do not require the same level and type of security measures as are required for male offenders (TFFSW, 1990) and the subsequent development of a unique security management model to address these qualities illustrates an organizational commitment to serving women's needs as they define them. Thus far, this tactic has co-opted and distorted the feminist critique of correctional risk assessment and risk management practices. The fact that women are now constructed as "high need" as opposed to "high risk" makes little substantive difference in their correctional management. Increasingly, needs are being treated in the same manner as risks in terms of defining carceral responses to women. (p. 88)

Frames, Lenses, and Maps

Keeping the broader picture in mind requires paying attention to what Stephanie Covington referred to in her presentation as our "mental maps." As she noted every field or discipline carries its own assumptions, and, especially as we work for a long period in one area, these can often go unexamined. In turn, individuals tend to look at issues through a particular "lens" and that chosen in any given instance has a profound effect on how related problems are defined. Historically, criminal justice issues have tended to be seen through the lens of men's eyes. Whether one chooses to emphasize the "criminal," "cognitive therapy," or "addiction," said Covington, will likewise lead one down certain routes and simultaneously away from others. Her own chosen lens—and one shared by many conference participants—of "women's lives" leads clearly in a holistic direction in assisting female offenders.

In short, one challenge is to be aware of the contours of our own "maps," including both their strengths and limitations.

But being reflexive about our own approaches is only one part of the challenge. We also need to be aware of the contours of the "maps" that are actually at work within the system. In particular we need to be reflexive about the contours of the actuarial map and its emphasis on risk. The reflections offered in this article are a very modest step in this direction. What is needed is more empirical research on how these relatively new instruments are actually being used, and how they differentially impact people in corrections on the basis of gender, ethnicity, class, and so on.

Another challenge facing us, and especially as researchers on female offenders, is to keep the complexity of related issues front and center stage. There seemed to be a feeling at the conference that researchers should be able to deliver clear and unequivocal guidelines about how to proceed. For example, Richard Billack, who was serving as President of the ICCA at the time of the conference, stated, "We want the research community to give us *tools*" (emphasis added). The actuarial approach, by sidestepping or ignoring issues of the broader workings of the criminal justice system, appears most able to deliver in response to this request. But, as has been argued, this is done at the expense of considering the strong tendency of the criminal justice system to focus on those who are already vulnerable. Aiming to simply provide tools arguably turns researchers into technocrats and turns them away from considering the nuances of given situations.

Perhaps the job of the academic researcher is primarily to bring the contours of dominant "maps" more clearly into focus so that in turn we can all better address the various principles, perspectives, and moral issues that are involved in definitions of, and responses to, crime. This is not to say that academic researchers cannot suggest plans of action. For, as the conference presenters showed, they certainly can. What is different is that the plans of action offered are far clearer in articulating their presuppositions, the context of the actions required, and their potential consequences. In short, there are no magical tools, and the task of the social scientific community is to articulate the complexity of social problems as well as suggesting potential directions in responding to them.

CONCLUSION

In conclusion, it seems to me that points of dissension and debate at the conference ultimately circulated around competing views about "ways of knowing" or "ways of seeing" female offenders and their behavior, and how to proceed in responding to them. In turn these ways of knowing seemed to divide into those that emphasized an intuitive, woman-centered and holistic approach as against those that emphasized a scientific and highly rational approach. The underlying debate then, might be described as art versus science.

How might this debate be advanced? Here the words of Leonid Ponomarev (1979) are useful, as he reflects on the strengths and limitations of science and art as two ways of knowing:

> It has long been known that science is only one of the methods of studying the world around us. Another—complementary—method is realized in art. The joint existence of art and science is in itself a good illustration of the complementarity principle. You can devote yourself completely to science or live exclusively in your art. Both points of view are equally valid, but, taken separately, are incomplete. The backbone of science is logic and experiment. The basis of art is intuition and insight. But the art of ballet requires mathematical accuracy and, as Pushkin wrote, "Inspiration in geometry is just as necessary as in poetry." They complement rather than contradict each other. True science is akin to art, in the same way as real art always includes elements of science. They reflect different, complementary aspects of human experience and give us a complete idea of the world only when taken together.... we cannot assess the degree of damage we undergo from a one-sided perception of life.

In attempts to assist female offenders our efforts can be aided by intuitive insights coupled with scientific rigor. But to proceed only through one route or the other is to increase the danger of the penal system further oppressing women and girls who are already among those who are most vulnerable in our societies.

About the Author

Maeve McMahon, Ph.D., teaches in the Department of Law at Carleton University, Ontario, Canada. She is the author of The Persistant Prison? Rethinking Incarceration and Penal Reform *(University of Toronto Press, 1992).*

References

American Correctional Association, *The Female Offender* (American Correctional Association, 1992).

Andrews, D., "Criminal Recidivism Is Predictable and Can Be Influenced: An Update," 8 *Forum on Corrections Research* 42-44 (1996).

Andrews, D., Zinger, I., Hoge, D., Bonta, J., Gendreau, P. & Cullen F., "Does Correctional Treatment Work? Clinically Relevant and Psychologically Informed Meta-Analysis," 28 Criminology 369-404 (1990).

Bloom, B., "Beyond Recidivism: Perspectives on Evaluation of Programs for Female Offenders in Community Corrections." In M. McMahon (Ed.) *Assessment to Assistance: Programs for Women in Community Corrections* (pp. 107-138) (American Correctional Association and International Community Corrections Association, 2000).

Bonta, J., Pang, B. & Wallace-Capretta, S., "Predictors of Recidivism Among Incarcerated Female Offenders," 75(3) The Prison Journal 277-294 (1995).

Carlen, P., *Alternatives to Women's Imprisonment* (Milton Keynes: Open University Press, 1990).

Cayley, D., *The Expanding Prison: The Crisis in Crime and Punishment and the Search for Alternatives* (House of Anasi, 1998).

Chesney-Lind, M. "What to Do About Girls?" In M. McMahon (Ed.), *Assessment to Assistance: Programs for Women in Community Corrections* (pp. 130-170) (American Correctional Association, 2000).

Chesney-Lind, M. & B. Bloom, "Feminist Criminology: Thinking About Women and Crime," in B.D. MacLean & D. Milanovic (Eds.) *Thinking Critically About Crime* (Collective Press, 1997).

Cohen, S., *Visions of Social Control* (Polity, 1985).

Covington, S. S., "Helping Women to Recover: Creating Gender-Specific Treatment for Substance-Abusing Women and Girls in Community Corrections. In M. McMahon (Ed.), *Assessment to Assistance: Programs for Women in Community Corrections* (pp. 171-234) (American Correctional Association and International Community Corrections Association, 2000).

Currie, E., *Crime and Punishment in America: Why the Solutions to America's Most Stubborn Crisis Have Not Worked—and What Will* (Metropolitan Books, 1998).

Downes, D. & Rock, P., *Understanding Deviance: A Guide to the Sociology of Crime and Rule Breaking* (3rd ed., Oxford University Press, 1998).

Faith, K., *Unruly Women: The Politics of Confinement and Resistance* (Press Gang, 1993).

Federally Sentenced Women Program (FSWP), *Correctional Program Strategy for Federally Sentenced Women* (Correctional Service of Canada, 1994).

Foucault, M., *Discipline and Punish: The Birth of the Prison* (Pantheon, 1977).

Gendreau, P., "1998 Margaret Mead Award Address: Rational Policies for Reforming Offenders." In M. McMahon (Ed.), *Assessment to Assistance: Programs for Women in Community Corrections* (pp. 329-338) (American Correctional Association and International Community Corrections Association, 2000).

Gendreau, P., "The Principles of Effective Intervention With Offenders," in A. Harland (Ed.), *Choosing Correctional Options that Work: Defining the Demand and Evaluating the Supply* (Sage, 1996).

Hannah-Moffat, K., "Moral Agent or Actuarial Subject: Risk and Canadian Women's Imprisonment," 3(1) Theoretical Criminology 71-94 (1999).

McMahon, M. (Ed.), *Assessment to Assistance: Programs for Women in Community Corrections* (American Correctional Association and International Community Corrections Association, 2000).

Motiuk, L. L., & Blanchette, K., "Assessing Women Offenders: What Works." In M. McMahon (Ed.) *Assessment to Assistance: Programs for Women in Community Corrections* (pp. 235-266) (American Correctional Association and International Community Corrections Association, 2000).

O'Dwyer, J., Wilson, J. & Carlen, P., "Women's Imprisonment in England, Wales, and Scotland," in P. Carlen & J. Worrall (Eds.), *Gender, Crime and Justice* (Milton Keynes: Open University Press, 1987).

Ponomarev, L., "In Quest of the Quantum." Quoted in B. Edwards, *Drawing on the Right Side of the Brain: A Course in Enhancing Creativity and Artistic Confidence* (J.P. Tarcher, 1979).

Rothman, D., *Conscience and Convenience: The Asylum and Its Alternatives in Progressive America* (Little, Brown, 1980).

Skotnicki, A., *Continuity and Change in the Pursuit of Criminal Justice* (Presentation to the ICCA conference, 1998).

Stern, V., *A Sin Against the Future: Imprisonment in the World* (Penguin, 1998).

Task Force on Federally Sentenced Women (TFFSW), *Report of the Task Force on Federally Sentenced Women*, (Ministry of the Solicitor General, 1990).

Chapter 3

Penal Policies and Women Inmates in the 1990s

by Candace Kruttschnitt, Ph.D. and Rosemary Gartner, Ph.D.

INTRODUCTION

How the United States has come to incarcerate more people than anyone else in the industrialized world, and continues to do so at alarming rates, has been the subject of much scholarly and public debate (Tonry, 1999). What has been lost in this debate, however, is the question of how this change in penal policy has impacted inmates, especially female inmates whose rate of imprisonment has increased more quickly than men's each year over the past two decades. In this brief chapter, we provide a glimpse of the answer to this question by presenting some results from a survey we conducted of 1,821 women currently serving time in two of the five prisons in California that house women: the California Institution for Women (CIW) and Valley State Prison (VSP).

In our study of female inmates, we chose to focus on the California penal system for several reasons. First, the California prison system is the largest in the western world, larger than any western nation's system and the Federal Prison System. Thus, a substantial proportion of the total female prison population in the United States is incarcerated in the prisons we studied. Second, most of the major trends in California prisons foreshadow trends in prison systems throughout the United States and in other countries (Zimring,

---

Note: An earlier version of this chapter appeared in Women, Girls & Criminal Justice, *Vol. 2, No. 2, February/March 2001.*

1992). Some scholars have even suggested that familiarity with the California prison system is essential to understanding the American prison system as a whole (Silberman, 1995). Third, many of the factors we believe may have affected women's prison experiences are not unique to California. In particular, a number of changes in criminal justice policies, practices, and philosophies and in women's lives have occurred throughout the United States and in many other developed nations.

THE NEW PENALITY: THE SHIFT FROM REHABILITATION TO RETRIBUTION AND RISK MANAGEMENT

California's primary response to the rising female inmate population has been prison construction. Between 1980 and 1995, the female prison population in California grew from 1,300 to almost 9,000 (a 500% increase) and four new prisons for women were opened. This growth in the number of women's prisons, combined with the move toward gender equity in corrections, means that more women are now incarcerated in physical surroundings and subjected to disciplinary regimes unlike women's prisons of the past and more similar to men's prisons. Female offenders, once viewed as maladjusted and in need of treatment, are now viewed as dangerous and in need of strict control (Faith, 1993). These transformations have produced a radical and rapid shift away from the rehabilitative and therapeutic approaches that gave women's corrections a coherence and distinctiveness for most of the century. Simply put, the character and meaning of women's imprisonment have fundamentally changed, and in ways that are unparalleled in men's imprisonment.

Old School vs. New School Corrections

In order to understand how these changes in penality may be affecting women inmates, we chose to contrast women's experiences in CIW with women's experiences in VSP. VSP is a product of the new penal philosophies that emphasize retribution and risk management (Feeley & Simon, 1992). Opened in 1995, VSP has the prototype modular design typical of new men's prisons. It houses eight women per cell, is headed by a male warden, and has a capacity of 2,500 inmates. Yet at the time we conducted our research, the prison population exceeded this capacity and was housing approximately 3,600 women.

In contrast, CIW was opened in 1952. For 35 years, CIW was the only prison for women in California. It has a traditional campus-style architecture, houses two women per cell, is headed by a female warden, and has a population goal of 1,650 (less than its current population of approximately 1,800 but twice the population it was built to hold). CIW also has a long institutional history and culture. Some current inmates and staff were at CIW when it was the only prison for women in California and recall when inmates wore their own clothes and decorated their cells with personal belongings, and when female correctional officers did not wear uniforms and male correctional officers had little contact with inmates. In contrast, VSP has no history and is only beginning to develop a culture—one that presumably will reflect different influences from those that have shaped the culture of CIW.

Despite their differences, both of these institutions are dealing with the American "crisis in penality." Both are facing growing populations of women who are serving longer sentences; shrinking budgets for programs and services; and a general thrust toward classification, control, and standardization in institutional operations. We suspected that these differences in the history and culture of each prison would influence whether and how

Table 3.1: Selected characteristics of the Inmate Populations at California Institute for Women (CIW) and Valley State Prison (VSP)

	CIW (N = 887)	VSP (N = 934)
Custody Level		
Level I	62%	49%
Level II	17%	24%
Level III	10%	14%
Level IV	11%	13%
Parole/Probation Violators	55%	46%
Age at First Institutional Commitment		
19 and younger	32%	36%
20 to 29	41%	39%
30 and older	27%	25%
Number of Prior Years in Jail/Prison		
None	28%	31%
1	35%	32%
2 or more	37%	37%
Family Members in Jail/Prison	65%	64%
Prior Alcohol/Drug Problem		
Alcohol	30%	29%
Drugs	76%	78%
Mental Health Treatment	29%	31%

these changes in penality influenced institutional operations and inmates' experiences (Lynch, 1998).

Institutional Differences

In order to understand how women in these two different institutions are responding to prison life, it is important to note at the outset that, while the populations of the two prisons differ substantially in size, they do not differ in the types of women they house. In large part this is because at the time we conducted this survey California had still not instituted an official system for classifying female inmates. Both VSP and CIW are considered to be level 1-4 (minimum to maximum security) prisons, but efforts were underway to transform CIW into a level 2 or "soft" level 3 institution (Dykes, 1995). These efforts include sending "troublemakers" from CIW to VSP or to the Central California Women's Facility (CCWF) at Chowchilla.

Table 3.1 provides a brief profile of the women who responded to our survey at each prison. In this table we concentrate on the criminogenic aspects of the populations at each prison because (1) in early work we established that there are virtually no substantial differences in the demographic profiles of the women at these two institutions (Kruttschnitt & Gartner, 2000), and (2) it is well known that certain pre-prison experiences, such as crime, previous institutionalization, history of drug use, and mental illness affect responses to imprisonment (Mandaraka-Sheppard, 1986).

STRIKING SIMILARITIES IN POPULATIONS AND CRIMINAL JUSTICE EXPERIENCES

Generally, we found remarkable similarities in the experiences of women housed at both CIW and VSP. While CIW houses slightly more probation or parole violators and women with minimum custody levels than VSP, there are few differences in the criminal justice, substance abuse, and mental health backgrounds of the two groups of women. As Table 3.1 shows, at both prisons approximately one-third of the women had their first prison commitment at age 19 or younger and, not surprisingly, just over one-third spent two or more years incarcerated before their current sentence. Most of these women also have had a family member who has spent time in jail or prison. In fact, at both institutions, almost two-thirds report that a family member—most often this is a brother—has been incarcerated. There is also no evidence that women with prior drug, alcohol, or mental health problems are more likely to be in one of these facilities than the other. In fact, at both CIW and VSP, the vast majority of women report having a drug problem. While the proportion of the prison populations with reported drug problems may largely reflect statutory changes that have resulted in more drug convictions and prison sentences for drug law violations (Blumstein & Beck, 1999), this cannot account for any noted differences in women's responses to incarceration across institutions.

THE INMATE EXPERIENCE: A STUDY IN CONTRASTS

How, then, do these women, who have very similar experiences with the criminal justice system and related social agencies, respond to these two institutions? At this point it is important to remember that CIW and VSP differ on a number of dimensions that are perhaps best reflected in their physical layouts and architectural features. CIW has the traditional campus layout and is more reminiscent of an old high school campus than a prison. Layers of security have been added over the years, including guard towers and barbed-wire, but one still gets the sense that this is a more relaxed institution that is less concerned about the inmates wandering the tree-lined courtyard than the smell and flies from the adjacent farms that pervade the institution in the summer. VSP is a model of the new prison technology where primacy is given to efficient regulation and management of inmates. Each prison has fenced yards and inmates must wait for electric gates to be opened in order to pass from one yard into the next. A perimeter guard patrols the prison just outside of the electric fences. Trees are largely absent on the grounds as they would obscure the view of inmates from the guard tower.

Women's Response to Aspects of Doing Time

In our survey, we asked women to respond to a number of aspects of doing time. While we cannot reproduce all of the findings here, we draw attention to some of the more significant differences we observed. First, we indicated to women that we were aware that "no one likes doing time but there can be some good things that come out of it." We asked the women to indicate, on a list of forced-choice responses, all of the things that had been good for them. About one-half of the women at both institutions felt that "getting off drugs" was a positive aspect of doing time, and over two-thirds also found "having time to think about their life" was beneficial. One notable difference, however, occurred in the number of women who indicated that "establishing important and personal relationships" was one of the good aspects of doing time. Over one-third of the women at CIW checked this item, only one-quarter at VSP. Similarly, women at CIW were far more likely to indicate that this prison experience had "boosted their self-esteem" than were women at VSP (45% vs. 27%).

We also asked women to indicate what they found to be the most difficult aspects of adjusting to prison. Again, we used a set of forced-choice response categories and permitted women to check all of the items they found difficult. Here we found that on measures of deprivation from what might be considered indicators of "life on the outside" there were few differences between the women at CIW and VSP. Virtually all of the women (90% at CIW and 92% at VSP) indicated that the absence of home and family was very difficult. Sizeable proportions of the population at both prisons also noted that the absence of social life and friends on the outside (72% at CIW and 73% at VSP), the poor quality of food (59% at CIW and 63% at VSP) and the lack of adequate medical care (81% at CIW and 88% at VSP) were also difficult aspects of doing time.

Larger Populations Increase Strain on Inmate and Staff Relations

By contrast, perceptions of the difficulty of specific aspects of dealing with other inmates and the prison administration differed depending upon where women were located. For example, fewer than one-half of the women at CIW (46%) but almost two-thirds (59%) of those at VSP cited having to deal with other inmates as a difficult aspect of prison life. And while the majority of women at both prisons complained about overcrowding and the lack of privacy, it was clearly more troublesome for a larger proportion of the women at VSP (roughly 90%) than the women at CIW (approximately 70%). No doubt this difference reflects the relative size of the inmate populations at each institution and the fact that women at VSP are crammed into living quarters designed to hold four women but which in fact house eight.

Relative to the women at CIW, VSP inmates also expressed having more difficulty with the correctional officers (40% vs. 62% respectively) and the rules and regulations (24% vs. 38% respectively). Differences between the two prisons in perceptions of the staff, and in particular the even-handed application of rules and regulations, appeared and reappeared throughout our results. For example, when we asked the women whether most correctional officers "go by the rule book" when dealing with inmates, over one-half of the women at CIW agreed, relative to only 44% at VSP. We suspect that these institutional differences are linked to the fact that the two prisons have very different "work groups." As noted at the outset, many staff at CIW have worked in this institution all of their lives. They have seen tremendous change in the wardens and periodic dramatic fluctuations in the size of the inmate population. But the stability of the institution has given them a sense of security and purpose and a seemingly very professional demeanor. VSP, by contrast, is filled with young new correctional officers. For many this is their first job, or their first job in a female institution. They impart a no-nonsense military aura and, while they all indicate that moving from the violent atmosphere of a men's prison to the relative calm of a woman's prison is a relief, they still want you to know that they take their work seriously and they are ready for any problems the inmates might present.

Availability of Programs

Finally, the majority of women at both institutions bemoaned the lack of programs in the prisons. We compiled a list of programs from our interviews with women at both prisons who were serving on the inmate council, and from our interviews with staff. Although not all of these programs were simultaneously available or well staffed, they included the following: schooling/correspondence courses, vocational training, religious programs, parenting groups, individual counseling, peer counseling, abuse survivors group, 12-step chemical dependency programs, arts and crafts, community service, athletic teams, inmate council, and the literacy program. The availability of any given program and inmate participation in programs varied dramatically between the two prisons. At CIW close to one-half of our survey respondents indicated that they had participated in schooling (including correspondence courses), vocational training (including both job-related skills, such as electronics and data processing, and institutional maintenance, such as janitorial services), religious programs, 12-step programs for chemical dependency, and athletic teams. At VSP, the only program that the majority of women indicated they had participated in was religion.

We suspect that there are several reasons why women at CIW were more active participants in the available programs and complained less about their availability than the women at VSP. First, the greater participation of CIW inmates in a variety of programs is probably directly related to the fact that more women are serving life sentences at CIW (24%) than at VSP (11%). "Lifers" simply have more time to sample what is available in the institution and since most still hope to get released some day, and programming impresses the parole board, keeping busy is a high priority for them. Second, differences in the sheer size of the prison populations affects accessibility to programs. With some 3,600 inmates at VSP, it is extremely difficult for women to gain access to the available programs. In fact, when we asked why women hadn't enrolled in programs they expressed interest in, the majority of women at VSP indicated that it was because they were "waiting to get in them." By contrast, women at CIW indicated that the reason they were not taking a particular program of interest was because "they had no available free time." Finally, the difficulty of getting into programs may present a particularly acute problem for women at VSP who share their living quarters with seven other women, as opposed to the women at CIW who have only one cellmate.

CONCLUSION

What do we make of these obvious differences in the way female inmates are responding to prison life? In her influential book on the history of women's prisons in the United States, Nicole Rafter (1990) argued that the most powerful influence on women's prisons over the past two decades has been the rapid population increase and the concomitant crisis management approach. We agree. However, we would also add that this crisis management approach does not have the same effect on all institutions and all inmates. For those who have a vested interest in maintaining the status quo, it is unlikely that the applications of new rules and regulations will be complete or effective. At CIW, an institution disproportionately populated with "lifers" and with an entrenched group of correctional officers and administrators, there is little incentive to drastically disrupt practices that have been in place for a long time. So while the administration complies with the imposition of new rules from the Department of Corrections on, for example, inmate appearance (hair length, makeup, and clothing), they still maintain a fairly relaxed attitude about who is in the yard with inmates and the inmates' behavior on the yard. Simply put, they are much more willingly to treat the inmates as "individuals," and the inmates reciprocate in their individualization of correctional officers, noting that some are "very good" at their job. VSP has no such "buffer zone" for dealing with various aspects of the "new penology." With two new wardens in five years, a larger contingency of new correctional officers and administrators, and a much larger population of inmates, there is little or no room for individualization. These findings, showing contextual variation in response to changes in penality, are further supported by our analysis of the interviews we conducted with inmates at each prison (Kruttschnitt et al., 2000) and they suggest that we take seriously the observations of scholars who have suggested that both rehabilitative and managerial philosophies are operating, albeit to different degrees, in today's prisons. Perhaps, however, these contradictions remain more apparent in institutions for women where reforms are rarer and more often uneven in their application.

About the Authors

Candace Kruttschnitt, Ph.D., is Professor and Chair of the Department of Sociology at the University of Minnesota, Minneapolis. Rosemary Gartner, Ph.D., is Professor and Director of the Centre for Criminology at the University of Toronto.

References

Blumstein, A. & Beck, A.J., "Population Growth in U.S. Prisons, 1980-1996," in M. Tonry & J. Petersilia, (Eds.), *Prisons. Crime and Justice,* Vol. 26, pp. 17-61 (University of Chicago Press, 1995).

Dykes, R., Personal communication with the Associate Warden of the California Institution for Women (Frontera, Ca, July 17, 1995).

Faith, K., "Media, Myths, and Masculinization. Images of Women in Prison," in E. Adelberg & D. Currie, (Eds.), *Conflict With the Law: Women and the Canadian Criminal Justice System,* pp. 174-211 (Press Gang Publishers, 1993).

Feeley, M.M. & Simon, J., "The New Penology: Notes on the Emerging Strategy of Corrections and its Implications," 30 *Criminology* 449-474 (1992).

Kruttschnitt, Gartner, C. & Gartner, R., *Women in Prison in the 1990s: A Temporal and Institutional Comparison* (Final Report for the Law and Social Science Program, National Science Foundation, proposal #SBR-9617285, 2000).

Kruttschnitt, C., Gartner, R. & Miller, A., "Doing Her Own Time? Women's Responses to Prison in the Context of the Old and the New Penology, " 38 *Criminology* 681-718 (2000).

Lynch, M., "Waste Managers? The New Penology, Crime Fighting and Parole Agent Identity," 32 *Law and Society Review* 839-869 (1998).

Mandaraka-Sheppard, A., *The Dynamics of Aggression in Women's Prisons in England* (Gower, 1986).

Rafter, N.H., *Partial Justice: Women, Prisons and Social Control* (Transaction, 1990).

Silberman, M., "Review of the Rise and Fall of California's Radical Prison Movement," 24 *Contemporary Sociology* 94-95 (1995).

Tonry, M., "Why Are U.S. Incarceration Rates So High?" 45 *Crime and Delinquency* 419-437 (1999).

Zimring, R., *Prison Population and Criminal Justice Policy in California* (Institute of Government Studies Press, University of California Berkeley, 1992).

Chapter 4

Prisoner Reentry: Social Capital and Family Connections

by Creasie Finney Hairston, Ph.D. and James Rollin, Ph.D.

INTRODUCTION

Historically, policy debates on prisoners and criminal offenders have focused on their individual deficits and negative attributes and the problems they present for the general society. Recent policy discussions have broadened to include concerns about the concentration of large numbers of former prisoners in specific communities and the expected return home of hundreds of thousands of individuals imprisoned during the 1990s war on drugs to these same communities. The importance and urgency of the matter is heightened by the high recidivism rates among former prisoners and evidence that building more prisons is an extremely expensive policy option. Policymakers and program planners are, therefore, giving attention to identifying factors that may reduce recidivism and lessen the negative impact that returning prisoners have on their communities and to examining prisoners' strengths as well as deficits. In so doing, former prisoners' social capital has emerged as a topic of interest.

Generally, social capital refers to the ability of people to secure benefits by virtue of their membership in social networks or other social structures. (Portes, 1998). Discussions of prisoners' community reentry also use this broad definition and focus on identifying formal organizational structures and community services that can be used in the post-release environment to increase post-release success. Some researchers have observed that prisoners' families and friends are integral parts of their social networks and that net-

---

Note: An earlier version of this chapter appeared in Women, Girls & Criminal Justice, *Vol. 4, No. 5, August/September 2003.*

work development and asset building (social capital) after incarceration is not independent of the social assets that existed and were developed and maintained during incarceration.

Families and friends provide returning prisoners with basic necessities that are often the primary sources of emotional support and of information about community norms and activities, as well as how to get help (identification cards, bus passes, Medicaid) from other sources. Families' roles during incarceration are also significant. Several research studies indicate that men who maintain strong family ties during incarceration have higher rates of post release success than those who do not have such ties. In addition, those men who assume responsible family roles following incarceration have higher rates of post release success than those who do not assume those roles. (Hairston, 1988, 1991). Research also indicates that family functioning influences females' post release success. (Dowden & Andrews, 1999). At the same time family structures, bonds, and commitments are complex and diverse and change over time. Moreover, some family networks and living environments place returning prisoners at high risk of returning to prison on a technical violation or new criminal charge.

STUDY OF FAMILY CONNECTIONS DURING IMPRISONMENT

The central role that social capital occupies in newer ways of thinking about community reentry and the relevance of families and friends in the formation and use of social capital indicate the need for sound information about prisoners' family networks. At a minimum, social policies and programs ought to be informed by the realities and implications of prisoners' family connections or lack thereof. Toward this end, this study examines one aspect of prisoners' social capital, namely family connections during imprisonment. The study's focus is prisoners' visits, telephone calls, and mail and the extent to which these connections differ by race and gender.

Data for the study were obtained from the Bureau of Justice Statistics 1997 surveys of State and Federal prisoners ("Surveys of Inmates in State and Federal Correctional Facilities," 2000). Data for the surveys were collected from a nationally representative sample of prisoners during the months of June through October 1997. During personal interviews prisoners provided information about their criminal history, family background, prior drug and alcohol use and treatment, participation in prison activities, and contacts with children and other individuals external to the prison.

Our analysis is based on the responses of state prisoners only and includes men and women and black, white, and Hispanic respondents. This sample includes 12,633 individuals, 80% of whom were male and 20% female. Almost half (49%) were black; about a third (35%) were white and 17% were Hispanic. Most were not married at the time of the survey, and had never been married. Only 17% were currently married; 3% were widowed; 6% were separated for reasons other than incarceration, 19% were divorced, and 55% report never having married. Most (58%) had at least one minor child, more women (65%) than men (55%) had a minor child.

VISITING CONNECTIONS

Using visiting as an indicator of the strength of an individual prisoner's social assets, it is apparent that many prisoners lack the type of social capital that could provide a strong base of support upon release. Most prisoners do not see their families and friends on a regular basis. When asked how many visits, other than with attorneys, they had in the past month, about two-thirds indicated that no one had visited them. Although there were racial and gender differences, the majority of all races and of both men and women reported that no one had visited them in the past month. Men fared worse than women and whites were better off than other racial groups. Sixty-five percent of males and 62% of females did not have visits in the past month; 59% of whites, 67% of Hispanics, and 68% of blacks did not have visits in the past month. Only 52% of white women had no visitors. Black men (67%), Hispanic men (67%), and Hispanic women (68%) were the groups with the highest numbers of individuals who had no visitors.

In sharp contrast to the large number of prisoners who had no in-person contact at all with individuals from the "free world" is a small number of individuals who maintained regular and frequent contact with families and friends via prison visits. About 9% reported four or more visits (an average of one a week) in the past month. The number ranged from 6% to 13% and was highest for white women and lowest for Hispanic women. Other percentages were: white men, 10%; Hispanic men, 8%; black men, 7%; and black women, 7%.

Children as a Factor Determining Visits

Having minor children appears to be a social asset as the frequency of visits is related to prisoners' parental status. Sixty-two percent of prisoners with minor children, compared to 67% with no children, reported that they had not had a visit in the past month. With the exception of white women, prisoners with minor children in all categories of race and gender had the highest percentage of individuals who had received at least one visit in the past 30 days. (A higher percentage of white women with no children [53%] had at least one visitor than those with minor or adult children [47%].)

Impact of Prison Policies and Location

Visiting is shaped not only by individual preferences, but also by prison policies. Prison rules determine whether, and how often, prisoners can visit; who can visit; and the visiting schedule. Some prisons permit weekly visits on more than one day a week. Others restrict visiting to weekends or alternate weeks or days. Prison rules also dictate the placement of prisoners. Many prisons are located in remote locations that are inaccessible by public transportation; some prisoners are placed hundreds of miles away from their homes. The study data did not provide a means for assessing the influence of rules on visiting frequency. Information was provided, however, on how far prisoners were from their homes.

The distance prisoners were from their homes influenced the extent to which they saw family and friends. The farther prisoners were from their homes, the higher the percentage who had no visitors in the month preceding the survey. Of the prisoners whose homes at the time of their arrest were within 50 miles of the prison where they were placed, 46% did not have any visitors—compared with 56% who lived from 50 to 100 miles away; 70% who lived 101 to 500 miles away, and 84% who lived over 500 miles away. Those whose homes were closest to the prison had the most visits. Of the prisoners who lived within 50 miles of the prison, 20% reported having four or more visits compared with 12% for those living 50 to 100 miles away, 5% for those living 101 to 500 miles away, and 2% for those living more than 500 miles away. The negative association between miles from home and number of visits held for men and women as well as for different racial groups.

CONTACTS WITH CHILDREN

Incarcerated parents' visits with their minor children throughout imprisonment mirror the findings of the past months' contacts with any visitors. Most parents with minor children (54%) had never seen any of their children since they had been incarcerated. The number of parents who had not seen at least one of their children since entering prison is probably even higher given research which indicates that an incarcerated parent with two or more children often has different relationships with the different children. A parent may never see one child even though he or she communicates regularly with a second child who resides in another household (Hairston, 2001).

Females reported slightly higher contact with their minor children via visits than males. Fifty-five% of females, compared with 58% of males, indicated they had not seen their children since admission to prison. In contrast with no visits, 25% of females and 22% of males had visits at least monthly. Blacks visited more regularly with their children than other groups. Fewer blacks than other racial groups reported never having had a visit with their children since admission. The percentages of individuals reporting no visits were: blacks, 55%; whites, 60%; Hispanics, 61%. Among blacks, 24% had at least monthly visits versus 21% for Hispanics and 20% for whites. Black females had the highest percentage of at-least monthly visits with their minor children (28%), and white males the lowest (19%).

The majority of prisoners with minor children had been in contact with their children at least once by telephone since they had been committed. Women talked with their children more than men and blacks talked with their children more than other racial groups. Although prisoners must usually make telephone calls collect to the receiving party and the calls are very expensive, many families communicate regularly by telephone. Fifty-two percent of females and 42% of males had contact by telephone at least monthly. A little over one half (51%) of blacks, 39% of whites, and 36% of Hispanics talked with their children at least monthly. Twenty-five percent of males and 37% of females had weekly phone calls, as was the case with 32% of blacks, 25% of whites, and 21% of Hispanics. In contrast is the substantial number of parents of minor children who had never spoken with their children by telephone since being committed to prison. This number includes a higher percentage of males (41%) than females (31%) and a much higher percentage of Hispanics (49%) than whites (44%) or blacks (32%).

Communication by letter is the predominant mode of communication for many prisoners with 67% of females and 50% of males sending and/or receiving mail from their children at least monthly. There are slight differences among racial groups with 56% of blacks, 51% of whites, and 52% of Hispanics reporting monthly mail contact with children.

RETURNING HOME

Prisoners' personal situations and contacts with families and friends differ considerably. A small number of prisoners appear to have a strong social capital base upon which to draw when they are released from prison. They have maintained consistent contact with at least one relative or friend who has demonstrated care and concern for them. Evidence of that caring is reflected in the expenditure of the emotional, financial, and social resources required for visits, phone calls, and mail. These connected prisoners probably have some knowledge of family news and changes and of community life as experienced by those that they know intimately. They probably have a home to which to go. Time and resources have been invested in them and on their behalf and in that sense they have assets and working capital. With that investment, however, comes commitments and obligations and probably assumptions that upon their return home they will contribute to, rather than subtract from, family well being.

Many others, a majority, have not maintained community ties with any regularity and are likely to be in a very different situation upon release. If they have not burned their bridges, they will start in a very different place than their connected peers in rebuilding family and community ties. Their social assets, related to family connections, may be in a deficit situation. Their families have been either unwilling or unable to provide support during imprisonment and may be similarly disposed when the prisoner gets out.

The different levels of social capital that these different groups of returning prisoners have will, no doubt, demand different levels and types of support from the formal social organizations and governmental agents planning for prisoners' community reentry.

About the Authors

Creasie Finney Hairston, Ph.D., is Dean of the Jane Addams College of Social Work at the University of Illinois at Chicago. She received her doctorate in Social Welfare from Case Western Reserve University. She conducts research on the impact of incarceration on families and children. James E. Rollin, Ph.D., is an Assistant Professor at Jane Addams College of Social Work, University of Illinois at Chicago; he holds a doctorate from the Joint Program in Social Work & Social Science at the University of Michigan and is retired from Saginaw (Michigan) Police Department.

References

Dowden, C., & Andrews, D. A., "What Works for Female Offenders: A Meta-Analytic Review," 45(4) *Crime and Delinquency* 438-452 (1999).

Hairston, C. F., "Family Ties During Imprisonment: Do They Influence Future Criminal Activity." 52(1) *Federal Probation* 48-52 (1988).

Hairston, C. F., "Family Ties During Imprisonment: Important to Whom and for What?" 18(1) *Journal of Sociology and Social Welfare* 87-104 (1991).

Hairston, C. F., "Fathers in Prison: Responsible Fatherhood and Responsible Public Policies," 32(3/4) *Marriage and Family Review* 111-135 (2001).

Langan, P. A. & Levin, D. J., *Recidivism of Prisoners Released in 199,* (Report No. NCJ 193427), (Bureau of Justice Statistics, National Institute of Justice, U.S. Department of Justice, 2002).

Portes, A., "Social Capital: Its Origins and Applications in Modern Sociology," 24 *Annual Review of Sociology* 1-24 (1998).

"Surveys of Inmates in State and Federal Correctional Facilities, 1997," (2000), [Computer Files]. U.S. Dept Justice, Bureau of Justice Statistics, and U.S. Dept of Justice, Federal Bureau of Prisons. (ICPSR 2598) Compiled by the U.S. Dept of Commerce, Bureau of the Census. ICPSR ed. Ann Arbor, MI: Inter-university Consortium for Political and Social Research, [producer and distributor].

Chapter 5

Sexually Abused Women in State and Local Correctional Institutions, 1980-2000

by Kristine Mullendore, J.D. and Laurie Beever, J.D.

INTRODUCTION

"That was not part of my sentence, to ... perform oral sex with the officers."
New York Prisoner Tanya Ross, November 1998 (Amnesty International, March 1999 citing November 1, 1998 Dateline NBC interview.)

Sexual abuse is a well-documented problem that is shared by male and female inmates of correctional institutions run by state and local governments (Amnesty International, 1999; Human Rights Watch, 1996; General Accounting Office [GAO], 1999). However, the treatment of female inmates and the conditions of their confinement present unique and complex problems for correctional administrators and staff.

This chapter originally appeared in Women, Girls & Criminal Justice, *Vol. 1, No. 6, October/November 2000.*

The generally perceived and expected risk of sexual assault in correctional institutions is converted into a fact of institutional life for too many of the women and girls who are confined in these institutions whether they are there serving sentences or are pretrial detainees awaiting trial. *Women Prisoners v. District of Columbia*, 93 F.3d 910 (D.C.Cir. 1996). The severity of this problem is heightened by the fact that the number of female inmates in state and federal prisons has nearly doubled since 1990 (Bureau of Justice Statistics, 2000).

The attempts of female inmates to use the federal court system to hold their sexual abusers accountable have met with little success mirroring their treatment within the criminal justice system. This chapter examines lawsuits that illustrate the sexual abuse of women in state and local correctional institutions to identify some of the legal and social factors that contribute to the correctional environment that fails to protect female inmates from sexual misconduct by correctional staff.

PRISON CONDITIONS

"There should not be male guards in women's prisons. There should not be a male superintendent of a women's prison. Our statutes should not be construed to require such a mechanical suppression of the recognition that in our culture such a relation between men in power and women in prison leads to difficulties, temptations, abuse, and finally to cruel and unusual punishment." *Jordan v. Gardner*, 986 F.2d 1521 (9th Cir. 1993).

Inmates inhabit a world with conditions that differ dramatically from those found in free society. The normal operations of a prison or jail are premised on the assumption that the inmate must be maintained in custody. Inmates are, therefore, subjected to many interactions with each other as well as with correctional staff and administration that would be considered severe violations of civil and criminal law if committed by persons living freely in society. *Women Prisoners v. District of Columbia*, 93 F.3d 910 (D.C.Cir. 1996). As convicted persons, or pretrial detainees, inmates are expected to comply with all institutional policies and directives of correctional officers, as long as these policies and directives are aimed at the legitimate penological objective of maintaining the security and order of the institution. *Turner v. Safley*, 482 U.S. 78 (1987). The care, custody, and control of the inmates is assumed by the institution and its staff. The power is removed from those that are kept and conferred on those who keep (Robertson, 1999). The institution, therefore, takes on a legally imposed duty to protect inmates from themselves and other inmates and from mistreatment by the staff, while adequately providing for their daily needs. Because this legal duty places discretionary control in the hands of correctional staff, the staff becomes even more dominant and powerful and the inmates more subordinate and dependent. The inequitable nature of this relationship creates a great potential for the abuse and mistreatment of all inmates and contributes to an environment that, all too often, results in the sexual abuse of female inmates by their male guards.

Intense surveillance is required to achieve the goals of care, custody, and control and that surveillance creates an environment where there is only a "de minimis" expectation of privacy. *Hudson v. Palmer*, 468 U.S. 517 (1984). Inmates are exposed to visual monitoring by correctional officers. *Timm v. Gunter*, 917 F.2d 1093 (8th Cir. 1990), *cert. denied,*

501 U.S. 1209 (1991). This visual monitoring includes viewing them in states of undress while changing their clothes, showering and performing other acts of physical hygiene, using toilet facilities, and sleeping (Jurado, 1998/1999). Surveillance is often done by correctional officers of the opposite sex due to successful employment discrimination suits brought by male and female correctional officers (*Forts v. Ward,* 621 F.2d 1210 (2d Cir. 1980); Amnesty International, 1999). According to a 40-state survey conducted in 1997, male correctional officers account for approximately 41% of the officers dealing with female inmates (Amnesty International, 1999). Summarizing the obvious problems that arise, Collins and Collins note, "[t]he problem of sexual abuse of female inmates . . . may be attributed to permitting male officers to work in contact with female inmates . . ." (Collins & Collins, 1996).

In addition to intense surveillance, the bodily integrity of inmates is subject to searches that range from frisks of clothed inmates to strip searches and even (under administrative order) body cavity searches where warranted. *Bell v. Wolfish*, 441 U.S. 529 (1979). In fact, in one case where a male inmate challenged a random, visual body cavity search performed by two officers, the search was upheld as an appropriate institutional procedure. *Covino v. Patrissi,* 967 F.2d 73 (2d Cir. 1991). This lack of privacy is extended also to inmate personal belongings which are similarly exposed to being searched by correctional staff. *Hudson v. Palmer*, 468 U.S. 517 (1984).

Daily exposure to these admittedly necessary invasions of personal privacy desensitize all involved to the nature of the invasion. Tolerance of these necessary surveillance behaviors creates an environment where the sexual abuse of women is also tolerated. The risk and occurrence of sexual abuse becomes an accepted reality, especially since confinement simultaneously limits female inmate contacts with any one other than correctional staff. The "caretakers" or "keepers" who are subjecting them to the abuse are part of the same social group to whom they would complain.

CORRECTIONAL INSTITUTIONS' RESPONSE TO INMATE COMPLAINTS

> The District of Columbia has the duty not only to train its officers in matters relating to sexual contact between prison guards and inmates, but also has the responsibility to actively devise and implement a system of supervision of its first level corrections officers in accordance with the law. *Newby v. District of Columbia*, 1999 U.S. Dist. LEXIS 10428 (D.C. 1999).

Correctional institutions have options as to what type of system should be used to respond to allegations of sexual abuse. Since inmates are confined and therefore restricted to having contact only with permitted visitors or correctional staff, the first step in whatever process is used must be the same. That first step is to make a complaint within the institution. The institution then becomes the initial investigator of the validity of the complaint. After that first internal complaint and investigation is complete, one process option is to continue to handle complaints internally through a formal institutional grievance and personnel process. Another option is to refer the complaint outside the institution to the criminal justice system for prosecution in the courts (Amnesty International, 1999). Both of these processes have been ineffective in protecting female inmates.

PROCESSES WITHIN THE CORRECTIONAL INSTITUTION

Lack of Communication

Interviews with female inmates reveal that they have never received information about the administrative grievance processes or are ignorant of their existence (Human Rights Watch, 1996). Even when aware of the processes, they are reluctant to use them because the inmates lack confidence in the system and feel vulnerable (Human Rights Watch, 1996). Often the abuse reporting procedure meant to assist inmates is not appropriate for a variety of reasons that are attributable to the nature of the prison environment (Human Rights Watch, 1996). For example, during an Amnesty International visit to the California Valley State Prison for Women in 1998 inmates expressed reluctance to use prison drop boxes because of the appearance that they may be reporting other prisoners' misconduct (Amnesty International, 1999).

Perceived Failure to Respond

The perceived failure of prison officials to respond to complaints of staff-on-inmate sexual abuse contributes to the lack of inmate confidence in the prison complaint procedures (Amnesty International, March 1999). Determining the efficacy of the system's response to those complaints is further complicated because there is no systematic documentation of the sexual abuse complaints that are made. According to a General Accounting Office report, the "U.S. correctional systems still do not adequately capture or track data related to such allegations [of sexual misconduct]." This absence of data regarding sexual misconduct also hinders future attempts by correctional administrators to effectively handle cases of inmate abuse (GAO, 1999).

Fear of Retaliation and Feelings of Vulnerability

"[M]any sexual relationships appear to be unreported due to the presently widespread fear of retaliation and vulnerability felt by these women." This fear on the part of female inmates is well founded. Evidence demonstrates that female inmates have been subjected to sexual and physical assaults, intrusive searches, threats of physical or sexual abuse, and false reports of inmate misconduct after complaining of sexual abuse (Amnesty International, 1999). This risk is exacerbated by grievance processes, which often require that the inmates confront their abusers. (Human Rights Watch, 1996).

Reluctance to Report

Court cases confirm that female inmates are reluctant to come forward with allegations of sexual abuse. Abused inmates make comments to correctional staff or to other inmates in unofficial, informal contexts, but as a general rule they do not directly invoke the formal complaint procedure. In *Barney v. Pulsipher,* 143 F.3d 1299 (10th Cir. 1998), two female inmates brought an action under Section 1983 of the Civil Rights Act, 42 U.S.C.§1983 ("Section 1983"), against a correctional facility for sexual assault. One of the two plaintiffs, Barney, informed her drug counselor of her rape by the male correctional officer. The counselor then informed Barney's probation officer, who subsequently reported it to correctional administrators. Only after this report of Barney's assault, did the facility subsequently learn of the other plaintiff's earlier assault by the same officer. Similarly, in *Carrigan v. Delaware*, 957 F. Supp. 1376 (Del. 1997), a female inmate told another female inmate that a male correctional officer had raped her when he found her alone and asleep in her cell. The other female inmate assisted the inmate in bringing her complaint to the institution's attention. In *Thomas v. Galveston County*, 953 F. Supp. 163 (S.D.Texas 1997), a male correctional officer repeatedly engaged in the sexual assault of a female inmate including forcing her to perform oral sex over a five-month period before she reported it to a female correctional officer. This report triggered an investigation that revealed that other female inmates had also been sexually assaulted, but none of them had ever reported it to the jail administrator.

CRIMINAL JUSTICE RESPONSES

Studies indicate that when correctional institutions refer complaints to criminal law enforcement, the institution's internal investigation then ceases (Amnesty International, 1999; Human Rights Watch, 1996). Since no internal investigation continues, remedying the problem is left entirely in the hands of law enforcement officials (Human Rights Watch, 1996). In many cases, the substantiation of sexual abuse ultimately rests solely on the word of the female inmate against the word of the male officer denying it (Amnesty International, 1999). A female inmate in a Massachusetts's prison described the dilemma of reporting abuse by stating, "Most officers will tell you, 'go ahead and tell—it's your word against mine. Who are they gonna believe? I'm an officer, I have a badge on, I'm in a superior position to you'" (October 16, 1998 WBUR, Boston University, radio interview as quoted in Amnesty International, 1999). In addition to the fear of retaliation, female inmates fail to report sexual abuse because of the difficulty of proving that the abuse took place (Amnesty International, 1999).

Criminal prosecution is inhibited by the generally held belief that female inmates, who have been labeled the "bad girls" by society, have consented to the sexual activity. Often female inmates have incorporated society's bad girl label into their own self-images making them unlikely candidates to be effective users of the prison complaint procedures and these complaint procedures are the first step that triggers criminal prosecutions (Baro, 1997). Even in the context of a correctional environment that inhibits complaints, there is evidence of a "non-response" by the criminal justice system to those complaints that are made. A General Accounting Office study reveals that three of the four prison systems studied, the Federal Bureau of Prisons, and the state systems of California, and Texas, (the District of Columbia was the fourth), received over 500 internal allegations of sexual abuse during 1995 to 1998 of which only 92 resulted in some form of staff discipline or termination. According to prison officials, a "lack of evidence" (medical and physical) and false allegations explain the overall low percentage of sustained allegations of sexual abuse. Despite the fact that all four of the studied jurisdictions permitted the options of both criminal prosecution and employment termination, only the Federal Bureau of Prisons reported any criminal convictions and only 14 incidents resulted in convictions during the time frame under review (GAO, 1999).

Some states have amended their penal laws by eliminating one barrier to criminal prosecution through the removal of consent as a defense to claims of sexual relations between correctional officers and inmates, others have changed their treatment of this behavior as a crime by elevating its status from a misdemeanor to a felony. However, many states have not responded in this fashion. Legislation concerning sexual misconduct has failed in at least four states and no reforms in this area have been instituted in another 13 states. Michigan and Iowa, for example, proscribe the conduct as criminal, but classify it as a misdemeanor (U.S. Department of Justice, 1996). In Michigan, proposed legislation is under consideration which would amend its criminal sexual conduct code to make this behavior, previously classified as a two-year circuit court misdemeanor, a 15-year felony of criminal sexual conduct in the second degree (Michigan Penal Code, 750.520e, 1996; 2000 Michigan HB 4881).

Even when this type of proactive legislation has been enacted, meaningful change is not guaranteed. Prosecutors must still decide to bring charges, fact finders must decide to convict, and judges must seek to impose appropriately severe sentences (Baro, 1997). Addressing the cumulative effect of the failures of state officials to respond appropriately by creating, classifying, charging, convicting, and sentencing correctional officers who engage in this conduct as serious violators of criminal law is a crucial piece that is all too often missing in efforts to prevent the sexual abuse of female inmates.

CIVIL LITIGATION AND SEXUAL ABUSE CASES

The issue concerns the realities of human nature in situations where one individual occupies a position of substantial authority relative to another. The situations or, more accurately, relationships are myriad: supervisor to employee, military officer to soldier, guard to pre-trial detainee. Whatever the relationship, it is abundantly clear that our society is beginning to recognize these as potentially volatile situations [citations omitted]. *Scott v. Moore*, 114 F.3d 51 (5th Cir. 1997).

The use of civil litigation avoids many of the problems inherent to internal administrative complaint procedures and criminal prosecution. Perhaps the single most significant advantage to the use of civil litigation to remedy sexual abuse of female inmates is that the inmates, as the named plaintiffs, are able to exercise control of legal strategies. Also, unlike correctional grievance processes that are designed, staffed, and operated by correctional staff, the judicial branch offers an independent forum free of conflicting self-interest. And, unlike criminal cases, the female inmate is a named party whose claimed injuries to her legal interests are being determined by the court.

Plaintiffs in the federal courts have employed several legal theories to redress the sexual abuse of female inmates. These theories are presented under two causes of action: (1) Section 1983 of the Civil Rights Act of 187, 42 U.S.C. §1983 and (2) state tort laws. These causes of action have been brought before the federal courts with varying degrees of success.

Section 1983

Courts have recognized that female inmates have "a constitutional right to be secure in their bodily integrity and free from attack by prison guards." *Hovater v. Robinson*, 1 F.3d 1063, 1068 (10th Cir. 1993). Inmates may bring federal constitutional tort claims based on alleged violations of their First, Fourth, Eighth, and Fourteenth Amendment rights under Section 1983. In order to establish a Section 1983 claim, a plaintiff must establish the following three elements:

- That a person or persons,

- Acting under color of state law,

- Has deprived the plaintiff of one or more federally protected rights. *Thomas v. Galveston County*, 953 F. Supp. 163 (S.D. Texas, 1997).

Under Section 1983, female inmates can also allege that the sexual abuse they experienced at the hands of correctional staff was a violation of their constitutional rights, specifically:

- Their unlawful seizure as an excessive use of force in violation of the Eighth Amendment, *Hudson v. McMillian*, 503 U.S. 1 (1992);

- An invasion of their privacy, Jordan v. Gardner, 968 F.2d 1521 (9th Cir. 1992); and

- A violation of the Eighth Amendment cruel and unusual punishment prohibition when the sexual harassment creates conditions that fall below the "minimal civilized measures of life's necessities." *Farmer v. Brennan*, 511 U.S. 825 (1994); *Boddie v. Schnieder*, 105 F. 3d 857 (2d Cir. 1997).

In Eighth Amendment conditions of confinement claims, the unlawful condition of confinement must meet the same two-part objective and subjective standard used to evaluate any condition of confinement:

- A constitutional deprivation must be established that is sufficiently serious to justify court response by an objective standard; and

- The official being sued must have a sufficiently culpable state of mind. Farmer v. Brennan, 511 U.S. 825 (1994); *Boddie v. Schnieder,* 105 F. 3d 857 (2d Cir. 1997).

For sexual harassment cases to meet the first part of this standard, a single occurrence must be shown to be of sufficient severity, or there must be a repetitive nature to the conduct. *Harris v. Zappan,* 1999 U.S. Dist. 8404 (E.D.Pa. 1999); *Boddie v. Schnieder*, 105 F. 3d 857 (2d Cir. 1997).

To date, verbal sexual abuse alone, consisting of sexual innuendoes and gestures without any physical contact or other aggravating incident, has not been found to establish a sexual harassment claim for either male or female inmates. *Poe v. Haydon,* 853 F.2d 418 (6th Cir.1988); *Adkins v. Rodriguez,* 59 F.3d 1034 (10th Cir. 1995); *Blueford v. Prunty,* 108 F.3d 251 (9th Cir. 1997).

Under the second part of the *Farmer* standard, referred to as the subjective standard, a culpable state of mind may be established by "any relevant evidence" and can be demonstrated by proof either that an official had actual knowledge or through a showing of "deliberate indifference." *Farmer v. Brennan,* 511 U.S. 825, (1994). Deliberate indifference on the part of an official, which is a lesser degree of culpability than either knowing or purposeful conduct, can be proven by establishing the absence of proper supervision, training, and discipline. *Thomas v. District of Columbia*, 887 F. Supp. 1 (D.D.C.1995). It should be noted that this type of deliberate indifference is not equivalent to the deliberate indifference that must be shown in a qualified immunity defense by municipalities and other organizational entities.

Diversity and Pendent Claims Based on State Tort Law

Another theory is available under state tort laws, although litigated in the federal courts. Here inmates advance traditional law claims of personal injury for the sexual assault and battery as permitted by each state's tort laws. Since the state tort law claims may be brought within federal courts under federal diversity of citizenship and pendent jurisdiction theories, state courts have not played a significant role in inmate litigation. These state tort theories have been successfully employed to recover damages in federal court, even after losing under other claims made under federal law. *Downey v. Denton County,* 119 F.3d 381 (5th Cir. 1997). The state tort claims have a better chance of success then their federal counterparts under state law where states have waived their traditional common law immunity from liability for intentional acts. Since the time that the federal courts became active in hearing inmate lawsuits, they have been the court of preference for most inmate claims, a situation which contributed to the political drive to enact restrictions on access through Prison Litigation Reform Act of 1996 [PLRA] (42 U.S.C. §1997e). The success of these state tort claims in federal court further reinforces an inmate preference for bringing all potential claims in federal court.

PLRA has significantly impacted federal court access for inmate lawsuits for both state and federal inmates. Whatever the advantages with civil litigation, inmates may not elect it as their sole option. Under the PLRA, inmates are required to exhaust available grievance processes before filing a civil law suit. The PLRA also states that the federal courts can dismiss cases where immunity would prevent recovery of monetary relief. Therefore, the PLRA along with the qualified immunity doctrine present significant potential obstacles to female inmate's civil claims, especially since they face a difficult task of proving the abuse or harassment has violated a "clearly established right." *Galvan v. Carothers,* 855 F. Supp. 285 (Alaska, 1994).

LIMITED JUDICIAL REMEDIES

While prison officials are able to consent or agree to all types of reforms aimed at combating the problem of sexual abuse of female inmates, courts do not have the same freedom to remedy sexual abuse as do the parties themselves. The dilemma faced by the courts is that of how to remedy abuse while not usurping the government's function of running correctional institutions. Although courts are not in the business of running these institutions, they must ensure that the institutions do not violate the constitutional rights of inmates. The courts's task is complicated by the fact that court orders remedying abuse may need to be monitored yet the courts themselves cannot interfere with the government's authority to operate its prisons. The challenge to remedying abuse within the constraints of their powers is illustrated by *Women Prisoners v. District of Columbia,* 877 F. Supp. 634 (D.D.C. 1994). Here, female inmates complained, among other claims, that prison guards had sexually assaulted them. The District Court characterized the District of Columbia's Department of Corrections's (DCDC) lack of response to the inmates' allegations of sexual misconduct as "most disturbing" in finding that the defendants were deliberately indifferent to the sexual harassment of female inmates in violation of the Eighth Amendment. Evidence revealed that the prisoners who complained of abuse had "little cause for hope because investigations are not taken seriously." Defendants responded "slowly and superficially" to inmate complaints and failed to keep the complaints confidential. The court determined that the policies and procedures dealing with sexual misconduct had "little value" because of the DCDC addressed "the problem of sexual harassment of women prisoners with no specific staff training, inconsistent reporting practices, cursory investigations and timid sanctions." For example, the DCDC would require written reports from inmates regarding their allegations of sexual abuse. As the court aptly noted, this presents "an obstacle for illiterate women who wish to file a complaint." Due to the DCDC's pattern of deliberate indifference to the sexual harassment of inmates, the district court ordered the following: implementation of specific inmate grievance procedures, prohibition of officer retaliation for inmate reports of sexual harassment, and appointment of a Special Officer from the district court staff to monitor allegations of abuse.

While the District of Columbia conceded to the fact that they had failed to protect female inmates from abuse, they appealed the appointment of a Special Officer of the district court monitoring sexual harassment complaints as an abuse of the court's discretion. *Women Prisoners v. District of Columbia*, 93 F.3d 910 (D.C.Cir. 1996). Specifically, the DCDC accused the District Court of performing a non-judicial, local government function when it ordered that a Special Officer of the district court investigate complaints of inmate sexual harassment within the prison. The appellate court agreed that the District Court overstepped its authority and subsequently vacated the portion of the order that directed the appointment of a Special Officer.

Although a court's remedies for sexual abuse may be somewhat limited, courts still have the ability to make corrections officials accountable for their failure to comply with the spirit of court orders. In *Newby v. District of Columbia*, 1999 U.S. Dist. LEXIS 10428 (D.C. 1999), the court found the District of Columbia guilty for violating the Eighth Amendment as a matter of law (without a trial) based on its continued maintenance of "a government custom of sexual harassment in the three D.C. correctional facilities" even though there were "existing official policies prohibiting such behavior" (p. 5). The *Newby* case, which was decided after *Women Prisoners*, relied on the fact that the District of Columbia was under an existing court order to "take remedial steps to put an end to, and prevent in the future, the gross abuses of the rights of female prisoners."

In *Newby*, evidence revealed that the DCDC male guards continued to engage in unlawful sexual activity with female inmates just seven months after the district court had ordered changes in prison policies and procedures to remedy such abuse. The evidence of ongoing sexual abuse came to light when an inmate, Jacquelyn Newby, filed a Section 1983 claim against the DCDC alleging that male guards forced the inmates to participate in strip-shows and exotic dancing. Although the *Newby* court acknowledged the DCDC's compliance with the district court's order to implement specific policies and procedures to combat the abuse complained of in *Women Prisoners,* it found that the District of Columbia "did little else to ensure the cessation of guards engaging in proscribed activities with inmates."

In finding, as a matter of law, that the District of Columbia violated the inmates' constitutional rights the court in *Newby* declared that the District had either "endorsed such violative activities or actually participated in them by failing to actively supervise its prison facilities." As a result of the violation of the inmates' rights, the court submitted only the issue of monetary damages to a jury. The court's decision in *Newby* relied heavily on the District of Columbia's failure to take affirmative steps to correct the abuse of inmates despite its awareness of the problem of sexual abuse in its correctional facilities.

Federal courts also acknowledge the importance of taking into account the state prison officials' awareness of, and reaction to, allegations of sexual abuse of female inmates by male guards. One example is when inmate Amy Fisher brought a civil suit against the prison officials at Albion in New York State, claiming that they did not follow up on her allegations of sexual abuse by male prison guards. *Fisher v. Goord,* 981 F. Supp. 140 (W.D.N.Y.1997). Fisher's motion for a preliminary injunction against the prison officials was denied because the court failed to find Fisher to be a credible witness. In the course of its rulings, however, it detailed many aspects of the correctional administrator's actions that caused the court to find conditions at the Albion prison to be "not right." Evidence was admitted from credible sources indicating that voluntary sexual relations between inmates, and between inmates and staff, were common at Albion and that male correctional officers "grope inmates while frisking." The court specifically stated that the denial of Fisher's motion "should not be viewed as a ringing endorsement of the situation at Albion." In its decision, the court stressed "how important it is for the defendant prison officials to investigate fully and thoroughly these matters and to take immediate and appropriate remedial action, where required."

MERE NON-COMPLIANCE WITH INTERNAL POLICIES NOT ACTIONABLE

While courts will hold prison officials accountable for not responding to inmate allegations of sexual abuse, officials' mere noncompliance with the institution's own policies may not be used as evidence that officials knew of a risk of abuse to inmates. In *Hovater v. Robinson*, 1 F. 3d 1063 (10th Cir. 1993), an inmate prevailed at trial by arguing that the institution's escort policy (requiring that a male guard not be permitted to have unsupervised care of a female inmate) was in itself evidence of the institution's knowledge of the risk to female inmates of assault from male correctional officers when left alone together. However, the appellate court overruled the trial court, finding that there was no evidence on the record to support the conclusions that a female inmate is always at risk to her "bodily integrity" when the two are left alone. The court clearly stated that the "mere existence of the policy at issue does not establish an obvious risk that females left alone with male guards are likely to be assaulted" and noted that constitutional violations cannot be established by a reliance on unsupported assumptions.

Similarly, in *Barney v. Pulsipher*, 143 F. 3d 1299 (10th Cir. 1998), female inmates claimed that the correctional institution's policy of "requiring two jailers to be present when female prisoners were removed from their cell. . . [reflected] . . . defendants' understanding that a substantial risk of sexual misconduct to female inmates existed when only one male jailer was present." Again, the court of appeals rejected the argument that an institution's policy alone could be used to prove defendants' knowledge of a substantial risk of harm to inmates in violation of the Eighth Amendment. The court stressed the need for evidence of a risk to inmates if left alone with jailers or evidence of past sexual misconduct by the jailers to prove defendants' knowledge of a substantial risk of harm.

Although courts will not rely on "unsupported assumptions" as proof of evidence of an obvious risk of sexual abuse to inmates, courts have shown a willingness to look outside to expert witnesses to establish evidence supporting inmate claims. In *Jordan v. Gardner*, 986 F. 2d 1521 (9th Cir 1992), female inmates brought a civil suit against the officials at the Washington Corrections Center for Women (WCCW) under Section 1983 after the WCCW implemented a new policy "requiring male guards to conduct random, nonemergency, suspicionless clothed body searches on female prisoners." The District Court found that the WCCW policy violated the inmates' Eighth Amendment rights and issued a permanent injunction enjoining the routine cross-gender pat down. The appellate court, in upholding the district court's decision, discussed at length the testimony presented by psychologists, social workers, and others on the "psychological impact of forced submissions' to the male guards." Social science experts played a crucial role in establishing evidence for the inmate sexual abuse claims. The appellate court noted that the female inmates' histories of sexual or physical abuse by men supported the district court's finding that female inmates react differently than male inmates to cross-gender searches. Due to this testimony on the impact of the pat-down searches on female inmates the court found a high probability of harm to some inmates even if the searches are "properly conducted." As a result of the *Jordan* case, the Washington State Correction's policy on "pat-down" searches now requires routine searches of female inmates to be conducted by female officers except in defined cases of an emergency (National Institute of Corrections, 1998.)

Ironically, the Washington Corrections Center for Women instituted the cross-gender pat-down searches complained of in *Jordan* to avoid potential litigation by female correctional officers who had traditionally conducted all such searches. *Jordan v. Gardner*, 986 F. 2d 1521 (9th Cir 1992). One year prior to the implementation of the cross-gender pat-down policy, female guards had filed a grievance against the same-gender search policy because the female guards, who were the only ones who could conduct the routine searches, were disturbed during meal breaks to perform these searches. The administration's fear of a lawsuit by female guards may have been based in part on the fact that the female guards could have claimed a violation of the Equal Protection clause, since the Equal Protection clause requires public institutions to treat male and female officers in a like manner when the gender-based groups are similarly situated (Stollman, 1994).

STATE PROHIBITION OF SEXUAL RELATIONS BETWEEN INMATES AND CORRECTIONS STAFF

Judicial treatment of the power discrepancy between inmates and correctional officers in civil lawsuits appears to be strongly influenced by the individual state criminal laws regulating sexual relations between guards and inmates. In *Fisher v. Goord*, 981 F. Supp. 140 (W.D.N.Y. 1997), the judge specifically noted that, while he agreed that the differential of power between inmate and guard should be considered as a factor in sexual abuse claims of female inmates, he was aware of no case law or statutory authority that an inmate could not consent as a matter of law. He noted that a law making this conduct statutory rape had been enacted by New York after the time frame when the sexual conduct involving Amy Fisher occurred and found this to be an indication that inmates could consent to sexual contact before the law was passed. The judge indicated his agreement with the public policy behind such criminal laws stating that it

> ...draws a "bright line" between acceptable and unacceptable conduct. Sexual interaction between correction officers and inmates, no matter how voluntary, are totally incompatible with the order and discipline required in a prison setting. Further, the Court is disturbed by the notion that an inmate might feel compelled to perform sexual favors for correction officers in order to be on the officer's "good side." Such quid pro quo behavior is inappropriate,

despicable and serves no legitimate penological purpose. *Fisher v. Goord*, 981 F. Supp. 140, 175 (W.D.N.Y. 1997)

Freitas v. Ault, 109 F. 3d 1335 (8th Cir. 1997), supports the conclusion that a government statement that this conduct is prohibited by criminal law and punished at the felony level as a serious crime will positively impact on a court's determination of the seriousness of the underlying conduct. In *Freitas*, a male inmate sued a female correctional officer in a Section 1983 action. The court found that since the sexual behavior was consensual it did not establish an Eighth Amendment claim. However, it is of interest to note that at that time Iowa, where the institution was located, graded such conduct in its criminal code as only an aggravated misdemeanor (U.S. Department of Justice, November 1996). The *de minimis* view of the injury to the male inmate is a reflection of the *de minimis* view of the nature of the crime that the state had identified.

CONCLUSION

Defendants claim that there is no evidence regarding minimal standards of privacy and decency for a woman inmate. The court finds this statement to be fantastic. Though prisoner's rights must give way to valid penological concerns, plaintiff's status as an inmate impacts not the least on the minimal standards of privacy and decency in the area of sexual harassment. [Citations omitted] The court finds that minimal standards of privacy and decency include the right not to be subject to sexual advances, to use the toilet without being observed by members of the opposite sex, and to shower without being observed by members of the opposite sex. *Galvan v. Carothers*, 855 F. Supp 285, 289 (Alaska,1994)

Despite the efforts of advocates for female inmates sexual abuse in U.S. correctional facilities remains unabated. Media reports of both civil and criminal pending litigation as well as governmental agency investigations of the abuse of female inmates discloses the vast nature of this continuing violation of human rights.

Civil law suits permit female inmates to maintain control of the legal strategy in the suits rather than having to rely on the abilities and discretionary choices of a public prosecutor. When this control is coupled with the lower standard of burden of proof in civil lawsuits, some of the obstacles to developing successful litigation strategies are removed and the chances of success increased.

Advocates for female inmates should continue to work for state legislation criminalizing this behavior at the felony level as well as for the removal of consent as a defense to these charges. As discussed earlier, the courts use such criminal laws as public policy statements in applying sexual abuse and harassment laws to female inmate lawsuits. Where these criminal laws do not reinforce protection of the female inmate, civil litigation is undermined.

The most critical area for reform by correctional administrators is internal grievance procedures. The unduly burdensome provisions of the PLRA, which require an inmate to exhaust the seriously flawed internal grievance procedures before external remedies can be pursued, serve to defeat many inmates before their cases have ever been heard by independent tribunals. Until reforms are instituted, other methods which provide access to the courts may have to be employed. In fact, recent inmate lawsuits have prompted (by settlement or court order) various prison systems to implement new procedures for reporting and responding to allegations of staff-on-inmate sexual abuse (Amnesty International, 1999). For example, the Federal Bureau of Prisons now provides the Inspector General's telephone number to all inmates so that sexual abuse can be reported to an office outside the prison itself (Amnesty International, 1999). The District of Columbia Department of Corrections now provides a 24-hour hotline to report, in confidence, staff-on-inmate abuse (GAO, 1999). These innovative alternative approaches have started to improve female inmate access to the justice system.

Improved documentation of inmate allegations and the official follow-up, including imposition of employee sanctions, and initiation of criminal prosecution, where appropriate, would serve the dual purpose of improving the integrity of the internal grievance procedures in the eyes of the aggrieved inmate and changing the cultural tolerance of this behavior. Inmate complaints should be confidential. Claims of sexual abuse should be investigated immediately, before evidence is lost, as they are when investigated in a free society. Similarly, investigators of these complaints should be appropriately trained in evidence gathering and the interviewing techniques that are unique to this type of crime. Hearing officers should be external to the correctional institution and should also be trained to understand how sexual abuse impacts the victim.

If all of these reforms are instituted then, perhaps, the historical problem of sexual abuse and institutional victimization of female inmates may be abated. It is only through such concerted efforts that any long lasting changes will be effected. Sexual abuse should not be accepted as just one of those risks that comes with incarceration.

About the Authors

Kristine Mullendore, J.D., is a professor at the School of Criminal Justice/Legal Studies at Grand Valley State University, Grand Rapids, Michigan. Laurie Beever, J.D., an attorney living in New Hampshire, is currently an at-home mother.

References

Amnesty International's Campaign on the United States, *Not Part of My Sentence: Violations of the Human Rights of Women in Custody*, (March 1999).

Baro, A., "Spheres of Consent: An Analysis of the Sexual Abuse and Exploitation of Women Incarcerated in the State of Hawaii,"8(3) *Women and Criminal Justice* 61-84 (1997).

Bureau of Justice Statistics, "Prison and Jail Inmates at Midyear 1999," (NCJ 181643) (U.S. Department of Justice, April, 2000).

Collins, W. & Collins, A. W., "Women in Jail: Legal Issues," (National Institute of Corrections, U.S. Department of Justice, December, 1996).

General Accounting Office (GAO), "Women in Prison: Sexual Misconduct by Correctional Staff," (GAO/GGD-99-104) (U.S. Government Printing Office, 1999).

Human Rights Watch, *"All Too Familiar: Sexual Abuse of Women in U.S. Prisons,"* (1996).

Jurado, R., "Essence of Her Womanhood: Defining the Privacy Rights of Women Prisoners and the Employment Rights of Women Guards," 7 *Am. U. J. Gender Soc. Pol'y & L* 1-51 (1998/1999).

National Institute of Corrections, "Current Issues in the Operation of Women's Prisons,"(September, 1998).

Robertson, J. E., "Cruel and Unusual Punishment in United States Prisons: Sexual Harassment Among Male Inmates," 36 *Am. Crim. L. Rev* 1–585 (1999).

Stollman, D. J., "Comment: *Jordan v. Gardner*: Female Prisoners' Rights to be Free From Random, Cross-Gender Clothed Body Searches," 62 *Fordham L. Rev.* 1877-1910 (1994).

United States Department of Justice, "Sexual Misconduct in Prisons: Law, Agency Response, and Prevention," (November, 1996).

Chapter 6

The Impact of the Drug War on Women: A Comparative Analysis in Three States

by Marc Mauer, M.S.W., Cathy Potler, J.D. and Richard Wolf, J.D.

INTRODUCTION

In November, 1999, The Sentencing Project published a report, "Gender And Justice: Women, Drugs and Sentencing Policy," which contains the findings of a multi-year study we conducted on how the criminal justice system has responded to drug abuse and crime by women. That report, the key findings of which are summarized here, includes a national overview of the issues as well as a focus on three states. This chapter reports on the trends we found in New York, California, and Minnesota.

While national data are revealing in discerning trends, they can obscure what may be considerable variation among individual cities and states. Crime and the response to crime

---

This chapter originally appeared in Women, Girls & Criminal Justice, *Vol. 1, No. 2, February/March 2000.*

are local phenomena in many respects and communities and policymakers in different parts of the country may adopt different approaches to these issues.

The three states examined have been selected for a variety of reasons. They are geographically diverse and so provide some sense of the variation in approach to these issues nationally. They also have adopted distinctive legislative approaches to sentencing, which may affect the issues being examined here. In New York, the "Rockefeller Drug Laws" enacted in 1973, have long been regarded as among the nation's harshest. They eliminate most judicial discretion in sentencing by requiring lengthy mandatory minimum sentences for many first-time offenders, and are augmented by other provisions that call for enhanced mandatory minimum sentences for second- and persistent offenders. For example, sale of two ounces or possession of four ounces of a narcotic drug are felonies subject to a mandatory minimum sentence of 15 years. This penalty applies regardless of an offender's role in the drug trade or any other extenuating circumstances.

Under California's determinate sentencing format, adopted in 1976, judges have limited discretion. The legislature has set three fixed-term sentence-length options for each offense. The presumptive sentence is the mid-length term, but judges may impose either the higher or lower option upon finding aggravating or mitigating circumstances. In 1994, California adopted a "three strikes and you're out" law which is the broadest and harshest such policy in the nation. Under its provisions, conviction on any felony following two prior serious felony convictions can result in a sentence of 25 years to life. The law also requires that conviction of a second felony results in a doubling of the prison term. The U.S. Supreme Court recently declined to review a California three strikes case of an offender serving 25 years to life for the theft of a $20 bottle of vitamins from a grocery store. Although most of the data analyzed for our study reflect cases brought prior to the adoption of the three strikes law, the law is now having a substantial impact on sentencing patterns and inmate populations.

In 1980, Minnesota established a sentencing guidelines system under which sentences are determined through a sentencing "grid" based upon the severity of the offense and the offender's prior record. Designed to enable the state to control the growth of the prison system, the guidelines system restricts judicial discretion but does not eliminate it. Judges may depart from the presumptive sentence for an offender if they can document the aggravating or mitigating factors giving rise to the departure.

Our findings are summarized in Exhibit 6.1, and detailed in the sections that follow.

NEW YORK: DRUG-DRIVEN CRIMINAL JUSTICE SYSTEM OFFERS STARK CHANGES FOR FEMALE ARRESTEES AND OFFENDERS

Of the three states examined in this study, and quite likely of all states, New York presents the starkest picture of a criminal justice system driven by drug policies for the period 1986–1995. The 10-year period is marked by dramatic changes in women's rates of arrest, conviction, and incarceration, the vast majority of it fueled by drug arrests and sentences. Further, the female drug offenders entering the criminal justice system are virtually all members of racial and ethnic minorities. By the close of the 10-year period, twice as many women were being arrested for drug offenses. Those women arrested for drug offenses were substantially more likely to be convicted and for those convicted, the odds of receiving a prison term rose dramatically. In 1986, one of every 20 women arrested for a drug offense was sentenced to prison. By 1995, that ratio had increased to one in seven.

Exhibit 6.1: Key Findings of the Sentencing Project's Report

Drug Offenses and Women's Incarceration Drug offenses accounted for half (49%) of the rise in the number of women incarcerated in state prisons from 1986 to 1996, compared to one-third (32%) of the increase for men.

The number of women incarcerated in state prisons for a drug offense rose by 888% from 1986 to 1996, in contrast to a rise of 129% for non-drug offenses. Drug offenses account for a dramatic proportion of the rise in the number of women sentenced to prison from 1986 to 1995:

- 91% of the increase in New York

- 55% of the increase in California

- 26% of the increase in Minnesota

Women drug offenders in 1995 were more likely to be sentenced to prison than in 1986. In contrast to a rise in drug convictions of 256% and 177% in New York and Minnesota respectively, the increase in prison sentences for drug offenses was considerably higher, 487% in New York and 400% in Minnesota.

State Variations

Whereas drug offenses accounted for 63% of the increase in women's arrests in New York from 1986 to 1995, they represented just 10% of the rise in Minnesota. In New York, Hispanic women constituted 44% of women sentenced to prison for drug offenses in 1995, compared to only 14% of the state's population, while in California, Hispanic women represented 25% of the drug prison sentences compared to their 31% share of the total population.

Minority Women and Drug Offenses

Minority women (black and Hispanic) represent a disproportionate share of the women sentenced to prison for a drug offense:

- New York: 91% of prison sentences for drugs compared to 32% of state population

- California: 54% of prison sentences for drugs compared to 38% of state population

- Minnesota: 27% of prison sentences for drugs compared to 5% of state population

82% of the Hispanic women sentenced to prison in New York in 1995 were convicted of a drug offense, as were 65% of black women and 40% of white women.

Increase in Drug Arrests

During the study period, nearly two million people were arrested for a felony offense in New York, of whom 13% (245,000) were women and 87% (1.7 million) men. Women's arrests rose at more than double the rate for men from 1986 to 1995, 31% versus 13%. The impact of drug offenses can be seen in the fact that while total arrests increased by 15% from 1986 to 1995, drug arrests rose by 61% during this period.

While drug arrests rose for all demographic groups the rate for women increased at nearly double the rate for men. The number of women arrested for a felony drug charge grew by 98%, from 4,263 in 1986 to 8,432 in 1995, while the rate for men increased by 55%, from 29,964 in 1986 to 46,429 in 1995. Overall, drugs constituted nearly two-thirds (63%) of the increase in female arrests from 1986–1995.

Among the women arrested for drug offenses, the vast majority, 86%, were racial and ethnic minorities. Black women constituted 52% of drug arrests and Hispanic women 34%. Among minority women, drug offenses represented the most substantial category of arrests: half (49%) of all Hispanic women's arrests were for drugs and a third (31%) of black women's arrests, compared to 17% of white women's arrests.

Increase in Drug Convictions

While one would expect the number of women's drug convictions to have risen along with the increase in arrests over this 10-year period, in fact women's drug convictions rose at a substantially faster rate. The number of women convicted of drug offenses rose by 256%, from 873 to 3,108, compared to the 98% rise in arrests (and an increase in male drug convictions of 148%). Of the total increase in women's convictions from 1986 to 1995, drug offenses accounted for 82%.

For the period as a whole, black and Hispanic women accounted for nine out of 10 (89%) female drug convictions, 47% and 42% respectively. The dramatic impact of the drug convictions on Hispanic women can be seen in the fact that drug offenses account-ed for 77% of all felony convictions of Hispanic women during this period.

Prison Sentences

In parallel with the rise in the number of women in earlier stages of the justice system, the number of women sentenced to prison in New York increased dramatically as well during this period. By 1995, 156% more women received prison sentences than in 1986, compared to a 49% increase for men during this time. For the entire 10-year period, black and Hispanic women represented 87% of all female commitments. Perhaps most dramatic is the role of drug offenses in the rising women's prison population, with drug offenses con-stituting 91% of the 1,114 additional prison commitments in 1995 over 1986. While the men's prison sentence increase also resulted almost exclusively from drug offenses, the scale of the increase for women was more than double that of men, 487% rise in female drug commitments over 10 years compared to a 203% increase for men. Overall, drug offenses as a proportion of all female commitments rose from just over one in four (29%) in 1986 to two in three (67%) by 1995. The corresponding increase for men was from one in five (21%) to two in five (44%).

The racial and ethnic impact of drug policies in New York can be seen most dramati-cally in sentencing patterns for women drug offenders. Four out of five (82%) Hispanic women sentenced to prison in 1995 were convicted of drug charges, as were two out of three (65%) black women. Drug offenses accounted for a substantial portion of commitments for white women as well—40%—but not on the same scale as for minorities. Overall, black women accounted for 47% of female drug sentences and Hispanic women for 44%.

As a result of the cumulative impact of law enforcement and sentencing policies, New York's prison population grew substantially in the study period and reflected the increasing emphasis on prosecuting drug offenders. By January 1, 1997, there were 69,646 inmates in the state prison system, of whom 5.4% (3,735) were women. One in three (32%) male prisoners were serving drug sentences, but six of every 10 (61%) women in New York state prisons were serving sentences for drug convictions. Overall 77% of Hispanic women inmates were incarcerated for a drug crime, 59% of black women, and 34% of white women.

Impact of Sentencing Policies

The combination of New York's Rockefeller Drug Laws and repeat felony offender laws have had a dramatic impact on women. Since women offenders in New York are more likely than men to have been convicted and imprisoned for a drug offense, they are more likely to be subject to the state's harsh mandatory sentencing laws. Further, minority women are disproportionately affected since, as we have seen, the overwhelming majority of women sentenced to prison for drug offenses are black and Hispanic.

CALIFORNIA: GETTING TOUGH ON CRIME AND GREATLY EXPANDING THE PRISON SYSTEM

The 1986–1995 period was a significant one for criminal justice policy in California. Building on an increasingly "tough on crime" political environment that began in the early 1980s, the state engaged in a massive expansion of its prison system that resulted in a 532% increase in its inmate population, from 25,000 in 1980 to 158,000 in 1997—nearly double the national increase of 278%. The influence of drug offenses, though significant, was not nearly as overwhelming as in New York, although the growth of the numbers of women offenders in the system far outpaced that of men, and drug offenses disproportionately contributed to that rise.

The pattern for minority women diverges significantly from that seen in New York. Black women experienced a substantial rise in the criminal justice system during this time period but Hispanic women far less so. Further, in some regards, the growth in the number of white women entering the criminal justice system for drug offenses is most divergent from trends in other states.

Increase in Drug Arrests

Women accounted for 15% of California's total of 5.5 million arrests during the 10-year period. Women's arrests rose at nearly three times the rate of men's, by 40% compared to 14%. While the total number of arrests in California increased at approximately the same rate as in New York (17% compared to 15%) from 1986 to 1995, the increase in California was not primarily fueled by drug offenses, which rose by only 7%.

A gender breakdown again reveals the disproportionate impact that the drug war has had on women. While drug arrests overall increased by 7% in the 10-year period, the rate of increase for women was 10 times that for men, a 31% rise for women compared to 3% for men. Drug offenses accounted for 24% of the increase in women's arrests over this period, compared to 6% for men. Further, drug offenses constituted 31% of women's total arrests for this period, compared to 26% for men.

A racial/ethnic breakdown of women's drug arrests reveals patterns significantly different from those found in New York. While minorities represent half of female drug arrests for the period, this is not nearly as pronounced as in New York. Further, while arrests of African Americans are clearly disproportionately high—black women represent 7% of the female population but 27% of drug arrests—the figures for Hispanic women show that they are arrested at lower rates (20%) than their 30% share of the female population. The most substantial growth in female drug arrests over the period is for white women, who experienced a 48% increase, compared to 20% for Hispanic women and 6% for black women.

Prison Sentences

Over the course of the 10-year period, the number of offenders sentenced to prison each year more than doubled, from 31,265 to 65,939. The increase for women far outpaced that for men, 149% increase compared to 108%. For the entire study period, minority women represented nearly two-thirds (63%) of all female prison sentences.

The impact of drug sentences on these trends is quite significant as well. While the total number of women sentenced to prison between 1986 and 1995 increased by 149%, the number sentenced for a drug offense increased by 316%, compared to an increase of 223% for men. Given that drug arrests rose by only 31% over these 10 years, we see a remarkably increased propensity to incarcerate women for drug offenses, rising fully 10 times faster than the increase in arrests.

Overall, drug offenses accounted for half (55%) of the increase in the number of prison terms for women, compared to 46% for men, and represented 40% of all female prison commitments for the study period. By 1995, drug offenses constituted 43% of women's prison sentences compared to 34% for men.

The rate of increase in prison terms for drug offenses was very dramatic for black and white women—635% and 408% respectively—but considerably less so for Hispanic women (157%). For the 10-year period as a whole, black and Hispanic women comprised 60% of all prison commitments for drug offenses. By 1995, more than two out of five (43%) women sentenced to prison had been convicted of a drug offense: 46% of white women, 39% of black women, and 47% of Hispanic women.

On December 31, 1997, women represented 7% (10,281) of the total of 152,225 inmates in the California prison system. About 70% of all inmates were minorities. Women were significantly more likely than men to be serving a prison term for a drug offense, with 42% of women and 26% of men incarcerated for a drug offense. Of the women imprisoned for drug offenses, 58% were black or Hispanic.

Impact of Sentencing Policies

One of the most striking aspects of the changes in the criminal justice system in California as it applies to women in the decade under review is the dramatic 316% increase in the number of women sentenced to prison for drug offenses, 10 times the rate of increase for women arrested for these offenses. Thus, increases in offending do not explain the change that we observe, but rather a greatly increased likelihood that arrests and convictions will lead to a prison term.

The adoption of determinate sentencing in California in the 1980s has been a key factor in contributing to increased imprisonment rates for women. Criminologist Meda Chesney-Lind describes how, in establishing norms for sentencing in such a system, data rely on the overwhelming number of men in the court system and then apply these standards to women, without any consideration that there may be justifiable reasons for different punishments imposed on men and women. She noted that the determinate sentencing law "used the averaging approach, one consequence of which was to markedly increase the sentences of women—especially for violent offenses."

Within the determinate sentencing structure there are three sentencing options for judges: low, middle, and high terms for each offense. Judges are expected to sentence at the middle level unless they find aggravating or mitigating circumstances in the case.

An analysis of sentencing practices in drug cases for the period reveals that minority women were more likely than white women to be sentenced at the lowest permissible level for drug offenses, 64% compared to 56%. This was true for men as well, although men were somewhat less likely to be sentenced at the lower level: 59% for minority men and 48% for white men.

The lesser sentences imposed on minority women could be evidence of greater leniency in the courts, but could also be a consequence of other factors. As criminologist Michael Tonry has documented, "Urban black Americans ... have been arrested, prosecuted, convicted, and imprisoned at increasing rates since the 1980s, and grossly out of proportion to their numbers in the general population or among drug users." If more blacks are arrested for drug offenses it is likely that on average they will represent increasingly less serious offenses. This is because the number of drug "kingpins" is relatively modest, while there are far more lower-level users and sellers who may become targets of law enforcement. If this is the case then at the time of sentencing minority women's convictions for possessing or selling drugs may on average involve smaller quantities of drugs than for whites and so result in lower level sentences. Similar dynamics could be at work in the contrast between male and female drug sentences. A host of factors relating to the severity of the offense, prior record, and individual circumstances would need to be evaluated to make a full assessment of this issue.

MINNESOTA: CRIMINAL JUSTICE SYSTEM ALLOWS FOR LOW INCARCERATION LEVELS

For quite some time Minnesota's criminal justice policies have been characterized by a degree of moderation that is not found in most other states. The sentencing guidelines adopted by Minnesota in 1980 represent a policy-driven approach to prison growth that has attempted to reconcile sentencing practices with available prison space. While the prison population in the state has increased in recent years, the state's rate of incarceration remains well below the national average.

Overall, two findings are worth noting in regard to drug offenses and women offenders in Minnesota. First, drug offenses comprise a much smaller portion of the court and prison population in the state than in the two other states in this study. Second, the racial disparities in this area are quite extreme in Minnesota, although the small number of cases suggests that a degree of caution is necessary in interpreting these results.

Increase in Drug Arrests

Of the 1.4 million arrests (misdemeanor and felony combined) during the study period, women accounted for 20% of the total. Arrests for both men and women increased most rapidly here, of the three states, although, again, more so for women (60% compared to 37% for men). Arrests for drug offenses increased at a much more rapid pace from 1986 to 1995, rising 174%, compared to an overall arrest increase of 41%.

While the number of women arrested for drug offenses is relatively small, they experienced a 279% increase in the 10-year period, from 438 to 1,661, considerably greater than the 162% increase for men during this time. Since women's arrests for all offenses increased at a faster rate than for men, drug offenses accounted for 10% of the rise in women's arrests, compared to 18% for men.

Unfortunately, the available data for Minnesota do not permit a breakdown in arrests by both race and gender combined. Looking at rates of arrest by race for both men and women, we find that the black proportion of drug arrests increased from 10% in 1986 to 26% in 1995. This compares to the 3% black share of the state's population. (Separate data are not maintained for Hispanics in Minnesota.)

Increase in Drug Convictions

As the number of drug arrests rose in the state, so did the number of drug convictions for both women and men during this period, by 177% and 162% respectively. Drug offenses accounted for 24% of the increased number of convictions for women and 34% for men. Black women accounted for one-quarter (26%) of the total drug convictions for the period. While the overall figures are small, the scale of the increase for black women is quite dramatic, an 878% increase from nine convictions in 1986 to 88 in 1995; the increase for white women was 84%.

Prison Sentences

Minnesota sends fewer offenders to prison than most other states, but nonetheless experienced a significant increase in the number of women receiving a prison sentence from 1986 to 1995. The number of women sentenced to prison rose by 139%, from 66 to 158, compared to a 75% rise for men, from 1132 to 1978. The proportional increase in the number of drug offenders receiving a prison term was quite substantial for both women and men (400% and 610% respectively), but the overall numbers are still very modest—a women's rise from six to 30 and a men's rise from 41 to 291. Overall, drug offenses accounted for 26% of the increased number of prison terms for women and 30% for men. By 1995, 19% of women's prison sentences were for drug offenses, and 15% of men's.

While the number of women being sentenced to prison for drug offenses in Minnesota is quite small, black women are considerably overrepresented. For the 10-year period as a whole, black women constituted 36% of all women's drug sentences to prison. In 1995, 18% of white women sentenced to prison had been convicted of drug offenses and 15% of black women.

Of Minnesota's 5,327 prisoners in 1998, 4.7% (253) were women. Overall, just over 10% of inmates were serving drug sentences. While African-Americans represented 2.7%

of the state's population, they constituted 36.6% of the state's inmates.

Impact of Sentencing Structure

Minnesota's sentencing guidelines system was established to generally place greater emphasis on the use of prison space for violent offenders and to seek non-prison sanctions for many non-violent offenders. Although legislators have made alterations to this structure over the years, the overall impact of law enforcement and sentencing policies continues to result in considerably fewer imprisoned drug offenders than in the other states.

Under the guidelines system judges have sentencing discretion within a specified range to determine if aggravating or mitigating circumstances warrant a departure from the presumptive sentence. "Dispositional departures" result in an otherwise prison-bound offender being sentenced to a non-incarcerative sentence, or vice versa, and "durational departures" serve to increase or decrease the presumptive sentence length.

While mitigation may be employed for a range of circumstances, research on the use of departures under conditions of prison overcrowding has revealed that there are negative consequences for women. Criminologists Lisa Stolzenburg and Stewart D'Alessio examined sentencing practices in Minnesota for the years 1980-1992 and concluded that in times of high prison crowding men were considerably more likely than women to receive mitigating departures at sentencing, even though the state women's prison was considerably more crowded than the men's system. The researchers theorize that during periods of overcrowding judges seek to bring the system within its mandated capacity by sentencing more offenders to non-prison terms. Since there are considerably more male inmates in the system, reducing the number of men sentenced to prison will have a greater overall impact on the population.

ASSESSING THE TRENDS

Assessing the trends in women's involvement in the criminal justice system over the 10-year period of 1985–1995 demonstrates both the substantial impact that criminal justice policies have had on women's involvement in the system as well as the complex ways in which this manifests itself. Because much of the legislative and policy changes during this period focused on drugs, women have been affected more than men since they are more likely to come into the criminal justice system on a drug offense. While the national data portray a compelling picture of the impact of drug and sentencing policies on women offenders, the state-level analysis illustrates the range of how these trends may be affected by decisions made by state and local policymakers.

About the Authors

Marc Mauer, M.S.W., is Assistant Director of The Sentencing Project. Cathy Potler, J.D., and Richard Wolf, J.D., consultants to The Sentencing Project, are attorneys with the New York Board of Correction.

References

Chesney-Lind, M., "Patriarchy, Prisons and Jails: A Critical Look at Trends in Women's Incarceration," 71(1) *The Prison Journal* (1991)

Stolzenburg, L., & D'Alessio, S.J., "The Impact of Prison Crowding on Male and Female Imprisonment Rates in Minnesota: A Research Note," 14(4) *Justice Quarterly* 793-809 (December 1997).

Tonry, M., *Malign Neglect—Race, Crime and Punishment in America* (Oxford, 1995).

Chapter 7

Exploring Alternatives to Incarceration for Minnesota's Bulging Women's Prison Population

by the Minnesota Department of Corrections' Alternatives to Incarceration—Female Offenders Committee of the State Advisory Task Force on Female Offenders

This chapter originally appeared in Women, Girls & Criminal Justice, *Vol. 5, No. 3, April/May 2004.*

Editor's Note: The following chapter is adapted with permission from a report released in February 2004 through the Minnesota Department of Corrections. Entitled "One Less Bed: A Report on Alternatives to Incarceration for Female Offenders at MCF-Shakopee," the report takes an important step in examining some possibilities for reducing the size of its women's prison population. In recent years, several states have become concerned about the number of women they imprison, especially when such practices create overcrowded facilities. As far as I know, however, this report from Minnesota is the only written report that has come from a serious effort to examine options other than building new prisons, squeezing women into facilities designed for other purposes, transporting women to other states far from their families and support systems, and other irresponsible approaches that have characterized the treatment of women in the criminal justice system over the years. (Full copies of the report, which include an executive summary as well as various statistical charts and tables, can be obtained from the Minnesota Department of Corrections website at www.corr.state.mn.us/pdf/one percent20less percent20bed_1.pdf.)

INTRODUCTION

At the end of January 2003, Minnesota Commissioner of Corrections Joan Fabian met with State Advisory Task Force on Female Offenders representatives, who described the work of the Task Force and suggested that alternatives to incarceration exist for women who are committed to MCF-Shakopee, the state's women's prison. In light of the state's budget crisis and its increasing prison population, Commissioner Fabian requested that a Task Force should organize a work group to analyze the state's female prison population and to return with recommendations addressing these alternatives.

There are good reasons to explore alternatives to prison for women convicted of crimes. Minnesota has experienced an unprecedented growth in its female prison population. Minnesota's female prison population growth largely paralleled national trends until 1994, when Minnesota's rates declined. Starting in 1996, however, the growth in the female prison population in Minnesota became even more pronounced when compared to national rates. This increase is remarkable on its own accord, but also in comparison to growth in the men's prison population. The growth of the female prison population in Minnesota rose dramatically, from 77 women in 1985 to 450 in 2003 (a 484% increase). The men's population rose from 2,246 to 8,623 (a 195% increase) during the same time frame.

In November 2003, the bed capacity at MCF-Shakopee was 409, but the actual population count in the facility was 423 and the total number of women under commitment status was 450. A construction project is currently underway that will remodel and expand the facility's Independent Living Center unit, which will house an additional 48 women, bringing the maximum bed capacity to 457. In addition, the facility will have the ability to convert day rooms into bedrooms, thereby adding 94 overflow beds to temporarily handle any future overcrowding. Despite this expanded bed capacity, the Alternative to Incarceration committee recognized that it can be expensive to house offenders in a state correctional facility, both financially (the FY03 per diem was $86.99) and in social, economic, and psychological terms. The marginal costs that would be saved by not having a committed female offender serve her incarceration at MCF-Shakopee is considerably less than $86.99, even when amortized capital costs are included.

This assignment started out simply enough: explore those existing alternatives that might reduce the state's reliance on incarcerating women. In the end, however, the task became more complex. As committee members learned more about the women in the prison, sentencing and revocation practices, criminal justice policies and practices, and societal influences, still more questions emerged. In the end, the committee had to finish its work recognizing that this is just the beginning. A great deal more must be studied in the years ahead. Hopefully, this report represents a good beginning of a very important and worthwhile endeavor.

STUDY PROCESS AND PREPARATION

The Working Group

The State Advisory Task Force on Female Offenders working group was entitled the Alternative to Incarceration—Female Offenders Committee and met from February to December of 2003. The members and resource people in the working group included: Danette Buskovick, Research Unit, Minnesota Department of Corrections (DOC); Mark Carey, Warden, MCF-Shakopee; Claudia Fercello, Research Unit, Minnesota Department of Corrections; Kim Greer, Sociologist, Minnesota State University at Mankato; Mickey Kopfmann, Program Director, MCF-Shakope; Anne McDiarmid, Ramsey County Community Corrections; and Sharen R. Southard, Hennepin County Community Corrections.

During this study period, the working group reviewed national and state prison trends and examined the existing profile of women committed to MCF-Shakopee. Assumptions about possible prison alternatives were tested through an analysis of the data. Recommendations were formed using criteria such as public safety, program effectiveness, cost efficiencies, and public sensibilities.

National Trends

The working group used the National Institute of Corrections Information Center and other sources to examine national prison trends, which indicated that states were considering a variety of strategies to address the number of women being incarcerated, including the following:

- New York and other states (reducing sentences for low level drug offenders);

- Kentucky, California, Oregon, Arkansas, and Indiana (reducing sentences for non-violent offenders);

- California, Maryland, and other states (dealing with elderly inmates differently);

- Arkansas, Kentucky, and Indiana (releasing inmates close to release dates);

- Washington, Oklahoma, Connecticut, Oregon, and Nevada (reducing length of parole and altering policies to reduce parole violations returned to prison);

- California (increasing its use of "good time");

- Ohio, Illinois, Michigan, and Florida (closing prisons);

- Washington, Kansas, New York, Oregon, and Missouri (modifying sentencing practices); and

- Arizona, the Federal Bureau of Prisons, Colorado, Wyoming, and Pennsylvania (building more prisons).

National trends were compared with state and local trends to develop some initial premises as to which alternatives to incarceration might be most promising for Minnesota. While state trends do not necessarily mirror national conditions, they can spark ideas about where to look for possible improvements in practice or efficiencies.

Population Profile Information

The following profile information serves as additional background on the women incarcerated at MCF-Shakopee:

- Most are single and Caucasian, although a disproportionate percentage are non-Caucasian compared to the general public;

- Those released from prison commit new felony offenses less frequently than their male counterparts; according to the 2000 Annual Performance Report, the average three-year reconviction rate for men released from prison between 1990 and 1997 was 25%; the average three-year reconviction rate for women during this same time period was 22%;

- No significant differences were evident in the length of incarceration of men and women convicted of crimes against persons, but women were significantly more likely than men to be incarcerated for one year or less as a result of a property crime; and

- Women are more likely than men to be released on supervised release and less likely to be placed on Intensive Supervised Release (ISP); this should not be surprising given that men are more likely to be convicted of a personal offense and the ISR program is designed to provide intensive surveillance for those offenders who pose the greatest public risk.

In order to better understand where potential alternatives to incarceration exist, the committee examined the process by which an offender received a prison sentence length. In general, there are three areas where the committee described the ways women enter and leave prison and devised alternatives that could affect the length of their stay:

- Events leading up to sentencing (such as prior record, sentencing practices, laws, sentencing guidelines, revocation practices, etc.);

- Discipline procedures that might lead to extended incarceration; and

- "Early release" programming such as work release, medical release, or the challenge incarceration program.

A profile analysis was conducted on the MCF-Shakopee population. Some of its findings and recommendations are woven throughout this chapter. There are seven recommendations, two being "processed" or recommended for study to better understand issues and trends that might lead to further improvements in finding incarceration alternatives and five being concrete steps that could be taken immediately. The article is divided into three major sections of analysis, covering the most promising recommendations, topics warranting further study, and subject areas not deemed to be promising.

MOST PROMISING RECOMMENDATIONS

Reestablish a Residential Program for Pregnant Offenders

MCF-Shakopee had a Community Alternative for Mothers in Prison (CAMP) program in place from 1988 to 2001 (totaling 29 participants during those years). The CAMP program was designed for pregnant women and their newborn children. From eight to 12 state-incarcerated women are pregnant on any given day. The CAMP program provided an opportunity for some women who gave birth during their term of incarceration to remain with and care for their newborn infants. Offenders who give birth within six months of their release date and who will parent upon release were being screened for eligibility. They completed their sentence at a residential facility in the community and attended parent education classes through a selected vendor. Through these programs the mothers learned parenting skills as they bonded with their infants.

In such a program, if reestablished, women would be selected from the MCF-Shakopee population based on the following eligibility criteria:

- Completion or exemption from chemical dependency directive;

- Six months or less until supervised release date;

- Acceptable institutional discipline record;

- Approval from county child protection (if applicable);

- Medium or minimum classification; and

- Signs a participant agreement.

A selection committee consisting of the facility medical director, the parenting/family program director, and the case manager would determine which women are eligible for the program. The Program Review Team would make the final approval. The eligibility criteria take into account factors such as the woman's medical and programming needs, likelihood of success in community living, and institutional history. The case manager would also contact sentencing judges to gain input before accepting women in the program.

Prisoners who participate in the program would live at a community facility that has demonstrated its ability to work effectively with women and their children. Vendors with community-based services would provide support/education groups free of charge to the CAMP program participants.

The Minnesota Department of Corrections would pay per diem costs to the residential service provider. This vendor will facilitate the mothers' applications for county financial assistance for their infants. The per diem is estimated at $68.50, a figure that does not include the additional $13.84 cost per day for health care and central office support. Based on the average number of pregnant women incarcerated in past years and past participation rates, it can be expected that CAMP will serve four to six women and their infants per year. The range of participation will depend on the actual number of eligible women, their length of stay, and available funds. For purposes of initial budgeting, it is estimated that approximately $30,000 would allow an average of five women to participate in the program annually for an average of 90 days per stay.

All agencies that were involved with the previous program have expressed excitement and enthusiasm at the prospect of reinstating this program and are committed to working on this joint venture. It is recommended that the CAMP program be reinstated and that the Research and Evaluation Unit of the Minnesota Department of Corrections should conduct a program evaluation of the success rate of past and future participants in terms of recidivism and parenting outcomes.

Expand Challenge Incarceration Program and Use of Gender-Responsive Programming

Minnesota women are more often incarcerated than men for property and drug offenses. Men are incarcerated for personal offenses twice as much as women (39% vs. 21%). The Challenge Incarceration Program (CIP) is designed primarily for drug offenders and a larger percentage of women than men meet its eligibility criteria. Women represent 6% of the total Minnesota prison population, yet make up 17% of current CIP beds. At some point, the department will maximize its use of CIP beds for women. Given their offense profile and completion rates, it is recommended that the DOC should continue to test that upper limit of referrals.

So far, 1,458 women and men have entered the CIP. Overall, 45% of these participants have successfully completed the entire program. Women are more likely to complete the program than men (53% vs. 44%).

Female offenders are more likely to be eligible for CIP given the offense type than are male offenders and are more likely to successfully complete the program As such, it is recommended that the current plan to expand the number of CIP beds for women should be supported. In addition, the CIP program should make improvements in its gender responsivity.

Technical Assistance to Examine Admissions Due to Revocation

An additional factor that may be leading to the high use of revocation is the lack of resources available to the courts and probation/supervised release officers in finding alternatives for offenders. The DOC should request technical assistance to examine the frequency of technical violations of probation and supervised release conditions resulting in a prison admission. Prison populations have risen dramatically in nearly every state over the past decade, so have the number of releasees who might be returned to prison for a revocation. Recent data from the federal government reveals that one-third of all prison intakes across the United States are due to parole/supervised release technical violations as opposed to new crimes. In Minnesota, the releasee return rate for technical violations is slightly lower, at 27% with no significant differences between male and female returnee rates.

An incredible 61% of female prison admissions are due to probation or supervised release violations. This compares to 53% for the male prison admissions due to probation or supervised release violations. The distinguishing factor between the different revocation admission rates is the significantly higher rate of probation revocations leading to prison commitments for women.

There are many reasons for the gender-based variation in probation revocation rates due to technical violations, including county-by-county variations in offense and offender profiles, corresponding differences in conditions of probation set by local courts, and different policies about when revocations are pursued. A concern expressed by the committee is the degree to which local correctional agencies have implemented gender-specific programs and case management to address the unique needs and barriers faced by women.

An explanation the committee has ruled out is that of more serious female offenders being placed on probation initially. In general, it is believed that Minnesota retains higher-risk offenders locally, thereby increasing the likelihood that probation would be revoked for noncompliant behavior. According to the Minnesota Sentencing Guidelines Commission, only 16% of the women on probation who were revoked and sent to prison were originally allowed to remain on local supervision when the guidelines indicated that a prison term was presumptive.

No matter the reason, the difference in revocation rates for stays of imposition/execution is significant and important to address if reductions in prison intakes are going to become a reality. The comparatively high revocation rates in Minnesota are having a significant impact on bed space, especially for women. This fact alone warrants immediate attention, if only because of the financial significance of the revocation issue. At an average cost of $86.99 per day to confine a woman in a Minnesota prison, the revocation practice is costing the state $31,751 per year per bed. While the committee is not questioning the need to provide prison as a backstop for local correctional practice, it must be asked whether the use of prison is needed in all of these cases, why there is such a disparity between the revocation rates of men and women on probation, and whether the cost is worth the perceived outcome.

Probation revocations are costing Minnesota millions of dollars per year. While it is recognized that many of those revoked could not be retained locally due to public safety risks and that there are local costs involved in retaining these offenders at the non-prison correctional level, certainly some cost savings could be attained through alternative interventions that are applied locally.

An additional factor that may be leading to the high use of revocation is the lack of resources available to the courts and probation/supervised release officers in finding alternatives for offenders facing a revocation and prison incarceration. While the prison population has been steadily growing, from 2,244 in 1985 to 7,579 in 2003, the number of state-funded prison alternatives (halfway houses, work release, intensive community supervision, challenge incarceration program, and day reporting centers) is believed to have dropped significantly. No data is available to verify or disprove this belief, but it is commonly discussed as a factor in recent trends. Some of this drop has been "recouped" in the past three years by an increase in funding for work release beds spurred on by the fact that the per diem for work release is lower than the per diem for prison. Offenders who might have accessed these resources are no longer able to do so with the same frequency as in the past. Additional halfway house capacity, for example, has not been funded since the early 1970s. The recent upsurge in bed use, however, simply brings the level of work release access up to levels that existed in the years prior to 2001 and does not fully restore the use of work release that once totaled 220 beds on an average day. In the past three years, the number of alternative bed days has dropped slightly, from 289 to 282 bed days on average. While there is reason to believe that the average daily population of the total alternative programs will increase, this increase will not come close to mirroring the total prison population increase of the past 10 to 15 years.

The reasons for the decrease in alternative prison programs are numerous, including funding constraints and budget reductions, perceived changes in public/elected official sentiments opposing offender release, and zoning challenges. The capacity and use of these programs has changed over the past three years (the only years the DOC has reliable data on). Women in halfway houses have declined from four to one; women on work release have more than doubled from 14 to 32; no women have participated in the day reporting center in any year; and CIP participation remains stable, with approximately 16 women active in the program each year.

Exacerbating this revocation issue is the caseload size of probation/supervised release officers. Despite the infusion of new funds for probation officers in the late 1990s, the average case load size has not changed much because of the increased number of offenders ordered to be supervised and the overall length of probation increasing due to sentencing enhancements and public opinion. New legislative mandates have expanded the roles and duties of the supervising agents. In addition, government has reduced services due to recent budget cuts. It is perceived that this high workload and reduced services at the local level has resulted in less ability to meet offender needs, thereby causing a loss of support for retaining offenders at the local level. There are at least two theories on the impact these high caseloads have on revocations. One is that agents have less time to provide individualized responses to offender needs, less ability to respond quickly when warning signs appear, and are more likely to resort to revocation as an acceptable response to violations of supervision conditions. The second is that agents are less likely to revoke an offender's supervision because detection of misbehavior is lessened due to fewer face-to-face appointments, home/work visits, and other collateral contacts. Until a study is conducted, however, much of this is speculation.

In the past, the National Institute of Corrections (NIC) has supported technical assistance in working with jurisdictions seeking to examine and to alter revocation practices. Part of this technical assistance includes a review of trends and practices, as well as policy and program solutions. While NIC is no longer providing this assistance, a number of consultants are available with extensive experience in this area.

Since the prison population has been increasing while the level of programming alternatives has been decreasing, probation/supervised release agent workloads continue at high levels and recent revenue shortfalls have negatively affected local/state budgets and services. Accordingly, there is reason to believe that these trends are contributing to the use of revocations on technical violation cases resulting in prison stays. The number of revocations leading to prison may be reduced through a concerted effort. This is particularly important for the female offenders given the high percent of intakes caused by probation revocations. The DOC should therefore establish a state/local partnership to seek technical assistance in examining revocation patterns and policies that may determine possible alternatives.

Review and Reduce Sanctions Affecting "Good Time"

MCF-Shakopee has a number of options available for use in handling offender discipline matters. Three of them can result in longer prison stays than the minimum required due to extended incarceration or loss of good time.

The discipline options that do not affect length of stay are:

- *Disciplinary Loss of Privileges (DLOP)*. When an offender receives a DLOP, she loses recreational and social activities; she may also be confined to her own cell/room/bunk during non-working hours;

- *Restitution*. An offender may be required to pay for damage to property and/or expenses related to injuries incurred as a result of her actions; and

- *Confiscation*. In addition to a discipline penalty, unauthorized money or property may be seized.

In addition to these sanctions, an informal Loss of Privileges (LOP) may be applied without the case going through the discipline route.

The discipline options that can affect length of stay are:

- *Disciplinary Segregation*. This sanction requires that the offender serve a specified number of days of confinement in a room/cell following either the signing of a waiver or finding of violation;

- *Restrictive Disciplinary Segregation*. A more restrictive form of disciplinary segregation limited to a maximum of 10 days in a 15-day period; and

- *Extended Incarceration*. An offender sentenced for an offense committed after August 1, 1993, is subject to extended incarceration equal to the disciplinary confinement period imposed by the hearing officer.

The work committee measured which sanctions were used at what rate on two different days (February 23, 2003, and April 3, 2003). DLOP sanctions increased in number from 10 (2.4%) to 31 (7.5%). LOP sanctions stayed exactly the same at 26 (6.2%). Use of segregation moved slightly from 21 (5%) to 25 (6%). Overall, sanctions increased from 57 women (13.6%) on the first day to 82 women (19.8%) on the second. Attempts to compare this usage with the male facilities were unsuccessful due to the differences in how sanctions are applied, for which offenses, and how infractions are defined and categorized. And, attempts to find patterns of discipline usage were dismissed due to the amount of time it would take to manually find and analyze the data.

MCF-Shakopee has made adjustments to make the best use of the diminishing ratio of segregation beds to general population. These adjustments include:

- Running cases concurrently on discipline offers instead of consecutively;

- Offering restrictive segregation instead of discipline segregation to reduce the number of days of extended incarceration and loss of good time;

- Offering DLOP sanctions instead of segregation or extended incarceration when an offender's discipline history is positive; and

- Providing for the possibility for some discipline to be handled informally for some offenses thereby preventing the use of extended incarceration.

MCF-Shakopee staff discussed the possibility of applying a more varied and restorative set of interventions, such as "community" work service, accountability classes, apology letters, and programming requirements. These alternatives would likely be more meaningful in that they would give women a more structured way of learning from their infractions, repairing any damage that their behavior may have caused. However, these alternatives would also be time intensive to administer and recent staffing and budget cutbacks have reduced the ability of the facility to consider these options. In addition, the centralization of policies and procedures across all facilities to improve consistency and professionalism limit the ability of one facility to embark on an effort that does not apply to other institutions.

It is estimated that a fair number of bed days were expended with added sanctions (extended incarceration or loss of good time) in the course of the year 2002 at MCF-Shakopee. However, this data cannot be acquired without a significant amount of manual record sorting.

Two recent department-wide changes will possibly reduce the number of bed days filled because of previous discipline practices:

- Effective August 13, 2003, the standard penalty for Mandated Treatment Failure was significantly reduced from 90 days extended incarceration to 45 days (with only 30 days being applied to those who sign an agreement); and

- Currently, a committee out of central office has been meeting and reviewing discipline penalties at all facilities that result in extended incarceration and loss of good time for possible revision.

A significant amount of research has been conducted in recent years indicating that long-term, pro-social behavior can be improved through positive reinforcement and modeling, and that punishment and negative reinforcements are poor motivators for long-term change. Prisons are designed around control and fair, humane treatment. Discipline is almost exclusively negative in its orientation. It stands to reason that little learning occurs through these discipline procedures. Yet, social learning theory suggests a more rigorous use of rewards and cognitive restructuring techniques to bring about change.

Despite progress made through recent departmental efforts, it is conceivable that doing the following could make further reductions in costs to the state:

- *Add a discipline alternative function to staff duties* by diverting some of the marginal cost savings from lessened use of extended incarceration and discipline leading to loss of good time. Creative means of holding the offender accountable might be put in place if a staff member had the time to administer both the restorative process and the implementation of the response; and

- *Provide incentives for women to earn lost good time.* North Carolina, for example, has established various alternatives such as "gain time," "earned time," and "meritorious time," and these incentives can be tied to restorative and cognitive restructuring techniques so that long-term learning occurs.

Minnesota prides itself on its rehabilitation mindset and supports a host of services designed to bring about long-term behavioral change. Programs in Minnesota prisons appear comprehensive and effective. However, current discipline practices do not promote learning and are costing the state in longer prison stays. Existing efforts to revamp discipline procedures should be supported and additional, alternative means of holding offenders accountable should occur through the use of social learning theory techniques, funded through savings from the reduced use of extended incarceration.

Support Initiatives to Assist the Mentally Ill/Chemically Dependent

Practitioners and scholars in the field of criminal justice are increasingly turning their attention to the growing number of mentally ill persons being incarcerated in the nation's prisons and jails. Approximately 280,000 mentally ill individuals were incarcerated in prisons and jails at the end of the 1990s. Additionally, in excess of 540,000 adults reporting prior mental health treatment were supervised in the community; nearly a third of mentally ill offenders had a dual diagnosis.

Offenders with co-occurring disorders have been described as "full service customers" because they require an array of services, including supportive housing. Approximately 49% of mentally ill jail inmates are back in jail within one year. Such individuals tend to cycle between release from incarceration, community re-entry, and re-incarceration.

Women offenders are at risk of high rates of mental illness, substance abuse, and co-occurring disorders because of past experiences of abuse and trauma. The intersections among mental health, trauma, and substance abuse are critical for women. Further highlighting this convergence, women who use drugs are more likely to be involved in crime. Substance abuse is also linked to issues of trauma and mental health. While mental illness and substance abuse serve as "pathways to prison" for women, mental illness contributes to disciplinary problems within institutions. Such problems have the potential of lengthening the time served for offenders if it results in the loss of "good time" or the imposition of "extended incarceration." The women at MCF-Shakopee face serious chemical and mental health challenges that affect their ability to find and maintain adequate housing. Fifty percent have mental illness, 40% take psychotropic medications, and 85% are chemically dependent.

As the committee discussed incarceration alternatives for the MI/CD offender at MCF-Shakopee, it discovered that appropriate housing for these women is a major problem in transition planning. A departmental work group on housing has proposed statewide scattered site housing with a case management component that could greatly enhance community supervision of the MI/CD offender. Although the DOC has recently hired mental health release planners to work with persistent chronically mentally ill offenders at MCF-Shakopee to establish community re-entry case plans, housing is frequently a barrier to successful community re-entry. In addition, the Department of Human Services (DHS) and the Minnesota Housing Finance Agency have a collaborative partnership working to provide access to mental health services, stable housing, and economic support for people who have a mental illness and are involved in the criminal justice system. A primary goal of this collaborative is to secure housing that is targeted for the needs of the individual. The DOC and DHS State Operative Services have been working on several collaborative efforts for the past five years. Ideally, these two agencies could provide an appropriate housing initiative for this population. These efforts, along with the State Advisory Task Force on Female Offender's decision to establish a subcommittee to work on housing, enhances the opportunity for establishing some appropriate housing for the MI/CD offender.

There are vendors interested in providing appropriate housing for the mentally ill and chemically dependent female offenders. A model for this housing and services suggests what can be done. Ideal women's MI/CD services provided with financial and administrative support from the Department of Corrections might include the following:

• Integrated Dual Diagnosis Treatment (currently in place);

- MI/CD specific housing unit (assign a unit to MI/CD housing with full time support specialist committed to this population);

- Open-ended counseling/case management (currently in place);

- Long-term aftercare/continuing care (currently in place);

- Full-time nursing services (increase nursing services to full time); and

- On-site psychiatric consultation and medication management (still needed).

Given the high prevalence rates of mental illness and chemical abuse/dependency among the committed female offender population, extra attention should be devoted to removing barriers to successful reentry. Two of the most difficult obstacles for a releasee to overcome are that of gaining housing and mental health services. It is therefore recommended that the DOC support the housing initiatives put forth by the housing workgroup in the Minnesota Department of Corrections to assist the releasee. The State Advisory Task Force on Female Offenders has proposed establishing a sub-committee to investigate appropriate housing for mentally ill/chemically dependent women leaving MCF-Shakopee.

AREAS IN NEED OF FURTHER STUDY

Conduct a Flowcharting Study Process

This chapter documents differences between male and female incarcerated offenders. Yet, currently, no practical method exists for examining how different incarcerated populations (male vs. female, offenders with different offense types, etc.) respond to their correction's system experience.

Developing an electronic flow chart model that tracks and documents offenders' demographic information as well as their movements and activities from the time they enter prison through supervision discharge would provide the DOC with valuable information on how offenders' personal or group characteristics impact outcomes. This information would be extremely useful for policy and programming decision-making as well as for focusing resources to have the greatest benefit. It should be noted that such a study might require a reworking of the COMS systems and an extensive review or modification of existing records.

The DOC should create an "informational flow chart framework" to evaluate the impact interventions have on offenders depending on the various characteristics present in individuals and facilities. It should be recognized, however, that while this process should yield helpful information to maximize the use of limited resources, it would require considerable up-front resources.

Conduct a Study on Geographic Differences in Sentencing

Significant differences exist in commitment sentencing patterns across judicial districts, ranging from 14% to 39% for men. The number of women who received a dispositional departure downward across judicial districts also varied. However, the numbers in some districts were too small to use for comparison purposes. No significant disparity of departures for drug offenses was found. However, when gender is considered as a factor statewide, the disparity was pronounced.

The reasons for this sentencing disparity can range from differences in the availability in local resources to community attitudes, values, and tolerance to the type of crimes committed. The availability of gender-specific programming may not be as prevalent in areas where the number of women offenders is too few to justify the cost of conducting female-only programs. If the goal is to examine prison referral rates for the purpose of devising strategies to retain offenders on the local level and avoid the high cost of state incarceration, then a more thorough examination of sentencing practices based on geographical differences and causes would be beneficial in the development of strategies to impact incarceration rates.

AREAS NOT DEEMED TO BE PROMISING

Reducing Prison Lengths for Female Offenders

Analysis shows that there are some significant differences between men and women's incarceration lengths. Women tend to serve shorter lengths of time for the same offense. While more than half of men and women are incarcerated for two years or less, more men than women are incarcerated for significantly longer periods of time. This should not be surprising given the fact that the men are more likely to be committed to the Commissioner of Corrections for personal or violent offenses than women, offenses for which a longer sentence is indicated in the Minnesota Sentencing Guidelines.

In addition to shorter sentence lengths, women offenders are more likely to receive downward (mitigating) departure rates than men. The compelling fact is that women are significantly less likely to receive a prison sentence than men when the sentencing guidelines call for prison. Moreover, when they are committed, women serve less time in prison than men (likely due to the lower severity of their offense). And, women are less frequently revoked and returned to prison than men for supervised release technical violations.

Given this set of facts, there does not appear to be a lot to be gained by seeking strategies to reduce sentence length. Women already are less likely to serve a prison term and more likely to serve less time than men. The more promising intervention is likely around revocation rates.

Setting Up a Geriatric Care Center or Release Mechanism

As correctional agencies across the country begin to explore ways to cope with overcrowded prisons and shrinking state government budgets, an obvious prison population to consider for some type of alternative to incarceration is elderly (geriatric) inmates (55 years or older). This group of individuals is a likely population to target for possible cost savings because of the expense associated with providing medical services to older inmates. However, this does not seem to be a viable possibility for cost savings at MCF-Shakopee given the rather small number of elderly women currently incarcerated there.

The vast majority of offenders incarcerated at MCF-Shakopee are between the ages 22 and 50, with the most frequent age being between 31 and 40. Near the end of October 2003, there were 18 women (4%) at Shakopee who were 50 years or older. The committee members felt this group of offenders did not represent a promising target population for this project, simply because they represented such a small percentage of the institution's total population.

Diverting Female Offenders From Prison

As noted previously, the committee explored three areas where members thought the committed female offender intake might be impacted: at the point of court commitment, during incarceration through extended stays, and upon release and possible return. After reviewing data provided by the Minnesota Sentencing Guidelines Commission, the committee members concluded that we would most likely not be able to further impact the number of women being sentenced to prison. According to the information we received, women offenders in Minnesota already receive a 56% downward departure rate.

Chapter 8

Prison Overcrowding in Alabama's Women's Prison: Real Solutions for Real Problems

by Tim Roche

INTRODUCTION

This chapter discuesses recommendations the Justice Policy Institute made recently to the Honorable Myron H. Thompson, who is presiding over an unconstitutional conditions case regarding the Julia Tutwiler Prison for Women in Wetumpka, Alabama. These concrete steps are designed to help the Alabama Department of Corrections (ADOC), the Alabama Parole Board and/or other Alabama criminal justice system officials to remedy, in a safe and thoughtful manner, unconstitutional conditions at the women's prison. While much of what follows related to Alabama laws, policies, and conditions, the information is generally suitable for application in other jurisdictions.

In preparing the original report, I had access to information about Alabama prison policies and practices, including Judge Thompson's original court order, the State of Alabama's response to Judge Thompson's December, 2002, order, and ADOC materials on classification and disciplinary procedures, as well as a September, 2002, validation study report by James Austin, Ph.D., of George Washington University, regarding the DOC's security classification system.

Still, critical information was lacking about the population at Julia Tutwiler Prison for Women and other institutions housing female prisoners. Absent specific demographic, criminal history, and other data pertaining to the female population, I used national data

---

This chapter originally appeared in Women, Girls & Criminal Justice, *Vol. 4, No. 4, June/July 2003.*

on female prison populations and my previous experience in women's prisons to make certain assumptions about Alabama's female prison population. I am aware of no reason why the inmate population at Tutwiler should be viewed or treated as more dangerous or crime-prone than the rest of the female prison population across the country.

Accordingly, I consulted the U.S. Department of Justice's Bureau of Justice Statistics data on women prisoners, which reports pertinent characteristics that define the female inmate population nationally, including the following:

- More than one-fourth of all women sent to state prison are convicted of larceny or fraud;

- Approximately one-third of female inmates were on probation when they were committed to state prison, suggesting that a significant number of them were returned to prison for violations of probation—often for technical violations rather than for the commission of a new offense;

- Seventy percent of female state inmates have minor children;

- In 1996, 17% of all female state prison admissions were for violent offenses, 36% were for property offenses, 39% were for drug offenses, and 8% were for "other" offenses;

- Of those women committed to state prison for "violent" offenses, 75% committed simple assault;

- Fifty percent of women in state prison were using alcohol or drugs at the time of the offense; and

- Sixty percent experienced physical or sexual abuse in the past.

I believe these data serve as an accurate barometer against which to judge the relative risk and need of the population of female prisoners in Alabama. It is important to note that while Dr. Austin's classification study provides demographic data on the female population that helps assess the predictive value of the institutional adjustment of inmates, this study should not be confused with an analysis of who among the inmate population would be good candidates for supervised release into less secure settings. Dr. Austin's report nevertheless contains compelling information that supports the position that large numbers of female inmates can be found in Tutwiler and at other ADOC facilities that are very low risk and, with the proper support and structure, could do well in a less restrictive setting. Among the more notable references in the report are the following:

- Property crimes were the most common offenses for men and women inmates (33% and 44% respectively). Drug-related crimes constituted the second largest offense category (34% of the women, 27% of the men). Twenty-four percent of the males and 13% of the females were incarcerated for person-related crimes.

- Sixty-three percent of the women had sentences less than five years. About 14% of the inmates (19% female, 13% male) had sentences of one year of less.

- Eighty-five percent of the women when initially classified had no (48%) or only one (37%) prior felony conviction.

- When reclassified, 93% of the women had no history of institutional violence; 65% had low (23%), low/moderate (33%) or moderate (9%) rates of current offense severity; 96% had no low or low/moderate prior assaultive offense histories; the most severe disciplinary reports during the previous 18 months was none (46%), low/moderate (7%), or moderate (20%).

- Excessive use of overrides was found (27% of the female admissions were over-ridden or scored to recommended security). The majority of these overrides (20% for males, 17% for females) were to a higher security level. The override rates were higher for the daily population (33% and 38% for males and females respectively from scored to recommended levels). Most of these overrides were to a higher custody level.

Although it is not my intention to critique the specific elements of Alabama's proposed plan, I believe that the plan fails to squarely address the single most pressing issue at Tutwiler—the overpopulation of non-violent women. While the DOC's proposed plan addresses some of the pressing physical plant improvements needed at Tutwiler, as well as increasing correctional officer staffing, it is my purpose here to put forth some ideas for substantially reducing the overpopulation of non-violent female offenders for whom the DOC already has the authority to safely and skillfully transition back into the community with ample supervision.

The ADOC has at its disposal several mechanisms through which a significant number of women could be safely transitioned out of the prison and into community settings. What I attempt to do here is provide a series of suggestions that could be used in a court order, or a correctional plan, to compel the state to safely and swiftly address conditions the court has deemed unconstitutional.

COMMUNITY PUNISHMENT AND CORRECTIONS PROGRAMS

Perhaps the most obvious mechanism for safely and swiftly preparing Tutwiler women to transition out of the facility is through *The Alabama Community Punishment and Corrections Act* (1991, No. 91-441). Through this act community punishment and corrections programs (CPCPs)were established statewide for the purpose of providing accountable punishment options for both misdemeanor and felony offenders in the communities from which they come.

Since its enactment, 29 community punishment and corrections programs have been established and authorized around the state. These programs represent an enormous resource for a thoughtful depopulation effort that gives state planners the advantage of not needing to pass any new legislation in order to implement a population reduction effort.

These programs are staffed by trained professionals who are experienced in working with correctional officials, judges, community members, and different types of offenders to design and to monitor strict community-based conditions of a sentence as viable alternatives to costly and crowded prisons. These programs currently serve more than 1,300 would-be prisoners and others who have been released from prison to the specific conditions of a community punishment plan.

The ADOC was an active supporter in the passage of this Act and has complied with an agreed reimbursement mechanism for those inmates who were successfully diverted or removed from state prison and maintained per the conditions of a community punishment plan developed by CPCP staff. The provisions of this Alabama statute contain the legal elements of a safe, thoughtful, and effective means by which the ADOC could enlist the support and aid of professionals around the state to help improve the intolerable conditions at Tutwiler. Section 15-18-172 (d) of the Act states:

> A state inmate incarcerated in a state facility may be approved by the department for participation in a community punishment and corrections program established under this article and be assigned to a program in such county from which he was sentenced if a community punishment and corrections program under this article has been established in such county and if the sentencing judge of such county authorizes the inmate to participate in the program. An inmate may be assigned to a community punishment and corrections program in another county if the presiding judge of the other county and the sentencing judge agree to such assignment and if the county has agreed in the contract to accept inmates originally sentenced in other counties. In the event the sentencing judge is unavailable due to death, retirement, or any other reason, the presiding judge from the sentencing circuit shall act in the sentencing judge's stead.

Under this provision, the ADOC could enlist the support of CPCP professionals to develop community punishment plans on behalf of women prisoners for presentation to the original court of jurisdiction to consider as a means of modifying the prisoner's sentence. To exercise this provision of the Act, ADOC officials would simply have to express their desire for CPCP staff to begin interviewing a segment of Tutweiler's population and to develop community punishment plans for consideration by the sentencing judge. Alabama is fortunate to have at its disposal this degree of community corrections sophistication across the state and the extended legal jurisdiction the act allows sentencing judges, in effect, to modify the terms of a prison sentence in light of such factors as a prisoner's rehabilitative progress in the institution since the original sentence was imposed, the availability of community-based resources that may not have been present or known to exist at the time of sentencing, and countless other changed circumstances, including but not limited to the conditions of confinement at Tutwiler.

In light of this, Justice Policy Institute made the following recommendations:

1. The ADOC should, within one week, produce a list of all female inmates at Tutwiler and in all other ADOC facilities who meet the following criteria:

   - Most serious committing offense is a non-violent offense (excluding simple assault and technical parole violations);

   - Their sentence is not more than 15 years; and

   - They have no rule violations of the "highest severity" or "high severity" during the previous four months.

2. This list should be provided to Plaintiffs who would in turn provide it to CPCP officials based on the region of the state in which the offense occurred.

3. ADOC officials should allow access by CPCP staff to interview inmates appearing on the list to assess the inmate's amenability to, and interest in, participating in and complying with a community punishment plan. Access should be consistent

with rules pertaining to attorney/client interviews and should be allowed to occur between the hours of 7:00 a.m. and 9:00 p.m., seven days a week.

4. ADOC officials should allow access to all relevant institutional records pertaining to inmates whose names appear on the list and who have expressed their desire to participate in the development of a community punishment plan.

5. The ADOC should compensate CPCPs, consistent with existing reimbursement agreements, for any community punishment plans that are submitted on behalf of a female inmate and accepted, in whole or in part, by the sentencing court resulting in the inmate's release.

SUPERVISED INTENSIVE RESTITUTION

In addition to the CPCPs, ADOC officials administer several other programs through which inmates can be transferred out of institutional settings and placed under strict supervision in the community. Among the most notable of these programs is Supervised Intensive Restitution (SIR) and Pre-Discretionary Leave (PDL; discussed in the next section). Programs such as these exist in virtually all departments of corrections and have proven to be effective population management tools. Not only do such programs reward and encourage good behavior in the institution, but they also help to safely manage the reduction of inmate populations when/if overcrowding becomes a problem within a prison system. For such programs to be effective, however, they must be designed with a reasonable degree of flexibility so as to allow inmates who have demonstrated their suitability to participate to take full advantage of the rehabilitative opportunities the programs present.

The SIR program is designed to allow appropriate prisoners to move under close supervision, out of institutional settings and into the community. As described in the ADOC Classification Manual, "The SIR program is designed for non-violent, low-risk offenders." Several criteria must be met for ADOC inmates to be eligible for SIR consideration. First among these is the requirement that eligible inmates must be within four years of parole review date or end of sentence. To participate in SIR, inmates cannot have been convicted of certain, mostly violent, offenses. Two of the 12 excluded offenses are Sales or Trafficking in Drugs, and Assault (felony conviction). Information is not immediately available about how many prisoners at Tutwiler and other ADOC facilities are eligible for SIR. Also unavailable is information on the number of inmates who are excluded from SIR eligibility due to convictions for the two noted offenses, or as a result of allegations of drug trafficking despite convictions to lesser offenses. But one can assume, given that 39% of female inmates nationally are imprisoned for drug offenses and three-quarters of those committed for violent offenses were sentenced for simple assault, that a significant number of women are ineligible for these reasons.

Additional SIR criteria require that an "inmate must have no major disciplinaries in past three months." The ADOC classification manual's "Disciplinary Severity Scale" reflects four severity categories—Highest Severity, High Severity, Low Moderate Severity, and Low Severity. It is not clear which of these constitute "major disciplinaries" and are therefore exclusionary.

All inmates who participate in the SIR program must also have a "suitable sponsor," which is defined in the classification manual as immediate family, e.g., spouse, children, father, mother brothers, sisters, grandparents, and persons *in loco parentis*. Aunts and uncles may also be considered if they are approved by the SIR officer and appear on the inmate's visitors' list and have visited the prisoner during incarceration. The classification manual offers no rationale for why a sponsor must be a member of the inmate's family. Friends, neighbors, ministers, AA sponsors, former employers, and others could serve as valuable supports for those reentering the community from prison and should not be excluded from consideration because they are not direct members of the inmate's family.

The SIR program, like many other similar programs across the country, is capable of providing a valuable service to the ADOC, prisoners, and the community at large. Unnecessarily restrictive criteria, however, often limit the effectiveness of such programs. I believe that for some of the reasons noted above, SIR is unnecessarily underused and of marginal benefit.

With a few adjustments, the utility and benefit of the SIR program could be greatly enhanced. ADOC's proposed plan observes, "*275 female inmate files were randomly selected for review by the Central Review Board (CRB) to check for inmates who might be eligible for early release and to further check for 'over classification.' Four (4) inmates were found to be eligible for early release via PDL (Pre-discretionary Leave) or SIR (Supervised Intensive Restitution).*" By more aggressively planning for the potential transition of inmates from institutional settings into the community through SIR, a greater number of low-risk prisoners who currently fill beds in the ADOC facilities could be safely monitored in the community.

Therefore, Justice Policy Institute said the ADOC should immediately take steps to exercise its authority by taking fuller advantage of the SIR program, and made the following recommendations:

1. Within a week, the ADOC should prepare a comprehensive list consisting of the name of every female inmate in ADOC custody who meets the existing criteria for SIR, as well as those who would meet the criteria if exceptions were granted to those convicted of simple assault or low-level drug charges despite unproven allegations of more serious involvement. Further, the list should include those inmates who, under existing policy, are excluded from participation due to violations of what are described in the ADOC classification manual as "low moderate" and "low severity" institutional infractions.

2. Once a list has been compiled, a copy should be provided to plaintiffs who should in turn share the list with officials from CPCP. Inmates should be interviewed by CPCP staff based on their geographic location around the state and be allowed access to all relevant institutional information necessary to develop a comprehensive community punishment plan that augments the requirements of SIR.

3. Multiple classification committee teams should be assembled and hearings should be held continuously until each of the eligible inmates is heard.

4. CPCP officials should be allowed to attend the entire classification hearing at which each inmate's SIR eligibility is determined so as to fully explain the elements of the proposed community punishment plan to committee members and advocate for the inmate's release on SIR pursuant to the conditions set fourth in the plan. (Generally speaking, corrections staff do not see their mission as facilitating the release of inmates, no matter how well planned the release might be. The persistence of severe overcrowding at Tutwiler over the past several years serves to

illustrate the challenge faced by the ADOC to manage even the most well-designed reduction of its inmate population. It is for this reason that credible forces from outside the ADOC must be allowed to play a meaningful role in the expeditious planning for transition of low-risk inmates. CPCP officials from around the state are an ideal vehicle for this purpose.)

5. Community punishment plans would include a suitable place of residence, substance abuse, mental health, family counseling, and vocational/educational services as appropriate. Plans could also include additional support in the form of mentors and advocates who would engage the inmate on a regular basis in the community to enhance their likelihood of success.

6. Classification committee decisions should be made and announced at the time of the hearing.

7. All inmates placed in the SIR program are assigned a SIR officer to help monitor their compliance with the conditions of their release. The work of the SIR officer will in most cases be augmented by volunteers supplied in each plan developed by CPCP staff. It should, therefore, be unacceptable for any inmate to be denied SIR status due to a lack of SIR officers. To the extent that a shortage of SIR officers is viewed as a barrier by the ADOC to placing eligible inmates on SIR, then the Defendants should be compelled to hire additional SIR officers, detail officers from non-essential posts to this function, or allow CPCP staff to fill this function.

8. For each eligible inmate who is denied SIR status, a detailed, individualized memorandum should be drafted describing the rationale for denial. Completed denial memos should be provided to the Court and to the Plaintiffs along with a copy of the community punishment plan submitted on the inmate's behalf. A mechanism for appealing all denials to the office of the Director should be established and pursued at the discretion of each inmate.

9. For each inmate released on SIR after a community punishment plan is developed and submitted on his/her behalf, the CPCP responsible for preparing the plan should be compensated by the ADOC in a manner consistent with agreements between CPCP and the DOC regarding diversions of prison-bound defendants.

10. Eligible "sponsors" should be expanded to include individuals other than family so long as they are of good moral character and are willing and able to provide the support necessary to assist in the successful transition of the inmate back to the community.

11. Inmates granted SIR status should be released to the conditions of their plan within one week of the decision.

12. SIR officers are typically assigned to work out of one or more release facilities. It is not clear to what extent inmates are excluded from consideration because their potential residences are located a considerable distance from such facilities. But this should not be allowed to serve as a barrier to participation. By allowing CPCP offices and other locations as points of contact for each inmate, the same purpose can be served as that of a work release facility. The Community Punishment and Corrections Act provides for offenders from any county to complete their com-

munity punishment plan in any other county that has an operating CPCP, assuming the sentencing judge and the presiding judge in the receiving county concur.

PRE-DISCRETIONARY LEAVE

The PDL program is described in the ADOC Classification Manual as, "Placement which allows selected inmates to return to placement with approved sponsors when they are within the final portion of their commitment to the ADOC in order to secure employment, housing, training, etc. to ease their adjustment for return to society." Like SIR, PDL is a constructive tool available to the ADOC for thoughtfully transitioning appropriate inmates back to the community as they approach the end of their sentence or parole. Close examination of the criteria for PDL participation, however, reveals some of the same unnecessary barriers to eligibility that are seen in the SIR program. By placing greater emphasis on helping qualify inmates for participation in the program, rather than eliminating from consideration those who technically fall just outside of eligibility requirements, the ADOC could very likely ease the unacceptable level of overcrowding at Tutwiler without compromising public safety, while also lending meaningful assistance to inmates for a successful return to their communities as productive citizens.

Justice Policy Institute found that PDL represents another administrative mechanism available to the ADOC to control and thoughtfully manage its inmate population. By evaluating women housed at the Tutwiler Prison and other ADOC facilities for inmates who are or could be made eligible for PDL, this administrative mechanism could be used to aid in safely easing the level of overcrowding at Tutwiler Prison. Therefore, it was recommended that:

1. The ADOC should produce, within one week, a comprehensive list of all female inmates at the Tutwiler Prison and other ADOC facilities who are eligible for PDL based on the criteria described on page 42 of the ADOC Classification Manual. The list should also include a special section for those inmates who would be eligible if the slight adjustments to existing criteria described below.

2. As with SIR, inmates are excluded from participation in PDL if they have received a "major disciplinary" in the past four months. As noted above, it is not entirely clear what constitutes a "major disciplinary." Therefore, for purposes of compiling the list of PDL eligible inmates, only those guilty of "highest severity" and "high severity" disciplinaries should be excluded.

3. Exclusionary offense criteria include those convicted of Felony Assault on Police Officer, Trafficking in Drugs, Felony DUI, or a sex crime. It is further noted that, "current policy requires that the details of a drug offense be used rather than how the crime may have come to be titled." Therefore, even if an inmate was allowed to plead a trafficking case down to a less serious offense such as distribution, sales, or possession, that individual is not eligible for consideration for community custody. Inmates should not be excluded from participation in a valuable program such as PDL based on alleged behavior.

4. Inmates must also be "within 12 months of their end of sentence (EOS) or parole." The classification manual does not make clear if this reference includes those who are within 12 months of parole eligibility or within 12 months of an established

parole date. It is recommended that the ADOC exercise its discretion and apply PDL program benefits to those inmates who are within 12 months of EOS or parole eligibility.

5. Because the PDL program is specifically designed to aid inmates in the securing of employment and housing, they should have the full benefit of CPCP staff who specialize in designing community-based plans and securing needed resources for offenders. CPCP staff should be allowed to interview and examine the institutional files of all female inmates whose names appear on the list described in #1 above to help prepare community punishment plans for presentation the community review board. CPCP staff responsible for developing the plans should be allowed to attend the entire community review board hearing at which PDL access is determined. CPCP staff should be allowed to make a formal presentation to the Central Review Board (CRB) to describe in detail the specific elements of the plan and the rationale for why they believe the plan is appropriate for the particular inmate.

6. Decisions by the CRB should be reached and announced at the close of each hearing, but under no circumstances should a decision be delayed for more than 24 hours.

7. Denials should be accompanied by a detailed written description as to precisely why the inmate was deemed inappropriate for access to PDL in spite of the individualized community punishment plan submitted on their behalf.

8. Denials should be appealable to the Director of the ADOC.

9. CPCP staff should be compensated for their work in developing each plan that is accepted by the CRB in accordance with the agreement that exists between the DOC and the CPCP relative to the diversion of prison-bound offenders.

10. Institutional delays between CRB decisions and actual release should be eliminated by requiring that inmates granted access to PDL be allowed to exit the Tutwiler Prison or any other DOC facility in which they are housed and reenter the community to embark on the elements of their plan within no more than one week of the decision.

WORK RELEASE

Correctional systems operating at or above capacity are forced to function in a highly interdependent manner. When one facility is operating over capacity, it invariably has a ripple effect on other facilities that are dependent on the smooth operation of those facilities where prisoners are typically moved. This interdependence is very likely at play for the ADOC, particularly relative to the efficiency of its work release facility for women.

There is a common tendency within departments of corrections to retain compliant and relatively high-earning prisoners at work release facilities, rather than move them into supervised, independent living situations so room can be created for those who remain backed-up at institutions. In part because work release prisoners contribute a percentage of their income, and because it is more desirable for correctional staff to manage a facility filled with compliant inmates who know the rules and are known not to violate them, work release facilities are ripe for "hoarding" "good" inmates. This practice creates an obvious backlog in the system because those most likely to do well in the community, i.e., those who have been successful in work release for six or more months without a violation, are not allowed to transition to their homes or other community placements, freeing up a work release bed in the process.

I witnessed a very similar situation when working with the ADOC as a consultant for the Edna McConnell Clark Foundation during the early 1990s. To remedy the situation I led an effort to convene a mass reclassification effort of all the inmates at the ADOC work release facility for men in Jefferson County, Alabama. Four or five tables, each with four chairs, were arranged in a large room far enough from each other to provide for some measure of confidentiality. At each table sat a correctional counselor from the work release facility and one or more members of the Jefferson County Alternative Sentencing Project. Work release inmates from each counselor's caseload were brought to a table one at a time, along with their institutional folders, and each was assessed for SIR or PDL eligibility/consideration. Community punishment plans were developed on behalf of the inmates who were seemingly good candidates to enhance standard SIR or PDL conditions. This exercise, which was fully supported and endorsed by Morris Thigpen, who was then the Commissioner of Corrections, produced a reduction in the work release population of approximately 20%. This reduction allowed for eligible inmates housed in more secure prisons to be transferred to the work release program. A similar review of female inmates in work release facilities across the state should be conducted and could almost certainly produce even better results.

Specifically, I would recommend a thorough and independent review of practices within the Alabama DOC work release facilities for women with specific regard to length of stay, release planning, and eligibility/appropriateness of the population for movement out of the facilities and into less restrictive setting. This review should be undertaken immediately and completed without delay so its findings can be acted upon promptly to further relieve the stress of overcrowding. Should the review reveal that there are a significant number of female inmates languishing in work release, an effort should be conducted without delay to that is similar in design and function to what was done in Jefferson County a decade ago.

About the Author

Tim Roche was Executive Director of the Justice Policy Institute when this chapter was written. Currently, he is President of New York State Youth Advocate Programs.

Part 2

Juvenile Justice Issues and Programs

In the juvenile justice system, as with the adult criminal justice system, movement in programs, practices, and policies is often guided—or coerced—under the darkening cloud of one perceived crisis or another. Without such crises, it is too often the case that little or only exceptional guidance is delivered from proactive planning initiatives instigated by sage administrators, soundly-operated agencies, or innovative legislators or other oversight bodies.

At the moment, for instance, we are hearing more and more about the rise of "violent girls" entering the juvenile justice system and its institutions. As was not the case during past "moral panics," some seemingly accurate data is now being posited for those interested in discussing the matter, but still too little attention is directed toward deciphering what these data mean in the real activities of girls' lives.

The six chapters in this section directly address, and hopefully will help to shape, the form of juvenile justice interventions that affect girls and young women:

- Francine T. Sherman, J.D., who directs the Juvenile Rights Advocacy Project at the Boston College School of Law, describes the pathways and processes that involve excessive numbers of girls in the juvenile justice system, as well as those that might divert girls from detention to less restrictive program and sanctioning options.

- Kristi Holsinger, Ph.D., a criminologist at the University of Missouri, Kansas City, challenges the "mismatch" of delinquent girls in intervention programs designed for boys, and reports results of a study of girls in Ohio's juvenile detention facilities that establish a footing for programs designed specifically for girls and their particular needs.

- Scott K. Okamoto, Ph.D., who currently teaches social work at Arizona State University, and Meda Chesney-Lind, Ph.D., who worked with Okamoto on this project when they were both at the University of Hawaii, pierce girls' relational aggression, describing it as a response to powerlessness.

- Hawaiian researchers Konia Frietas, M.A., and Meda Chesney-Lind examine how practitioners talk about and assess the problems and processes of working with girls in the juvenile justice system, including girls' relationships, their distrust of adults, the challenges of cross-gender supervision, and coping with girls' troubled family relationships.

- Veteran juvenile justice researcher Rebecca Maniglia, M.A., who is now working on her doctorate in Chicago, reviews the importance of "talk" and "listening" in working with juvenile girls.

- And, Lyn Mikel Brown, Ed.D., who teaches at Colby College in Maine, and Meda Chesney-Lind provide a short essay on the trivialization of girls' anger, an essay that ends with Brown's "Twelve Ways to Prevent Girlfighting and Build Allies Instead."

Chapter 9

Promoting Justice for Girls in an Unjust System

by Francine T. Sherman, J.D.

An earlier version of this chapter originally appeared as a three-part article in Women, Girls & Criminal Justice, *Vol. 3, Nos. 4, 5, and 6, June/July 2002, August/September 2002, and October/November 2002.*

INTRODUCTION

Angela (a composite of many of the girls I have known over the years) entered the juvenile justice system at age four, entered foster care at age six, was separated permanently from her brother at age seven, was sexually abused beginning at age eight, lost her mother to drugs at age 12, became a prostitute at age 13, had a child at age 15, and lost her child to adoption at age 17. Along the way she lived in 15 foster homes, and eight group homes, was hospitalized four times, and attended eight different schools. She had at least 15 different case workers; was found delinquent for shoplifting, prostitution, and aggravated assault; and ran away from placements more than 30 times.

Angela is Latina and has long, wavy, brown hair. She writes poetry and, when she is feeling good about herself, goes to church and reads spiritual books. She is very emotional and devoted to friends. She engages people easily, saying hello to passersby on the street and chatting with people everywhere she goes. When I meet with her she asks how I am doing before launching into the issue of the day. She is smart and quickly grasps everything I say and offers solid suggestions. She is disorganized and impulsive and seems to live in the moment. She quickly becomes caught up in disputes and difficulties on the street and, although she has big plans, she has difficulty following through on most things.

Above all else, Angela is resilient. Her story may sound extreme, but it is not. In fact, it is remarkably typical of girls in the justice system. Lawyers for girls around the country describe similar cases of early victimization combined with gross system failure and inconsistency beginning in the child welfare system and moving up through the delinquency and criminal justice systems. Recent research describes girls in the system with histories of multiple incidents of sexual and physical abuse, current school failure, and unmet educational and mental health needs. We know that girls enter the delinquency system disproportionately for misdemeanors or misbehavior, and remain in the system due to probation and parole violations, and running away (*Justice by Gender*, 2001).

PROBLEMS BETWEEN GIRLS AND THEIR LAWYERS

In its groundbreaking report, *A Call for Justice*, the American Bar Association's Juvenile Justice Center identified disposition and post-disposition practice as critical areas for lawyers representing delinquent youth (Puritz, 1996). The report is clear that quality representation should extend beyond delinquency proceedings into ancillary legal matters such as special education (Puritz, 1996). This is true for girls. Education and mental health advocacy may prevent system recidivism and offer girls the best chance of developing into healthy young women. Girls particularly need representation across system boundaries: from delinquency to child welfare, from education to mental health. Attorneys for girls must pay particular attention to detention, disposition, and post-disposition stages of the delinquency case, to reduce girls' time away from their communities without appropriate services, and increase their access to appropriate services.

Unfortunately, many delinquency lawyers describe their female clients as demanding and describe working with them as draining. This attitude is perpetuated in programs and probation departments. When the juvenile probation department in Baltimore, Maryland, developed its Female Intervention Team, e.g., probation officers were offered a caseload reduction to devote their attention to female probationers. Probation officers made their feelings about the difficulties of working with girls clear, agreeing to trade 10 boys' cases for one girl's case. (Daniel, 1999).

The first step toward appreciating and successfully working with girls is to understand their development, from which many of their expectations for counsel arise. A girl client's expectations for relationships with counsel and others is based in her development and socialization, yet they can make it difficult for lawyers to establish and maintain professional boundaries. While a female lawyer might identify closely with girls' experiences, male attorneys may be uncomfortable with the sexual abuse that is often part of the girl's background and find it difficult to maintain a healthy and appropriate relationship. Both need to be conscious of transference and role reversal in their relationships with girl clients (Chesney-Lind & Freitas, 1999).

In addition to their developmental needs, girls can be difficult to work with because there are so few services for girls—and those that exist are difficult to access. Moreover, girls are uniquely affected by social factors like pregnancy and sexual assault, which raise complex psychological and service challenges for advocates.

Girls have high expectations for counsel and are disappointed when those expectations are not met. In one California study girls interviewed believed that their lawyers did not take the time to know their cases, did not work hard enough to obtain a good result, and did not care or respect them (Acoca & Dedel, 1998). Girls interviewed in Cook County echoed this negative assessment but also described disappointment with lawyers who, they felt, "didn't care" about their cases and were "not really involved." In assessing both probation officers and lawyers, "good" meant caring about the case, demonstrated by talking to those in power (judge) and achieving their desired disposition. In addition to caring as a major theme, Cook County girls equated good lawyering with being in control of the case and the courtroom. (Cook County findings are based on interviews on file with the author.)

In a study done by the Juvenile Rights Advocacy Project in Massachusetts, girls in the justice system had a favorable assessment of their lawyers' legal abilities but a poor assessment of their lawyers' abilities outside of the courtroom. Thus, while girls in the Massachusetts system could generally agree that their lawyers cared about their traditional legal needs, they felt their lawyers did little to help them at disposition and post-disposition. Lawyers did not help obtain services, work with multiple agencies, or work on girls' educational plans. Moreover, echoing the theme of "caring," the girls in Massachusetts thought their lawyers did not establish relationships with them, did not call them regularly or stay in contact. (These findings are reflected in an evaluation of the Juvenile Rights Advocacy Project's girls' representation initiative and are on file with the author.)

Lawyers representing girls must be familiar with adolescent female development and understand the impact of early trauma. Moreover, lawyers must be careful to follow-through and not establish expectations they are unable to meet. Inconsistency and disappointment in relationships already characterize the lives of the majority of the girls in the delinquency system.

PATHWAYS OF GIRLS IN THE JUSTICE SYSTEM

Victimization

A history of physical or sexual victimization is one of the most common characteristics of girls in the justice system. Seventy percent of women in prison report that they were physically or sexually abused as children (Amnesty International, 1999). Two-thirds of girls interviewed in a study of girls in the justice system in Duval County, Florida, reported being abused or neglected (Acoca, 2000). A staggering 92% of girls interviewed in four California counties in 1998 had suffered some form of abuse: 88% suffered emotional abuse; 81% reported physical abuse; and 56% report one or more form of sexual abuse (40% reporting at least one incident of forced sex and 17% reporting more than five incidents of forced sex) (Acoca & Dedel, 1998). Chronically delinquent girls studied by the Oregon Social Learning Center experienced an average of 4.28 forms of severe sexual abuse, with an average age for the first abuse of 7.43 years (Chamberlain & Moore, 2002).

Education Failure

Even more than for boys, negative attitudes toward school and school failure are powerful predictors of delinquency in girls (Harris & Jones, 1998). School failure (in the form of truancy, suspension, poor grades, or expulsion) was the most statistically significant risk factor for girls who were repeat offenders in Duval County, Florida (Acoca, 2000). Girls are particularly vulnerable to school failure during pre- and early-adolescence (Acoca & Dedel, 1998). In Duval County, Florida, 39% of girls whose case files were reviewed and 90% of girls interviewed had histories of school suspension. Twenty-five percent of girls interviewed indicated a need for special education services and 36% of the case files reviewed indicated special education needs. It is likely these numbers under-represent the level of educational need, because education-related data was missing from a significant percentage of the case files: further evidence of the systems' failure to attend to the education of those girls (Acoca, 2000).

Multiple System Involvement

Due to histories of victimization, many girls in the delinquency system are already in the custody of the child welfare system as dependent children or status offenders. Children in multiple systems are often disadvantaged by poor cross-system communication, the tendency of the dependency system to "pass off" a youth when she becomes involved in delinquency, and the absence of a parent at detention and disposition hearings. A 1998 study by the Vera Justice Institute (*Adolescent Pathways*, 1998) highlighted the costs, to youth and the public, of the lack of coordination between the child welfare and juvenile justice systems. That study estimated that 1,000 foster children were in the criminal or juvenile justice systems in New York City in 1997. The study found that 15% of youth entering detention from mid-December 1996 to mid-February 1997 were foster kids, which was eight times the rate of foster children among the New York City general population. Yet the foster children in detention were not committing serious offenses that might account for their significant presence in detention. The study concluded that lack of coordination between the juvenile justice and foster care systems was largely responsible, because foster kids were less likely to have an adult present at any stage of the proceeding, thereby reducing their chances of release. Moreover, juvenile justice personnel had difficulty even determining whom in the child welfare agency to call when a foster child was arrested. Significantly, foster children were far more likely to be arrested at "home" than other youth. Once in detention, foster kids typically lost their foster placements, further reducing their chances of release and increasing their instability.

GIRLS' EXPERIENCE IN THE JUSTICE SYSTEM

Poorly Served and Mistreated

Girls arrive in detention in a particularly vulnerable state. Overwhelmingly, girls in the justice system have been victims of physical and sexual violence, often in their homes and often throughout their childhoods. They suffer from eating disorders, abuse alcohol and drugs, and they are sexually active at a young age (often with much older men as their sexual partners). They become pregnant and parents as young teens. Quietly, they fail in school, internalizing their failures and suffering from depression and post-traumatic stress. Many girls in the system have attempted suicide. Delinquent girls typically have dependency system histories of family separation, multiple foster home placements, and running away. Teenage girls' self images depend on healthy relationships, yet these girls' abuse histories, school failures, and system involvement are destructive of relationships and the development of positive identities and success.

In detention, girls are re-victimized by demeaning and sexually abusive language used by staff. Girls are sexually assaulted by staff and then re-traumatized by the use of restraints and isolation. Girls interviewed in the California Youth Authority described being called "hood rat," "slut," and "little hooker;" one girl described a teacher threatening to "kick her ass" (Acoca & Dedel, 1998). In one Massachusetts detention center, girls reported being called "whore" and "trash" by the director who, when the girls were slow to line up for the bathroom, would say "if the line was for dime bags, you'd come running." (These are some of the findings of an investigation conducted by the Juvenile Rights Advocacy Project, Massachusetts Department of Youth Services and Massachusetts Office of Child Care Services and are on file with the author.) A girl in Chicago reported, "The staff … cuss at you, they yell at you, they put you down…." This use of demeaning, sexual epithets by detention staff toward girls is a clear violation of their human rights and national standards (*see* Amnesty International, 1999; 1998).

Girls also report physical and sexual abuse by male staff in detention centers and residential programs. At least 26 states have statutes aimed at protecting youth in custody by imposing criminal penalties for sexual misconduct by staff with prisoners either explicitly or implicitly including minors in detention and programs. Some statutes explicitly reference juveniles, such as the Iowa sexual misconduct statute prohibiting "Sexual misconduct with offenders and juveniles …[by]…(2) An officer, employee, contractor, vendor, volunteer, or agent of a juvenile placement facility." Iowa Code Ann. § 709.16(2) (West 1993 & Supp. 2000). Others statutes use general language, implying inclusion of juveniles. Moreover, statutory rape laws are available for prosecution in many cases in which girls are under the age proscribed by statute. Statutory rape eliminates consent as a defense to rape, reflecting the vulnerability inherent in minority (*see generally*, Oberman, 2000).

Though girls in programs talk of sexual contact with male staff as a common occurrence, the small number of reported cases suggests that a relatively small percentage of these cases are prosecuted. It is clear that the power imbalance inherent in any custodial relationship, and the age difference between girls in custody and male staff together, are inherently coercive elements to which girls with histories of victimization are particularly vulnerable. [*See, e.g., State v. Martin*, 561 A.2d 631, 636 (N.J. Super. Ct. App. Div., 1989) (upheld conviction for sexual assault, official misconduct, and sexual conduct against male staff member at youth shelter holding that his supervisory role was the sort of power imbalance that the law was designed to address and that the 17-year-old girl's consent was not a defense); *Tennessee v. Halton*, 1988 WL 105722, at *5 (Tenn. Crim. App. 1988) (upholding convictions for rape and sexual assault of two juvenile girls by male Detention Center staff).]

Restraints and isolation are common mechanisms for controlling behavior in detention, and are used more frequently when facilities are overcrowded (Burrell, 2000). Jurisdictions are inconsistent in training staff in gender-appropriate restraint methods for girls, some of whom are pregnant and many of whom relive the trauma of sexual abuse when restrained and placed in isolation. Isolation increases the risk of suicide in adolescents and, given that twice as many girls as boys attempt suicide, is a dangerous practice.

Development Negatively Impacted

Even for girls without trauma histories, detention and incarceration interferes with healthy development. Developmentally, adolescent girls are preoccupied with fairness and can be outspoken and demanding in their efforts to correct unfairness they see. Girls in the system are aware that as girls they have fewer programs and poor conditions. They resent these inequities, impeding their progress and reducing their trust in the ability of the adults to help and support them. Adolescent girls build healthy identities from feelings of success in which they learn that they are loved and capable. For girls, who see women in society as less powerful than men and who have seen their mothers victimized in abusive relationships, developing a sense of mastery and control is particularly important (Beyer, 2000). Detention makes girls feel powerless. The most common complaint among girls in detention is of being kept in the dark by caseworkers, lawyers, and probation officers who do not contact them, yet have complete and unfettered control over placement and service decisions. Girls express confusion about the reasons behind their moves in and out of programs and detention, who the players are in the system, and what roles they play. This lack of control generates frustration at not having a voice in decisions about their lives and does not meet their developmental needs to feel in charge.

"You just sit there basically and wait until when they feel like taking you out or switching you to another place and you just wait. It's structured and everything and you have rules, but there's nothing there to help you. There's no therapy, there's no groups, nothing. You just sit and that wasn't helping me at all. That was making me worse."

GIRLS ARE EXCESSIVELY DETAINED

Nationally, girls are being detained at higher rates than boys, with the use of detention for girls increasing dramatically through the 1990s. From 1988 to 1997, the rate of delinquency cases involving detention increased 65% for girls as compared with 30% for boys. This increase was across all offense categories, with a 156% increase in the use of detention for girls in person cases and a 63% increase in public order cases (Porter, 2000). Interestingly, e.g., among chronically delinquent youth in a study conducted by the Oregon Social Learning Center, boys had an average of 14.2 prior offenses and girls an average of 11.8 prior offenses, yet boys had averaged 72 days in detention while girls had averaged 131 days (Chamberlain, 2002). This inequity and increase in detention rates for girls is likely the result of a number of factors including an increase in female arrest rates, the practice of detaining girls to provide them with services, and excessive lengths of stay for girls due to lack of programs.

As with boys, minority girls are disproportionately confined. This is consistent with national data indicating that African-American girls the fastest growing population in the delinquency system and African-American women the fastest growing adult incarcerated population. Nationally, African-American girls comprise nearly half of all those in secure detention, and Latinas constitute 13%. Although Caucasian girls constitute 65% of the population at risk, they account for only 34% of girls in secure detention. Seven of every 10 cases involving Caucasian girls are dismissed, compared with three of every 10 cases for African-American girls (*Justice by Gender*, 2001). In one jurisdiction where African-American girls comprised 31% of youth admitted to detention and Latinas 6%, advocates said that while resources are scarce for girls generally, they are virtually nonexistent for girls of color. There are few culturally-specific girls' programs, and one of the limited residential treatment resources had a history of declining placements of black girls whose behavior in programs can be misunderstood without an understanding of the developmental and cultural context.

A review of data on detention return for girls indicates both the significant roles played by probation violation, warrants, and program failure as offenses, which bring girls back into detention, as well as the gender gap in detention recidivism for these reasons. Across sites studied in the mid-1990s, girls returned to detention for warrants, probation or parole violation, or program failure in greater percentages than boys and that gap increased with each detention return. Thus, across the sites, of youth who returned to detention once within one year, 53% of girls as compared to 41% of boys did so for warrant, probation or parole violation, or program failure. Of youth returning twice within one year, 66% of girls as compared with 47% of boys did so for warrant, probation or parole violation, or program failure. Moreover, of youth returning to detention three times within one year, 72% of girls as compared with 49% of boys did so for warrant, probation or parole violation, or program failure. The gender gap increased 7% between the first and second detention return and 11% between the first and third (*Juvenile Detention Alternatives Initiative*, 1994-1997).

It is clear that advocates for girls must take into account both the needs girls present and the ways in which they are affected by systemwide inequities.

HOW GIRLS GET BOOTSTRAPPED INTO THE SYSTEM

Bootstrapping, which is turning a status offense into delinquency and confinement through contempt, minor delinquency charges, or probation violations, contributes to detention overcrowding and its corresponding harms for girls and may reach into the adult criminal justice system making incarceration as an adult woman more likely. Contempt continues to be used to change status offenses to delinquency, allowing juvenile courts to detain girls for behavior that would otherwise not be criminal. Girls are far more likely than boys to be incarcerated as a result of contempt. Although defense lawyers have observed this for years, a study of contempt practices in Florida in the early 1990s confirmed the practice. The Florida study found that while the typical male offender had a 3.9% chance of incarceration, which increased to 4.4% if he was found in contempt, the typical female offender had a 1.8% chance of incarceration, which increased to 63.2% if she was held in contempt (Bishop & Frazier, 1992). Juvenile courts are more likely to use the contempt sanction for girls and when they do, the sanction is very likely to result in detention. In many cases, courts use contempt to detain girls when they run away, and arrests of girls for running away exceed those of boys. In 1999, although girls were only 27% of the juveniles arrested overall, they accounted for 59% of juvenile arrests for running away and 54% of arrests for prostitution (Snyder, 2000).

The Juvenile Justice and Delinquency Prevention Act (JJDP Act) prohibits incarceration of status offenders absent a valid court order (VCO). In 1974, Congress passed the Juvenile Justice and Delinquency Prevention Act, 42 U.S.C. §5633 (12)(A), which among its four mandates prohibited the incarceration of status offenders. This deinstitutionalization of status offenders (DSO) prohibition was partially a response to accounts of girls being incarcerated for disobeying their parents and running away from troubled families. In 1980, the JJDP Act's DSO mandate was amended to provide an exception for those cases in which the youth violates a VCO. That exception provides the authority for courts to exercise their contempt powers, or use specific state VCO statutes, and detain girls who run from their homes or from placements for status offenses. The practice of confining a female status offender for contempt has become known as bootstrapping.

Some states allow status offenses to be bootstrapped into delinquency through the contempt finding. States have varied approaches to allow contempt for violations of juvenile court orders generally or specifically in status cases. Some have general juvenile contempt statutes and have not prohibited contempt in status offense cases. Many states have explicitly authorized the use of contempt in status offense cases through case law. Some of those states allow the practice, but restrict it by requiring courts to consider alternatives first and use contempt sparingly. In Florida, the legislature responded to a 1992 case holding that although the juvenile court had the authority to adjudicate contempt, it did not have the authority to order secure confinement for juveniles in contempt, without a statute specifically authorizing confinement in a secure facility for "a child who commits direct contempt of court or indirect contempt of a valid court order." Fla. Stat. ch. 985.216(1) (2000). Other states have approached the issue through case interpretation of existing contempt statutes. The Supreme Court of Hawaii, e.g., held that the family court might adjudicate status offenders for criminal contempt for violations of court orders. In its holding the court balanced "…the policies of 'deinstitutionalizing' status offenders, on one hand, and ensuring effective administration of the family court's function, on the other." *In the Interest of Jane Doe*, 96 P.3d 562, 568 (Haw. 2001). In some states, such as California, the courts have used statutes giving juvenile courts contempt authority to allow secure confinement for status offenders who violate court orders while maintaining that this practice does not constitute "bootstrapping" because it does not elevate the status offense into delinquency. *In re Ricardo A.*, 38 Cal. Rptr.2d 586, 591 (Cal. Ct. App. 1995).

Behind these findings of contempt is judicial frustration at the lack of a mechanism to enforce court orders in the face of status offenders, many of whom are girls, who repeatedly defy them by running away in direct violation of court orders. New York's family courts struggled with this issue in a series of three cases in which three family court judges determined separately that delinquency confinement for criminal contempt was lawful as a sanction for violations of PINS orders: *Asia H.*, 705 N.Y.S.2d at 874; *Jennifer G.*, 695 N.Y.S.2d at 884-85; *Kimberly A.P.*, 678 N.Y.S.2d at 869. In these cases family court judges expressed outright exasperation at girls who violate PINS orders by running away from home in the belief that the court is powerless to compel their compliance. The matter was finally resolved against contempt authority by the Appellate Division. *In re Naquan J.*, 727 N.Y.S.2d 124 (2001).

A minority of states hold that their juvenile courts do not have, or have only limited, authority to find a status offender in contempt and use secure confinement as a sanction. These states prohibit the use of contempt to securely confine status offenders. In a series of cases of status offenders who run away from placement, Pennsylvania courts have reiterated the distinctions between delinquency and dependency systems and prohibited the use of contempt to transform dependency into delinquency. *In re R.B.*, 621 A.2d 1038, 1040-41 (Pa. Super. Ct. 1993). Similarly, in 1999 the Massachusetts Supreme Judicial Court held that the juvenile court does not have the power to issue contempt orders against juveniles for failing to comply with conditions of status offense custody. In reaching this decision the court noted the juvenile court's longstanding inability to enforce its orders in status offense cases and asked the legislature to address this issue. *Florence F.*, 709 N.E.2nd 418, 422 (Mass. 1999). The Appellate Division in New York eventually settled the issue, as noted in the preceding paragraph. Like Massachusetts, the Appellate Division invited the legislature to correct this defect in the state law. *In re Naquan J.*, 727 N.Y.S.2d 124, 125,128 (2001).

Among states that specifically do allow the use of contempt to punish status offenders who violate court orders, some limit its use to repeat violators of court orders or allow confinement only if there is no less restrictive alternative. South Carolina specifically allows confinement of status offenders for contempt but limits the term of confinement to not more than 90 days. S.C. Code Ann. § 20-7-7810(F) (Law. Co-op. 1976); *In re Tonisha G.*, 520 S.E.2d 807, 808 (S.C. 1999). Other states allow the practice but refer to the requirements for delinquency dispositions to prevent secure placements except in the most serious cases of repeat offenders.

The Juvenile Rights Advocacy Project (JRAP) has been representing girls across legal actions and administrative systems for the last five years. According to JRAP data for this period, 67 girls represented through the project were involved with 265 legal or administrative cases (an average of four cases for each girl). These cases included delinquency, status offenses, special education, school suspension, dependency, post-disposition, and civil legal matters. Success for girls requires better coordination across systems and legal strategies that are comprehensive, hold systems accountable for efficiently providing services, and meet girls' needs.

DISPOSITION ADVOCACY FOR GIRLS

[N]othing was being dealt with and … I was dealing with everything by myself and just sitting there and having all that time on my hands and just wondering why I'm sitting here and why I'm not … these are people that are supposed to help me and … nothing was being done and when it got close to me being 18 and they wanted to lock me up … again for another year. I was like they just, I'm going to have no preparation for when I'm 18 out in the world by myself. They were going to just do nothing to help me. They were just, 18 and then I'm done. I would have walked out the doors and have nowhere to go and I would have been all by myself and not have known what to do.

—Quotation from an interview with a girl in the Massachusetts delinquency system.With this as a backdrop, this article, and one in the next issue, will present some potential areas for effective legal advocacy for girls.

Using the Adoption and Safe Families Act

Although the federal Adoption and Safe Families Act of 1997, Pub. L. No. 105-89, 11 Stat. 2115 (amending 42 U.S.C § 671 (a) (ASFA)), has resulted in permanent removal of children from many incarcerated girls and women, it also may be used to support the use of child welfare and community resources for delinquent girls. ASFA, passed in 1997, places requirements on states in order to receive Title IV-E reimbursement for juveniles in eligible foster care. Chief among those requirements are strict time frames for permanent plans for children in care. Advocates for incarcerated women and girls have criticized ASFA and its state counterparts for prompting the permanent removal of children from incarcerated mothers without family resources. In many cases ASFA's time frames have resulted in parental rights being terminated and children being placed in the foster care system without identified adoptive families and with little practical chance of adoption.

However, because ASFA's requirements apply to delinquent and status offending youth as well as dependents and youth in foster care under voluntary placement agreements, it may be a tool to reduce the time a youth spends out of home and prompt probation, the juvenile justice agency, and the dependency agency to work together to provide the most appropriate services to the juvenile and her family. To fulfill ASFA's mandate that states make reasonable efforts to prevent removal from the home, a girl who would otherwise be placed in detention or a delinquency program, might be placed into eligible foster care. States that collect Title IV-E funding for delinquent youth have the greatest incentive to comply with its requirements and should have the judicial and administrative structure in place to comply with ASFA's provisions in delinquency cases.

States may collect Title IV-E reimbursement for delinquent youth who are in eligible foster care only when they satisfy ASFA's time frames and requirements for findings that reasonable efforts have been made to prevent removal from the home, and that remaining in the home would be contrary to the welfare of the child.

Virtually every state has incorporated some aspect of ASFA into their state child welfare system either through statute, court rule, or regulation. According to the U.S. General Accounting Office (2000), as of 1998, 22 states applied for and received the Title IV-E reimbursement for youth in their delinquency systems (Alabama, Alaska, California, Colorado, Delaware, Indiana, Kentucky, Louisiana, Maryland, Minnesota, New Hampshire, New York, North Dakota, Ohio, Pennsylvania, Rhode Island, South Dakota, Tennessee, Texas Utah, Virginia, and Wyoming). States can be reimbursed for both the placement and associated administrative costs.

ASFA requires specific findings and conditions upon removal of the child from the home. ASFA provides that states may receive Title IV-E reimbursement for youth in an eligible foster home or childcare institution for a defined period within which the custodial agency must provide a permanent plan for a youth in custody. The client must have been eligible to receive public assistance at the time of removal or six months prior to removal. In reimbursed cases, the court must find that the agency made reasonable efforts to prevent removal of the child from the home, and that remaining in the home would be contrary to the welfare of the child. Regardless of whether the client's initial placement is in eligible foster care or whether you would predict her eventual placement in eligible foster care, judges must make these determinations at the first placement in any kind of substitute care (including detention) for ASFA benefits to be available later in the case. The statute sets out detailed time frames and requirements for permanency hearings, case planning, and case reviews.

Reasonable efforts to prevent removal might include assessments for special education services, assessments for mental health and other therapeutic services, family-based prevention work, use of community based detention alternatives, and placements with family or friends. Because many steps should be taken prior to detention to satisfy the "reasonable efforts" requirements, ASFA may offer a tool to courts and counsel who become frustrated with a lack of human services to minor delinquency offenders with significant social services needs.

Seeking the Least Restrictive Alternative

Courts are guided by statutory standards such as "least restrictive alternative" in ordering dispositions. Disposition is a critical opportunity to argue the package of services that will best meet the needs and support the strengths of young women in the system and that are most likely to return them to their communities. Planning for disposition is a central part of delinquency, gender-sensitive, community-based services, that can both meet the needs of the girl and insure community safety, while offering solid alternatives to secure placement. Disposition planning should begin early in the case and should actively include the client, her family, and potential service providers.

Typically, disposition standards are statutory and allow significant judicial discretion. Most state statutes have some language referring to rehabilitation, the minor's interests, or least restrictive alternatives. Juvenile courts in Alaska, for example, must consider the best interests of the minor and the interests of the public. Alaska Stat. §47.12.120(d) (Michie, 2001). Indiana focuses on fostering family connections and services, providing that the disposition order must be consistent with the safety of the community and the best interests of the minor and, within those parameters, must be the least restrictive alternative, close to the parents' home, consistent with family autonomy, least disruptive of family life, impose the least restraint on the child's freedom, and provide reasonable opportunity for family participation. Ind. Code §31-37-18-6 (1998). States also draw on the purpose clauses of their Juvenile Court Acts in assessing placements. Purpose clauses, which reference "rehabilitation," "best interests and welfare," or the restorative justice concept of increasing competency, may form the basis for arguments in favor of gender responsive services.

It should also be noted that a few states have reduced discretion in disposition decisions and introduced legislatively mandated disposition grids into their systems. In these states the court's discretion is exercised within a grid based on the seriousness of the offense and the offense history, limiting opportunities for alternatives.

Disposition plans promoting gender responsive services and community-based, non-system resources are alternatives to removing girls from their communities. Because so few state delinquency placements provide gender responsive services for delinquent girls, disposition statutes and purpose clauses can be used to support a well-developed disposition plan which provides gender-sensitive programming focusing on girls' strengths and needs. Creative disposition planning should draw on community programs for girls, which may be found in churches, community centers, and community-based non-profits rarely used by the justice system. These community-based resources are diverse and provide alternatives to typical justice system deficit-based programming, which removes girls from their communities. Disposition planning should focus on girls' strengths and needs.

ADVOCACY ISSUES THROUGHOUT THE POST-DISPOSITION PHASE

Once the juvenile court has imposed its disposition, the case moves into what maybe its longest and most critical phase: post-disposition. Post-disposition advocacy is critical for all delinquent youth and particularly for girls. During the post-disposition phase, advocacy should:

- Ensure the juvenile justice agency does, in fact, provide the services mandated by the courts and statutes;

- Promote the girl's return to her family and community as soon as possible;

- Provide aftercare access to community and system resources to reduce the likelihood of the child's return to the delinquency system.

Shared Post-Disposition Authority

Post-disposition authority is typically shared between the judiciary and administrative agency. In most states, statutes set out the general contours of shared authority, but challenges to agency decisions have been common and courts struggle to apply general statutory frameworks to specific cases of disputes over placement, services, and parole. Virtually all state systems for making post-disposition decisions have some elements of judicial decision-making and some elements of administrative decision-making. Three factors present in most state statutory schemes determine the degree to which a state is judicial or administrative in its approach post-disposition:

- Whether the juvenile court has continuing jurisdiction after disposition;

- To what extent the agency must report to the court post-disposition;

- To what extent the court has authority to order particular placements or services.

State approaches vary. Massachusetts, e.g., is one of the most administrative systems with juvenile court jurisdiction ending upon a youth's commitment to the Department of Youth Services. Commitments can last until age 18 or 21 and during the commitment, the Department of Youth Services has authority to place and service the juvenile as it sees fit with no clear statutory access to the courts for review of these decisions. On the other extreme, in Pennsylvania the committing court continues to have supervisory authority over the delinquency case post-disposition. The court commits a juvenile to a specific placement, which must seek court consent to transfer the juvenile.

A majority of courts, however, retain jurisdiction over delinquency cases post-disposition. The clear majority of jurisdictions have statutes providing for retained jurisdiction in the juvenile court post-disposition until the juvenile's 18th or 21st birthday. Typically, these states provide for retained jurisdiction regardless of whether custody of the juvenile is transferred at disposition to a placement or delinquency agency. However, juvenile court jurisdiction may be restricted when the juvenile is committed to the State Department of Corrections. Those states with more administratively driven post-disposition systems might provide for continuing jurisdiction with the courts, yet specify that after commitment to the agency, the juvenile is subject to agency control. For example, statutory provisions in New Mexico indicate that once legal custody is transferred to an agency, the court's jurisdiction ends and the court has no authority to mandate placements, although the court may make suggestions regarding the rehabilitation of the child. N.M. Stat. Ann. § 32A-2-19 (2000).

Required Agency Reporting

Courts require agencies to report on post-disposition services to varying degrees. Regular reporting to the court as well as access to judicial hearings post-disposition are safeguards which some states impose on agencies responsible for post-disposition delinquency placements and services. Some states allow for frequent judicial review of disposition orders in which the juvenile court may modify its original disposition order upon a showing that the child is not being properly rehabilitated. Some states provide post-disposition judicial review upon motion of the parents or the juvenile. In many states, post-disposition review is structured statutorily as modification of the original disposition with a range of rules concerning what evidence the court may consider.

Yet, even with regular access to courts, the authority of the courts to order specific services and placement can be limited. Kansas, for example, provides that juvenile court jurisdiction terminates 60 days after a commitment to the juvenile correctional facility. After the 60 days, the commissioner of the agency has authority to choose the facility, but must provide notice to the court. While the court may recommend a specific placement, the agency makes placement decisions. Kan. Stat. Ann. §§ 38-1604, 38-1671 (2000). In Tennessee, the agency determines placement once the court grants it custody of the delinquent youth. The agency determines whether to discharge the youth and must review the child's progress quarterly. The court retains jurisdiction to hear matters relating to whether the youth is placed at home, and must be given notice of the department's decision to discharge a youth to the community. Tenn. Code Ann. § 37-1-137 (2000).

Power to Order Particular Placements

The power to order particular placements or services for delinquent youth post-disposition is a critical determinate of post-disposition authority. Whether a state's post-disposition system is primarily administrative or judicially driven depends on which branch has authority to make post-disposition decisions about services and placements. The District of Columbia and Massachusetts are extreme, with neither continuing juvenile court jurisdiction nor reporting requirements post-disposition. The administrative agency exercises almost total control over the juvenile post-disposition. In the District of Columbia the court has authority in its original disposition order to specify a particular placement. However, after the initial disposition and commitment to the custody of the department, the court relinquishes its authority to determine the appropriate measures needed to insure rehabilitation, once the agency has complied with the order. In Massachusetts, child welfare cases, which are handled much like delinquency post-disposition, the juvenile court may not overrule a residential placement decision made by the Department of Social Services unless the judge finds the decision is arbitrary, capricious, or amounts to an abuse of discretion. *In re Jeremy*, 646 N.E.2d 1029, 1031 (Mass. 1995); *In re Isaac*, 646 N.E.2d 1034, 1036 (Mass. 1995). When an agency is given permanent custody of a child in the child welfare context, it may place that child as it chooses, subject to a petition for review, which cannot be filed more than every six months. Similarly, once a delinquent youth is committed to the Department of Youth Services, juvenile court jurisdiction ends and the agency has sole authority to determine placement and services. There is limited administrative process surrounding these decisions and no access to counsel or court to challenge agency decisions post-disposition.

On the other hand, in a minority of states, the court commits the juvenile to the juvenile justice or corrections agency, giving the agency custody and control over placements and treatment with limited or no judicial oversight. In some states, the judicial review of agency decisions is restricted significantly, where relevant statutes provide for a rigid division of responsibility between the agency and the judiciary once courts grant custody to the agency. South Dakota has perhaps gone the farthest in articulating autonomy for its department of corrections. The South Dakota statute provides that the committing court may not specify a placement and "No juvenile has any implied right or expectation to be housed in specific facility, participate in a specific program, or receive specific services." S.D. Codified Laws § 26-11A-4 (Michie, 2000).

Even in states with continuing jurisdiction or some degree of reporting from the agency to the court, agencies can have fairly autonomous authority over the details of post-disposition decisions. One step away from purely administrative states are those states that allow juvenile courts to exercise some degree of oversight over agency decisions, although these statutory schemes do not usually allow juvenile courts to dictate the specific placement of a juvenile. In Vermont, the statutory view of judicial authority allows the juvenile court to accept or reject specific placement decisions of the agency, but does not allow the court to dictate the general parameters of a specific placement. Vt. Stat. Ann. c. 33 §5529 (2000); *In re G.F.*, 455 A..2d 805, 808 Vt. 1982). With a different emphasis, in Arkansas the juvenile court has the authority to order placement in a state agency, but not to direct placement in specific programs within the department. *Arkansas Dept. of Human Servs. v. State*, 894 S.W.2d 592, 593 (Ark. 1995). Decisions involving specific programs are within the agency's discretion, and although the court is allowed to recommend placements, the ultimate decision is statutorily reserved for the agency. Nonetheless, there are mandatory judicial reviews of dispositions every six months. Ark. Code Ann. § 9-27-337 (Michie, 1987) (amended 2001).

In some states decisions about the details of services post-disposition are more shared with the agency determining the child's specific placement, constrained by the type of placement, which is directed by the court.

Shared Authority Leads to Tension

Tension between the agency and court is common in states with shared post-disposition authority. Tensions arise under many state statutory schemes that provide for shared authority of post-disposition decisions. Courts look to the entire disposition and post-disposition statutory scheme to determine legislative intent as to the scope of shared post-disposition authority across those branches of government. The North Carolina Supreme Court, for example, upheld a juvenile court decision preventing the release of a juvenile unless he received specific sex offender treatment, which the court had ordered along with the youth's commitment to the Division of Youth Services. North Carolina statutes specify that commitment to the agency transfers physical custody but jurisdiction is retained in the court. *In the Matter of William Doe*, 407 S.E.2d 798, 802-03 (N.C. 1991). In a similar challenge to a court order placing a delinquent girl under the care of the juvenile justice agency and ordering that agency to place her in a specific psychiatric treatment hospital, the court relied on the statutory scheme that precluded such dual orders. In overturning the disposition, the court relied on the statutory scheme but noted that the court's disposition order was designed to force the agency to fund the psychiatric placement, which may be contrary to their mandate to balance the needs of all youth within a finite budget. *In the Interest of D.F.*, 367 A.2d 1198, 1200-01 (N.J. Super Ct. App. Div. 1976).

These challenges to judicial authority to order the juvenile justice agency to provide specific treatment are decided against a backdrop of separation of powers. Specifically considering that argument, the North Carolina Supreme Court held that there was a "functional overlap" in the authority of the juvenile court and the agency in delinquency and child welfare, and the "principle of cooperation" supported a court order for specific treatment, particularly because the statutory scheme continued jurisdiction in the juvenile court *William Doe*, 407 S.E.2d at 804.

Access to Counsel

Access to counsel during the post-disposition phase is critical to effective implementation of services and placements. In *A Call for Justice* (Puritz, 1996), the American Bar Association Juvenile Justice Center found that a significant number of delinquent youth do not have access to counsel post-disposition. One reason is that many public systems do not pay attorneys for representation once the youth has received a disposition in court. Because many girls find themselves stuck in the system post-disposition, access to counsel, at this stage of the delinquency process is particularly critical. In response to the lack of access to counsel, a few public defender services have initiated post-disposition enforcement units, two of which were elements of settlements in conditions cases.

A youth's right to counsel post-disposition stems originally from *Bounds v. Smith*, 430 U.S. 817, 828 (1977), which provided that adult prisoners are entitled to meaningful access to the courts. In *Morgan v. Sprout*, 432 F. Supp.1130, 1159 (S.D. Miss. 1977), a federal district court in Mississippi provided that juveniles incarcerated in state training schools were constitutionally entitled to access to the courts indistinct from that provided constitutionally for adults. In *Germany v. Vance*, 868 F.2d 9 (1st Cir. 1989), the Court of Appeals for the First Circuit affirmed the right of juveniles in the delinquency system to access to the courts. However, that case is restricted somewhat by its facts. In *Germany*, the juvenile's Department of Youth Services' caseworker withheld information from the juvenile post-disposition that would have exonerated her. The failure of the caseworker and her supervisor to disclose this information resulted in the juvenile's continuing confinement for a year. Here the court referred to *Bounds* and held that the constitutional right of access to the courts applies to juveniles in Department of Youth Services custody, but the court was most concerned with the impact on adjudication that the exculpatory evidence would have had.

In *John L. v. Adams*, 969 F. 2d 228, 232-33, 235 (6th Cir. 1992), the Court of Appeals for the Sixth Circuit affirmed the principle of access to the courts for incarcerated juveniles and restricted that principle to constitutional and civil rights matters. The court further held that while the state could not erect barriers to court access in civil matters it did not have an affirmative duty to provide access through counsel to pursue matters of education and treatment on behalf of incarcerated youth.

Due Process

Post-disposition decisions by agencies require procedural due process. States that defer to administrative agencies for placement and treatment decisions, whether or not they provide for judicial review, must provide due process safeguards for those administrative decisions. *Morrissey v. Brewer*, 408 U.S. 471 (1972). Without basic procedural due process these administrative decisions, which may involve increased restrictions on the girl's liberty, are made by the juvenile justice agency without the benefit of alternative points of view and without the development of a record for later judicial review. A record of the basis for the agency's decision is critical, as later judicial review of agency placement and treatment decisions may be held up to an "abuse of discretion" standard that is difficult to satisfy.

EFFECTIVE ADVOCACY FOR GENDER RESPONSIVE PROGRAMMING

In 1992 the Juvenile Justice and Delinquency Prevention Act (JJDP) required states to analyze their juvenile justice system's provision of "gender specific" services to juvenile female offenders and develop a plan to deliver gender specific treatment and prevention. The Act further made funding available under "Challenge E" to prevent gender bias and provide access to a full range of gender specific services for girls. From 1995 to 1998, Challenge E was the most popular challenge area, accounting for almost 20 percent of applications among the ten challenge areas. (Chesney-Lind & Sheldon, 1998).

Despite the precipitous rise in attention to girls in the justice system and development of models for gender responsive services, the majority of services and programming for girls is not culturally competent and gender responsive, and girls do not have access to the range of programs available to boys. Gender responsive programming is not only consistent with the JJDP Act, but is also constitutionally mandated as a part of an equal and individualized juvenile justice system. The following is an overview of Equal Protection, Title IX, and state Equal Rights Amendment theories that support equal access to programming for girls and gender responsive program design.

Equal Protection Issues

Equal protection has historically been used to challenge gender-based juvenile justice statutes. Historically, protective attitudes towards girls were expressed through statutes defining the jurisdiction of the juvenile court over status offenses and delinquency. For example, the PINS statute in New York defined its jurisdiction over boys until age 16 and girls until age 18. N.Y. Family Law § 712(b) (McKinney 1998) (amended 2001). Similarly, the juvenile court statutes in Alabama, Oklahoma, Illinois, and Texas defined delinquency jurisdiction to offer girls greater protection than boys in the juvenile justice system (until 18 for females and 17 or 16 for males).

State courts overturned both unequal status offense and delinquency jurisdiction statutes in the 1970s on equal protection grounds. Some courts used strict scrutiny analysis no longer available to assess equal protection claims based on gender. However, in New York the PINS statute was overturned because the age/gender difference in jurisdiction bore no reasonable relation to the object of the legislation. Although the court postulated that the classification stemmed from a concern for reducing teen pregnancy, they concluded that even that rationale did not justify excluding boys, who are responsible for the pregnancies. Moreover, if that had been the concern, the statute might have been written narrowly to control sexual misconduct. Rather, the court concluded that the age/gender classification reflected "… the imputation that females who engage in misconduct, sexual or otherwise, ought more to be censured, and their conduct subject to greater control and regulation, than males." *A. v. City of New York*, 286 N.E.2d 432, 435 (N.Y. 1972).

Individual equal protection challenges to delinquency dispositions are difficult to establish. Few individual equal protection challenges to disposition or transfer decisions have been reported, and those that have been were unsuccessful due, in part, to the broad discretion given courts in making juvenile disposition and transfer determinations. As a result of that latitude, appellate courts have held that trial courts' disposition decisions were based on a range of legitimate grounds rather than gender. For example, in *In re Gwenette D.*, 237 Cal. Rptr. 41 (Ct. App. 1st Dist. 1987), a juvenile challenged her commitment to a locked facility for girls following a delinquency finding for theft. Gwenette argued that the commitment violated equal protection because there was no intermediate facility available to girls while there was for boys. Had she been a boy in the same situation, she argued, she would not have been committed to a locked facility. The California Court of Appeals, however, found that although there was no intermediate facility for girls, its absence was not a factor in the juvenile court's decision, which was based on her record in prior placements and the probation officer's recommendation. Similarly, in *Montana v. Spina*, 982 P.2d 421, 437 (Mont. 1999), the defendant challenged the application of the Montana waiver statute in her case arguing that the lack of secure placements for a female juvenile offender within Montana, and consequent cost of incarcerating her as a juvenile out-of-state, factored into the court's waiver decision in violation of equal protection. The Supreme Court of Montana upheld the lower court's waiver decision, holding that the decision was based not on the lack of in-state placement but on the allowable criteria of the difficulty of rehabilitating Spina before majority.

Both *Gwenette* and *Spina* failed on equal protection grounds because the record provided reasons other than gender for the courts' decisions and thus did not support the conclusion that these girls were treated differently due to gender. However, these cases leave open the possibility of an equal protection challenge if the trial court were to find that the lack of a particular program for girls was the reason for its decision. In denying Gwenette's appeal the court did note that, "…although it is facially plausible that the county's failure to maintain an intermediate unlocked facility for girls as it does for boys violates the constitutional rights of a girl placed in a locked facility as a result of this failure, the facts of this case do not place Gwenette within the affected class." *Gwenette*, 237 Cal. Rptr. at 43.

Like Spina, the juvenile in *Toomey v. Clark*, 876 F.2d 1433 (9th Cir. 1989), challenged a state court decision to waive jurisdiction to the adult court saying that it was impermissibly based on gender, in the form of her pregnancy. This case is distinguished from the two above because the Court of Appeals found there was no lack of available programs in the juvenile system for pregnant girls like Toomey. In fact, there was testimony that a facility was available in the juvenile system in Washington for pregnant girls. Rather, according to the Court of Appeals, the trial court based its waiver decision, in part, on testimony that Toomey's pregnancy would interfere with the treatment she needed for rehabilitation and therefore make it unlikely that she could be rehabilitated before majority. The court concluded that consideration of the impact of her pregnancy on her prospects for rehabilitation was rationally related to the public protection purpose of the waiver law.

Like the other two cases, flexibility in the waiver decision, in which the court considered all the *Kent* factors, allowed the Appeals Court to uphold that decision.

Discrimination based on pregnancy can constitute gender-based discrimination. Treatment of pregnant girls and women in the justice system has been the successful basis of conditions litigation and civil rights claims. In *Women Prisoners of the District of Columbia*, 968 F. Supp. 744, 747 (D.D.C. 1997), the court found that the use of physical restraints on pregnant women prisoners violated the Eighth Amendment. Moreover, when harm resulted from mistreatment of a pregnant woman or girl in an incarcerated setting, individual civil rights claims were available. According to Amnesty International (1999), abuses of pregnant women in prisons and jails are widespread in the United States and there is anecdotal evidence that pregnant girls suffer the same conditions.

Courts have been reluctant to decide cases on equal protection grounds. Though there are no reported systemic equal protection challenges to inadequate juvenile programs for girls, such challenges have been brought by adult women prisoners. These claims are difficult to establish and must overcome the federal judiciary's reluctance to intervene in the operation of state institutions and the impediments posed by the Prison Litigation Reform Act.

Equal protection challenges to conditions in women's prisons struggle to establish that women prisoners are similarly situated to male prisoners receiving greater programs and benefits. To make out an equal protection claim, the plaintiffs must establish a similarly situated comparison group and government action in which these similarly situated groups are treated dissimilarly. In determining whether groups are similarly situated courts look at the size of the population, security level, types of crimes, length of sentence, and special characteristics of the population. Theoretically, the broader the comparison, the more likely a court may be to find groups similarly situated. However, a challenge to a very narrow policy (e.g., the way in which the agency makes programming decisions in male and female facilities) might also satisfy the threshold requirement that females are similarly situated to males for the purpose of the challenged action.

The need to prove that girls are similarly situated to boys is a legal box that is difficult to reconcile with the notions of gender difference and gender responsive programming that have been the focus of advocacy for girls in the juvenile justice system. In *Klinger v. Department of Corrections (Klinger II),* the plaintiffs alleged discrimination in programs and services between the only women's prison in Nebraska and the maximum security men's prison. In finding that the men and women were not similarly situated, the court relied on the facts that the women's prison had fewer inmates, a shorter average length of stay, was minimum security, and that women prisoners have distinguishing social characteristics making them different from men, "... ranging from the fact that they are more likely to be single parents with primary responsibility for child-rearing to the fact that they are more likely to be sexual or physical abuse victims." 31 F.3d 727, 732 (8th Cir. 1994).

The inquiry as to whether groups are similarly situated also turns on the alleged governmental action. In both *Klinger II* and *Women Prisoners*, plaintiffs did not allege discrimination in funding and the courts pointed out that more was spent on the women's prisons than the men's. In addition, they did not and could not challenge the lawful practice of segregating men and women in prisons. They did not argue gender-based classifications, but argued that the programs and services in the women's prisons were inferior to those of the men. Due to differences in the male and female prisons and the deference accorded prison officials in operating their systems, the courts refused to compare program for program.

Title IX Challenges

Beginning in the 1980s women prisoners brought claims for gender discrimination in vocational and educational programming under Title IX of the Education Amendments (20 U.S.C. §§ 1681-1688), which provides: "No person in the United States shall, on the basis of sex, be excluded from participation in, be denied the benefits of, or be subjected to discrimination under any education program or activity receiving Federal financial assistance…." Though Title IX goes on to list certain exceptions, neither prisons or juvenile facilities are included in the exceptions and therefore are included under Title IX protection.

While prison education programs seem to fall under the protection of Title IX, it is unlikely that work details, prison industries, recreation and religious programs, or counseling are covered. In *Women Prisoners*, the Court of Appeals reversed the District Court's finding of Title IX violations concluding that the women and men were not similarly situated; however, educational (academic and vocational) programs were not parts of that appeal. Therefore, the District Court's findings that the women prisoners were discriminated against under Title IX in academic and vocational programs stands and the District Court's final order included 18 paragraphs addressing disparity in those areas. *Women Prisoners*, 968 F. Supp. 744, 747-749 (D.C. Cir. 1997).

Courts hearing Title IX claims differ on whether an initial finding that the programs are similarly situated is required. In *Women Prisoners*, the Court of Appeals for the District of Columbia found that, like equal protection claims, claims under Title IX require an initial finding that the two groups are similarly situated. On that basis the Court of Appeals for the District of Columbia reversed the District Court's findings as to all Title IX claims that were the subject of the appeal. On the other hand, the 8th Circuit in *Klinger II*, held that Title IX does not require an initial determination that the men and women are similarly situated. Rather, the inquiry under Title IX is whether male and female participants, within a given federally funded program, are being denied equal educational opportunities "on the basis of sex." Under this standard the court relies on the finding that the male and female prisons were strikingly different ("… comparing the programs at NSP to those at NCW is like the proverbial comparison of apples to oranges," *Klinger II*, 31 F. 3d at 733 (8th Cir. 1994)). Because the facilities were not factually comparable, the court could not conclude that educational programs were being denied "on the basis of sex" as required under Title IX.

State Equal Rights Amendments

Propelled by efforts to eliminate the detrimental economic and sociological effects that past governmental discrimination had on women, Equal Rights Amendments (ERAs) have been adopted by 14 states: Pennsylvania, Massachusetts, New Mexico, Maryland, Washington, Texas, Virginia, Alaska, Illinois, Colorado, Hawaii, Montana, New Hampshire, and Connecticut. To prevail under a state ERA claim, the plaintiff must show that state action resulted in sex-based discrimination, that such discrimination does not fall under the physical-characteristics exception, and that the discrimination fails the state's judicial-scrutiny test.

To establish discrimination, the plaintiff must show that similarly situated groups are being treated dissimilarly by the challenged statute or practice. Some states, such as Texas,

Massachusetts, and New Mexico, recognize discriminatory impact as sufficient to establish discrimination. In addition, the plaintiff must establish that the disparate classification does not fall under the physical characteristics exception, in which case the challenged governmental action would be considered valid. Most states require that differential treatment based on unique physical characteristics be linked to the purpose of the statute in order to be valid.

After a showing of discriminatory intent or impact, the state's standard of judicial scrutiny is applied to determine constitutionality. Four standards of judicial review have been recognized among the 14 states that have adopted an ERA. These differing standards mirror the intermediate scrutiny standard of judicial review afforded by the equal protection clause of the 14th Amendment, and require a stricter level of scrutiny. Maryland and Washington State apply absolute scrutiny, the strictest standard of judicial review. Under an absolute scrutiny standard, to the extent that the equal rights clause specifically prohibits discrimination, the court will not consider any justification and the state's discriminatory classification is unconstitutional, unless it is justified by an actual physical difference between the sexes. Courts in these states have reasoned that dissimilar language in state provisions that have federal counterparts supply a compelling reason for expanding federal protection of individual rights. A second group of states, including Massachusetts, New Hampshire, New Mexico, Texas, Illinois, Connecticut, Pennsylvania, and Hawaii, apply strict scrutiny, whereby the discriminatory statute or practice is presumed invalid unless it can be shown that the statute or practice serves a compelling state interest, is narrowly drawn to protect such compelling interest, and no alternative means can adequately protect this interest. Courts in this second group reason that, because the state has adopted the ERA in addition to the equal protection clauses in the state and federal constitutions, they meant the ERA to afford a higher level of protection of individual rights than afforded under the 14th Amendment.

A third and fourth group of states apply a standard that either mirrors the federal equal protection standard or, in some states, actually affords less protection. Colorado follows the federal equal protection standard in sex-based discrimination cases applying intermediate scrutiny, in which a statute or regulation treating males and females differently violates the ERA unless the classification serves an important government objective and is substantially related to achievement of that objective. Finally, Virginia, Montana and Alaska apply a rational basis test, in which the court's function is to decide whether the purpose of the legislation is legitimate and whether the particular enactment is designed to accomplish that purpose in a fair and reasonable way.

CONCLUSION

As we learn more about the needs of girls in the justice system and the inequities in their processing and programming, it is incumbent on attorneys representing girls to step up efforts in those areas in which girls are particularly affected. Attorneys for delinquent girls should pay particular attention to the detention, disposition, and post-disposition phases of the case, and to cross-system advocacy strategies. Data suggests that once girls enter the system they have difficulty returning to their communities but are poorly served in the system, which lacks adequate, gender-responsive programming. Though the lack of adequate girls programming is frustrating, attorneys for girls should be creative, working with community-based alternatives to incarceration whenever possible.

About the Author

Francine T. Sherman, J.D., is Director of the Juvenile Rights Advocacy Project at Boston College Law School.

References

Acoca, L., *Educate or Incarcerate: Girls in the Florida and Duval County Juvenile Justice* (National Council on Crime and Delinquency, 2000).

Acoca, L. & Dedel, K., *No Place to Hide: Understanding and Meeting the Needs of Girls in the California Juvenile Justice System* (National Council on Crime and Delinquency, 1998).

Adolescent Pathways: Exploring the Intersections Between Child Welfare and Juvenile Justice, PINS, and Mental Health (Vera Institute of Justice, 1998) [Available online at www.vera.org/pathways.pdf]

Amnesty International, *Betraying the Young: Human Rights Violations Against Children in the U.S. Justice System* (Amnesty International Publications, 1998).

Amnesty International, *"Not Part of My Sentence": Violations of the Human Rights of Women in Custody* (Amnesty International Publications, 1999).

Beyer, M., *Recognizing the Child in the Delinquent* (Practicing Law Institute, Litigation and Administrative Practice Course Handbook Series, Criminal Law and Urban Problems, PLI Order No. C0-0016, Children's Law Institute 2000, (2000).

Bishop, D. & Frazier, C., "Gender Bias in Juvenile Justice Processing: Implications of the JJDP Act," 82(4) *J. Crim. L. & Criminology* 1162-1186 (1992).

Burrell, S., *Pathways to Juvenile Detention Reform: Improving Conditions of Confinement in Secure Juvenile Detention Centers* (Annie E. Casey Foundation, 2000).

Chamberlain, P., presentation at *National Training Conference on Juvenile Detention Reform*, Portland, Oregon, January 26, 2002).

Chamberlain, P. & Moore, K., "Chaos and Trauma in the Lives of Adolescent Females With Antisocial Behavior and Delinquency," in R. Greenwald (Ed.), *Trauma and Juvenile Delinquency: Theory, Research and Interventions* (Haworth Press, 2002).

Chesney-Lind, M. & Shelden, R. G., *Girls, Delinquency, and Juvenile Justice* (2nd ed.) (West/Wadsworth, 1998).

Chesney-Lind, M. & Freitas, K., *Working With Girls: Exploring Practitioner Issues, Experiences and Feelings*, Hawai'i Girls Project, (The Center for Youth Research Pub. No. 403, June, 1999).

Dale, M. J. et al., *Representing the Child Client* (Matthew Bender, 1987).

Daniel, M. D., "The Female Intervention Team," VI *Juvenile Justice* 1, 14 (October, 1999).

Fullwood, P. C. et al., *The New Girls Movement: Implications for Youth Programs* (Ms. Foundation for Women, 2001).

Harris, P. W. and Jones, P. R., "The Female Delinquent" (*ProDes: The Program Development and Evaluation System*, Crime and Justice Research Institute and the Division of Juvenile Justice Services, Department of Human Services, Philadelphia, PA, 1998).

Hemrich, V., *Applying ASFA to Delinquency and Status Offender Cases* (American Bar Association, 2000).

Hughey, M. L., "Holding a Child in Contempt," 46 *Duke L.* 353-430 (October 1996).

Justice By Gender: The Lack of Appropriate Prevention, Diversion and Treatment Alternatives for Girls in the Justice System (American Bar Association & National Bar Association, 2001).

Juvenile Detention Alternatives Initiative (Annie E. Casey Foundation, 1994-1997).

Oberman, M., "Regulating Consensual Sex With Minors: Defining a Role for Statutory Rape," 48 *Buffalo L. Rev.* 703, 2000).

Peters, S. P. et al., *Guiding Principles for Promising Female Programming: An Inventory of Best Practices* (Office of Juvenile Justice and Delinquency Prevention, 1998).

Porter, G., *Detention in Delinquency Cases, 1988-1997* (OJJDP Fact Sheet, Office of Juvenile Justice and Delinquency Prevention, Office of Justice Programs, U.S. Department of Justice, 2000).

Puritz, P., *A Call for Justice: An Assessment of Access to Counsel and Quality of Representation in Delinquency Proceedings* (American Bar Association, 1996).

Snyder, Howard, *Juvenile Arrests 1999*, Washington, D.C.: U.S. Department of Justice (2000).

United States General Accounting Office, *HHS Should Ensure That Juvenile Justice Placements Are Reviewed* (GAO/HEHS-00-42), Washington, DC: U.S. Printing Office (2000).

Chapter 10

Services for Girls: What They Need—What They Get

by Kristi Holsinger, Ph.D.

THE MISMATCH: DELINQUENT GIRLS AND PROGRAMS DESIGNED FOR BOYS

Correctional programs and services for youth have, in large part, been designed to meet the needs of the male delinquent. Girls are expected to fit into programming that has not been developed with their specific experiences and needs in mind. In general, girls' deviant behavior has been easier to ignore due to their lower rates of involvement and the less serious nature of the misbehavior. When girls are not being ignored, their delinquency is conceptualized in ways far different from that of boys. Explanations of girls' delinquency are more frequently linked to their sexuality and inadequate gender role socialization. The general approach suggests that returning girls to their "proper" gender role will eliminate their deviant behavior.

In many cases, this approach is used by correctional facilities. One British study found that girls are encouraged to engage in activities that will enable them to become successful wives and mothers. For example, girls were offered programs emphasizing emotional development and cooking skills, while boys were encouraged to participate in sports (Gelsethorpe, 1989). Often, existing programs are based on stereotypical gender roles of girls and fail to provide them with adequate skills to support themselves post-release (Morash, Harr, & Rucker, 1994).

An earlier version of this chapter originally appeared in Women, Girls & Criminal Justice, *Vol. 4, No. 4, June/July 2003.*

Females typically have had fewer vocational, educational, and recreational programs than males. Many of these long-standing concerns are reflected in a recent statewide study of official reports of residential facilities for youth in Missouri (Kempf-Leonard, Peterson, & Sample, 1997). Facilities serving girls were found less likely than those serving boys to provide treatment services for youth with physical health problems, disruptive and/or violent behavior, mental health problems, and sexual victimization histories. Facilities for girls also provided less aftercare, shorter programs, and fewer certified teachers on staff. Similarly, Wells (1994) found that girls received half as many treatment services as boys, waited longer for treatment services to begin, and had less intensive treatment options, which were shorter in duration. In effect, many of the best correctional intervention practices have not been implemented for girls.

Since the 1990s, however, increased attention has been given to the treatment of girls in the juvenile justice system. Whether the attention has come from increasing rates of female incarceration or from practitioner-level concern over how little is known about how to effectively intervene in girls' lives, more research is being conducted on girls' lives and correctional interventions specific to girls are now being explored. Research and theoretical perspectives about these "gender-specific services" are still in their early stages of development. Regardless, a good deal of consensus exists as to what the key components of gender-specific services should be.

Many scholars in this area have come to the conclusion that delinquent girls should be actively involved in developing and evaluating treatment programs (Fejes & Miller, 2002; Greene, Peters & Associates, 1998). By listening to girls' voices, Artz (1998) noted that during the time of her study the girls were not involved in fights, which may have indicated the benefits of being listened to and treated with respect as a way to counteract violence. This was consistent with findings from focus groups in Ohio with system-involved girls, who made repeated comments about their need to be listened to and respected (Belknap, et al., 1997).

In another study on the subculture of incarcerated juveniles, Zingraff (1980) also found that youth, both girls and boys, were more likely to engage in an oppositional subculture that worked against the goals of the correctional facility when they were denied participation in determining some of the operations of the facility.

STUDY OF GIRLS IN OHIO DYS FACILITIES

Study Population

In order to assess programs desired and received, 163 surveys were completed by girls who were incarcerated by the Department of Youth Services (DYS) in the state of Ohio. One DYS institution, Scioto Village, housed the majority of delinquent girls. The survey was also given, however, to a small group of girls held at Freedom Center, a minimum-security facility. No surveys were excluded for being incomplete or for suspicion of untruthful responses. At Scioto Village, a small (undetermined) number of girls were unable to participate since they were being processed, having visitors, or receiving programming. The survey took approximately one hour to complete. The girls were made aware that participation was voluntary and they were given assurances of confidentiality and anonymity.

Measurement Instrument and Programs Measured

The 15-page measurement instrument was the result of an extensive review of research on delinquent girls and gender differences in delinquency etiology, processing, and treatment, as well as information gleaned from qualitative focus group data (Belknap, et al., 1997). The vast number of variables in this survey allowed for an examination of the broad range of the issues girls are likely to face (e.g., sexual abuse, pregnancy, sexism in processing) and how the girls can be better served with new programs and broader implementation of existing programs. The survey concluded with a final section asking the youth to identify the services they would like to receive as well as services that they actually had received. Findings presented here relied on these data.

Seventeen programs were examined in the survey. Most of the listed programs come out of a literature based on the programmatic needs of system-involved girls. This list of programs was presented to ascertain what programs incarcerated girls want to participate in. Respondents were also asked to report whether they had received (past or present) any of the 17 programs. The services that were included on the survey were:

- Three education-related programs (sex education, learning to be a better student, general health education);
- Three relational training programs (problem-solving skills training, anger management training, learning how to have good relationships);
- Three independent living programs (learning how to live on one's own, learning how to be a parent, learning job or career skills);
- Three abuse-related counseling programs (sexual abuse counseling, physical abuse counseling, emotional abuse counseling);
- Three general counseling programs (family counseling, individual counseling, help with depression or other mental problems);
- One specific treatment program (drug and alcohol treatment); and lastly,
- Sports, health, and/or fitness training.

FINDINGS

Demographic Characteristics

The sample in this study was 48% African-American, 36% white, and 16% other (girls describing themselves as Native American, Hispanic, Puerto Rican, Spanish, Asian South African, or biracial). The sample ranged in age from 12 to 20 years old with a mean age of 16. In order to measure socioeconomic status, girls were asked whether their family had ever received welfare. Approximately two-fifths of the girls reported that their families had received welfare, although 21% did not know the answer to this question.

Desired Programs and Services

Programs were listed on the survey along with the question, "Would you like to participate in any of the following services?" Many of the girls indicated an interest in education-related programs. Forty-nine percent wanted sex education, 54% desired general health education, and 61% of the girls wanted to become better students.

As a group, programs focusing on relational training were rated even higher. Fifty-six percent of the girls wanted to obtain problem-solving skills, 62% hoped to learn how to better manage their anger, and 69% wanted to learn how to have good relationships.

However, independent living skills received the highest numbers, in terms of the type of programming girls most wanted to receive. Given the young ages of the girls, it is interesting to note that 45% of them desired to learn how to parent. Learning how to live independently was desired by 64%.

The most frequently desired programming was services teaching job or career skills. Seventy-two percent of the girls felt they could benefit from this type of program. Several programs included on the survey addressed abuse-related counseling programs. About one-third of the girls wanted counseling for physical abuse, a slightly higher number (35%) desired sexual abuse counseling, and 43% wanted counseling to address emotional abuse they experienced.

General counseling programs were also rated highly. Nearly half of the girls (46%) wanted services to deal with depression or other mental health issues. Over half (54%) wanted family counseling, and 58% desired individual counseling. Drug/alcohol treatment was desired by 44% of the girls. Sports, health and/or fitness training also proved to be frequently desired, with 66% of the girls responding in the affirmative.

Few racial differences were found when comparing the responses of African-American and white girls. For all but one program, there were no significant differences between the two groups. However, services to help the girls learn to become better parents were more frequently requested by African-American girls (54%) than white girls (34%).

Programs and Services Received

On the survey, the girls were able to note "I already do or have" received a particular type of service, indicating programs that they had already received at some time in the past or programs they are currently receiving. The program most frequently received was drug/alcohol treatment. Twenty-four percent of the girls reported having received this type of programming at some point. Sex education was received by almost as many girls (21%), however, whether they received this type of program while incarcerated is unclear. Individual counseling was also reported as received by 21% of the girls. Family counseling was reported by 14% and help with depression or other mental problems was reported by 12%.

Every other program mentioned on the survey was received by less than 10% of the girls. They were:

- Learning how to be a better student (3%);

- General health education (8%);

- Problem-solving skills (9%);

- Anger management training (9%);

- Learning how to have good relationships (5%);

- Learning how to be a better parent (4%);

- Learning how to live on their own (5%);

- Job or career skills (9%);

- Sexual abuse counseling (9%);

- Emotional abuse counseling (8%);

- Physical abuse counseling (8%); and

- Sports-related training (6%).

Programming Gap

Clearly, there is a profound disjuncture between services desired and those received. Many of the girls were unlikely to receive the types of programs they most desired. In order to examine this discrepancy, percentages of girls receiving a particular program were subtracted from the percentage of girls who desired that program. Therefore, in the lists below the larger the number, the greater the discrepancy between programs desired and received. The programs that showed a gap greater than 50% included:

- Learning to have good relationships (65%);

- Job/career skills (63%);

- Sports, health and/or fitness training (60%);

- Learning to live on my own (59%);

- Learning how to be a better student (58%); and

- Anger management training (53%).

The programs that showed a gap between 30% and 50% were:

- General health education (46%);

- Learning how to be a parent (41%);

- Family counseling (40%);

- Individual counseling (37%);

- Emotional abuse counseling (35%); and

- Help with depression or mental problems (34%).

The final group of programs, showing a gap of under 30%, showed the least desired/ received discrepancy. Yet, each of these programs were still requested by a greater percentage of youth compared to what they had received:

- Drug/alcohol treatment (28%);

- Physical abuse counseling (26%); and

- Sexual abuse counseling (26%).

More racial differences existed when examining the services girls received. White girls were significantly more likely than African-Americans to have received sex education (28% vs. 12%), drug/alcohol treatment (30% vs. 14%), individual counseling (26% vs. 12%), and treatment for depression or mental health issues (17% vs. 5%). These findings suggest that racial disparity exists on some level in the provision of services for incarcerated girls.

CONCLUSIONS

Correctional programming for girls is at a crossroads, as many states begin to look at the unique needs of female offenders. As this research is being conducted, along with newer ways of theorizing about female delinquency, gender-specific services are just beginning to take shape. As these services develop, it is crucial that girls' voices are heard and that their desires help shape the types of programs offered.

Among other things, the results of this research suggest that girls want to participate in programs while incarcerated. The program that was desired by the fewest girls was requested by just over one-third of the respondents. With rates ranging from 34% to 72%, it is clear that incarcerated girls are interested in improving themselves and their lives.

Girls want programs that have not been available to them due to gender stereotypes about what girls need. Girls' interests do not always match the perceptions of professionals who work with them. For example, girls are more interested in sports and fitness programs than estimates by professionals (Belknap, et al., 1997). Some of the programs most desired by girls are the ones that have been most lacking for them—job/career skills, learning how to live independently, and sports or fitness training. These are the very programs girls need to give them the tools to succeed upon release. Unfortunately, these programs and services are not currently being delivered on a large-scale basis.

Another finding from the gender-specific literature is that girls do better in programming that is relationship-oriented, rather than the more traditional, male model of behavior modification. The current study supports this suggestion, with over two-thirds of the girls reporting that they want to learn how to have good relationships. Well-trained correctional staff could be appropriate and available models to assist girls in developing these skills. Sadly, most research on staff notes their dislike for working with girls, who are typically perceived to be harder to work with than boys.

Given the assumption that all correctional facilities for youth are charged with providing a basic education, it is disheartening to see that only 3% of the girls report receiving skills training to help them succeed as students. Without a doubt, academic success is a protective factor to help girls avoid further delinquency. The girls seem to recognize this fact, with 61% desiring services that would help them become better students.

In the past, both equal treatment and unequal treatment have worked to the disadvantage of girls. Equal treatment has meant that the specific needs of girls were ignored by a system based on boys' needs. Unequal treatment has been based on stereotypical ideas about what the needs of girls are. It is important that equality be defined as providing opportunities, some different, some the same, to both girls and boys (Belknap, et al., 1997). Learning what those services should be requires listening to girls.

About the Author

Kristi Holsinger, Ph.D., is an assistant professor in the Department of Sociology/Criminal Justice and Criminology at the University of Missouri-Kansas City.

References

Artz, S., *Sex, Power, and the Violent School Girl* (Trifolium Books Inc., 1998).

Belknap, J., Holsinger, K. & Dunn, M., "Understanding Incarcerated Girls: The Results of a Focus Group Study," 77(4) *Prison Journal* 381-404 (1997).

Fejes, K.E. & Miller, D., "Assessing Gender-Specific Programming for Juvenile Female Offenders: Creating Ownership, Voice and Growth," 53(2) *Journal of Correctional Education* 58-64 (2002).

Gelsethorpe, L., *Sexism and the Female Offender* (Gower Publishing, 1989).

Greene, Peters, & Associates, *Guiding Principles for Promising Female Programming: An Inventory of Best Practices* (Office of Juvenile Justice and Delinquency Prevention, 1998).

Kempf-Leonard, K., Peterson, E.S.L. & Sample, L.L., *Gender and Juvenile Justice in Missouri* (Missouri Department of Public Safety, 1997).

Morash, M., Harr, R.N. & Rucker, L., "A Comparison of Programming for Women and Men in U.S. Prisons in the 1980s," 40(2) *Crime and Delinquency* 197-221 (1994).

Wells, R.H., "America's Delinquent Daughters Have Nowhere to Turn for Help," 19(11) *Corrections Compendium* 4-6 (1994).

Zingraff, M.T., "Inmate Assimilation: A Comparison of Male and Female Delinquents," 7(3) *Criminal Justice and Behavior* 275-292 (1980).

Chapter 11

Girls and Relational Aggression: Beyond the "Mean Girl" Hype

by Scott K. Okamoto, Ph.D. and Meda Chesney-Lind, Ph.D.

> Girl 1: You are a total prostitute.
>
> Angela: Hey, that's how things really are. You just don't know because you're this pampered little suburban chick.
>
> —American Beauty (1999)

INTRODUCTION

Are girls mean? Are they meaner than boys? If one is watching television or reading the papers, it is hard not to note the flood of stories on the latest bad girl. A veritable torrent of books on the topic have suddenly appeared as well, including Rachel Simmons's *Odd Girl Out* (2002), Sharon Lamb's *The Secret Lives of Girls* (2001), and Rosalind Wiseman's *Queen Bees and Wannabes* (2002). While most of these books are forgettable, there are aspects of recent psychological research on aggression that are important to those working with girls (see Chesney-Lind, 2002).

To understand girls' aggression, it is first important to understand what "aggression" is and how this psychological concept relates to common sense understandings of aggression, which is often conflated with fighting and other forms of violence. Early research on aggression has concluded that, as a group, boys exhibit significantly higher levels of aggression than girls (see Crick & Grotpeter, 1995, for review). This is consistent with statistics illustrating higher rates of violent crime (i.e., murder, forcible rape, robbery, and

An earlier version of this chapter originally appeared in Women, Girls & Criminal Justice, *Vol. 3, No. 6, October/November 2002.*

aggravated assault) for male versus female youth (Snyder, 2001). The perception that males are more aggressive, however, might be more of a factor of *how* aggression is defined, which historically tended to reflect more overt manifestations. Increasingly, in both the empirical and popular literature, the concept of girls and "relational aggression" has been discussed. This concept has implications for how we work with boys and girls in terms of violence prevention and intervention in the community and school settings.

CONCEPT OF RELATIONAL AGGRESSION

The concept of relational aggression relates to a repertoire of passive and/or indirect behaviors (e.g., rolling eyes, spreading rumors, and ignoring) used with the "intent to hurt or harm others" (Crick & Grotpeter, 1995; Crick et al., 1998). As such, the concept of relational aggression expands the range of behaviors that are typically considered aggressive in nature. On one end of the spectrum are covert, non-physical forms of aggressive behaviors, while on the other end are overt, physical forms of aggressive behaviors.

Does relational aggression occur more frequently with girls and boys? Research addressing this question has been mixed. Crick and Grotpeter (1995), for example, found that girls in their sample of third- through sixth-grade students were significantly more relationally aggressive than were boys. They found that these youth were significantly more disliked and lonelier than nonrelationally aggressive peers. Bjorkqvist and Niemela (1992) found that when types of verbal aggression (e.g., gossiping or spreading rumors) were included in their overall measurement of aggression, gender explained only 5% of the variance. This suggests that, by using a broader definition of aggression, both boys' and girls' unique forms of aggression were accounted for in their study.

Other research, however, has found no difference in the frequency of relational aggression between boys and girls (e.g., Gropper & Froschl, 2000; Tiet, et al., 2001). In these studies, however, researchers coded observations of aggression, while in the Crick and Grotpeter (1995) study, peer nomination was used as the data collection procedure. This suggests that manifestations of relational aggression may be difficult to detect by adult observers, and may need to be identified by members of the youth peer group. Because of the relatively indirect nature of behaviors related to relational aggression, Crick and Grotpeter (1995) state that "it might be difficult for those outside the peer group to reliably observe and evaluate [this form of aggression] in naturalistic settings" (p. 712).

PRACTICAL IMPLICATIONS

Violence Intervention

Why is relational aggression important from a practice perspective? First, it is likely that girls in delinquency prevention and intervention programs have considerable problems with relational aggression, since it has been shown to be related to internalizing problems, peer rejection, and depression (Crick et al., 1998). Second, while girls' aggressive behavior often remains relational in nature, overt manifestations of aggression are often preceded by relational aggression. This phenomenon is evident in both the school and group home settings for girls. Often, the rationale for a physical fight is, "She's talking behind my back," or "She's after my boyfriend." By addressing the relational aspect

---

Table 11.1: Challenges of Male Practitioners Working With Female Youth Clients*

1. Sexual abuse allegations from the youth directed at the practitioner.

2. Practitioners' fear of liability/litigation.

3. Practitioners' boundary setting with youth.

4. Practitioners' sexual feelings toward youth.

5. Managing sexual behaviors from the youth directed at the practitioner.

6. Managing transference from the youth (i.e., managing the youth's initial perception
   that the male practitioner is sexually and/or physically abusive, similar to men in her past).

7. Rage of the youth directed at the practitioner.

*Findings adapted from Okamoto (2002; 2003), Okamoto & Chesney-Lind (2000), and St. Germaine & Kessell (1989).

---

of aggression early and often, practitioners working with youth are in essence conducting overt violence prevention. The significance of this process extends to boys as well. The massacre at Columbine High School, for example, might have been prevented if the relational aggression associated with the ostracism and ridicule extended to Eric Harris and Dylan Klebold by their peers were addressed. In other words, relational aggression, while seemingly insignificant, can lead to serious consequences if left unaddressed by youth practitioners.

Effective Intervention Strategies

Second, research suggests that relational aggression is one of the factors contributing to the stereotype that "girls [are] more difficult to work with" for practitioners. Using in-depth interviews, Freitas and Chesney-Lind (2001) describe how difficult it is for practitioners to watch girls be "mean" to other girls and boys, and the challenges for practitioners associated with being targets of relational aggression themselves. Okamoto (2002) describes the unique challenges that male practitioners face in working with female youth clients. Male practitioners in this study stated that one of these challenges, sexual abuse allegations, was used by female youth clients as a form of aggression toward them (for a more extensive list of the challenges faced by male practitioners working with girls, see Table 11.1). These findings suggest the importance in training practitioners how to appropriately respond to relational aggression, and the need for ongoing practitioner support and supervision.

RELATIONAL AGGRESSION AS RESPONSE TO POWERLESSNESS

Having said all this, there are a couple of other perspectives that need to be kept in mind regarding the "hype" around mean girls. First, alternative aggressions are, fundamentally, weapons of the weak. As such, they are as reflective of girls' powerlessness as they are of girls' meanness. Historically, women and other oppressed groups have not been permitted direct aggression (without terrible consequences). As a result, in certain contexts, and against certain individuals, relational aggressions were ways the powerless punished the bad behavior of the powerful. This was, after all, how slaves and indentured servants—female and male—got back at abusive masters, how women before legal divorce dealt with violent husbands, and how working women today get back at abusive bosses.

Second, a myopic focus on girls doing this to other girls tends to blur the fact that girls exist in a world that basically ignores them and marginalizes them—all the while empowering young boys. Certainly, we want to change much about girlhood, and we want to stop girls from hurting other, weaker girls, but even in a perfect world, girls will need to know something about how to "do" relational aggression. After all, it was Machiavelli who first taught us that while all are supposed to be good, if one wants to be successful politically, and one is forced to make a choice, it is much safer to be feared than loved. The world, even the male world, is not a perfect place, and girls need many and varied skills to survive it.

Finally, we need to keep in mind that there are some problems with a concept of "aggression" that is so inclusive that such disparate behaviors as rolling your eyes at a stupid remark and murder fall within it. While an understanding of all forms of aggression is important, the degree of harm involved in such behavior is important to keep in mind as well. Some aggression makes us depressed and sad for a day, and some we do not survive. The media hype surrounding the discovery of girls' meanness seems to imply that this "new" attribute makes them about as bad as boys or worse. That is not the case, as virtually all girls' aggression is non-violent. This does not mean that girls are perfect, but we should keep our perspective. Boys are still over 80% of those arrested for serious crimes of violence, and it is boys' violence, not girls' gossip, that gives the United States the highest rate of firearm-related deaths among youths in the industrialized world (U.S. Surgeon General, 2001).

About the Authors

Scott K. Okamoto, Ph.D. is an assistant professor at the School of Social Work, Arizona State University. Meda Chesney-Lind, Ph.D. is Professor, Women's Studies Program, University of Hawai`i at Manoa.

References

Bjorkqvist, K., & Niemela, P., "New Trends in the Study of Female Aggression," in K. Bjorkqvist & P. Niemela (Eds.), *Of Mice and Women: Aspects of Female Aggression* (Academic Press, 1992).

Chesney-Lind, M., Review of *Odd Girl Out* by Rachel Simmons, 1(1) *Youth Today Review of Books* (Fall 2002).

Crick, N. R., & Grotpeter, J. K., " Relational Aggression, Gender, and Social-Psychological Adjustment," 66 *Child Development* 710-722 (1995).

Crick, N. R., Werner, N. E., Casas, J. F., O'Brien, K. M., Nelson, D. A., Grotpeter, J. K., & Markon, K., "Childhood Aggression and Gender: A New Look at an Old Problem," in D. Bernstein (Ed.), *Gender and Motivation*, pp. 75-141 (University of Nebraska Press, 1998).

Freitas, K., & Chesney-Lind, M., "Difference Doesn't Mean Difficult: Workers Talk About Working With Girls," 2(5) *Women, Girls, & Criminal Justice*, 65-78 (August/September 2001).

Gropper, N., & Froschl, M., "The Role of Gender in Young Children's Teasing and Bullying Behavior," 33(1) *Equity & Excellence in Education* 48-56 (2000).

Lamb, S., *The Secret Lives of Girls* (The Free Press, 2001).

Okamoto, S. K., "The Challenges of Male Practitioners Working with Female Youth Clients," 31(4) *Child and Youth Care Forum* 257-268 (2002).

Okamoto, S. K., "The Function of Professional Boundaries in the Therapeutic Relationship Between Male Practitioners and Female Youth Clients," *Child and Adolescent Social Work Journal* 303-313 (August, 2003).

Okamoto, S. K. & Chesney-Lind, M., "The Relationship Between Gender and Practitioners' Fears in Working With High-Risk Youth," 29(6) *Child and Youth Care Forum* 373-383 (2000).

Simmons, R., *Odd Girl Out* (Harcourt, 2002).

Snyder, H. N., *Law Enforcement and Juvenile Crime* (Rep. No. 191031) (Office of Juvenile Justice and Delinquency Prevention, 2001).

St. Germaine, E. A., & Kessell, M. J., "Professional Boundary Setting for Male Youth Workers With Female Adolescent Clients," 18(4) *Child & Youth Care Quarterly* 259-271 (1989).

Tiet, Q. Q., Wasserman, G. A., Loeber, R., McReynolds, L. S. & Miller, L. S., "Developmental and Sex Differences in Types of Conduct Problems," 10(2) *Journal of Child and Family Studies* 181-197 (2001).

U.S. Surgeon General, *Youth Violence: A Report of the Surgeon General* (U.S. Department of Health and Human Services, 2001).

Wiseman, R., *Queen Bees and Wannabes* (Crown Publishers, 2002).

Chapter 12

Difference Doesn't Mean Difficult: Practitioners Talk About Working With Girls

by Konia Freitas, M.A. and Meda Chesney-Lind, Ph.D.

INTRODUCTION

Theorists have generally ignored girls or portrayed them in a shallow and stereotypical manner (Belknap, 1996; Chesney-Lind & Sheldon, 1992; Campbell, 1981). The most profound implication of this cognitive void can be seen in the way that girls are processed in juvenile and criminal justice systems. "Research shows that many of the same themes advanced by traditional theories of delinquency to subordinate girls, discriminate against them via their processing in the system as well" (Holsinger, 1999, p. 4). For example, numerous scholars have documented that the higher prevalence of female status offenses and harsher treatment for girl status offenders in comparison to boys indicates the heightened focus on girls' sexuality. Likewise, the effect of violating gender-role stereotypes or

An earlier version of this chapter originally appeared in Women, Girls & Criminal Justice, *Vol. 2, No. 5, August/September 2001.*

acting out of the culturally acceptable feminine role has resulted in harsher punishments for females (Holsinger, 1999; Girls Incorporated, 1996).

Furthermore, once girls are processed out of the juvenile justice system they are placed into programs that are modeled for delinquent boys. A study of 443 delinquency program evaluations completed since 1950 shows that 34.8% of these programs only served males and 42.4% served primarily boys. Conversely, only a paltry 2.3% of delinquency programs served only girls, and 5.9% served primarily girls (Lipsey, 1990). A more recent review of "potentially promising programs" identified by the Office of Juvenile Justice and Delinquency Prevention (Howell, 1995) cited 24 programs specifically for boys and only two programs specifically for girls. Ironically, the one program for incarcerated parents was a program for teen fathers—there was no counterpart for teen mothers (Girls Incorporated, 1996). Understanding the concerns girls have is a crucial step towards providing appropriate services.

Given the void of research on girls' issues and gender-specific programs, it comes as no surprise that virtually no research exists on the experiences of professionals who work with girls. This chapter highlights the feelings, experiences, and views of professionals who work with adolescent girls on a daily basis in either gender-specific or coed programs in the state of Hawaii. This data was gathered through a series of neighbor island interviews (n = 4) and O'ahu Island Focus Groups (n = 9) conducted in March and April 1999. Two focus groups were conducted in April 1999. Participants came from a wide variety of agencies and geographic regions, and most, but not all, were female. The program services represented by the participants fell into four broad categories: residential treatment, case management, prevention, and intervention. The majority of participants had previous work experience with male and female adolescents either as teachers, counselors, or therapists in Hawaii or in the continental United States. Between all the participants there was a range of four to 15 years of work experience with adolescent youth.

RESEARCH ON ISSUES IN WORKING WITH GIRLS

Important gender differences in adolescent development coupled with the lack of gender-specific programming places a heavy burden on the shoulders of the professionals who work with girls. Perhaps it is not surprising to note that there is virtually no research or studies that document the experiences of youth workers. Among the research that does exist, youth workers commonly lament that girls are more difficult to work with (Belknap et al., 1997; Baines & Adler, 1996; Kersten, 1990). Chief among their conclusions was that the confrontational and negative aspects of relationships between workers and young women combined with the lack of appropriate services and facilities may produce detrimental outcomes for young women.

Other studies have found that professionals had clear ideas about the problems in the juvenile justice system and perceived differences in the nature of boys and girls. Further, they identified lower program availability, specific needs of girls, and parents as a significant part of the problem (Belknap et al., 1997). Professionals varied a great deal in their attitudes and experiences with female delinquents. While some professionals demonstrated tremendous amounts of dedication to girls and significant insight into the special problems that girls faced, others appeared to stereotype girls and blame them and their parents for all their problems (Belknap et al., 1997).

Our research considered both worker perceptions about the unique problems of the girls they work with and, as we discuss in the following sections, the particular challenges they experienced working with this population.

GIRLS' STRESS AND PRESSURE

The youth workers generally felt that girls today are under a tremendous amount of "stress" and "pressure." Some workers stated that while everyone has experienced pressure during adolescence, the confusion that girls face today is different from what the workers recall having encountered during their youth. These youth workers felt that the pressure and stress are fueled by confusion about being female, about sex, stressful home life, boyfriends, work, and school.

> *It's the case that the girl, given her history [of sexual and physical abuse], can't figure out how to relax. She's always anxious, tense. Now we have an awake staff in the house, they will always be up and if the girl needs something they are there.*

> *Generally the teenagers that I work with are under tremendous amount of stress. Stress has a lot to do with confusion of our times. So they have a lot of confusion around sex, being female, their roles. Their struggling with parental disapproval around how they're being different girls from how their mothers were, or that their fathers are used to. There's the struggle of not being dependent on a male whereas a lot of us are trained to find the perfect man and he'd take care of us forever. So there's still that confusion around who am I and what am I, but it's a little different flavor from when I went through it.*

ARE GIRLS MORE DIFFICULT TO WORK WITH?

Most participants in this study did not regard girls as more difficult. In fact, quite a number observed that they *like* working with girls. Reasons varied (girls are more verbal, girls are less violent, and there are fewer girls over all). In general the practitioners recognized that girls were indeed different to work with in comparison to their male counterparts and this distinction required different techniques and approaches.

> *For me it was easier to work with girls. A lot easier. I think because I am female there's a different dynamic between myself and the client. They reach out to you more as a role model whereas the boys just look at you differently because I'm female. I think it's easier to connect with a female because I am. It was completely different for me.*

> *Like it, [they are] more open minded, able to sit and listen and hear what you're proposing to them, [they are] less accusational toward staff. Boys will say that it's her (staff) fault, they are doing this to hurt me, they don't like me.*

The girls are survivors, they are strong. I'm privileged to work with them. They are able to communicate appropriately. The are very capable of living, but need to channel energy to not endanger themselves.

It is easier to work with girls. They are not as violent, there is less ego. Girls are manipulative, controlling—e.g. "don't worry I won't tell," those kinds of things but sometimes these kinds of things that girls do is really the way that these girls have learned to survive.

I find that girls are easier to talk down, but I don't necessarily have a lot of people going nuts on me.

Staff want to work with the girls because there are less of them.

It takes longer to get to the core of what's bothering them, there are signals to know though. Not with boys, they say something, I did this, then that happened and that's it . . . whereas with girls you get cues and they are consistent with all the staff. They will act the same way and give the same cues to everyone. To the girls the staff is all the same, you are all the same.

GIRLS AND RELATIONSHIPS

Some youth workers stated that the value that girls place on relationships (particularly with peers) helps them in their programs. The emphasis that girls place on peer relationships means that creative workers can access key girls within networks to promote healthy messages. However, the practitioners were quick to note that it was important to be aware of the "ebb and flow" of girls' relationships since the intimate clique dynamics of girls can polarize quickly and turn against staff.

We are in prevention. We use that constantly, bring in girls who are leaders, we recruit. If we can turn them to the positive, and get them excited to be drug free, they can have a huge influence over a large amount of girls that we can't touch. We use that.

There's an ebb and flow to the relationships. Can't take it for granted that relationships are always going to be positive. You have to pay real close attention to them. In the same week you can pull a couple of girls together, mobilize them, and use them to get out a good prevention message or engage other girls and in that same week you cross them the wrong way or something happens and that same group of 15 could create a ripple effect of people not coming up because then a rumor start up about the staff . . . . It makes our job easier when we are tuned in to that "ebb and flow." When we exploit it to the advantage of our program and to the advantage of that group and we mend it as quickly as possible if we see it going in the other direction.

DEALING WITH DISTRUST OF ADULTS

Workers indicated that the challenges they faced with girls centered around issues of trust and authority. Often, the girls that they work with come from abusive households so they look at the world through distrustful eyes, particularly when it comes to adult women. Recall that for many of these girls, the adult betrayal begins with the adult male abuser and, then, it is sadly followed by the failure of their mothers, in many instances, to side with them and protect them from abuse.

> *Girls need patience, guidance, nurturing and it takes a lot to deal with this. These kids realize that once you start getting close they need to push you away because you can't be trusted, this is all they know, and this is what we have to deal with.*

> *Before, I would be threatened and scared to work with these types of kids, but not any more. I remember my first case . . . she sat in a circle with a pillow in front of her, and slightly above her mouth and she just stared at me, her eyes glaring, very standoffish type. This stuff does not faze me because I think wow, you must really be hurting.*

> *If I say to them "what are you doing?" then I'm the mom, I'm the authority. So the authority issues sometimes get in the way because they see me as: you're older, you're the enemy, instead of [I'm here to help] and I can hear what you say because I trust, because I know that you care about me. And that's sometimes really frustrating for me.*

DEALING WITH GIRLS' CHOICES

Another issue is when the choices that girls make are personally challenging for workers. Issues that evolve around pregnancy decisions surface here, but there are also worker reactions to passive/aggressive "games" that girls have cultivated living in worlds characterized by exploitation and victimization. Workers felt that here were two sides to victimization and exploitation. On the one hand, many of the girls were being exploited, particularly by adults; but on the other, the young girls were, in turn, often exploiting other girls or boys. While practitioners were clear in a desire not to blame the victim, some of the clique dynamics in girls' behavior were often difficult to deal with, as were some decisions about sexuality and pregnancy.

> *It's not every single girl, the games they play "here's some dumb guy we're going to go make 'A' out of." I felt really bad, I want to warn them, but on the other side there are some guys who are like "hey are you going to score with this one" and you've got the innocent girl. The game play that's around exploitation feels ugly to me.*

> *I'm hearing more about high school age girls working in strip bars. Kids you wouldn't expect, apparently they are being "employed." I'm hearing that more . . . I think they get paid cash and when the cops are going to come or when they [the owners] feel [that it's getting too risky] then they let them go. . . . They don't hold it at all as prostitution, or as their job, it's a total choice that they're doing, it's the kind of work that they want to do. Before we knew it as survival. . . . It's really sad to me that they are being "employed."*

> *Sometimes it's painful to watch and I feel sad for the girls who are in a sense being victimized by their own sisters. I used to see it in other programs I work in.*

What's more is that other counselors or teachers will blame the girl. They'll say "well you know she was sort of laughing so she brought it on herself," or "she's not serious," or "oh forget it, she's going to go right back." That for me is really difficult. I try to explain to them. I can understand their position, too, because I feel frustrated, too.

There have been other times where there was someone who wanted that choice [abortion] and asked that I go with them. My worry as a counselor is that I couldn't do that because then I'd have to call a parent . . . and so I felt really torn.

I know that there are some girls who use abortion as a birth control method and that is really hard for me personally to look at.

WORKING WITH GIRLS IS SAFER

Virtually all of the practitioners agreed that girls were not as physically aggressive or violent as boys, thus, being with girls created a much safer working environment. Furthermore, there are no sexual overtones for women working with girls in contrast to boys.

Sometimes dealing with boys is peculiar because of the anger issue and the violent way in which they express their anger and given their strength and their body mass it can be quite frightening sometimes. They'll break a door and pick up a weight or they'll throw something.

Girls are not sexually explicit in talk, when we talk about their past week and I ask them did they get angry many will say "yes"; and if things got physical it was because someone was "talking sh--" about them. Boys just fight with anyone, girls don't fight as much, they are not proud or as boasting; they won't fight for anything. They are more communicative.

When we are dealing with the boys' group we usually have a male and female. There is a lot of posturing with the boys, a lot of sexual comments, the boys will give positive strokes to each other for displaying aggressive behavior. They are proud to be brutal.

In a mixed group situation, though, this is what I notice, boys are more talkative, so girls are either not as talkative or they become very aggressive. If a boy says something the girl will just say "f--- you."

CHALLENGES OF CROSS-GENDER SUPERVISION

Practitioners described the difficulty they have with determining the role of men in a predominantly all-female program or environment.

This is always an issue [we're]. . . looking at having male staff, and it's always such a hard thing to figure out what would be most appropriate for the girls. I do know that it would be extremely healthy for them to develop an appropriate relationship with a male . . . where they can count on a male and feel close to a male and that there isn't any sexuality involved. . . . At the same time ... what I feel from the girls, is that they don't feel as comfortable when males are there . . . and when the males work, they come to me afterwards and they say the girls just cling to them and attack him or they are just constantly on them. So it's really hard to figure out what's appropriate for them.

. . . for the [male] staff it's really difficult. He said he felt very uncomfortable and he didn't want to be left alone. He was real concerned about being left alone and if they would say something or do something to get him into a precarious situation where he had to defend himself. So he felt so uncomfortable that he asked not to work there anymore.

The female participants noted the difficulties that the male staff experience with female clients.

For male staff it is very hard, they have to watch what they do, what they say, everything. It is harder for them to make relationships with the girls. The girls will do male bashing, blame the male staff for everything, accuse them of things, make charges. It is very hard for male staff. He has to be aware of where he sits, what he says. For boys, it's a matter of "who's in charge" vs. girls who are manipulative or controlling.

It is easier for female staff. For the male staff it's harder, they must keep shifting and figure [the girl] out. The male staff will see a girl as being manipulative or trying to get around things, or being controlling. In staff meetings the female staff can note the cues more carefully versus male staff. Female staff will tell the male staff it may be that the girl is being manipulative or controlling but it could also be a reflection of a survival skill or coping strategy that the girl is using because this is all she has come to know about how to survive. We have to remind the male staff.

Our male staff is really young, just recently out of college. The girls relate to him in a more sexual way. They flirt a lot with him. Female staff notice that way of relating to him. So the relationship between girls and male and female staff is very different. Sometimes they might even see you as competitive, you know, in that sense, and they relate to the male staff in a more sexual or flirtatious manner.

The male participants tended to agree that boundary setting was indeed difficult but that the issue was complicated by gender role reversal. One practitioner noted that in order for a male to work successfully in this field he must have "a sense of himself and a sense of his own boundaries and be able to verbalize that with the girls."

A lot of people only get to the point of being uncomfortable and they don't know how to handle this, "I've never been uncomfortable in my work, I'm uncomfortable, it's not me, it's my situation and I'm going to remove myself from the situation."

Definitely there's a role reversal. . . . Men may be more "comfortable," for lack of a better word, to be seen as a victim in a situation with other guys than to be felt like a victim . . . because in the dynamic we are conditioned to think that we are in control of the situation and we set the rules and we can break them if we want and this is how we do it. If you turn it on us, now what are we going to do? It's foreign territory right there.

. . . it's a whole different process and for a whole lot of men they have to be sensitive to that and be willing to be more verbal, more articulate, and more in tune to secure boundaries and watching for transference issues.

However, boundary setting was not an issue reserved solely for male youth workers. One female participant felt that it was difficult trying to negotiate how to deal with girls. Another female indicated that in order to deal with girls you must not take anything personally.

Walking into work at the boys' house it was second nature, but walking to the girls' house I'd be like "I wonder what they're like" or "I wonder if they're going to think I'm a bitch" or "how am I going to approach her about it." . . . I guess hurting them is the thing, you don't want to say something and they internalize it.

Anger directed at me . . . this sounds so elementary, but do not take it personally. If we get into our small ego self, "do they like me, or not like me." I just picture them laying stuff down on the table, and if I pick it up then I make it mine.

COPING WITH GIRLS' TROUBLED FAMILY RELATIONSHIPS

Most of the practitioners acknowledged the importance that family has in a girl's life. Some practitioners were cognizant of the fact that they must be very careful to help the girl question why she is in a particular situation vis à vis the role of the parents. For staff negotiating familial loyalty and the individual, this was deemed difficult. There were also other compounding factors, such as culture, that made family roles and staff work more challenging.

. . . all the role modeling they ever had was those two things [screaming and punching] but you're teaching them another way, which they'll own.

Parents should be mandated to learn skills that kids are being taught. Kids learn skills but can't use them with parents because parents feel belittled or think that kid is talking back to them . . . some kids will come back and tell me, you know, that skill just didn't work with the parent or the adult. [We] need to teach families communication skills all together, not just the kid.

We're talking about alcohol, ice, crack cocaine. It's usually in that order. Some of my kids say, before mom and dad just smoked pot. Before the ice they [mom and kids] used to do all kinds of things together, go out, shopping, go to the mall. Mom and dad used to be more mellow when they smoked pot, but pot is hard to find so now they use ice because there's plenty. All of a sudden mom would give them money to go out, or call someone to pick the kids up so mom can do drugs at home. She just gives them money to get them out of the house. She doesn't spend time with them anymore. So here are kids with lots of money and they are alone. And it sucks. Dad is already gone, he's out doing his "trip" and now mom is trying to get rid of the kids. So these kids are alone. They have money, time and there's nothing to do.

WORKER RELATIONSHIPS

Some participants have had formal training in social work, others had none. Most seemed to agree that theories or techniques are either confirmed or refuted on the job and on the job training is just as valuable if not more valuable, than formal schooling or training. Some workers felt more training was necessary in their programs. Interestingly, many workers stated that they spent a lot of time "bouncing" ideas off of each other because feedback from co-workers helps the most. Outside training helps with categorizing, for one, but feedback from peers was the most helpful. In this sense the relationships that workers foster among themselves on the job mirrors the value that girls place on their own relationships with peers.

Often times it's [theory, methodology] either confirmed and supported on the job or totally ripped apart on the job. So the job is the validator of the things that you get [through formal education or training].

The ongoing support, being able to bounce it off with staff, to say "Hey I'm having a problem with Cindy, is anyone else having a problem with her, or am I just rubbing her the wrong way?" and it helps to hear "No, last week she told me to f--- off too, so don't worry about it."

We spend a lot of time talking about our experiences.

Training helps you to put names on things.

SUSTAINING YOURSELF IN THIS TYPE OF WORK

The role that these practitioners play in young girls' lives is paramount to the future well being of these young people. There were a variety of reasons given as to how these practitioners sustain themselves in this type of front-line work. All participants agreed that they were not in this line of work "for the money" (a comment that elicited a lot of laughter from the participants). Some cited philosophical reasons for being in this job, because there is constant growth and learning. In working with girls, these workers felt a definite sense of personal fulfillment. Others felt that it was a privilege to be someone in the lives of young people and be someone who could effect change. Others found young people to be dynamic and noted the small but positive outcomes and successes with youth that make the job worthwhile. Another person felt that she had to be faithful to kids and not "bail out" because adults were so transitory in these young people's lives.

Of course people get burned out. People are getting paid $7.00 an hour to be told that they are sh-- and take all this stuff from the kids but when the kid runs away and they are tired and hungry they will call and ask if someone can come pick them up.

We get paged and called, [we] deal with crisis.

Dealing with the vast differences requires having a vast repertoire of techniques. You use whatever you got in your back pocket that will keep the moment because you can't just say the one thing. I do a tremendous amount of therapy for myself and retreats and counseling and workshops just to keep my tool chest full so that I can do things a bunch of different ways.

You learn a lot of theory but until you practice it for a few years you don't get the hang of it and there will be those who just won't. It's almost I think intuitive working with kids. Some people get the connection and others won't make that bridge and move on to something else. I don't know, it takes a certain personality, certain belief system that enables you to do this work.

It's not easy. [I do] not have the right answer. I tell kids I don't know, though sometimes this is more frustrating. I'm not here to be important . [I] maintain a distance; I still hug the kids, we are warm to each other, they don't expect me to fix things. I also have a life outside of work, that helps me too.

LACK OF PROGRAMMING

When asked what resources are available for girls the most common response from practitioners was "none." Many voiced frustration at the lack of programs for girls. However, if a program existed, it was not holistic in their view. Those areas specifically mentioned for gaps in services were: post-incarceration services, gay and lesbian counseling programs, and eating disorders.

Not having enough resources for them. I wish programs were more holistic.

The gap I find is with post incarceration. . . . They might do some time, but then they go right straight out. There's a huge gap. They're not interested in programs because they see that as being incarceration. For me personally that transitional window is a huge gap in services.

Girls do get the short end of the stick, programs are designed for boys, but the girls do OK. There needs to be more specialized girl treatments but when work gets crazy I back off on these kinds of ideas. . . . Wish I could do more but then my family would suffer, and I'm working 60 hours a week already.

Recognizing the lack of support by schools and parents to the emotional well being of an adolescent relative to academic well-being.

The court systems are brutal.

Part of my thing is what doors can I open. . . . I would have taken [the girl] out of a home in a second, but it takes CPS a week to get there. If I call my friend then it will be handled differently. That's a little bit of the plus of being around a while.

Sometime it might be wise for us to look at alternatives to punishment. You don't put addicts in prison, or people with communication problems or social skills. You have to teach them and give them purpose.

No, not enough [options for girls]. We tend to group them with the boys. Once I had a girl who needed help, gay and lesbian counseling, but there was none. Or I had a kid who needed to go to Alanon but the sessions were only offered in the day when the kid is in school.

WRAPPING UP

The workers we spoke with reported that they liked working with girls, and could see advantages to working with this population. Chief among the positives included girls' willingness to communicate, the importance of relationships in girls' lives, and the relative safety of working with girls. Frustrations were voiced about the lack of programming available for girls, the low pay for this kind of "frontline" youth work, and the sometimes disappointing choices that marginalized girls made, particularly in their relationships with other girls and boys. The study clearly indicates the need for specialized training in the area of working with girls, including gender identity and female development, including lesbian and transgender issues; and cross-gender staff/client interactions. Policy implications for agencies that work with girls were also suggested. These suggestions included:

- Providing networking opportunities for staff to reflect and discuss;

- Re-examining existing services for girls and advocating expansion where necessary;

- Encouraging agency responsiveness to gender; and

- Expanding research on young women, particularly among different cultural; and socioeconomic groups.

About the Authors

Konia Freitas has a Master's Degree in Urban and Regional Planning and is a researcher at the Social Science Research Institute, University of Hawaii at Manoa. Meda Chesney-Lind, Ph.D., is on the Advisory Board for Women, Girls, and Criminal Justice *and teaches in the Women's Studies Program, University of Hawaii at Manoa.*

References

Baines, M. & Alder, C., "Are Girls More Difficult to Work With? Youth Workers' Perspectives In Juvenile Justice and Related Areas, " 42 *Crime and Delinquency* 3 (July 1996).

Beal, C. R., *Boys and Girls: The Development of Gender Roles* (McGraw-Hill, Inc., 1994).

Belknap, J., Holsinger, K. & Dunn, M., "Understanding Incarcerated Girls: The Result of a Focus Group Study, " 77 *The Prison Journal* 4 (December 1997).

Belknap, J., *The Invisible Woman: Gender, Crime, and Justice* (Wadsworth Publishing Company, 1996).

Boyle, P., "Are Girls Getting Worse, or Are Adults Getting Scared?" 8(2) *Youth Today* 1, 16-18 (Febuary, 1999).

Campbell, A., *Girl Delinquents* (St. Martin's Press, 1981).

Chesney-Lind, M. & Rodgriquez, N., "Women Under Lock and Key, " 63 *Prison Journal* 47-65 (1983).

Chesney-Lind, M. & Sheldon, R. G., *Girls Delinquency and Juvenile Justice* (Brooks/Cole, 1991).

Federal Bureau of Investigation, *Crime in the United States 1995* (Government Printing Office, p. 213, 1996).

Girls Incorporated, *Prevention and Parity: Girls In Juvenile Justice* (Office of Juvenile Justice and Delinquency Prevention, 1996).

Greene, Peters and Associates, *Guiding Principles for Promising Female Programming: An Inventory of Best Practices* (Office of Juvenile Justice and Delinquency Prevention, 1998).

Holsinger, K., "Challenging Delinquency Theories and Sexist Processing, " Paper presented at the Annual Meeting of the American Society of Criminology, Washington DC. (November 1999).

Howell, J.C., Ed., *Guide for Implementing the Comprehensive Strategy for Serious, Violent and Chronic Juvenile Offenders* (Office of Juvenile Justice and Delinquency Prevention, 1995).

Katz, L.F., Kramer, L., & Gottman, J.M., "Conflict and Emotions in Marital, Sibling, and Peer Relationships," in C. Shantz & W. Hartup, Eds., *Conflict in Child and Adolescent Development*, pp. 122-152 (Cambridge University Press, 1992).

Kersten, J., "A Gender Specific Look at Patterns of Violence in Juvenile Institutions: Or Are Girls Really 'More Difficult to Handle'?" 18(4) *International J. of Sociology of Law* 473-493 (1990).

Lipsey, M.W., *Juvenile Delinquency Treatment: A Meta-analytic Inquiry into the Variability of Effects* (Russell Sage Foundation, Research Synthesis Committee, 1990).

Maniglia, R., "Appropriate Gender Specific-Programming for Female Offenders and Girls At-Risk: Standards for Operation," *Ka Mana o No Kaikamahine: The Power of the Girls Conference,* Tokai University Pacific Center, Honolulu, Hawaii (October 29, 1998).

Chapter 13

Working With Girls: The Need for Talk and the Art of Listening

by Rebecca Maniglia, M.A.

INTRODUCTION

One of the foundations of providing appropriate services for young women who are at risk or involved in the juvenile justice system is the clear understanding of the role relationships play in their lives. As common experience with girls reveals and research confirms, relationships are truly, in the words of Carol Gilligan, "the glue that hold girls' lives together" (Gilligan & Brown, 1998). For so many of the young women who come to the attention of the juvenile courts across the country, it is their support of and involvement with others that brings them there in the first place. While the circumstances are varied—girls holding drugs or guns for boyfriends, girls shoplifting or drinking with friends, girls becoming violent in response to years of abuse by adults—the theme of relationships is ever present.

But understanding the role relationships play in girls' personal and criminal lives must also extend to acknowledging the role relationships must play in their treatment after they enter public or private service delivery systems. Just as relationships with peers, boys, and family are often causal in the girls' involvement in the system, it is their relationships with probation officers, case managers, and residential treatment staff that have the potential to teach them alternatives to past behavior, show them self-respect and self-esteem, and enable them to leave the system as healthy human beings.

An earlier version of this chapter originally appeared in Women, Girls & Criminal Justice, *Vol. 1, No. 6, October/November 2000.*

One of the key aspects of understanding this need for positive relationships with adult treatment staff is to recognize the role ongoing dialogue plays in building and sustaining these relationships. The fulfillment of this need is so foundational in the lives of young women that it has been acknowledged by both the psychological literature on female development and the analysis of service needs of young women involved in the juvenile justice system.

When the Valentine Foundation (1990) published the results of one of the first forums discussing the need for gender specific services in the country's justice system, this need for meaningful conversation was addressed in its recommendations.

The discussion of girls' need for ongoing dialogue with adults is a complex one, involving issues from women's verbal history as a people to the very structure of the female brain. Therefore, this is not meant to be a comprehensive examination of this need, but instead a short summary of the main issues involved in understanding young women's need for verbal communication with adults and the implications of this need on our service delivery systems and for those working in them.

GIRLS AND TALK

More Than an Information Exchange

To begin to understand girls' need for talk, one must recognize the purposes for which women and girls in general use communication. According to Deborah Tannen (2001) and John Gray (1992), two of the gurus in the field of communication studies, women generally use dialogue to build relationships with other people while men generally use communication to solve problems and take stands on issues. The first step in honoring a girl's need to talk, therefore, is to realize that the conversations staff have with young women, regardless of topic, are, for the girls, as much about establishing rapport as they are about giving or receiving information.

Building on this basic premise, staff must begin to comprehend their conversations with young women as being about establishing trust, working through issues, and creating relationships. Only when the unintended purpose for the discussion is clear, can staff begin to truly dialogue effectively with young women. For instance, when a probation officer can begin to see the probation interview as an opportunity not just to gather information, but also to establish a relationship, the nature of the dialogue changes dramatically. Suddenly the off-topic rambling of a young woman can be understood as an attempt to establish trust, to verify boundaries, and to check for responses and encouragement from the listener. Instead of silencing girls by providing them with easy and sometimes obvious solutions to their problems, staff can begin to understand the girl's need for a detailed discussion of a situation's interpersonal dynamics. The exploration of the fight with her mother is more important than finding her an alternative manner of transportation to her groups.

Impact on Juvenile Justice Systems

The ramifications of this discussion on the regular system of doing business in juvenile justice are many and complicated. There must be opportunities built into the residential daily schedule that allow girls the opportunity to have meaningful conversations with staff, in one-on-one situations as well as during group times. This does not just mean talk that is focused on a treatment topic, but a more general understanding of the need for dialogue. For instance, a group, which happens immediately after the school day, must allow for the girls to have a brief period of time to process the educational and social experiences of the day, both with one another and with staff. Ignoring this need often puts staff in the position of fighting the girls to pay attention to the topic of the group. As an alternative, when girls are given specific, reliable times and structures in which to talk with one another and staff, their panic around always trying to corner staff to get them to listen diminishes significantly, thus allowing for a much smoother program structure.

Further, as more probation units move toward single gender caseloads, it must be stated that, in most cases, a probation officer working exclusively with young women cannot handle as large a caseload as those working with both genders or working just with young men. While there are exceptions, often the female need for dialogue as a way of building rapport and the staff need to honor that dialogue as a way of building trust cause probation interviews with young women to take a longer period of time than those with young men. While allowing for single-gender caseloads has many benefits for the female clients, usually providing them with a probation officer who desires, and has the skills necessary, to work with girls, the issue of dialogue and the time involved must be addressed if such caseloads are to be successful.

THE ROLE OF LISTENER

Having described the importance of honoring the female need for meaningful conversation in the context of ongoing relationships, the role of the listener becomes an inherent and critical part of this discussion. Judith Jordan (1991) has said, "Voice is shaped by the quality of the listening provided." Yet in the discussion of providing gender specific services, too often honoring girls' voices, stops with the acknowledgment of their need to talk and does not extend to staff's need to learn to listen and listen to learn. If staff members are truly to honor girls' need for verbal dialogue, they must discover what it means to really listen.

Accounting for Filters

The discussion of how to effectively listen begins with the acceptance that one's own individual experience is the filter through which one is able to hear the voices of others. Too often, listening to girls is hampered by the listener's preconceived notions of female behavior, personal beliefs about effective service delivery, and/or specific ideas about the young woman's treatment needs or background. As staff (or as researchers) we must ask: How often are questions asked to which the staff believe they already know the answers? Do staff catch themselves finishing the sentences of the girls because they think they know what is coming? Does this effect staff's ability to hear what girls are saying? Is that truly listening or truly honoring a girl's need to talk?

In *Between Voice and Silence* (Taylor et al., 1995), the authors discuss at length the need for researchers to constantly acknowledge how their culture, race, ethnicity, social class, and position of authority flavor the answers young women give to their research questions. If this is true of strangers interviewing young women, how much more true it becomes when there is some type of relationship between the questioner and the answerer. For instance, young women will speak of not telling their probation officers vital pieces of information because they are not sure if they trust officers. Likewise, a probation officer who approaches a young woman with only an air of authority is likely to get very different answers (and to hear those answers differently) than one who works to establish mutual care and concern with a client.

Once staff recognizes and challenges its own listening filters, it becomes necessary to understand listening as going beyond hearing spoken words. In *Mother Daughter Revolution* (Debold et al., 1993), the authors examine how listening is as much about watching for body language and paying attention to the expression of feelings as it is listening for verbal clues. The listener must notice and work to interpret reasons why the girl is slow to speak, seems nervous, is excessively aggressive or defensive in tone. How a young woman says what she says is as important as the words she uses.

MORE THAN ADVICE

Listening is not just about giving advice to young women. Even when staff members are not jumping to find quick solutions for a girl's problems, they sometimes don't listen long enough before imparting wisdom. While it is true that young women need the guidance of older adults with whom they have a relationship, the time for advice is often much further into the conversation than found in a typical staff to girl conversation. As Debold, Wilson, and Malave (1993) explain it, "Listening to learn isn't just about giving advice—at least not until asked—but about trying to understand exactly what someone means, how it is that someone looks at and feels about her particular situation. Listening to learn is a conspiracy—which literally means a 'breathing together'— in which one person breathes in the words and feelings of another" (p. 146).

Finally, listening designed to honor the female need to talk must also sometimes include action. When young women describe the injustices of the world or the system or their very lives, staff must be willing to acknowledge the feelings behind those expressions and then, when possible, to join with these girls to bring about change, both internally and externally. In a system that praises conformity in behavior and attitude, perhaps this is the most difficult aspect of truly listening to young women. As Taylor et. al (1995) write, "To listen to girls whose voices are ordinarily met with silence in the larger world is to invite disruption, disturbance, or dissolution of the status quo" (p. 203).

Despite the risks, listening in a way that honors the female experience and the feminine need for verbal expression must still be foundational to the establishment of gender appropriate services throughout the juvenile justice system.

About the Author

Rebecca Maniglia, M.A., formerly an Assistant Contract Director and Regional Manager for Community Research Associates, a technical assistance provider with the U.S. Office of Juvenile Justice and Delinquency Prevention, is currently Director of RLM Associates in Lakewood, Colorado.

References

Debold, E., Wilson, M. & Malave, I., *Mother Daughter Revolution* (Bantam Books, 1993).

Gilligan, C., & Brown, L.M., *Meeting at the Crossroads* (Ballantine Books, 1998).

Gray, J., *Men Are From Mars, Women Are From Venus* (Harper Collins, 1992).

Jordan, J., Kaplan, A.G., Miller, J.B., Stiver, I.P. & Surrey, J.L., *Women's Growth in Connection* (Guilford Press, 1991).

Tannen, D., *You Just Don't Understand: Women and Men in Conversation* (Perrenial Currents, 2001).

Taylor, J.M., Gilligan, C. & Sullivan, A.M., *Between Voice and Silence: Women and Girls, Race and Relationship* (Harvard University Press, 1995).

Valentine Foundation, *A Conversation About Girls* (1990).

Chapter 14

"Bad Girls, Bad Girls, Whatcha Gonna Do?"

by Lyn Mikel Brown, Ed.D. and Meda Chesney-Lind, Ph.D.

Suddenly the world is filled with nasty girls. "Girls just want to be mean," the *New York Times Magazine* announced last year as a slew of new books on girls' relational aggression told us how "to tame them," to use the *Times*' own words (Talbot, 2002).

Girls will be (backstabbing, catty) girls—the latest flavor du jour of the American media's love affair with "bad" girls. Hardly a new idea in a country that grew up reading Longfellow's poem about his daughter: "when she was good, she was very very good, but when she was bad she was horrid."

Now comes the ultimate girl fight in living color. Full-scale "savagery in the Chicago suburbs," *Newsweek* called it (Meadows & Johnson, 2003). Junior girls from the privileged

---

An earlier version of this chapter originally appeared as two separate articles in Women, Girls & Criminal Justice, *one by both authors, in Vol. 4, No. 6, October/November 2003 and the other (on the 12 ways to prevent girlfighting) by Lyn Mikel Brown alone, Vol. 5, No. 2, February/March 2004.*

Glenbrook North High School paid for the right to be hazed by seniors at the annual pow-der puff football game. After the beatings and humiliations ended, five girls were sent to the hospital, one with a broken ankle, another with a concussion so serious it caused mem-ory loss, another to receive 10 stitches in her scalp.

TRIVIALIZATION OF GIRLS' ANGER

As authors who write about girls' anger, aggression and violence, we are troubled, for reasons that are obvious and some that are less so. Violence that girls perpetrate on other girls, whether it's emotional or physical, is cause for concern. But the media frenzy that greeted the lurid and voyeuristic video of girls fighting other girls is also problematic. In fact, it signals another major issue for those concerned about girls' development. Girls grow up in a world that has long encouraged them to turn their rage against one another—and then taken a front row seat in the audience for the fight. Like the Glenbrook parents, they might even supply the beer.

Girls' anger has a long history of being dismissed ("she's just a bitch," "it must be PMS") and trivialized ("you're beautiful when you're angry"). Girls' violence is gener-ally either ignored entirely or sensationalized and sexualized. Girlfighting, in particular, is often presented as a spectacle (consider mud or Jello wrestling), enjoyed for its eroti-cism as much as its entertainment value (think Jerry Springer).

The hazing we watched up-close and personal, over and over again, was horrifying, but questions about how and why the episode gripped the nation are at least as troubling. Who was it watching the events unfold on the field? Why was it caught on videotape to begin with? How was it passed on to cable and network television? Who made the deci-sion to run it repeatedly? Why was it international news?

Girlfighting as spectator sport. Again.

Why, when boys perpetrate 80 percent of serious violence in the U.S., is this the story that captivates us and helps define a generation of girls?

ISSUES OF POWER AND SUBORDINATION

In the shock and awe, we've missed the point. The school principal suggests this is just kids with "old scores to settle." That doesn't tell us enough and, worse, it fudges the real issues.

This was girls fighting over boyfriends and popularity. The seniors used words like "bitches," "wimps," and "sluts" to shame the juniors into staying on the field. In what many think of as post-feminist America, it's not popular to raise issues of power and sub-ordination, but the fact that girls are fighting other girls in front of videotaping boys is hardly insignificant. That girls used sexist and misogynistic language to control other girls during and after the event and that their fights were primarily for boys' attention and favor is a symptom of deeper cultural problems. As with many girl fights, boys are both the "cause" of girls' violence and the real audience.

We need to ask harder, more critical questions about why girls are fighting. Why embrace insults that ratify the sexual double standard? Why is strength in women always devalued as "bitchiness?" Why the endless competition among girls for male approval? And why fight each other instead of fighting against a culture still rife with sexism and violence toward women?

Girlfighting gets acted out horizontally on other girls because this is the safest and easiest outlet for their outrage and frustration. Girls are essentially accessing and mimicking the male violence they sometimes know all too well; and they are choosing victims that are societally approved—other girls. This pattern of horizontal aggression has long characterized subordinate groups, since it manages the inevitable anger in the group being controlled without jeopardizing the overall structure of male privilege.

Girls' violence also served one additional purpose. It's not uncommon for the targets of that violence to be, themselves, the group members that are challenging the rigid norms of girlhood. Why, for example, wouldn't the girlfighters go after those "girly girls" that the media continuously tells them are weak, vapid, and stupid? From the evil head cheerleaders in the Disney Channel's *Kim Possible* and *Lizzie McGuire*, to *The Man Show*'s Juggy Squad on Comedy Central, to *Thong Song* wannabes, these girls make easy targets.

Girls who take out other girls for being "dykes," "hos," and "bitches" can prove they are different, worth taking seriously, a force to contend with. No wimps, wusses, or victims here. But this posturing is short-lived protection at best, because selling out other girls this way only continues a climate of misogyny, and any wrong move can quickly turn the perpetrator into a victim

A PROBLEM OF THE GENERAL CULTURE

The problem is not girls, but rather a culture that denigrates, commodifies, and demoralizes women and then gets a kick out watching the divide-and-conquer consequences.

There's an old saying, "Men kill their weak, women kill their strong." If we would give girls legitimate avenues to power, value their minds as much as their bodies, they'd be less likely to go down those nasty, underhanded, or openly hostile roads, less likely to take their legitimate rage out on other girls. Let's face it, "meanness" and other covert aggressions are, in the final analysis, weapons of the weak; horizontal violence ultimately ratifies boy not girl power. When we join with girls to create real pathways to power and possibility, we'll have a lot less to videotape and we'll have a lot more to be proud of both in ourselves and in our daughters.

TWELVE WAYS TO PREVENT GIRLFIGHTING AND BUILD ALLIES INSTEAD

1. Do Your Own Work

We cannot help girls see or deal with girl bullies or offer them constructive ways to respond to their own and other girls' anger and aggression unless we can negotiate these things ourselves. This means exploring the roots of our own anger, disappointment, jealousies; refusing to engage in slander and gossip, confronting the fears and anxieties that standing up for ourselves, speaking truth to power, or feeling excluded or talked about invoke.

2. Read the School Culture Critically

Helping girls read the school culture and the messages it conveys about power and privilege (who is important and who is not) can give them some critical distance and explanatory power so that they don't take sexist messages personally. Providing safe spaces for girls to discuss the climate of their schools is important; more important is encouraging them to develop ways to move beyond discussion and give them room and power to initiate change.

3. Encourage Discriminating Tastes in Friendships

We need to rid ourselves of the fiction that girls should like and be friends with everyone. Encourage girls to choose people as friends who are affirming, who listen to them and treat them well. It's okay not to be friends with someone as long as you treat that person respectfully. Most important, mistreatment is *not* a quality of friendship.

4. Address Girlfighting When You See It

Talk with girls about relational and physical violence. Relational aggression has very real consequences and often precedes physical aggression. There is, however, little training for teachers and school administrators to spot and understand the near invisible cycles of popularity and isolation among girls. Encourage your school to provide teacher education on relational as well as physical forms of aggression and to understand how and why girls and boys express their anger and aggression differently.

5. Engage Girls' Anger and Hone a Sense of Fairness and Justice

To express anger and aggression is human. Used constructively, both can be real sources of power. Girls need guidance about how to stay clear and centered in their disagreements and they need support for not giving up their convictions to maintain a false relational harmony. Help girls to know and own the real sources of their strong feelings and to make considered choices about how to express them and to whom.

6. Foster Solidarity Between Girls, Between Women, Between Women and Girls

Avoid a "girls will be girls message" when what you really mean to say is that all girls are petty, mean, or back-stabbing or that all girls engage in exclusive cliques and clubs. Instead, affirm girls' relational strengths and the potential for collective action and help girls identify things that they can change to make their environments better places. Model healthy, honest, committed relationships with women.

7. Develop "Hardiness Zones" and Safe Spaces for Girls

Hardiness is a concept that describes people who thrive in stressful circumstances. Offering girls opportunities to develop ideas, to take action on issues that really matter to them, to experience the challenge of changing their schools and communities for the better, develop hardiness. Provide safe spaces for girls to get together to practice their critique of a media rife with damaging stereotypes and negative voices. In these spaces girls can talk, plan, and organize for social change, write poetry, critique sexism, and practice sisterhood.

8. Question the Traditional Romance Story

The usual story of heterosexual romance places girls in subordinate relationship with boys. When you see such stories, question them. Question connections between male desire and violence; refute the line that boys chase, hurt, kick girls because they like them. Question double standards about sexual activity and prevailing assumptions that boys only want sex and girls only want relationships, or that boys are ruled by their hormones and so it's up to girls to control them. Talk with girls about what they want.

9. Develop Media Literacy

Provide girls with the language and tools to be critical of the things they watch and read and hear. Practice the four-step model proposed by Dr. Janie Ward (2000) in her book *The Skin We're In*:

- *Read it*—Help girls break down racist/sexist/classist experiences by exploring the images/situation with them. Help them make connections and see larger patterns.

- *Name it*—Acknowledge the presence of racism/sexism/class bias and bring its reality into full consciousness, however painful this might be.

- *Oppose it*—Help girls consider constructive forms of resistance tied to a healthy and positive sense of themselves and their values.

- *Replace it*—Help girls put something new and affirming in the place of the feeling, attitude, or behavior being opposed. Encourage them to take a stand for fairness and justice, reinforce personal integrity, and the power of acting on their beliefs.

10. Encourage Girls to Play Sports and Build Physical Strength

Awareness of and comfort with our bodies centers us, connects mind and body. Fully inhabiting our bodies as subjects rather than objects radically alters our relationship to the public world. Sports, self-defense classes, and martial arts offer girls a chance to know their strength, instill confidence and full awareness of what their bodies can do, and encourage girls to take up space.

11. Practice Voice, Encourage Activism

Provide girls with different venues and opportunities to voice their thoughts and feelings: drama, debate clubs, discussion groups, book clubs, mentoring programs. Civil rights teams can be great places to expand consciousness and work toward justice. Connect with non-profits that do programming for girls, offer alternatives to media images, and encourage girls to be strong, independent, and confident.

Girls who appreciate that the world is bigger than the social dynamics of their school are less likely to be devastated by the vicissitudes of peer rejection. Rather than spend time playing girl-targeted video games in which girls shop, decorate a house, or design clothes, encourage them to investigate who makes the clothes they wear and what their lives are like. Rather than read magazine articles that encourage dieting or looking perfect, encourage girls to do something to support those who "go without" in their community. Connect them with human rights organizations to find out how they can make the world a better, more caring, and just place.

12. Tell the Truth

What happens when women and girls get together to fight sexism or other related "isms"? Can they cross race and class lines? Can they address heterosexism and homophobia? Can they make real changes? The truth is both that it's very hard *and* that it's worth the struggle. The truth is that there are consequences—real dangers—to taking yourself seriously and challenging the status quo. Telling girls the truth about *our* lives, choices, and actions helps them understand their choices, prepares them for the consequences of their actions, and reminds them that conflict and disagreement is not only inevitable but important.

About the Authors

Lyn Mikel Brown, Ed.D., is an associate professor of education at Colby College in Waterville, Maine and author of Raising Their Voices: The Politics of Girls' Anger *(Harvard University Press 1998) and* Girlfighting: Betrayal and Rejection Among Girls *(New York University Press, 2003). Meda Chesney-Lind, Ph.D., is a professor of women's studies at the University of Hawaii at Manoa and co-author of* Girls, Delinquency and Juvenile Justice *(Wadsworth, 2003),* The Female Offender *(Sage, 2003) and* Female Gangs in America *(Lakeview Press, 1999).*

References

Meadows, S. & Johnson, D., "Girl Fight: Savagery in the Chicago Suburbs." *Newsweek*, May 19, 2003, p. 37.

Talbot, M., "Mean Girls and the New Movement to Tame Them." New York Times Magazine, February 24, 2002, pp. 24-29, 40, 58, 64-65.

Ward, J., *The Skin We're In* (The Free Press, 2000)

Part 3

Mothers and Children

Incarcerated women, as well as women under community corrections supervision, are often mothers and it is important to note that their children are deeply affected by such parental confinement and restriction. Motherhood issues for women involved with the criminal justice system are often two-edged swords. Women are frequently castigated for how their behavior affects their children. Sometimes, their motherhood is overlooked; other times, they are simply blamed as "bad mothers." Less often are motherhood matters given serious attention. Nonetheless, they have been given more attention than other important matters, such as addictive behavior or mental health care. Accordingly, the role of motherhood in the lives of women in conflict with the law is something that is more readily, and even more easily, discussed in various policy and program settings. It is reasonable to say, then, that "mothers and children" are topics that are more likely to occur in criminal justice or correctional conversations. Still, it is far from clear that the general recognition of these matters is given sufficiently granted resources and implemented services.

In the 12 chapters in this section, various academics, advocates, and practitioners map out an array of policy issues and program concerns about incarcerated mothers and their children:

- Gail T. Smith, an attorney and the long-time director of Chicago Legal Aid to Incarcerated Mothers (CLAIM), a venerable advocacy group, provides an early description of the generally worsening impact of the Adoption and Safe Families Act of 1997 on incarcerated mothers and their children.

- Patricia Allard, a Canadian now working in the United States with the Brennan Center for Justice at the New York University School of Law, examines the unintended victims (e.g., children and others) of the lifetime welfare ban that was part of another troubling piece of federal legislation, the Personal Responsibility and Work Opportunity Reconciliation Act of 1996.

- Pennsylvania attorney Amy E. Hirsch takes a state-specific look at the impact of 1990s welfare reform on women with drug convictions.

- Chicago attorney Susan M. George reports statistical information from Illinois on the economic and social characteristics of incarcerated mothers and their children.

- Criminologist Joycelyn M. Pollack reports an in-depth, comprehensive national survey of parenting programs, including special visiting areas, furloughs, community facilities, overnight visitation, prison nurseries, and other options, that are available to women imprisoned in state facilities.

- Independent researcher Kelsey Kauffman reports on the slow process of establishing nurseries in women's prisons, with detailed emphasis on a nursery opened on the grounds of the Ohio Reformatory for Women in 2001.

- Sociologist Maureen Norton-Hawk finds patterns of intergenerational dysfunction in her Massachusetts survey of incarcerated mothers and their children.

- Arkansas practitioner Susan Phillips describes local processes of connecting and building relationships between child welfare and corrections agencies.

- Karen V. Chapple, E. Paula Cox, and Jamie MacDonald-Furches describe Summit House, an alternative program in North Carolina for incarcerated mothers and their children.

- Practitioner Jennifer A. Lynch reports on the YMCA Character House in Sarasota, Florida, which cares for juvenile justice-involved girls and their babies.

- Retired corrections researcher Ann Jaede discusses the importance of community-based services for federally sentenced women.

- Finally, Californians Lt. Kris Anderson and Julie Harmeyer describe the MOMS Program located at the Alameda County Sheriff's Community Re-Entry Center.

Chapter 15

Adoption and Safe Families Act of 1997 and Its Impact on Prisoner Mothers and Their Children

by Gail T. Smith, J.D.

INTRODUCTION

The dramatic growth in the women prisoner population has a critical impact on our collective future because of women's role as mothers and the effect their incarceration has on the lives of their children. As more mothers are locked up, more children are joining the burgeoning population of foster children in a system widely recognized to be a disaster. The question whether these children will be reunited successfully with their mothers, be adopted, or grow up in the system has always depended as a practical matter on a number of factors, including the length of the mother's sentence, the nature of her offense, her participation and progress in rehabilitative programming, the age of the child, the quality and

This chapter originally appeared in Women, Girls & Criminal Justice, *Vol.1, No.1, December/January 2000.*

strength of the mother's relationship with the child, and the attitudes of the case worker and foster parent toward the mother. The hope of reuniting their families is acknowledged by addictions specialists, corrections officials, and researchers as a primary motive for women to change their lives for the better. The fear—or reality—of permanent loss of her children can send a mother into a downward spiral of relapse and recidivism.

The dilemma for imprisoned women who have minor children has gotten worse. The Adoption and Safe Families Act of 1997 (AFSA; PL 105-89), has made it far more likely that mothers of children in foster care will lose their children permanently. While ASFA is intended to provide permanency for children in foster care, its likely impact for many children, in particular older children who are less adoptable, will be to make them legal orphans who have neither ties to their birth parents nor permanent homes. As more children grow up in foster care with no relationship with their mothers, the conditions of their lives put them at risk of becoming part of the prison population. If the law provided resources and focused on assisting mothers with addictions instead of so quickly giving up on them, it could help families in a meaningful and lasting way. ASFA fails families on that score. This chapter explores ASFA and its implementation in the states, and suggests ways to preserve families in spite of it.

FUNDAMENTAL CHANGES IN FOSTER CARE POLICY

ASFA makes four important changes to foster care policy at the federal level. First, it removes the requirement for states to provide reasonable efforts to reunite foster children with their parents under specified circumstances, and it emphasizes that the child's health and safety shall be the paramount concern when providing reasonable efforts. Second, it hastens the process of permanency planning and court proceedings, and mandates reasonable efforts to find a permanent placement for the child in cases when reasonable efforts to reunite the family are not required. Third, it imposes a mandate for states to move to terminate parental rights in certain circumstances, with a shorter timeline for parents to complete services and regain custody or face termination. If a child has been in foster care for 15 of the past 22 months, the state must move to terminate the parent's rights except under certain circumstances. Fourth, it provides financial incentives for states to increase the number of adoptions completed annually. AFSA also provides for criminal records checks for prospective foster and adoptive parents, calls for documentation of agency efforts to locate an adoptive or other permanent homes, and promotes resources for cross-jurisdictional adoptions and permanent placements of children across state and county lines.

Push Toward Terminating Parental Rights

Under ASFA, reasonable efforts to preserve and reunify families are not required when a parent has:

- Subjected the child to aggravated circumstances such as abandonment, torture, or abuse;

- Committed, or had any criminal accountability in, the murder or manslaughter of a child or the child's other parent; or

- Committed felony assault resulting in serious bodily injury to the child or the other parent.

While this would seem a reasonable provision to insure child safety, its application, for example, to battered mothers who have acted to protect themselves and their children against abuse by the other parent and who then are held criminally culpable will likely result in severe injustices against mothers and children in the aftermath of domestic violence, since they could be separated under the Act.

Further, ASFA removes the requirement of reasonable efforts to reunify families if the parent's rights to a sibling have been terminated involuntarily. Mothers who have lost children permanently for reasons not related to any mistreatment of the children, including the mere length of time in foster care, face the risk of losing any children they ever have in the future. For any mother who has struggled with addiction and relapse for several years before she was able to turn her life around, this poses the ongoing risk of state intrusion and removal of her children even when she is stable in recovery. The perceived unreasonableness of this policy can lead mothers to desperate acts such as forgoing prenatal care or trying to give birth out-of-state.

Even more troubling, states are required by ASFA to file or join a petition to terminate the parent's rights not only in the above circumstances but whenever a child has been in foster care for 15 of the most recent 22 months. There are three exceptions to this termination requirement:

- The state has placed the child in the care of a relative;

- The state has documented a compelling reason why a termination petition would not be in the child's best interests; or

- The state has not provided the family with services necessary for the child's return, in cases when such services are required.

Disparate Impact on Prisoner Mothers

The ideology of family reunification, which some commentators believe has been applied too broadly, never has been applied with enthusiasm to prisoner mothers. This is in part due to the distance foster care caseworkers must travel to provide visits for children with mothers in prison, and caseworkers' unfamiliarity with prison regulations, resources, programming, and staff. It is also due in large part to a widespread bias against reuniting children with a mother who has been to prison. The gap between the policy of family reunification and the practice in reality is stark. Despite the generous efforts of non-profit agencies and volunteers, the dearth of resources to preserve the families of imprisoned mothers is a national shame, particularly since most were convicted of petty offenses.

The push toward termination of parental rights based strictly on a 15-month timeline will likely have the worst impact on the largest number of families of imprisoned mothers. For a mother serving even a relatively short sentence, meeting the new time frame imposed by ASFA will present an extraordinary hurdle at best, and in many cases will be impossible. When one considers the number of months, or even years, spent in pre-trial detention in large metropolitan criminal court systems, it is quite possible that even a mother found not guilty of a criminal charge could lose her children permanently while awaiting trial on a case. To avoid losing her child permanently, within 15 months of the child's placement in foster care or adjudication as a ward of the court, the mother must establish a household and a source of legal income to support the child, recover from any addiction she may have, and complete all other required services, which usually include parenting classes, counseling, and a psychological evaluation. Put this scenario in context of the hardships faced by most women as they re-enter the community after prison, including the severe lack of services or resources to aid their transition from prisoner to self-supporting community member, and it is clear that they face nearly insurmountable odds in their hope of reuniting with their children in foster care.

STATE RESPONSES MIRRORING THE FEDERAL STATUTE

Forty-eight states have passed legislation in response to ASFA. By the end of the year 2000 only Hawaii and Vermont had not amended their state laws. The mandate to file termination of parental rights petitions when children have been in placement for 15 of 22 months was added to 35 state statutes, and five other states added provisions that may make the time frame for termination even tighter than that.

Illinois, for example, added provisions echoing ASFA and three additional grounds for termination of parental rights that specifically target imprisoned parents; there is a rebuttable presumption that a parent is depraved (and therefore unfit) if:

- The parent has been convicted of at least three felonies under any state, federal, or territorial law, and at least one conviction took place within five years of the filing of the termination petition;
- The child is in custody, the parent is incarcerated at the time of the filing of the petition, prior to incarceration the parent had little or no contact with the child or provided little or no support, and incarceration will prevent the parent from discharging parental responsibilities for more than two years after the petition is filed;
- The child is in custody, the parent is incarcerated at the time of filing, the parent has been repeatedly incarcerated as a result of criminal convictions, and the incarceration has prevented the parent from discharging parental responsibilities for the child.

These grounds look both at past conduct and prospective availability of the parent. A mother who is working hard in rehabilitative programs and turning her life around is out of luck if her past fits within this profile. So is a mother who is serving a first-time sentence of more than two years and who—in her addiction, for example—was out of touch with her children before her arrest. Given the turnover not only of foster care workers but even foster care agencies overseeing services, it is not easy to keep in touch. The state, however, puts the burden squarely on the mother to do so.

CREATING MORE OFFENDERS: THE PATH FROM CHILD WELFARE TO THE CRIMINAL JUSTICE SYSTEM

The recent growth in the foster care system, combined with the proliferation of foster care agencies, can be connected with the anticipated continued growth of the prison-industrial complex. The path from foster care to delinquency, the juvenile justice system, and prison is all too familiar to service providers and advocates working with prisoners. Children in foster care are subjected to multiple placements that forever affect their relationships, sense of self-worth, and ability to function as adults. This author has noted a high proportion of clients who were foster children before they were prisoners, many of whom had their first experiences of alcohol, drugs, and sexual abuse in their foster homes. Approximately one in four foster children are abused in foster care. The loss of family connections also means loss of potential family resources for young adults when hard times hit, and thus foster care in childhood has been connected with homelessness in adulthood. The General Accounting Office in its 1995 Foster Care Overview noted a study finding that two to four years after leaving foster care, 40% of youths had been on public assistance, incarcerated, or posed other costs to the community (U.S. General Accounting Office, 1995). This is no surprise, and it should make us question the motives of those policymakers who favor severance of family ties over family preservation.

Goal of Increasing Adoptions Not Met

The stated goal of ASFA was to increase the annual number of adoptions of children in foster care. In 1996 there were over 30,000 more children whose parents' rights were terminated than there were children adopted. However, neither ASFA nor the majority of state statutes requires adoptive parents to be identified before a child is permanently cut off from the parents. State foster care budgets depend on federal reimbursement for children in foster care, and since ASFA's financial incentives for increasing adoptions over the annual mean is small in relation to these payments, it is all the more likely that the expansion of termination of parental rights will result in an ever-larger population of children who will grow up in foster care and never have an opportunity to live with their mothers again, nor to be adopted.

The media storm surrounding several horrifying cases of child abuse in recent years has led to increased removal of children whose parents were suspected to be caring for them inadequately, flooding the foster care system and therefore rendering it even less able to serve children and families. The number of children in foster care has almost doubled in the past 10 years, and in many cases, their placement is not due to child abuse. Child welfare advocates widely recognize that the parent-child separation in itself is severely damaging to children's well-being, yet services to prevent the need for foster care or to help parents remedy problems early on have never been sufficiently available, of uniformly good quality, or adequately funded. In fact, the availability of substance abuse treatment has actually declined, and other resources designed to keep children at home are almost nonexistent. If preventive services were widely available, and provided in a manner that respected mothers and built on their family strengths, many women in prison today would have addressed their problems before they were ever arrested.

Separation From Mother Likely to Seriously Affect Children

For children who have lived with their mothers, know and remember them, and have bonded with them, AFSA's 15-of-22-month provision is likely to be devastating. Older children are far less likely than babies to be adopted; even when they are adopted, the failure rate of adoptions of older children is disheartening. As mentioned above, most states do not require any showing that adoptive parents have been found prior to terminating a parent's rights. On the contrary, the rationale is that when a child is "freed" for adoption it will be easier to find an adoptive placement. For older children, this is simply not realistic. Thus, state and federal law operate to create legal orphans. The legal and practical effect of terminating rights is to completely sever the mother-child relationship. After termination is ordered, the mother and child have no further visitation rights; indeed, the agency may decline even to tell the mother the child's whereabouts or news of the child's well being.

WORKING TO PRESERVE BOND BETWEEN INCARCERATED MOTHERS AND CHILDREN

It is possible for incarcerated mothers to continue their relationship with their children in some cases. The best way for a family to avoid termination of the mother-child relationship is to avoid having the children placed in foster care in the first place, if at all possible.

Use of Community-Based Programs

Community-based sentencing for mothers convicted of nonviolent offenses should be made widely available to prevent the separation of the family. Day programs for women to take part in rehabilitation while living with their children should be the preferred sentencing option whenever the woman poses no risk of flight or harm to her family or community. Residential mother-child programs in which mothers care for their babies and young children have been highly successful in reducing repeat offenses, and at the same time prevent the destruction of the family.

Community-based sentencing alternatives to keep the family intact are most crucial for very young children and infants who are still in the process of bonding with their mothers, but increasingly should be explored as well to prevent older children from permanently losing the mothers with whom they are bonded. About 16 states already are operating such programs to keep families with very young children together and provide treatment, but only for a tiny fraction of eligible women. There is a provision in ASFA for demonstration projects to provide substance abuse treatment to mothers while they care for their infants, and such programs have been highly successful in helping women to attain and maintain recovery.

Providing for Legal Guardianship if Mother Imprisoned

For mothers who must serve their sentences in prison, private guardianship should be considered if the children are not already in the foster care system. The advantages of guardianship are that children stay with a familiar person who loves them, and usually benefit from regular contact with their mother. Many states provide for private guardianships through the probate court or similar provisions. In Illinois, e.g., the mother can appoint a short-term guardian for up to 60 days without any court involvement; full legal guardianship can be established in probate court. With written parental consent, an appropriate caregiver—a relative or simply a trusted friend—can be appointed as the minor's guardian by the court in a fairly simple proceeding.

Legal service practitioners can assist the family in establishing guardianship, and many caregivers represent themselves in court with assistance from the clerk of court or a volunteer lawyer project. Legal aid providers can help the family set up a smooth transition for the children, caregiver, and mother by drafting a co-parenting agreement and by counseling the parties about the exact nature of guardianship, the mother's residual rights, and the process for resuming custody upon her release. Ethical considerations require that the written representation agreement include a provision stating the parties' understanding that if a conflict of interest were to arise between the guardian and the mother, the lawyer would withdraw and refer each to separate counsel.

In many instances where guardianships have been arranged, the mother moves in with the guardian (often her own mother) and children after serving her sentence. This assists not only her process of reunification with children but also her re-entry into her community.

Kinship Care Arrangements

A somewhat similar provision is possible on a practical if not a legal basis under the foster care system: kinship care. A major difference, as compared to guardianship, is that while the mother may continue a relationship with her children, she is far less likely to regain legal custody of them. The provision of foster care by a relative has many of the advantages for children that private guardianship provides, except that the state intrudes into the family's decisions. As noted above, an exception to the mandate to terminate parental rights exists when children are in kinship care, and many states have enacted that exception in their state laws.

The practical workings of kinship care depend a great deal on the caseworkers' training and professionalism. There have been circumstances in which relatives have been bullied to adopt children or else lose them, when the relatives strongly believed the children needed ongoing relationships with the mothers. In other cases, relatives have been threatened that if they did not adopt, the children would be scattered to strangers' homes, although the relatives were firmly dedicated to providing a permanent home. Post-adoption services for children with special needs are commonly denied, although mandated, making it more difficult for relative caregivers to adopt. It is hard to imagine how termination of parental rights in such cases is in children's best interests. States that have statutes governing open adoption contracts may present one more option for mothers who face permanent loss of their children but hope to have some continued communication with them.

CONCLUSION

ASFA has exacerbated the plight of women prisoners and their children in foster care. It will take dedication, creativity, and determination to fight its destructive impact, and imprisoned mothers, their advocates, and service providers will need every bit of ingenuity, compassion, strength, and creativity they can tap to handle the crisis.

About the Author

Gail T. Smith, Esq., is executive director of Chicago Legal Aid to Incarcerated Mothers (CLAIM).

References

U.S. General Accounting Office, Child Welfare: Complex Needs Strain Capacity to Provide Services, GAO/HEHS-95-208, (U.S. Government Printing Office, 1995).

Chapter 16

Unintended Victims of the Lifetime Welfare Ban for Drug Offenders

by Patricia Allard, M.A., LL.B.

INTRODUCTION

In 1996, the federal government replaced its 60-year-old social welfare system, Aid to Families with Dependent Children (AFDC), with the Personal Responsibility and Work Opportunity Reconciliation Act of 1996 (Welfare Reform Act). Under the Welfare Reform Act, a federal block grant program, Temporary Assistance for Needy Families (TANF), imposes time limits and work requirements on welfare recipients. Section 115 of the Welfare Reform Act stipulates that persons convicted of a state or federal felony offense involving the use or sale of drugs are subject to a lifetime ban on receiving cash assistance and food stamps. This provision applies only to those convicted of drug offenses.

This chapter originally appeared in Women, Girls & Criminal Justice, *Vol. 3, No. 3, April/May 2002.*

Table 16.1: State Implementation of Lifetime Welfare Ban as of December, 2001

State	Denies Benefits Entirely	Partial Denial/ Term-Denial	Benefits Dependent on Drug Treatment	Opted Out of Welfare Ban
Alabama	X			
Alaska	X			
Arizona	X			
Arkansas		X		
California	X			
Colorado		X		
Connecticut				X
Delaware	X			
District of Columbia				X
Florida		X		
Georgia	X			
Hawaii			X	
Idaho	X			
Illinois		X		
Indiana	X			
Iowa		X		
Kansas	X			
Kentucky			X	
Louisiana		X		
Maine	X			
Maryland			X	
Massachusetts		X		
Michigan				X
Minnesota			X	
Mississippi	X			
Missouri	X			

This chapter documents the impact of the lifetime welfare ban on women and their children in the 42 states now enforcing the ban in full or in part. An estimated 92,000 women are affected by the ban in the 23 states for which we were able to obtain data. The ban also places over 135,000 children in these states at risk of neglect and involvement with the criminal justice system due to the prospect of reduced family income support. Further, significant potential societal costs are associated with the ban in the areas of criminal justice, health, and child welfare.

The intersection of the drug war, the criminal justice system, welfare reform, and other social policy arenas creates a disparate impact on African-American women and Latinas. The lifetime welfare ban has a disproportionate impact on mothers of color for two reasons. First, racially biased drug policies and enforcement practices account, in large part, for the rapid growth in the numbers of African-American and Latina drug offenders under criminal justice supervision. Second, race- and gender-based socioeconomic inequalities

Table 16.1: *(Cont'd)*

State	Denies Benefits Entirely	Partial Denial/ Term-Denial	Benefits Dependent on Drug Treatment	Opted Out of Welfare Ban
Montana	X			
Nebraska	X			
Nevada			X	
New Hampshire				X
New Jersey			X	
New Mexico	X			
New York				X
North Carolina		X		
North Dakota	X			
Ohio				X
Oklahoma				X
Oregon				X
Pennsylvania	X			
Rhode Island		X		
South Carolina			X	
South Dakota	X			
Tennessee	X			
Texas		X		
Utah			X	
Vermont				X
Virginia	X			
Washington			X	
West Virginia	X			
Wisconsin			X	
Wyoming	X			
U.S. Total	**22**	**10**	**10**	**9**

make African-American and Latina mothers highly susceptible to poverty and dispro-portionately represented in the welfare system.

IMPLEMENTATION OF THE LIFETIME WELFARE BAN

The drug provision of the welfare reform act applies to all states, unless a state legis-lature elects to either modify or opt out of the provision. As of December, 2001, 42 states enforce the ban in full or in part, and only eight states and the District of Columbia have opted out. As seen in Table 16.1, as of December, 2001, 22 states had adopted the drug pro-vision in full, while 20 states have modified it. (*Editor's note:* Table 16.2 shows how the states look as of January, 2005, to update our readers.)

Table 16.2: State Implementation of Lifetime Welfare Ban as of January, 2005

State	Denies Benefits Entirely	Partial Denial/ Term-Denial	Benefits Dependent on Drug Treatment	Opted Out of Welfare Ban
Alabama	X			
Alaska	X			
Arizona	X			
Arkansas		X		
California		X		
Colorado		X		
Connecticut				X
Delaware			X	
District of Columbia				X
Florida		X		
Georgia	X			
Hawaii			X	
Idaho		X		
Illinois		X		
Indiana	X			
Iowa		X		
Kansas	X			
Kentucky			X	
Louisiana		X		
Maine				X
Maryland			X	
Massachusetts		X		
Michigan				X
Minnesota			X	
Mississippi	X			
Missouri	X			

Of the states that have modified the ban, several limit ineligibility for welfare benefits to persons convicted of particular drug offenses, such as manufacturing or distributing illegal substances. Some states have replaced the lifetime ban with a one-year or six-month ineligibility period. In yet other states a drug conviction will lead to the denial of either food stamps or TANF benefits but not both. In December, 2001, Massachusetts modified the lifetime ban, to eliminate the ban on eligibility for food stamps for those individuals convicted of drug offenses. However, those who serve a prison term for a felony drug offense will be denied cash assistance for the first 12 months following their release, unless they meet specific exemptions. Those exemptions include pregnancy, care of a disabled child or child under the age of two, or if a woman qualifies for a domestic violence waiver. Persons with a drug conviction remain eligible for food stamps. In several partial opt-out states, mothers remain eligible for TANF and food stamps provided they

Table 16.2: *(Cont'd)*

State	Denies Benefits Entirely	Partial Denial/ Term-Denial	Benefits Dependent on Drug Treatment	Opted Out of Welfare Ban
Montana	X			
Nebraska	X			
Nevada			X	
New Hampshire				X
New Jersey			X	
New Mexico				X
New York				X
North Carolina		X		
North Dakota	X			
Ohio				X
Oklahoma				X
Oregon				X
Pennsylvania				X
Rhode Island		X		
South Carolina			X	
South Dakota	X			
Tennessee			X	
Texas	X			
Utah			X	
Vermont				X
Virginia	X			
Washington			X	
West Virginia	X			
Wisconsin			X	
Wyoming	X			
U.S. Total	**16**	**11**	**12**	**12**

participate or enroll in, or successfully complete, a drug treatment program, while in other states, such as Wisconsin, drug treatment is not required but mothers are subject to random drug tests; mothers who test positive for drugs lose their eligibility immediately.

Some states deny benefits only for certain drug offenses. In Arkansas, Florida, and Rhode Island, benefits are denied as a result of the sale of drugs only. However, in Colorado, purchasing drugs with food stamps benefits will result in that person's becoming ineligible for food stamps. Illinois limits welfare-benefits ineligibility to persons convicted of the sale of drugs or possession of a large quantity of drugs. However, those same individuals remain eligible for food stamps. In Louisiana, eligibility is subject to a one-year waiting period after release from custody or conviction date, while in North Carolina, the waiting period is six months. In addition, ex-offenders in North Carolina are required to either have successfully completed a drug treatment program or be participating in one to have their eligibility restored. In Texas, persons convicted of possession or sale of drugs are ineligible for food stamps only. In Wisconsin and Minnesota, persons convicted of drug offenses are not required to enter drug treatment programs to receive their benefits, but they must submit to regular drug tests.

IMPACT OF LIFETIME WELFARE BAN

Number of Affected Women

Our analysis of the impact of the welfare reform act is drawn from state sentencing and correctional data compiled by various law enforcement, corrections, and court agencies. The figures provided here are estimates, in light of reporting problems in different states. Some state agencies, for example, provided data for incarcerated women drug offenders, but not for those on probation. In other jurisdictions, state officials were not able to avoid "double-counting" some felony drug offenses; e.g., a woman convicted of a drug offense in 1997, and therefore subject to the ban, may be counted twice if convicted of another drug offense in 1999.

Although 42 states implement the ban, we selected for review the 28 states imposing immediate and lifetime ineligibility for welfare benefits following a conviction. These include the 22 states with a complete lifetime ban as well as the six states that either limit the ban to certain types of drug convictions, or deny food stamps or cash assistance but not both. In the remaining 14 states, eligibility is either denied for a specific period of time or dependent on a person's participation in a drug treatment program. Of the 28 states that met our criteria, we obtained data from 23. Breakdown by race and ethnicity is provided where possible. The data compiled covers the period from 1996 to 1999.

Table 16.3 presents our findings on the current impact of the lifetime welfare ban, providing totals for 23 states. Of the states covered here, 19 deny cash assistance and food stamps for possession or sale of drugs, three restrict the lifetime ban to sale offenses, and three deny either cash assistance or food stamps, but not both. Using state conviction and

Table 16.3: Women Affected by Welfare Ban, 1996-1999

State	Number of Women	State	Number of Women
Alabama	1,339	Maine	71
Alaska	481	Mississippi	2,480
Arkansas	5,132	Missouri	6,429
Arizona	1,394	Montana	146
California	37,825	North Dakota	273
Delaware	323	Pennsylvania	3,068
Florida	485	South Dakota	156
Georgia	8,608	Tennessee	1,837
Idaho	931	Texas	4,700
Illinois (Cook County)	10,298	Virginia	3,686
Indiana	1,281	West Virginia	123
Kansas	1,231	**Total**	**92,297**

corrections data, we estimate that more than 92,000 women in 23 states that enforce the ban in full or in part have had a felony drug conviction since the adoption of the legislation and will be affected by the lifetime welfare ban. There is at this writing no national data on the number of women who have actually been denied benefits as a result of the ban. The figure of 92,000 represents the number of women who are now ineligible to receive benefits for the rest of their lives.

The national figures represent a conservative estimate of the number of women affected by the ban. For instance, data was not compiled for the states (Louisiana, Massachusetts, and North Carolina) that impose only a time limit rather than a lifetime ban. However, the impact of denying welfare assistance on the rehabilitative efforts of women reentering their communities for even a year should not be underestimated. In addition, some women who are eligible for welfare benefits have been improperly denied benefits by state welfare agencies either for misdemeanor convictions or for conduct prior to August 22, 1996, the implementation date of the ban.

Those states in which welfare assistance depends on women's participation in drug treatment programs were also not included. However, the national shortage of drug treatment programs that serve mothers and their children can be expected to result in a significant number of women in these states being denied TANF and food stamps. We also note that in seven states officials were not able to provide data that eliminates any double-counting of women who may have had a felony drug conviction in different years. Our findings include:

- Over 92,000 women are currently affected by the lifetime welfare ban.

- The ban after only five years was already having a dramatic impact in a number of states: in California, 37,825 women are affected; in Illinois, 10,298; and in Georgia, 8,608. While there are no overall data on the children of these offenders, using Bureau of Justice Statistics, we estimate that 135,000 children will potentially be affected by the lifetime welfare ban.

Racial and Ethnic Impact

Table 16.4 provides a racial and ethnic breakdown of the number of women affected by the ban in the 21 states for which we were able to obtain data. It documents that:

- More than 44,000 white women, nearly 35,000 African-American women, and almost 10,000 Latinas are affected by the ban.

- Forty-eight percent of the women affected are African-American or Latina.

- In five states African-American women represent the majority of women subject to the ban—Alabama (61%), Delaware (65%), Illinois (Cook County) (86%), Mississippi (54%), and Virginia (63%).

- In Pennsylvania and Texas, African-American and Latina women represent more than 50% of the women affected by the ban.

- Of the states we examined, the number of Latinas affected by the ban is particularly high in some, including Arizona (26%) and California (21%).

Table 16.4: Women Convicted of Felony Drug Offenses by Race and Ethnicity

State	White	Black	Hispanic
Alabama	526	813	–
Alaska	315	64	14
Arkansas	3,991	1,066	–
Arizona	774	199	364
California	19,168	8,471	7,772
Delaware	102	211	10
Florida	278	207	–
Georgia	4,320	4,182	68
Idaho	832	8	57
Illinois (Cook County)	1,029	8,820	432
Indiana	648	587	28
Kansas	903	245	61
Mississippi	1,054	1,339	12
Missouri	4,613	1,713	60
Montana	121	0	4
North Dakota	214	2	11
Pennsylvania	1,334	1,227	407
Tennessee	904	907	–
Texas	1,795	2,283	622
Virginia	1,313	2,304	53
West Virginia	91	29	2
Total	**44,325**	**34,677**	**9,977**

Effect on Lives of Women and Children

U.S. Department of Justice data show that nearly 30% of women in prison nationally had been on welfare in the month prior to their arrest, and as such we anticipate a significant number of women will require public assistance immediately upon their release from prison. The lifetime welfare ban will have a serious effect on these women's ability to overcome addiction, to raise their children, find work, and access drug treatment services. The combined effect of the ban and other recent social policies—public housing and post-secondary financial aid restrictions—will also diminish these women's ability to access education opportunities and housing.

Welfare assistance, a pivotal transitional mechanism for poor and low-income families who face economic insecurity, is dependent on two components: (1) transitional income assistance for daily living; and (2) concrete anti-poverty resources, such as education, sustainable employment, living wages, and drug treatment.

Lack of Transitional Income. Under welfare reform, women convicted of drug offenses are not offered any transitional benefits, and immediately lose access to TANF and food stamps for life. A mother's ineligibility and loss of benefits will put a severe strain on household resources and her ability to support and care for her children. For women released from prison, this burden may be insurmountable.

Inability to Meet Life's Basic Necessities. Women denied benefits because of a drug conviction are likely to face similar economic barriers to those encountered by low-income and poor families, as well as those who have recently left welfare. A 1992 study (U.S. Department of Commerce, 1995) showed that the proportion of persons unable to pay, in full, either their rent or mortgage and their utility bills was significantly higher for AFDC (29% and 41% respectively) and poor families (26% and 32% respectively) than non-poor families (8% and 10% respectively). Poor families were four times more likely than non-poor families to have their gas or electricity services cut off, whereas AFDC families were fives times more likely.

For many women subject to the lifetime welfare ban, and especially for African-American and Latina women, reliance on social networks will not be an effective support alternative. Economic hardships are disproportionately visited upon African-American and certain Latino communities, including Puerto Rican, Mexican, and emerging communities from Central and South America. Research shows that "Blacks have fewer resources than whites do, and the resources they do have are often less effective. The social networks of African-American women are often made up of others in similar structural positions."

Family Dissolution. U.S. Department of Justice research shows that 63% of white women and 67% of African-American and Hispanic women incarcerated in state prisons have minor children. Many of the children separated from their mothers due to incarceration will only interact with their mothers in correctional environments or through letters or telephone calls, while others will have no contact for many years.

With fewer financial resources available, some mothers subject to the ban may be compelled to place their children in the care of others. More fortunate mothers may be able to place their children in the care of friends or relatives, but some mothers may be forced to resort to foster care. A Wisconsin study found that "five percent of mothers cut off from federal assistance had to 'abandon' their children."

Other families are likely to be separated by child welfare services. The reduction of family income increases the likelihood that children will be characterized as neglected, which is likely to result in child welfare services intervention. Mothers unable to secure housing for their families may turn to shelters as a last resort. Children may have to be separated from their fathers to secure housing, while young male teens may be forced to leave their families and fend for themselves at an early age or be placed in foster care until the age of 18.

Housing Difficulties. Housing difficulties are likely to surface when reduction in family income limits the funds available for rent. For mothers living in large urban areas with higher rents, finding affordable and safe housing with reduced cash assistance may prove to be very difficult.

In 1996, the federal government implemented the "One Strike Initiative," authorizing local Public Housing Authorities (PHAs) to obtain from law enforcement departments criminal conviction records of adult applicants or tenants, for screening and eviction purposes. Local PHAs also have broad discretionary power to deny housing to or evict a person they determine is illegally using controlled substances.

Many mothers released from prison turn to the relatives and friends who cared for their children during their prison term for help upon release. As most of the incarcerated mothers come from impoverished communities, it is likely that many of their friends and relatives live in public housing complexes. Under the One Strike Initiative, a mother wanting to move in with a relative or friend, and possibly with her children, while she gets back on her feet may not be able to do so.

The lifetime welfare ban is likely to force mothers to leave or expose their children to very precarious environments. Grandparents and siblings caring for children may not have the necessary financial resources, or the emotional or physical capacity, to fulfill the needs of children in their care. Relatives or friends taking on the guardianship of the children may already have their own families, leading to overcrowded households with limited resources, where the needs of the children may not be met.

Mothers who do not have the support network to provide continued shelter for their children may be at risk of homelessness. Others may cohabit with an abusive partner or engage in illegal activity, leading to toxic family environments where substance abuse, violence, and neglect are daily occurrences. Some mothers will be forced to move in with friends or relatives and live in overcrowded households to avoid homelessness.

Mental Health and Educational Difficulties. Children exposed to stressful family environments are more likely to perform poorly in school and to experience emotional and behavioral problems. An Urban Institute study (Moore & Vandivere, 2000) found that 31% of children living under stressful family conditions had low levels of educational engagement, compared to 17% of other children, and 15% of children aged 6 to 11 who lived in stressful family environments had high levels of emotional and behavioral problems, whereas only 4% of other children experienced similar problems.

As mothers subject to the lifetime welfare ban struggle to make ends meet, they may be less able to provide the parental supervision and quality attention that is needed by children. An Office of Juvenile Justice and Delinquency Prevention (OJJDP) study (Browning et al., 1999) conducted in Rochester, New York found that "[e]conomic hardship and stressful life events led to a lack of parent-child involvement, attachment, and control over adolescents" (p. 2). The study concluded that the lack of parent involvement in their children's lives increases the risk of delinquency.

Research clearly shows that the well-being of children is intimately linked to the well-being of their parents. The impact of maltreatment and family dissolution on the well-being of children is a clear indication that the lifetime welfare ban, although ostensibly targeted only at adults, not only punishes mothers, who are entitled to well-being in their own right, but their children as well.

Transitional financial assistance represents only one step toward providing women subject to the lifetime welfare ban with the necessary tools to overcome the barriers they will face upon returning to their communities. In order for cash assistance and food stamps to be a temporary source of support, women will need access to anti-poverty resources enabling them to eventually become self-sufficient and productive members of their communities. Most women subject to the lifetime welfare ban will need access to at least three critical services—education, vocational training and drug treatment.

A significant number of women under criminal justice supervision have a history of low educational attainment, thus reducing their prospects of finding work with living wages following a conviction. Forty percent of women on probation, and 44% of women in state prison, have not graduated from high school or received a GED, and only 21%

of women on probation and 17% of women in state prison have some college education.

Glaring racial and ethnic differences in educational opportunity highlight the employment and wage disparity between women of color and white women. According to the Bureau of Justice Statistics, 59% of Hispanic mothers and 50% of African-American mothers in state prison have not graduated from high school or received a GED, compared to 27% of white mothers. Only 7% of Hispanic mothers have any schooling beyond high school, compared to 15% of African American mothers and 20% of white mothers.

Since incarcerated people have limited educational opportunities while in prison, few women will have the necessary qualifications to successfully compete in the labor market immediately upon their release from prison. Although correctional institutions have increased the number of general education programs (i.e. adult basic education, GED, high school) available to prisoners since the 1970s, as of 1996 only 52% of correctional facilities for women offered post-secondary education. Access to college education was further limited in 1994, when prisoners were declared ineligible for college Pell grants, leading to the inability of an increased number of incarcerated women, especially low-income women and women of color, to overcome their socioeconomic disadvantages prior to their release. Even women who received educational training report that the skills acquired have proven inadequate upon release from prison.

The pervasive low levels of educational attainment among women in the criminal justice system, and the impact this has on their employment prospects signals an urgent need for increased educational opportunity for women subject to the lifetime ban. Of particular concern are the higher levels of economic insecurity that African-American and Latina women are likely to face following the imposition of a lifetime welfare ban compared to their white counterparts if they are not afforded the time and support necessary to pursue educational opportunities.

Many people lacking competitive employment skills return to school to improve their skills, but for low-income women convicted of drug offenses, the lifetime welfare ban, job training programs excluding former substance abusers, and federal legislative changes limit educational opportunities.

Although the ban on cash assistance and food stamps does not prohibit women from taking part in educational and vocational programs and services offered by Departments of Human Services, the likelihood of these women accessing such services once they have been taken off welfare rolls is minimal. Studies documenting the experiences of those families who have left welfare show that few are able to access vital welfare programs and services, for which they remain eligible.

Women subject to the welfare ban who are informed of educational and vocational programs may still not be able to take advantage of these programs because of a lack of transitional income to support them during the program period. Some job training programs do not admit women with a recent history of drug addiction and require women to wait at least two years after their recovery to be entitled to access these services.

Women's reentry prospects are further limited by a 1998 amendment to the Higher Education Act mandating that anyone with a drug conviction cannot receive federal financial aid to enroll in a post-secondary institution. The amendment provides that federal financial aid (grant, loan, or work assistance) will be delayed or denied to any person convicted of a drug offense.

UNDERSTANDING EX-OFFENDER WOMEN'S EMPLOYMENT HURDLES

A criminal record significantly impairs a person's ability to find stable and legal employment, as well as to develop earning potential. As employers are generally hesitant to hire someone with a criminal record, particularly former inmates, prior convictions limit employment opportunities for many ex-offenders to low-wage and low-skill markets where employers cannot be as selective about a criminal record.

Ex-offenders' employment opportunities are further curtailed by government policies. A woman's felony conviction subjects her to a lifetime public employment ban in at least six states—Alabama, Delaware, Iowa, Mississippi, Rhode Island, and South Carolina. Although other states do not impose an automatic ban, state statutes provide for broad and discretionary powers increasing the likelihood that ex-offenders will be denied public employment in those states. Most states further prohibit ex-offenders with felony convictions from obtaining certain types of occupational or professional licenses in fields commonly pursued by women, including childcare, social work, nursing, dentistry (dental assistant), health, and accounting.

Mothers who have a felony conviction, but were sentenced to probation, fare better in the job market than those who served a prison sentence. This is particularly significant for African-American and Latina women who, in 1998, accounted for 37% of adult women on probation, but represented 63% of the state female prison population and 67% of women in federal prison.

A significant number of women under criminal justice supervision experienced high levels of low-wage work, underemployment, and unemployment prior to their arrest. Only half of the mothers in state prison reported employment in the month before their arrest (of these, 79% reported full-time employment, 18% part-time, and 4% sporadic employment). A racial and ethnic breakdown shows that mothers of color experience significantly higher rates of unemployment than white mothers. Latina women as a group experience the highest rates of unemployment, followed by African-American and white women. Fifty-eight percent of all Hispanic mothers of minor children did not have a job or business prior to their arrest, compared to 52% of African-American women and 44% of white women.With respect to mothers who were employed prior to their arrest, white women were more likely to be employed full-time than were African-American or Latina women. Eighty-four percent of white mothers incarcerated in state prison who reported employment before their arrest indicated they were employed full-time, while 76% of black mothers and 71% Hispanic mothers were employed full-time.

Due to limited employment opportunities, women under correctional sanctions experienced high rates of poverty prior to their arrest. As African-American and Latina mothers face greater employment insecurity, they are more likely than white women to have lower pre-arrest incomes. Once again, a racial and ethnic breakdown shows that a disproportionate number of African-American and Latina women relied on welfare as a source of income prior to their arrest. Thirty-six percent of black mothers and 31% of Hispanic mothers were welfare recipients, whereas 20% of white mothers were dependent on welfare benefits.

Like former welfare recipients, women subject to the lifetime welfare ban will encounter significant spells of unemployment resulting from labor market conditions, poor employment histories, or inability to meet work-related expenses, including affordable and safe child care and transportation. Studies documenting the employment status of former TANF recipients have found that approximately one-half of those who have left welfare in most states report no earnings in the calendar quarter in which they left the rolls.

Recent studies documenting the occupations of parents leaving welfare show that most found employment in similar fields to those for which incarcerated women are being trained, and continue to experience significant poverty. The wages earned by those who have left the welfare rolls ranged from the minimum wage at the low end to eight dollars per hour at the high end. Although many parents engage in long work weeks (30 to more than 50 hours per week), studies still find that employed parents leaving welfare are still poor.

The economic insecurity of incarcerated African-American and Latina women is comparable to that of women of color generally, suggesting that the employment and wage prospects of African-American and Latina mothers and white mothers subject to the lifetime welfare ban will differ significantly. Although the employment rates of Puerto Rican and Mexican women increased between the 1970s and 1990s, while those of African-American women remained relatively stable during this period, the employment gap between women of color and white women widened significantly during this same period.

Given the barriers women face as a result of poor employment skills, criminal histories, and the racialized and gendered labor market, women should be afforded the time and assistance needed following a criminal conviction to build marketable skills. This will require vocational training in areas where women with a criminal record are not automatically excluded, and challenges to such exclusions, as well as training for the types of jobs that provide living wages along with employment benefits.

The availability of transitional assistance while women engage in substantive vocational training ensures that they are able to house and feed themselves and their children as they devote themselves full-time to gaining employment skills that will enable them to eventually become self-sufficient. For many women, vocational training may be insufficient to reach self-sufficiency, and increased access to educational opportunities for women, especially African-American and Latina women, who are returning to their communities, may be necessary.

WOMEN'S DRUG TREATMENT PROSPECTS

Seventy-four percent of women entering the criminal justice system reported using drugs regularly prior to their arrest. While some women are initiated into the world of drugs by their peers, others turn to drug use as a response to the emotional, physical, or sexual abuse they suffer during their childhood and/or as adults.

Unlike middle-class women who experience addiction, most low-income women and women of color do not have the financial resources to address their personal hardships or abuse with costly prescription drugs and/or therapy, and as such many will use drugs to self-medicate, which places them at risk of coming in contact with the criminal justice system. Half the women incarcerated in state prisons described themselves as daily drug users, and 60% reported using drugs in the month before their arrest. For many women drug addiction is intimately linked to involvement in criminal activity—prostitution, theft, drug sales—which is often engaged in to support their addiction. Thirty-three percent of women in state prison reported that they committed the offense for which they were incarcerated to support their addiction, and 40% reported using drugs at the time of their offense. Women on probation have slightly lower rates of addiction, but 38% of women reported being daily drug users, and 12% said they were under the influence at the time of the offense.

While 74% of women prisoners have a history of drug use, only 25% of state and federal prisoners participate in either drug treatment or other drug abuse programs. Racial and ethnic disparities persist in access to treatment programs, with Hispanics and African-Americans less likely than their white counterparts to receive substance abuse treatment or to access substance abuse programs. Women on probation are even less likely than prisoners to receive any form of drug treatment. In 1995, 50% of probationers had to submit to drug testing, but only 17% received drug treatment during their probation sentence, further demonstrating the government's overemphasis on punitive rather than rehabilitative measures in addressing drug addiction.

Given the limited availability of drug treatment programs for low-income people, many women who are subject to the lifetime welfare ban will encounter even greater obstacles in overcoming their addictions. The ban forces women overcoming addiction into the workforce, which, according to substance abuse counselors, undermines women's recovery efforts. In addition, the ban will impact the availability of drug treatment programs for low-income women.

Drug treatment staff report that cash assistance and food stamps are critical for the successful recovery of low-income women because women who try to maintain employment in the early phases of recovery are likely to relapse and quit or lose their job. According to one drug treatment counselor, "the combination of the stress and frustration of low-wage employment with the demands of childrearing and the fragility of early recovery is extremely difficult, particularly for women whose coping skills are limited" (Hirsch, 1999, p. 48).

The ban will also affect the availability of drug treatment programs. The Conference of Mayors and the National League of Cities strongly oppose the ban because of its effect on drug treatment prospects for those most in need of substance abuse treatment. In their opposition to the ban, the two groups assert that the drug provision makes "drug addicts ineligible for any of the effective drug treatment programs that are being developed by the States and federal Government." They argue that the ban will undermine treatment programs developed by community health centers across the nation that help mothers reenter the job force and reunite with their families. Such programs "will be off limits to the people who need them most." Furthermore, since many residential drug treatment programs rely heavily on mothers' welfare benefits to cover their operating expenses, low-income and poor women's access to treatment may be further diminished.

For many women released from prison, residential treatment programs constitute a critical step in their recovery process, and toward successful reintegration into society. Women who are unable to find affordable and safe housing may find that residential drug treatment programs provide a viable temporary alternative for them and their children. Many residential treatment programs also provide a panoply of life skills building programs—employment, education, medical care, parenting skills, and therapy—as well as a structured living environment.

At present, there are limited numbers of residential drug treatment programs accommodating women and their children. Since the client base of family-centered residential programs is primarily composed of low-income and poor women, these programs are likely to be the hardest hit by the lifetime welfare ban. For women whose release from prison or probation status is contingent on their participation in a residential drug treatment program, a reduction in family-centered residential programs may force women to be separated from their children in order to enter an adult-only treatment program.

RECOMMENDATIONS

During this welfare reform reauthorization year [2002], Congress has the opportunity to review the effectiveness of its decision to deny welfare benefits to people convicted of drug offenses and to consider the following recommendations to prevent future harms:

1. Repeal federal lifetime welfare ban:

- Congress should repeal Section 115(a) of the Welfare Reform Act (lifetime welfare ban).

- Congressional hearings should hear from various actors directly and indirectly affected by the ban.

2. Make state modifications to include services for women:

- State governments should opt out of the ban or at least modify it, as provided for under Section 115(d) of the Welfare Reform Act. Some states have limited ineligibility to women with drug sale convictions; other states maintain eligibility for a person enrolled in or participating in a state approved drug treatment program.

- Since not every woman convicted of a drug offense has a substance abuse problem, states should provide alternative programs, such as job training or GED programs, to allow women to maintain welfare benefits.

3. Repeal post-incarceration sentences: Policymakers should repeal legislation that delays or denies access to social benefits such as education, housing, and employment to ex-offenders. Women's inability to access various social entitlements in some states undermines efforts to turn their lives around, to provide for their families, and to become more effective contributing members of their communities. These include:

- *Restrictions on post-secondary financial aid.* During the 2000-2001 school year, Section 483(f) of the 1998 Amendments to Higher Education Act of 1965, which delays or denies any form of federal financial aid for post-secondary education to persons convicted of a drug offense, affected over 43,000 students. A substantial number of studies have shown that providing prisoners or ex-offenders with educational opportunities significantly reduces recidivism, and thus increases public safety and reduces costs associated with criminal behavior.

- *Public housing restrictions.* The federal government's One Strike Initiative has the potential of leaving many women subject to the lifetime welfare ban, along with their children, homeless—exposing them to an inordinate number of precarious situations, including those likely to involve criminal activity. The inability to access public housing constitutes an enormous barrier to finding work and receiving social benefits, further exacerbating the efforts of low-income women and women of color subject to the ban to become active social participants, as well as subverting efforts to create safe communities.

- *Employment bans.* Policymakers should reconsider the effectiveness of state and federal statutes that call for the imposition of mandatory or permissive lifetime bans on government jobs or professional and occupational licenses for drug offenders. A lifetime-ban policy fails to recognize that people can overcome addiction and make important social contributions.

4. Increase access to and quality of education and employment opportunities:

- State welfare agencies should develop strategies aimed at informing women who are denied cash assistance and food stamps of other benefits and services such as Medicare, job training, and educational programs.

- Access to educational opportunities for women should be a priority. Emphasis should be placed on increasing access to non-traditional fields where higher earning potential and better working conditions are likely to improve the reentry possibilities of mothers and to reduce the need for social assistance.

- Educational and training opportunities should be provided without restrictions. Many women in the criminal justice system have very limited educational attainment, and are likely to require more than the maximum 12-month period TANF-eligible women now have to fare better in the labor market and to become self-sufficient.

5. Increase availability and quality of drug treatment: Drug treatment not only saves lives, but also reduces a variety of social problems associated with substance abuse, and saves tax dollars. A study found that for every dollar allocated to drug treatment, taxpayers save $7.46 in social costs. Therefore:

- Federal anti-drug funding policies, which allocate two-thirds of the budget to law enforcement and incarceration, should increase the proportion of funds for treatment programs.

- More treatment slots should be made available for mothers requiring treatment. The shortage is of particular concern in states where eligibility for welfare benefits depends on a mother's participation in drug treatment.

[*Editor's note:* As of March 2005, none of the recommended changes had been made on the federal level, but the 109th Congress is considering Welfare Reauthorization. A bill introduced by the 108th Congress, "Second Chance Act of 2004: Community Safety Through Recidivism Prevention," requests many reforms related to reentry, including an examination of the impact of PCP, primarily in the form of studies. For an overview of changes on the state level, compare Tables 16.1 and 16.2.]

CONCLUSION

A disproportionate number of women under criminal justice supervision face serious socioeconomic barriers prior to their contact with the criminal justice system. Many lack the resources to overcome poverty and abuse, and often turn to illegal means to survive.

Overwhelmingly, women who come in contact with the criminal justice system seek to turn their lives around for themselves and their children. Yet, the lifetime welfare ban, along with other punitive social policies, makes the possibility of women returning to their communities as productive members more difficult than before their conviction.

The lifetime welfare ban has an impact that goes well beyond the effects on or barriers created for individual women. Since the inception of the "war on drugs," children have been some of the most affected innocent causalities of misguided drug policies, and the welfare ban is yet another example of such misguided policies. Children are increasingly at risk of neglect and of irreparable damage to their family environment. Societal costs associated with the lifetime welfare ban will extend to the criminal justice and health care systems, as well as child welfare services.

Racial disparities in the criminal justice system, education, and employment exacerbate the effects of the lifetime welfare ban on African-American women and Latinas. Only a multi-pronged approach to these issues, which recognizes and addresses the intricate links between socioeconomic barriers, drug policy, and the criminal justice system will successfully reduce the disproportionate number of women of color sentenced to a lifetime of poverty.

About the Author

Patricia Allard is a former Policy Analyst with The Sentencing Project. Currently, she is Associate Counsel, Criminal Justice, at the Brennan Center for Justice in New York City.

References

Moore, K. A. & Vandivere, S., *New Federalism: National Survey of America's Families*, "Stressful Family Lives: Child and Parent Well-being," (Urban Institute, June 2000, p.2).

Browning, K., Thornberry, T. P. & Porter, P. K., *Highlights of Findings from the Rochester Youth Development Study* (Fact Sheet) (U.S. Department of Justice, Office of Juvenile Justice and Delinquency Prevention, April 1999, p. 2).

Hirsch, A. E., "Some Days are Harder Than Hard": Welfare Reform and Women with Drug Convictions in Pennsylvania (Center on Crime, Communities and Culture, October, 1999, p. 48).

U.S. Department of Commerce, "Current Population Reports—Beyond Poverty, Extended Measures of Well-Being: 1992" (U.S. Department of Commerce, November 1995, Table 2).

Chapter 17

The Impact of Welfare Reform on Women With Drug Convictions in Pennsylvania: A Case Study

by Amy E. Hirsch, J.D.

INTRODUCTION

A small but vulnerable group of women in recovery from drug addiction are facing an additional obstacle in their efforts to move forward with their lives. They are trying to stay clean, to rebuild relationships with their children and families, to recover from sexual and physical abuse, and to get the skills they will need to find and keep a job. Yet they are banned from ever receiving cash assistance or food stamps, no matter what they do or how hard they try, because they have felony drug convictions, often for only $5 or $10 worth of drugs.

This chapter originally appeared in Women, Girls & Criminal Justice, *Vol. 1, No. 3, April/May 2000.*

Federal law allows states to opt out of the ban, but requires them to pass legislation in order to do so. At least 31 states, including New York, New Jersey, Illinois, Connecticut, and Ohio had taken the option to support women in recovery, and have eliminated or modified the ban as of September, 2002. Before Pennsylvania's legislature lifted the ban, approximately 1,100 women in Pennsylvania were convicted each year.

[*Editor's note:* Pennsylvania enacted legislation lifting the lifetime ban on TANF and Food Stamp benefits, Act 44 of 2003, December 2003, which became effective February 21, 2004. Act 44 passed the Senate by a vote of 49-0, and passed the House by a vote of 185-15. Bipartisan leadership on the bill was provided by Representative Frank Oliver and Senator Jane Earll. Act 44 lifts the ban for all affected residents of Pennsylvania, and requires the welfare department, after approving benefits, to refer all affected individuals for assessment and drug and alcohol treatment, if available and appropriate. It was strongly supported by the Pennsylvania District Attorneys' Association, which describes the bill as "an important anti-crime measure" and "sensible anti-crime" legislation, and a wide range of over 100 groups from across the state.]

THE WOMEN AT ISSUE AND THE BENEFITS BAN'S IMPACT

Women with drug convictions, criminal justice staff, and drug treatment providers in four counties in Pennsylvania were interviewed for this study. In addition, data from the Philadelphia Criminal Court system, women's drug treatment programs, and state and federal agencies, was analyzed to put together a picture of the women, their life histories, and the impact on their future and the future of their families, the community, as well as on the criminal justice system, if they are permanently denied benefits.

Each of these sources provided different types of data, and a different window through which to view issues around women's drug usage and criminal activities. Yet they also provided a surprisingly consistent picture of the women themselves, their lives and criminal histories, and the barriers they have faced and continue to face in their struggles to recover from addictions and abuse. In spite of, or because of, all they have been through, these women struggle to develop and maintain healthy relationships with their children, families, and friends, and to move forward with their lives. The picture that emerges is quite striking:

- The overwhelming majority of the women had no prior drug convictions, and their felony convictions were for very small quantities of drugs (often only $5 or $10 worth).

- They began their drug usage as young children or teenagers, often in direct response to sexual and/or physical abuse they were experiencing, or when they ran away to escape the abuse.

    When I was a child, my father used to rape me. It started when I was nine.... After I ran away, I wanted somebody to want me. I ran into this guy, he was older, and I wanted him to want me. He gave me cocaine. I was 13. (Tanya, interviewed 7/9/98)

- The women have limited education and literacy, employment histories in short-term low-wage jobs, histories of homelessness and prostitution, multiple physical and mental health problems needing treatment, and have survived repeated and horrific violence as adults.

  They don't understand how she could have used drugs; they don't understand how much physical and emotional pain she was in—she had broken ribs, broken arms. The abuse this woman endured from her husband, I would have written prescriptions for myself too—she was in such pain. (non-urban jail staff member, interviewed 12/15/98)

- These are mothers with children about whom they care very much, and with whom they have had very troubled relationships as a result of their drug addictions. They are trying to build and maintain healthier relationships with their children.

  My son is happy I'm not using drugs no more. I'm here for him. He always was with me but my body was just there—my mind wasn't. Now my body and mind are both there. I spend more time with him, show him love, take him places, and do things with him. (Tanya, interviewed 7/9/98)

- Jail was the first place anyone had talked to them about the abuse they had experienced, or offered them drug treatment.

  I started using alcohol and pills when I was 13. I was raped when I was 12, my father was an alcoholic, my mother was using pills. He used to beat her up all the time—it was pretty crazy. No, no one helped me. This [drug and alcohol treatment program in jail] is the first place anyone talked about it. (Cindy, interviewed 9/22/98)

  [In jail] they had all different kind of classes—about being raped in the street, about being raped in your family. I needed both those classes. (Maria, interviewed 2/25/98)

  This is my first time in treatment. I couldn't get medical assistance so I couldn't get treatment. Now I'm court-stipulated, so I can get treatment. (Wendy, interviewed 4/28/98)

- The ban is likely to increase recidivism and relapse. Taking away benefits—the additional strain of severe poverty—makes it harder for a woman to stay clean and to stay out of jail. As one woman put it, "Now it matters because I'm trying to do the right thing" (Sharon, interviewed on 4/28/98).

- It also results in additional costs for the child welfare system, and harm to the children. An unintended consequence of the ban is that the children of these convicted felons will be placed in foster care, or remain in that placement longer because their mothers can not afford housing. The drug treatment programs which, in turn, depend on food stamps and cash assistance to feed and house women and children in treatment programs, suffer a loss of funding and cannot financially meet their commitments.

> The whole nature of an addiction is that it is a disease—the point of treatment is to try to cure that disease. Then you have a well person, a different person. If we want to create well women, how can we deny them help because of a mistake they made while they were sick? (Linda Mathers, Director, Intensive Supervision, Adult Probation Department, Court of Common Pleas, Philadelphia, PA, interviewed 5/6/98)

POLICY RECOMMENDATIONS

Allow Women Access to Subsistence Benefits

There are several recurring themes in these interviews with women in recovery and with drug treatment, criminal justice, and public health staff about what we need to do to support women in recovery, prevent recidivism and relapse, and to help them care for their children and move forward with their lives.

It appears from data collected by the Federal Bureau of Justice Statistics that approximately 61,000 women were convicted of felony drug offenses in state and federal courts in the U.S. during 1996 (Brown, Patrick et al., 1999; Brown & Langan, July 1999). The Legal Action Center (1997) surveyed 17 drug and alcohol treatment programs for women with children around the country, and found that 21% of the mothers receiving welfare in those treatment programs had felony drug convictions. The number of women denied benefits would grow each year, as the cumulative impact of the ban increases.

The women who were interviewed for the current study talked about different ways in which the denial of cash assistance or food stamps would affect them. There were five recurring themes:

- The inability to work because of illness and disability;

- The need for temporary help until women can get back on their feet, particularly given the difficulties of early recovery and of finding work with a criminal record;

- The lack of financial support to women in treatment, and help to sustain their recovery;

- The availability of benefits as an alternative to staying in or returning to abusive relationships or engaging in illegal activities; and

- The absence of support and assistance to reunify or to keep a family together.

The same themes emerged in the interviews with drug treatment, health department, and criminal justice staff. The women's plans for building a new, productive life had three parts: taking care of their children, maintaining recovery, and looking for work. Access to welfare benefits was a critical factor for all three pieces. In addition to talking about the material difference welfare makes—the ability to pay rent, buy food, clothing, and other necessities, several of the women talked about the ways in which welfare helps them feel connected to civil society:

> We still need welfare until we are strong enough to get on our feet. Trying to stay clean, trying to be responsible parents and take care of our families. We need welfare right now. If we lose it, we might be back out there selling drugs. We trying to change our lives. Trying to stop doing wrong things. Some of us need help. Welfare helps us stay in touch with society. Trying to do what's right for us. (Tanya, interviewed 7/9/98)

Increase Outreach, Remove Barriers, and Improve Access to Treatment

One of the most disturbing findings in this study is the lack of outreach for drug treatment prior to arrest. Of the 26 women interviewed, 17 (65%) first received treatment through the criminal justice system. Six (23%) were referred through a friend or relative and one (4%) called her HMO. Only one (4%) woman was referred to treatment by the child welfare system; and only one (4%) was referred to treatment by the shelter system. The criminal justice system should not be the first place a woman is offered treatment!

The National Center on Addiction and Substance Abuse (1996) at Columbia University estimates that "less than 14% of all women and 12% of pregnant women" (p. 7) in need of drug or alcohol treatment get it. The reasons for this acute lack of treatment are varied, a shortage of treatment slots, especially for women with children; women's family responsibilities; doctors' failure to properly diagnose addiction in women; and the greater stigma surrounding addiction in women. A survey of state alcohol and drug agencies by the Legal Action Center (1997) found that only an average of 24% of the women who were eligible for publicly funded drug treatment were actually served, as the need for treatment far outstripped the funds available.

OUTREACH AND TREATMENT ISSUES UNIQUE TO WOMEN

In addition to the overarching issues of lack of funding for treatment and inadequate numbers of facilities for women and children, there are some additional outreach and treatment issues particular to women, reflecting both the levels of violence women have been subjected to and their role as caretakers of children.

Support and Services With No Strings Attached

We need to offer services and support to women with no strings attached, as we do at senior citizen centers and at mental health centers run by consumers. Women who are on the street, women who are prostitutes, and women who are not yet ready to commit to a treatment program should all be targeted for these benefits. Similar suggestions were made by women drug users who were interviewed for an Atlanta study (Sterk, 1999). Offers of drop-in services can be used to develop a relationship of trust with women. These individuals are looking for a refuge from the violence and degradation of the street: a safe place to sit, to get a cup of coffee, to use a bathroom, to take a shower, to wash clothes, all without fear of assault and without fear of losing their children.

Gender-Specific Programs

Voluntary, confidential, gender-specific drug and alcohol treatments (e.g., treatments for women that addresses the violence and abuse women have experienced, as well as addressing their needs as mothers) should be offered to every woman who interacts with the child welfare system (Nelson-Zlupko, et al., 1995).

Improved Integration and Proximity of Court System and Drug/Alcohol Treatment Facilities

Dependency court, which hears child welfare (abuse and neglect) cases should have drug treatment evaluation and placement staff co-located at the court, so staff can immediately provide referrals for parents in need of treatment, and assistance in actually getting to the treatment facility. Staff at every social service and educational agency should be trained to offer treatment in a sensitive and non-judgmental manner, and how to access treatment immediately for women who want it.

We need to increase the number of treatment facilities for women with dual diagnoses, severe and persistent mental illness, as well as drug addiction. Also greater resources for mental health treatment for women in drug treatment who have less severe mental illness are required.

We should build on the existing network of women and women and children's treatment programs to increase the number of facilities providing gender-specific treatment, to include families with multiple children and/or older children, especially adolescents, and to provide family therapy involving members of the woman's family who are not in the treatment program. A prime example is the OPTIONS program in the Philadelphia County Jail. This program has recently expanded its Forensic Family Therapy Treatment Program so that a woman's therapist can continue to work with her and her family after she leaves jail and enters a drug-treatment program in the community.

Treatment issues for younger women, aged 18 to 25, are especially difficult. The creation of specialized programs for women in this age range, who are less likely to succeed in traditional women's treatment programs, would address the unique problems facing this population. Similarly, non-English speaking treatment resources for Spanish speaking women, and women of other ethnic groups, especially women with children, have been absent from the available rehabilitation options and should be established.

Response to Violence Against Women and Girls

The women interviewed in this study experienced pervasive violence, and responded to battering and rape with drug usage as self-medication. Twenty-one (81%) of the 26 women who were interviewed disclosed having been abused as children and adults, or both. Twenty (77%) of the 26 women interviewed disclosed having been battered by a husband or boyfriend. Eighteen (69%) of the 26 women who were interviewed disclosed having been abused physically and/or sexually abused as children. Twenty-one (81%) out of the 26 women began their drug usage before the age of 20. Of those 21 women, 19 (90%) began using in the context of severe abuse, and two (10%) began using in the context of pre-existing mental illness. For 19 (90%) of the 21 women who disclosed childhood and/or adult abuse, jail or a women's drug and alcohol treatment program was the first place anyone had talked to them about the abuse they had survived, or helped them try to deal with it.

Therefore, our response to violence against women and girls must be improved in several key respects. First, we need to pay attention to the violence that women who are charged with or convicted of crimes have survived. When domestic violence advocates have focused on the criminal justice system it has more often been in the context of improving police or prosecutorial response to women complainants. This study, and other recent studies of incarcerated women, has demonstrated the long-term, pervasive consequences of violence in these women's lives, and the close connections between that violence and the women's criminal activities.

Second, improvements to outreach on domestic violence and sexual assault to women who are in active addiction, to women who are working as prostitutes, and to women who are living on the street are critical. Unlike some other large cities, Philadelphia has no programs to assist prostitutes.

> Women who are working as sex workers have no resources, no ability to protect themselves, they're in violent relationships. They seek help at the needle exchange, but not about the abuse. We see women with visible bruises. They're not in contact with domestic violence organizations or resources. We…[used to have] a drop-in center. Women needed a break. They could come in for coffee, a few safe minutes. (Julie Parr, Executive Director, Prevention Point Philadelphia, interviewed 12/3/98)

Third, increased emphasis must be placed on prevention and the appropriate response to child sexual abuse as well as intervention to prevent drug addiction as a response to that abuse. Elementary school children and young teenagers should be targeted by outreach programs. Adults must end the silence about childhood sexual abuse; abusers must be challenged to stop the abuse and seek treatment. Men and boys should be taught that physical and sexual abuse is unacceptable behavior and the childhood sexual abuse many male perpetrators of sexual violence against women experienced as boys should be explored. ("We adults — not our children — must shoulder the burden of stopping the cycle of abuse." STOP IT NOW! P.O. Box 496, Haydenville, MA 01039). Our inquiry into domestic violence, dating violence, child abuse or child sexual abuse in any studies of children at risk, should include both boys and girls.

A report sponsored by the Pennsylvania Commission on Crime and Delinquency (Diagnostics Plus, 1997) illustrates the failure of many of these studies to explore domestic violence and abuse. This survey appears not to have asked questions about the topics highlighted above, and focused on violence at school rather than violence at home. The only data broken down by sex in the report are on use of smokeless tobacco by boys. Similarly, a federal report on juvenile justice and drug usage breaks none of its data down by gender, and does not acknowledge the role of sexual and physical abuse in children's drug usage (Office of Juvenile Justice and Delinquency, 1998).

Last, both domestic violence and drug and alcohol treatment programs should change their foci to recognize the connections between domestic violence and drug usage by women, integrate both issues into their programs, and find ways to provide ongoing support for women after leaving the programs. Treatment program staff noted that women struggle with violence in relationships even after treatment is completed, and that domestic violence is a major trigger for relapse, especially if the abusive partner is still using drugs.

Increase the Supply of Safe, Affordable Housing

The lack of safe, affordable homes for women and their children is a major barrier to recovery from drug addiction and a prime precipitant of relapse. Of the 26 women interviewed, 23 (88%) had either been homeless or lived in very unstable housing before being arrested. A total of 24 (92 %) of the 26 women interviewed identified the need for safe housing as a major concern facing them when they completed treatment. They viewed housing as an overwhelming issue in maintaining recovery, protecting their children, extricating themselves from abusive relationships, and reuniting their families. The fear of having nowhere else to go leads women to stay in or return to abusive relationships. The difficulty of finding appropriate housing for women leaving jail or treatment programs was raised in almost every interview, as was the role of unsafe housing and homelessness in women's drug usage and exposure to violence. "If I could get welfare, it would make a lot of difference to me. I wouldn't have to ask nobody for anything. I'd have something of my own" (Linda, interviewed 6/25/98).

Assist Women in Getting Education and Job Skills

Education was repeatedly identified by women and by staff as critical to sustaining recovery and finding jobs that will last. Of the 26 women interviewed, 19 (73%) had less than a high school education; 14 (54%) had less than a tenth grade education. The overwhelming majority of women did not have high school degrees and, despite having miserable memories of failure in school, were nonetheless eager to learn. The combination of limited education and the loss of skills during years of active addiction, physical abuse, and living on the street left them at a terrible disadvantage in seeking work now. They need adult basic education, GED classes, and job skills for employment that is not closed to them as a result of felony drug convictions. A state law barring those with drug convictions from holding jobs in health care and child care, has closed these women out of jobs in those two areas which traditionally have held employment opportunities for low income women. Education is essential to any hope of employment that will enable these women to stay off of drugs and out of jail, and to support themselves and their children.

CONCLUSION

The overwhelming consensus among the professional drug treatment, public health and criminal justice staff who were interviewed, was that the ban on benefits is counterproductive and should be eliminated. Denying women cash assistance and food stamps does nothing to prevent drug usage or sales; instead it increases the chances of recidivism and relapse, harms women and their children, and makes it harder for them to reconnect with society and to rebuild their lives.

The data from this study clearly leads to the conclusion that Pennsylvania and other states should join the 27 states that have taken the option to support women in recovery by allowing them access to cash assistance and food stamps.

About the Author

Amy E. Hirsch, J.D., is a supervising attorney at Community Legal Services in Philadelphia, PA.

References

Brown, J. M., & Langan, P.A., *Felony Sentences in the United States, 1996* (175045 NCJ, Table 2) (Bureau of Justice Statistics, July 1999).

Brown, J. M., Langan, P.A. & Levin, D.J., *Felony Sentences in State Courts* (173930 NCJ, Tables 1 & 5) (Bureau of Justice Statistics, May 1999, revised July 30, 1999).

Diagnostics Plus, *A Generation at Risk: Alcohol, Tobacco, Other Drugs, Weapons, Violence and Pennsylvania's Youth, The 1997 Survey* (Pennsylvania Commission on Crime and Delinquency, 1997).

Legal Action Center, *Making Welfare Reform Work: Tools for Confronting Alcohol and Drug Problems Among Welfare Recipients*, (Author, September 1997.)

National Center on Addiction and Substance Abuse, *Substance Abuse and the American Woman: Foreword and Executive Summary* (NCASA, June 1996).

Nelson-Zlupko, L., Kauffman, E. & Morrison Dore, M., "Gender Differences in Drug Addiction and Treatment: Implications for Social Work Intervention with Substance-Abusing Women," 40(1) *Social Work*, 45-54 January 1995.

Office of Juvenile Justice and Delinquency Prevention, *Drug Testing and Identification in the Juvenile Justice System* (167889 NCJ) (OJJPD, May 1998).

Sterk, C.E., *Fast Lives: Women Who Use Crack Cocaine* (Temple University Press, 1999).

Chapter 18

Incarcerated Mothers and Their Children: A Decade Long Overview

by Susan M. George, J.D.

INTRODUCTION

U.S. Department of Justice statistics indicated a few years ago that, on any given day, approximately 84,000 women are in federal and state prisons and nearly 70,000 additional women are incarcerated in county jails (Greenfeld & Snell, 2000; Beck & Karberg, 2000; Rafter, 1990). Since 1980, the number of women imprisoned in the United States has increased at roughly a 10% annual rate. At this rate, the female prison population is doubling every seven to eight years. During 1999, women incarcerated in federal and state prisons or in county jails were mothers to about 250,000 children (Greenfeld & Snell, 2000). Most of these children were less than 10 years old and about 20% were under the age of five (Mumola, 2000).

Despite the escalating numbers of incarcerated mothers entering and exiting prison, very little information is available about this population. In particular relatively little is known about their economic prospects, their ability to function as parents, or the consequences that prison and their lives leading up to prison have for their children. Such

---

This chapter originally appeared in Women, Girls & Criminal Justice, *Vol. 4, No. 5, August/September 2003.*

information is essential in order to guide the design and assessment of appropriate interventions to improve the outcomes for these mothers and their children.

U.S. Department of Justice statistics indicated that incarcerated women are in worse economic circumstances than either incarcerated men or other economically disadvantaged women (Mumola, 2000). The vast majority of incarcerated women are high school dropouts. Only one-half had any type of employment in the month before they were arrested. One in five was homeless during the year prior to arrest. One in five also has a history of mental illness. Finally, most women in state prisons report a drug or alcohol addiction.

A study, *Incarcerated Mothers and Their Children,* was conducted at the Harris School of Public Policy Studies at the University of Chicago. The first phase of this research project used state level administrative data, available through collaborative relationships with the Illinois Department of Corrections and the Chapin Hall Center for Children at the University of Chicago. With these data the study is tracking, for the years 1990-2000, the histories of the approximately 14,000 women admitted to prison in the state of Illinois, and their estimated 35,000 children, as they move through the criminal justice system, foster care, welfare programs, and the legitimate labor market.

The results reported in this chapter come from an analysis of the Illinois Department of Corrections admissions and exit files covering a 12-year period between 1990 and 2001 that examines the characteristics of a large sample of female prisoners. The demographic information in these files includes information on these women's ages, when they were admitted to prison, ethnicity, educational attainment, country of residence, number of children ever born, and whether the woman reported a substance abuse problem at the time she entered prison. In addition, these files contain precise information on these women's offenses, time served, and whether they had been in prison before.

POPULATION CHARACTERISTICS

Generally

This study of incarcerated women is based on an analysis of the admission and exit files from the Illinois Department of Corrections (IDOC) Offender Tracking System. The IDOC creates these files annually to contain information on individuals who enter and exit the Illinois state prison system during each fiscal year. These files include information on a woman's name, age, the primary offense for which she is incarcerated, the dates that she was incarcerated, educational achievement, length of sentence, time served, county of residence, ethnicity, and self-reported information on substance abuse. The information on substance abuse reports whether the individual acknowledged a substance abuse problem, with either drugs or alcohol, at the time she entered prison. The IDOC files also include information on the number of children ever born. The IDOC files do not contain information on whether the mother was the custodial parent when she was admitted to prison.

Women who have been incarcerated in Illinois prisons possess several characteristics that indicate they are likely to have difficulty becoming economically self-sufficient once they leave prison:

- They have low levels of schooling;
- They report a substance abuse problem; and

- They are single mothers.

Female inmates, like male prisoners, have very low levels of schooling. In Illinois, the majority of prisoners have less than a high school education. Further, these low levels of educational attainment have changed little among the inmate population since 1990. The percentage of new inmates who were high school dropouts stood at 62% in 1990 and was 64% in 2000.

Substance Abuse/Dependence

The majority of incarcerated women admit to having a substance abuse problem when they entered prison. During the period studied, approximately 65% of these women acknowledged that they had a substance abuse problem. This percentage rose during the decade. During 2000, nearly 70% of all women exiting prison identified themselves as having a drug or alcohol problem when they entered the system.

Incidence of Single Motherhood

Another indication that incarcerated women are economically disadvantaged is that most are unmarried mothers. Two-thirds of female inmates report that they never married. Another 20% report that they are divorced. At the same time, more than 80% report that they have had at least one child and about 25% report having had four or more children. Further, the share of female inmates with four or more children has increased from 19% in 1990 to 28% in 2000. This category of women is the fastest growing segment of the female prison population in Illinois. These women are likely poor and, absent substantial intervention, are likely to remain so after they leave prison.

Drug and Property Offenses

The frequent histories of self-reported substance abuse among the female prison population also is consistent with the frequency of drug offenses and of property-related crimes that are likely drug-related among this group. In terms of broad categories of offenses, the IDOC files reveal that nearly 45% of female inmates committed a drug offense. Many of these offenses appear to be for small-scale sales of controlled substances. Further, the average annual increase among inmates who were convicted of drug offenses has been about twice the rate of growth for the female prison population as a whole. Accordingly, the proportion of female inmates serving time for drug convictions has risen from about one-fifth in 1993 to nearly one-half of the total female prison population by 2000.

Another 35% of incarcerated women committed a property-related offense. Among these crimes, the most common offense was retail theft of less than $150. Although we can not determine the reason for these offenses from the IDOC data, based on the Department of Justice's survey, we suspect that many of the property-related offenses were related these women's addictions to crack/cocaine and other drugs.

Other Offenses

By contrast, person-related crimes, sex-related crimes, and other categories of criminal behavior together constitute about one-sixth of the offenses for the remaining population of female inmates. These figures support the contention that incarcerated women are usually not violent compared to their male counterparts. Nationally, incarcerated women are about one-half as likely to be in prison for a violent offense (Mumola, 2000). Further, studies indicate that, unlike men, about three-quarters of women incarcerated for violent offenses had committed simple assault—a category that usually means that there was no bodily injury to the victim (Greenfeld & Snell, 1999).

THE CHILDREN OF INCARCERATED WOMEN

Economically Disadvantaged

The IDOC data suggest that the children of incarcerated mothers have as mothers women who are among the most economically disadvantaged of the female prison population. To see this point, consider that incarcerated women who have given birth to the most children are likely the most disadvantaged among the prison population. Women who have had four or more children are more likely to have served time for a drug-related offense than are women with fewer children. Consistent with this finding, they are more likely than other female inmates to self-report a substance abuse problem and they are more likely to be high school dropouts than other female offenders.

The implications of these findings from IDOC records are twofold. First, having given birth to four or more children predicts diminished prospects for economic self-sufficiency. Second, the incarcerations that affect the most children likely involve the most disadvantaged mothers. About one-fourth of mothers have four or more children, and nearly 45% have three or more. These figures imply that children with incarcerated mothers likely have mothers who have had many children:

- More than one-half of the children of incarcerated mothers have mothers who have had four or more children, and

- Nearly three-quarters of these children have mothers who have had three or more births.

This evidence suggests that children of incarcerated mothers come from especially disadvantaged backgrounds even relative to the backgrounds for the entire population of female inmates.

A Growing Challenge to Social Welfare System

We can use these figures on the number of children ever born to women entering Illinois state prisons to estimate how many children in Illinois had a mother serve time in prison between 1990 and 2001. To compute this estimate, we simply add up the number of children ever born to each of the 14,724 women who served at least one spell in prison. This computation indicates that nearly 35,000 children in Illinois had a mother who spent time in prison. Because most of these children have mothers who are the most economically disadvantaged among the population of incarcerated women, these children are likely especially challenging to social and child welfare professionals.

Our 35,000 figure probably understates the magnitude of the current and future challenge for state authorities. As discussed above, the number of incarcerated women has increased sharply during the period studied. Further, the number of incarcerated women with four or more children has increased even faster. Therefore, looking into the future we expect that more children will have had a mother who spends time in prison during their childhood than has been the case in the past.

Another way to understand the importance of mothers' incarceration for children is to ask how many Illinois children can expect to have a mother who spent time in prison during their childhood? To get a sense of how many children this might be consider the following calculation. During fiscal year 2000, approximately 7,500 children had a mother who spent time in prison. Approximately one-half of these children had mothers who were admitted to prison for the first time. Each year new children are born and other children "age out" of childhood. For simplicity, we assume these numbers are approximately the same. Then we estimate that each year there are 3,250 children born in Illinois who will have a mother who will be sent to state prison at least once by the time they reach age 18.

The foregoing calculation underscores the point that it is relatively rare for a child to have a mother serve time in prison. Each year there are approximately 200,000 babies born in Illinois. This figure implies that approximately 1% to 2% of the state's newborns will have a mother who spent time in prison during their childhood. The reason to study these children is not because their experiences are common, but because they are unusual and at the same time likely pose a disproportionately large burden on the child and social welfare systems. Further, although these percentages are small, the magnitude of the burden for child and welfare agencies is substantial. Even if the numbers and characteristics of the female prison population do not change, during the years ahead Illinois authorities can expect at any one time there to be as many as 60,000 minor children whose mothers spent time in state prison while they were a child.

CONCLUSION

The IDOC data indicates that female ex-offenders' prospects for economic self-sufficiency are very poor. If they are to become self-sufficient, they likely require a comprehensive program including life skills, substance abuse treatment, education, and job training and placement (Topics in Community Corrections, 2000). Despite the escalating numbers of incarcerated mothers returning to the community, very little information is available to guide the design and assessment of appropriate interventions to improve the outcomes for these mothers and their high-risk children. Future research should contribute to our understanding of the context in which these interventions might take place and under what circumstances they might be successful.

About the Author

Susan M. George, Ph.D., is a research associate with the Irving B. Harris Graduate School of Public Policy Studies, University of Chicago.

References

Beck, A. & Karberg, J., *Prison and Jail Inmates at Midyear 2000* (Bureau of Justice Statistics Bulletin, (NCJ 185989) (U.S. Department of Justice, 2001).

Greenfeld, L. & Snell, T., *Women Offenders,* (Bureau of Justice Statistics Special Report, NCJ 175688) (U.S. Department of Justice, 2000).

Mumola, C., *Incarcerated Parents and Their Children* (Bureau of Justice Statistics Special Report, (NCJ 182335) (U.S. Department of Justice, 2000) .

Rafter, N.H., *Partial Justice: Women, Prisoners, and Social Control* (Transactions Books, 1990).

Topics in Community Corrections, *Responding to Women Offenders in the Community,* (National Institute of Corrections, 2000)

Chapter 19

A National Survey of Parenting Programs in Women's Prisons in the U.S.

by Joycelyn M. Pollack, Ph.D., J.D.

This chapter originally appeared in Women, Girls & Criminal Justice, *Vol. 2, No. 4, June/July 2001.*

INTRODUCTION

In order to conduct a national survey of parenting programs in women's prisons, in the spring of 1998, I sent letters to the central offices of correctional agencies in all 50 states. The letters were directed to either the director of corrections, requesting that it be assigned to an appropriate staff person, or to the person primarily responsible for women's programming. In my letter, I informed them of the survey and established the parameters for what would be considered a "parenting program." Parenting programs, I noted, were those that addressed the woman's role as mother, facilitated her performance in this role, or helped develop parental skills. These programs could range from parenting classes of a few hours to nurseries where imprisoned women and their infants can live together during the term of imprisonment. A state was determined to have a parenting program if one of theses wide range of classes existed in at least one prison.

In addition to the letter, I included a questionnaire that requested information about:

- Changes in the women's prison population since 1995;

- The demographics of women prison populations;

- The children of incarcerated mothers; and

- The availability and description of parenting programs.

The letter also explained that I would call telephone respondents to discuss the questionnaire or to obtain answers. By the end of the summer, 40 states had responded, either by mail or by phone. In 10 states, agencies refused to participate or the appropriate staff persons did not return repeated telephone calls.

MOTHERS IN PRISON AND THEIR CHILDREN

High Percentage of Incarcerated Mothers

At least 70% of women in prison have at least one child under 18, and incarcerated women have an average of two or three children (Gabel & Johnston, 1995; Immarigeon, 1994; Bloom & Steinhart, 1993; Pollock, 1998). One study in Maryland even found that 80% of the women in prison had children and averaged three children each. These children are usually young, with 34% of them in preschool and 55% of school age (Block & Potthast, 1997). A conservative estimate of the number of children under 18 with mothers in prison is 119,000, although some authors estimate the number is much higher (Gabel & Johnston, 1995). Contrary to the common belief that mothers in prison abandoned their children prior to imprisonment, research shows that many women were the primary caregivers before their imprisonment and they expected to regain custody of their children upon their release.

Where Children Live During Mother's Incarceration

What happens to these children when their mother is imprisoned? State corrections departments do not collect information about the children of incarcerated mothers (or fathers). We know from a few states and national samples, however, that about 10% of these children enter foster care (Immarigeon, 1994; Pollock, 1998). In this study, I found in the six states that recorded such data that from 3% to 38% of the incarcerated women's children were in foster care.

Of those women who retained custody of their children during imprisonment, most place their children with relatives, usually the maternal grandmother (Grossman, 1984; McGowan & Blumenthal, 1978; Hungerford, 1993; Baunach, 1985; Bloom, 1995; Bloom & Steinhart, 1993). In this study, as many as 85% of the children were reported living with maternal or paternal grandparents. According to other studies, only a small fraction of these children live with fathers. In this study, the figures ranged from a low of 3% (Indiana and Mississippi) to a high of 21% (Pennsylvania).

Pregnancy During Incarceration

This study found, as in other reports, that about 10% of women in prison were pregnant on any given day (Muse, 1994). These pregnancies are often high risk, since women in prison may have been drug users, avoided or neglected medical treatment, or had difficult previous pregnancies (Woolredge & Masters, 1993). One report, for instance, indicated that 77% of imprisoned women had exposed their fetuses to drugs (Johnston, 1995). Some research indicates a higher than average rate of miscarriages for women in prison, part of which is because women must be transported to outside hospitals for delivery and for medical emergencies (Bloom, 1995: 23; Amnesty International, 1999). In all but a few states, the inmate-mother must arrange custody, relinquish her infant, and return to prison 24 to 48 hours after birth.

DIFFICULTIES IN MAINTAINING THE MOTHER-CHILD BOND

Lack of Mother-Child Contact

Some women in prison never see their children (Immarigeon, 1994, Couturier, 1995). Visits are difficult because of the long distances between the prison and home and the expense of traveling. Also, there may be hesitancy on the part of caregivers to take the children to a prison or anger at the mother for her actions that led to her incarceration. Many social workers, who often feel it is traumatic for children to see their mothers in prison, resist accommodating such visits. Finally, the mother herself may not want her children to see her in prison, or to have them be subjected to the search and admission procedures required for visitation. She may feel guilty and ashamed about her imprisonment and refuse to let her children see her in such a setting. Furthermore, visits necessarily include saying good-bye, an experience that is so painful to both mother and child that many women prefer to avoid it (Henriquez, 1996; Gaudin, 1984; Bloom & Steinhart, 1993).

Estimates vary on the number of women who never see their children. While some reports indicate about one-half of women in prison have at least one visit during their prison sentence, other reports indicate the number is higher. Bloom and Steinhart (1993) found that 54% of mothers in a national sample reported no visits; this compares to only 2% of those surveyed in a 1978 study who reported no visits. Reasons why women receive fewer visits today include restriction of prison telephone privileges to collect calls only, the construction of new women's prisons in rural areas, and lack of financial support from social service agencies for travel.

Effect of Separation on Children

Imprisonment separates mothers from their children. In some cases, this separation may not be traumatic (i.e. if the child had been living with and attached to other caregivers), but in some cases, the effects of imprisonment are severe.

Research from child development and psychology explains that part of healthy development involves becoming "attached" to a caregiver. If some separation occurs after an attachment has formed, the child is affected negatively (Ainsworth, 1973; Bowlby, 1952/1969; Rutter, 1979 & 1995). The loss of the mother or primary caregiver will result in whining, crying, aggressive behavior reflecting anxiety and distress, perhaps a regression in toilet training, and delayed development in verbal skills. If the separation occurs between the ages of six to 10, learning problems may result or the child may become withdrawn and may have sleeping problems (Ainsworth, 1973; Woolredge & Masters; 1993; Sheridan, 1996). Children can form attachments to more than one person (i.e., father or maternal grandmother or baby-sitter). Separation is less traumatic for those children who have formed other attachments and more severe when there has been only one primary attachment. Factors affecting the consequences of separation include:

- The age of child;

- Whether the separation is temporary or permanent;

- The length of the separation;

- Whether it occurs in familiar or unfamiliar surroundings;

- Whether it is ameliorated by visits from mother;

- Whether there is a substitute mother figure;

- The kind of child-mother attachment that preceded the separation; and

- The kind of interaction characteristic of mother and child after the reunion (Ainsworth, 1973).

After reviewing the research, it seems clear that separation effects may be traumatic, but they may not be immutable. Further, the severity of the separation is related to other circumstances, i.e., the presence of other attachment relationships.

Most studies find negative effects for the children of incarcerated mothers. Some studies note that maternal separation may cause emotional problems, discipline issues, learning difficulties, hyperactivity, aggressiveness, "acting out" behavior, excessive crying, withdrawal, sleep disturbances, impaired concentration, and anxiety (Block & Potthast, 1997; Hairston, 1991; Gaudin, 1984; Stanton, 1980; Jose-Kampfner, 1995; Johnston, 1995). These symptoms can be predicted by the child development literature on maternal separation. The parent-child relationship is extremely important in healthy child development and separation or lack of attachment affects future relationships and emotional development (Rutter, 1995).

While attachment is the relationship of the child to a caregiver, bonding occurs in the caregiver "toward" her child. Research indicates that mothers are not necessarily predisposed to love their newborn. Love or "bonding" occurs over the period of time immediately after birth. There is biological evidence to indicate that the hormones released with breast-feeding actually influence the development of loving feelings of the mother toward the infant. There is also evidence to indicate that mere closeness and responding to the needs of the infant create the "bond" or maternal love that characterizes healthy mother-child relationships. Research indicates that when mothers and their babies are separated after birth (due to medical problems), then it is harder for women to "bond" with their babies. There is even evidence to indicate that child abuse is more frequent among those mother-child pairs that experienced such a separation (Ainsworth, 1973; Walsh, 1991).

CORRECTIONS' ROLE IN FOSTERING BETTER PARENTING

How do correctional systems across the country help women in their role as parents? Parenting programs range from prison nurseries to parenting classes and include nurseries, overnight visits, community facilities, furloughs, special visiting areas or programs, and parenting classes. These programs provide enriched or expanded visitation or contact with children or actively help the mother improve her parenting skills.

Meeting Mothers' Needs

The first thing to note is that many women in prison are not generally "bad" mothers. In the few attempts to measure parental effectiveness, studies indicate that prison mothers score in the low normal range on parent attitude surveys (Baunach, 1984; Gabel & Johnston, 1995). However, they do face problems. In one review, their needs were listed as including adjustment and mental health counseling, legal protection of parental rights, prenatal health services, financial assistance for families, substance abuse/addiction counseling, employment training and placement services, and re-entry and family re-unification assistance (Gabel and Johnston, 1995). Thus, programs for incarcerated mothers should provide good parenting skills, including life skills to earn a decent wage and the tools necessary to stay drug-free.

Meeting Children's Needs

Children of incarcerated parents suffer a unique form of separation, since the prison sentence carries with it stigma, guilt, and shame for family members, as well as the incarcerated parent. In some cases, family members may project shame and anger toward the incarcerated parent onto the child (Breen, 1995; Fritsch & Burkhead, 1981). Children worry over what is happening to their parent in prison, they worry that if they share their activities with the parent during visitation that the parent will be sad, and they sometimes have unresolved feelings of anger and resentment toward their mother and her abandonment of them. It should also be noted, however, that imprisonment may provide a relief to the child. If the imprisoned mother subjected her child to a life filled with parental absences, substance abuse, domestic violence, police contacts, arrests, and other disruptions, her absence may be, in some ways, a relief. Of course, children may then experience guilt over feeling better off without their parent. Thus, programs should allow children to have expanded visitation with their mothers in a natural setting, to talk with those who understand what it is like to have a parent in prison, and to receive support for issues and problems in the child's life that incarcerated mothers can do nothing about.

SURVEY FINDINGS

Past Surveys

A number of national surveys have determined the range and extent of programs for mothers in prison. In one review of past studies, Gabel and Johnston (1995) found few numbers of women were involved in any meaningful parenting programs. Only 14% of women prisoners were enrolled in parenting classes, less than 10% of all prisoners were enrolled in drug treatment, only 10% were enrolled in any psychological counseling, and only 5.3% of all prisoners were enrolled in employment training programs.

In Clement's (1993) survey of 43 states, 36 reported that they had some type of parenting program. However the length of the program varied from four to eight weeks in 13 states to 20 weeks in one state, and ranged from one to two hours per week in 16 states to 24 hours a week in one state. Clement reports that the average parenting program was a four- to nine-week program, two hours a week, accommodating 25 or fewer women per class. Fifteen of the programs were modeled after Systematic Training for Effective Parenting (STEP), while 23 used no particular model. Only 12 used correctional staff and the rest of the programs used outside staff or volunteers.

Present Survey

In this study I found that most prisons (90%) have some form of parenting classes, either as part of a general life skills program, or separately. The range of length, intensity, and coverage of such programs, however, is extreme. In more comprehensive programs, parenting classes are offered as part of a total package of services that includes enriched visitation and other programs. In others, classes are short modules in a "life skills" offering. It is hard to estimate the value of programs that last only a few hours or the reach of classes given to only a few women.

Special Visiting Areas. Many prisons (73%) have special visiting rooms or separate days for children to visit their mothers. These accommodations are designed to lessen the intimidation of a visit to a prison and to provide a more natural setting. The time for visitation may be longer and fewer rules may govern movement, touching, and activities. One problem women mention is the difficulty of taking care of "adult business" in front of children. Thus, some prisons use volunteer inmate aides who will play with the children for a short period of time so that adults can talk freely. Again, a wide range of visiting opportunities exist, from simple "Sesame Street" corners with toys in traditional visiting rooms, to separate buildings with playgrounds used for day-long visits between mothers and children without caregivers present.

Availability of Furloughs. Over 50% of the institutions reporting in Boudouris' (1996) survey used furloughs, or had them available, to maintain family bonds, but this was a decline from a previous survey in 1985. In this survey, 55% of the states reported having furloughs available, but they noted that these may be "on paper" only and are not seriously considered as viable tools to maintain parental bonds. The value of the furlough is the opportunity to be with children in a natural, non-intimidating environment. In these programs, the mother is typically the one who travels, as opposed to the caregiver and children. The children are not subjected to the negative and frightening elements of a prison visit. However, the distance and the expense involved in travel is still a barrier for the mother and furlough programs have been drastically curtailed across the country.

Presence and Utilization of Community Facilities. About one-third of the states (35%) had one or several community facilities that allowed mothers to live with their children while serving some portion of their sentence, all of their sentence, or part of parole immediately after release. Boudouris (1996) reported that 17 states had community facilities in 1996 (up from five states in 1985). In the present study, of the 40 states that responded, 14 had community facilities. Some state reporters, however, were not aware of private facilities that were available for prisoners as well as clients sentenced directly from the court. California, for instance, contracts with private providers for a half-dozen community facilities for women with infants and young children to six years of age. In California, a state corrections staff person is responsible for overseeing the operation of these facilities and all state rules involving visitation and contraband are followed. These facilities also provide drug treatment and a range of other services and programming.

Option of Overnight Visitation. Boudouris (1996) reported that 31 of 86 responding institutions (in 21 states and provinces) allowed overnight visits between mothers and children. He also reported that the use of overnight visits had declined, as had children's centers or daycare centers. In this study, 11 states reported overnight visits were available. Again, however, availability may not necessarily mean many inmates were able to use the program. In one state, for instance, only five inmates were cleared for overnight visits with children.

Overnight visits can take place in trailers or cabins on the prison grounds, or even in the mother's cell or room. Camping programs may allow mothers to meet with their children on or off the grounds of the prison for a weekend camping experience. The value of overnight visitation is that it allows mother and child uninterrupted time to talk and interact away from the caregiver and away from the restrictions often placed on regular visiting room visits. These visits are distinct from "family" visits, which involve husbands, mothers, and other relatives, as well as children, who spend up to 48 hours with the incarcerated woman in an isolated apartment or trailer. Often mothers must complete parenting classes, or remain in parenting classes, to take advantage of such visits. No studies have so far evaluated these programs as to their value in easing the transition back to full parenthood.

Presence of Prison Nurseries. Although several state prisons had accommodations for babies in the early part of this century, only California, Nebraska, New York, and South Dakota continue to allow women to spend any length of time with their newborns today (Brodie, 1995). The Bedford Hills Correctional facility in New York State is the only prison in this country that has continuously provided a nursery since the early 1900s. California has recently opened the first of several small institutions that accommodate mothers and infants, sentenced directly from the court. Nebraska's program was modeled after New York's. South Dakota has a modified nursery program that allows the mother to return from the hospital with her infant for a "bonding period" of 30 days. After that time, other arrangements must be made.

The argument for prison nurseries is that bonding and attachment between mother and child outweigh any operational or cost concerns of creating prison nurseries. State officials familiar with nursery programs point out that few, if any, security incidents have occurred.

Availability of Other Programs. Several unique programs exist alone or in combination with others. "Mother Read," for instance, allows a woman to read a story into a tape and the tape is given to the child. The program is said to assist in literacy improvement for both the mother and the child, and to help to maintain the tie between the mother and child, even if there is no opportunity for visitation. "Girl Scouts Behind Bars," also available in several states across the country, allows the daughters of imprisoned mothers to organize as a girl scout troop and those involved can visit the mother at one or two meetings a month (other meetings take place outside the prison). This program provides counseling and support to the daughters of imprisoned mothers as well as allows the mothers inside to spend more time with their children and to meet in support groups themselves (Moses, 1993).

CONCLUSION

Little or no commitment will be given to providing services to incarcerated mothers and their children if correctional administrators and policy makers treat incarcerated mothers solely as individuals with no effort to help them with their responsibilities as mothers. This is a shortsighted approach, since much anecdotal evidence suggests the stress of being released from prison involves a woman's fears and anxieties about her role as mother. As with previous surveys, this survey shows that most women in prison are unable to access comprehensive, enriched programs to help with their parenting role. Some states have different parenting programs, but these states also have very large female prisoner populations, so only a fraction of imprisoned women are able to access such programs. Some states have virtually no parenting programs available. Although most prisons for women have parenting classes, they merely provide "content" on parenting, with no real opportunity to have extended contact with children or the opportunity to implement what is learned in class. Nor do such classes offer assistance or support in maintaining bonds to children. Few studies explore the claim that parenting programs strengthen bonds or improve the lives of the children of incarcerated mothers. One study, however, found that a parenting program that incorporated an enriched visitation opportunity not only showed measurable effects on the bonds between mothers and children, but also participation in the program seemed correlated with a reduction in recidivism (Martin, 1997). In general, however, we have learned that states offering an integrated combination of classes and extended visitation, with perhaps overnight visitation programs as well, seem to provide the best continuum of services to women and their children.

About the Author

Joycelyn M. Pollock, Ph. D., J.D., is a professor at Southwest Texas State University, in the Department of Criminal Justice.

References

Amnesty International, *"Not Part of my Sentence" : Violations of the Human Rights of Women in Custody* (Amnesty International, 1999).

Ainsworth, M., *Patterns of Attachment: A Psychological Study of the Strange Situation* (Lawrence Erlbaum, 1973).

Baunach, P., *Mothers in Prison* (Rutgers/Transaction Press, 1985).

Block, K. & Potthast, M., "Living Apart and Getting Together: Inmate Mothers and Enhanced Visitation through Girl Scouts" (Paper presented at Academy of Criminal Justice Sciences, March 1997).

Bloom, B., "Imprisoned Mothers." In K. Gabel & D. Johnston, Eds., *Children of Incarcerated Parents* (pp. 21-30) (Lexington Books, 1995).

Bloom, B. & Steinhart, D., *Why Punish the Children? A Reappraisal of the Children of Incarcerated Mothers in America* (National Council on Crime and Delinquency, 1993).

Boudouris, J., *Prisons and Kids* (American Correctional Association, 1985/1996).

Bowlby, J., *Attachment and Loss*, Vol. 1 (Basic Books, 1952/1969).

Breen, P.A., "Advocacy Efforts on Behalf of the Children of Incarcerated Parents," In K. Gabel & D. Johnston, Eds., *Children of Incarcerated Parents* (pp. 292-298) (Lexington Books, 1995).

Brodie, D.L., "Babies Behind Bars: Should Incarcerated Mothers Be Allowed to Keep Their Newborns With Them in Prison?" 16 *University of Richmond Law Review* 677-692 (1995).

Clement, M., "Parenting in Prisons: A National Survey of Programs for Incarcerated Women," 19(1) *Journal of Offender Rehabilitation* 89-100 (1993).

Couturier, L., "Inmates Benefit From Family Services Program," 57(7) *Corrections Today* 100-107 (December 1995).

Fritsch, T. and Burkhead, J., "Behavioral Reactions of Children to Parental Absence Due to Imprisonment" 30(1) *Family Relations* 83-88 (1981).

Gabel, K. & Johnston, D., *Children of Incarcerated Parents* (Lexington Books, 1995).

Gaudin, J., "Social Work Roles and Tasks With Incarcerated Mothers," 53 *Social Casework* 279-285 (1984).

Grossman, J., *Female Commitments 1982*, (New York State Department of Correctional Services, 1984).

Hairston, C., "Family Ties During Imprisonment: Important to Whom and For What?" 18(1) *Journal of Sociology and Welfare* 87-104 (1991).

Henriquez, Z., "Imprisoned Mothers and Their Children: Separation-Reunion Syndrome Dual Impact," 8(1) *Women and Criminal Justice* 77-97 (1996).

Hungerford, G., "The Children of Incarcerated Mothers: An Exploratory Study of Children, Caretakers and Inmate Mothers in Ohio" (Ph.D. dissertation, Ohio State, 1993).

Immarigeon, R., "When Parents Are Sent to Prison" 9(4) *National Prison Project Journal* 5 (1994).

Johnston, D., "Effects of Parental Incarceration," In K. Gabel & D. Johnston, Eds., *Children of Incarcerated Parents* (pp. 59-88) (Lexington Books, 1995).

Jose-Kampfner, C., "Post Traumatic Stress Reactions in Children of Imprisoned Mothers," In K. Gabel & D. Johnston, Eds., *Children of Incarcerated Parents* (pp. 89-100) (Lexington Books, 1995).

Martin, M., "Connected Mothers: A Follow-Up Study of Incarcerated Women and Their Children," 8(4) *Women and Criminal Justice* 1-23 (1997).

McGowan, B. & Blumenthal, K., *Why Punish the Children? A Study of Children of Women Prisoners* (National Council on Crime and Delinquency, 1978).

Moses, M., "Girl Scouts Behind Bars: New Program at Women's Prison Benefits Mothers and Children," 55(5) *Corrections Today*, 132-135 (August 1993).

Muse, D., "Parenting From Prison," 72 *Mothering* 99-105 (Fall 1994).

Pollock, J., *Counseling Women in Prison* (Sage Publications, Inc., 1998).

Rutter, M., "Maternal Deprivation, 1972-1978: New Findings, New Concepts, New Approaches," 50 *Child Development* 283-305 (1979).

Rutter, M., "Maternal Deprivation," In M. Bornstein, (Ed.), *Handbook of Parenting* (pp. 3-31) (Erlbaum, 1995) .

Sheridan, J., "Inmates May Be Parents Too," 58(5) *Corrections Today* 100-103 (August 1996).

Stanton, A.M., *When Mothers Go To Jail* (Lexington, 1980).

Walsh, A., *Intellectual Imbalance, Love Deprivation and Violent Delinquency* (Charles C. Thomas, 1991).

Woolredge, J. & Masters, K., "Confronting Problems Faced by Pregnant Inmates in State Prisons," 39(2) *Crime and Delinquency* 195-203 (1993).

Chapter 20

Prison Nurseries: New Beginnings and Second Chances

by Kelsey Kauffman, Ed.D.

INTRODUCTION

In April 2001, Ohio became the fourth state to open a prison nursery for incarcerated mothers and their newborns. The nursery at the Ohio Reformatory for Women in Marysville is part of what appears to be an important new trend in the treatment of mothers in prison in the United States. With more than 1.5 million children under 18 in the U.S. who have at least one parent in prison, correctional administrators are grappling with ways to nurture rather than sever parental bonds, especially maternal bonds.

During most of the second half of the twentieth century, New York was the only state that permitted incarcerated mothers to keep their infants with them in prison. Yet prison nurseries were once common in the United States and are currently found throughout the rest of the world. A survey of 70 nations conducted by the United Nations in 1987 found that the United States, Suriname, Liberia, and the Bahamas were the only countries that routinely separated incarcerated mothers from their babies (Alliance of NGOs on Crime Prevention and Criminal Justice, 1987). Since then, however, Nebraska, Washington, and Ohio have opened prison nurseries, and more states are considering doing so.

This chapter originally appeared in Women, Girls & Criminal Justice, *Vol. 3, No. 1, December/January 2002.*

THE OHIO PROGRAM

The Ohio Reformatory for Women (ORW) dates back to the early 1900s. Prior to 1953, inmates gave birth on grounds and were allowed to stay with their babies in a small nursery for one week after delivery. After that, babies remained in the nursery, visited daily by their mothers, until relatives or agencies from outside were able to come and collect them. A small nursery remained open until the early 1980s, when it gave way to the crush of new inmates. As in the rest of the nation, the inmate population at ORW increased dramatically over the next two decades and by 2001 was home to 1,700 inmates and many new buildings.

The current ORW nursery program is open to healthy mothers convicted of non-violent crimes who give birth while in the custody of the Ohio Department of Rehabilitation and Correction and have less than 18 months remaining on their sentence. The program is housed in a separate wing of one of the newest buildings on grounds, which also houses the prison's boot camp and assisted living units. The nursery wing contains double occupancy rooms for up to 20 mothers and their babies, as well as a recreation area, laundry, and the unit's own childcare center.

A pregnant inmate who qualifies for the program participates in an orientation at the prison nursery before being transferred to the prenatal unit in Columbus, where she receives a full array of prenatal services and instruction. Each mother is encouraged to have a "birthing support person"—usually the father or other family member—during labor, which, contrary to the practice in some states, she undergoes without the humiliation and impediment of shackles. If there are no complications, mother and child leave the hospital together and go directly to the ORW nursery.

Promoting the Mother-Child Bond

The bond between mother and child is at the heart of the ORW nursery. As the official "Program Rationale" states:

> Infants are severely impacted by being separated from their mothers in the crucial first months of life. Child development experts have long identified that certain developmental tasks must be achieved through bonding or serious and intractable ramifications for the child will result.
>
> Rather than allowing incarceration to negatively impact these infants, the Ohio Reformatory for Women offers a program which allows the non-violent, short-term offender to maintain custody of her baby while she serves her sentence. The needs of her infant are primary, and every intervention is employed to address the physical, intellectual and emotional needs of the mother and child. (Ohio Reformatory for Women, undated)

Once in the nursery, mother and child are given ample opportunity to become acquainted and begin the bonding process, while the mother receives instruction in basic infant care and development. Once they are settled in, the mother participates in work, educational, and therapeutic programs and parenting instruction while her baby or toddler is cared for by other mothers, trained inmate caregivers, or staff in the unit's childcare center. Throughout their time in the unit, the centerpiece remains intensive involvement of each mother with her child under the watchful and supportive eye of trained correctional and childcare staff.

Positive Responses From Mothers and Administrators

Babies have the potential to transform the prison environment. The first mother to arrive at the nursery at ORW with her infant in her arms recalled the welcome she received: "It was very overwhelming for me—all of the attention I got from the staff and from the other inmates. They were all very happy and excited as well as I was. It was like I was having the baby for everybody. It was nice. It wasn't coming home to my family, but it was close. It made me feel good. It made me feel like I was wanted." She reflected on the impact that the babies in the program had already had not only on the mothers and staff in the nursery, but also on inmates and staff in the adjoining assisted living unit. "They love the babies. I think it's good for them, too.... I think babies bring out the softer side in people."

The first mothers admitted to the nursery were ecstatic about the program. In interviews conducted for this article, each one recalled her depression when she found herself pregnant, in prison, and anticipating separation from her newborn. A young first-time mother remembered her terror at the thought that her daughter would go to a foster home. "I was sick to my stomach. I felt like, well, I'm losing my baby and that's it. I was very depressed." Another mother who had two children on the outside reflected on the prospect of losing her baby, "I believe that the first beginnings of a baby's life is more important than any part. I wanted to really bond with my baby. I didn't just [want to] have him and send him off. It really rips you apart more than anything!" A third mother described her fear that her baby would go to foster care as "crushing." Like the other mothers, she was overjoyed when she heard about the new prison nursery. In recognition of her and her baby's sudden change in fortune and the opportunities that had been opened up for both of them, she named him "Chance." "This is our 'chance.' That's why he got his name."

The prison's administrators also declared themselves pleased with the program's first months. Not only had the mothers and babies thrived, but the babies had also had a joyful effect on what is often a grim and contentious world. Furthermore, based on the reports of other prison nurseries, ORW administrators had sound reasons to predict that the program would lead to "decreases in misconduct reports while having an overall calming effect on the institution" (Ohio Reformatory for Women, undated report). Although it is certainly too early to tell, prison administrators also hope to see significant reductions in recidivism among mothers who are graduates of the program.

OPERATIONAL VARIATIONS AMONG NURSERY PROGRAMS

While the nursery at ORW is itself in its infancy, it may be useful to correctional professionals contemplating opening a nursery to compare the ORW program to other prison nurseries in the United States and overseas on five key variables: eligibility of mothers, eligibility of children, length of stay, integration into the prison, and integration into the community.

Eligibility of Mothers

The ORW program is relatively restrictive regarding eligibility of mothers. They must (1) be convicted of a non-violent offense, (2) have no current or previous charges concerning child endangerment, (3) be healthy, and (4) have 18 months or less to serve at the time they give birth.

In contrast, none of these restrictions automatically apply to inmate mothers at New York's Bedford Hills Correctional Facility. Instead, eligibility there is determined on a case-by-case basis. Approximately two-thirds of the mothers who apply are approved including, in rare cases, mothers who are serving lengthy sentences for crimes of violence. Although most of the mothers leave the prison with their babies, others must stay behind for months or even years.

The prison nursery at Washington Corrections Center for Women, located in Gig Harbor, Washington, takes a different approach. There, maintaining continuity in the parent-child relationship is considered paramount. Any pregnant inmate who has a minimum-security classification and who will, upon her release, be the primary caregiver of her child, can apply for the program. Thus, on the one hand, a mother must have a release date that allows her to leave at the same time as her baby (up to four years if she spends part of her sentence in pre-release and work release centers); on the other hand, she may be eligible for the program even if she has had a poor parenting record with previous children. As one of the program's directors observed, "If they are going to be parents on the outside, they should be in our program."

Eligibility of Children

All four of the prison nurseries in the United States at this writing require that participating babies be born after their mothers have already arrived in prison. If a mother gives birth the day before she goes to prison, she and her baby are ineligible for the nursery and must be separated during her incarceration, even if she is serving a sentence of only a few months.

Most prison nurseries worldwide, however, consider the time and place of birth to be less important than the need to sustain the bond between baby and mother. Of the 70 nations surveyed by the United Nations (Alliance of NGOs on Crime Prevention and Criminal Justice, 1987) (66 of which had prison nurseries), 57 allow mothers to bring infants or very young children to prison with them. It is worth noting that this figure includes 12 of 14 Western European nations, as well as Canada and Australia, which are, in most respects, the nations with prison systems closest to our own. As well, Norway forbids the incarceration of any woman who is pregnant, nursing, or has recently given birth unless the woman herself requests that she begin serving her sentence and has the permission of the prison director to do so.

Length of Stay

Ohio, New York, and the Nebraska Correctional Center for Women in York, Nebraska, require babies to leave the prison nursery by the age of 18 months. Washington, on the other hand, permits mothers and babies to stay in the prison nursery for up to two years, at which point they can transfer to one of two pre-release centers and/or work release for an additional two years.

The length of time that children can remain in prison with their mothers varies widely overseas, from just a few months to 18 years. Of the 57 nations in the United Nations (Alliance of NGOs on Crime Prevention and Criminal Justice, 1987) survey that permit mothers to bring children to prison with them, approximately one-third require babies to leave by the time they are 18 months old (often with short extensions possible). Another third allow children up to two or three years old. Most of the rest require children to leave at age six, although a few countries (mostly in South America) permit older children to stay as well.

While infants may be blissfully unaware that they are in a prison setting, school-aged children generally are not. The imposition of age limits for children in prisons reflects fears that at some point children will be harmed by their unnatural surroundings. To some extent, age limits are correlated with the degree to which the prison world deviates from the world outside. For example, a maximum-security prison in the United States may be a far more deviant environment for an American toddler than a "village style" prison is for a child in Bolivia, where the entire family may move to the prison to be with the mother (Kauffman, 1997).

One of the most creative solutions to this problem in the western world can be found at Preungesheim prison in Frankfurt, Germany. Mothers with children up to 18 months old are housed in a separate building on the grounds of the old maximum-security prison. Mothers who are not considered to be security risks can then move with their pre-school-aged children to a modern facility just off grounds, which faces onto a quiet residential street. Once children are old enough to go to school, they must leave the prison to live with relatives. Even then, the tie between mother and child can be maintained: If her children live in Frankfurt and the mother is eligible for work release, she can leave the prison daily to work for her own family (Kauffman, 1997).

Integration Into the Prison World

Prison nurseries around the world differ considerably in their degree of isolation from the general inmate population. Most institutions provide a separate wing or building for the mothers and babies, but many allow—and some even encourage—mothers and babies to have contact with other inmates. In times past in the United States babies born in some prisons had the benefit of many mothers. One woman I interviewed, who was born in a Midwest prison in the 1940s, recalls that she was the only baby in a unit with 20 inmates, all of whom cared for and adored her: "My mother said that having me there gave her sanity. It gave the other inmates something gentle. It softened them. They loved to take care of me. It made a big difference in their lives. It made a connection to what is important, what was real. They were wonderful…. When I was born, I was everybody's baby."

Although none of the four prison nurseries in the United States at this writing permit such informal parenting to take place, they have different conceptions of the role of the nursery in the wider prison community. Perhaps because it is still new, the ORW unit discourages all contact between babies in the nursery and inmates outside it, except for trained child care workers. The rule book given to mothers stipulates, "All areas designated for children and where children are congregated are off limits to ALL inmates except the program mothers and the inmate caregivers. The main institution is off limits to infants at ALL times" (Ohio Reformatory for Women, April 2001). In contrast, the nursery in Washington, which houses about 20 mothers and children, is part of a unit housing 90 inmates that is, in turn, part of a larger compound with 360 inmates. Mothers can take their children to the dining hall and can be seen strolling their babies through the compound as other inmates stop to chat and coo. The unit supervisor of the Washington nursery observed, "All of the women are so protective of the program and the babies. It's had a calming effect on the whole compound" (Kauffman, 2001).

Integration Into the Community

Prisons, by their nature, isolate their inhabitants from the wider community. Prison nurseries are no exception. To some extent, that isolation can be an advantage as it presents an opportunity to focus each mother's attention on her baby, away from the distractions of drugs, gangs, and other negative influences outside. But the unnatural isolation can also be a problem, not least when mother and child leave the prison and attempt to survive together in what will be for many of them a much more hostile and less supportive environment.

In the 1970s, California opened the first of a series of residential community programs for convicted mothers and their children and it has recently added residential treatment programs for addicted mothers and babies, although the latter are locked institutions. Massachusetts, Indiana, and several other states also have community residential programs for female offenders and their children. However, the number of women and children eligible for these programs is small, and most women participating in them must serve some portion of their sentences in prison without their young children before moving to the community programs. As noted earlier, mothers and babies in Washington Corrections Center for Women's prison nursery can transfer to a pre-release or work release center for the last two years of the mother's sentence, providing a gradual transition from prison to community without ever separating mother and child.

The prison in Preungesheim, Germany, appears to have the best integrated program. There, mothers and their babies progress from a "closed mother-child house" within the prison to an "open mother-child house" just outside from which mothers and toddlers can go out into the surrounding residential community for strolls, picnics, shopping, and even trips to the nearby zoo. Integration into the community is nearly complete for mothers at the prison whose work release job is to care for their school-aged children who live and go to school in Frankfurt.

PRISON NURSERIES SERVE CRITICAL NEEDS

More than 90,000 women are currently in state and federal prisons in the United States; 80% of them mothers. They leave behind more than 125,000 children under the age of 18. Nearly half were the sole parent in the home at the time of arrest. Six percent were pregnant on arrival. Most of them retain or will regain legal custody of their children and will someday resume their role as primary parent, if not for the children that they left behind, then for others they conceive after release. These children, in turn, have a greatly enhanced chance that they, too, will go to prison someday.

Prison nurseries are one means of responding to this challenge. They are founded on the well-documented premises that parenting is a learned skill and that the strength and continuity of the bond between a mother and her baby is critically important for both of them. Prison administrators who oversee nurseries almost universally report that they run smoothly, that the mothers and babies in them thrive, and that the presence of the nurseries contributes to the overall well-being of the institution, including both staff and inmates. Retrospective surveys suggest that recidivism rates are much lower for women who have been able to keep their babies with them in prison than they are for the general population.

However, no longitudinal research has been done that systematically tracks mothers and babies after they leave the nurseries or attempts to compare their experiences with those of mothers and babies who were separated during the mother's incarceration. Without that research, it is difficult to answer key questions regarding the long-term effects of prison nurseries:

- Do mothers and babies thrive after leaving the nurseries?
- Do most of the mothers continue as the primary custodial parent?
- Do the mothers have lower recidivism rates?
- Do their children have lower incidence of criminality as they grow up?

Answers to these questions would help administrators decide which mothers and babies to allow in their programs, for how long, and under what conditions.

About the Author

Kelsey Kauffman, Ed.D, is an independent researcher and writer. She has visited women's prisons and prison nurseries in North America, South America, Europe, Asia, and Australia.

References

Alliance of NGOs on Crime Prevention and Criminal Justice, *Children in Prison with Their Mothers* (Author, 1987).

Kauffman, K., "A Cross-National Perspective on Residential Programs for Incarcerated Mothers and Their Children." In C. Blinn, Ed., *Maternal Ties: A Selection of Programs for Female Offenders*, (pp. 159-165) (American Correctional Association, 1997).

Kauffman, K., "Mothers in Prison," 63(1) *Corrections Today*, 62-65 (February 2001).

Ohio Reformatory for Women, *ABC: Achieving Baby Care Success,* (Author, undated, p. 1-2).

Ohio Reformatory for Women, *ABC's Resident Handbook* (Author, April 2001, p. 8).

Chapter 21

Forgotten Victims: The Children of Incarcerated Mothers

by Maureen Norton-Hawk, Ph.D.

INTRODUCTION

A nationwide concern for the physical and psychological well being of children has swept across America. Anxiety over emotional and psychological injuries has led to the increased use of therapeutic and pharmacological interventions for children (Leo, 2002). The "zone of privacy" that families once enjoyed is being breached as authorities take action to defend children from the physical, emotional, and sexual harms that can occur in the home (Horn, 1998). Clergy, scout leaders, and athletic coaches are considered as potential threats to youthful innocent. Programs like "stranger danger" educate young children on how to avoid abduction. Government agencies urge the availability of portfolios that include children's pictures, imprints of their fingerprints, and dental records in case a child is abducted (Hubler, 2002). Experts have even called for the implantation of microchips that will allow us to track missing children.

In sharp contrast, little attention has been paid to the extreme stress suffered by the children of incarcerated mothers. The number of young Americans with an imprisoned mother has increased rapidly from 64,000 in 1991 to 126,000 in 1999 (Mumola, 2000). Little public sympathy has been expressed for these "forgotten victims." These children are stigmatized by the moral, legal, and financial failings of their parent. They are the offspring of parents who represent the worst qualities of the urban underclass. Their mothers

---

This chapter originally appeared in Women, Girls & Criminal Justice, *Vol. 4, No. 1, December/January 2003.*

are poor, unmarried, uneducated, inner city lawbreakers. These families are viewed as the "undeserving poor"—bad seeds who are not worthy of our protection or do not merit our time, sympathy, or tax dollars (Kasarda & Williams, 1989; Wilson, W.J., 1981).

These children only become politically visible when they grow old enough to come into conflict with the law. The public then demands that something be done about gang violence, drive-by shootings, teen prostitution, "babies-having-babies," school drop out rates, and teenage drug use. Longer jail terms, "just say no" drug education programs, and faith-based education are advocated as the cure for these social ills.

STUDY OF INCARCERATED MOTHERS AND THEIR CHILDREN

This study of the children of incarcerated mothers suggests that such policies will be counterproductive and succeed only in producing another generation of deviants and lawbreakers. A coordinated approach involving many social service agencies will be necessary.

Research Method

Both qualitative and quantitative questions were included in intensive face-to-face interviews with 70 mothers awaiting trial in Boston, Massachusetts, between June and September of 1999. Maternal demographic information, drug-use history, and criminal involvement were gathered. Separate surveys were then completed for each of the children. Data were collected on each child's demographics, placement, custody, education, life experiences, prenatal health and drug exposure, and physical as well as psychological problems. Finally information was gathered on the nature of services that mothers would consider beneficial.

Results

The Mothers. Even by the most generous of interpretations, these women fail to approximate society's image of the ideal mother. The majority of these incarcerated mothers are poorly educated and completely lacking vocational skills that would allow them to properly provide for their children. Two-thirds of the sample failed to complete high school; 24% had no formal schooling beyond the ninth grade.

These women have little experience in the legitimate job market. Only 13% of the respondents held even a part-time job at the time of their arrest. The largest number (40%) were supporting themselves and their children primarily through illegal means, most commonly prostitution.

Incarcerated women rarely have the advantages provided by a stable partner. Over two-thirds of the respondents in this study have never been married (67%). Many of the women gave birth at an early age, the youngest being 13 years; 27% had had their first child by age 17; 41% by age 18 and 53% by the time they were 19 years old.

Drug use is endemic within this population. Almost all the women have tried a variety of both legal and illegal addictive drugs—80% have used alcohol, 89% cigarettes, 80% marijuana, 74% powder cocaine, 64% crack cocaine, and 44% heroin. Drug use began early. The median age of first use of cigarettes is 14 years; alcohol and marijuana: 15; powder cocaine: 18 years; crack cocaine: 21; and heroin: 25. Ninety percent report daily use of illegal drugs or alcohol. Daily use of alcohol is reported by 21%, 34% for marijuana, 36% for powder cocaine, 44% for crack cocaine, and 36% for heroin.

Because of their need to finance expensive drug habits, a large percentage of these women engage in criminal behavior resulting in lengthy arrest records. The median number of incarcerations is three. Twenty-four percent of the women were arrested for drug offenses; 40% faced more serious charges such as assault, larceny, and auto theft. One was awaiting trial for a murder that resulted from a violent dispute over payment for sexual services. The remaining 16% are awaiting trial for probation violations.

The Children. The 70 women in this study have been pregnant a total of 296 times, resulting in 174 live births. Slightly less than one-half of the failed pregnancies resulted from miscarriages; the rest were the result of abortions. Only children under the age of 18 were included in this study, resulting in a sample of 144 offspring. Seven was the average child's age, with males slightly outnumbering females.

The children reflect many of the problems faced by their mothers. The risks to these children's well being began prior to birth. Twenty-four percent of the mothers continued to use alcohol frequently and 73% of the women continued to smoke during pregnancy. Forty-eight percent of the children were frequently exposed to illegal drugs during the prenatal period. This is more than four times the national figure of 11%. The exact consequences of *in utero* exposure to these drugs are still uncertain but a number of studies (e.g., Gingras et al., 1992; Chasnoff et al., 1985) have found serious negative short- and long-term consequences. The youthfulness of the mother, poor prenatal nutrition, drug use during pregnancy, emotional stress and a generally unhealthy lifestyle resulted in 29% of the children being born prematurely.

Lack of a stable, nurturing home environment during childhood may further exacerbate the problems faced by these children. Most of the children were born out of wedlock. The transitory nature of these women's relationships with men is illustrated by the fact that in less than half of the cases is the biological father also the father of any of her other children. African-American children were particularly likely to lack a stable father figure; 31% of the black fathers have never been involved with their biological child as compared to 14% for whites.

Home is not a safe place for many of these children. The mothers report that 41% of the children have experienced physical neglect; 25% have been emotionally abused; 21% have been physically abused; 14% have been sexually abused; and 9% have been raped. The Massachusetts Department of Social Services (DSS) has been involved in 45% of the children's lives. Thirty-one percent of the children have been placed in foster care at least once.

Significantly more white children (57%) have been involved with the DSS than African Americans (34%). Differences in DSS involvement eventually leads to differences in the likelihood of foster care placement (white, 38%; black, 22%). Reliance on the extended kinship system is part of a longstanding African-American tradition (Enos, 1998). Consistent with earlier studies, African-American women are much more likely to rely on a sibling, a member of their extended family, or a friend to provide childcare (U.S. Department of Justice, 1994; Bresler & Lewis, 1986). White women are more likely to rely on grandparents or foster/state care.

Considering the lack of a stable home, parental drug use, and the likelihood of physical and sexual abuse, it is not surprising that mothers describe 52% of the children as suffering from at least one major psychological disturbance. The most common disorder is anxiety (31%), followed by depression (21%) and hyperactivity (19%). Many of the psychological problems appear to go untreated. Only 26% of the children have been treated professionally for their psychological problems.

The children's physical and psychological problems make it difficult for them to succeed in school. Of those currently enrolled, 33% have had to repeat a grade and 35% have been in special education classes because of emotional issues such as attention deficit disorder and other forms of psychological maladjustment. Many of these children also exhibited more extreme forms of misbehavior, such as aggression and violence. This pattern of academic failure combined with impaired mental and physical health makes it unlikely that they will become successful adults without early intervention by social service agencies.

CONCLUSION

This study finds a clear pattern of intergenerational dysfunction. Incarcerated mothers have a wide variety of severe psychological and behavioral problems—often stemming from their own childhood—that impedes their parenting capabilities. These deficiencies include poly-drug addiction, inadequate education, lack of job skills, and family instability. The chaotic lives of the mothers are reflected in the emotional and physical symptoms displayed by their children.

These children are the innocent victims not only of a home life that is in disarray but also of legal, educational, and social service institutions that lack the resources and coordinated approach necessary to deal with their complex needs. Programs must be developed that are specifically designed to compensate for the limitations of their childhood environment. By failing to design effective interventions for this rapidly growing population, America is setting the stage for much greater troubles in the future, because the pattern of intergenerational dysfunctional will continue to expand.

About the Author

Maureen Norton-Hawk, Ph.D. is a professor in the Department of Sociology at Suffolk University, Boston, MA.

References

Bressler, L. & Lewis, D.K., "Black and White Women Prisoners: Differences in Family Ties and Their Programmatic Implications," 63 *The Prison Journal* 116-122 (1968).

Chasnoff, I. J., Burns, W. M., Schnoll, S. H. & Burns, K. A., "Cocaine Use in Pregnancy," 313(11) *New England Journal of Medicine* 666-669 (1985).

Enos, S., *Mothering From the Inside: Parenting in a Women's Prison* (State University of New York Press, 1998).

Gingras, J. L., Weese-Mayer, D. E., Hume, R. F. & O'Donnell, K. J., "Cocaine and Development: Mechanisms of Fetal Toxicity and Neonatal Consequences of Prenatal Cocaine Exposure," 31 Early Human Development 1-24 (1992).

Horn, M., "Shifting Lines of Privacy," *U.S. News and World Report* 57-59 (October 26, 1998).

Hubler , E., "Escape School Offers Kids Lessons in Fleeing Danger," *Denver Post*, March 6, 2002, p. B1.

Kasarda, J.D. & Williams, T., "Drugs and the Dream Deferred," 6(3) *New Perspectives Quarterly*, 16-21, (Summer 1989).

Leo, J., "American Preschoolers on Ritalin," 39(2) *Society* 52-61 (2002).

Mumola, C. J., "Incarcerated Parents and Their Children," Report No. NCJ 182335 (Bureau of Justice Statistics, U.S. Department of Justice, 2000).

U.S. Department of Justice, "Women in Prison," Report No. NCJ 145321 (Bureau of Justice Statistics, 1994).

Wilson, W.J., "Race, Class and Public Policy," 16 *American Sociologist* 125-134 (1981).

Chapter 22

Mother-Child Programs: Connecting Child Welfare and Corrections Agencies

by Susan Phillips, LMSW

INTRODUCTION

Between 1985 and 1994, the number of women in jails and prisons in the United States increased by 153%, compared to a 96% increase in the number of men incarcerated during that same period. Given the different roles that men and women typically play in the lives of their children, it is not surprising that the arrest of a mother should have different consequences for children than the arrest of a father. Studies suggest that the arrest and incarceration of a mother is more disruptive to children because mothers are more likely than fathers to have been primarily responsible for their children before being arrested (Bloom & Steinhart, 1993). Also, children whose fathers are incarcerated typically remain with their mothers before, during, and after their fathers go to prison. In comparison, when mothers are arrested it is not the children's fathers but grandparents, aunts, and uncles who most often care for their children (Johnston, 1995b).

With the rise in the number of mothers serving time, there has been an increasing interest in corrections programs that address women's roles as mothers. A number of prisons offer parent education classes. Others are working to improve the quality of visitation between children and their mothers by creating "child-friendly" visitation areas and providing structured programs to promote positive mother-child interactions (Boudouris,

---

This chapter originally appeared in Offender Programs Report, *Vol. 1, No. 6, March/April 1998.*

1996). At the same time, the child welfare community has been urged to recognize the vulnerability of children whose mothers are incarcerated and to shape meaningful responses (Marcus, 1995).

RATIONALE FOR CORRECTIONS-BASED PROGRAMS

Strong Family Relationship and Recidivism

The rationale for correctional programs that promote positive mother-child interactions is twofold. First, advocates for family programs argue that there is a link between parole success and strong family ties (Mustin, 1994). Programs that maintain and improve the relationship between mothers and children may be valuable for their potential in reducing recidivism. Recidivism is costly to taxpayers, burdensome to the criminal justice system, and damaging to the children of offenders.

Reducing Inter-Generational Effects of Mother's Incarceration

Another reason for the growing interest in programs of this nature is their potential for preventing children whose mothers are incarcerated from following in their mothers' footsteps. Many children with incarcerated mothers will end up being arrested themselves. Nationally, the U.S. Bureau of Justice Statistics has found that over half the children in state-operated facilities had experienced the incarceration of a parent. In Ohio, a study found that four out of 10 boys between the ages of 14 and 17 whose mothers were incarcerated had been adjudicated delinquent (Hungerford, 1996). The life experiences of these children are often characterized by chronic exposure to traumatic and stressful experiences such as abuse and neglect, witnessing violence and parental substance abuse, recurring parent/child separations, bereavements, and repeated changes in residence and caregivers (Johnston, 1995a).

Current research is beginning to recognize a connection between childhoods characterized by such ongoing stressors and future criminality (Widom, 1997; Johnston, 1995a). A number of studies show that a significant number of children of incarcerated mothers have behavioral, emotional, or academic problems that are warning signs of potential delinquency (Harm & Thompson 1995; Bloom & Steinhart 1993).

SUPPORT FOR CAREGIVERS OF CHILDREN

Given the potential for preventing recidivism among mothers and reducing the chance of inter-generational involvement in the criminal justice system, it is important that the corrections community expand programs for families of female offenders to include the relatives who care for the mothers' children. Likewise, public and private organizations that have traditionally served children and families must also recognize the increasing frequency with which children are experiencing the incarceration of their mothers and shape meaningful responses to support the incarcerated mothers' family members who care for the children.

Creation of "Family Matters"

Faculty from the School of Social Work at the University of Arkansas at Little Rock assessed the needs of family members who were caring for children whose mothers were incarcerated in the Arkansas Department of Corrections. The findings from this assessment were used by Centers for Youth and Families, a behavioral health care organization, as the basis for creating a program, called "Family Matters." This program provides support groups for caregivers and concurrent therapeutic groups for children whose mothers are involved in the criminal justice system. Referrals for more intensive services are made as needed. In addition to group support, case managers help relatives overcome barriers to services necessary to help them meet the needs of the children in their care.

Building Cooperative Relationships

For the Centers for Youth and Families, the over-arching lesson learned in working with these families has been the need to build cooperative relationships between the child welfare community and the criminal justice system. This is not something that happens overnight, but is a process in which systems come to understand other systems' missions that are mutually compatible and develop respect for their assets and limitations. The list below suggests ways these communities can begin to build these relationships:

1. *Ask women if they have children that will need to be provided for when they are arrested, when they are booked, when they are arraigned, and while they are incarcerated.* When a mother is arrested she may not volunteer that she has children for fear that they will be taken from her. Having accurate, understandable information about child welfare laws can help alleviate unnecessary fears and help mothers make plans for the care of their children.

2. *Have the local child protective agency develop written information that can be given to mothers who have been arrested.* This information should note specific details of any laws that apply in cases where mothers are incarcerated, and should be easily understandable by someone with no background in child welfare. Also, ask the agency to provide periodic in-service training to staff who work with female offenders.

3. *Provide information to relatives about what is happening with the mother.* People have a tendency to fill in the unknown with the worst case scenario. Relatives need to know, among other things, the release date for the mothers, the sentencing date, visiting hours, the rules about children visiting their parents, how children will be searched, and where the mother will be housed. Providing this knowledge not only relieves the relatives of unnecessary worry—so that they have more emotional energy to devote to helping the children cope with their mother's arrest—but also lets them provide the children with information so that they will not imagine the worst.

4. *Help mothers to be realistic about their prospect of serving time.* Another human tendency is to distort or deny difficult situations. When a mother is facing jail or prison time, she may want to believe a miracle will happen. This can prevent mothers from making necessary arrangements for their children or prevent children from having an opportunity to say good-bye to their mothers.

5. *Give relatives information about community resources that can help them meet the needs of the children.* Many agencies that serve children and families will have a list or directory of local resources. Relatives will need help with everything from food to diapers to clothing and medicine. Determine who is caring for the mother's children and send them a copy of the list or information about where to get a directory. Also, develop a pool of mental health professionals from agencies that serve children and invite them to take turns being available during visitation to explain their services to relatives.

6. *Encourage caregivers.* Taking responsibility for someone's children is a major disruption to employment, marriage, and other children in the caregiver's home. It is an overwhelming experience. Not only are relatives' lives turned upside down, but they may be angry with the mother, blame themselves for the situation, be unrealistic about the mother's chances of being released, and be exhausted from trying to fill in as parent to children who are in emotional crisis. They may feel isolated and alone, ashamed to let other family and friends know of the arrest.

Studies show that children cope better with crisis when the person caring for them copes well. Support groups where relatives can talk with others who are in similar situations can have a powerful impact. They provide caregivers an opportunity to discuss their feelings and concerns with persons who will understand through experience the situation. The support groups also give caregivers the opportunity to share information and learn ways of coping from each other. (Information about how to start a caregiver support group is available from the AARP Grandparent Information Center, 601 E Street, N.W., Washington, D.C. 20049, (202) 434-2296; (e-mail) member@aarp.com. Also, contact Legal Services for Prisoners with Children, 100 McAllister Street, San Francisco, CA 94102, (415) 255-7036 (phone); (415) 552-3150 (fax); http://www. igc.org/justice/cjc/lspc/manual/cover. html.)

7. *Help the children's mothers prepare to resume caring for their children.* Without intervention, mothers may leave jail or prison no better off than before being arrested. In fact, their criminal records may make it even more difficult for them to find housing and employment to support their children. Parent education classes, substance abuse treatment, domestic violence education groups, and employment assistance are important to help female offenders be in a better position to resume the care of their children when they return to the community.

CONCLUSION

The influx of women into the criminal justice system creates new challenges for both the criminal justice system and the child welfare community. One of those challenges is finding ways to work with grandparents, aunts, uncles, or other relatives who are caring for a female offender's children. The suggestions presented here are far from exhaustive. They represent initial steps that can be taken to bring groups together to meet the challenges of the growing population of women who are involved in the criminal justice system. The number of children who experience the arrest and incarceration of a mother as part of their formative childhood experience is increasing. The steps we take to reach this vulnerable group of children by helping their mothers and extended family will make a difference to this generation of children and to generations to come.

About the Author

Susan Phillips, LMSW, is the Community Resource Development Coordinator for the Parenting from Prison program operated by the Centers for Youth & Families in Little Rock, Arkansas. She is also the coordinator for Arkansas' efforts on behalf of the national "Mothers in Prison, Children in Crisis" Campaign.

References

Bloom, B. & Steinhart, D., *Why Punish the Children: A Reappraisal of the Children of Incarcerated Mothers in America* (National Council on Crime & Delinquency, 1993).

Boudouris, J., *Parents in Prison: Addressing the Needs of Families* (American Correctional Association, 1996).

Harm, N. & Thompson, J., *Children of Incarcerated Mothers and Their Caregivers: A Needs Assessment* (Centers for Youth and Families, 1995).

Hungerford, G., "Caregivers of Children Whose Mothers Are Incarcerated: A Study of the Kinship Placement System," 24(1) *Children Today* 23-27 (1996).

Johnston, D., "Effects of Parental Incarceration," in K. Gable & D. Johnston, Eds., *Children of Incarcerated Parents* (Lexington Books, 1995a, pp. 59-88).

Johnston, D., "The Care and Placement of Prisoners Children," in K. Gable & D. Johnston, Eds., *Children of Incarcerated Parents* (Lexington Books, 1995, pp. 103-123).

Marcus, S., "Child Welfare System Policies and the Children of Incarcerated Parents," in K. Gable & D. Johnston, Eds., *Children of Incarcerated Parents* (Lexington Books, 1995b, pp. 285-291).

Mustin, J., Ed., "Families of Offenders: A Key to Crime Prevention," 1 *Family & Corrections Network Report* (1994).

Widom, C.S., "Child Victims: In Search of Opportunities for Breaking the Cycle," in *U.S. Department of Justice, Perspectives on Crime and Justice: 1996-1997 Lecture Series* (National Institute of Justice, 1997).

Chapter 23

Summit House: Alternative to Prison for Mothers, Better Future for Kids

by Karen V. Chapple, M.A., E. Paula Cox, Ph.D. and Jamie MacDonald-Furches, B.A.

INTRODUCTION

A mother imprisoned is a family fractured. Incarcerating mothers and pregnant women goes far beyond the direct impact on the mother as the children become unwitting victims of their mother's debt to society. In North Carolina 78% of all incarcerated women are mothers and 83% of the mothers are single parents. The mothers must relinquish physical custody of their children. Perhaps more unfortunate are the cases of pregnant women who are forced to give up their newborns within 24 to 48 hours after birth, taking away the opportunity for that initial and valuable bond with their children. During 1993, over 150 pregnant women were admitted to the North Carolina Correctional Institution for Women. On any given day, over 1,400 women are incarcerated in the state of North Carolina, leaving over 3,000 children without their mothers. The issue of justice becomes a double-edged sword as the children bear both edges, a mother incarcerated and a family separated.

This chapter originally appeared in Community Corrections Report, *Vol. 4, No. 6, September/October 1997.*

When a mother is sentenced to prison, she faces the reality of losing direct involvement in her child's life during her incarceration. This separation can severely affect the mother-child bond for infants and younger children, and can result in behavior problems for older children. The likelihood of problems increases when the source and quality of custodial care for the child are inadequate or inconsistent. Sadly, the children of incarcerated parents face an increased likelihood of being involved in deviant activity as juveniles or adults.

Summit House seeks to avoid this family disintegration and to stop the cycle of crime by keeping mothers and children together, while strengthening family ties through extensive treatment and rehabilitation.

MAKING FAMILY AND LIFE-SKILLS TRAINING PART OF PROBATION

Summit House Program

The Summit House program was conceived by a group of community leaders concerned about the implications for the family when a mother goes to prison. Of equal concern was the status of the children who are usually placed in foster care or with extended family members whose care can be of lower quality than foster care and fraught with the same risk factors which affected the mothers. Therefore, the issue of the care of the children became paramount.

Summit House is a non-profit, community-based sentencing and corrections program where mothers and pregnant women who have been convicted of nonviolent felonies receive residential and/or day-reporting services. These mothers who would otherwise be sentenced to prison come to Summit House as a condition of their probation. Mothers admitted to the Summit House residential program live there with their children.

The purpose of Summit House is to strengthen the mother-child bond, and to change the behaviors and attitudes that relate to committing crimes by providing a closely supervised and highly structured program of therapeutic intervention and rehabilitation. At Summit House, the woman must address major life issues such as parenting, substance abuse, life trauma, relationship skills, child and maternal health, education, employment, financial management, and other crucial life skills.

Genesis and Growth of the Program

In the 1970s the need for an alternative to prison for mothers and pregnant women was discussed by the Greensboro Commission on the Status of Women. As a result of these discussions, the Commission created Another Way, Inc., a program designed to outline the need for the vision of an alternative to prison. In the 1980s, a steering committee was established to address the needs verified by Another Way, Inc. This group evolved into a Board of Directors, which created a program that included residential and day-reporting elements. In 1987 the program was incorporated as the "Guilford County Residential/Day Center." The residential program was designed to enroll women for at least 11 months, providing a structured context in which counseling services, life skills training, and parenting classes were offered. Both the residential and day-reporting programs opened in January 1988. True to its mission, the residential and day-reporting programs allowed the female residents to retain primary care of their children. Thus the vision was born and the philosophy was becoming a reality. In January 1989, The Guilford County Residential Day Center changed its name to "Summit House." More importantly, three residents became the first graduates of the residential program, and state government provided funds for the programs operation.

Growing Pains Overcome. Even with increased support, the program experienced growing pains. In 1988, the day center closed due to transportation difficulties. In 1990, the residential program closed for five months because of a financial shortfall. Nonetheless, a strong commitment to the vision remained. Clients were referred to other programs, or released and continued on probation. When Summit House reopened, a behavior modification program based on the Teaching Family Model of the Bring It All Back Home agency in Morganton, NC, was implemented to address the women's behavior while they lived in the residential setting. As program changes occurred, the program strengthened. In 1991, the Z. Smith Reynolds Foundation funded an evaluation of Summit House— one of two evaluations to occur that year. The evaluation results were extremely positive. That same year, new management was hired and Summit House received substantial state funding. In 1992, the local Junior League funded the Women's Learning and Resource Center, the program's day-reporting component, to be located beside the residential facility in Greensboro.

Expansion to Provide Statewide Service. In 1993 expansion plans were approved for developing residential programs in Charlotte and Raleigh, and reopening of a full Day-Reporting and Resource Center in Greensboro. A committee of volunteers reorganized Summit House into a true statewide agency. A Board of Governors was formed as the overall policy making board, and each site continued to be governed by a local Board of Trustees. Two representatives of each local Board were chosen to serve on the Board of Governors. The Greensboro Women's Learning and Resource Center (WLRC) opened in early 1994. This innovative program was the first day-reporting center in North Carolina. In April 1995, the residential programs in Charlotte and Raleigh accepted their first families as Summit House recognized state growth.

Due to the expansion of programs in North Carolina, by 1997 Summit House was striving to provide services to approximately 21 women and 35 children in the residential programs across the state, and 65 active day-reporting clients annually in Greensboro. Summit House recognizes the strong need for day-reporting services since at least 725 women are on probation in the local service area. [*Editor's Note:* As of spring 2005 Summit House has three facilities, in Greensboro, Charlotte, and Raleigh, serving 54 women and children.]

NEW SENTENCING LAWS CREATE MORE NEED FOR SUMMIT-TYPE PROGRAMS

North Carolina's structured sentencing laws, enacted in October 1994, were intended to place increasing numbers of nonviolent offenders into local community treatment programs, thereby reserving prison for violent and repeat offenders. However, since the enactment of structured sentencing, North Carolina has witnessed an alarming increase in convictions mandating prison sentences for women who are repeat offenders. (Formerly, these women would have spent a few days in jail and been released.) This rise in the need to serve prison-bound women offenders is a definite call to action for developing more community programs like Summit House.

HOW THE RESIDENTIAL PROGRAMS WORK

Program Goals

Each of the Summit House residential programs operates in a home-like setting. Dwellings with multiple bedrooms in residential communities provide women and children with housing that models a neighborhood setting. If space in a given residence allows, each Summit House client and her children share a bedroom with another resident and her children. A sense of community and cooperation is fostered as the women and their children share meal preparation and dinner times, and take turns with chores and other day to day responsibilities.

The goals of the Summit House program are to:

- Improve parenting skills;

- Identify and manage self-defeating behaviors;

- Practice self-supporting behaviors by developing long-term goals, life planning, education and training, financial management/budgeting, and employment;

- Develop a healthy sense of self, family, and competency in relationships with others.

Behavior Modification and Empowerment

Summit House provides a structured approach that blends a comprehensive selection of services. Each woman's progress is guided by a behavior modification and empowerment model where behaviors are rewarded or discouraged relative to goals set by the woman and Summit House staff. The program utilizes many local agencies, professionals, and schools to provide services. Elements of service include therapeutic intervention; classes and workshops are provided on major life issues such as positive parenting skills, good health practices and status for mother and child, addiction education and addiction-free living through 12 step programs such as Narcotics Anonymous, formal academic education, family relationships enhancement, self-management skills, job-seeking and employment skills, and social skills training and practice.

The rehabilitation program at Summit House borrows from the most successful applications of learning and immediate reinforcement. Staff members serve as positive role models for appropriate behavior thereby giving clients the opportunity to observe and practice positive behaviors. Staff members establish a therapeutic relationship with clients wherein unconditional positive regard is balanced with a supportive environment, which encourages clients to take responsibility for the consequences of their behavior. The staff-client relationship is built on the principles of empowerment where staff members support and facilitate self-sufficiency and success in clients at whatever level is needed for any given situation.

The program and management staff at Summit House are dedicated to individualized treatment where service and rehabilitation are tailored to the specific needs of each mother and her children. This provides an element of empowerment to the woman entering

Summit House, encouraging her to participate in setting goals relevant to her needs and the needs of her family. Since each client and her children have a unique set of goals, no absolute length of stay is set for women residing at Summit House. Depending on each woman's rate of progress, it takes between one and two years to achieve the requisite skills for graduation.

Clear, Tough Standard Requirements

Alongside her own individual goals for achievement, each client must attain a standard set of expectations held by Summit House for her. During their involvement in the Summit House program, clients must:

- Obtain a GED (if they do not already have a high school diploma);

- Attend college or vocational training;

- Participate in substance abuse counseling/treatment and counseling on victimization;

- Learn parenting, financial management, relationship, mediation, and coping skills;

- Play an active part in the daily operations of the home and eventually share in the management of the day-to-day operations of the home, including Family Conference (the Summit House "self-government" system);

- Obtain employment with earnings above the present minimum wage in order to be self supporting;

- Obtain appropriate housing for themselves and their children preferably outside of public housing and not with family members whenever relationships tend to be dysfunctional;

- Begin paying restitution; and

- Perform community service.

CONCLUSION

Summit House is committed to serving the needs of women offenders and their children through the provision of a comprehensive battery of services. The major long-term benefits that Summit House offers are: assisting society to break the cycle of poverty and crime; offering prenatal medical care for at-risk mothers with substance abuse problems, therefore modifying their behaviors; and allowing them to become productive members of society in the future, and better parents to their children. The Summit House program provides a balance of treatment factors, including those known to be effective with offenders in general, while addressing at the same time the individual needs and dynamic characteristics of the women served. Rehabilitation involves treatment of offenders as women and mothers within larger systems of family and community.

The women who attend Summit House are a unique group of individuals. While they come with a lifetime of factors that have put them on a trajectory of crime and self-denigration, and come with a history of significant nonviolent offenses, they are truly a testament of the human desire to rise above adversity. They come primarily for the sake of their children, who have paid the highest price for their mothers' addictions and criminal behaviors. These women come willing to live in the highly structured environment, and under great demands placed on them for self-enhancement and successful living. They come seeking better lives for, and better relationships with, their children. Often they feel tempted to leave Summit House, but love for their children anchors their stay.

Our message is simple and strong—preserve the family; rehabilitate, not merely habitate; and look toward the future for these children by decreasing their likelihood toward criminal behavior. Summit House strives daily to accomplish these goals as it reaches out to preserve the outcomes of its clients—the women and their children. The significant investment in the people at Summit House serves brings the greater return of self-sufficiency and empowerment for a promising, productive future.

About the Authors

Karen V. Chapple, M.A., is the Vice President of Criminal Justice Services at Coastal Horizons Center, Inc., in Wilmington, NC. Previously, she was the Chief Executive Officer of Summit House in Greensboro, NC. E. Paula Cox, Ph.D., is the former Director of Training and Evaluation, and Jamie MacDonald-Furches, B.A., is a Public Relations Consultant for Summit House.

Chapter 24

Girls and Their Babies: "Time" Together at Florida's YMCA Character House

by Jennifer A. Lynch, B.S.

Sarah (not her real name) is 14. She comes from the northern part of Florida. She is in the ninth grade and has missed 20 days of school so far this year. She has violated her probation, again. Her probation officer finally found her staying at a new boyfriend's house and brought her to the local detention center. She has always had problems with her stepfather. In fact, that is what got her into the system in the first place: She was charged with battery against him.

This time, Sarah's stepfather caught her with drugs and threatened to call the police. She ran out the door. She had been gone for two weeks before the officer found her. Although she has been in other "programs" since entering the juvenile justice system at age 12, she has never been to the YMCA Character House in Sarasota, Florida. That is because Sarah was never pregnant before this.

This chapter originally appeared in Women, Girls & Criminal Justice, *Vol. 3, No. 3, April/May 2002.*

USING TIME INSTEAD OF DOING TIME

Group Home for Teen Mothers

The YMCA Character House is a 20-bed residential group home under contract to Florida's Department of Juvenile Justice. It opened its doors in 1996. The Character House has successfully graduated more than 90% of its residents. Character House has one of the lowest recidivism rates in the state. In addition, youth improve their academics achievement levels by an average of one and one-half grade levels in both math and English. The program serves adjudicated pregnant teens and teen mothers from around the state. It is the only program of its kind in the state where young delinquent mothers have the opportunity to keep their newborns with them, developing the critical baby-mother bond, while they complete their commitment time in a juvenile justice program. Instead of "doing time," Sarah and other young girls in the same predicament are given the opportunity to change by learning character development, behavior modification, and parenting skills.

The Character House accepts girls ages 12 to 18 from all over the state. Ethnic backgrounds of the girls who have resided in Charter House include black, Hispanic, white, and Asian. Most are from low- to middle-income families. In some cases, these girls have been raised by one parent or a grandparent. In other cases, parents are divorced and re-married and there is a stepmother or stepfather present, as in Sarah's case.

The Character House derives its name from emphasis on the YMCA of the USA's Four Core Values: respect, responsibility, caring, and honesty.

The program uses a positive behavior management approach with supportive counseling services. It is designed to increase the probability of successful socialization by increasing resiliency to substance abuse, minimizing risk of additional unwanted pregnancies, and assisting each youth in making better life choices and avoiding future delinquent acts.

Program Basics

Living Arrangements. Residents live in a structured environment with people who care. Twenty-four-hour "behavior coaches" work directly with the youth and infants on activities of daily living. The youth participate in daily upkeep of the house including cleaning, food inventory, shopping, and food preparation.

Individualized Treatment Plans. Case management, health care, counseling, education, and behavior management services are combined to formulate an individualized treatment plan. Sarah's treatment plan, e.g., will incorporate anger management, impulse control, decision making, dealing with past life choices, a plan for advancing to the tenth grade, family counseling, and learning age-appropriate behaviors with a focus on alternatives to drugs. The individualized treatment plan will guide her to successful completion of the program and teach her how to be a law-abiding individual.

THE PROGRAM IN PRACTICE

Sarah's Program Goals

After her initial treatment team meeting, when her program goals will be established with input from her, Sarah will meet with the treatment team two times per month to discuss and review how she is progressing on those goals. Her goals can be amended or discontinued as determined by the treatment team and, as always, with input from her.

Learning Appropriate Behavior

The case manager together with the residential manager will help Sarah learn the aspects of the behavior management system including the different levels. She will realize the importance of learning that she will start on the Trainee level and then move to Bronze, then Silver, then Gold, and finally, when she is almost ready to graduate, she will earn Platinum Status. Her behavior is what will determine how quickly she moves through the levels because the Character House is a behavior-based program, not time-based. The average length of stay for a youth is six months and if Sarah stays on track, works on her goals with the treatment team, and incorporates effective parenting techniques, she will earn her graduation from the program and return home "on schedule." If Sarah takes an unusually long time adjusting, denies that she has issues to work on, or has a setback due to inappropriate behavior, she may remain in the program as long as one year. While she is moving through the level system, Sarah will be evaluated daily for appropriate behavior. If her behavior is not appropriate, she will earn consequences that could move her projected release date further back. The behavior management system focuses on immediate consequences for all behaviors. Appropriate behaviors are rewarded with special privileges as the youth progresses through the level system.

Care for the Body and the Mind

Health Care. Health care is a major aspect of the program. Sarah will receive specialty health care delivered by an on-site registered nurse, a certified nurse midwife, and an OB-GYN physician. She will be examined by the nurse practitioner/midwife with increasing frequency as her pregnancy progresses, and the medical doctor will be consulted or examine her as needed. During labor and delivery, a certified doula (a labor and postpartum support person who assists a pregnant or postpartum woman) will tend to Sarah, in addition to the nurse practitioner. Lab tests and other diagnostic procedures are used routinely, as the nurse practitioner/midwife and physician deem necessary for a safe pregnancy, labor, delivery, and recovery period. On a day-to-day basis, the registered nurse will be available to Sarah to evaluate any health complaints or concerns for her or her baby.

The local health department will provide well-baby and sick-baby care, a family planning clinic, the WIC program (nutritional supplements and counsel), and STD clinic, and an immunization clinic for Sarah and her infant. In the event those basic health care providers cannot meet Sarah's or her baby's needs, she will be referred to a specialty provider or in the event of an emergency, the local emergency room is utilized.

Counseling and Education. Another important aspect of the program is counseling. Sarah will be assigned to one of two master's level counselors in the program. In counseling, she can work on her mental health and substance abuse issues. In addition, therapeutic group sessions are available that target specific issues such as anger management, self-esteem, character development, and healthy relationships.

There is a "second chance" classroom within the walls of the facility. Education is emphasized and promoted for the future of all residents. Sarah will be mandated to attend school for five hours each day, excluding weekends. Ten residents attend school in the morning, while the other 10 are in the house caring for the infants. In the afternoon, the groups switch places, and school and daycare activities resume.

Residents vary in their academic levels. The education coordinator enrolls each youth in appropriate course work with the local school board. In addition to standard subjects such as math, reading, history, and science, Sarah will learn about parenting, peer counseling, and culinary arts. Residents are given an opportunity to earn high school credits or work towards their GED, as appropriate.

COMMUNITY AND FAMILY INVOLVEMENT

Community resources are abundant. Parenting education, Planned Parenthood, Alcoholics/Narcotics Anonymous, and PWA (People with AIDS speakers bureau) are just some of the groups that Sarah will attend and learn about. Local theater companies donate tickets to theatrical performances, the library provides a lending service for girls to take out books for leisure reading, and local businesses offer the opportunity for these youth to work off their community service hours.

Family involvement is encouraged whenever possible. Parents are invited to participate in the treatment team meetings and family counseling sessions are offered when the individual counselor determines they are a necessary component of treatment. On the day of delivery, Sarah may have three immediate family members in attendance at the birth of her child, unless this is contraindicated as determined by the treatment team, or prohibited by the Department of Juvenile Justice.

Prior to discharge, the case manager contacts the "conditional release" or "aftercare" probation officer so that appropriate arrangements for home-placement can begin. After graduation, residents usually return home to live with their families. Occasionally residents will return to foster care or enter a transitional living program with their babies.

Once she is home, Sarah will be given court mandates such as a curfew, school attendance, and counseling that she must follow prior to being discharged from the juvenile justice system. She will be monitored by the aftercare probation officer and must have regular contact with him/her for approximately four to six months.

SUCCESSFUL MOTHERS, HEALTHY BABIES

At Character House, the overall goal for Sarah and other teen girls will be change. All aspects of the program and all staff members will focus on providing Sarah with an environment that is conducive to change. She will learn how to reframe old patterns so that she achieves future success. She will work through her issues so that she is better able to handle life situations for herself and her child. Academic classes will provide for rapid progress and a chance to make up for past academic failure. Sarah can be successful and she will be given the tools to make the decision to reach that success.

The YMCA established the Character House based on the belief that mothers bonding with their infants would mitigate factors against child abuse, prevent neglect and abandonment, decrease subsequent unwanted pregnancies, and decrease recidivism. Sarah will learn the importance of the baby-mother bond and that she has an opportunity that only a few delinquent, pregnant Florida girls are given.

Sarah is scared but will start to realize that this is the best place for her right now. Although youth always think "home" is better, the YMCA Character House is the best place for her to have her baby at such a young age. When graduation comes, Sarah will be ready for home . . . and another girl just like Sarah will be joining the Character House family.

About the Author

Jennifer A. Lynch, B.S., is the Program Director at the YMCA Character House, YMCA, Children, Youth & Family Services in Sarasota, FL.

Chapter 25

Federal F.O.R.U.M.—Helping Federal Women Prisoners to Stay in Touch With Their Children

by Ann Jaede

A MOTHER'S INCARCERATION, A FAMILY'S SENTENCE

Mary Gaines is from Minneapolis, Minnesota. She was in a federal prison in Pekin, Illinois, for almost eight years. She has three children; at the time of her imprisonment they were eight, nine, and 11 years old. She did not see them for the entire time she was in prison. Many children whose parents are sent to prison are placed in foster care. Mary's children were luckier than most; they were cared for by her sister while she was gone. However, prison rules allowed Mary, her sister, and her children to talk for only 15 minutes every month by telephone. The impact of their mother's absence on Mary's children was severe and predictable: her daughter became pregnant at age 16, dropped out of school and was on the edge of delinquency during her adolescence; her two sons stayed in school, but are now struggling with the aftermath of Mary's absence. All of her children have had trouble accepting her authority and are angry at her absence.

Mary is a product of the War on Drugs and the federal response to drug offenses (Anderson & Harmeyer, 2000). Mary's crime was "holding drugs" for an acquaintance who happened to be an informant of the Drug Enforcement Administration, a violation of 21 U.S.C. § 846 (conspiracy) and 21 U.S.C. § 841(a)(1) (aiding and abetting). Mary does not deny her guilt. She was given a mandatory minimum sentence required by federal law based on history and offense. She served 7.5 years.

This chapter originally appeared in Women, Girls & Criminal Justice, *Vol. 2, No. 3, April/May 2001.*

CHILDREN OF INCARCERATED MOTHERS SUFFER PROFOUND EFFECTS

In 1999 the estimated number of female federal prisoners was 5,100—up from 2,900 in 1991 (Federal Bureau of Prisons, 1999). These women had 10,600 children, or approximately two children per offender (Mumola, 2000). As of January 2000, the Federal Bureau of Prisons reported there were 127 Minnesota women in federal prisons. But Minnesota does not have a federal prison for women. The closest prison is in Pekin, Illinois, 600 miles away from Minneapolis, where Mary's children lived.

Research suggests that the effects of parental arrest and incarceration on a child's development are profound (Johnston, 2000; see Figure 25.1) and because two-thirds of incarcerated mothers were the sole caretaker of children prior to their arrest, the effects on children are most disruptive when the imprisoned parent is the mother. Children suffer from multiple psychological problems including trauma, anxiety, guilt, shame and fear. Negative behavioral manifestations can include withdrawal, low self-esteem, decline in school performance, truancy and use of drugs and alcohol and aggression. Caregivers have also cited teen pregnancy as a problem among these children. It is difficult for incarcerated women to maintain contact with their children and more than half of all incarcerated mothers do not receive any visits from their children. The single most significant reason for lack of contact is the children's distance from their mother's prisons, many of which are located far from major population centers (Simmons, 2000). For federally incarcerated mothers and their children, this problem is often exacerbated because the mothers may be imprisoned in federal prisons in other states and federal sentences, particularly for drug-related crimes, are generally quite long.

A CREATION OF SUPPORT SERVICE FOR FAMILIES

While Mary was in prison, she vowed that upon her return to the community she would start a program that would strengthen the ties between mothers and their children so that the relationships could survive the long years of imprisonment. In 1997, Mary, along with several other women who had been in federal prison, designed Federal F.O.R.U.M. (Females Organizing and Restoring Unity for Mothers). The thrust of the program is to:

- Provide a support network for children and their imprisoned mothers;
- Assist the women upon their return to the community; and
- Build ongoing job training and placement, as well as supply housing run by the women themselves with community support.

The Adoption and Safe Families Act of 1997 (ASFA), which requires that children be placed for adoption if not reunited with their parent within one year, did not affect Mary's imprisonment. However, the impact of ASFA is great among the women with whom Mary works. The law requires physical contact with a child within a year (Smith, 2000). Because federal sentences are long and the federal prison is a long distance from Minnesota, many mothers lose custody of their children during their imprisonment. Mary has worked with women being sentenced to prison and judges to try to seek family adoptions so that relationships with the children have a better chance to succeed. There is no data on how often

Figure 25.1 Possible Developmental Effects of Children of Parental Crime, Arrest and Incarceration

Developmental Stage	Developmental Characteristics	Developmental Tasks	Influencing Factors	Effects
Infancy (0 - 2 years)	Total dependency	Attachment and trust	Parent-child separation	Impaired parent-child bonding
Early childhood (2 - 6 years)	Increased perception and mobility; incomplete individuation from parent	Sense of autonomy, independence, and initiative	Parent-child separation; trauma	Anxiety, developmental regression, acute traumatic stress, survivor guilt
Middle childhood (7 - 10 years)	Increased independence, ability to reason, importance of peers	Sense of industry, ability to work productively	Parent-child separation; enduring trauma	Acute traumatic stress, and reactive behavior
Early adolescense (11 - 14 years)	Increasing abstract thinking, future-oriented behavior, aggression, puberty	Ability to work productively with others; control of emotions	Parent-child separation; enduring trauma	Rejection of limits on behavior, trauma-reactive behaviors
Late adolescense (15 - 18 years)	Emotional crisis and confusion, adult sexual development, abstract thinking, independence	Achieves identity, engages in adult work and relationships, resolves conflicts with society and family	Parent-child separation enduring trauma	Premature termination of parent-child relationship; intergenerational crime and incarceration

Source: Johnston (Simmons, 2000)

this happens or the impact on the children or their mothers. It was not easy to start or continue this program. To our knowledge, there have been no community programs for male or female federal offenders to use as models. We believe this is the first. There is no good data source for information about federal offenders that is specific to Minnesota. The Bureau of Prisons has been helpful with special runs. It has been difficult to build interest in the funding community to support a program like this: the numbers are small and the impact unknown.

BUILDING COLLABORATION

Federal F.O.R.U.M. devoted the first year to building a core of ex-prisoners who wanted to make life better for their "sisters." There has been much in-kind support from local churches and other community organizations, but volunteers, especially Mary, do the core work. Community and church groups have donated clothing, provided transportation for job interviews, and held activities for the identified children. But it has been mostly Mary who has spent the entire three years (at this writing) since her release taking her cause to the community. Sister Rita Steinhagen, whom Mary met after her return from federal prison, has assisted Mary in her work. Sister Rita herself served a federal sentence, for civil disobedience. She and her order, the Sisters of St. Joseph, have been helpful in getting other religious organizations to take an interest in Federal F.O.R.U.M..

Mary's charisma and perseverance have paid off. The Shadow Convention, an alternative to the 2000 Republican National Convention, invited Mary and a group of young people whose mothers were in federal prison to come to Philadelphia to explain the pain and anger of separation caused by their mothers' incarceration. Their way was paid by the Drug Policy Foundation, the Rand Smith Foundation, and Arianna Huffington. The young people were an instant hit. They wrote a song and a play about their lives that they performed to an appreciative audience.

In August, 2000, after several years of communication back and forth, the authorities at the federal prison in Pekin, Illinois, gave permission for Federal F.O.R.U.M. to bring 20 children and their caregivers to visit their moms. Six mothers took advantage of the opportunity. A local community agency and a county organization, along with a loan from a Federal F.O.R.U.M. board member, provided the last minute funding for the trip. *The Minneapolis Star Tribune*, which has been a supporter, went along (Kumar & Griesdleck, 2000). One girl was quoted as saying, "I'm dying without my mom. I miss everything about her." Her mom said, " I think Lyndsey is a lot angrier than she would be. She's an unhappy and angry little girl who thinks she got ripped off…. And she did get ripped off." Lyndsey replies, "I'm glad she's in prison because otherwise she would've been dead or something. She's learned her lesson, so she won't do it again." "But I didn't need eight years to figure that out," her mother is quoted, adding, "The real punishment here isn't the fence, but being away from your kids and family. But their suffering is probably more than mine." (Additional interviews with the children and their mothers can be heard on the web site: http://www.star tribune.com/news/variety/prison/openhearts.html.)

Federal F.O.R.U.M. has come a long way in its first three years. It has a board of directors, a majority of whom are ex-offenders; it is seeking 501(c)(3) status—not easy without money—and continues to be a visible organization for female federal offenders, particularly those with children. The organization has provided services to over 50 women returning from federal prison by assisting them in finding jobs, by arranging housing, by giving them clothes and transportation to job interviews. It has given the opportunity to children and mothers to stay connected and has allowed caregivers to have a network that had not existed before.

About the Author

Ann Jaede, now retired, is past research director for juvenile corrections, Minnesota Department of Corrections, and a board member of Federal F.O.R.U.M.

References

Anderson, K., & Harmeyer, J., "Forging a Separate Peace: The Alameda County 'MOMS' Program," 1(4) *Women, Girls & Criminal Justice* 1 (June/July 2000).

Federal Bureau of Prisons, Statistical Reporting Section, Office of Research and Evaluation, U.S. Department of Justice, January 21, 1999.

Johnston, D., *Effects of Parental Incarceration* (Simmons, 2000).

Kumar, K. & Griesdleck, J., "News from Home," *The Minneapolis Star Tribune*, September 30, 2000, p. E1.

Mumola, C. J., *Incarcerated Parents and Their Children* (Bureau of Justice Statistics, U.S. Department of Justice, August 30, 2000).

Simmons, C. W., "Children of Incarcerated Parents" (California Research Bureau, California State Library, March 2000).

Smith, G.T., "Adoption and Safe Families Act of 1997 and Its Impact on Prisoner Mothers and Their Children," 1(1) *Women, Girls & Criminal Justice* 3, (December/January 2000).

Chapter 26

The Alameda County MOMS Program

by Kris Anderson and Julie Harmeyer

HIDDEN CASUALTIES OF THE WAR ON DRUGS

The celebrated War on Drugs—conducted at such high cost with such questionable results—has devolved into a de facto War against Families. Consider these facts:

- Mandatory prison sentencing requirements, particularly for drug offenses, have significantly affected the incarceration of women by eliminating judicial discretion in sentencing. While women customarily fill lower-level roles in the drug distribution hierarchy and are consequently more susceptible to arrest on the streets, their minimal involvement leaves them without much information to provide prosecutors in exchange for reduced plea bargains.

- Over one-third of all women in prison are serving sentences for drug offenses.

- From 1980 until 1997, the number of women in prison increased six-fold, and women today find themselves incarcerated at twice the rate of men.

- In 1998 alone, an estimated 3.2 million women were arrested, comprising about one-fifth of all arrests. Of these, there were more than 250,000 female drug arrests, or about 18% of all drug law violation arrests (Greenfield & Snell, 1999).

This chapter originally appeared in Women, Girls & Criminal Justice, *Vol. 1, No. 4, June/July 2000.*

- Altogether, about 951,900—about 1% of all adult females in the U.S.—were under the care, custody, or control of the criminal justice system, with about 84,427 women actually in prison (Greenfield & Snell, 1999).

- Approximately 70% of these incarcerated women have children younger than 18 (Family and Corrections Network, 1986). Whereas the majority of California's female prison population is single (an estimated 42.9% have never been married), almost 80% of these single women have an average of two dependent children (Bloom, 1993).

The scope of the problem becomes clearer when one realizes that as recently as 1991 there were an estimated 1.5 million children with incarcerated parents, with an estimated 125,000 children under the age of 18, having mothers behind bars on any given day (Center for Children of Incarcerated Parents, 1992). This is particularly sobering in light of studies that estimate that the children of inmates are five to six times more likely to become incarcerated themselves (Bloom, 1993).

If we agree that these jail-orphaned children are perhaps the hidden casualties of the War on Drugs, then certainly there has been forged on the local level in California what many criminal justice professionals are beginning to tout as a "separate peace": The Alameda County Sheriff's Office "MOMS" Program (Maximizing Opportunities for Mothers to Succeed).

COLLABORATION BETWEEN COUNTY AND COMMUNITY AGENCIES

Sheriff Charles C. Plummer, in collaboration with other county agencies and community partners, is pioneering a new and innovative approach to reuniting mothers with their children and reducing recidivism in Alameda county jails in California's Bay Area. MOMS is a cooperative effort among many county and community agencies delivering health, mental health, substance abuse, social, law enforcement, and educational services. Key partnerships include, under subcontract to MOMS, three collaborating agencies:

- *BOSS (Building Opportunities for Self-Sufficiency).* Since its beginnings in 1971, BOSS has grown to become one of the Bay Area's premier providers of services to the homeless, the disabled, and low-income families.

- *Second Chance, Inc.* A non-profit counseling and recovery center, Second Chance operates the Phoenix Program. Phoenix focuses upon substance-related problems experienced by pregnant, post-partum, and parenting mothers.

- *Eden Information and Referral.* Eden I&R provides information regarding countywide affordable housing and human services.

PROGRAM GOALS

MOMS' goals are twofold:

- Promote the healthy development of children by increasing the capacity of their incarcerated mothers for self-sufficiency and parenting skills, with an emphasis on successful parent-child bonding; and

- Reduce recidivism among incarcerated pregnant women and incarcerated mothers of young children.

As its primary outcome, MOMS seeks to demonstrate a replicable, community-oriented criminal justice model for assisting incarcerated pregnant women and incarcerated mothers of young children toward self-sufficiency, family reunification, and reversal of previous adverse behaviors. MOMS is fortunate to have as its evaluator Dr. Barbara Bloom, a nationally renowned criminal justice consultant.

ADDRESSING THE PROBLEMS OF MOTHERS IN JAIL

Anyone familiar with the custodial setting knows how commonplace it is for mothers, by virtue of their incarceration, to effectively forfeit all bonding opportunities with newborn infants surrendered shortly after birth. Lamentably, it is also not atypical to see them lose custody of their older children as another direct consequence of incarceration. During the time mothers spend in jail, their children will often find themselves placed in any number of questionably protective foster environments. Most protective environment caregivers tend to do little or nothing to facilitate ongoing family contact while mother is doing time.

An ongoing concern among criminal justice professionals is the paucity of any meaningful resources available to single mothers in custody. It is suggested that the greatest loss many women experience while in custody is the loss of bonding between themselves and their children (Morton & Williams, 1998). The incarcerated woman must face a succession of seemingly insurmountable hurdles if she truly desires to be reunited with her children. Without adequate resources, she all too frequently finds herself powerless upon release to re-establish and maintain any meaningful contact with her children, much less regain actual custody.

A woman's inability to access community assistance, obtain safe housing, or attain any meaningful degree of economic self-sufficiency also works to preclude her successful re-entry into the community, thereby conspiring to doom her efforts to achieve family reunification. Released with little or no money and often homeless, many mothers have already lost track of their children's whereabouts.

Cost-Effective Approach

During an action planning workshop facilitated by Attorney General Janet Reno (the December 1999 "National Symposium on Women Offenders," sponsored by the U.S. Department of Justice), delegates from local detention facilities pointed out the incongruity of directing resources toward the reduction of recidivism only after a woman finds herself trapped in the long-term prison setting. Recognizing that the "decarceration" of female offenders incarcerated for drug and property crimes would not pose any significant threat to public safety, it was suggested to the Attorney General that some of these resources might be more cost-effectively brought to bear at the local, short-term custody level. It seems penny-wise and pound-foolish to allow family groups to disintegrate, when women could instead be diverted at the front end from lengthier, more expensive incarcerations in prison.

For this reason, the MOMS' agenda "to provide effective pre- and post-release assistance to incarcerated pregnant and parenting women" seems particularly unique. To our knowledge, no comparable jail-based program exists for incarcerated mothers in any other local detention facility in the United States.

Yet from a cost-benefit perspective, given the fact that female offenders are the fastest-growing segment of the incarcerated population, MOMS makes sense. It is recognized that the female offender population has significantly different needs than the male population, and that the female offender is usually the victim of some form of sexual or physical abuse. Further, women need vastly different types of health care, with the actual amount of medical services per inmate being higher for women than for the traditional male inmate (Gondles, 1998). Women substance abusers are typically more difficult to treat than their male counterparts, because they have more abuse issues and more physical problems (Kerr, 1998).

Overcoming the Culture of Custody and Preconceived Notions of Staff

One problem of considerable scope, which had to be overcome when initiating the MOMS program, was the culture of custody itself. Preconceived notions among staff about the questionable value of inmate programming presented formidable hurdles. Correctional officers and law enforcement personnel, finding themselves consistently exposed to "manipulative" behaviors of people in confinement, tend to become jaded about the suggestion that offering inmates meaningful rehabilitative programming has any real value.

Predictably, the first reaction of most law enforcement professionals to the notion of reunification is also an emotional one. To the police officer who must routinely place children in protective custody upon their mother's arrest, the very idea of reuniting a child with a substance-dependent parent is almost anathema. "Why would you want to give a crack baby back?" is a sentiment not uncommon among seasoned officers. "Perhaps the children are better off away from their dope-fiend mothers" is another typical response. Unfortunately, these seemingly reasonable gut reactions are based upon stereotypes, and fail to take into consideration the less than desirable consequences inherent to most care giving alternatives.

Focus on Bonding Between Mother and Child

The fact of the matter is that the incarcerated female is much more likely to be her child's primary caregiver than is the incarcerated male, dramatically increasing the impact of the mother's incarceration upon both child and inmate (De Constanza, 1998). However unconventional the family setting offered by the mother may be, and however lacking her parenting skills, it is vitally important to remember that to the child she is still mother. Unless her ministrations are grossly abusive, whatever limited parenting the mother does offer will generally still be preferred by the child to the offerings of even the kindest, most conscientious stranger.

Ironically, the single mother is far less likely to have an opportunity to interact meaningfully with her child while in custody than her single male counterpart. Statistically, the male will more probably enjoy some continued interaction with his offspring, simply because the primary caregiver is more likely to be the mother or some other family member emotionally invested in facilitating such encounters.

This syndrome was graphically illustrated to the author during an interactive parent/child bonding opportunity hosted in the custody setting by the Alameda County Sheriff's Office. Out of an inmate population approaching 4,500 at any given point, about 70 inmates are enrolled in the Sheriff's parenting program. Parents who faithfully participate in these weekday parenting classes are afforded the opportunity on Saturdays to interact with their children on a contact-visit basis inside the jail setting. This privilege is contingent, of course, upon the willingness of family members or foster care providers to transport the children to the jail. Of 40 men enrolled in the program, 35 typically interacted with their children. Conversely, of the 30 women enrolled, only three were able to interact with their youngsters. No one was willing to bring the remaining children to visit their mothers.

Remembering that emotional vacuums in childhood invite sociopathy in adult life, it is particularly troubling that the children of single mothers stand in far greater jeopardy of losing any sense of family whatsoever than do children from two-parent homes. It is estimated that about 64% of female state prisoners with minor children lived with the children prior to imprisonment. Conversely, only about 44% of imprisoned men actually lived with their children before going to prison, despite the fact that male prisoners have almost 15 times as many minor children as do female prisoners (Greenfield & Snell, 1999).

Once crucial windows of opportunity for bonding have been forfeited during the time that these mothers must languish in jail or prison, these opportunities do not come again. Instead, we read of, e.g., nearly 11,000 children murdered by parents and stepparents between 1976 and 1997, half of these murders having been committed by mothers and stepmothers. It seems particularly relevant in terms of missed bonding opportunities that mothers tended to murder their infants, whereas fathers generally killed their children at age eight or older (Greenfield & Snell, 1999).

It is this hidden, hellish ecology that MOMS seeks to identify and address. MOMS attempts to insert bonding opportunities into the custodial setting, and creates a bridge for re-entry back into the community through the provision of wraparound services. The continuity of ongoing pre-release and post-release case management is the program's key to success. The availability of case management and housing assistance, provided while the woman is in jail, is coupled with access to a range of community-based resources upon the woman's release, including primary care, substance abuse treatment, and mental health services.

CURRICULUM ENCOURAGES INCLUSION AND CONTINUUM OF SERVICES

Given its short-term custody mandate, MOMS' curriculum centers on 30-day "crash course" modules. Graduates of the first 30-day, Core One, module, which covers basic parenting and life skills, are eligible to enroll in a second 30-day, Core Two, skills application module. Given the time constraints, the MOMS Program is of necessity one of inclusion rather than exclusion. MOMS cannot afford a waiting list, and no one is "classified" out of the program. Staff are encouraged to find reasons for bringing women into the program, and every effort is made to facilitate each single mother's participation.

The Core Two module has proven to be the most exciting aspect of the MOMS Program. Upon being sentenced, MOMS women are eligible for transfer from the main county jail to the Sheriff's alternative custody facility, the Alameda County Community Re-Entry Center. An unlocked facility, the Center houses approximately 230 in-custody residents at any given time, 40 of these being women. (Of the approximately 4,500 inmates in Sheriff's custody, about one in 10 are women.) Recognizing that successful programs are positively correlated with respectful and compassionate staff (Bill, 1998), the Center strives to create more of a homelike, less-institutionalized environment.

One truly unique aspect of the program has been its capability to temporarily release MOMS residents so that they may participate in off-site community-based program opportunities. Once established at the Community Re-Entry Center, MOMS participants are entitled to leave the Center on day-furlough passes for the purpose of attending various parenting classes in the community as part of the Core Two application phase. In these non-custodial settings, MOMS participants have the opportunity to interact with their children, who will have been brought to the community settings for this purpose by family or foster care providers.

Research suggests that many women fear getting out of custody, experiencing tremendous pressure and a sense of hopelessness over such issues as housing, employment, transportation, and parenting, all the while trying to refrain from further criminal offenses (deGroot, 1998). One of the side benefits of the MOMS' community networking approach, therefore, has been that upon release women are encouraged by their assigned caseworkers to continue using these community-based parenting resources. In this way, relationships between the client and the respective service provider can become well established by the time the woman leaves custody.

A STEP TOWARD MAKING A DIFFERENCE

Will the MOMS model make a significant difference? The program at this writing only was in operation about six months, and it was still too early to determine statistically whether MOMS will have the hoped for effect in terms of reducing recidivism. Similarly, any measurable impact in terms of facilitating the bonding experience between participants and their children may not be discernible for years, if ever.

Still, the motivation behind MOMS is not unlike that of the seashore stroller who saw the need to save stranded starfish. The story is told of an elderly beachcomber, observed in the early morning as he stooped every few steps to pick up starfish washed ashore in the night. The old man would then flick each creature, in Frisbee fashion, back into the surf. Asked why he bothered, the old man explained that he performed this mercy daily lest hundreds of starfish perish under the heat of the coming sun.A passerby chided the old man, reminding him that since hundreds of thousands of starfish are similarly washed ashore on the world's beaches all the time, his futile rescues made no conceivable difference."Oh yeah?" said the man as he picked up yet another starfish and threw it back into the water. "Made a difference to that one!"

About the Authors

Lt. Kris Anderson is the Director of the Alameda County Sheriff's Community Re-Entry Center. Julie Harmeyer is the MOMS Program Manager.

References

Bill, L., "The Victimization and Re-Victimization of Female Offenders," 60(7) *Corrections Today*, 106, December 1998.

Bloom, B., "Incarcerated Mothers and Their Children: Maintaining Family Ties." In *Female Offenders: Meeting Needs of a Neglected Population* (Chapter 11) (American Correctional Association, 1993).

DeConstanza, E., "Why Women Offenders?" 60 (7) *Corrections Today*, 82, December 1998.

deGroot, G., "A Day in the Life," 60(7) *Corrections Today*, December 1998.

Family and Corrections Network, Proceedings of the First National Leadership Conference on Families of Adult Offenders (Author, 1986). (Available online: www.fcnetwork.org/.)

Gondles, J. A., "Addressing the Needs of the Female Offender," 60(7) *Corrections Today*, December, 1998.

Greenfield, L. & Snell, T., *Women Offenders* (Bureau of Justice Statistics Special Report, December, 1999).

Kerr, D., "Substance Abuse Among Female Offenders," 60(7) *Corrections Today*, 114, December 1998.

Morton, J. & Williams, D., "Mother/Child Bonding," 60(7) *Corrections Today*, 98, December 1998.

Part 4

Gender-Specific Classification, Risk Assessments, and Programming

Some years ago, a state corrections system greatly enhanced its security apparatus around maximum-security institutions for men; in the process, undoubtedly fearing a "discrimination" suit, the state made similar enhancements for its women's prison (which held maximum-security women) even though there was little evidence that the enhancement was actually necessary. Shifts in practice that affect men prisoners often also affect women prisoners. So, as women's prison populations have increased in recent decades, and as more attention is given to researching the conditions of women in confinement, management tools, such as risk and need assessments or classification procedures—that are used for men are generally transferred into use at women's prisons, again without regard to need, or even utility.

In recent years, some researchers, as well as some state and federal agencies, have begun to explore the possibilities and the feasibility of risk and need assessments, or classification procedures, that are more specifically applicable to and suitable for women. A key issue raised in the course of this work is whether these processes should be used simply to stir resources among incarcerated women, or whether they should be used to divert women from incarceration to community-based programs. Clearly, however, gender-specific assessments or classifications categories are being used to (potentially) connect women with program options of various sorts.

The eight chapters in this section are written by some of the key participants in the work that has been done in this area in recent years. Collectively, they cover a range of important issues that merit further detail and attention in the years to come. In these articles, we see the following:

- Russ Immarigeon argues that too many women are imprisoned, too few programs exist for women in either community- or institution-based corrections, and classification and risk assessment are most useful when they adequately link women with treatment options, especially when they divert women from more to less restrictive settings.

- British criminologist Pat Carlen examines the ability of gender-specific (and cross-national) projects for women to survive over time and identifies a series of important characteristics of such programs, including flexible organization, holistic approaches, and a realistic grasp of drug rehabilitation processes and possibilities.

- California-based criminal justice researchers and program developers Barbara Bloom, Barbara Owen, and Stephanie Covington report findings from their National Institute of Corrections-sponsored research on the theory, policy, and guiding principles of gender-specific principles and practices.

- Michigan practitioners Karen Woods and Julie Jenkins describe how to involve women prisoners in the development and operation of gender-specific planning and practices.

- Canadian criminologists Margaret Shaw and Kelly Hannah-Moffat explore the offender classification literature and develop feminist arguments for a women-centered approach to assessment procedures.

- Researchers Christopher Lowenkamp and Edward Latessa, both from the University of Cincinnati, review mega-analyses of risk/need predictors, assess whether separate instruments are needed for men and women, and argue that the causal factors behind criminogenic needs are different for each gender.

- Patricia Van Voorhis, also of the University of Cincinnati, and Lois Presser, of the University of Tennessee, report the under-use of validated risk instruments for women offenders and the disconnect between such instruments and decision-making on offender housing and program placement.

- Mary Grace, Jenny O'Donnell, William Walters, Walter Smitson, and Mary Carol Melton, all Ohioans, describe the substance abuse- and mental health-oriented women's assessment project operated in Cincinnati's probation department.

Chapter 27

Can Classifying Women Offenders Give Greater Priority to Community Corrections?

by Russ Immarigeon, M.S.W.

> In a risk society, that is a society, which is no longer, oriented towards positive ideals and solidarity but towards a negative solidarity of shared fears, justice gets an "actuarial" character.
> —Rene van Swaaningen, (van Swaaningen, 1999, p. 16)

ISSUES IN CLASSIFICATION OF FEMALE OFFENDERS

The development and use of risk- or need-based classification scales or schemes for criminal offenders or convicted prisoners has a rather long, albeit dispersed and fractured, history. One deficiency of this history is the paucity of effort that has gone into the development of specifically female-centered scales or schemes. Accordingly, now is a very good time to start exploring what, if anything, should be done about the classification of female offenders.

Several points can be made to begin this exploration:

This chapter originally appeared in Women, Girls & Criminal Justice, *Vol. 1, No. 4, June/July 2000.*

- Much more attention has been given the classification of female offenders in recent years.

- The use of male-oriented classification schemes for female offenders is widely seen as inappropriate.

- The nature and success of female-oriented classification schemes are uncertain, untested, and unclear.

- The common purposes for classifying female offenders are often inappropriate and probably incomplete.

- The classifying of female offenders, to the extent it happens, occurs too late in the criminal justice and corrections process, and is too narrowly constructed, forestalling the possibility of certain non-security-oriented objectives.

- The classification of women offenders is largely disconnected from the fiscal resources and actual programming necessary for the classification of women to have meaningful utility.

THE BASIC PROBLEM: TOO MANY WOMEN IMPRISONED

In the U.S., the number of incarcerated women has soared, even in states with relatively small correctional populations. The basic problem is that too many women in our correctional, i.e., jail and prison, systems should not be there. I have never visited a corrections facility where officials could not think of offenders who would be more appropriately served by community corrections or a less restrictive alternative. There are many other responses to offender crimes or circumstances that are more constructive for local communities and our general societies as well as for individual women. In short, we imprison too many women and we do not do enough to provide for non-incarcerative options. This stream of thought provided an undercurrent for discussions at the December 1999 National Symposium on Women Offenders, sponsored by the U.S. Department of Justice in Washington, D.C., for 54 state and local jurisdictional teams of policymakers.

Fifteen years ago, or thereabouts, I attended a Cropwood Conference gathering at Cambridge University on women and the prison system. At one point in the workshop discussions, an elderly male Crown Court judge said (more or less) the following: "I know I'll get in trouble for saying this, but I think women's place is on the pedestal." At this point, Chris Tchaikovsky, the head of Women in Prison, a lobbying group, sitting across the table from the judge, said, "Even women with tattoos." The judge, stiffly but assuredly, affirmed, "Yes." I repeat this story only to suggest that if there is need for a pedestal, and a pedestal may serve the useful function of keeping an issue at the forefront of our attention, the proper occupant of the pedestal should be the concept that too many women are imprisoned and not enough is done to do otherwise. Let's keep that in mind. It too frequently slips away from our vision when we speak about correctional policy matters. This is unfortunate not only because it is a decent reform notion, but also because it is, or at least should be, a key component of correctional planning and programming.

In saying that too many women are imprisoned, I suggest two problems:

1. If we are to establish a feminist, or women-centered, classification system, or simply a classification scheme that is responsive to the unique (or non-unique) needs of women, what can be done with the idea that many women are unnecessarily, improperly, or wrongfully imprisoned? How does this affect the nature of the classification procedures, processes, and products we are thinking about?

2. Once we conclude that some or many women do not belong in jail or prison, what processes should be established to place them elsewhere? Would a classification scheme be helpful in this endeavor or are there means better suited for this task?

WHY CLASSIFY?

Classification can be done for many reasons. Many years ago, I worked for a New York City agency that asked me to determine the equipment and other nonpersonnel-related needs of "free medical clinics" in the city. The purpose of my survey was to see who needed what so that the city could dispense some extra funds accordingly. As it happened, I went to a Catholic Worker House on the Lower East Side. Ostensibly, Catholic Worker Houses, part of the movement started by Peter Maurin and Dorothy Day, gave food and shelter to "Bowery Bums" and the alcoholic homeless. But in fact, they gave food and shelter to anyone who needed food and shelter. When I entered the Catholic Worker House, I was brought upstairs and introduced to Dorothy Day herself. I was a bit nervous, as I recognized her, although she wasn't introduced to me as Dorothy Day. With the objective of completing my assignment, I asked such questions as "How many people come here?" and "How much food or shelter do you give people?" She dismissed my questions completely, and said: "When someone comes here looking for a bowl of soup, we give him a bowl of soup. When someone wants a bowl of soup and a blanket, we give him a bowl of soup and a blanket. If somebody doesn't want anything, we don't give him anything."

Dorothy Day's response has made me think many times over subsequent years. The basic concerns she raised are: What are you doing what you are doing for? And, what can you do once you know what you want to do? These concerns, in brief, are matters of purpose, need, and resources.

CORRECTIONAL OBJECTIVES VS. CORRECTIONAL RESOURCES

I'm not certain how often, if ever, prison systems have the resources to do what they want beyond incapacitation and housing, and even here, where overcrowding exists, these objectives usually fall short of the mark. California offers a good example of the dilemma I am trying to identify. In the mid-1990s the California Senate commissioned a report on female inmate and parolee issues. In reading the Commission's final report (1994), several observations came to mind about female classification:

- *No Correlation Between Females' Classification and Placement.* The classification levels in California's prisons correspond to the behavior of male inmates. Male inmates are therefore housed according to their security-based classification levels.

These levels reflect the relative levels of risk various inmates are expected to pose, based on a variety of background and institutional behavior factors. However, similar correlations between classification levels and female inmate behavior do not exist. In theory, these classification levels are used for determining eligibility for community-based programming. In the prisons, different classification levels are actually housed together.

- *After Classification, Little Appropriate Programming.* California has been toying with the idea of using community-based programs for greater numbers of women offenders, in part because these women are suitable for such programs and in part because the state needs more prison space for male inmates. So, and I'm guessing here, a female inmate group of some size has been classified for such programs. But only some of the proposed programs are authorized and in place. Furthermore, the programs in place are underutilized.

  Such underutilization of community-based options for women is common elsewhere in the U.S. In New York, for at least some years, there was a large contingent of female prisoners who were eligible for work release programs but were not sent to them because too few work-release beds were available in the community, even when the state resorted to "double-bunking" work-release beds.

- *Over-Classification.* Despite the lack of security-related issues with female offenders, women inmates in the state are still often prohibited from participating in community-based drug treatment, mother/infant, and community work service programs because they have classification levels that suggest they are a security risk—even though the state acknowledges that they are classified according to male standards, not female ones. Also, despite higher classification levels, they are apparently safe enough to house with women of lower classification levels. They are, in other words, over-classified.

Such classification schemes get curiouser and curiouser, and drift quickly away not just from the interests of female offenders but, I would suspect, even from those of the corrections system. This California example, nonetheless, gives a glimpse at some of the difficulties involved in American corrections with the idea of diverting or displacing women (and other) offenders from incarceration.

KEY CONCERNS: TIMING AND PLACEMENT

Classification as an information-gathering and screening device for housing, program, or security purposes most often occurs late in the criminal justice process. This raises several concerns that involve timing and the in/out question. Put another way, when should classification (information-gathering) schemes be applied and which women should be incarcerated? In general, I think classification is done too late in the criminal justice process, *after* sanctions are given. Classification should be emphasized *before* such decisions are made. In my mind, these two concerns—timing and the in/out question—are connected because factual information about risks and needs, as well as the availability of resources to address these risks and needs, can be packaged in such a way as to reduce the use of confinement in U.S. jails and prisons. In doing this, we alter the context within which we would be addressing female prisoners, including considerations about the how, why, and when of classifying them in one way or another.

In short, if prison is an option of last resort, the gathering and organizing of information on female—as well as male—offenders should be done earlier in the system. Greater emphasis should be given to pre-sentence planning; and such pre-sentence planning can be later useful for either community programming or institutional confinement purposes. Classification, as I am broadly conceiving it, would be more useful if seen as part of a continuum of information-gathering activities, from initial police and pretrial activities to criminal court and corrections activities.

It is important to acknowledge the larger context within which classification schemes of any sort are developed and how these schemes are related to diversion or displacement concerns. When speaking of diversion or displacement, it is also important to focus on fiscal resources as well as individual women, because money wasted on unnecessary confinement eats away at funds that might otherwise be available for community-based options.

If women are to be incarcerated, classification may have an important role to play. But before incarcerating women, what role can classification—or information gathering as I am reconceiving it—play in assuring that women are not needlessly imprisoned? This is a major policy concern; one too often neglected. It is a question that must be routinely addressed. If I go to a women's prison today, I must ask not just which section(s) of the prison should these women be moved to, but also whether it is best, with reference to both needs and risks, for these women to be here at all. Where else might they better be? This concern challenges the status quo, I think, but in the end it produces a better classification scheme. What happens, after all, when classification suggests that something should be done that cannot be done, at least in jail and prison settings?

THE PROBLEM OF WOMEN'S IMPRISONMENT

Too often, decisions that affect women's imprisonment, from decisions to incarcerate to decisions about the availability of programming, are made without considering the background and characteristics of women offenders.

Nancy Harm (1992) has observed that prior to the 18th century incarcerated men, women, children, the mentally ill, first offenders, repeat offenders, debtors, and felons were not separated from each other. They were simply thrown together in large rooms. Through the reformist efforts of women such as Dorothea Dix, female offenders were eventually separated from male offenders, mainly, however, to maintain administrative discipline or to avoid sexual scandals. As Harm notes:

> The issue was not exclusively better treatment of women by their separa-
> tion from men or better protection of women from abuse and mistreatment
> by men. Rather, the prevailing rationale seemed to be that female criminals
> were more depraved than were male criminals and therefore influenced male
> inmates to commit sexual improprieties; thus, male criminals could better
> be reformed without the presence of female inmates. (p. 93)

This problem of submitting women to ill-fitting procedures or processes occurs outside the prison system too. Several years ago, Lani Guinier, Michelle Fine, and Jane Ballin (1997) surveyed students at the University of Pennsylvania Law School. They found that the pedagogy of teaching at the law school ill suited female law students. It did not fit who they were or address their needs. As a result, these students tended to lose much, from their confidence to their career focus, in the course of their legal education. In a more recent speech, however, Guinier (1998) noted that the problem with legal education for women was not an individual problem of the women themselves, but an institutional problem of the ways law schools conduct their educational business. In short, those aspects of female students—such as the ability to listen, a preference for teamwork, or the tendency to say things only when they are clearly formulated or need saying—may be a failing part of their law school career, but a key part of their success in later legal practice.

In a similar vein, the problems inherent in discussions of female classification may be less those of female offenders than of female correctional systems. If this is the case, then it must be addressed as such.

WHY BASE CLASSIFICATION ON WEAKNESSES RATHER THAN STRENGTHS?

In much, if not all, of the research on prison classification, offenders are already in prison, and thus it is simple, practical, and within job descriptions or research assignments not to address whether something other than incarceration is appropriate. Thus, researchers look at negative dimensions, such as levels of dangerousness or of social, economic, health, or family needs.

Why can't we reverse this assumption, and assume, at least for the time being, that the purpose of predictive, or risk and need, studies is to estimate what resources are needed in the community to maximize a jurisdiction's ability to provide community-based programming for as many offenders as possible, so as to reduce reliance on incarceration. Furthermore, why can't we begin to examine female offenders through what social workers call a "strengths perspective?" The correctional approach generally relies on "locking down" deficits, with the routine result that missing pieces remain missing. The strengths perspective builds upon what already exists, as a matter of past experience, available skills, and so forth. The correctional approach assumes that all is broken, while the strengths perspective assumes that some things simply need fixing while other things can, in fact, help fix them.

WHAT DOES CLASSIFICATION HAVE TO DO WITH PROGRAMMING?

Classification procedures clearly have some benefit for institutional credibility. Administrators and policy makers alike can claim, "We have our inmates sorted out. We have successfully classified them." Thus, the correctional system has the appearance of orderliness. But does this have anything to do with the availability, not to mention the success, of correctional programming? Moreover, do classification procedures improve the ability of institutions to identify who needs what type of treatment?

In the U.S., the National Center on Addiction and Substance Abuse at Columbia University estimates that 81% of women in prison are substance abuse-involved offenders (Peugh & Belenko, 1999). Moreover, there are gender-specific aspects of women's substance abuse problems. Peugh and Belenko offer as one example:

Even more so than for men, the ability of substance-involved women inmates to earn a living may be essential to avoid returning to lives of drug use and dealing, theft, and prostitution. Because women often enter substance abuse treatment with greater feelings of helplessness to change their present conditions than do males, it is crucial to provide vocational testing, skills assessment, and career and educational guidance to give them the skills, resources, and confidence to support themselves and their families.

A process that simply identifies a woman's substance abuse problem is incomplete as a form of classification. Yet a process that identifies women with substance abuse problems and connects them to appropriate substance abuse services is completely useful, particularly when those services are indeed available. I do not wish to posit the categorization of these differences as being a choice that has to be made between correctional and social work approaches. This would miss my point. The strengths perspective, as only one possible alternative, can refer to many disparate approaches, many of them having little to do with boosting the presence and power of professional social work. For instance, Aboriginal approaches, as I understand them, build not just upon the individual strengths of offenders, victims, family members, and extended kinship networks, but also the collective strengths of Native communal formations.

It is also worth noting some empirical realities. Several years ago in the U.S., Merry Morash and Tim Bynum at Michigan State University surveyed state-level administrators, prison superintendents, and jail wardens about female offender programming. One-quarter of the state-level administrators said, "Classification and screening didn't provide needed information, were not adapted to women, and were not useful in matching women's needs to programming" (Morash & Bynum, 1998, p. 30). Jail administrators also gave rare instances of using classification procedures to match women offenders with correctional programming (Ibid., p. 30).

SUGGESTED NEW DIRECTIONS FOR THE CLASSIFICATION FOR WOMEN

Several new directions with regard to the way we approach the classification of female offenders and women prisoners have already been inferred in my comments so far.

Before addressing the classification of women prisoners, it is necessary to assess, probably more thoroughly than has been the case, whether these women should be prisoners at all. This is, obviously, not simply the task of prison staff. In fact, they should probably be the least involved of all because they are, much like female offenders themselves, the subject of executive, legislative, probation, and court decisions made previous to their introduction to those women who come before them in their custody and for their supervision. This concern is a broad, systemwide matter. All these other parties, plus community-based advocates, offenders' families and extended family-members, and program liaisons to the criminal justice system, must be more integrally involved with the development of information about female offenders that can be used by different decision-making bodies to reduce the frequency with which women enter the correctional system at either the local, state, or federal levels. In particular, it is important to focus on how different mechanisms, from probation pre-sentence reports or defense-based sentencing plans to family group conferences, can improve their capacity to obtain and process information that helps to divert or displace women who are otherwise likely to receive a term of imprisonment.

Also, to what extent does concern about the classification of women offenders or prisoners delay, divert, or displace attention from perhaps more important concerns, such as the planning of actual programming, the provision of financial resources to establish and continue such programming, and the ability to have qualified staff present to interact with women in need of certain services? At this point, classification's role as a control mechanism becomes increasingly clear. Many schools, themselves total institutions, have about as many students as correctional institutions have prisoners. Yet, other than by crude distinctions such as gender, grade level, or grade scores, students are left unadorned by sophisticated (or unsophisticated) classification levels. Still, services, or at least a modicum of services, are provided them, according to expressed or observed need. Obviously, this is not a completely sound approach, as can be witnessed in current American rhetoric about school violence, and it creates a vacuum within which decidedly arbitrary, scatterbrained "proposed remedies" can rattle around until they self-destruct or result in (un)usually bad public policy. And the lack of classification—risk/need—scales for students does not mean adequate student services are not in fact provided them, but, as with prisoners, it is not clear either that classification would in turn result in more services, more appropriately delivered, to individual students.

Other suggestions, not so immediately clear from what I've said so far can also be made. While dramatic increases in the incarceration of women have been noted, less has been said about the racial and ethnic make-up of this population increase. In the U.S., Mauer and Huling (1995) found that black women have become imprisoned, over the past two decades, at a rate higher than white women, black men, or white men; Latina women fall somewhere between black women and white women. More globally, Tonry (1997) observes: "Members of *some* disadvantaged minority groups in every Western country are disproportionately likely to be arrested, convicted, and imprisoned for their violent, property, or drug crimes" (p. 1). Accordingly, it is essential that we be not just racially or ethnically sensitive, but also cognizant of the fact—the reality—of racially and ethnically skewed prisoner populations. Diversion and displacement schemes must not be similarly disproportioned. Community-based resources and targeting strategies that direct themselves to the characteristics, needs, and strengths of these populations must also be consciously empowered, identified, and financed.

More research is required. Recently, several qualitative case studies have appeared that demonstrate the relevance of process to outcome in the measurement of criminal justice efforts. In particular, works by McMahon (1999), who has examined the official response to instances of sexual assault and harassment in a Canadian jail and criminal justice training center, and by Lynch (1998), who has examined the office and practice culture of a local California parole office, suggest that, regardless of the ideal of particular measures, the implementation of these measures is another matter, and one that significantly affects the outcome. Accordingly, it is important that we invest more time in assessing the construction and carrying out of the risk/need classification scales we use now, or might use in the future. A broader understanding of who does what and how, may be as important as, or more important than, what is done and where.

About the Author

Russ Immarigeon, M.S.W., is the editor of Women, Girls and Criminal Justice.

References

California Senate Concurrent Resolution Commission, *Female Inmates and Parole Issues* (Author, June 1994).

Guinier, L., "Lessons and Challenges of Becoming Gentlemen," 24(1) *New York University Review of Law & Social Change* 1-16 (1998).

Guinier, L., Fine, M., & Ballin, J., *Becoming Gentlemen: Women, Law School and Institutional Change* (Beacon Press, 1997).

Harm, N.J., "Social Policy on Women Prisoners: A Historical Analysis," 7(1) *Affilia*, 90-108 (1992).

Lynch, M., "Waste Managers? The New Penology, Crime Fighting, and Parole Agency Identity," 32(4) *Law & Society Review* 839-869 (1998).

Mauer, M. & Huling, T., *Young Black Americans and the Criminal Justice System: Five Years Later* (The Sentencing Project, 1995).

McMahon, M., *Women on Guard: Discrimination and Harassment in Corrections* (University of Toronto Press, 1999).

Morash, M. & Bynum, T., *Findings From the National Study of Innovative and Promising Programs for Women Offenders* (Michigan State University, 1998).

Peugh, J. & Belenko, S., "Substance-Involved Women Inmates: Challenges to Providing Effective Treatment," 79(1) *The Prison Journal* 23-44 (March 1999).

Tonry, M., "Ethnicity, Crime, and Immigration," in Tonry, Ed., *Ethnicity, Crime, and Immigration: Comparative Cross-National Perspectives* (Crime and Justice: A Review of Research, Volume 21) (The University of Chicago Press, 1997).

Van Swaaningen, R., "Reclaiming Critical Criminology: Social Justice and the European Tradition," 3(1)*Theoretical Criminology* 5-28 (1999).

Chapter 28

Questions of Survival in Gender-Specific Projects for Women in the Criminal Justice System

by Pat Carlen, Ph.D.

INTRODUCTION

Widespread international concern is urging various governments to develop and co-ordinate gender-specific policies for female offenders to slow down the rate of their offending and imprisonment or to engender flexible programs that reduce the destructive pain and psychological damage of time spent in custody. However, a main problem has been development of projects that survive for more than a year or two. The primary reason projects close down (or change their role) is usually financial, though funding problems often mask a range of other shortcomings, such as changing objectives, poor or adverse publicity, loss of gender-specificity, non-use by the courts, and inappropriate expectations or evaluations by funding agencies. One of the objectives of my current, ongoing cross-national research into women's imprisonment and its alternatives, therefore, has been to investigate projects for female lawbreakers which, while remaining true to their gender-specific and reductionist objectives, continue to thrive at least two years beyond their inception.

Here, I first outline the priority of concerns or issues raised by agency managers in the United States, the United Kingdom, Scotland, and Israel when discussing the necessary con-

This chapter originally appeared in Women, Girls & Criminal Justice, *Vol. 2, No. 4, June/July 2001.*

ditions for surviving without the loss of integrity as gender-specific projects. Then, I raise three of the more difficult issues discussed by these managers.

CRITICAL SURVIVAL CHARACTERISTICS OF GENDER-SPECIFIC PROJECTS

In my interviews, the managers of a range of custodial and non-custodial gender-specific projects suggested that, in order to survive without losing identity, integrity, and effectiveness, gender-specific criminal justice projects for women should ideally have at least the following seven characteristics:

1. *Evolutionary and Flexible Organization.* All respondents stated that projects should constantly monitor the relationship between the services offered by the program and the varied or constantly changing situations of the women actually attending the project at a particular time. Furthermore, they argued that organizational needs should come second to the needs of program participants, thereby ensuring that the form and structure of the organization is appropriate to the delivery of services tailored for whom it was set up to serve.

2. *Democratic Ownership of Innovation.* Democratic ownership of innovation—i.e., when all staff members are involved in the evolution of new ideas and ways of operating—was mentioned in varying types of projects and was seen as especially important in custodial settings, where disciplinary staff frequently feels excluded from more innovative types of decision-making. A democratic mode of policy formation was viewed as an essential prerequisite to high staff morale, which, in turn, was seen as essential for the success of project innovation and survival.

3. *Holistic Approach to Women's Needs, Inter-Agency Working Relationships, and the Spatial Proximity of Multi-Agency Service Delivery.* A holistic approach to service delivery was seen as desirable in both custodial and non-custodial settings, with a priority of successful inter-agency or multi-agency communication. In custodial settings, the stress was on building effective working relationships with agencies in the community, but always under the auspices of an approach that sees project participants not as "female offenders" but as "women who break the law." Several of the most impressive project managers pointed to the geographical clustering of multi-agency services as being integral to the success of their service delivery because it eases women's access to useful services and minimizes both inter-professional distrust and the accidental subversion of each others' endeavors by agencies which share the same clients.

4. *Insistence on a Realistic Approach to Drug Rehabilitation.* Agency managers insisted on the importance of those providing financial resources recognizing the realities of drug rehabilitation common to all projects. Although they were generally prepared to require drug-free environments, project workers almost always insisted on giving relapsed participants "as many chances as it took." This resulted, however, in their calling for, and devising, much more sensitive and complex "accountability" evaluations.

5. *Resistance to Erosion of Gender-Specificity.* Because of the relatively small numbers of females eligible to take part in some women-only noncustodial projects, there was often pressure to extend the facilities to men. This pressure was felt particularly in smaller jurisdictions, where it was feared that spare capacity might result in the loss of funding. However, there was general agreement that facilities for women should be "ringfenced" (i.e., have narrowly defined, strict, and often legal, limitations placed on the purposes for which funds can be used). Shared-site provision (however arranged) is either underused or (subsequent to its underuse) ends up being revamped as a male-only facility. This is because women's histories of male physical and sexual abuse make them reluctant to put themselves at risk of male violence or harassment in mixed projects. Similarly, workers insisted that programs developed in other countries or for men (such as cognitive skills acquisition) should not be parachuted into projects as prisoner-processing packages with a universal application; instead, they should be gender-assessed and adapted to the very specific histories and attributes of the actual women currently attending the project.

6. *Explicit Principles of How Human Beings Should Be Treated.* Despite project leader claims that a main concern was crime reduction, they all admitted to a more fundamental philosophy—a vision of the equal treatment of all human beings, including lawbreakers and crime victims. At the most fundamental level, therefore, they often saw that a project's relative longevity depends on its continuing success at convincing courts, the public, crime victims, and criminal justice professionals of a common interest in reducing future re-offending through improvements in the quality of women's lives in the present.

7. *Excellent Public Relations.* All interviewees took seriously the importance of educating the public policymakers and the courts. Larger agencies employed specialist public relations officers, but innovative project directors—for example, sheriffs in the United States, a prison governor in Scotland, and Rehabilitation Authority officials in Israel—all welcomed opportunities to address public fears about offending behavior and program risk and to spread word about both the low risk presented by the majority of women who come before the courts and the often incredibly complex and gender-specific social and health issues that must be addressed in order to reduce the risk of their re-offending.

QUESTIONABLE SURVIVAL STRATEGIES FOR GENDER-SPECIFIC PROJECTS

In addition to the seven agreed upon survival strategies, program managers also talked about three strategies about which they expressed more ambivalence. Managers repeatedly mentioned two strategies, while I raised the third, which I will discuss first.

Employment of Ex-Drug Users or Lawbreakers

All of the noncustodial projects I visited cited the employment or other involvement of former drug users or lawbreakers as an organizational strength and, in some cases, the fulfillment of a stipulation for funding. Yet, none of the projects had developed education, training, or career plans for these "nonprofessional" and non-salaried or poorly paid helpers. As a result of conversations on this very issue with many ex-lawbreakers, I suggested two difficulties with the prevalent ideology that the employment of ex-offenders in rehabilitation projects is unambiguously to the benefit of all involved—though there is no doubt that, as the managers claimed, the projects are usually the beneficiaries of such authoritative, committed, and cheap assistance.

First, although it is often asserted that the employment of ex-clients can confer legitimacy on an organization's claims to therapeutic authority, some offenders are often initially wary of "going to projects run by people no better than myself."

The second, more serious issue, however, concerns the desirability of having rehabilitated ex-prisoners or drug-users embracing the "ex-offender" role and, most seriously of all, of exploiting (outside a proper career and salary structure) the goodwill and experience of those who have suffered multiple disadvantage in the service of professional counselors and state officials. In raising this question, I am well aware that some of the most successful noncustodial projects for female offenders owe their existence and persistence to the vision and commitment of people who themselves were once addicts or prisoners. These visionary leaders, however, are exceptional and usually they rise above the label "ex-prisoner." However, even here, no doubt should exist that they should (but seldom do) receive proper recompense and recognition for their labors.

Protection by an Official or Umbrella Organization Versus Independent, Visionary, and Project-Specific Leadership

A majority of the managers I interviewed ruminated on the age-old question of the merits and demerits of charismatic leadership versus organizational stability; most of them (whether part of a larger organization or not) eventually concluded that their own projects would not have lasted so long had they not been blessed with some very strong campaigning or lobbying leadership during the first few years when a recurring challenge was the need to establish the need for gender-specific women's projects. However, those who were part of a larger organization also claimed that, because the leadership of the parent organization had been supportive in principle, belonging to it had offered them a measure of protection against critics and funding problems.

A minority of the managers said a main reason for their survival was their favorable position as part of a larger service provider or as members of an umbrella organization. However, they continually had to fight for recognition of women's different requirements when they were part of an organization (e.g., a mixed prison site) that also served males.

All respondents, however, pointed to the dual need for committed, strong, and innovative leadership *and* for the stability of established organizational structure, while recognizing inevitable tensions between the two. Evolutionary and democratic structures were developed, then, to cherish innovation, avoid organizational stagnation, and protect leaders from burnout. Nonetheless, it seems that, in every country visited, the most common threat to gender-specific projects in the early stages of their development was posed by the overlong hours worked by project leaders driven to deliver a holistic and very demanding service outside of any effective official recognition that the social, economic, and health burdens of women in trouble with the law are, at the present time, usually much more complex than those of males.

Accountability as Measurement Versus Accountability as Quality

Project leaders and staff centered on the ways they should or could account for their work and satisfy employers and/or those providing funding that they were getting value for their money. All of the managers recognized the moral obligation and practical necessity (i.e., project-survival) of accountability for the money spent, yet all, without exception, felt that financial backers and employers entertained unrealistic or inappropriate expectations of the job that must be done and how it could be adequately assessed.

Those individuals or groups providing financial resources, including the general public, had *unrealistic* expectations which were the easiest to deal with, and gradually could be changed in an appropriate direction by increasing information about the histories and experiences of the project-clients and the difficulties of rehabilitating women with a myriad of social and economic difficulties.

Expectations that project workers felt inappropriate were generally related to scepticism that the quality of their work was amenable to quantitative measurement. However, because such expectations resulted in the annual reporting requirements being simply comprised of measurements of output and performance upon which, in turn, the continuation of their funding/existence depended, they also exercised the minds and ingenuity of project leaders a great deal.

Carter, Kein, and Day (1992) point out that it is usually impossible to measure the impact on society of specific social policies, for three primary reasons:

1. The problem of multiple objectives;

2. The difficulties of specifying and understanding the relationships between intermediate outputs and output measures; and

3. The inevitable time lag between input and impact, especially in programs "where the benefits only become fully apparent over decades."

Attempts to measure the output of rehabilitation projects for women fall afoul of all three strictures. Paper and other routine organizational outputs tell nothing about either the quality or the relative importance of audited activities in reducing future recidivism or in improving the quality of life of program participants and their children.

Project leaders, however, have to meet the challenge of presenting their work in measurable form. The most favored method was to compare the cost of custodial and noncustodial programs for women, with special emphasis on the hidden costs relating to childcare when a woman goes to jail or prison. The second method, especially popular with project leaders running innovative (and maybe comparatively costly) projects in custodial (or semi-custodial) settings, was to develop indicators demonstrating women's increased "accountability," "self-knowledge," and so forth, all put forward as factors conducive to reducing risk to the community in the future.

A third approach, however, took the line that the agency or program should be entrepreneurial about relevant assessment criteria. These more critical strategy sets out to develop qualitative indices of the following:

- The necessary conditions for maintaining client services;

- Organizational strength (staff recruitment, retention, and qualifications);

- Community support, relationships with other organizations (especially the media and the formal criminal justice system), range of visitors, and academic and other citations;

- Evidence of innovatory qualitative capacity (the ability to meet the changing needs of clients and the criminal justice system);

- Qualitative annual growth factors (not just a numerical assessment but also a measure of increased quality of service, such as more productive time spent with clients); and

- Developed arguments about the amelioration of client need and community risk (sometimes related but not always the same thing).

Limits to the quantification of qualitative measures, however, became most apparent when projects were explicitly committed to making and sustaining qualitative changes not amenable to measurement, and when the assessment of at least some of the success of those changes called for moral rather than quantitative evaluations. Many project workers expressed the view that when they are faced with women on the edge of despair, or even death, one prerequisite for the preservation of life and the maintenance of staff morale is official recognition that qualitative inputs are necessary. Such qualitative information is not amenable to measurement as *performance indicators*. Moreover, time-consuming but life-supporting, responses (*inputs*) that involve listening, kindness, and comfort, together with other *nonprogrammable* therapies may be *good in themselves*.

CONCLUSION

For me, the huge gap between the knowledge and experiences of workers in gender-specific projects for women and that of their various publics sharply suggested that, despite the increase in public rhetoric about women's difference, a need still exists for vigorous campaigning about the complexity of the relationships between social and criminal justice for women.

About the Author

Pat Carlen, Ph.D., is a professor of sociology at the University of Bath School of Social Sciences.

References

Carter, H., Klein, R., & Day, P., *How Organizations Measure Success: The Use of Performance Indicators* (Routledge, 1992).

Chapter 29

Gender Responsive Strategies: Theory; Policy; Guiding Principles and Practices

by Barbara Bloom, Ph.D., Barbara Owen, Ph.D. and Stephanie Covington, Ph.D.

This chapter originally appeared as two separate articles in Women, Girls & Criminal Justice, *Vol. 4, No. 6, October/November 2003 and Vol. 5, No. 2, February/March 2004.*

INTRODUCTION

In reviewing current knowledge of the ways gender shapes behavior and life experience, this chapter offers a review of the characteristics of women offenders, current criminal justice practice, theoretical perspectives, and the gendered effects of current policy. We examine the context of women's lives and their involvement in the criminal justice system, to provide the empirical and theoretical foundation for developing gender- and culturally responsive policy and practice. A central finding is that recognizing and responding to the differences between male and female offenders improves effectiveness in managing women offenders in community and institutional settings.

We also describe the need for a gender-responsive vision for the criminal justice system, wherein the behavioral and social differences between female and male offenders are seen to have specific implications for policy and practice. "Gender-responsive" means creating an environment through site selection; staff selection; and program development, content, and material that reflects an understanding of the realities of women's lives and addresses the issues of the participants. These approaches are multi-dimensional and they are based on theoretical perspectives that incorporate women's pathways into the criminal justice system. They address social and cultural factors as well as therapeutic interventions. Therapeutic approaches address issues such as abuse, violence, family relationships, substance abuse, and co-occurring disorders. They provide a strength-based approach to treatment and skill building. The emphasis is on self-efficacy. Here, we outline guiding principles, general strategies, and implementation steps for the development of gender-responsive policies, practices, programs, and services.

As the criminal justice system becomes more responsive to the issues of managing women offenders, it will be more effective in targeting the pathways to offending that both propel and return women into the criminal justice system. Gender-responsiveness improves outcomes for women offenders because it considers their histories, behaviors, and life circumstances. An investment in gender-responsive policy and procedures produces dividends in the long run for the criminal justice system, the community, and women offenders and their families.

The research conducted for this project reviewed multidisciplinary research literature, including topics in health, family violence, substance abuse, mental health, trauma, employment, and education. Additional data pertinent to managing women offenders within the criminal justice framework was collected through national focus groups and interviews with experts representing various criminal justice agencies, as well as women in the criminal justice system. Official and technical reports concerning women offenders, policies and procedures, and existing academic research and other materials relevant to these topics were then collected and analyzed. Finally, an advisory group representing community corrections, jail, prison, and parole professionals reviewed multiple drafts of these findings.

Overall, the research found that consideration of the differences in male and female pathways into criminality, their differential response to custody and supervision, and their differing realities can lead to better outcomes for both men and women offenders. Policies, programs, and procedures that factor in these empirical, gender-based differences in behavior and response to supervision can make the management of women offenders more effective; enable more suitable staffing and funding; decrease staff turnover and sexual misconduct; improve program and service delivery; decrease the likelihood of litigation against criminal justice agencies; and increase the gender-appropriateness of services and programs.

CHARACTERISTICS OF WOMEN IN THE CRIMINAL JUSTICE SYSTEM

The first step in developing gender-responsive criminal justice policy and practice lies in understanding gender-based characteristics. In addition to offense and demographic characteristics, the specific life factors that shape patterns of offending should be included in gender-responsive planning. Current research shows that women offenders differ from their male counterparts regarding personal histories and pathways to crime. Women offenders are more likely to have been the primary caretaker of young children at the time of arrest, for example. They are also more likely to have experienced physical and/or sexual abuse and they have distinctive physical and mental health needs. They are also more likely to be a substance abuser and far less likely to be convicted of a violent offense. They pose less of a danger to the community.

Women Offender Demographics

Women offenders are disproportionately women of color, low income, undereducated, and unskilled with sporadic employment histories. They are less likely to have committed violent offenses and more likely to have been convicted of crimes involving drugs or property. Often their property offenses are economically driven, motivated by poverty and/or the abuse of alcohol and other drugs. Women confront life circumstances that tend to be specific to their gender, such as sexual abuse, sexual assault, domestic violence, and primary caregiver of dependent children. Approximately 1.3 million minor children have a mother who is under criminal justice supervision and approximately 65% of women in state prisons and 59% of women in federal prisons have an average of two minor children. The characteristics of criminal justice-involved women thus reflect a population that is marginalized by race, class, and gender. For example, African-American women are over-represented in correctional populations. They comprise only 13% of women in the United States; however, nearly half of women in prison are African American and they are eight times more likely than white women to be incarcerated.

The majority of women in the criminal justice system are on probation or parole. Eighty-five percent of women offenders are under community supervision. In 2000, over 844,697 women were on probation and 87,063 were on parole. Women represented an increasing percentage of the probation and parole populations in 2000 as compared to 1990; 22% percent of all probationers in 2000 (vs. 18% in 1990) and 12% of those on parole (vs. 8% in 1990) were women.

In contrast to women in jail, prison, and parole, nearly two-thirds of women on probation are white. Women under institutional supervision are more likely to be women of color. Nearly two-thirds of those confined in jails and prisons are African American, Hispanic, or other (non-white) ethnic groups. About 60% of women on probation have completed high school; 72% have children under 18 years of age. Despite the fact that the greatest number of women offenders are under community supervision, there is far less information available on their characteristics than on those in custodial settings.

Women Offenders' Backgrounds

Family History. Women in the criminal justice system are more likely than women in the general population to grow up in a single parent home. Incarcerated women are more likely than are men to have at least one family member who has been incarcerated.

Abuse History. The prevalence of physical and sexual abuse in the childhood and adult backgrounds of women under correctional supervision has been supported by the research literature; abuse within this segment of the population is more likely to occur than in the general population. Probation statistics show a dramatic gender difference in that over 40% of the women, compared to 9% of the men, reported being abused at some time in their lives. Women in prison are three times more likely to have a history of abuse than men in prison.

Substance Abuse. The link between female criminality and drug use is very strong. Research consistently indicates that women are more likely to be involved in crime if they are drug users. Substance abuse is also linked to trauma and mental health issues. Approximately 80% of women in state prisons have substance abuse problems. About half of women offenders in state prisons had been using alcohol, drugs, or both at the time of their offense. On every measure of drug use, women offenders in state prisons reported higher usage than their male counterparts—40% of women offenders compared to 32% of male offenders had been under the influence of drugs when the crime occurred.

Physical Health. Women frequently enter jails and prisons in poor health and they experience more serious health problems than do their male counterparts. Such poor health is often due to poverty, poor nutrition, inadequate health care, and substance abuse. It is estimated that that 7% to 10% of men go to prison sick call daily compared to 20% to

35% of women. The specific health consequences of long-term substance abuse are significant for all women, particularly if they are pregnant.

Mental Health. Many women enter the criminal justice system having had prior contact with the mental health system. When compared to women in the community, women in prison have higher incidents of mental disorders. One-quarter of women in state prisons have been identified as having a mental illness. The major diagnoses of mental illness are depression, post-traumatic stress disorder (PTSD), and substance abuse.

Children and Marital Status. Approximately 70% of all women under correctional supervision have at least one child under the age of 18. Two-thirds of incarcerated women have minor children; about two-thirds of women in state prisons and half of women in federal prisons had lived with their young children before entering prison. It is estimated that 1.3 million minor children have a mother who is under correctional supervision and more than a quarter million minor children have mothers in jail or prison.

Women under correctional supervision are more likely than the general population never to have been married. In 1998, nearly half of the women in jail and prison reported that they had never been married; 42% of women on probation reported that they had never been married.

Education and Employment History. In 1998, an estimated 55% of women in local jails, 56% of those in state prisons, and 73% of women in federal prisons had a high school diploma. Approximately 40% of the women in state prisons reported that they were employed full time at the time of their arrest. Most of the jobs held by women were low-skill, entry-level jobs, with low pay. Women are less likely than men to have engaged in vocational training prior to incarceration.

Offense Characteristics

Accompanying this increase in population are several questions about women offenders. Why has women's involvement with the criminal justice system increased so dramatically? Are women committing more crimes? Are these crimes becoming more violent? The data on arrests demonstrates that the number of women under criminal justice supervision have risen disproportionately to arrest rates. For example, the total number of arrests of adult women increased by 38.2% between 1989 and 1998, while the number of women under correctional supervision increased by 71.8%. Overall, women have not become more violent as a group. In 2000, women accounted for only 17% of all arrests for violent crime. About 71% of all arrests of women were for larceny-theft or drug-related offenses.

Women on probation have offense profiles that differ somewhat from those of incarcerated women. Nationwide, almost half of women on probation have been convicted of property crimes (44%). Public order offenses represent 27% of female probationers, drug offenses represent 19%, and only 9% committed violent crimes.

U.S. Bureau of Justice Statistics data indicate that violent offenses are the major factor in the growth of the male prison population; however, this is not the case for women. For women, drug offenses represent the largest source of growth. In 1998, approximately 20% of women in jails or prisons had been detained for, or convicted of, violent offenses. The majority of offenses committed by women in prisons and jails are nonviolent drug and property crimes.

WOMEN OFFENDERS AND CRIMINAL JUSTICE PRACTICE AND PROCESSES

Gender makes a difference in current criminal justice practice. Differences in supervising women in the community and managing them in correctional settings have significant implications for criminal justice policy and practice.

Two key findings emerged from our research. First, the overwhelming number of male offenders often overshadows the issues relevant to women offenders. This lack of numbers of females relative to male offenders, however, must not be interpreted as an indication of their lesser importance. Second, the criminal justice system often has difficulty applying to women offenders policies and procedures that have been designed for male offenders.

Differences in women's pathways to the criminal justice system, women's behavior while under supervision or in custody, and the realities of women's lives in the community have significant bearing on the practices of the criminal justice system. There is significant evidence that the responses of women to community supervision, incarceration, treatment, and rehabilitation differ from those of men. These differences between men and women under community supervision and in custody been documented in terms of the following:

- Lower levels of violence and threats to community safety in their offense patterns;

- Responsibilities for children and other family members;

- Relationships with staff and other women offenders;

- Vulnerability to staff sexual misconduct;

- Programming and service needs, especially in terms of health, mental health, substance abuse, recovery from trauma, and economic/vocational skills; and

- Reentry into the community and community integration.

Many systems, however, lack a written policy on the management and supervision of female defendants, probationers, inmates, or parolees. In focus group interviews, many managers and line staff reported that they often had to manage women offenders based on policies and procedures developed for male offender. They also reported difficulties in modifying these policies to more appropriately develop an effective response to women's behaviors within the correctional environment.

Assessment and Classification Procedures

Traditionally and statistically based on experiences with male offenders, community assessment procedures and prison classification systems are often unable to accurately assess both the risk and needs of women throughout the criminal justice system. For example, since danger to the community and violence are a consideration for only a minority of women, the utility of applying these existing systems based on this male behavior is called into question. The purpose of community assessment procedures and classification systems for women offenders needs further investigation, both in the form of empirical exploration and work with jurisdictions concerned with more closely matching gender characteristics to criminal justice practice.

Women's Services and Programs

The salient features that propel women into crime include family violence and battering, substance abuse, and the struggle to support themselves and their children. Both in institutional settings and in community agencies, minimal attention has been given to the gender differences that maximize successful outcomes and the rehabilitation of women. In order to address female criminality, services and programs must be developed that address the histories, backgrounds, and experiences that promote this behavior. One approach to increasing both attention to these issues and the provision of women's services was suggested by many focus group participants and some of the written policies: Criminal justice agencies and systems should make planning, funding, and administering women's services an integral part of executive decision-making. Through the development of a "Department of Women's Services," or the creation of a high-level administrative position, women's services and programs could receive the appropriate level of support within a system dominated by the male offender.

Staffing and Training

Staffing and training are core issues in the appropriate management and supervision of women in the criminal justice system. A 1998 national survey of 40 prison systems found that over one-half of them did not have specialized training on the female offender. Specialized training for practitioners working with female offenders is justified on the basis of real differences between male and female offenders along three dimensions: demographics, needs, and personalities. Community corrections staff, institutional staff, and senior management need appropriate information, attitudes, skills, and guidelines to enhance their work with women offenders.

Staff Sexual Misconduct

During the past 10 years, the problem of staff sexual misconduct has received significant attention by the media, the public, and many correctional systems. Misconduct can take many forms, including inappropriate language, verbal degradation, intrusive searches, sexual assault, unwarranted visual supervision, denying of goods and privileges, and the use or threat of force. It includes disrespectful, unduly familiar or threatening sexual comments made to inmates or parolees. It is also important to note that female officers have also been involved in this serious misconduct, although the more publicized pattern focuses on male staff with female inmates.

Staff sexual misconduct can be aggravated by poor grievance procedures, inadequate investigations, and staff retaliation against inmates or parolees who "blow the whistle." Standard policies and procedures in correctional settings (e.g., searches, restraints, and isolation) can have profound effects on women with histories of trauma and abuse, and they often act as triggers to retraumatize women who have PTSD. A focus group respondent noted that staff sexual misconduct should be defined as a security issue, in that such behavior damages the safety and security of staff and inmate alike.

Staff sexual misconduct has gained most of its publicity and research attention in the prison setting, but there is also significant concern within community corrections and jails. The issue plays out differently due to the community location and the interaction between women offenders and community corrections staff.

THE CONTEXT OF WOMEN'S LIVES: A MULTIDISCIPLINARY REVIEW OF RESEARCH AND THEORY

Our discussion of the implications of gender within the criminal justice system is based on a simple assumption: Responding to the differences between women and men in criminal behavior and their antecedents is consistent with the goals of all criminal justice agencies. These goals are the same for all offenders, whether male or female. Across the criminal justice continuum, the goals of the system typically involve sanctioning the initial offense, controlling behavior while under its jurisdiction and, in many cases, providing interventions, programs, and services to decrease the likelihood of future offending. At each stage in the criminal justice process, the differences between female and male offenders affect behavioral outcomes and the ability of the system to address the pathways to offending and thus achieve its goals and management practice.

Understanding the context of women's lives in the general population and under criminal justice supervision is an important step in developing gender-responsive policy and practice. The multidisciplinary review of research and practice documents the ways in which gender differences shape the lives of women and men and specifically how gender influences their behavior and programming in the criminal justice system. In particular, such an examination provides a greater understanding of the factors that impact women offenders and their experiences in the criminal justice system.

Research on the differences between women and men suggests that social and environmental factors, rather than biological determinants, account for the majority of behavioral differences between males and females. While purely physiological differences influence some basic biological processes such as health and medical care and a range of reproductive issues, many of the observed behavioral differences are the result of differences in gender socialization, gender roles, gender stratification, and gender inequality.

Race and class can also determine views of gender appropriate roles and behavior. Differences exist among women based on race and socioeconomic status or class. Regardless of their differences, they are expected to incorporate gender-based norms, values, and behaviors of the dominant culture into their lives.

Contemporary theorists note that most theories of crime were developed by male criminologists to explain male crime. Historically, theories of women's criminality have ranged from biological to psychological and from economic to social. Social and cultural theories were applied to men, while individual and pathological explanations were applied to women. Until recently, most criminology theory ignored the dynamics of race and class and how these factors intermixed with gender to influence criminal behavior patterns. Across groups of women, class differences, often interwoven with racial and ethnic differences, also emerge in forms such as poverty, disease patterns, and treatment responses. Contemporary theorists argue for the integration of race, class, and gender in any analytic framework to study the experiences of women in the criminal justice system. Without such a framework, it is impossible to draw an accurate picture of the experiences of women offenders.

The Pathways Perspective

Research on women's pathways into crime indicates that gender matters significantly in shaping criminality. Among women, the most common pathways to crime are based on survival of abuse and poverty, and substance abuse. Recent work on women's lives establishes that women are at greater risk for certain experiences because of their gender: sexual abuse, sexual assault, domestic violence, and the responsibility and care of their children. Pathway research identifies key issues in producing and sustaining female criminality: histories of personal abuse as girls and women; mental illness and substance abuse; economic and social marginality; homelessness; and relationships.

Relational Theory and Female Development

Relational theory increases our understanding of gender differences and the different ways in which women and men develop psychologically. The importance of relational theory is reflected in the recurring themes of relationship and family in the lives of female offenders. Disconnection and violation, rather than growth-fostering relationships, characterize the childhood experiences of most women in the correctional system. In addition, these women have often been marginalized because of race, class, and culture, as well as by political decisions that criminalize their behavior (e.g., the war on drugs).

The role of relationships provides a key difference in the lives of female and male offenders. The dominant theme of connections and relationships threads throughout lives of women offenders. When criminal justice policy ignores this theme, the ability to improve women's lives through correctional intervention is significantly diminished. Additionally, when the concept of relationships is ignored in the correctional environment, the ability of the system or agency to operate effectively is undermined. Thus, a relational context is critical to success in addressing the reasons women commit crimes, their motivations and the ways they change their behaviors, and their reintegration into the community.

Trauma Theory

The terms "violence," "trauma," "abuse," and "PTSD" are often use interchangeably. One way to clarify these terms is to think of trauma as a response to violence. Over the past 100 years, a number of studies have investigated trauma, and various experts have written about the process of trauma recovery. It is now understood that there are commonalities between rape survivors and combat veterans, between battered women and political prisoners, between survivors of concentration camps and survivors of abuse in the home. Because the traumatic syndromes have basic features in common, the recovery process also follows a common pathway.

Addiction Theory

A generic definition of addiction that is helpful when working with women is the chronic neglect of self in favor of something or someone else. This view conceptualizes addiction as a kind of relationship. The addicted woman is in a relationship with alcohol or other drugs, a relationship characterized by obsession, compulsion, non-mutuality, and an imbalance of power. The relational aspects of addiction are also evident in the research that indicates that women are more likely than men to turn to drugs in the context of relationships with drug-abusing partners in order to feel connected through the use of drugs. In addition, women often use substances to numb the pain of non-mutual, non-empathic, and even violent relationships. Therefore, it is important to integrate trauma theory and relational theory when developing substance abuse services for women.

THE GENDERED EFFECTS OF CURRENT POLICY

Gender is also important in examining the differential effect of national and state drug policy. Nationwide, the number of women incarcerated for drug offenses rose by 888% from 1986 to 1996. Compelling evidence exists to support the contention that much of the increase in criminal justice control rates for women is a result of the war on drugs. Inadvertently, the war on drugs became a war on women, particularly poor women and women of color. The emphasis on punishment rather treatment has brought many low-income women and women of color into the criminal justice system. Women offenders who would have been given community sanctions in past decades are now being sentenced to prison. Mandatory minimum sentencing for drug offenses has significantly increased the numbers of women in state and federal prisons.

While attention on the impact of the war on drugs has mostly focused on the criminal justice system, policy changes in the areas of welfare reform, housing, and other social policy arenas have combined to create a disparate impact on drug-abusing women and women of color. Important policy areas that affect the lives of women offenders and their children include welfare benefits, drug treatment, housing, education, employment, and reunification with children.

Our multidisciplinary review of the context of women's lives concludes that contemporary perspectives of female criminality can provide a solid foundation for the development of a gender-responsive criminal justice system. The current theories have particular strengths. First, a focus on women's lives and their personal histories highlights the connections among crime, substance abuse, violence, and trauma. Second, the pathways perspective applies a variety of research methods in the search for explanations of criminal behavior. Third, the pathways and relational explanations offer specific targets for correctional intervention. These descriptions are particularly useful for developing an empirical framework for gender-responsive principles, policy, and practice.

A NEW VISION

We put forth the following guiding principles and strategies to improve management, operations, and treatment of women offenders in the criminal justice system. Evidence drawn from a variety of disciplines and effective practices suggests that addressing the realities of women's lives through gender-responsive policy and programs are fundamental to improving outcomes in all phases of the criminal justice process.

The following principles and strategies offer fundamental building blocks to criminal justice policy and a blueprint for the development of a gender-responsive approach:

- *Gender:* Acknowledge that gender makes a difference.

- *Environment:* Create an environment based on safety, respect, and dignity.

- *Relationships:* Develop policies, practices, and programs that are relational and promote healthy connections to children, family, significant others, and the community.

- *Services and Supervision:* Address the issues of substance abuse, trauma, and mental health through comprehensive, integrated, culturally relevant services and appropriate supervision.

- *Economic and Social Status:* Improve women's economic/social conditions by developing their capacity to be self-sufficient.

- *Community:* Establish a system of community supervision and reentry with comprehensive, collaborative services.

The following strategies should be used in putting principles into practice:

- *Adopt:* Each principle is adopted as policy on a system-wide and programmatic level.

- *Support:* Principle adoption and implementation receives full support of the administration.

- *Resources:* An evaluation of financial and human resources occurs to ensure adequate implementation and allocation adjustments made to accommodate any new policies and practices.

- *Training:* Ongoing training is essential to the implementation of gender-responsive practices.

- *Oversight:* Oversight of the new policies and practices is included in management plan development.

- *Congruence:* Procedural review is essential in order that procedures are adapted, deleted, or written for new policies.

- *Environment:* Ongoing assessment and review of the culture/environment occur to monitor attitudes, skills, knowledge, and behavior of administration, management, and line staff.

- *Evaluation:* An evaluation process is developed to consistently assess management, supervision, and services.

Acknowledge That Gender Makes a Difference

The first and foremost principle in responding appropriately to women is to acknowledge the implications of gender throughout the criminal justice system. The criminal justice field has been dominated by the "rule of parity," but equal treatment does not necessarily mean the same treatment is appropriate for women and men. Supervision, services, and treatment should be appropriate to gender. The data is quite clear as to distinguishing aspects between women and men. Women come into the criminal justice system through different pathways; respond to supervision and custody differently; have differences in terms of substance abuse, trauma, mental illness, parenting responsibilities, and employment histories; and represent a different level of risk within the system. In order to address services, supervision, and treatment for women, these gender differences must first be acknowledged.

The differences between women and men are well documented across a variety of disciplines and practices. Increasing evidence shows that both social and environmental factors account for the majority of these differences. Physiological differences can influence some basic biological processes related to health such as reproduction issues. However, many observed behaviors are the result of gender-related differences such as socialization, gender roles, gender stratification, and gender inequality. The nature and extent of women's crime and the way they respond to supervision reflects such gender differences. These differences include:

- Women and men differ in levels of participation, motivation, and degree of harm caused by their criminal behavior;

- Female crime rates, with few exceptions, are much lower than male crime rates. Women's crimes tend to be less serious than men's crimes. The gender differential is most pronounced in violent crime statistics, where women's participation is profoundly lower;

- The interrelationship between victimization and offending appears more evident in women's lives. Family violence, trauma, and substance abuse contribute to women's criminality and shape their offending patterns; and

- Women respond to community supervision, incarceration, and treatment differently than male counterparts. Women are less violent while in custody, but have higher rates of disciplinary infractions. They are more influenced by their responsibilities and concerns for their children as well as their relationships with staff and other offenders.

Implementation steps:

- Make women's issues a priority;

- Allocate both human and financial resources to create women-centered services;

- Designate a high-level administrative position responsible for oversight of management, supervision and services; and

- Recruit and train personnel and volunteers interested and qualified to work with women under criminal justice supervision.

Create an Environment Based on Safety, Respect, and Dignity

Research from a range of disciplines, including health, mental health, and substance abuse, shows that safety, respect, and dignity are fundamental to behavioral change. Therefore, a safe and supportive setting for supervision is critical in order to improve behavioral outcomes for women. The profile of women in the criminal justice system, discussed earlier, indicates that many of them have grown up in less than optimal family and community environments. In interactions with women offenders, criminal justice professionals must be aware of the significant patterns of emotional, physical, and sexual abuse that the women may have experienced. The criminal justice setting should not re-enact earlier life experiences. A safe, consistent, and supportive environment is the cornerstone of a corrective process. Because of a low risk to public safety and lower levels of violent crime, women should be supervised, wherever possible, with the minimal amount of restrictions required to meet public safety guidelines.

Research from the field of psychology, particularly trauma studies, indicates that environment cues behavior. We now have a better understanding of what a woman's environment needs to reflect if it is to affect the biological, psychological, and social consequences of trauma. The corrections culture, influenced by punishment and control, is often in conflict with the culture of treatment. Corrections is based on a control model, while treatment is based on a model of behavioral change. Both models should be integrated to produce positive outcomes for women offenders. Such an integration should acknowledge the following facts:

- Substance abuse professionals and literature report that women require a treatment environment that is safe and nurturing as well as a therapeutic relationship that is one of mutual respect, empathy, and compassion;

- A physically and psychologically safe environment produces positive outcomes for women;

- Studies in child psychology demonstrate that the optimal context for childhood development consists of a safe, nurturing, and consistent environment. Such an environment is also necessary for changes in adult behavior;

- Safety is identified as a key factor in effectively addressing the needs of domestic violence and sexual assault victims;

- Custodial misconduct has been documented in many forms including verbal degradation, rape, and sexual assault;

- Classification and assessment procedures often do not recognize the lower level of violence by women in their offense and behavior while under supervision. This can result in women's placement in higher levels of custody in correctional institutions and inappropriate assessment of risk in the community; and

- Low public safety risk suggests that women can be managed in the community; their needs for personal safety and support suggest the importance of safe and sober housing.

Implementation steps:

- Conduct a comprehensive review of the institutional or community environments wherein women are supervised to provide an ongoing assessment of the current culture;

- Develop policy that reflects an understanding of the importance of emotional and physical safety;

- Understand the effects of childhood trauma in order to avoid further traumatization;

- Establish protocols for reporting and investigating claims of misconduct; and

- Develop classification and assessment systems that are validated on samples of women offenders.

Develop Policies, Practices, and Programs That Are Relational and Promote Healthy Connections

The role of relationships in women's lives is fundamental to an understanding of the connections and relationships that weave their way throughout female offenders' lives. When the concept of relationship is incorporated into policies, practices, and programs, a criminal justice system's or intervention agency's effectiveness is enhanced. This concept is critical when addressing the reasons women commit crimes; the impact of interpersonal violence on their lives; the importance of children; the relationships between women in an institutional setting; the process of women's psychological growth and development; the environmental context needed for programming; and community reentry challenges.

A basic difference in the way women and men "do time" is related to their ability to develop and maintain relationships. Studies of women offenders highlight the importance of relationships and the fact that criminal involvement often develops through relationships with family members, significant others, or friends. This is qualitatively different than the concept of "peer associates," which is often cited as a criminogenic risk factor in assessment instruments. For many females, it is the connection to significant others that is often key to their involvement in crime. Interventions must acknowledge and reflect the impact that these relationships have on women's current and future behavior. Important relationship findings include:

- Developing mutual relationships is fundamental to women's identity and sense of worth;

- Women suffer from isolation and alienation created by discrimination, victimization, mental illness, and substance abuse;

- Studies in the substance abuse field indicate that partners, in particular, are an integral part of women's initiation into substance abuse, continuing drug use, and relapse. They can also influence retention in treatment programs;

- Theories that focus on female development posit that the primary motivation for women throughout life is the establishment of a strong sense of connection;

- The majority of women under criminal justice supervision are mothers of dependent children. Many women try to maintain their parenting responsibilities while under community supervision or while in custody and many plan to reunite with one or more of their children upon release from custody or community supervision; and

- Studies have shown that relationships among women in prison are also important. Women often develop close personal relationships and pseudo families as a way to adjust to prison life. Research on prison staff indicates that correctional personnel are often not prepared to provide an appropriate response to these relationships.

Implementation steps:

- Develop training with relationships as a core theme for all staff and administrators. Such training should include importance of relationship, staff-client relationship, professional boundaries, communication, and the mother-child relationship;

- Examine all mother and child programming through the eyes of the child (i.e., child-centered environment, context) and enhance the mother-child connection and the connection to child caregivers and other family members;

- Promote supportive relationships among the women; and

- Develop community and peer support networks.

Address Substance Abuse, Trauma, and Mental Health

Substance abuse, trauma, and mental health are critical, interrelated issues in the lives of women offenders. These three issues have a major impact on a woman's experience of community correctional supervision, incarceration, and transition to the community, in terms of both programming needs and successful reentry. Although therapeutically linked, these issues historically have been treated separately. One of the most important developments in health care over the past several decades is the recognition that a substantial proportion of women have a history of serious traumatic experiences that play a vital, and often unrecognized, role in the evolution of a woman's physical and mental health problems.

The salient features that propel women into crime include family violence and battering, substance abuse, and mental health issues. The interconnections between substance abuse, trauma, and mental health are numerous. For example, substance abuse can occur as a reaction to trauma or it can be used to self-medicate symptoms of mental illness; mental illness is often connected to trauma; and substance abuse can be misdiagnosed as mental illness. Other considerations include:

- Trauma, particularly in the form of physical or sexual abuse, is closely associated with substance abuse disorders in women. A lifetime history of trauma is present in 55% to 99% of female substance abusers;

- Women who have been sexually or physically abused as children or adults are more likely to abuse alcohol and other drugs, and may suffer from depression, anxiety disorders, and PTSD;

- Regardless of whether mental health or substance abuse disorders are considered primary, co-occurring disorders complicate substance abuse treatment and recovery. An integrated treatment program concurrently addresses both disorders through treatment, referral, and coordination;

- Gender differences, as well as race and ethnicity, must be considered in determining appropriate diagnosis, treatment, and prevention; and

- Treatment programs are better able to engage and retain women clients if they are targeted to their culture.

Implementation steps:

- Service providers need cross-training in substance abuse, trauma, and mental health;

- Resources, including skilled personnel, must be allocated;

- Service delivery environments must be closely monitored for emotional and physical safety; and

- Service providers and criminal justice personnel need training in cultural sensitivity so they can understand and respond to issues of race, ethnicity, and culture.

Improve Women's Self-Sufficiency by Improving Their Economic and Social Conditions

Addressing both the social and material realities of women offenders is an important aspect of correctional intervention. The female offender's life is shaped by her socio-economic status; her experience with trauma and substance abuse; and her relationships with partners, children, and family. Most women offenders are disadvantaged economically and socially, which is compounded by trauma and substance abuse histories. Improving outcomes for women requires that they receive preparation through education and training to support themselves and their children.

Most women offenders are poor, undereducated, and unskilled. Many have never worked, have sporadic work histories, or have lived on public assistance. Other factors that impact their economic/social condition include:

- Most women offenders are female heads of household. In 1997, nearly 32% of all female head-of households lived below the poverty line;

- Research from the domestic violence field has shown that material and economic needs such as housing and financial support, educational, and vocational training, and job development are essential to women establishing separate lives from their abusive partners;

- Research on the effectiveness of substance abuse treatment has noted that, without strong material support, women presented with economic demands are more likely to return to the streets and cease treatment; and

- Recent changes in public assistance (Temporary Assistance for Needy Families) affect women disproportionately and negatively impact their ability to support themselves and their children. In approximately half of the states, convicted drug felons are ineligible for benefits. When eligible, they still may not be able to apply for benefits until release from custody or community supervision. They cannot access treatment or medical care without Medicaid. Additionally, their conviction can also preclude them from being eligible for public housing or Section 8 subsidies.

Implementation steps:

- Allocate resources for comprehensive, integrated services within community and institutional correctional programs that focus on the economic, social, and treatment needs of women. Ensure that women leave prison and jail with provisions for short-term emergency services (subsistence, lodging, food, transportation, clothing);

- Provide traditional and non-traditional training, education, and skill opportunities to assist women in earning a living wage; and

- Provide sober living space in institutions and in the community.

Establish a System of Community Supervision and Reentry With Comprehesive Collaborative Services

Women offenders face specific challenges as they reintegrate back into the community from jail or prison. Women on probation also face challenges in their communities. In addition to the female offender stigma, they may carry additional burdens such as single motherhood, decreased economic potential, lack of services and programs targeted for women, responsibilities to multiple agencies, and a general lack of community support. Navigating through myriad systems that often provide fragmented services and conflicting requirements can interfere with supervision and successful reintegration. There is a need for "wraparound" services—a holistic and culturally sensitive plan for each woman that draws on a coordinated range of services located within her community. The types of organizations that should work as partners in assisting women that reenter the community include mental health systems; alcohol and other drug programs; programs for survivors of family and sexual violence; family service agencies; emergency shelter, food, and financial assistance programs; educational organizations; vocational and employment services; health care; the child welfare system, child care, and other children's services; transportation; self-help groups; consumer advocacy groups; organizations that provide leisure options; faith-based organizations; and community service clubs.

Challenges to successful completion of community supervision and reentry for women offenders have been documented in the research literature. They can include housing, transportation, child care, employment, reunification with children/families, peer support, and fragmented community services. There is little coordination among community systems that link substance abuse, criminal justice, public health, employment, housing, and child welfare. Other considerations for successful reentry and community supervision include:

- Substance abuse studies have found that women's issues are different than that of men and comprehensive services should include, but not be limited to, life skills, housing, education, medical care, vocational counseling, and assistance with family preservation;

- Studies from fields such as substance abuse and mental health have found that collaborative, community-based programs offering a multidisciplinary approach foster successful outcomes among women;

- Substance abuse research shows that an understanding of the interrelationships among the women, the program, and the community is critical to the success of a comprehensive approach. Comprehensive also means taking into consideration a woman's situation and desires related to her children, other adults in her family or friendship network, and her partner(s);

- Data from female offender focus groups indicate that the following needs, if unmet, put women at risk for criminal justice involvement: housing, physical and psychological safety, education, job training and opportunities, community-based substance abuse treatment, economic support, positive role models, and a community response to violence against women. They are critical components of a gender-responsive prevention program;

- Research has found that women offenders have a great need for comprehensive community-based wraparound services. This case management approach has been found to work effectively with women, as it addresses their multiple treatment needs; and

- Relational theory indicates that approaches to service delivery based upon ongoing relationships that make connections among different life areas and work within women's existing support systems are especially congruent with female characteristics and needs.

Implementation steps:

- Create individualized support plans and wrap the necessary resources around the woman and her children;

- Develop the one-stop shopping approach for community services. The primary service provider should also facilitate access to other needed services; and

- Use a coordinated case management model for community supervision.

POLICY CONSIDERATIONS

As agencies and systems examine the impact of gender on their operations, policy-level changes are a primary consideration. A variety of existing policies developed by the National Institute of Corrections Intermediate Sanctions for Women Offender Projects, the Federal Bureau of Prisons, the American Correctional Association (ACA), the Minnesota Task Force on the Female Offender, and the Florida Department of Corrections contain crucial elements of a gender-appropriate approach. Gender-responsive elements derived from this analysis are:

- Create parity;

- Commit to women's services;

- Review standard procedures for their applicability to women offenders;

- Respond to pathways;

- Consider community; and

- Include children and family.

IMPLICATIONS FOR PRACTICE

After policy development, the next step concerns the specific ways that gender-appropriate policy elements can be incorporated into practice to improve service delivery and day-to-day operations and procedures. A critical step is to identify the problems created by the lack of knowledge about women offenders and the problems created by gender-neutral practice. Important factors for gender-responsive practice are discussed below:

Building Community Support

Building community support is an important factor in effective community corrections. In order to improve the circumstances of women offenders and their children, a gender-responsive approach particularly emphasizes community support. There is a critical need to develop a system of support within our communities that provides assistance to women (housing, job training, employment, transportation, family reunification, child care, drug and alcohol treatment, peer support, and aftercare) who are returning to their communities. Women transitioning from jail or prison to the community must navigate myriad systems that often provide fragmented services, and this can pose a barrier to their successful reintegration.

Prevention is another aspect of building community support. In focus groups conducted for this study with women in the criminal justice system, participants identified a number of factors when asked how things could be different in their communities to help prevent them from criminal involvement.

Restorative Justice

Restorative justice is an important vehicle for building community support for criminal justice services. The framework for restorative justice involves relationships, healing, and "community," factors that are common with female psychosocial developmental theory. Restorative justice focuses on mechanisms such as victim-offender mediation, family group conferencing, and community circles of support, rather than on punishment and retribution. This perspective is consistent with both the level of harm represented by women offenders and the need to target their pathways to offending. Social support, including intimate relationships, social networks, and communities, is a key variable in a range of effective interventions.

Women offenders are good candidates for restorative justice and community corrections. Because women commit far fewer serious or violent offenses and pose less risk to public safety than male offenders, they are in a preferred position to take the lead in participating in programs of restorative justice. Similarly, because of their suitability for community correctional settings, women offenders may be in a better position to model the significant benefits to the community that may be achieved through effective restorative justice programs.

Reentry and Wraparound Services

Reentry programs can serve as a model for enhancing community services. All offenders confront the problem of reentry into the community and conventional institutions. The obstacles and barriers faced by women offenders are, however, specifically related to their status as women. In addition to the stigma attached to a criminal conviction and a likely history of substance abuse, women carry additional burdens as a result of individual level characteristics such as single motherhood, decreased economic potential, and structural characteristics, such as the lack of services and programs targeted for women, responsibilities to multiple agencies, and lack of community support for women in general. Often, women in the larger community confront this same harsh reality. Service systems in most communities and institutions are fragmented and lack coordination, with the goals and values incompatible among various programs.

Considerations for Gender-Responsive Programs and Services

The development of gender-responsive programs and services involves a number of factors. For women who are in the system, a gender-responsive approach would include services both in context, which includes structure and environment, and in content, i.e., are comprehensive services that relate to the reality of women's lives. Programs need to consider the larger social issues of poverty, abuse, race, and gender inequalities, as well as the individual factors that impact women in the criminal justice system. Services also need to be responsive to the cultural backgrounds of women. Culture may be defined as a framework of values and beliefs and a means of organizing experience. Cultural sensitivity is sensitivity to the differences in ethnicity, including language, customs, values, and beliefs, in order to create a sense of inclusiveness.

Programming that is gender- and culture-responsive emphasizes support. Service providers need to focus on women's strengths, and to recognize that a woman cannot be treated successfully in isolation from her social support network (relationships with her partner, family, children, and friends). Coordinating systems that link a broad range of services will promote a continuity-of-care model. Such a comprehensive approach would provide a sustained continuity of treatment, recovery, and support services, beginning at the start of incarceration and continuing through the full transition to the community.

Program Evaluation

Program evaluation is another step in building gender-responsiveness. As the vision of gender-responsiveness evolves, documenting the effectiveness of gender-responsive practice addresses the need for empirical research on the outcomes of gender-responsive programs. Process evaluation identifies the fit between the principles of gender-responsivity and program implementation. This type of evaluation measures the environments within which programs operate. Process evaluation measures the unique "culture" of individual programs, such as the relationships between staff and women offenders, relationships between women, and rules and regulations so as to determine how these factors may impact the program. It is also important to gain the input of the women participants in terms of their feedback on the services provided. Outcome evaluations describe measures of program success or failure. They examine the short- and long-term impact of the intervention on program participants. Ideally, outcome measures used in evaluations should be tied to program mission, goals, and objectives. Also, outcome measures should go beyond the "traditional" recidivism measures to assess the impact of specific program attributes on the pathways to female criminality.

CONCLUSION

This chapter raises the importance of understanding and acknowledging differences between female and male offenders and the impact of those differences on the development of gender-responsive policies, practices, and programs in the criminal justice system. This analysis has found that addressing the realities of women's lives through gender-responsive policy and practice is fundamental to improved outcomes at all phases of the criminal justice system. We maintain that consideration of female and male pathways into criminality, their differential response to custody and supervision, and their differing program requirements can result in a criminal justice system that is better equipped to respond to both male and female offenders.

About the Authors

Barbara Bloom, Ph.D., teaches at the Department of Criminal Justice Administration at Sonoma State University in Rohnert Park, California. Barbara Owen, Ph.D., teaches at California State University, Fresno. Stephanie Covington, Ph.D., teaches at the Center for Gender and Justice in La Jolla, California. Note: Copies of the full report, Gender-Responsive Strategies: Research, Practice, and Guiding Principles for Women Offenders (June 2003), on which this chapter is based are available from the National Institute of Corrections Information Center, 1960 Industrial Circle, Suite A, Longmont, CO 80501, (303) 682-0213 or (800) 877-1461, (e-mail) info@nicic.org; (website) www.nicic.org.

Chapter 30

Involving Women Prisoners in Gender-Specific Planning for Girls

by Karen A. Woods, M.S.W. and Julie Jenkins, M.A.

REFOCUSING SERVICES IN MICHIGAN

In 2000, the Michigan Bureau of Juvenile Justice hired a Gender Specific Specialist to focus more attention on services to girls in the juvenile justice system. To assist the specialist, a Gender Specific Task Force was created. This task force, which meets regularly, is comprised of representatives from public and private residential treatment agencies, courts, schools, prosecutors' offices, and community organizations. As a result of this increased focus, several institutions have retooled their programming for girls, but more still needs to be done for their benefit.

The Gender Specific Task Force was developed in response to federal initiatives and state law, especially 1997 legislation that mandated advocacy for and development of community-based alternatives to detention for delinquent youth. Early in this process, Michigan also became involved with the National Institute of Corrections, which was developing gender-specific and female-responsive curricula for program and treatment services. Michigan also wanted to minimize the detention of girls becoming involved with the state's courts. Throughout this process, little funding was available, especially in recent years when the state's budget crisis has been most severe. In this context, the Michigan Family Independence Agency, a child welfare rather than a corrections agency, has been offering technical assistance and resources to local communities.

Research provided by the Office of Juvenile Justice and Delinquency Prevention (OJJDP, 1998, 2000) through curricula and publications, recommends that gender-specific program providers listen to girls. Listening to girls' verbal and nonverbal communication

---

This chapter originally appeared in Women, Girls & Criminal Justice, *Vol. 5, No. 2, February/March 2004.*

can help program staff learn more about girls' lives. Listening to girls also entails including them in the development, implementation, and refinement of programs.

Staff recruitment, selection, and training are critical to gender-specific programming. Staff should represent the diversity of the girls they serve. Staff should also be aware of the individual needs of girls, including the importance of relationships to girls, the impact of victimization, and the ways in which girls hurt themselves and others. Staff should be trained in ways that engage girls in healthy, appropriate relationships.

In Michigan, many professionals—social scientists, social workers, researchers, educators, and juvenile justice administrators—are asking a variety of focus groups what can be done to enhance services in the juvenile justice system for females. They are also asking how to reduce recidivism and/or the escalation of girls into the adult correctional system. We decided that significant information could be accessed if we interviewed former "customers/consumers" of the juvenile justice system who are now incarcerated as adults.

On May 30, 2003, we posed the following question to 14 inmates at the Scott Correctional Facility in Plymouth, Michigan: "What can the juvenile justice system do to prevent female juvenile offenders from entering the adult system?" Their answers were not new to us. In fact, their answers mirrored what we have come to understand as "best practices" in the juvenile justice system and female gender-specific programming, namely that we must listen to, and be responsive to, the needs of girls. Females, unlike their male counterparts, have a resounding need for relationships.

SURVEY POPULATION AND RESEARCH METHOD

These women (all volunteers) were selected out of the total prison population at the Scott Correctional Facility, which houses 850 medium- and high-security female inmates, with the caveats that they (1) must have spent time in a Michigan juvenile facility (either residential treatment or detention) and (2) not be emotionally or mentally challenged.

The women ranged from 18 to 41 years old. Ten were between 18 and 24. All of the participants had entered the juvenile justice system before their fourteenth birthday. Thirteen of the women were African American and one Caucasian. Four of the women had been in foster care and each had experienced multiple placements in the foster care system. These women's crimes included passing bad checks, carjacking, and murder. Their sentences ranged from three years to life. None of the women were legally married; 11 had children. One-half of their children were living with relatives, the other half were in foster care.

We interviewed the women in two groups, with seven women in each. We asked the same open-ended question in each group: "What can the juvenile justice system do to prevent female juvenile offenders from entering the adult corrections system?" Each group interview lasted two hours. Responses were recorded during the interviews.

FINDINGS

The inmates were very candid with their responses. Tears were shed during both sessions. The women demonstrated genuine care and concern for the young female offenders and were very willing to speak with the girls in residential treatment. They did not want to use the "Scared Straight" model, but rather to share experiences and the wisdom of their years with the girls.

The themes that ran through the interviews included the following:

- *Don't send kids to prison.* They only learn to be "better" criminals. One girl said, "Kids need to be rehabilitated if possible." Another added, "Crime is glorified in prison. It fills the pockets of the greedy. It provides immediate gratification. It makes you look good among your peers, until you get caught."

- *Don't scare me, help me.* Dig deep into the individual's psyche. Get to the root of the problem. Therapy/counseling is valuable. Individualize treatment. Motivate the youth to talk. Create avenues through which young girls feel safe enough to share what is inside them. Use skilled social workers or therapists who know how to handle people.

- *Deal with the inmates' personal victimization.* Help the individual understand that it's not her fault that she is in or was in foster care. All of the participants are angry with their mothers because their mothers did not protect them from the physical, emotional, and sexual abuse they experienced as children.

- *Do a better job with dysfunctional families.* Early identification of family needs and the prevention of familial dysfunction is important.

- *Substance abuse medicates the pain of not "fitting in."* One girl noted, "It heals the pain."

- *Ensure that mothers and their children maintain contact and relationships.*

The most significant finding, however, was that these women just wanted to be cared for and loved. They needed to be able to trust the individuals in their environment. They looked for "love" everywhere. They ran from home "looking for love," they ran from placements "looking for love," they assisted boyfriends in crime "looking for love." They had children, "looking for love."

PRISONER SUGGESTIONS FOR THE CRIMINAL JUSTICE SYSTEM

The women surveyed had several suggestions for criminal justice professionals:

- *Teach independent living skills.* Teach these skills at the learner's level of understanding. Follow up with practical experiences. Teach tangible things that can be used in life.

- *Recruit lots of mentors.* "There's got to be a somebody for everybody who is willing to be helped." Ensure a good match between mentor and youth for a positive outcome.

- *Teach confidence and self-esteem.* Help young women build their confidence and self-esteem.

- *Don't lock girls up.* Keep them in the community with lots of community support. Include their families in treatment services. "Lock-ups are artificial environments. Make it real!" said one girl. If a girl has been locked-up, follow up with her for at least a year after she's been released from a facility.

- *Provide girls and families with necessary resources.* Employment and education are key.

- *Staff should listen attentively.* Teach staff to listen. Recruit people who care about girls, not people who are there simply to get a paycheck.

- *Provide around-the-clock supervision.* Staff or mentors should be available 24 hours a day.

- *Individualize treatment.* Reward and reinforce positive behavior.

- *Show youth the positives of life.*

- *Do not do co-ed programming.* Most girls are just going to try to get a boyfriend and will not pay attention to what's being offered.

- *Provide structured treatment or redirection in detention facilities.*

- *Illustrate reality.* Get some "before and after" pictures of criminals who were "dope" (riding high); and then show the same person disabled, dead, or in prison.

- *Provide support groups for victims of sexual assault, grieving, sexual molestation, abandonment and loss, substance abuse.*

- *Don't work in a vacuum.* Include boyfriends or significant others in the treatment.

- *Take advantage of experience.* Use folks who "have been there" to teach the youth.

- *Focus on the positive.* Adults should help a youth develop the "light at the end of the tunnel."

- *Help girls feel safe!*

CONCLUSION

We have a long way to go. All of us are in this thing called "life" together. We've got to reach out, listen, and love if we're ever going to see a brighter future. Let's do it!

About the Authors

Karen A. Woods, M.S.W., is the Female Gender Specific Specialist and Julie Jenkins, M.A., is the Director of Reintegration Services for the Michigan Family Independence Agency.

References

Office of Juvenile Justice and Delinquency Prevention, *Beyond Gender Barriers: Programming Specifically for Girls* (US Government Printing Office, 2000).

Office of Juvenile Justice and Delinquency Prevention, *Guiding Principles for Promising Female Programming: An Inventory of Best Practices* (NCJ Publication No. 173415) (US Government Printing Office, 1988) Available online at http//ojjdp.ncjrs.org/pubs/principles/contents.html.

Chapter 31

Risk Assessment in Canadian Corrections: Some Diverse and Gendered Issues

by Margaret Shaw, Ph.D. and Kelly Hannah-Moffat, Ph.D.

INTRODUCTION

Recently, in Canada, actuarial risk and need assessment has become a major aspect of the federal correctional system which is responsible for all those sentenced to two years or more. In 1994, an elaborate risk and need classification and assessment process (the Offender Intake Assessment, or OIA) was instituted across the system. This affects all prisoners as well as those on parole. Actuarial techniques are also being used in some provincial correctional systems, notably Ontario.

These developments stem primarily from the work of a group of Canadian psychologists, working both inside and outside the correctional system, who have been actively promoting the revival of the concept of rehabilitation. On the basis of a series of meta-analyses, they argue that appropriately targeted treatment programs, using techniques based on cognitive psychology, reduce recidivism. This work, vigorously promoted inside and outside Canada, has achieved a high profile in a number of countries including the United States, and some correctional services are actively adopting the treatment approaches and adapting risk assessment tools and instruments to their clientele (see e.g., Holt, 1996; Aubrey & Hough, 1997; Davey & Lane, 1999; Mair, 1999).

There are, however, a number of concerns about the rush to implement such risk assessment instruments and treatment programs. In spite of the claims made for their veracity, most of the work on which they have been based is partial. It has been developed on the

This chapter originally appeared in Women, Girls & Criminal Justice, *Vol. 2., No. 1, December/January 2000.*

basis of male, and usually white, correctional populations. It is un-gendered and has maintained that issues such as race and ethnicity as well as gender are inconsequential (e.g., Bonta, 1989; Andrews, Bonta & Hoge 1990; Bonta, Pang & Wallace-Capretta, 1995). This chapter draws on a recent study of the implications of universal actuarial systems for women and minority groups (Hannah-Moffat & Shaw, 2001). It traces the development of classification systems and their specific application to federally sentenced women in Canada—those who receive sentences of two years or more. They represent only 2% of the federal prison population, around 360 women (compared with 12,600 men). They are also more diverse ethno-culturally than the male population. Aboriginal women in particular are heavily over-represented. Up to 25% of women in Canadian federal prisons are Aboriginal, compared with 2% in the Canadian population as a whole, and there is an increasing proportion of black women and other minorities.

EVOLVING APPROACHES TO CLASSIFICATION: CLASSIFYING MEN

Classification provides the fundamental basis for decision-making in the day-to-day lives of prisoners. In current correctional systems it affects the type of institution, the regime, program access, release decisions, and parole conditions. Its evolution shows that it has varied in both the purpose of classifying and in the methods used to classify. Early classification systems used the simple criteria of separation by gender, length, and type of sentence, and criminal history. These were used in some European countries to separate women from men and to allocate suitable work, and subsequently to separate the reformable from the recidivists. They enabled the nineteenth century penitentiary to maintain order and facilitate moral reformation.

Modern classification systems in most Western countries, however, have rarely considered gender or diversity. They have been designed to manage, control, and treat the larger, usually white, male prison populations. From the 1930s, as the numbers of treatment professionals such as psychologists and psychiatrists in prisons expanded, methods of classification and treatment allocation became more elaborate with the development of clinical assessments, checklists, and test batteries based on studies of male populations. In the 1960s there was a shift in the purpose of classification from sentence length to security in a number of countries, associated with notions of dangerousness and public safety (Price, 1999).

A further shift in both the purpose and methods of classification occurred in the mid 1970s. Prison and parole classification systems, particularly in the U.S., began to place greater emphasis upon risk and its prediction (e.g., of escape, risk to the public, to other prisoners, to staff, to institutions, to themselves) together with the development of very different methods of assessment. The clinical judgments and test batteries used for classification were characterized as "subjective" or "judgmental" and were replaced by "objective" tools and actuarial measurements which created standardized responses and risk profiles (Gottfredson & Tonry, 1987). What "objective" classification systems have in common is "the universal application of predetermined and weighted criteria which is combined in a mechanical or mathematical way to arrive at a custody determination" (Holt, 1996, p. 41). Proponents argue that actuarial tools eliminate subjective, arbitrary decision-making, bias, and prejudice and they lead to more efficient, effective, and impartial classification, and to more rational and just institutions and have better predictive capacity than do subjective methods. They are clearly directed at predicting risk and recidivism on the basis of statistical analysis of large data sets (Feeley & Simon, 1992 ; Castel, 1991).

The most recent shift has been that initiated largely by Canadian psychologists in the 1990s who have added the notion of need to that of risk, linked to rehabilitation and the effectiveness of particular types of treatment (Andrews, Zinger et al., 1990; Andrews, Bonta & Hoge, 1990). They argue that specific types of treatment (usually based on cognitive behavioral techniques) and targeted to the right categories of offenders, are effective in reducing reoffending. Thus in addition to risk-based security placement and release decisions, actuarial tools allocate level and types of treatment or supervision required, on the basis of what is now termed criminogenic need. Risk factors—or what they now refer to as static risk factors—are seen as characteristics predictive of re-offending which cannot be changed, such as age at first offense. Need factors—what they now term dynamic risk factors—are those which are predictive of re-offending, but are seen as susceptible to treatment, such as attitudes or substance abuse. Significantly, in the Canadian literature, therefore, need is no longer a statement of entitlements, or a service or treatment that a prisoner requests, or which might be seen by others as helpful or humane to provide. Not all needs are seen as criminogenic, only those which are predictively related to recidivism.

These developments have been criticised in relation to majority male populations on correctional, operational, and theoretical grounds (see, e.g., Sparks, Bottoms & Hay, 1996; McHugh, 1997; Ditchfield, 1997; Price, 1997). Actuarialism introduces a form of managerialism, which "appears to its practitioners to offer powerful tools for modernizing archaic practices, rationalizing the use of resources, and informing action by ever better and more precise information" (Sparks et al., 1996, p. 94). The extent to which actuarial models replace or displace subjective forms of clinical judgements and moral evaluations of an offender's behavior, however, is questionable. While the tools appear to be reliable and efficient and devoid of moralism, questions are raised about how they are used in practice, and they appear more aptly to identify social disadvantage (Hannah-Moffat, 1999; Hannah-Moffat & Shaw, 2001).

Further, actuarial measures have been developed and validated on large majority male populations. They have not been validated for women and minority groups. Many of the requirements for developing reliable and valid predictors of risk cannot easily be met by small populations. If a classification system, with all its diverse objectives, is based on expectations about the majority population, this may be inappropriate for minority populations with diverse backgrounds and experiences, and much greater heterogeneity.

CLASSIFYING WOMEN: EMERGENCE OF LITERATURE ON FEMALE OFFENDER CLASSIFICATION

Apart from the major differences in levels of women's offending compared with men's, and the much lower levels of violence, there are clear differences between men and women in prison. This includes women's treatment needs, their learning styles, and the characteristics of programs and holistic approaches best suited to them (see, e.g., Owen & Bloom, 1995; Bloom & Covington, 1998; Carlen, 1998). Women in prison have specific needs as women in terms of the centrality of relationships and the role that children and families play to their lives. In addition, the health needs of these women are both greater and different from those of male prisoners. They have had greater experience as the victims of violence and abuse from childhood. They generally have lower levels of education and job skills, and have different reasons for their use of alcohol and drugs.

But women also react very differently to being in prison (Hannah-Moffat & Shaw 2000; Liebling, 1994, Comack, 1996). They are more likely to injure themselves, and much less likely to be involved in serious violence against men. Beyond quantifiable differences lie major qualitative differences in the lives of women, in the social controls exercised over them and expectations about their roles and behavior. All of these issues underline the importance of specific classification and assessment.

Nevertheless, almost all modern studies of classification have ignored women and ethnicity apart from some concerns with the implications of sentencing guidelines on black populations (Gottfredson, 1987). No literature on classifying women emerged until the late 1970s. (see, e.g., Nesbitt & Argento, 1984). This work has consistently concluded that in most countries the small populations of women were classified using security/risk based systems developed for men. This resulted in women prisoners being routinely over-classified and held in conditions of higher security than necessary. Yet given their much lower levels of risk, significant numbers of women could be decarcerated (Burke & Adams, 1991). Further, their program and service needs were also consistently overlooked because of the overriding focus on security and risk. Some work on developing or adapting classification systems for women was begun, including a recognition of the need to take account of the context of women's violence, given that much of it was in response to domestic abuse (Alexander, 1988).

In the 1990s U.S. reviews confirmed that little progress had been made on revising this classification. As of this writing, most work on classification has continued to ignore issues of gender or race, or has promoted "gender-neutral" systems. In an American survey, male-based classification systems were still being used in prisons in 39 states, and in 50 out of 54 jails studied (Morash, et al., 1998). Only three states had developed a special classification system for women. Yet as Farr (2000) concludes many factors that predict risk for men are invalid for women. In England and Wales "the fetishism of prison security" resulting from concerns over male prison escapes has further impacted the conditions of women's imprisonment (Carlen, 1998). In Canada, as will be outlined below, a male-based system has been imposed on female and Aboriginal populations, in spite of a government commitment to recognize the different needs of women prisoners.

Overall, therefore, three approaches seem to have emerged over the past 20 years: (1) do nothing; (2) append women and diversity to existing practices by modifying and "fine-tuning" existing male systems to "fit" women; or (3) develop a women-specific classification model.

This last option could include using a behavior-based classification in which all women would be initially classified at the lowest level, and reclassified upward in the event of behavioral problems; and/or replacing risk with the concept of "habilitation" for women. The latter refers to the very marginal lives lived by many women prisoners in the community, and the need to increase their capacity to survive economically and socially by strengthening family, health and community-based programs (Brennan, 1998). Most initiatives, however, are still driven by the requirements of the male population, although some attempts are being made to move to woman-based systems.

RISK AND NEED AND THE CANADIAN MODEL OF WOMEN-CENTERED PRISONS

In Canada, classification is a legal requirement. All federal prisoners must be assigned to a security classification of maximum, medium, or minimum, and allocated to an appropriate institution (defined in terms of their potential for escape, their institutional conduct, and their risk to the public). They will then "cascade" to lower security levels until eventual release. For women this has been an ambiguous requirement. Until the opening of new regional prisons from 1995 to 1997, all federally sentenced women were housed in one maximum-security institution, the Prison for Women (P4W) or in provincial prisons under exchange of service agreements. While officially described as a multi-level security institution, P4W was effectively maximum security, and from the 1980s classification within the institution used male-based instruments for security and release decisions as well as case-management (e.g., the Wisconsin Case Management Strategy).

In 1990, the Task Force on Federally Sentenced Women set out a new women-centered philosophy for women's prisons responding to the different and specific needs of women prisoners and recommended the construction of new regional prisons, including a Healing Lodge for Aboriginal women (*Creating Choices*, 1990). The core principles of the new model were to be:

- Empowerment;

- Meaningful and responsible choices;

- Respect and dignity;

- A supportive environment; and

- Shared responsibility.

Women were to live in self-sufficient small cottage housing units without perimeter fences, apart from those needing enhanced security on a temporary basis (Shaw, 1993). *Creating Choices* argued that women presented low risks in or outside prison compared with men, and were more likely to injure themselves than others. They had high needs and required support rather than security. It advocated assessment of treatment needs, not classification, and argued that classification criteria discriminated against Aboriginal women in particular given their heavy over-representation in the population. It was argued that women's treatment needs were interrelated, requiring a holistic rather than a hierarchical approach to program provision. The government accepted all the recommendations.

In the implementation phase attempts were made to develop a women-centered assessment system. An offender-management classification system based partly on that used in Shakopee women's prison in Minnesota was proposed (Hannah-Moffat, 1999). This incorporated gender-specific factors into security classification within the institution, and established performance expectations for reclassification. A women-centered assessment tool was developed in one prison. Following the implementation of the OIA in all federal prisons, a guideline for its use in women's prisons was prepared. These took some account of the differences in the experiences of women compared with men—for example, full time work at home was to be assessed as full time employment.

Following the opening of the new facilities from 1995 to 1997, however, these were replaced by the OIA system developed on the male population. The research and managerial demands of this system, the goals of eliminating diversity and overrides, of ensuring that everyone is classified and assessed in the same way to facilitate predictive validation, appear to drive the process. A number of problems are evident, all of them suggesting a wide divergence from the women-based prison philosophy accepted in 1990.

- Examination of scale components suggests that women are likely to be assessed poorly since the tools have been developed on men. Considerable sections of the needs assessment domains are either irrelevant to women or fail to take account of their experiences as women. For example, pathways to substance abuse for women are different, use of medical and outpatient services are higher among women than men, they are much less likely to have "stable" employment patterns. Similarly, no account is taken of differential cultural experiences or seasonal work patterns such as Aboriginal trapping lines.

- Further, while *Creating Choices* emphasized the low security risks but high treatment needs of women, the redefining of need as a dynamic risk predictor has major implications for both their management within the prison and for release decisions. It suggests that women may be denied re-classification and release on the grounds that they have not addressed their needs, even though women as a whole represent much lower security risks to the public than men. A desire to receive counseling for family violence, for example, may become a requirement to attend a course on anger management, before re-classification or parole is granted.

- Additional problems stem from the absence of programs for women in the community given their small numbers. If no treatment program or appropriate services can be located in the community, then women will be unable to meet parole requirements associated with identified dynamic risks or needs.

- A further problem of the male-derived system is that not all needs are seen as criminogenic. The emphasis on appropriately targeted treatment means that only needs predictively related to re-offending should form part of the treatment plan. Since prediction has been conducted on male and majority populations, those needs identified by women or minorities which do not fit predictive patterns (e.g., individual counseling for sexual abuse or trauma; culturally specific programs) may be excluded from treatment plans.

GENDER AND DIVERSITY ISSUES

The Canadian classification and assessment tools have been developed on the basis of studies of white male populations (Motiuk, 1997). Their literature on rehabilitation and the effectiveness of treatment is based almost exclusively on meta-analyses of male adult and young offender programs (Andrews, Zinger, et al., 1990; Andrews, Bonta & Hoge, 1990). What is of particular significance is that the characteristics of programs thought to be ineffective in reducing recidivism in this literature include precisely those that women prisoners have themselves found helpful, or which are recommended in the literature on women-specific programs. This includes individual therapy and counseling that is not rigidly structured (Kendall, 1993; Bloom & Covington, 1998). This research raises issues of subjectivity, individual pathology, treatment proscription, and the slippage between risk and need.

Over the past five years these researchers have begun to examine samples of women and Aboriginal offenders, while continuing to argue that race and gender are, overall, irrelevant. A number of papers have attempted to validate classification tools on federally sentenced women although without much success (e.g., Bonta, Pang & Wallace-Capretta, 1995; Blanchette & Motiuk, 1995; Blanchette, 1997; Motiuk & Blanchette, 1998). They are not concerned with developing separate women-specific tools. There is also an attempt, however, to identify the specific characteristics in the female population, such as suicide attempts or self-injury, which predict violent re-offending—this on the basis of a minute population of women, many of whom are Aboriginal. The language of actuarial assessment is also far removed from that used by those proposing gender-specific approaches, it is about systems improvement, not individual diversity (c.f., Motiuk & Blanchette, 1998; McMahon, 1999). While a more recent attempt has been made to consider the effectiveness of women-specific programs on the basis of historical information (Dowden & Andrews, 1999), this is particularly problematic given the broad cultural variations and the difficulties of measuring the impact of programs on small and diverse populations.

Most of this research, like the literature on classification, does not question the underlying assumptions on which classification is based, the concept of risk itself, or the objectivity of actuarial approaches. In arguing that male-based systems be adapted or validated for women, such researchers still assume that subjectivity has been eliminated. Risk assessment is seen to be objective and neutral, and gender and race are treated as factors to be added in without requiring further contextualizing. While checklists, training manuals and programs, and additive assessments may appear to be objective, they in fact depend upon multiple judgments made by classification officers, line managers, frontline and other prison staff, or by probation or parole officers (Hannah-Moffat & Shaw, 2001). Such assessments do not require the broader context of women's (or men's) lives and offending to be taken into account, and still treat individual factors (job history, relations with family, discipline infractions) as "flat" and of equal weight for men and women, Aboriginal and non-Aboriginal, black and white. Gender blindness—a major characteristic of gender-neutral systems—is not eliminated by the adaptation of male-derived actuarial measures to women.

The same applies to systems that are blind to race. Monture-Angus (2000) argues that risk scales are individualized instruments which fail to account for the significance of colonial oppression in the lives of Aboriginal men and women, and that the individualized nature of law obscures systemic problems in the court process as well as classification and risk assessment. Being Aboriginal, female, and poor presents a special context of difference (Jackson, 1999). Black women in Canada, and those from other minority groups have also experienced direct and indirect racism and discrimination (Pollack, 2000).

Part of the problem also stems from the specific disciplinary perspective—cognitive psychology—which forms the basis for the Canadian research. This places greater emphasis on individual pathology than on contextual and institutional factors in explaining events or behavior. In the Canadian context, the incorporation of feminist language into the correctional setting has also had a number of consequences (Hayman, 2000; Hannah-Moffat & Shaw 2000; Hannah-Moffat, 2003). The language of empowerment has been reinterpreted in terms of the "responsibilization" of women. This is a term that is used in the literature on risk to refer to patterns of governing by the state or others, and implies that individuals are now expected to be responsible and accountable for their own risk management and "self-governance." Thus it is their responsibility to take programs and to change, and their responsibility to take those seen by others as likely to reduce their offending. This is not the model of empowerment allowing women to make choices and gain control over their lives that was envisaged by the Task Force. Second, as this chapter has suggested, the incorporation of gender-specific information into actuarial assessments has placed women in a more vulnerable position, turning their needs into risk factors requiring program completion—what has been termed "slippage" (Hannah-Moffat, 1999). As has been seen, women are generally seen as presenting low risks but high needs, but since needs in this literature are *dynamic risks*, this has major consequences for release decisions.

MORAL DIMENSION TO ASSESSMENT CATEGORIES

There is also a strong moral dimension to the categories used in assessment with implications about how people should behave and think (scale items in the OIA, for example, include not having a bank account or collateral, having no hobbies, a poorly maintained residence, inappropriate sexual preferences, not being conscientious). Given the history of over-regulating the behavior of women in (and out of) prison, women may still be over-regulated by actuarial approaches. For example, there are indications that Canadian federal sentenced women are more likely to have their parole revoked for technical violations than men. Staff in some of the women's prisons were concerned about judgmental attitudes about minority women who may be seen to be too assertive and outspoken, or too submissive. For the very small group of women in Canada classified as high risk and high need (between 20 and 30), there are huge barriers to release when issues such as self-injury and suicide are claimed as predictive of violent recidivism. There are clearly many different contextual factors associated with their violent offending and their self-injury when compared with violent offenders in the male population. These are women seen as difficult to manage and those with mental health needs, and around half of the women classified as maximum security are Aboriginal (Kendall, 2000).

A number of other writers have begun to explore some of these issues in relation to black and Aboriginal offenders (e.g., Bhui 1999; Davey & Lane, 1999; Dawson, 1999; Mair, 1999). Australian studies raise the moral, ethical and empirical problems of adopting actuarial tools from other cultures and countries. Dawson (1999) argues that actuarial tools should not be constructed on the premise of ethnic neutrality—that factors found to be predictive of offending among probationers or parolees in North America cannot be used to predict re-offending among indigenous populations. For example, risk assessments which incorporate measures of employment history, and numbers of job or address changes are bound to discriminate against Aboriginals when levels of unemployment in Aboriginal communities are around 38% compared with 11% among the general Australian labor force. She also questions the cultural relevance of attitudinal judgments such as "motivation to change/willingness to accept responsibility for the offence"—given the very different experiences of justice among Aboriginal and non-Aboriginal populations. Mair (1999) questions the use of gender- neutral tools on female and black probationers in Britain. Bhui (1999) raise issues of the discriminatory assessment of black mentally disordered offenders, and the importance of understanding cultural difference.

CONCLUSION

The problems outlined in this paper relate both to the implications of using actuarial tools based on large-scale prediction studies of majority populations for women and minority offenders, as well the as a more general methodological critique of the assumptions underlying risk-based classification systems. The latter have included:

- Their failure to recognize the significance of gender, race and social disadvantage;

- Their inability to view problems holistically or in the broader context of women/ minorities' lives;

- Their restriction of information to apparently objective "facts" which do not take account of the context of events or situations, including regime factors;

- Their underlying subjectivity; and

- The dominance of particular subjects and explanations.

In addition for Canada, there is the problem of addressing the needs of a very small and diverse population in the context of a wider correctional system that focuses on the concerns of incarcerated men. There remain many unresolved questions about correctional research in spite of its claims for the 'validity' of tools and the effectiveness of proscribed treatment. Among some practitioners working with women there is awareness of these issues, but they are not likely to be resolved by tinkering with male-based tools.

About the Authors

Margaret Shaw, Ph.D., teaches in the Department of Sociology, Concordia University, Montreal. Kelly Hannah-Moffat, Ph.D., teaches in the Department of Sociology, University of Toronto. An earlier version of this chapter was published in the United Kingdom in the Fall 2000 issue of Probation Journal. *The authors are grateful to Status of Women, Canada, for supporting the research project on which this chapter draws and to participants in a workshop on risk that was held in Toronto, Canada, in May 1999.*

References

Alexander, J., *Working Paper XVI: Initial Security Classification Guidelines for Females.* (New York, Department of Correctional Services, 1988).

Andrews, D., Bonta, J., & Hoge, R.D., "Classification for Effective Rehabilitation," 17 *Criminal Justice and Behaviour*, 19-52 (1990).

Andrews, D., Zinger, I., Hoge, R.D., Bonta, J., Gendreau, P., & Cullen, F.T., "Does Correctional Treatment Work? A Clinically Relevant and Psychologically Informed Meta-Analysis," 28(3) *Criminology* 369-404 (1990).

Aubrey, R. & Hough, M., *Assessing Offenders' Needs: Assessment Scales for the Probation Service*, Research Study No. 166. (British Home Office, 1997).

Bhui, H.S.,"Race, Racism and Risk Assessment: Linking Theory to Practice With Black Mentally Disordered Offenders," 46(3) *Probation Journal* 171-181 (1999).

Blanchette, K., "Classifying Female Offenders for Correctional Interventions," 9(1) *Forum on Corrections Research*, 36-41 (1997).

Blanchette, K., & Motiuk, L., *Female Offenders Risk Assessment: The Case Management Strategies Approach*. Paper presented at the Canadian Psychological Association Annual Convention, Charlottetown, Prince Edward Island, Canada (1995).

Bloom, S., & Covington, S., *Gender Specific Programming For Female Offenders: What is Important and Why it is Important*. Paper presented at the American Society of Criminology meetings, Washington, D.C., (November, 1998).

Bonta, J., "Native Inmates: Institutional Response, Risk, and Needs," 31(1) *Canadian Journal of Criminology* 49-60 (1989).

Bonta, J., Pang, B., & Wallace-Capretta, S.,"Predictors of Recidivism Among Incarcerated Female Offenders," 75(3) *The Prison Journal* 227-293 (1995).

Brennan, T., "Institutional Classification for Females: Problems and Some Proposals for Reform." In R.T. Zaplin (Ed.), *Female Offenders: Critical Perspectives and Effective Interventions* (pp. 179-204) (Aspen, 1998).

Burke, P., & Adams, L., *Classification Handbook for Women Offenders in State Correctional Facilities: A Handbook for Practitioners* (National Institute of Corrections, U.S. Department of Justice, 1991).

Carlen, P., *Sledgehammer: Women's Imprisonment at the Millennium* (Macmillian Press, Ltd., 1998).

Castel, R., "From Dangerousness to Risk," In G. Burchell, C. Gordon & P. Miller (Eds.), *The Foucault Effect: Studies in Governmentality*, (pp. 281-289) (University of Chicago Press, 1991).

Comack, E., *Women in Trouble*, Halifax, (Fernwood Publishing, 1996).

Creating Choices, Report of the Task Force on Federally Sentenced Women (Correctional Service Canada, 1990).

Davey, D., & Lane, R., "Actuarially Based 'On-Line' Risk Assessment in Western Australia," 46(3)*Probation Journal* 164-170 (1999).

Dawson, D., *Risk of Violence Assessment: Aboriginal Offenders and the Assumption of Homogeneity*, Paper presented at the Australian Institute of Criminology conference, Adelaide, Australia (October 1999).

Ditchfield, J., "Actuarial prediction and risk assessment," 113 *Prison Service Journal* 8-13 (1996).

Dowden, C., & Andrews, D. A., "What Works for Female Offenders: A Meta-Analytic Review," 45(4) *Crime and Delinquency* 438-452 (1999).

Farr, K., "Classification for Female Inmates: Moving Forward," 46(1) *Crime and Delinquency*, 3-17 (2000).

Feeley, M., & Simon, J., "The New Penology: Notes of the Emerging Strategy for Corrections and its Implications," 30(4) *Criminology* 49-74 (1992).

Gottfredson, D. M., & Tonry, M. (Eds.), *Prediction and Classification: Criminal Justice Decision Making*, Vol. 9, Crime and Justice: A Review of Research, (University of Chicago Press, 1987).

Gottfredson, S. D., "Prediction: An Overview of Selected Methodological Issues," In D. M. Gottfredson & M. Tonry (Eds.) *Prediction and Classification: Criminal Justice Decision Making*, Vol. 9, Crime and Justice: A Review of Research (pp. 21-52) (University of Chicago Press, 1987).

Hannah-Moffat, K., "Moral agent or actuarial subject," 3(1) *Theoretical Criminology* 71- 94 (1999).

Hannah-Moffat, K., *Punishment in Disguise: Penal Governance and Federal Imprisonment of Women in Canada*. (University of Toronto Press, 2003).

Hannah-Moffat, K., & Shaw, M., *"Taking Risks": Gender, Diversity, Security Classification and Assessment with Canadian Federally Sentenced Women* (Status of Women Canada, 2001).

Hannah-Moffat, K., & Shaw, M., *An Ideal Prison? Critical Essays on Women's Imprisonment in Canada* (Fernwood, Canada, 2000).

Hayman, S., "Prison Reform and Incorporation: Lessons From Britain and Canada," In K. Hannah-Moffat & M. Shaw (Eds.), *An Ideal Prison? Critical Essays on Women's Imprisonment in Canada* (pp. 41-51) (Fernwood Publishing, 2000).

Holt, N., *Inmate Classification: A Validation Study of the California System* (California Department of Corrections, 1996).

Jackson, M., "Canadian Aboriginal Women and Their 'Criminality': The Cycle of Violence in the Context of Difference," 32(2) *The Australian and New Zealand Journal of Criminology* 197-208 (1999).

Kendall, K., *Programme Evaluation of Therapeutic Services at the Prison for Women* (Correctional Service Canada, 1993).

Kendall, K., "Psy-ence fiction: Governing Female Prisons Through the Psychological Sciences." In K. Hannah-Moffat & M. Shaw, *An Ideal Prison? Critical Essays on Women's Imprisonment in Canada,* (pp. 82-93) (Fernwood Publishing, Canada, 2000).

Liebling, A., "Suicide Among Women Prisoners." 33(1) *Howard Journal of Criminal Justice* 1-9 (1994).

Mair, G., "It's a Man's Man's Man's World: Risk/Need Assessment in England and Wales," Paper presented at the Workshop on Risk Gender, Diversity and Classification in Federally Sentenced Women's Facilities, Toronto, Canada (1999).

McHugh, M., "Risk assessment and management of suicides in prison." 113 *Prison Service Journal*, 4-8 (1997).

McMahon, M., Paper presented at the *Workshop on Risk Gender, Diversity and Classification in Federally Sentenced Women's Facilities*, Toronto, Canada (1999).

Monture-Angus, P., "Aboriginal Women and Correctional Practice: Reflections on the Task Force on Federally Sentenced Women." In K. Hannah-Moffat & M. Shaw (Eds.) *An Ideal Prison? Critical Essays on Women's Imprisonment in Canada*. (pp. 52-60) (Fernwood Publishing, Canada, 2000).

Morash, M., Bynum, T., & Koons, B.A., *Women Offenders: Programming Needs and Promising Approaches,* Research in Brief (National Institute of Justice, 1998).

Motiuk, L., "Classification for Correctional Programming: The Offender Intake Assessment (OIA) Process," 9(1) *Forum on Corrections Research* 18-22 (1997).

Motiuk, L., & Blanchette, K., "What Works in Assessing Female Offender Risk and Need." Paper presented at the International Community Corrections Association 6th Annual Research Conference, Arlington, Virginia (1998).

Nesbitt, C., & Argento, A., *Female Classification: An Examination of the Issues* (American Correctional Association, 1987).

Owen, B., & Bloom, B., *Profiling the Needs of California's Female Prisoners* (National Institute of Corrections, 1995).

Pollack, S., "Dependency Discourse as Social Control." In K. Hannah-Moffat & M. Shaw (Eds.) *An Ideal Prison? Critical Essays on Women's Imprisonment in Canada,* (pp. 72-81) (Fernwood Publishing, Canada, 2000).

Price, D., "Spies, Dickie, and Prison Security: A Short History of Security Classification in the English Prison System." Paper presented at the British Criminology Conference, Liverpool, England (1999).

Price, R., "On the risks of risk prediction." 8(1) *Journal of Forensic Psychiatry* 1-4 (1997).

Shaw, M., "Reforming Federal Women's Imprisonment." In E. Adelberg & C. Currie (Eds.) *In Conflict With the Law: Women and the Canadian Justice System* (pp. 50-75) (Press Gang Publishers, Canada, 1993).

Shaw, M. with Rodgers, K., Blanchette, J., Hattem, T., Thomas, L.S. & Tamarack, L., *Paying the Price: Federally Sentenced Women in Context*, User report 1992-13. Ottawa: Ministry of the Solicitor General (1992).

Sparks, R., Bottoms, A. E. & Hay, E., *Prisons and the Problem of Order* (Oxford University Press, 1996).

Chapter 32

Assessing Female Offenders: Prediction Versus Explanation

by Christopher T. Lowenkamp, M.S. and Edward Latessa, Ph.D.

INTRODUCTION

Every day in the criminal justice system scores of decisions are made about what can be done with individuals who commit criminal offenses. From pre-trial release through disposition and beyond, community supervision officers, case managers, prosecutors, defense attorneys, and judges try to make decisions that will ensure public safety. The control and management of persons charged with or convicted of crimes is too great and the costs to society are too high for these practitioners to make poor decisions regarding what to do with them or where to place them.

Empirical research indicates that the efficacy of decision-making is heightened by the use of empirically grounded and validated risk assessment instruments (for a review of this literature see Andrews & Bonta, 1999; Bonta, 1996). While the importance of empirical risk assessment is now accepted in many areas of the criminal justice system, concerns remain regarding the use of these assessments for so-called special offender population groups. For example, potential issues exist around the applicability of risk assessment instruments that are developed on male-based data and subsequently used on women or girls. This concern is based on the assertion that the predictors of deviant behavior differ for men and women (Chesney-Lind, 1989, 1997; Funk, 1999; Mazerolle, 1998). If this assertion is correct, instruments based on existing research, which is dominated by male sample groups, may prove to be faulty in their application to women or girls.

This chapter originally appeared in Women, Girls & Criminal Justice, *Vol. 3, No. 4, June/July 2002.*

STUDIES OF RISK FACTORS AND RISK ASSESSMENT

This section summarizes the relevant literature on risk factors and risk assessment, paying special attention to males and females. This review leads to the conclusion that there may be some differences in the causes of criminogenic factors for men and women. The criminogenic factors, however, are largely the same. The major implication of this finding is that differences in causes of criminogenic factors are irrelevant for prediction, but are of paramount concern for intervention programs and strategies.

Meta-Analysis of Predictors of Adult Recidivism

Given the vast amount of research on criminality, researchers have increasingly applied the technique of meta-analysis to criminological literature. This technique provides a mathematical summary of certain relationships that exist in these studies. The summaries generated by meta-analyses, because they are based on many individual studies, are usually fairly stable and review a large amount of literature.

Gendreau, Little, and Goggin (1996) conducted a comprehensive meta-analytic review of predictors of adult offender recidivism. This analysis included individual predictors (such as antisocial peers or antisocial attitudes) as well as actuarial instruments (composite scores from empirically based risk assessments). The authors identified 131 studies for inclusion in their analyses. These studies generated 1,141 relationships between hypothesized predictors and future criminal behavior.

The Gendreau et al.'s results indicated that certain types of factors are more important than others when predicting future criminal behavior. More specifically, dynamic factors (characteristics that can change) have greater predictive ability; compared to static factors (historical characteristics or characteristics that do not change over time). Within the dynamic group of predictors, criminogenic needs had the greatest predictive ability; criminal history measures had the greatest predictive ability in the static group. The most potent predictors in the dynamic group are companions, an antisocial personality, and other criminogenic needs, such as family and employment.

As would be expected, the predictive ability of actuarial assessments, which combine several individual risk factors from both the static and dynamic category, is greater than any single predictor. While this meta-analysis did not calculate separate effects for male and female offenders it is comprehensive and covers a wide range of predictor variables and actuarial measures of risk. Other meta-analyses have been conducted with similar results. The most potent risk factors are antisocial peers, antisocial associates, an antisocial personality, and a history of antisocial behavior (Andrews & Bonta, 1999). Only a small percentage of general criminological studies, as well as these meta-analyses, are based on sample groups of women or girls. Given the high percentage of male-only studies in the meta-analyses, it is reasonable to ask if we could be missing the importance of some gender-based risk factors and over-emphasizing the importance of other gender-based risk factors, disadvantaging women, if not men, in the process.

Meta-Analysis of Male vs. Female Risk Factors

Meta-analyses have been conducted to determine whether or not the risk factors associated with male criminality are equally important to the prediction of female criminality.

In one such analysis, Simourd and Andrews (1994) focused solely on youthful offenders and included 464 relationships from 60 studies. Their analysis indicated that, for both male and female youthful offenders, antisocial peers and attitudes were the strongest predictors, followed by temperament or misconduct problems and then by educational difficulties. Similarly, those factors relatively unimportant to the prediction of male delinquency were also found to be unimportant for female delinquency. Simourd and Andrews conclude, "[T]he general risk factors that were important for male delinquency were also important for female delinquency" (p. 28).

Simourd and Andrews (1994) also did some exploratory analyses on other categories of variables not included in their initial eight categories of risk factors (lower social class origins, family structure or parent problems, personal distress, minor personality variables, poor parent-child relations, educational difficulties, temperament or misconduct problems, and antisocial peers). While the numbers of studies in this exploratory analysis were limited, some promising relationships (lack of attachments to convention and criminality and sexual behavior and criminality) were identified.

Female-Only Studies

In a more recent meta-analysis Hubbard and Pratt (2002) look at some of these "other" categories mentioned in the Simourd and Andrews study. Hubbard and Pratt's analysis focused solely on female youthful offenders. The authors analyzed data on 13 variables across four categories of predictors (major predictors identified in previous meta-analysis, plus social-structural and socio-demographic, social interaction, and general behavioral, attitudinal, and personality predictors). Their results indicate that antisocial peers, history of antisocial behavior, and school relationships are the strongest predictors, followed by a history of sexual/physical abuse, antisocial attitudes/beliefs, and family relationships. Self-image and social adjustment are also identified as moderate to moderate-low predictors. The authors conclude that poor school relationships and history of sexual or physical abuse may be important predictors specific to female delinquency and overlooked in previous research. Furthermore, family relationships and IQ are potentially of concern with females. This is not to say that these factors are necessarily unimportant for predicting offending in males, but the research for both sexes has previously been lacking.

Summary

To review, several meta-analyses covering hundreds of studies and thousands of relationships indicate that the strongest predictors of recidivism are a history of antisocial behavior, antisocial peers, antisocial attitudes, and antisocial personality or temperament. Meta-analyses looking at how these factors differ by sex indicate that overall the major factors for males are also major factors for women although the rank ordering may change. In addition, it appears that some additional factors not previously researched, or discarded as unimportant for males, may be important for females.

The question that still lingers is whether these empirical differences equate to differences in the prediction of behavior. While the meta-analyses indicate some subtle differences in risk predictors between males and females, are these differences substantial enough to require separate risk assessment instruments for men and women?

ARE SEPARATE RISK ASSESSMENT TOOLS NECESSARY?

To answer this question we will review some of the existing research on the application of risk assessments to females and discuss how it is that an instrument developed on male-based data can predict equally well for females.

There is no doubt that research into the development of risk assessment instruments has historically focused solely on males. Several years passed before the Salient Factor Score (SFS), developed on male offenders but used for both men and women, was validated with a female population. Nonetheless, this gender-specific validation demonstrated its ability to satisfactorily predict risk for females (Hoffman, 1982).

More recently, correctional agencies' expanded use of the LSI-R as the risk assessment has led to renewed interest and concern as to whether this instrument is equally valid for females. Table 32.2 summarizes some of the correlations regarding the LSI-R. As noted, there are now a handful of studies that assess the ability of the LSI-R to predict recidivism for females. First, note that the last two studies are meta-analyses and are dominated by studies of the LSI-R's ability to predict male offending. Second, note that the individual relationships reported between the LSI-R and future criminality are at least equivalent to or higher than these summary scores provided by the meta-analyses. In essence, what

Table 32.1: Correlations Between Risk Factors and Criminal Behavior

Risk Factor	Simourd and Andrews, 1994		Gendreau et al., 1996	Hubbard and Pratt, 2000
	Males	Females	Mixed	Females
Parent Child Relations	.22	.20	.14	.17
Educational Difficulties	.24	.23	—	.25
Temperament	.36	.35	.18	.21
Antisocial peers or attitudes	.40	.39	.21*	.53*/.18**
History of Antisocial Behavior	—	—	.17	.48

* Companions only   ** Attitudes only

Table 32.2: Correlations Between LSI-R and Criminal Behavior

Study	Sample	Relationship
Coulson, Nutbrown, Giulekas, Cudjoe, and Ilacqua 1992	Female	.51
Kirkpatrick 1999	Female	.41
Rettinger 1998	Female	.58
Lowenkamp, Holsinger, and Latessa 2000	Female	.37
Gendreau, Little, and Goggin 1996	Mixed*	.35
Gendreau, Goggin, and Smith 2001	Mixed*	.38

* Indicates meta-analysis

this means is that the relationships between the LSI-R and criminal behavior for females are as good as or better than the typical relationship identified through the meta-analyses on the LSI-R.

Figure 32.1 illustrates the correlations between various outcome measures and the LSI-R composite score. This data is from offenders in a residential community based program in a large urban area in the mid-western U.S. This data has been reported in detail elsewhere (Lowenkamp, et al., 2001), however, a brief review of those findings seems relevant. Note that the correlations for female offenders are larger than those observed for male offenders. This is the case on each of the outcome measures. And while the correlations for absconding and successful program completion are smaller than anticipated, the correlations for the prediction of re-incarceration are at least as large as the correlations found elsewhere. The correlation between the LSI-R and re-incarceration for females is especially encouraging, as it is in the predicted direction and the value of r (r or Pearson's Correlation Coefficient indicates the degree to which [size of the coefficient] two variables are related and how [negative or positive] they are related) is relatively large.

While the number of studies on female offenders is limited, the studies that have been conducted support the use of the LSI-R with female offenders. Based on this limited information, however, we are comfortable concluding that an assessment developed on sound research—field tested by practitioners, validated, and tested for reliability and shaped by existing data and principles of assessment—can be equally valid for males and females.

DIFFERENCES IN RISK ASSESSMENT BETWEEN MALE AND FEMALE

We would be remiss if we left from our discussion differences we have noted between male and female offenders in our research on risk assessments. In a series of studies (Lowenkamp & Latessa, 2001a, 2001b, 2002) we reviewed the subcomponent scores and composite score for males and females on the LSI-R. In two of these studies (Lowenkamp & Latessa, 2001b and 2002), comparisons were made with male offenders from the same jurisdiction.

First, in each of these studies the alpha reliabilities (alpha reliabilities are a measure of how well a number of individual items measure one concept—for example how well 10 items together measure antisocial attitudes) for each domain and the composite scores were within normal limits of those alpha reliabilities published elsewhere. (For a list of alpha reliabilities used as comparisons consult Andrews & Bonta, 1999). Second, we found, as expected, that men scored higher than women when comparing their composite scores (total LSI-R score). Lastly, while overall women scored lower than men in terms of risk, they scored higher on such items as those pertaining to mental health problems, family problems, financial problems, and having a criminal spouse or partner.

This discussion serves as a potential explanation as to why risk assessment instruments, when properly developed, can be valid for males and females. At the left side of Figure 32.2, the two boxes contain some factors sited as potential predictors specific to female offenders. While we do not deny this to be the case, it is our contention that these factors operate through other criminogenic needs that will be captured on properly developed risk assessment instruments. The implications of this are that, for the purposes of prediction, we do not need to assess the factors listed in the two boxes at the left of Figure 32.2 if clear and detailed measures of criminogenic needs are included on the risk assessment instrument in question.

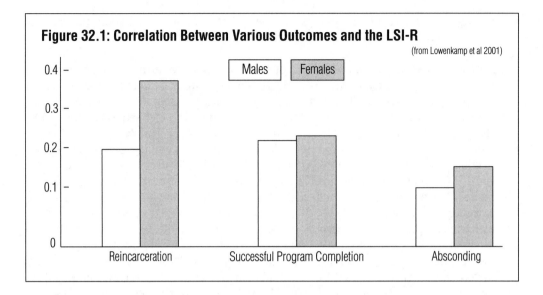

Figure 32.1: Correlation Between Various Outcomes and the LSI-R

(from Lowenkamp et al 2001)

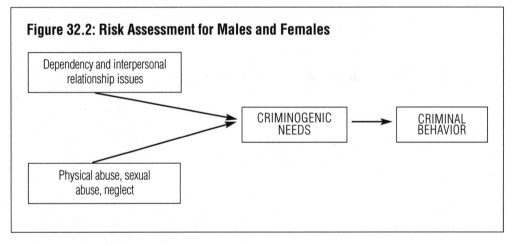

Figure 32.2: Risk Assessment for Males and Females

This is the case, as the factors listed in the two boxes at the left of Figure 32.2 operate and effect criminal behavior through criminogenic needs. If someone is physically or sexually abused, it is likely to lead to substance abuse, emotional problems, or possibly relationship problems (Lowenkamp et al, 2001). These factors are in turn directly related to criminality. Having this knowledge, assessors may need to consider expanded circumstances or explore additional background areas when assessing females to ensure that the necessary information is obtained to assess the offender and subsequently an accurate measure of risk is obtained.

It should be noted that the underlying causes or precursors of criminogenic needs must be understood and explored. This is of particular importance for female offenders as this is where differences between the two sexes might be seen. The information garnered through this process of exploring the causes of criminogenic needs has little bearing on prediction and need not be quantified or numerically measured. However, it has significant implications for treatment and offender adjustment. For example, it would be important to know that an offender's substance use and abuse started because of physical or sexual abuse rather than simply because of recreational activities with friends. While both need substance abuse treatment, the underlying causes that led to the abuse are different and may call for different types of additional counseling to prevent abuse in the future.

CONCLUSION

In conclusion, it seems that risk assessment instruments that are based on theory and properly developed through extensive testing and revisions are capable of assessing risk for males and females. While the average level of risk or the presence of a problem differs between males and females, these differences are expected to exist given information about male and female offenders in general. As a rule, risk assessors need to be aware of and note the causal factors behind criminogenic needs. This is where substantial differences between male and female offenders will be seen.

About the Authors

Christopher T. Lowenkamp, M.S., is a research associate at the University of Cincinnati, Division of Criminal Justice. Edward J. Latessa, Ph.D., is Professor and Head, University of Cincinnati, Division of Criminal Justice.

References

Andrews D.A., & Bonta, J., *Psychology of Criminal Conduct*, 2nd ed. (Anderson Publishing, 1999).

Bonta, J., "Risk-Needs Assessment and Treatment," in A. Harland (Ed.), *Choosing Correctional Options That Work: Defining the Demand and Evaluating the Supply* (pp. 18-32) (Sage Publications, 1996).

Chesney-Lind, M., "Girls' Crime and Woman's Place: Toward a Feminist Model of Female Delinquency," 35 *Crime and Delinquency* 5-29 (1989).

Funk, S., "Risk Assessment for Juveniles on Probation," 23 *Criminal Justice and Behavior* 427-439 (1999).

Gendreau, P., Little, T., & Goggin, C., "A Meta-Analysis of the Predictors of Adult Offender Recidivism: What Works!" 34 *Criminology* 575-607 (1996).

Hoffman, P., "Females, Recidivism, and Salient Factor Score: A Research Note," 9 *Criminal Justice and Behavior* 121-125 (1982).

Hubbard, D., & Pratt, T., "A Meta-Analysis of the Predictors of Delinquency Among Girls," Journal of Offender Rehabilitation 1-14 (2002).

Lowenkamp, C., Holsinger, A., & Latessa, E., "Risk/Need Assessment, Offender Classification, and the Role of Childhood Abuse," 28 *Criminal Justice and Behavior* 543-563 (2001).

Lowenkamp, C. & Latessa, E., *A Profile of Offenders at the New Directions Program, Oklahoma City, Oklahoma* (University of Cincinnati, unpublished, 2001a).

Lowenkamp, C. & Latessa, E., *A Profile of Offenders in Idaho Using the LSI-R* (University of Cincinnati, unpublished, 2001b).

Lowenkamp, C. & Latessa, E., *A Profile of Offenders in Prison and the Community in North Dakota* (University of Cincinnati, unpublished, 2002).

Mazerolle, P., "Gender, General Strain, and Delinquency: An Empirical Examination," *Justice Quarterly* pp. 15, 65-91 (1998).

Simourd, L., & Andrews, D.A., "Correlates of Delinquency: A Look at Gender Differences," 6 *Forum on Correctional Research* 26-31(1994).

Chapter 33

Women Offenders and Prison Classification: A Paradox

by Patricia Van Voorhis, Ph.D. and Lois Presser, Ph.D.

INTRODUCTION

Since 1990, the number of incarcerated women offenders increased 108% while men accounted for a 77% increase (Beck & Harrison, 2001). Having overlooked female offenders for years, policy-makers are ill equipped to deal with these increases. Moreover, existing research provides only limited guidance, because it is nearly nonexistent (see Belknap, 2001; Bloom & Owen, 2002; Chesney Lind, 1997). In this context, serious questions need to be

This chapter originally appeared in Women, Girls & Criminal Justice, *Vol. 4, No. 1, December/January 2003.*

asked about the adequacy and availability of women's programs, services, and facilities.

Growth rates of this magnitude also underscore the need for sound strategies of classification and assessment (Beck & Mumola, 1999). Even though classification determines crucial aspects of one's prison sentence (e.g., living conditions, time to release, privileges, and program assignments) sources note that existing classification models may be irrelevant to women offenders (Morash et al., 1998). Like programs, classification approaches typically have been developed for men and applied to women with little attention to their effectiveness (Brennan, 1998; Morash et al.,1998).

In 1999, the Prisons Division of the National Institute of Corrections (NIC) sought to further explore the status of current strategies for classifying women offenders. This entailed a national assessment of correctional officials in the 50 states and the Federal Bureau of Prisons. This assessment was a component of two NIC initiatives to address issues pertinent to women offenders. They included two cooperative agreements to address and improve classification systems for women offenders and one pertinent to women's programs and services (for classification systems, see Hardyman, 2001; Van Voorhis et al., 2002; for programs and services, see Bloom & Owen, 2002).

Results of the assessment supported concerns regarding the validity, legality, and relevance of classification. They also provided some direction to NIC's efforts to work with states to improve these systems. This survey was essential in this regard, because extant literature was unclear about what the purpose of classifying women offenders should be, and there were so few validation studies involving women offenders that it was not possible to determine whether existing systems were meeting any purposes of corrections, e.g., custody, housing, or programming.

This chapter summarizes the results of our discussions with correctional officials across the United States. (A larger, more detailed report is available on the NIC website, www.nic.org.)

FRAMING ISSUES

Notwithstanding the dearth of research on the topic, several issues framed the scope of this study.

Foundation of Classification Systems

First, a search through an array of unpublished validation studies (all these studies are on file at the NIC Information Center, but, as we noted earlier, few involved women offenders) revealed that the foundation of most institutional classification systems were instruments that addressed custody and security. In most instances these involved variations of an NIC Model Prisons approach—a system for predicting prison disciplinary infractions. The earlier NIC intake and reclassification classification models contained mostly static variables (e.g., history of institutional violence, severity of current and prior convictions, escape history, current or pending detainers, prior felonies, substance abuse, assaultive behavior, age, and misconduct). Later NIC versions added dynamic variables, such as education, employment, and performance in programs.

Earlier surveys indicated that not all correctional officials agreed that women offenders were as dangerous as men (Burke & Adams, 1991; Morash et al., 1998). As shown in Figure 33.1 those few validation studies that sampled both men and women supported this

---

Figure 33.1: Percent Serious Prison Misconducts by Sex

Author	Males	Females
Hardyman, 1999	17%	7%
Austin, Chan, & Elms, 1993 (fighting)	8%	3%
Harer & Langan, 2000	19%	3%

---

assertion. Findings such as these also suggested that custody classification systems clearly were more important for men than women.

Relevance of Classification Variables

Some sources questioned the relevance of commonly used classification variables, such as static criminal history variables and stability factors (e.g., age, education, and employment) (Burke & Adams, 1991). This concern was underscored by research which identified additional, and perhaps more relevant, risk factors for women, including:

- Marital status and suicide attempts (Forcier, 1995);

- Family structure of the childhood home (Balthazar & Cook, 1984; Kruttschnitt & Krmpotich, 1990);

- Childhood abuse, depression, and substance abuse (McClellan et al., 1997);

- Single parenting and reliance upon public assistance (Bonta et al., 1995); and

- Dysfunctional relationships (Covington, 1998).

Validity of Models for Women

The issue of whether or not existing classification models were valid for women posed legal concerns (Brennan, 1998). It has long been considered unethical to apply *any* assessment to a population unlike the one used for its construction and validation (AACP, 2000; APA, 1992). Even so, agencies often neglect to validate risk and custody classification systems, much less do so for specific populations (Van Voorhis & Brown, 1996). This omission has been the subject of at least one class action decision awarded to women offenders in Michigan: *Cain vs. Michigan Department of Corrections*, 548 NW2d 210, 222, n. 30 (Mich. 1996). Rather than being unique to corrections, this situation has unfortunate parallels in the fields of education, mental health, and medicine. In such cases, the consequences adversely affected women, resulting in less accurate:

- College admissions and scholarships (Sternberg & Williams, 1997);

- Mental health assessments (Gilligan, 1993);

- Information regarding women's heart attacks and strokes (Arnstein et al., 1996); and

- Understandings of drug dosages and side effects for women (Martin et al., 1998).

All of these adversities started with the error of conducting most studies on men and prematurely generalizing the findings to women.

Over-Classification of Women

Officials and researchers feared that systems could easily over-classify women offenders, directing that they be assigned to higher security/risk classification than warranted. This could occur as an artifact of prediction to low base rates as well as the fact that high-risk women are not as dangerous as high-risk men, even though they are more dangerous relative to other women offenders (see Van Voorhis et al., 2002). High citation rates for irritable behavior (rather than serious behaviors) could also help to drive classification scores higher, especially in settings where staff were inadequately trained to work with women offenders.

Relevance to Treatment Decisions

It was difficult to see how custody classification models could assist efforts to make treatment-related decisions (Andrews & Bonta, 1998; Van Voorhis, 2000). Program decisions are best informed by needs assessments or checklists indicating whether inmates show problems related to substance abuse, physical health, mental health, education, employment, or family issues.

This could encompass those community correctional risk assessment models that simultaneously assess risk and needs by tapping "criminogenic needs," or dynamic predictors of future offending (Andrews et al., 1990). In either case, we saw no evidence of any systems which tapped problems most important to women offenders, such as victimization, child care, self-esteem, relationships, and substance abuse and mental health issues relevant to gender (Brennan, 1998; LIS, Inc., 1998; Morash, 1998). Moreover, the research was too limited to determine whether these needs may also have been related to risk of re-offending.

Discouragement Regarding Use of Gender-Specific Classification

Finally, whether for purposes of custody, risk, or needs assessment, the use of gender-responsive classification factors had been discouraged for

- Legal reasons, (e.g., equal protection concerns [see Brennan, 1998; Burke & Adams, 1991]; Burke and Adams [1991] attach a legal analysis conducted by Nicholas and Loeb [1991] that effectively dispels these concerns);

- Lack of research on women-specific predictors of institutional infractions;

- Ongoing disagreements concerning whether or not there are enough dangerous behaviors to predict; and

- Arguments concerning whether or not women *should* be classified according to risk (Stanko, 1997).

STUDY GOALS AND APPROACH

In sum, the existing literature raised a number of questions for further exploration by the national assessment. The assessment sought to understand the extent to which issues pertaining to validity, purpose, over-classification, and relevance typified current correctional practices and whether agencies had formulated approaches for resolving them. Further, the national assessment sought detailed descriptions of practices currently in use for women offenders, including both problematic areas and emerging strategies. We were interested in officials' perceptions of whether their systems "worked" for women and served as a tool for making custody, programming, and housing decisions. Finally, we explored the extent to which agencies found the classification needs of women offenders to be different from men's and were particularly attentive to states that had made changes to their systems.

These matters were addressed through telephone contacts with representatives from 50 state correctional agencies and the Federal Bureau of Prisons, which took place between February 29 and May 23, 2000. Most of the respondents (33) were state directors of classification; five were administrators of women's facilities; four were research analysts; one was a clinical director; and eight were serving in some other administrative capacity (e.g., regional administrators). Occasionally, we contacted a consultant or researcher known to have worked with the agency.

STUDY FINDINGS

Purpose of Classification

What should be the purpose of classifying women offenders? The overwhelming majority of respondents noted security and public safety as the central purpose to be served by incarcerating and classifying women offenders. The implication of such a response appeared to favor continued use of custody classification systems designed to predict prison misconduct. Even so, 15 respondents observed that existing custody classification models failed to assist in programming and case-management decisions and ignored needs that were unique to women. Needs, according to these respondents, were as important as custody for women offenders. Some respondents also asserted that their systems did not necessarily do a good job of addressing custody considerations, because they did not move less serious women offenders through the system quickly enough. In this sense, "custody" pertained as much to low-custody inmates as to high-custody inmates, but typically failed low custody women.

Are Women and Men Classified Differently?

Although many respondents discussed clear differences between men and women offenders in terms of needs and dangerousness, very few states had incorporated these differences into their objective prison classification instruments. For example, 21 states employed a system that was a based on the NIC Model Prisons instrument described above. The remaining states employed objective instruments that were developed by outside researchers or "in house." Reclassification was typically conducted every three to six months, however, 14 states reclassified women on an annual basis. Of course, for numerous women serving short sentences annual reclassification meant *no* reclassification.

When asked if the classification system was developed primarily for men, four respondents indicated that their systems were developed for men and then applied for women. Thirty-nine indicated that their systems were designed for both men and women. As will be seen short-ly, however, this in no way assured that it incorporated factors that were relevant for women or that the model had been validated on a sample of women offenders.

Separate Classification Procedures

Respondents from 12 states reported different classification procedures for men and women. The distinctions were as follows:

- Four states (Idaho, New York, Massachusetts, and Ohio) had a separate custody classification system for women. (We have since learned that Illinois has a separate system for women offenders. At the time or our survey, Illinois had switched from using a separate system for women to using the same system for all inmates. They have since changed back to separate systems for men and women.)

- Four states and the Federal Bureau of Prisons instituted different cut-off scores for men and women, representing an attempt to tie each custody level to a group of offenders with similar behavioral outcomes.

- Two states changed specific variables to better reflect the nature of women's offend-ing. For example, New York reduced points on a common variable, seriousness of the current offense, for women who murdered an abuser in self-defense.

- Four states expanded options on existing variables to accommodate the nature of women's risk factors and their infractions while in prison. Employment variables, for example, were changed to avoid classifying full-time parents/caregivers as unemployed. Escape variables were modified to provide lower scores for offend-ers who walked away from community or other non-secure settings. Misconduct counted for shorter time periods on reclassification instruments.

Validation Problems

At the time of this survey only 14 states reported having validated their custody classification systems on a sample of women offenders. An additional 11 states combined women and men in the same validation sample. Unfortunately, combined samples often failed to show that an assessment was valid for women because they contained far fewer women than men. The resulting statistics were thus driven by the majority of the sample—men. Since the survey, an additional six states have conducted validation studies. All studies found that existing sys-tems were invalid for women offenders; two states have implemented improvements.

Over-Classification of Women Offenders

In many cases, existing classification systems over-classified women offenders. That is, the classification system assigned too many women to unnecessarily high custody levels, which ultimately required officials to override the classifications to lower levels. Representatives from 10 states indicated that they overrode more than 15% of their classification scores (override rates ranged from 18% to 70% of their cases). In effect, these agencies (20% of the total) indicated that their systems were not working for women offenders.

Failure to Adequately Assess Needs of Women

Classification systems did not adequately assess women's needs; therefore they did not assist efforts to link women to needed programs. Responses to questions about women's programming and treatment needs strongly echoed recent writings on gender-responsive programming (e.g., see Bloom & Owen, 2002). Forty-nine respondents (92%) asserted that women have unique needs that should be addressed in correctional settings; yet only eight states reported use of a system that identified gender-specific needs. Respondents suggested the following needs for inclusion into new needs assessments for women: trauma and abuse (23), self-esteem/assertiveness (10), vocational needs (10), medical (21), mental health (14), parenting and childcare (33), and relationship issues (8).

Custody Classification Disregarded

Many states did not use the custody classification systems to make institutional or housing decisions for women offenders. Given the observation that public safety and security was their primary concern, it was surprising to learn that in 35 states women with different custody scores were housed together in at least one if not all of the state's facilities for women. That is, regardless of the assigned custody level, women, unlike men, were often assigned to an institution where custody did not impact housing, privileges, programming, or movement throughout the facility. Furthermore, this practice occurred without increased risk of prison misconduct or breaches of security. Custody scores could, however, affect whether a woman worked outside of the facility's perimeter, the types of restraints required during transportation, and, more importantly, whether or not she moved to a community placement.

CONCLUSION

We know from our own experience that, since this survey, at least six states have worked to validate and change their systems for classifying women offenders. In most instances their work is not yet complete. Notwithstanding these new projects, this assessment clearly identified urgent areas of need. From an agency perspective, a clear picture of vulnerability to legal consequences is portrayed by the finding that, as of 2000, 36 states had not, to the knowledge of their officials, validated their classification systems for women offenders. Our concern is underscored by the fact that, from our working experience, these systems are more likely to be invalid than valid.

On another note, respondents spoke both indirectly and directly to the concern that classification typically failed to facilitate management and programming decisions regarding women offenders. Otherwise, why were 35 states not using the classifications to base institutional or housing placements and why do the majority of the respondents relate that needs assessments fail to adequately inform case management and programming decisions?

From the perspective of women offenders, flawed classification systems precipitate flawed decision making with respect to programming, rewards, work assignments, and release. Moreover, irrelevant needs assessment strategies cannot link offenders to programs even when the programs may be exemplary.

Other reports speak to strategies for meaningful improvements (Hardyman, 2001; Van Voorhis & Presser, 2001; Van Voorhis et al.). These range from minimal changes to custody instruments to major ones. The reports also question correctional policies, e.g.:

- What is the role of custody in populations where so few members commit violent acts?

- What are the most important risk factors to consider in classifying women offenders and in programming for their release?

- Are staff adequately trained to supervise and manage women offenders?

Of course, when the underlying problem is really a matter of policy, it is not likely to be resolved by a classification system.

About the Authors

Patricia Van Voorhis, Ph.D., is a professor at the University of Cincinnati, in the Division of Criminal Justice. Lois Presser, Ph.D., is an assistant professor at the University of Tennessee, in the Department of Sociology.

References

American Association of Correctional Psychologists (AACP) (Standards Committee), "Standards for Psychology Services in Jails, Prison, Correctional Facilities and Agencies," 27(4) *Criminal Justice and Behavior* 433-493 (2000).

American Psychological Association (APA), "Ethical Principles of Psychologists and Code of Conduct," 47 *American Psychologist* 1597-1611 (1992).

Andrews, D., & Bonta, J., *The Psychology of Criminal Conduct*, 2nd ed. (Anderson, 1998).

Andrews, D., Bonta, J., & Hoge, R., "Classification for Effective Rehabilitation: Rediscovering Psychology," 17(1) *Criminal Justice and Behavior* 19-52 (1990).

Arnstein, P., Buselli, E., & Rankin, S., " Women and Heart Attacks: Prevention, Diagnosis, and Care," 21(5) *Nurse Practitioner* 57-69 (1996).

Balthazar, M., & Cook, R., " An Analysis of the Factors Related to the Rate of Violent Crimes Committed by Incarcerated Female Delinquents." In S. Chaneles (Ed.), *Gender Issues, Sex Offenses, and Criminal Justice: Current Trends* (pp. 103-118) (Haworth Press, 1984).

Beck, A. & Harrison, P. M., *Prisoners in 2000* (Bureau of Justice Programs, 2001).

Beck, A. & Mumola, C., *Prisoners in 1998: Bureau of Justice Statistics Bulletin* (Bureau of Justice Statistics, 1999).

Belknap, J., *The Invisible Woman: Gender, Crime and Justice* (Wadsworth, 2001).

Bloom, B. & Owen, B., *Gender-Responsive Strategies: Research Practice and Guiding Principles for Women Offenders* (National Institute of Corrections, 2002).

Bonta, J., Pang, B., & Wallace-Capretta, S., "Predictors of Recidivism Among Incarcerated Female Offenders," 75(3) *The Prison Journal* 277-294 (1995).

Brennan, T., " Institutional Classification of Females: Problems and Some Proposals for Reform," In R. Zaplin (Ed.), *Female Crime and Delinquency: Critical Perspectives and Effective Interventions* (pp 179-204) (Aspen, 1998).

Burke, P., & Adams, L., *Classification of Women Offenders in State Correctional Facilities: A Handbook for Practitioners* (National Institute of Corrections, 1991).

Chesney-Lind, M., *The Female Offender: Girls, Women, and Crime* (Sage, 1997).

Covington, S., "The Relational Theory of Women's Psychological Development: Implications for the Criminal Justice System." In R. Zaplin (Ed.), *Female Crime and Delinquency: Critical Perspectives and Effective Intervention* (pp. 113-131) (Aspen, 1998).

Forcier, M., *Massachusetts Department of Correction Female Offender Objective Classification Technical Assistance Project: Final Report* (National Institute of Corrections, 1995).

Gilligan, C., *In a Different Voice: Psychological Theory and Women's Development* (Harvard University Press, 1993).

Hardyman, P., (2001), *Validation and Refinement of Objective Prison Classification Systems for Women: The Experience of Four States and Common Themes* (National Institute of Corrections, 2001).

Kruttschnitt, C., & Krmpotich, S., "Aggressive Behavior Among Female Inmates: An Exploratory Study," 7(2) *Justice Quarterly* 371-389 (1990).

LIS, Inc, *Current Issues in the Operation of Women's Prisons* (National Institute of Corrections, 1998).

Martin, R., Biswas, P., Freemantle, S., Pearce, G., & Mann, R., "Age and Sex Distribution of Suspected Adverse Drug Reaction to Newly Marketed Drugs in General Practice in England: Analysis of 48 Cohort Studies," 46(5) *British Journal of Clinical Pharmacology* 505-511 (1998).

McClellan, D., Farabee, D., & Crouch, B., "Early Victimization, Drug Use, and Criminality," 24(4) *Criminal Justice and Behavior* 455-476 (1997).

Morash, M., Bynum, T., & Koons, B., *Women Offenders: Programming Needs and Promising Approaches* (National Institute of Justice, 1998).

Nicholas, S., & Loeb, A., "Legal Analysis." In P. Burke & L. Adams, *Classification of Women Offenders in State Correctional Facilities: A Handbook for Practitioners* (National Institute of Corrections, 1991).

Stanko, E., "Safety Talk: Conceptualizing Women's Risk Assessment as a 'Technology of the Soul,'" 1(4) *Theoretical Criminology* 479-499 (1997).

Sternberg, R. & Williams, W., "Does the GRE Predict Meaningful Success in the Graduate Training of Psychologists?" 52(6) *American Psychologist* 630-641(1997).

Van Voorhis, P., "An Overview of Offender Classification Systems," In P. Van Voorhis, M. Braswell, & D. Lester (Eds.), *Correctional Counseling & Rehabilitation*, 3rd ed. (pp. 81-108) (Anderson, 1999).

Van Voorhis, P. & Brown, K., (1996), *Risk Classification in the 1990s* (National Institute of Corrections, 1996).

Van Voorhis, P., & Presser, L., *Classification of Women Offenders: A National Assessment of Current Practices* (National Institute of Corrections, 2001).

Van Voorhis, P., Pealer, J., Presser, L., Spiropoulis, G., & Sutherland, J., *Classification of Women Offenders: A National Assessment of Current Practices and the Experience of Three States* (National Institute of Corrections, 2002).

Chapter 34

The Women's Assessment Project

by Mary Grace, M.Ed., M.S., Jenny O'Donnell, Psy.D.,
William Walters, Ph.D., Walter S. Smitson, Ph.D. and
Mary Carol Melton

INTRODUCTION

The Women's Assessment Project was undertaken as a pilot study in the fall of 1999 in collaboration with the Hamilton County (Ohio) Probation Department, Department of Pre-trial Services, and Central Clinic. The objective of the study was to determine the mental health and substance abuse status of women being sent to a locked residential community assessment facility. Women could be sent to this facility from either the pre-trial or post-conviction stage of their criminal justice system involvement. Data derived from this study could identify undiagnosed mental illness and substance abuse disorders among incarcerated women which could in turn suggest unmet system service needs. Based on this evidence, calls for proposals could be developed to meet these service needs. In addition, this data could be used to develop effective aftercare plans for women as they end a period of incarceration and attempt community reintegration.

This chapter originally appeared in Women, Girls & Criminal Justice, *Vol. 3, No. 4, June/July 2002.*

STUDY PROCEDURES

Women who were sent to the assessment facility were approached each morning by the project psychology assistant and asked to participate on a first come, first served basis. Participation was high. Over 80% of women approached agreed to participate in the project. The study was explained to each participant and consent obtained before the interviewing process began. Participation was voluntary for all women. No financial compensation was made for participation. Once a woman gave consent for participation, she was administered a battery of standardized self-report and interview based measures by the psychology assistant. Several days later she received an extensive diagnostic assessment from a licensed psychologist who had previously reviewed the findings from the standardized assessments.

MEASURES

A battery of standardized assessments was used in this study to provide a comprehensive assessment of mental health and cognitive functioning. A brief description of each of these measures follows.

- *WASI:* The Wechsler Abbreviated Scale of Intelligence (WASI) is an interviewer-administered assessment of intelligence divided into two areas of Verbal and Performance subtests, yielding a Verbal IQ, a Performance IQ and a full scale IQ. Individual participant scores are interpreted against national norms of above average, average, low average, borderline, and mentally retarded.

- *WRAT-3:* The Wide Range Achievement Test (WRAT-3) is an interviewer-administered measure of a participant's level of academic achievement normed against the performance of other individuals in the participant's age group. Three subscales of Reading, Spelling, and Arithmetic are derived and data is presented in terms of standar:d scores, percentiles, and grade level achieved (i.e., 9th grade level).

- *BASIS-32:* The BASIS-32, a standardized, self-report problem behavior and symptom identification assessment tool, was developed in 1987 by the McLean Hospital (Belmont, Massachusetts) Department of Mental Health Services and is currently in broad use in both the public and private mental health services arena. The tool is scored in five specific domains of mental health functioning including relationships, depression and anxiety, daily living skills, impulsiveness and addictive behavior, and psychosis. In addition, the tool yields an Overall Impairment Score. Outpatient and inpatient norms have been established in large samples for the BASIS-32, which will allow the development and use of cutoff scores to determine likely cases of psychiatric illness.

- *TESI:* The Traumatic Events Screening Inventory (TESI) is a self-report measure that captures the occurrence of a number of traumatic life events in the participant's, life. These include sexual, physical, and psychological abuse, natural and man-made disasters, death, and injury. Comparative data are available from patient and non-patient samples.

- *SCID for DSM IV:* The Structured Clinical Interview for Diagnosis (SCID) was developed as a clinical interview designed to elicit the presence or absence of each of the AXIS I psychiatric disorders contained in the American Psychiatric Association's *Diagnostic and Statistical Manual*. Symptoms of each psychiatric disorder are investigated in a standardized way. Disorders are grouped into modules including substance abuse/dependence disorders, anxiety disorders, mood disorders, and psychotic disorders. At the completion of the SCID, a comprehensive diagnostic report is electronically rendered for each client. The SCID is widely used in research studies of psychiatric disorders.

FINDINGS

Demographic Characteristics

Forty women participated in this pilot project from October through December 1999. Women participants were, on average, 32 years old. Over three-quarters of these participants were African American, 90% were unmarried, 48% had less than a high school diploma, and over 67% had children, although only 30% of women with children had custody of their children. At the time of incarceration, 40% of the women reported working full time and an additional 32% reported working part time.

Forensic Status

Women in this sample were at the pre-trial or post-conviction stage of the criminal justice process in almost equal measure (42% vs. 58%). Over one-half of the women were incarcerated for misdemeanor offenses. Ninety-five percent of the women had a prior legal history, 45% for misdemeanors only.

Cognitive and Psychiatric Status

Scores on the WASI IQ test indicated that only 45% of participants had an average IQ; 17% were low average, 25% borderline, and 13% mentally retarded. The WRAT-3 academic achievement test indicated that 55% of the women had reading skills below the 9th grade level, 65% had spelling skills below the 9th grade level, and 95% had arithmetic skills below the 9th grade level.

The SCID identified Axis I psychiatric disorders in 75% of the women participants; 38% of the group had combined substance abuse and at least one other Axis I psychiatric disorder. Thirty one percent of the women had only a substance abuse/dependence diagnosis. Among the women with psychiatric disorders in addition to substance abuse, 35% had mood disorders, 23% had anxiety disorders, and 13% had post traumatic stress disorder (PTSD).

The BASIS-32 measure of behavioral and symptom distress indicated that, while the group as a whole reported only mild symptoms of distress on average, women who had psychiatric disorders had overall distress scores at the same level as psychiatric outpatient norms reported nationally. When the total sample is divided into women without any psychiatric diagnosis, women with a substance abuse diagnosis only and women with dual diagnosis, clear differences among groups appear on the BASIS-32. Women with dual psychiatric diagnoses report over twice the impairment as those with no diagnosis. Women with substance abuse diagnoses only also report significantly less distress than women with dual diagnoses.

Trauma History

The average number of traumatic events that have occurred in these women's lives is nine. Abuse of all sorts is a common occurrence: 53% report physical abuse, 55% report sexual abuse, and 63% report psychological abuse.

DISCUSSION OF FINDINGS

Serious Mental Health Problems and Educational Deficits

Results of this pilot study reveal significant levels of psychiatric diagnoses in addition to substance abuse/dependence diagnoses in the group of women incarcerated at the assessment facility. Behavioral and symptom distress scores for those women with psychiatric disorders exceeded large, published outpatient sample scores. In addition, this study found a serious lack of intellectual capacity and educational achievement in many of the women interviewed. Numerous traumatic events, particularly sexual, physical, and psychological abuse, were common. These findings, taken together, suggest the need for programming that addresses underlying psychiatric and substance abuse diagnoses, which may be contributing to women's involvement in the criminal justice system. The data also suggest that programming needs to be targeted to a woman's level of intellectual ability and readiness.

The population of the assessment facility would be seen as a relatively typical county jail population. The women were from a variety of situations, and varied demographically, socioeconomically, and educationally. These were not women who were thought to be in need of mental health services, and certainly were not flagged to receive any mental health services while in jail. Those women who were identified as needing mental health services, such as those who are not competent to stand trial, were already on psychotropic medications, were flagrantly psychotic, and were known to be involved in the local mental health system had already been screened out of this population. Women who behaved bizarrely, self-mutilated, or acted aggressively toward others were not housed at the facility and therefore were not included in this study.

However, despite the process of prescreening, this study revealed that the women at the assessment facility have significant histories of physical, sexual, and emotional abuse; cognitive deficits; and mental health needs. They also exhibited problems with achieving appropriate life milestones, maintaining jobs and stable housing, managing their parental responsibilities and substance abuse.

Programming Implications

This study allowed for a clinical assessment of a general population of incarcerated women so that future programming would meet the identified needs of this population, but it also provided an opportunity for the individuals who were evaluated to experience the potential benefits of counseling and mental health services. Several of the participants reported that they had never had an opportunity to discuss their histories, fears, and symptoms with anyone, and that they felt overwhelmed when trying to find out where and how to get appropriate services for their particular situation. Many of the women expressed a sense of relief and hopefulness at having been able to talk to mental health professionals, and were thankful for the opportunity to be heard. Several asked for information regarding community services that would be appropriate, and available to them when they were released, and how to access those services.

The women who participated in this study showed a clear need for treatment for academic underachievement and cognitive deficits; histories of physical, sexual, and emotional abuse and issues of grief and loss of loved ones; unmet expectations; and co-occurring mental health and substance abuse.

The academic needs of this population suggest that programming should be designed for those with significantly lower academic achievement that would particularly impact understanding written materials, being able to read without assistance, and being able to write or journal without assistance. Because of the cognitive deficits of this group, treatment planning and program design must be geared for individuals who will learn best from a model designed for their level of understanding. For example, information will be best learned in small chunks, using repetition. They will need information to be presented both verbally and visually, with repeated clarification. Regular checking with the participant for their interpretation of the information will help the facilitator recognize how much the participant has learned, and at what pace they can proceed.

This population identified several topics that could be treated through psychotherapy groups. The specific issues were sexual, physical, and emotional abuse as children and adults, as well as anger management, relationship issues, and stress management. These women were often still involved in abusive relationships and were unsure how to leave the relationships or how to avoid those relationships in the future. These issues result in ongoing depression leading to continued drug use. Breaking the cycle of trauma that continues to interfere with day-to-day mood and behavior is critical.

The specific needs to be addressed with regards to parenting issues are two-fold. Those women who still have custody of their children are in need of parent training and support groups that provide a safe place for them to process the frustration of parenting, and the feelings of being overwhelmed by their responsibilities. Those women who no longer have custody of their children often expressed anger, grief, hopelessness, and confusion about their situation and need to be able to learn to cope with those feelings without being incapacitated or turning to substances.

Clinical Implications

Most of the individuals with co-occurring mental health and substance abuse issues were higher functioning than those in a typical substance abuse/mental illness (SAMI) program. However, these women are still in need of a dual-diagnosis treatment model that can help them balance the need for medication with abstinence from other mood altering drugs while also teaching them to live with their mental illness and the day-to-day difficulties that may entail. Several of the women may also need an evaluation for appropriateness for medication once they have detoxified from their illicit drug use and have been sober for longer than 90 days.

The clinical implications of this study are that we need to develop an effective assessment model that allows prescreening to explore more of the behavioral/psychological/cognitive needs of the population. Many of these needs are not apparent in a brief conversation or interview that only addresses non-clinical issues. This assessment could utilize such tools as BASIS-32 or other self-report measures (i.e. asking about special education placement) that will flag the inmates with the more difficult to detect mental health needs that we found in this population. When such women are identified, there should be some provision made for more in-depth psychological assessments, either by a clinical interview or other psycho-metric measures administered by trained mental health forensic personnel. There should be a dedicated team of forensic mental health professionals conducting these assessments. We found that over time, as the population became more comfortable with the project, the women were more likely to be open and more revealing with the identified staff.

Discharge Planning

Lastly, discharge planning needs to begin the moment the inmate comes into the system. The complexity of getting connected to the cluster of services, and being reconnected to the outside world is more than most of these women are capable of doing, both emotionally and cognitively. A coordinated effort among the mental health providers, the social service agencies and the criminal justice system could be embodied in a transitional case manage-ment team. That team could then facilitate connecting these women with appropriate services, and hopefully provide them with the vehicle that they need to better manage their lives.

About the Authors

Mary Grace, M.Ed., M.S, is Outcomes and Quality Management Director of Hamilton County's Central Clinic in Cincinnati, Ohio. Walter S. Smitson, Ph.D., is President and CEO of Central Clinic. Mary Carol Melton is Vice President–Resource Development of Cincinnati: Union Bethel; previously, she was Assistant Director of Central Clinic. William Walters, Ph.D., is Assistant Director, and Jenny O'Donnell, Psy.D., is Research Assistant at the Hamilton Country Court Clinic.

Part 5

Drug Treatment, Health Care, and Mental Health Services

The extent and level of services being provided to women and girls in the criminal justice system has undoubtedly increased in recent years. In addition, our knowledge has improved about not just the conditions and circumstances of confinement and custody but also the backgrounds and the immediate and imminent needs of these women and girls. In many ways, this knowledge complicates our understanding of how we maintain custody of women and girls, reduce their confinement, or supervise them within community-based settings. This knowledge is challenging because it presents specific pictures of the often quite serious needs of this population. Where, then, are the willingness, resources, and skills necessary to address these needs in a least-restrictive environment?

The eight chapters in this section only begin to scratch the surface of these important questions. Nonetheless, among the approaches being taken to address these concerns are the following:

- Anthropologist Dorinda L. Welle and veteran drug researcher Gregory P. Falkin report the results of qualitative research on the self-described experiences of women drug users who "violate" or "turn it around," including a better understanding of a broader range of behavior these women experience in the course of their substance (ab)use and treatment.

- Maryland practitioners Joan Gillesce and Betty Russell describe several clinical approaches toward the provision of mental health and substance abuse treatment for incarcerated and community-based women.

- Drug researchers Nena Messina, William Burdon, Michael Prendergast, and Meredith Patten assess the psychological, physical, sexual abuse-related, and other needs of women receiving substance abuse treatment in therapeutic communities.

- Canadian researchers Cathy Fillmore and Colleen Anne Dell look at women's self-harming behavior in community and institutional settings, with emphasis on the needs, supports, and services of these women, especially Aboriginal women.

- Minnesota practitioner Lili Garfinkel examines the relationship between disabilities and other risk factors in the lives of female offenders and provides information about mandated special education services, especially for girls-at-risk or girls in the juvenile justice system.

- Veteran health researcher Nancy Stoller, a sociologist, delineates health problems facing women prisoners in California and offers several illustrative case studies on the impact of particular problems on women's lives.

- M. Katherine Maeve raises concerns about the inability of incarcerated women in Georgia to engage in self-care and self-medication.

- Diane Young and Liete Dennis also use case studies to illustrate the complex needs of mentally ill women confined in a local jail in upstate New York.

Chapter 35

Preventing "Violations" Through Drug Treatment

by Dorinda L. Welle, Ph.D. and Gregory P. Falkin, Ph.D.

REDEFINING "VIOLATIONS" AS VICTIMIZATION

In Project WORTH, we conducted a large study of women offenders receiving drug treatment in community and corrections-based programs in New York City and Portland, Oregon. In that study, many women offenders adopted the corrections language of "violations" and "turned it around" to illuminate their own experiences and to understand key relationships in their lives. By listening to how women defined and discussed "violations," the connections between discrete experiences of—and perspectives on—abuse and harassment become clearer. In addition, we can see how drug treatment provided a unique opportunity for women to address a range of "violations": not only the ones they had committed, but also the ones that they had experienced.

In the criminal justice system, women offenders may be mandated into drug treatment after having committed violations of their parole or probation. However, in the entire ethnographic study, not a single woman mentioned that she herself had actively "violated" the conditions of her parole; rather, women described "having been *violated by* [their] parole/probation officer."

At the same time that women described their parole/probation violations as a kind of victimization, they also detailed their own behavior as reasons for the violation. Typical reasons included testing positive for illegal drugs, failing to report to their parole officers (POs) as scheduled, and leaving or "splitting" a mandated drug treatment program. In the case of leaving a court-mandated drug treatment assignment, women reported splitting

This chapter originally appeared in Women, Girls & Criminal Justice, *Vol. 2, No. 6, October/November 2001.*

treatment after a relapse, splitting after discussing sexual abuse issues in women's groups or individual counseling, and leaving in order to return to partners or family members who were in crisis.

Some women experienced all three kinds of parole or probation violations. Women with multiple parole/probation violations reported the pattern of testing for illegal drug use, then being mandated into treatment, splitting treatment, avoiding their parole or probation officer, and eventually returning to drug use. These women were typically re-arrested and sentenced to serve prison time, and spoke bitterly of how often they had been "violated" by their POs.

EXPANDING THE CONCEPTUAL BOUNDARY

The Trauma Recovery Concept of Sexual Violations

Exposure to the notions of trauma and abuse in the course of drug treatment gave many women offenders a new "take" on the concept of violations. Primarily, drug treatment programs offering a range of gender-specific services provided women offenders with the opportunity to examine their own experiences of sexual "violations" (generally with less emphasis on physical abuse as a type of violation). While many of the drug treatment programs in the Project WORTH study provided services to address childhood sexual abuse (Welle, Falkin & Jainchill, 1998), women offenders expanded their definitions of sexual violations to include adult experiences of sexual assault/rape, sexual and economic exploitation by sex work clients or "johns," and sexual assault/rape by employers in the drug economy.

By and large, women offenders described violations by their significant others (SOs) as sexual in nature. In interviews and in support groups at their drug treatment programs, women survivors of domestic violence described their sexual encounters with abusive partners after being hit or beaten as a form of "violation" of dignity. In HIV education groups at the drug treatment programs, women offenders also treated intimate partners' refusals to use condoms as a kind of sexual violation. Extending the language of "being violated by a PO," women offenders in abuse survival and HIV education groups described various examples of "being violated by an SO." Through these similarities in terminology, it became apparent that many women offenders made linkages between the different kinds of violations they experienced from different types of people (e.g., POs vs. SOs), although these linkages were more or less explicitly articulated by individual women.

"Human Rights Violations"

In the context of their experiences in jail and prison, women offenders' definitions of "violations" proliferated and expanded in scope, using not only the concept of physical and emotional boundaries, but also the notion of human rights. In the ethnographic interviews, and in their interactions with drug treatment staff and corrections officers (COs) assigned to their treatment program units, women incarcerated in jail and prison described COs committing three types of violations: sexual violations, violations of dignity, and violations of human rights. Several women offenders described "being violated by [their] COs" sexually, citing examples of being expected to perform sexual favors, being denied privacy, and being submitted to routine and surprise strip searches in admissions, visiting rooms, and on their units. Emotional violations or violations of dignity included COs employing excessive shouting or screaming on the drug treatment unit, name calling and cursing, and assigning sanctions which were perceived as humiliating.

Women participating in drug treatment programs while incarcerated also described a range of deprivations as forms of violations of human rights. Drug treatment staff were sometimes accused of depriving individuals or the entire drug treatment unit of their phone privileges, and COs were variously accused of depriving women in the drug treatment units access to commissary. Some women perceived restricted access to commissary as a form of punishment or a way of leveling or reducing those inmates participating in "special" services while incarcerated (Welle, 1997). In addition, several incarcerated women reported that, at times, COs deprived inmates access to community-based drug treatment advocates: what women inmates considered a "violation of the right to get help." It should be noted that treatment advocates interviewed in the study reported their own frustrations in gaining access to both the general population inmates and to "the floor" of drug treatment units in jails and prisons.

THE DEMAND TO PREVENT RETRAUMATIZATION

These findings are significant in helping understand the impact and diffusion of drug treatment interventions into the various domains of women offenders' everyday lives, not only in community-based drug treatment facilities, but also at home and while incarcerated (Welle & Falkin, 2000). Through access to trauma recovery services, particularly incest survivor groups and domestic abuse survivor groups, women offenders are exposed not only to the notion of "violations" but also to the concept of "boundaries" and "rights." Based on the fundamental belief that no individual deserves to be sexually or physically violated, and reinforcing the fact that sexual and physical abuse are crimes, drug treatment interventions aiming to support abuse survival as part of the drug recovery process directly and indirectly provided women offenders with a conceptual framework and a set of terminology that enabled them to make links across diverse experiences of "violations." In addition, some women implicitly extended the notion of sexual abuse as a crime to inform an everyday notion of the victim's "right to recover," her "right to dignity," and "the right to get help." While these rights are not legally recognized, women offenders' assertion and defense of them illuminated numerous instances of perceived deprivation and mistreatment, and sustained a discourse about women offenders' needs in drug treatment and recovery.

In corrections settings, the fundamental principles of recovery from abuse, with an emphasis on the need to respect personal boundaries and prevent retraumatization, challenge the foundation of corrections practice which assumes an almost total access to the inmate. With implications for the retraumatization of inmates living with post-traumatic stress disorder (PTSD), corrections practices are employed within certain physical, sexual, and legal "boundaries" that may not recognize the violability of the individual or, at a more practical level, may not be accountable to the mental health needs of inmates in general population or drug treatment (as opposed to mental observation/psychiatric treatment) units. Through their appropriation of differently defined notions of violations, a number of women offenders in this study brought drug treatment interventions and corrections practice into conversation with each other.

On the ground, or rather, on the unit, the contradictions between these two ways of understanding violations become "material" for women offenders' efforts to demand and justify more humane treatment on the jail or prison floor. At times, when drug treatment staff was perceived as acting like correction officers, women offenders pointed a similar critique to their treatment staff. After being "taken off of phone privileges" for breaking a cardinal rule of the treatment program, e.g., one woman in a jail-based program shouted to her counselor, "Who are you, my treatment officer?" While these confrontations with corrections officers and "treatment officers" (TOs) remained isolated and localized, such conflicts were observed at all of the corrections-based drug treatment programs that participated in the study.

INTERVENING IN CYCLES OF "VIOLATIONS": APPLYING A TRAUMA MODEL TO DRUG TREATMENT AND CORRECTIONS PRACTICE

The findings reported here suggest the emergence of a social foundation for a unique critique of corrections practice which favor a more respectful approach to drug recovery and abuse survival, to the more traditional, punitive-oriented approaches to drug treatment. In many cases, women offenders are often labeled as "violators" of various laws and legal conditions before they have been identified by service programs as victims and survivors of a range of social and sexual violations. Women offenders' perspectives on violations by POs, COs, SOs, and TOs establish a range of implications for treatment effectiveness in correctional settings. Implied in the accounts of several women offenders in the study, the notion of human rights may in fact provide direction for the design of treatment services and treatment environments that can simultaneously support the goals of drug recovery and recovery from abuse, particularly within correctional settings. For women offenders in the WORTH study, talk about human rights in jails and prisons focused on "the right to get help," the right to remain in contact with loved ones and advocates, and the right to be treated with dignity and respect. While there are numerous problems with merging the roles of COs and drug treatment staff (Welle & Falkin, 1997), sensitivity trainings for COs which identify certain corrections practices as triggers of PTSD have the potential to enhance corrections-based treatment services (Welle, Falkin & Jainchill 1998). Innovative models of parole and probation that endeavor to provide a range of support services to women probationers and parolees may help establish the image of the PO as a resource rather than exclusively as a source of violations.

Intervening in the cycle of violations committed by women offenders' SOs others remains particularly challenging. However, drug treatment programs are uniquely positioned to play an empowering role during and after a woman offender's time in treatment. With increasing numbers of client referrals coming from the criminal justice system, the integration of legal services into the drug treatment repertoire has become a necessity, presenting a significant challenge to the design and delivery of community-based treatment services. Combined with abuse recovery services during treatment, the provision of parenting classes for women offenders with children, increased access to family counseling, and appropriate efforts to either involve SOs in the treatment process or to assist women who desire to establish independence from abusive partners all have the potential to enhance women offenders' drug recovery and prevent a range of violations. Aftercare services are especially crucial in providing support for women offenders in recovery attempting to manage new relationships with both SOs and POs.

CONCLUSION

Drug treatment professionals can exert multi-directional leverage in the prevention of violations in the lives of women offenders in drug recovery. By influencing best practices within the treatment program itself, by providing sensitivity trainings and staff coordination in corrections environments, and by maintaining pro-active linkages to local and state parole and probation departments, treatment programs serving women offenders can enhance the effectiveness of community-based and corrections-based drug treatment and can support the needs of women offenders who are increasingly organizing their drug recovery through the prevention of further violations in their lives.

About the Authors

Dorinda Welle, Ph.D., was the ethnographer for Project WORTH. She is currently Project Director with the Institute on Youth At Risk at the National Development & Research Institutes, Inc. (NDRI), and is Assistant Professor of Socio-Medical Sciences at Columbia University, Mailman School of Public Health. Gregory Falkin, Ph.D., was the Principal Investigator on Project WORTH, and is Deputy Director of the NDRI Institute for Treatment Services Research. The Project WORTH study was funded by National Institutes on Drug Abuse grant (5-RO1DA08688) awarded to Dr. Falkin, with additional support from NDRI.

References

Welle, D. L., *Invisibility Routes: Recovering Women in the American Carceral Network* (Doctoral Dissertation, New School for Social Research, 1997).

Welle, D. L., & Falkin, G. P., "Women Inmates in Drug Treatment: "Bio" Power and Bodies of Righting," 1(1) *Pre/Text: A Journal of Rhetorical Theory (Special Issue on Prison Literacy Cultures)*, 18(1-4): 144-163 (1997).

Welle, D. & Falkin, G., "The Everyday Policing of Women With Romantic Codefendants: An Ethnographic Perspective," 11(2) *Women & Criminal Justice* 45-65 (2000).

Welle, D., Falkin, G. P., & Jainchill, N., "Current Approaches to Drug Treatment for Women Offenders: Project WORTH," 15(2) *Journal of Substance Abuse Treatment* 151-163 (1998).

Chapter 36

Maryland's Programs for Incarcerated and Community-Based Women With Mental Illness and Substance Abuse Disorders

by Joan B. Gillece, Ph.D. and Betty G. Russell, Ph.D.

INTRODUCTION

The Maryland Department of Health and Mental Hygiene's Division of Special Populations (DSP) of the Mental Hygiene Administration (MHA) oversees programs for individuals with mental illness who may also have co-occurring substance abuse disorders or HIV/AIDS, be homeless and/or deaf, and are in the criminal justice system. To take part in DSP's programs, individuals must have both mental illness and criminal justice involve-

This article originally appeared in Community Mental Health Report, *Volume 1, No. 2, January/February 2001.*

ment. (MHA, of course, has other programs for individuals who are not in the criminal justice system.) As the number of women in jails has increased nationwide, there has also been a corresponding increase in female inmates in the detention centers in Maryland. While Maryland detention centers have been providing mental health services to inmates of both genders since 1992, their female inmates have not been the focus of specialized treatment until fairly recently.

The DSP began the Maryland Community Criminal Justice Treatment Program (MCCJTP) as a pilot program in four counties in 1992. Since that initial program, the Division has developed the program in 23 of Maryland's 24 jurisdictions. In 1995, the Division began to focus on treatment programs for women in response to the concerns of wardens about the special problems incarcerated women presented to correctional staffs, including increased suicidal threats; reclusive behaviors, i.e., women's refusal to be involved in activities, resulting in a lack of concern for personal hygiene and medical care; and the lack of ability to cope with their situations as inmates. In many cases, these behaviors resulted in institutional infractions.

In response to the wardens' concerns, the DSP and its partner, the Center for Mental Health Services Research (CMHSR) of the University of Maryland School of Medicine Department of Psychiatry, applied for two grants from federal agencies that would address these and related issues.

THE PHOENIX PROJECT

In 1997, the Substance Abuse Mental Health Services Administration (SAMHSA) of the United States Department of Health and Human Services requested grant applicants for demonstration sites that would divert individuals from jail to the community. The DSP applied for and received funding of $1,575,442 for a gender-specific grant for females with co-occurring serious mental illness and substance abuse disorders in rural Wicomico County, on the Eastern Shore of Maryland. Wicomico County has an estimated population of approximately 79,000. The major urban center is the city of Salisbury (population 21,827). This county was one of the original pilot counties in 1992. The local detention center holds approximately 600-700 inmates on any given day.

Determining Eligibility

To be eligible for the services of the Phoenix Project a woman must be 18 or older, have a severe mental illness as evidenced by a DSM-IV Axis I clinical diagnosis, and a substance abuse disorder. The woman must also face arrest for a misdemeanor or a nonviolent felony.

Before writing the grant, staff from the Division and CMHSR conducted a focus group with five women in the Wicomico County, Maryland, Community Criminal Justice Treatment Program. The women, who were inmates in the detention center at the time of the interviews, were asked what services could have helped them and their children. Each of the women had extensive substance abuse problems and all suffered from serious mental illnesses. The women spoke of their shame and desperation at the time of and following their arrest.

When determining the services and procedures that would be implemented in the Phoenix Project, the responses of the focus group were given great consideration. The police and mental health staff have been trained in recognizing symptoms of mental illnesses and substance abuse disorders and work with the Mobile Crisis Unit (MCU), which is available 24 hours a day. The MCU consists of a case manager, a sheriff's deputy, and a mental health professional. When police respond to a complaint, the MCU is called if a woman exhibits signs or symptoms of mental illness or a substance abuse disorder. The disposition of the case is a joint effort between the MCU and the police, contingent on multiple factors including the nature and severity of the offense, the mental status of the woman, her criminal history and her behavior and conduct. If she is eligible, she is diverted into the Phoenix Project and is not arrested.

Diversion and Case Management

A woman who is eligible for Phoenix and agrees to participate in the project will at that point either be diverted into emergency crisis housing where she will be further evaluated and stabilized, or will receive intensive case management and clinical interventions in her home. Her children will also remain with her. She and the children will be moved to transitional housing as soon as she is ready. In addition to transitional housing, if she is homeless, she will be eligible to access the Shelter Plus Care rental assistance available through the DSP's HUD grant.

A key component of the services available to the woman is a case manager who specializes in mental health and substance abuse. The case manager provides direct mental health/substance abuse treatment services and brokers other community services for the woman and her children as needed. With Maryland's entry into a managed public mental health fee for service care system, community services are most often reimbursable.

How the Program Will Be Evaluated

The evaluation of the Phoenix Project to be conducted by CMHSR features two major focuses. One is the compilation of a "learning history" that will explore how the various "communities of practice" within the Wicomico County mental health, substance abuse, and criminal justice systems learn to work with a jail diversion program. The Learning History is a special type of case study that employs a narrative approach to tell the story of the development of the program in the words of the participants who made it happen.

A second focus of the local evaluation is the use of Lifelines of the women in the Phoenix Project. The client reviews her life through the time of the interview by means of a chart that maps changes in life satisfaction to the present. The Lifeline will reflect "peaks" and "valleys." For each of these "turning points," the client is asked a series of questions. The answers reflect the interviewee's views of herself, others, and the events of her life. The Lifeline interview is administered at the time of admission to the project and again in12 months.

In addition to these primary studies, the evaluation will also focus on several secondary studies. These include the impacts on the children of these women and a study of the costs associated with developing and operating a jail diversion program. The evaluative component of the grant includes the director of the research project, three assistants, and various consultants.

The Phoenix Project had a late start-up due to issues at other sites involved in the SAMHSA grant. Wicomico County had its first woman enter the Phoenix Project in September of 1998. From October, 1998, through September 30, 2000, when the grant ended, 49 women were served. With the development of pre-booking diversion, women with co-occurring disorders and their children should be able to rejoin their communities and look to brighter futures.

THE TAMAR PROJECT

Trauma Issues Among Female Inmates

Women with histories of violence are not uncommon in local jails. A woman in one of the jails, e.g., told a staff member:

> I was raped when I was six by my mother's boyfriend and he kept on for the next two years until my mother threw him out. I thought I was just a bad person and deserved all of that. When I was 14, I started smoking grass and then ended up a heroin addict. I stole from everybody, passed bad checks, and worked the streets. No one told me that that stuff from the past was eating me up until I talked to another woman in here who had some of the same background but had gotten some help about it.

The DSP became concerned about trauma issues when staff members visited a substance abuse group in one of the detention centers in the MCCJTP program and listened to all of the women in the group describe the physical and sexual abuse they had suffered. When SAMHSA announced funding for a Women and Violence study in February, 1998, the DSP once again collaborated with the CMHSR at the University of Maryland at Baltimore to apply for funding. The TAMAR Project (*T*rauma, *A*ddictions, *M*ental health *A*nd *R*ecovery) is funded by SAMHSA and provides services for women who have histories of sexual and/or physical abuse, mental illness, and substance abuse disorders and who are in the criminal justice system. The project brings together agencies such as social services, mental health, substance abuse, domestic violence, and parole and probation in a collaborative to serve these women in a more efficient and beneficial way.

Development of Integrated System of Services

The three counties selected for the project represent various areas of Maryland. Dorchester County is a rural county on the Eastern Shore. Calvert County is in the southern part of the state and is rural as well as a bedroom community for upper management who work in the Washington, D.C., area. Frederick County is also a bedroom community for the District, but with a more middle-class population. There are still some rural areas in this county. The majority of women inmates in these three county jails may have received mental health and substance abuse treatment in the past, but this project allows the state to create an integrated system of services in each jurisdiction to serve this population more comprehensively.

Members of the Division and CMHSR once again went to the women who would be served by this project and asked them what services would have been of help to them. They were especially concerned about the importance of being able to discuss their difficulties with someone. They were concerned about their children and their inadequacies as mothers; they did not want to abuse their children. They admitted that they needed help both in the detention center and in the community upon release.

The DSP was notified that effective October 1, 1998, the Mental Hygiene Administration would be the only one of the 14 sites funded by SAMHSA for the Women and Violence study to serve women in correctional settings. Building on the Maryland Community Criminal Justice Treatment Program, the DSP has developed an integrated system to provide services for these women. Each of the three counties involved in TAMAR offered letters of support from numerous agencies that have a stake in the project. Meetings are held with agency representatives in each jurisdiction on a regular basis. The goal is to build a system that not only meets the needs of the women and their children, but also reflects that county's uniqueness (e.g., suburban vs. rural, available housing, and seriousness of crimes committed). This may produce three models with major commonalities but some variations that would be replicable by other similar jurisdictions.

Phase One of the grant, a two-year period, provided $1,139,430 and allowed each site to establish the programmatic services that would be provided. Although building on the existing MCCJTP, sites had to begin partnering with other agencies as a requirement of the grant. This necessitated the building of relationships that may have been perfunctory in the past. Many agency heads had never been in the same room together. Because of the time it took to build these networks, many months passed before the actual services were in place and women could begin to receive treatment.

Services Begin in Detention But Extend to Community

The women being served in this project are women with any mental illness and/or substance abuse disorder who have experienced violence at any time in their lives and who are or have been in the criminal justice system. Women in the detention center are assessed and diagnosed after arrest. A woman's condition may be identified either through the mental health or substance abuse counselor or through the medical personnel in the detention center. The trauma specialist will focus on safety and containment issues of symptom management through treatment groups within the detention center. Participation in the psycho-educational groups is voluntary. The trauma specialists, medical officer, mental health and substance abuse counselors and the classification officer of the detention center meet weekly to discuss providing the coordinated services these women need.

Upon release, these women will continue to meet in treatment groups that are developed by the trauma specialist in each county. Women also may be referred to the trauma specialist for community groups through parole and probation. A community team consisting of representatives from mental health, substance abuse, domestic violence, parole and probation, social services, and the trauma specialist meet weekly to coordinate community services.

An additional feature of the services offered is a community peer support group. Women from the Advocates Advisory Board are working in each of the counties to establish peer support groups that women can attend. The women in the groups will determine the groups' focuses. Funding is available to pay for transportation to the support groups as well as for child care while the groups meet so that the mother will not be distracted from the meetings.

The trauma specialist will also ensure that upon release, the woman and her children will be connected to a case manager and access any needed services. Services are available in Maryland to children but mothers are not included. The challenge is to expand services such as mental health and substance abuse to include the mother as well. To facilitate this integration, the DSP holds workshops and trainings on issues related to parenting and children's needs.

Clinical Supervision

To facilitate the work of the trauma specialists, a clinical supervisor (a Ph.D. in psychology with vast experience in trauma therapy) has been hired as a consultant. When the specialist is faced with a dilemma, the clinician is available to offer assistance. The clinician also meets with the three trauma specialists weekly to analyze specific cases. The clinician and the three trauma specialists designed the 12-week, three-hours-a-week curriculum that is being used in the groups. The curriculum includes journal writing and art therapy.

Professional Training Component

The DSP is also using grant funding to develop and implement training related to trauma. The Sidran Foundation, a private nonprofit publishing house that focuses on trauma issues, has conducted the training. All correctional officers within the detention center have received training in symptoms and trauma. A curriculum specifically tailored to the needs of correctional staff has been developed after consultation with the wardens of each county. The Maryland Correctional Officers Training Academy credits this as in-service training. The Academy will also be including a course in trauma as a part of training for new officers.

In addition to training those within the jails, there has also been training for representatives of the various agencies in the community that are providing services to the women in the TAMAR Project including social services, parole and probation, mental health, substance abuse, domestic violence, and children's services. Training is developed and delivered as needs and issues arise.

State-Level Oversight

A unique feature of the grant is the inclusion of a Director of Trauma Services at the state level who works in the Division of Special Populations. There are very few state level positions such as this nationally. The Division began providing the expansion of trauma services to male offenders in the summer of 2000, thanks to funding from the MHA.

How the Program Will Be Evaluated

Phase II of the Women and Violence grant will focus primarily on evaluation. The two areas of study are the process used to develop the integrated system and the effectiveness of integrated services. SAMHSA has developed evaluative measures that will be used cross-site. Maryland's local evaluation will use life stories and learning histories to determine the effectiveness of the integrated systems approach to treatment as well as the process of integrating various systems around the issues of trauma.

From September 1, 1999, until March 1, 2000, the first six months of the actual provision of services, 82 women had been served in the detention centers. Treatment groups in the community began on January 1, 2000, and 20 women had been served in the community by March 1, 2000. Peer support groups have been developed in each community. Preliminary interviews with 12 women indicated that the women were very enthusiastic about the provision of trauma services in the detention centers and the communities. All of the women currently incarcerated have stated that they will continue in the community treatment groups. There has been no formal evaluation of recidivism to detention centers or psychiatric hospitals in Phase I.

The Mental Hygiene Administration recently approved funding to provide trauma treatment for women and men in eight other detention centers in Maryland. Clearly, the issue of trauma is of paramount importance in serving individuals in the criminal justice system.

LESSONS FOR PROFESSIONALS

What have we learned so far? Though project evaluation is still underway for both the Phoenix Project and the TAMAR Project, several important lessons are already clear:

☐ *For Planners:*

- *Meet with agency heads individually prior to developing the project.* Explain your project and why their involvement will benefit them.

- *Interview the clients before beginning projects* such as those described above. Both of these projects included interviews with the women who would be served by them. Their experiences have provided them with a keen awareness of what would have helped them. Those lessons guided the services that are included in the projects.

- *It pays to hire the best.* Qualified personnel will save money in the long haul. Turnover will be less and better services will be provided for the clients.

- *Training and education are vital.* When everyone involved knows the issues, there is more cooperation among staff and better services for the clients. One warden even included the cooks on his staff in the trauma training for his facility.

☐ *For Supervisors:*

- *Support line staff.* Working with individuals such as those in these two projects is hard work. Include opportunities for your staff to take care of themselves. Provide stress workshops. Pat them on the back whenever you can. A complimentary comment often results in greater effort and more cooperation.

☐ *For Line Staff:*

- *Training is critical.* One of the keys to success of these two projects is training. Avail yourself of any training that you can. Mental health counselors should have backgrounds in substance abuse when working with individuals with co-occurring disorders. Social workers working with trauma issues should have strong clinical experience as well as extensive trauma education. Remember that you will often not see immediate results of the good things that you are doing.

☐ *For Everyone*:

- *Remember the Golden Rule.* What would you want if you were staff, the boss, or a client?

About the Authors

Joan B. Gillece, Ph.D., is Director, Division of Special Populations, Maryland Mental Hygiene Adminstration. Betty G. Russell, Ph.D., is Director, Trauma Services, Maryland Mental Hygiene Adminstration.

Chapter 37

Assessing the Needs of Women in Prison-Based Therapeutic Communities

by Nena Messina, Ph.D., William Burdon, Ph.D., Michael Prendergast, Ph.D. and Meredith Patten, M.S.

BACKGROUND

The number of incarcerated women in prisons more than doubled between 1990 and 1999, outpacing the rise in the number of incarcerated men (Beck, 2000). The growth in the female prison population is largely due to the increased use of incarceration for drug-related offenses, which also created an increased demand for appropriate drug treatment programs within prison settings. The therapeutic community (TC) treatment model has become a preferred method for substance abuse treatment and many TC programs were incorporated into American prisons throughout the 1990s.

Traditional TC programs were initially tailored to treat substance-abusing men and thus remain primarily male-oriented programs. However, recent treatment literature indicates that the treatment issues for women prisoners are quite different and more complex than those for men (Cranford & Williams, 1998). Thus, the extent to which traditional TC methods meet the treatment needs of drug-dependent women in prison is largely unknown. In fact, much of the knowledge regarding the treatment needs of drug-dependent women

This chapter originally appeared in Women, Girls & Criminal Justice, *Vol. 4, No. 3, April/May 2003.*

offenders has had to be pieced together from indirect sources, such as non-incarcerated women in community-based programs or incarcerated women who are not in treatment.

STUDY FOCUSED ON WOMEN INMATES

The research literature contains only two studies that directly compare the characteristics of incarcerated men and women in drug treatment programs (Langan & Pelissier, 2001; Peters et al., 1997). Both of these studies found that women were more likely than men to present greater challenges to treatment practitioners. For example, compared with incarcerated men in drug treatment, incarcerated women in treatment were significantly more likely to have severe substance abuse histories (e.g., using hard drugs, using more frequently, or taking drugs intravenously), to have grown up in homes where drug use was present, to have coexisting psychological and physical health problems, and to have been sexually and physically abused as children.

The purpose of this study is to generate a profile of women offenders entering institutional TC treatment in one state's prisons, and outline the specific needs of this group as they relate to prison-based substance abuse treatment and continued treatment in the community following their release to parole. Based on previous research in California testifying to the effectiveness of TCs (Jarmen, 1993; Prendergast et al., 1996), the California Department of Corrections (CDOC) designed an initiative to expand treatment opportunities for inmates. As part of this initiative, CDOC established TC treatment programs in designated housing units within many of its prisons, including all of the institutions that house women. Based on the findings of the above studies (Langan & Pelissier, 2001; Peters, et al., 1997), it was hypothesized that the needs of incarcerated women entering prison-based drug treatment programs would be substantially more complex than those of their male counterparts.

Methods and Data Collection

The data for this study were collected as part of the CDOC Prison Treatment Expansion Initiative. This initiative includes two five-year evaluation studies of drug treatment programs within the California state prison system. The University of California, Los Angeles (UCLA), Integrated Substance Abuse Programs (ISAP) was contracted by CDOC to evaluate these programs, with contract management provided by CDOC's Office of Substance Abuse Programs (OSAP). The two evaluation studies cover 15 substance abuse programs (SAPs) in 10 prisons, totaling approximately 3,300 beds (eight male programs totaling 1,600 beds and seven female programs totaling 1,700 beds). These SAPs became operational between July 1998 and December 1999 and include participants at all levels of security (Level I-Minimum through Level IV-Maximum). All of the SAPs provide treatment services using the TC model, as they are required to do under their contracts with CDOC.

Participation in these SAPs is open to inmates who have a documented history of substance use or abuse, and who have between six and 24 months left to serve on their current sentence. While inmates can volunteer for SAP treatment, those who meet these eligibility requirements are generally mandated into the treatment programs.

Client-level data were collected by the treatment providers upon admission into the SAPs using the Intake Assessment (IA) instrument. The IA is designed to assess a client's pre-treatment/pre-incarceration socio-demographic background, criminality, employment, and substance use, abuse, or dependence. Adopted from the Initial Assessment developed at the Institute of Behavioral Research at Texas Christian University (Broome, et al., 1996), the IA has been used extensively with criminal justice populations and provides information that is useful for both clinical and evaluation purposes.

Participants

The current study focuses on 4,509 women and 3,595 men who entered the participating SAPs between July 1998 and March 2001 and for whom intake data were available. Participants in the study were predominately white (39%) or black (31%), were 35 years old on average, and had completed approximately 11 years of education prior to their current incarceration. About half (45%) had never been married. Thirty-two percent were employed during the 30 days prior to their current incarceration, and 60% were parents. Participants reported an average of 15.8 arrests in their lifetime, and 57% were serving time for a drug-related offense at the time of their SAP admission.

Data Analyses

The analyses conducted for this study were primarily descriptive and were used to determine if gender differences relevant to prison-based substance abuse treatment exist and, if so, to outline the specific needs of drug-dependent women offenders. The large sample size substantially increased the likelihood of finding statistically significant differences at the $p < .05$ level. As a result, it was decided that "practical" significance was a more appropriate way to assess differences between men and women. For the purposes of this study, "practical" significance was defined as a difference of at least 20%age points on any categorical bivariate test and a difference of at least two points for continuous bivariate tests.

Logistic regression analyses were conducted to determine if gender was significantly related to a variety of characteristics that were thought to be relevant to the design of the substance abuse programs, while controlling for possible confounding factors.

STUDY RESULTS

Bivariate Comparisons

Table 37.1 displays the demographic characteristics for men (n = 3,595) and women (n = 4,509) participating in the prison-based substance abuse programs during the selected study period. Even though men and women had similar educational backgrounds, men were more likely than women to have been employed prior to incarceration (53% vs. 33%) and to report their job as their primary source of financial support (44% vs. 23%). Financial disparities were also evident from self-reported annual legal income. Although average annual incomes were below the poverty line for both men and women, men reported receiving nearly twice as much legal income as women in the year prior to their current incarceration ($14,000 vs. $8,000). Men were also more likely than women to report having children (74% vs. 54%). Women, on the other hand, were eight times more likely than men to report being sexually and physically abused as an adult (25% vs. 3%). Using the practical significance standard, no gender differences were found with regard to age, race/ethnicity, marital status, education, or sexual/physical abuse during childhood.

Table 37.1: Sample Characteristics at Treatment Admission, by Gender*

Characteristics	Men	Women	Total
	(n = 3,595)	(n = 4,509)	(N = 8,104)[a]
	percent M (SD)	percent M (SD)	percent M (SD)
Race/Ethnicity			
White	42	37	39
Black	32	31	31
Hispanic	20	21	21
Other	6	11	9
Marital Status			
Never Married	48	41	45
Married	6	24	25
Previously Married	26	34	30
Age at Admission	34.5 (8.9)	36.0 (7.6)	35.4 (8.2)
Years of Education	11.4 (2.0)	11.0 (2.2)	11.2 (2.1)
Employed 30 Days Prior to Incarceration	53	33	41
Source of Support 30 Days Prior to Incarceration			
Job	44	23	32
Mate/Family/Friends	13	24	19
Welfare/Public Assis./Unempl.	10	21	16
Illegal Activities	26	27	27
Other	7	5	6
Annual Legal Income Prior to Incarceration	$14,000	$8,000	$10,000
Have Children[b]	74	54	60
Provided Financial Support Prior to Incarceration	71	57	62
Plan to Provide Support Upon Release	81	65	71
Ever Sexually\Physically Abused as a Child[b]	14	25	22
Ever Sexually\Physically Abused as an Adult [b]	3	25	19
Treatment Referral Source			
Criminal Justice System (Mandated)	53	44	48
Self/Volunteer	47	56	52

*All bivariate analyses are *statistically* significant at $p<.001$.

[a] N's vary slightly due to missing data.

[b] Data collected from partial sample due to survey revisions (men = 801; women = 1,933).

This was mainly a stimulant-abusing sample; 35% of the participants reported methamphetamine/amphetamine as their primary drug problem and 28% reported cocaine/crack as their primary drug problem. Similar proportions of men and women reported daily use of methamphetamine 60 days prior to incarceration, but women were twice as likely as men to report daily use of cocaine/crack (36% vs. 16%) and opiates (44% vs. 22%). In addition, compared with women, men were younger at the age of first arrest (17.1 years vs. 21.3 years), had been arrested more often in their lifetime (17.4 arrests vs. 14.7 arrests), and had been incarcerated longer in their lifetime (5.5 years vs. 3.2 years). However, both men and women reported similar lengths of incarceration prior to program entry, were most likely to report being arrested for drug-related crimes and to be under the influence of drugs and/or alcohol at the time of their most recent arrest.

Significance of Variables

All logistic regression models control for the effects of age, race/ethnicity, marital status, and prior incarceration (not shown). Using the conservative alpha of $p < .001$ as the threshold for statistical significance, the difference between men and women was significant for 18 of the 21 dependent variables examined. The first eight regression models examined substance-using behavior and dependence prior to incarceration. After controlling for other related variables, the results showed that women were significantly different from men with regard to their drug-use patterns prior to their current incarceration. The odds of women using opiates or cocaine/crack on a daily basis prior to incarceration were approximately 20 times as great as those for men. The odds of women using two or more drugs on a daily basis were four times as great as those for men. The odds of women having a DSM-IV drug abuse/dependence disorder were 16 times as great as those for men. In contrast, women were almost three times less likely than men to have used marijuana on a daily basis prior to incarceration. There were no statistically significant differences between men and women with respect to daily use of alcohol or amphetamines.

Models 9 through 16 examined the psychological status of program participants. After controlling for related factors, the results showed that women were significantly more likely than men to have experienced some form of psychological impairment prior to entering the SAPs. Compared with men, the odds of women experiencing depression or tension/anxiety were 10 times as great, hallucinations: six times as great, trouble concentrating or remembering: eight times as great, and trouble controlling violent behavior: four times as great. The odds of women having serious thoughts of suicide or attempting suicide were 11 and 21 times as great as those for men, respectively. Finally, the odds of women taking prescribed medications were 18 times as great as those for men.

Models 17 and 18 examined gender differences relating to education and employment prior to incarceration. The results showed that women were at a significant disadvantage prior to incarceration. Compared with men, women were three times less likely to have completed high school or a GED prior to incarceration, and six times less likely to be employed. Model 19 examined gender differences for planned financial support of children upon release from prison. The model included only participants who reported having children prior to incarceration, and the results showed a significant difference. Compared with men, women were six times less likely to plan to support their children upon release from prison.

Finally, Models 20 and 21 examined gender differences with regard to sexual and physical abuse histories and found significant differences. The odds of women reporting sexual or physical abuse as a child were 13 times as great as those for men. Moreover, the odds of women reporting sexual or physical abuse as an adult were 104 times more likely than those for men.

IMPLICATIONS FOR PROGRAMMING

Consistent with the findings of Peters et al (1997) and Langan and Pelissier (2001), this study found that men and women entering prison-based substance abuse treatment differed in their substance abuse problems, psychological functioning, sexual and physical abuse histories, education and employment histories, and planned child support activity.

Women entering prison-based treatment were substantially more likely than men to be using hard drugs (i.e., cocaine/crack and heroin) on a daily basis and to be poly-drug users prior to their current incarceration. Women's severe drug-abusing histories, combined with their increased likelihood of having experienced some form of psychological impairment and use of prescription drugs for psychological or emotional problems, indicates the need for a more comprehensive diagnostic assessment of participants at intake as a means of informing treatment staff of the diverse substance use disorders and psychological needs of women entering prison-based treatment. These findings also indicate a need for developing more comprehensive and effective treatment plans. Furthermore, because treatment staff may not be adequately trained to handle or treat certain co-occurring psychological and medical conditions that women offenders present upon entry into prison-based substance abuse programs, suitable referral services for psychological and medical care should be in place within the institutional setting.

Multivariate analyses showed that women offenders entering prison-based substance abuse treatment were also significantly more likely than men to report being sexually and physically abused as children and as adults. The association between sexual/physical abuse, substance abuse, and crime, especially among women, suggests an urgent need for treatment components that address sexual/physical abuse and the mental health issues that often result from these forms of abuse. Substance abuse programs for women should also focus on developing strong interpersonal skills that will help the women confront and cope with past abuse while teaching them the appropriate skills for coping with future relationship issues.

In addition, treatment staff should be sensitive to women's histories of sexual and physical abuse so that the women can form trusting relationships with the staff. Training of treatment staff should include information about how to develop, nurture, and maintain relationships with clients that promote an effective therapeutic bond, while avoiding the appearance of impropriety. Gender specific staff can promote a strong therapeutic alliance and provide strong female role models, supportive peer networks, and attention to women's patterns of abuse from childhood to adulthood (Morash et al., 1998).

Women were also at a significant disadvantage with regard to educational and employment histories compared to men. Drug-dependent women in prison treatment were less likely than men to have graduated from high school, and often reported being financially dependent on family members and in need of public assistance (shown in Table 37.1). However, the majority of both men and women did not graduate from high school and less than half of the sample reported having a job prior to incarceration (41%). Moreover, only 32% of the sample reported that their job was their primary source of income, and both men and women reported annual legal earnings below the poverty line. These findings suggest that basic education, literary skills, and marketable vocational training are particularly important components of treatment programs for both men and women.

Exacerbating the need for appropriate education and vocational training is the finding that many drug-dependent offenders are parents. Incarcerated mothers are in need of activities that increase contact with their children and that strengthen the mother-child relationship. Moreover, the large percentage of drug-dependent offenders, male and female, who have children suggests that parenting programs should become a critical part of treatment for both men and women.

It should be noted that the current study relied on general intake data for a large sample of men and women entering prison-based treatment. Due to the overall scope of the CDOC initiative, the questions available on the IA instrument were limited in both range and depth. The IA instrument was not originally designed to capture detailed differences between men and women entering prison-based treatment. In addition, the findings generated by this study are limited to inmates who were selected for treatment participation and thus, cannot be generalized to general inmate populations in state prison. Nevertheless, the available data did reveal some important gender differences relevant to the design of institutional treatment programs.

A larger question, however, concerns the extent to which the traditional TC approach is appropriate for women inmates—or at least whether the TC model should be significantly modified to address the specific needs and learning styles of women offenders. Future post-treatment outcome analyses from this initiative could indicate which women might be at greater risk for relapse and in need of additional services.

About the Authors

Nena Messina, Ph.D., William Burdon, Ph.D., Michael Prendergast, Ph.D., and Meredith Patten, M.S., are affiliated with UCLA Integrated Substance Abuse Programs, Los Angeles, CA 90025.

References

Beck, A., *Prisoners in 1999* (Bureau of Justice Statistics Bulletin) (U.S. Department of Justice, Bureau of Justice Statistics, 2000).

Broome, K.M., Knight, K., Joe, G.W., & Simpson, D.D., "Evaluating the Drug-Abusing Probationer: Clinical Interview Versus Self-Administered Assessment," 23(4) *Criminal Justice and Behavior* 593-606 (1996).

Cranford, S., & Williams, R.,"Critical Issues in Managing Female Offenders," 60(7) *Corrections Today* 130-135 (1998).

Jarman, E., *An Evaluation of Program Effectiveness for the Forever Free Substance Abuse Program at the California Institute for Women, Frontera, California* (California Department of Correction, Office of Substance Abuse Programs, 1993).

Langan, N., & Pelissier, B., " Gender Differences Among Prisoners in Drug Treatment," 13(3) *Journal of Substance Abuse* 291-301 (2001).

Morash, M., Bynum, T., & Koons, B., *Women Offenders: Programming Needs and Promising Approaches* (Bureau of Justice Statistics Bulletin) (U.S. Department of Justice, Bureau of Justice Statistics, 1998).

Peters, R., Strozier, A., Murrin, M., & Kearns, W., "Treatment of Substance-Abusing Jail Inmates: Examination of Gender Differences," 14 *Journal of Substance Abuse Treatment* 339-349 (1997).

Prendergast, M., Wellisch, J., & Wong, M., "Residential Treatment for Women Parolees Following Prison-Based Drug Treatment: Treatment Experiences, Needs, and Services, Outcomes," 76(3) *Prison Journal* 253-274 (1996).

Chapter 38

Women and Self-Harm in Community and Institutional Settings

by Cathy Fillmore, Ph.D. and Colleen Anne Dell, Ph.D.

INTRODUCTION

Self-harm among women is a serious health concern. In recent years, a Canadian group, the Elizabeth Fry Society of Manitoba, recognized in its work with women in conflict with the law an alarming increase in the number of women who identified themselves as self-injurers. The group also recognized the need for expanded research and understanding.

The link between childhood experiences (of neglect and physical, sexual, and emotional abuse and violence) and self-harm is well documented in research literature (de Young, 1982; Green, 1987; Van der Kolk et al., 1991; Favazza, 1993). An unexamined focus, however, is the relationship between adult experiences of abuse and violence and self-harm (Babiker & Arnold, 1997).

This chapter originally appeared in Women, Girls & Criminal Justice, *Vol. 3, No. 2, February/March 2002.*

This chapter addresses two areas of self-harm that have received minor attention: (1) the needs, supports, and services of women in conflict with the law in both the community and institutional settings, and (2) Aboriginal women in conflict with the law.

WOMAN-CENTERED RESEARCH APPROACH

In our study, we employed data sources that offered a unique perspective to address these research concerns. These sources included interviews with women, both in the community and correctional institutions; a focus group with incarcerated women; community agency and correctional staff interviews; correctional staff surveys; and a review of community and correctional policies. The variety of methodologies contributed to the creation of a rich, in-depth, and complex data set. A total of 55 interviews and five surveys were conducted, spanning community women, incarcerated women, community staff, and correctional staff. Our study concentrated on women who self-harm in the Prairie Region of Canada (Alberta, Saskatchewan, and Manitoba).

We adopted a feminist approach to research methodology. Central to feminist methodology is the improvement of social conditions, rooted in the social inequality of women (Cook & Fonnow, 1990; Gelsthorpe, 1990; DeVault, 1996). Some ways in which we did this were by placing the women at the center of our research. To illustrate, an incarcerated woman and a woman in the community who self-harmed participated in the research process, including construction of the interview schedule. Additionally, following interviews with the women and staff, a package was supplied with information about self-harm and access to the Elizabeth Fry Society of Manitoba's toll-free number, other toll-free support networks, counseling and community agency services, and relaxation techniques and exercises. These are a few techniques of what feminist researchers Kirby and McKenna (1989) refer to as research being done by, for, and with people living on the margins of society.

Considerable insight and understanding have been gained in this research regarding the needs, supports, and services of women who self-harm while incarcerated and in the community. Special awareness has been attained in these areas regarding the importance of Aboriginal culture. An important outcome of this study is an examination of helpful and unhelpful responses to self-harm in these two settings. Although attention was paid to Aboriginal women's experiences of self-harm, a comparison to non-Aboriginal women's experiences was not possible due to the over-representation of Aboriginal respondents in the sample.

It is important to note that the narratives of the women in the community and correctional institutions were combined for the data analysis. The main reason for this is that all of the women, with one exception, had a history of being in conflict with the law, with the majority having experienced a period of incarceration. Particular attention was paid to Aboriginal women's experiences of self-harm. In addition, information gathered on community and correctional staff members was combined due to the limited number of staff respondents and the close similarity between the two groups. Where feasible, however, general references were made to denote whether a community or institutional context applied.

DEFINING SELF-HARM

Women's narratives, staff perceptions and accounts, and a review of the inter-disciplinary literature suggested the definition of self-harm that evolved in our research:

Figure 38.1: Holistic Model of Self-Harm

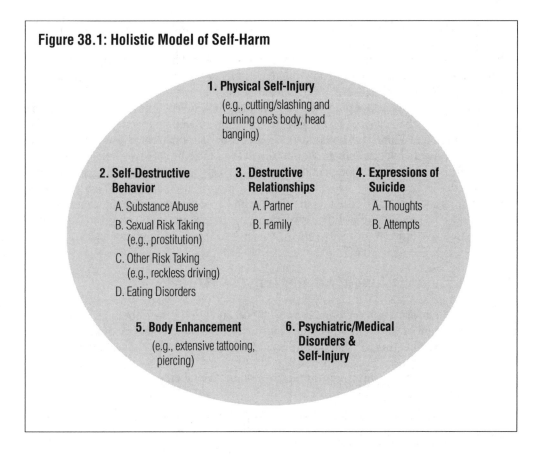

1. Physical Self-Injury

(e.g., cutting/slashing and burning one's body, head banging)

2. Self-Destructive Behavior

A. Substance Abuse

B. Sexual Risk Taking (e.g., prostitution)

C. Other Risk Taking (e.g., reckless driving)

D. Eating Disorders

3. Destructive Relationships

A. Partner

B. Family

4. Expressions of Suicide

A. Thoughts

B. Attempts

5. Body Enhancement

(e.g., extensive tattooing, piercing)

6. Psychiatric/Medical Disorders & Self-Injury

Self-harm—*Any behavior, be it physical, emotional, social, or spiritual, that a woman commits with the intention to cause herself harm. It is a way of coping and surviving emotional pain and distress, which is rooted in traumatic childhood and adult experiences of abuse and violence. It is a meaningful action, which fulfills a variety of functions for women in their struggle for survival.*

We found a diversity of women's experiences of self-harm and classified them into a Holistic Model of Self-Harm (See Figure 38.1). This model represents the inter-connected and complex nature of women's self-harm. This model is not generalizable to men's self-harm, which is reportedly different in nature and frequency. Research suggests that men have a lower incidence of self-harm in part because of other coping strategies, such as work, hobbies, and sports. These studies suggest that men may convert their feelings of emotional pain and anger through violence and abuse of others rather than inflicting harm on themselves (Graff & Mallin, 1967). However, while there is general agreement that self-harming behavior is especially prevalent among women in the general community, as well as in prison, little research has directly compared men and women self-injurers (Livingston, 1996).

Our findings suggest no clear boundaries in defining self-harm and no single explanation that can account for the complex nature of self-harm. Our model shows the wide range of conduct that involves the body in the expression of emotional pain and distress, from inflicting external physical forms of harm, such as slashing the skin, to less visible, internal forms of harm, such as substance abuse. The model is framed within a woman-centered approach and incorporates the connection between a woman's individual life experiences and her position in the broader social structure. This fills an important gap in the literature, which frequently decontextualizes and medicalizes women's emotional distress (Maticka-Tyndale & Bicker, 1996). Our study examines critical events in the women's childhood and adult lives that preceded their involvement in self-harm. These life experiences are typically characterized by marginalized statuses reflecting poverty, sexism, racism, and discrimination. Within this broader framework, our examination of how some women coped and survived violence and emotional pain in their lives by self-harming led to a view of self-harm as a necessary although unhealthy way of responding to distressing and oppressive conditions in the women's lives. This research demonstrates that only by beginning with the women's standpoints and situating their individual experiences within the context of the broader socio-economic and political structures, can we begin to uncover the complexities surrounding women's "choices" regarding self-harm as a coping response.

ORIGINS OF AND APPROACHES TO SELF-HARM

We gathered information on women's childhood and adult experiences and found that women had the greatest likelihood of self-harm when they had a history of highly unstable and unsupportive families. Such families were characterized by the following factors:

- Frequent moving and intermittent or permanent placements in foster and group homes;

- Absent, weak, or traumatic bonds with primary caregivers (especially the mother);

- Unmet emotional and social needs;

- Childhood abuse and violence (sexual, eaional, physical, and neglect); and

- Adult abuse and violence, primarily by a partner (sexual, emotional, and physical).

The majority of women in our study endured traumatic childhood and adult experiences. Staff also identified a relationship between highly unstable and unsupportive families and self-harm.

Coping and Survival Functions

The women expressed several functions of self-harm that helped them cope and survive their emotional pain and distress. Among these functions were:

- A need for attention and nurturing;

- A form of self-punishment and self-blame;

- A way of dealing with isolation and loneliness;

- A means of distracting and deflecting emotional pain;

- A response to an abusive partner;

- A cleansing and release of emotional pain;

- An attempt to regain a sense of reality and a feeling of "being alive";

- A communication or message signifying painful life experiences; and

- An opportunity to feel a sense of power and control.

Most of the functions of self-harm identified by community and institutional staff corresponded closely with those identified by the women. The main difference was in the degree of importance assigned to some of the functions of self-harm. Key departures of staff perspectives from the women's views included:

- A minimization of the women's need for attention and nurturing;

- An expanded interpretation of control to include the notion of women influencing others to take control for them;

- Less significance given to the role of isolation and loneliness in the women's lives;

- Lack of recognition of self-harm as a means to express painful life experiences; and

- The inclusion of self-harm as a form of manipulation.

Needs of Women Who Self-Harm

The women possessed a complex awareness of their needs and of the kinds of supports and services they required to address self-harm, including:

- Communication as an avenue to express emotional pain and distress;

- A sense of control and empowerment in their lives;

- Attention to issues of both childhood and adult abuse and violence;

- An understanding about their choice of self-harm as a way of coping with emotional pain and distress and exploring healthier and safer alternatives;

- Implementing an integrated and comprehensive care plan to promote healing; and

- A sensitivity to the role of Aboriginal culture in healing.

Women's Agency and Creative Ways of Coping and Surviving

The women in this study demonstrated a capacity for developing many creative and resourceful responses in attempting to find healthy alternatives to self-harm. Areas of individual ingenuity included:

- *Personal supports*, such as creative writing and journaling, rigorous physical activity, and attending to the needs of spirituality with daily smudging ("a ritual that involves a symbolic bathing with a sacred medicine, usually sage or sweetgrass, that is a holistic cleansing of the mind and body");

- *Informal supports*, for example, being more open and trusting with friends and partners as confidants; and

- *Formal supports*, such as taking the initiative for individual counseling, group therapy, and community programs.

Other supports could be categorized as activities that provided the women with opportunities to contribute to the well being of others, such as respite work for the elderly and babysitting.

RISK FACTORS FOR WOMEN'S SELF-HARM

Institutional Factors

The women and correctional staff identified considerably similar risk factors, although some differences were evident in their rankings of these risk factors. In general, the most important risk factors the women identified were personal losses and trauma, such as loss of children to child welfare agencies, followed by institutional conditions such as segregation. The staff's risk factors focused more on interpersonal factors and institutional conditions, such as stressful relationships with other incarcerated women and a lack of outlets for the women to communicate their distress.

Community Factors

The women and community workers also shared markedly similar assessments of risk factors and self-harm. Women in the community emphasized personal factors, while the community workers identified situational and social factors. The most important factor that the women identified was partner abuse, followed by personal losses, isolation, and loneliness. The central role of partner abuse in the women's self-identified risks is an important finding, as it is not highly recognized in the existing literature nor was it identified as a risk factor by staff in either of the two settings where we conducted our research. Community workers ranked lack of support as the central risk factor, followed by alcohol and drug abuse, unemployment, and poverty.

HELPFUL AND UNHELPFUL RESPONSES TO WOMEN'S SELF-HARM

On the basis of their knowledge and expertise, institutional staff and community workers identified the most helpful responses to women's self-harm, as well as some responses that were unhelpful. Insights were also gained from the women regarding helpful and unhelpful responses.

Helpful responses included:

- Endorsing a harm reduction and protection planning model based on the premise that it is inappropriate to completely remove a woman's sole means of coping with emotional pain and distress;

- Ensuring support, empathy, and active listening from staff;

- Providing programs and services that are based on empowering women;

- Establishing staff follow-through, which entails both on-going and long-term support, especially if a woman discloses childhood abuse and adult violence;

- Working with families of women who self-harm to broaden their basis of support and safety networks; and

- Incorporating an Aboriginal approach to healing, programs, and supports.

Conversely, some staff responses had a negative impact on the women, reinforcing their feelings of isolation, low self-worth, and loss of control. Unhelpful responses included:

- Physical restraints and segregation;

- A disrespectful and judgmental approach to women who self-harm;

- Unclear policy and guidelines regarding self-harm; and

- Lack of staff awareness of a general policy on self-harm.

A punitive approach also had negative repercussions for staff that was reflected in lower morale and increased work stress.

WORKING WITH WOMEN WHO SELF-HARM

The women and staff we interviewed in correctional institutions and in the community identified a series of recommendations to address the needs of women who self-harm. These recommendations are stated broadly to permit generalizability across various settings and contexts.

- Construct and increase awareness of policy and guidelines on self-harm;

- Adopt an integrated holistic approach to self-harm incorporating elements of harm reduction, protection planning, empowerment, and woman-centeredness;

- Implement a non-punitive approach which recognizes the dehumanizing and debilitating effects of physical and social isolation and the need to provide a nurturing and supportive environment;

- Create educational and training opportunities for staff;

- Recognize and provide tangible and intangible forms of support for staff;

- Ensure consistent, confidential, and non-judgmental counseling;

- Enhance access to peer support and healing activities;

- Increase availability of Aboriginal programming;

- Develop awareness of self-harm as an important health issue for women which requires a gender specific approach;

- Plan harm reduction strategies for prevention;

- Ensure extensive pre-release preparation and follow-through in the community;

- Provide information on community resources, especially drop-in centers or safe houses, and services designed for immediate crisis intervention including an initial contact person; and

- Address the larger social issues, such as poverty, education, job training, and safe, affordable housing.

POLICY RECOMMENDATIONS AND GUIDELINES

We were able to make several concrete policy and guideline recommendations based on our findings for women who self-harm in both correctional institutions and in the community. The women's discerning and perceptive reflections about self-harm as well as the staff's professional experiences helped form these suggestions, which are centered on the underlying theme of the empowerment of women. The suggestions are:

- A broader and more holistic definition of self-harm;

- An account of the origins/antecedents and functions of self-harm in education and training about self-harm;

- An identification of self-harm as a coping and survival function;

- An appreciation of the social portrait of women who self-harm;

- An evaluation of responses to self-harm and acknowledgment of helpful and unhelpful responses identified in this study and current research;

- An assessment of staff needs for additional supports; and

- The enhancement of Aboriginal culture in programs, supports, and services.

DIRECTIONS FOR FUTURE RESEARCH

This research project has uncovered significant findings as well as directions for future research. New knowledge was generated about the origins and functions of self-harm. Specifically, a relationship was found between self-harm and adult experiences of violence and abuse. One of the most important outcomes of the study was the development of policy recommendations on self-harm as a serious health concern for women within correctional institutions and in the community. There is a clear need for women-centered policies that account for women's specific histories and present circumstances that contribute to their "choice" of self-harm as a way of coping with emotional pain and distress.

We recognize that our research was exploratory and that further research is necessary to more fully understand women's self-harm in correctional institutions as well as in the general community. We plan to conduct additional research to expand the scope of our knowledge, including an increase in the representativeness of women who self-harm and of community agency workers. This will enable us to follow up and "test" certain relationships, patterns, and themes that have been reported in this article, such as the relationship between adult experiences of abuse, violence, and self-harm, in addition to official responses to self harm.

About the Authors

Cathy Fillmore, Ph.D., is an Assistant Professor at the University of Winnipeg, Department of Sociology and past board member of the Elizabeth Fry Society of Manitoba. Colleen Anne Dell, Ph.D., is an Assistant Professor at Carleton University, Department of Sociology and Anthropology and is the National Project Research Advisor with the Canadian Center on Substance Abuse.

References

Babiker, G., & Arnold, L., *The Language of Injury: Comprehending Self-Mutilation* (British Psychological Society, 1997).

Cook, J., & Fonnow, M., "Knowledge and Women's Interests. Issues of Epistemology and Methodology in Feminist Sociological Research," in J. McCarl (Ed.), *Feminist Research Methods. Exemplary Readings in the Social Sciences* (pp. 69-93) (Westview Press, 1990).

de Young, M., *The Sexualization Victimization of Children* (McFarland and Co., 1982).

DeVault, M., "Talking Back to Sociology: Distinctive Contributions of Feminist Methodology," 22 *Annual Review of Sociology* 29-50 (1996).

Favazza, A. R., *Bodies Under Seige, Self-Mutilation in Culture and Psychiatry* (Johns Hopkins University Press, 1993).

Gelsthorpe, L. "Feminists Methodologies in Criminology: A New Approach or Old Wine in New Bottles?" In L. Gelsthorpe & Morris, A. (Eds.), *Feminist Perspectives in Criminology* (pp. 70-84) (Open University Press, 1990).

Green, A.H., "Self-Destructive Behavior in Battered Children," 135 *American Journal of Psychiatry* 579-82 (1987).

Graff, H. & Mallin, R., "The Syndrome of the Risk-Cutter," 135 *American Journal of Psychiatry* 579-582 (1967).

Kirby, S. & McKenna, K., Methods From the Margins: Experience, Research, Social Change (Garmond Press, 1989).

Livingston, M., "A Review of the Literature on Self-Injurious Behavior Amongst Prisoners." In G.J. Towl (Ed.), *Suicide and Self-Injury in Prisons* (pp. 21-35) (British Psychological Society, 1996).

Maticka-Tyndale, E. & Bicher, M., "The Impact of Medicalization of Women." In B. Schissel & L. Mahood (Eds.), *Social Control in Canada* (pp. 149-173) (Oxford University Press, 1996)

Van der Kolk, B.A., Perry, C., & Herman, J., "Childhood Origins of Self-Destructive Behaviour," 148(12) *American Journal of Psychiatry* 1665-1671 (1991).

Chapter 39

Female Offenders and Disabilities

by Lili Garfinkel

INTRODUCTION

The risk factors for juvenile delinquency and criminal behavior are numerous, complex, and interrelated. They include a history of sexual and physical abuse, neglect, poverty, emotional and behavioral disorders, and a family history of criminal behavior. Emotional, behavioral, and learning disabilities that interfere with a youth's cognitive and behavioral functions can exacerbate the impact of other risk factors. While each of these risks is significant, their accumulated impact can increase the likelihood for involvement in criminal behaviors.

In 1999, 670,800 girls under the age of 18 (27% of the juvenile offender population) were arrested. Between 1988 and 1997, the number of delinquency cases involving girls increased by 83%. This increase was also observed across racial groups, with the highest increase among African American young women (American Bar Association, 2001). In addition, 25% of female arrests are for status offenses, such as running away, truancy, or curfew violations. For many girls who experience abuse and neglect, these actions represent their attempt to leave unsafe environments.

This chapter examines the relationship between the presence of disabilities and other risk factors in the lives of female offenders, provides information about mandated special education services, and makes recommendations for interventions that are more appropriate for girls at risk for or already involved in the juvenile justice system.

This chapter originally appeared in Women, Girls & Criminal Justice, *Vol. 2, No. 5, August/September 2001.*

DISABILITY CONNECTION TO OFFENDER STATUS

Recent research findings confirm that a high proportion of all youth in the juvenile justice system have one or more disabilities (Zabel & Robert, 2001). These include emotional and behavioral disorders including depression, attention deficit hyperactive disorder (ADHD), anxiety disorders, posttraumatic stress disorder (PTSD), and learning and developmental disabilities (Garfinkel, 2001). In addition, three-quarters of female offenders also have substance abuse disorders (Acoca, 1999).

Female offenders have a number of behavioral characteristics and histories in common. The most significant of these include physical, emotional, and sexual abuse; neglect; a history of multiple family problems; and dropping out of school. School failure is even higher among girls than boys and is also linked to the failure to identify underlying learning and mental health problems. As is evidenced by these characteristics, the impact of disabilities is considerable.

Studies conducted on groups of female offenders indicate that they share: lower grades and poorer scores on language and reading tests; higher rates of expulsion and suspension, often because of behavior or truancy; an average of one year less of school attendance; fewer problem solving and coping skills, possibly related to the presence of disabilities such as ADHD, depression and learning disabilities; behavior patterns characterized by poor self-esteem, dependency and ineffective survival strategies; a higher rate of mental health disorders (Ruffolo, Sarri & Goodkind, 2004; Widom, 2000); a higher number of episodes of depression; a higher rate of substance abuse problems; and a higher rate of suicide attempts. In addition, minorities are over-represented.

ABUSED AND NEGLECTED FEMALE OFFENDERS

Link to Depression

In order to understand female offenders more completely it is necessary to understand the impact of a disability and to promote strategies that can assist professionals in identifying needs in a more timely and effective manner. Abused and neglected female offenders often share many characteristics:

- Over 70% of the girls have experienced sexual or physical abuse;

- Nearly four out of five have run away from home, often in an effort to escape an abusive home environment. Abused and neglected girls are twice as likely to be arrested as other juveniles, and more than twice as likely to be arrested as adults (Widom, 2000);

- Abused and neglected women tend to have lower average scores on IQ and academic testing than non-abused and non-neglected women (Widom, 2000); and

- Victimized girls also experience more stressful life situations, a higher rate of suicide attempts, substance abuse, poor self-esteem, and difficulties in developing relationships with other women (Fejes-Mendoza et al, 1995).

Girls experience a sharp increase in the incidence of depression in middle school as compared with boys. Depression is a disorder that has many features, including anger and aggression. It is these expressions of depression that are thought to contribute to antisocial behavior (Obeidallah & Earls, 1999) because:

- Individuals who have depression withdraw socially and often have less interest in participating in activities or excelling at school;

- They are more critical of their friends, and, in turn, are more isolated;

- They seek friendships with other youths with problems where they feel more acceptance as an equal; and

- Their poor judgment in choosing friends is another risk factor for involvement in delinquency.

Link to Problems in School

Because depression is closely tied with a lack of interest in activities and learning, girls become less attached to school and are unable to consider education and relationships as valuable or necessary. They are more likely to take risks because they have such poor self-esteem and feelings of hopelessness (Obeidallah & Earls, 1999). Some of these risk-taking behaviors include substance abuse (a form of self-medication), early sexuality, and pregnancy.

MENTAL HEALTH/BEHAVIORAL DISORDERS

In one study it was found that, in addition to experiencing violence, the typical female offender had been hospitalized at least once for a psychiatric episode (usually a suicide attempt), had been violent in a school setting, and had a diagnosis of ODD (oppositional-defiant disorder). Because of girls' histories of abuse and violence it is likely that they also have abuse-related disorders such as PTSD, often confused with ODD or depression. Studies show that a large number of disorders are misdiagnosed (Ambrose, 2000).

Despite the high number of females thought to have ADHD, girls with ADHD may be underidentified and untreated. The research is based largely on a male population. Typically, girls with ADHD have more serious intellectual and functional impairment, higher rates of mood and anxiety disorders, and less hyperactivity and conduct disorder, which explains why they are not assessed in a timely manner (Biederman et al., 1999).

JUVENILE JUSTICE ISSUES

The impact of a disability on girls who have additional challenges can be far-reaching. Historically, female offenders were generally ignored by the juvenile justice system. Their criminal behaviors were considered to be victimless and self-destructive behaviors. Ironically, although much of female crime is a direct consequence of abuse and neglect, juvenile justice systems did not regard their behaviors as a cry for help. This attitude was reinforced by a number of factors:

- Inadequate information was available about the causes leading to girls' entry into delinquency and the juvenile justice system;

- Most female crimes were non-violent and status offenses including incorrigibility, drug offenses, curfew violations, prostitution, truancy, and running away;

- Historically, the juvenile justice system has been focused on males, as they comprise the largest population; and

- Few programs were established for female offenders.

As the number of girls in the juvenile justice system has increased, more questions must be raised about how best to serve a population with very different needs and experiences. An important early step is to identify the causes of problematic behavior when they impact their school performance. Under federal law, schools are mandated to address these issues through identification of disability need, meeting these needs with services and providing transition services.

Youth with disabilities have rights under several federal laws. These laws include the Individuals with Disabilities Education Act (IDEA), Section 504 of the Rehabilitation Act, and the Americans with Disabilities Act (ADA). Youth covered by IDEA also have rights under the other two laws. Youth who do not meet the eligibility criteria for special education under IDEA, but who do have a disability, may qualify for protections under Section 504 and the ADA. Evaluation determines eligibility and services.

Under IDEA, " a child with a disability" is a child who has been evaluated as having a specific disability and who, *because of the disability*, needs special education and related services. According to IDEA every youth who qualifies for special education services is entitled to free appropriate public education (FAPE). More than half of youth in the justice system are known to have one or more emotional and behavioral disorders. Children with emotional and behavioral disabilities may be entitled to services under IDEA using the category of "severe emotional disturbance." This right includes youth through age 21 who have been identified as having disabilities and who are involved in the juvenile justice system or who have been suspended or expelled from school (Burrell & Warboys, 2000). According to IDEA, each eligible youth must have an individualized education program (IEP) that describes the specific special education and related services and transition services to which the youth is entitled. Each state has the authority to identify specific criteria for the federal categories under which children are entitled to services.

Section 504 of the Rehabilitation Act, prohibits discrimination based on disability in any program that receives federal financial assistance. If a child with disabilities does not qualify for special education services under IDEA, he or she may receive the necessary accommodations, modifications or supplemental aids and services under Section 504. As is the case with IDEA, services under Section 504 must also be provided in state and county corrections facilities and programs that receive federal monies. The Americans with Disabilities Act (ADA) expands the power of Section 504 by including both entities that receive federal funds and those that do not.

STUDIES OF OUTCOMES FOR YOUNG WOMEN WITH DISABILITIES

Referrals for evaluation are most often made because of behavioral issues. Girls tend to internalize their frustrations and school difficulties. In contrast, boys are usually more aggressive and openly demonstrate their frustration with school. Consequently, they are more readily referred to special education when their behaviors become more challenging. Because girls are more passive, academic challenges are overlooked or even ignored. They are more likely to be labeled as moody or insolent when they act inappropriately.

Early studies have shown that young women with disabilities differ from young males and young women without disabilities in their post school outcomes:

- They were less likely to be identified as seriously emotionally disturbed and more likely to be identified as having mental retardation;

- They had more significant disabilities that interfered with day-to-day functioning;

- They were underrepresented in secondary school special education services;

- They were disproportionately over-represented by minorities;

- They were at greater risk for more problematic post-school and transition outcomes; and

- They dropped out of school at higher rates (Wagner, 1992).

RECOMMENDED STRATEGIES

The following recommendations can help improve practice and policy that concerns girls who have disabilities:

- Philosophical commitments that recognize, understand, respect, and support the differences in girls;

- Earlier identification of risk factors apparent in girls' lives together with supports and assistance to them and to their families;

- Early intervention for first-time offenders, including screening and comprehensive evaluations for disabilities and referral to special education services as warranted;

- Development of less punitive and disability sensitive correctional approaches that do not repeat the abusive experience;

- Creation of programs that promote individual strengths and encourage the development of problem-solving skills, social relationships, and employment skills;

- Programs for girls that include access to therapy, medication, crisis intervention, and strong individual supports;

- Access to culturally appropriate therapeutic and correctional programming with staff who could serve as positive role models;

- More user-friendly education for parents about characteristics of disabilities and mandated special education services;

- More education for advocates, judges, attorneys, educators, probation officers, and corrections staff about disabilities as they affect girls, and services mandated in schools through age 22 for those girls who qualify;

- Development of more community-based services for non-violent female offenders; and

- More research focused on characteristics of disabilities in girls in the justice system and those approaches that are most effective.

About the Authors

Lili Frank Garfinkel is Coordinator of the Juvenile Justice Project at the PACER Center in Minneapolis, MN.

References

Acoca, L., "Characteristics of Girls at Risk of Entering or Involved With the Juvenile Justice System: Investing in Girls: A 21st Century Strategy," 6(1) *Juvenile and Family Justice* (1999). Available online: www.ncjrs.org/html/ojjdp/jjjournal/1099/invest3.html.

Ambrose, A. M., & Simpkins, S., *Improving Conditions for Girls in the Justice System: The Female Detention Project*, American Bar Association Net: www.abanet.org/crimjust/juvjus/gji.html. (2000).

American Bar Association and the National Bar Association, *Justice by Gender: The Lack of Appropriate Prevention, Diversion and Treatment Alternatives for Girls in the Justice System*, 1-42 (May, 2001).

Biederman, J., Faraone, S. V., Mick, E., Williamson, S., Wilens, T. E., Spencer, T. J., Weber, W.; Jetton, J., Kraus, I., Pert, J., & Zallen, B., "Clinical Correlates of ADHD in Females: Findings from a Large Group of Girls Ascertained From Pediatric and Psychiatric Referral Sources," 38(8) *Journal of the American Academy of Child and Adolescent Psychiatry* 966-975 (1999).

Burrell, S. & Warboys, L. M., *Special Education and the Juvenile Justice System* (ED450515) (U. S. Department of Justice, Office of Juvenile Justice and Deliquency Prevention, 2000).

Fejes-Mendoza, K., Miller, D., & Eppler, R., "Portraits of Dysfunction: Criminal, Educational and Family Profiles of Juvenile Female Offenders," 18(3) *Education and Treatment of Children*, 309-321(1995).

Garfinkel, L. F., *Unique Challenges, Hopeful Responses: A Handbook for Professionals Working With Youth With Disabilities in the Juvenile Justice System*, (3d ed.), (PACER Center, Inc., 2001).

Obeidallah, D. A. & Earls, F. J., *Adolescent Girls: The Role of Depression in the Development of Delinquency* (A Research Preview) (U.S. Department of Justice, Office of Justice Programs, National Institute of Justice, 1999).

Ruffolo, M.C., Sarri, R., & Goodkind, S., "Study of Delinquent, Diverted, and High-Risk Adolescent Girls: Implications for Mental Health Intervention," 28(4) *Social Work Research* 240 (December 2004).

Wagner, M., *Being Female — A Secondary Disability?: Gender Differences in the Transition Experiences of Young People with Disabilities*, (Presentation to the Special Education Special Interest Group at the American Educational Research Association annual meeting, 1992).

Widom, C. S., "Childhood Victimization and the Derailment of Girls and Women to the Criminal Justice System." In Richie, B. E., Tsenin, K.,, & Widom, C. S., *Research on Women and Girls in the Justice System* (A Research Forum) (Department of Justice, Office of Justice Programs, National Institute of Justice, September 2000).

Zabel, R., & Nigro, F. A., "The Influence of Special Education Experience and Gender of Juvenile Offenders on Academic Achievement Scores in Reading, Language and Mathematics," 26(2) *Behavior Disorders* 164-172 (2001).

Chapter 40

Improving Access to Health Care for California's Women Prisoners

by Nancy Stoller, Ph.D.

INTRODUCTION

Maintaining and improving the health status of inmates, as well as providing preventive health care during incarceration, can substantially reduce the economic, social, and health care burden for parolees, their families, and the state. This chapter reports on a study that examined access to health care for women who are incarcerated in California state prisons. The study is based on the quantitative and qualitative analysis of a large database of interviews, medical records, legal documents, and judicial reports assembled in conjunction with inmate complaints over four years. The study's recommendations compare the California correctional health care model with "best practice" models for health care delivery to offer an empirical foundation on which to base deliberations on correctional health options.

The study reviewed 1,269 files of complaints made by women prisoners to various attorneys between 1996 and 1999. In all, we coded 269 files of complaints from women housed at California Institution for Women (CIW), 555 from California Correctional Women's

---

This chapter originally appeared in Women, Girls & Criminal Justice, *Vol. 2, No. 2, February/March 2001.*

Facility (CCWF), and 432 from Valley State Prison for Women (VSPW). In addition, we examined reports by the California Department of Health Services and the State Auditor, legal materials, and contemporary standards for medical care in prisons and jails. The research was supplemented with interviews with prisoners and health care specialists.

HEALTH CARE PROBLEMS OF WOMEN PRISONERS

Looking Beyond the Statistics to Real Impact on Women's Lives

"Marie Compton." Marie Compton suffered severe burns on over 50% of her body. When she was incarcerated, she had only one pair of custom-made pressure garments. Outside contacts attempted to send in other prescribed pressure garments, but these packages were refused and sent back. As a result, her burns began to show massive scarring. She was forced to wear the same garment for months without washing it. This is completely unhygienic and dangerous to her condition. It is likened to wearing the same pair of underwear for months on end. Ms. Compton was also denied physical therapy at the prison. As a result, her muscles tightened up and she was unable to walk. She spent most of her time in a wheelchair that was unsafe and difficult to maneuver on her own. When she was finally able to stand up, she could only do so on the tips of her toes because the muscles were too short. She also had extreme difficulty getting the medications she needed. Pain medications and lotions to help the burns heal were prescribed by outside doctors, but often they were never ordered. She wasn't even able to get olive oil to help loosen the skin.

"Kendra Brooks." Kendra Brooks has an extensive family history of breast cancer. She does self-exams quite regularly. When she found a lump in her right breast, she fought to get a mammogram done. Three months later, prison medical staff agreed to give her the mammogram. However, they kept putting her off and once even told her she'd have to go to the hospital because their machine was broken. She didn't actually get the mammogram until over a year later. When she went to get the results, the x-ray technician said there was no mammogram record in her file. She was told that they would have to do another one. She waited another three weeks for the results of the second mammogram. Then she was ducated [referred] to get another mammogram. When she questioned the technician about why she needed three mammograms, he said that they didn't see anything on the first one and so they were going to do it again. Ultimately she was told that the results were fine, but considering all the difficulties she had, she has trouble trusting them. She was very concerned because she has noticed that the lump is larger and there is now another small lump in her left breast. Ms. Brooks has also started having frequent dizzy spells where she sees black spots and stars. She was given a finger prick sugar test and was told that her blood sugar level is very low. They told her to eat more fruit to get her sugar levels up to par. Obviously this is a nearly impossible solution for her, since no one at the prison gets a special diet.

"Jessica Stacy." Although Jessica Stacy is a member of the Chronic Care Program, she has had great difficulty getting her Dilantin and Phenobarbital levels checked monthly, as she thought was required. Her levels were tested in November and then not again until May. She believes that the lack of testing has led to wrong levels of the medication in her blood, causing an increased rate of seizures. In May she estimates that she had three or four

Table 40.1: Health Care Problems of Women in California Prisons*

Diagnosis/Complaint	Frequency**	Percentage***
Latrogenic Problems	393	36.6
Gynecological/Reproductive	343	31.9
Miscellaneous Health****	278	25.9
Mental Illness	273	25.5
Respiratory	260	24.4
Injury	226	21.1
Miscellaneous Access	206	19.2
Orthopedic	203	19.0
Sex & Other Harassment	203	18.9
Gastrointestinal	149	13.9
Headache/Neurological	148	13.7
Liver Disease	130	12.2
Cardiovascular Disease	128	12.0
HIV/AIDS	116	10.8
Dental	112	10.4
High Blood Pressure	112	10.4
Seizures	109	10.2
STD	107	10.0
Cancer	94	8.9
Rheumatic Disease/Arthritis	80	7.5
Eye	70	6.6
Skin	60	5.7
Diabetes	60	5.6
Drug Abuse	53	4.9
Urinary	44	4.1
Ear	36	3.4
Hormonal (not reproductive)	33	3.1
Death	7	0.7
Throat	4	0.4

*California Institution for Women (CIW); California Correctional Women's Facility (CCWF); and Valley State Prison for Women ((VSPW).

**Total number of prisoner files reviewed (N = 1072) comes from CIW (N = 253), CCWF (N = 481), and VSPW (N = 338).

***Percentages add up to more than 100 because some prisoners report multiple problems (mean number = 3.92)

****Miscellaneous symptoms that were not diagnosed into a codable category of illness or disease.

seizures. During that month she went as long as six days without her meds and had two seizures during this delay. Beginning in March, her rate of seizures increased from one per month to one every two to three weeks.

Ms. Stacy was extremely concerned about a memo that was distributed informing prisoners that they would be charged $5 for each asthma attack or seizure. She attributes the distribution of this memo to the perception that prisoners are faking attacks or seizures. She believes that because of the delayed response time of prison officials to prisoner medical emergencies they often arrive after the attack or seizure is over and then accuse the women of faking. Ms. Stacey also has an artificial pin in her knee that slipped out of place. It is causing a bulge that can be seen from the outside. Although she has submitted at least 10 requests, she has not been able to see an orthopedist.

Types of Complaints in California

Table 40.1 indicates the primary health problems reported by California's women prisoners and further documented through available medical records. The following text further details our findings.

Problems of Access to Care and Medications. A large number of the health care problems of women prisoners involve access either to medications or to the type of care needed. The fact that "missed medications" was the most common complaint suggests that unavailability of medicines when needed is a serious problem. Nearly 22% of the women had missed important medications at least once, while many had missed them repeatedly. This was a common complaint from women with HIV/AIDS. Not ensuring proper and timely distribution of antiviral treatments can significantly shorten the lives and affect the quality of life of women with HIV/AIDS. Women with diabetes, asthma, heart disease, hypertension, cancer, and a host of other ailments are also put at grave risk when prescribed medications are missed. Overall, more than 19% of the women complained of at least one problem accessing the health care system.

Gender-specific health diagnoses also appear frequently in the lists of care problems for each institution. Thirty-two percent of the women report gynecological and reproductive health problems. Almost nine percent of the women complain about health care associated with a pregnancy. These rates point to the urgent need for accessible and expert specialist care in obstetrics/gynecology and other areas of women's health.

Other frequent complaints concern access to care for asthma, high blood pressure, heart disease, headache, insulin dependent diabetes, seizures, epilepsy, and orthopedic problems such as disc disease. These are all conditions that can be seriously debilitating, chronic, and in some cases, life threatening, if not treated properly.

Based on reports by prisoners, the health care that is available can actually be detrimental. For over 13% of the women, the care provided by medical staff was harmful to their health, sometimes very seriously.

Finally, almost 26% of prisoners in the sample suffered from a wide array of miscellaneous symptoms that were uncodable due to inadequate diagnostic information in their files.

Problems Related to the Prison System. Other health problems appear more related to prison deficiencies or abuse than to health care access issues. Among these are unintentional injuries, which are sufficiently commonplace to comprise the fourth most prevalent area of complaint among women in the sample. These injuries include broken bones, head injuries, and lacerations. Good public health practice, including the review and implementation of corrective safety measures in residential and work areas, could prevent many of these injuries.

Sexual harassment and abuse by guards is another important gender-specific issue. Sexual harassment was the "number one" complaint area from women at VSPW and it was reported at all three institutions studied. Over 14% of the women in the sample experienced some form of sexual harassment from staff or doctors.

CURRENT DEPARTMENT OF CORRECTIONS HEALTH CARE PRACTICE: MAJOR FINDINGS

Many of the reported access problems appear to result from the organization of health services at the women's prisons. The following aspects of the system of service were found to impede access to quality care:

- Inadequate management system;

- Medical grievances and appeals processes that are slow and uncertain in outcome;

- Lack of accredited services: none of California's prison health services are accredited;

- Dependence on Medical Technical Assistants (MTAs): MTAs are Licensed Vocational Nurses who also work as uniformed correctional officers. They are usually the medical staff of first contact, serving as gatekeepers to health care access, particularly during non-clinic hours. Their dual role compromises the independent medical function of a nurse in terms of confidentiality and priorities and, moreover, numerous complaints indicate that some MTAs make inadequate assessments and inappropriate decisions about emergency needs and urgent care;

- Restrictive policies resulting in sub-standard dental care, leading to a high rate of unnecessary tooth extractions (prisoners are not permitted root canal procedures or dental crowns);

- Restrictive policies that prevent access to community-based experimental treatment protocols for patients with HIV, HCV, and cancer (no system-wide Hepatitis C prevention, treatment, or counseling protocols exist);

- The co-pay system: prisoners must pay a $5 fee when seeking care, which discourages utilization of services, creates a bureaucratic burden to the health service and an economic burden to the very poor prisoner—and provides no documented economic gain to the department;

- Policies requiring physicians to perform unnecessary administrative, non-medical functions: physicians are required to authorize "chrono" forms which permit ongoing adjustments in schedule or access to special services, equipment, or housing needed for medical reasons. This paperwork function diverts physicians from direct clinical work and could be done by a non-clinical assistant;

- Inadequate translation services; and

- Inadequate preventive health services: routine screening for breast and cervical cancer is unavailable on a call-up basis; twice yearly dental prophylaxis is unavailable; HIV, STD, and HCV screening are limited. In addition, there is inadequate counseling, a lack of confidentiality, and visiting policies limit inmate interest in testing for HIV and then limit access to needed treatment.

RECOMMENDATIONS

We reviewed options for the organization of medical services in prisons and jails used in other states and by the Federal Bureau of Prisons. Based on this review, the following recommendations are proposed to improve care for women prisoners:

- *Clinical services should be provided by an independent non-profit agency.* Responsibility for structuring, managing, staffing, and improving the health care services of the California Department of Corrections should be transferred to another agency. Three possible options to achieve this goal include:

    1. *Placing oversight responsibility under the Department of Health Services (DHS) with contractual arrangements made for services in the different prisons.* This model is followed by the United States Bureau of Prisons (BOP), which utilizes the United States Public Health Service (PHS) as its primary provider for health care to prisoners. PHS clinical personnel are assigned to work within the BOP and report to the BOP Health Care Division.

    2. *Possible development of a program by the University of California to provide medical services to prisoners.* A growing number of public and private universities in the United States provide medical services to prisoners. The University of Texas Medical Branch (UTMB) at Galveston currently provides managed care to over half of Texas's prisoners, while a second medical school provides services to the rest. The University of Connecticut Medical Center provides managed care to Connecticut's prisoners. Yale University and Brown University have been active providers of HIV care for prisoners in New England. Possible advantages of this approach include access to quality staff, greater confidence on the part of the prisoners, a depth of experience and greater opportunity for ongoing education of staff in accord with current continuing medical education (CME) standards, training opportunities for interns and residents, and separation of custody and treatment functions. Potential problems with this approach include the difficulty of providing services throughout the state and the enormous expansion that the program would entail for the university.

    3. *Privatization of medical service delivery.* In the past 20 years, privatization has spread extensively in the United States correctional world. Private medical care provision has been a part of this growth. However, we do not recommend this option. A major concern with profit-based care is that an incentive exists to save money by providing less care or by paying low salaries, resulting in a significant reduction in the quality of service. We recommend that the state undertake detailed research to explore these and other options to transfer provision of clinical services. Important issues to consider are cost, quality, quality assurance

programs, ability to provide a local focus to the care, and provisions for close monitoring by state agencies.

- *Internal monitoring and quality improvement systems are necessary.* Quality management and improvement in any prison health care service requires ongoing review of procedures as well as key events (e.g., deaths). In a correctional system, continuous quality improvement is critical because of custodial pressures that can prevent rapid treatment or access to community resources. An independent unit of the state should conduct regular program review of the services and management in order to assure quality.

- *Location of ultimate authority for appeals concerning health care for prisoners should be moved out of the CDC to an independent agency.* The CDC is a correctional authority and not a medical system. Its primary goals are punishment, confinement, and security. California could consider an approach to health care appeals similar to that utilized in Florida, which has created the Correctional Medical Authority, an independent oversight commission.

- *California prisons should comply with national and international health care standards and be accredited by a national organization with expertise in prison health services.* The American Public Health Association (APHA), the National Commission on Correctional Health Care (NCCHC), the American Correctional Association (ACA), and the United Nations (UN) all have developed standards for health care in prisons. The UN standards are broadly focused on human rights minimums as the key to quality care. The APHA guidelines—which incorporate human rights, medical care, mental health, and public health concepts and include standards for adults and juveniles—are the most thorough of the United States standards. The NCCHC standards are part of a national accreditation program.

  California should also require that a national professional association experienced in evaluating prison health care services accredit all prison health services. Two appropriate options are:

  1. *The Joint Commission on Accreditation of Hospitals (JCAHO).* The U. S. Bureau of Prisons utilizes the JCAHO for its accreditation process.

  2. *National Commission on Correctional Health Care (NCCHC).* This organization was initially established by the American Medical Association and is a prime force in accreditation and improvement of care in jails and prisons throughout the United States.

- *Recruitment, retention, and further education of health care professionals should be improved.* Currently, the CDC has difficulty recruiting and retaining physicians and other health care providers sufficient to meet its needs. One solution is the provision of medical school scholarships, which would be forgiven in return for state service. A California scholarship recipient could work one year in a California prison or jail health service for each year of scholarship. A similar plan is used by the federal government to finance medical school in return for service in the Public Health Service (PHS), including assignments to the Indian Health Service, the Federal Prison System, and other underserved areas.

  Joint staff meetings, participation in local hospital CME and grand rounds programs could integrate prison medical staffs with the local medical community. CDC health service rules could mandate physician discussion with the specialist in every referral case. Additionally, medical department staff should be encouraged or required to attend CME programs in correctional medicine. All supervisory staff should be encouraged—and funded—to obtain credentials from the NCCHC as Certified Correctional Health Providers within two years of their appointment. They should be encouraged to join the Society of Correctional Physicians or the American Correctional Health Services Association and attend their meetings in order to be in contact with other providers and be able to hear about the latest developments in their field.

- *Separate the functions of custody and medical care.* Decisions about whether a medical situation is an emergency or needs urgent attention should be made by a registered nurse (RN). The licensed vocational nurse (LVN) training of MTAs is inadequate for diagnosis or triage. All national correctional health standards and accrediting bodies prohibit medical providers from having custody roles. If LVNs are to be used on the medical team they should not be members of the custody staff. Institutions could hire on-call RNs who are trained in triage to act as first responders in an emergency. Appropriate institutional staffing should include at least one RN at each skilled nursing facility or outpatient housing unit (OPHU) and a second one who could move around to see women in their housing units. The duties assigned to people in the current MTA position should be limited to those who are within the LVN scope of practices, such as taking vital signs and managing clerical tasks.

- *End the use of the co-pay system.* Until the co-pay system is dismantled, the money generated should be used to improve services for prisoners, including health education programs and preventive services.

- *Change the organization of local services so health clinicians are not performing non-medical functions.* Once a physician has indicated a particular health need in a medical record, the preparation of the appropriate authorization and paperwork should be handled by a non-clinical staff person.

- *Change the training of medical professionals hired by the CDC.* The training of medical professionals should be evaluated and upgraded to better meet the changing demands placed on the system.

- *Provide translation services.* Other jurisdictions provide needed translating through various combinations of on-site translators and assistance via telephone services. Other prisoners and custodial staff should not be used as translators.

- *Institute new services such as increased access to special diets.* Simple solutions like a low-fat, low-salt salad bar would assist prisoners with special dietary needs, relieve the food service of the burden of preparing individual trays, and allow otherwise healthy prisoners to live outside of special units.

- *Respond to the Hepatitis C epidemic.* It has been estimated that 40% of California women prisoners are HCV positive and that 30% of those with HCV are behind bars. The state should introduce a comprehensive screening program, provide access to testing for all prisoners at risk of infection, train its medical staff in the current treatment of HCV, institute broad education programs concerning HCV, and provide clinic services for patients with this illness.

- *Provide greater patient education and preventative care.* There is a broad need both for more patient education and for routine preventive services. Regular check-ups should be scheduled and reminders sent to patients. Women prisoners should be screened and treated according to community standards for breast and cervical cancer, dental prophylaxis (twice yearly), and routine tuberculosis testing (currently this is the only preventive screening which is on schedule at the studied institutions).

- *Expand peer education by HIV and HCV positive women.* Many studies have demonstrated that the most effective approaches to HIV prevention and motivation to survive are via peer education. Established peer education programs at the California Medical Facility at Vacaville and at other women's prisons (e.g., Bedford Hills in New York) have been very effective in helping prisoners make life-saving decisions about prevention and deal with difficulties of HIV medication regimens.

- *Establish protocols and policies to protect inmates from sexual harassment.* Given the potential for sexual exploitation of inmates as well as the high rates of previous sexual abuse that many women prisoners have suffered, the state should make strong efforts to hire female physicians for all direct clinical care. A corollary to this suggestion would be to end the practice of male correctional officers having contact with women prisoners in residential and medical areas.

- *Apply compassionate release more broadly.* Compassionate release should be considered part of providing overall medical care and as a palliative medical procedure similar to providing pain medications. Evaluation for compassionate release should be part of a prisoner's medical work-up and women with very serious illnesses should be frequently assessed for their eligibility. Not only is compassionate release humane, it is also cost effective and can save the state monies by placing gravely ill patients in more appropriate locations.

- *Promote alternatives to incarceration.* California's increase in incarcerate rates during the last 25 years has resulted in many problems, one of which is the imprisonment of thousands of people who are physically and mentally ill, as well as imprisonment of persons who could be more appropriately treated in alternative facilities.

  An increase in the use of community facilities for pregnant prisoners is greatly overdue. The state has long had legislation requiring the CDC to allow pregnant prisoners to reside in such facilities prior to birthing and to care for their infants there for up to a year and a half. However, the Department has restricted access to these programs, and the state has provided little funding. Consequently, they are almost unused. Instead, women give birth in prison where they undergo dangerous pregnancies and births. The infant is then separated from its mother within one day of delivery. Provision of community care in half-way houses for pregnant prisoners would greatly improve the quality of prenatal care for mothers and the first months of life for their babies, who would then have the opportunity to receive the health benefits of nursing and bonding with their mothers.

About the Author

Nancy Stoller, Ph.D., is in the Department of Community Studies at the University of California, Santa Cruz.

Chapter 41

Health Symptoms and the Inability to Engage in Self-Care and Self-Medication for Incarcerated Women

by M. Katherine Maeve, R.N., Ph.D.

INTRODUCTION

One of the greatest challenges faced by health care providers for women in jail is the seemingly endless number of health symptoms and complaints. Health care in jails (or prisons) is often polarized, with women on one side and health care providers on the other. Indeed, health care disputes are the leading cause of formal inmate complaints for women (and men). As health care costs soar, funding for health care provider positions diminishes, and provider burnout runs rampant, the costs of attending to these various symptoms and complaints becomes important.

For a number of years, my experience with incarcerated women was primarily as a nurse researcher. Subsequently, I also began a faculty practice providing nursing care that was not directly related to my research. When I first began to practice with incarcerated women in a local county jail, I was told "These are the sickest bunch of women you'll ever meet in your life." Though at first I believed this merely reflected the frustrations of that particular nurse on that particular day, I soon found I was beginning to feel the same way—every day. Not only do the women we incarcerate have numerous physical and psychological complaints, they are also particularly vocal and persistent in their complaints.

This chapter originally appeared in Women, Girls & Criminal Justice, *Vol. 1, No. 4, June/July 2000.*

On one level, the myriad complaints make complete sense. As a whole, incarcerated women do have increased incidences of chronic illnesses, infectious diseases, and mental health issues when compared to comparable groups of women in the free world. While conducting research in a large women's state prison, I was a first-hand observer of the practice of penal harm medicine so accurately described by Michael Vaughn and Linda Smith (Vaughn & Smith, 1999). Penal harm medicine (and by implication, penal harm nursing) refers to the idea that health care providers are co-opted into providing health care consistent with the notion that incarceration is meant to inflict pain in order to sufficiently punish offenders. Health care, then, becomes one more avenue by which to punish inmates. It was clear to me how other health care providers were socialized to view all complaints as forms of manipulation, thus discounting women and their symptoms. That, of course, could never happen to me.

Still, I now found women very often presented with complaints and symptoms that could not be explained, even after massive evaluative and diagnostic visits, including mental health evaluations. Additionally, women frequently requested emergency care for what seemed like medically trivial happenings. For example, I was once summoned to the women's unit for a woman who stated she was having chest pain, could not breathe, and believed she was having a heart attack. Having put all my other considerable obligations on hold, I found this 23-year-old woman, sitting at a table, playing cards and laughing with the other women. When I questioned her, she began to tell me how her chest was hurting because she was upset over an argument that happened some hours earlier. She equated having her heart broken by an argument with a friend, to having a "broken" heart—the kind of broken heart that ends up in a heart attack and death, requiring ambulances, and emergency room personnel. I confess that my already overtaxed amount of patience was at that point completely lost. This young woman was very angry with me, shouting, and calling me various unflattering names.

The officers on duty found this all somewhat amusing, and at least one was actually delighted that I was finally getting first hand experience of how petty women could be. (Of course, she was also seemingly ignoring the fact that I, too, was a woman.) I returned to the privacy of my office and reflected on how I was becoming guilty of the same biases I had so often condemned in others. My worst fears were being realized—I had gone from advocate to adversary. This was not the way it was supposed to be.

In an attempt to redeem myself, my practice, and ultimately the women I was caring for, I resolved to understand this better. In the process (and in conjunction with a new research project that involved following women after release from jail), I began to explore why women developed these demanding and, frankly, irritating illness behaviors while incarcerated. As a die-hard believer in the critical social theory and participative action research methodology I was using in my study, I had no doubt that together, we could figure some of this out. The following represents that exploration and some of the insights I have begun to develop and consider.

HEALTH SYMPTOMS AND INCARCERATION

A common belief exists in our society that women simply complain about their health more than men. Numerous studies have endorsed that belief. However, most of those studies were conducted on what were considered to be "healthy" populations. More recent studies, conducted in populations where an actual illness or disease is present, have demonstrated that women and men are equally likely to report symptoms, and some studies suggest that men are more likely than women to complain about severe symptoms. As previously indicated, incarcerated women do have increased incidences of numerous chronic and acute illnesses, including mental health illnesses. Therefore, it must be expected that women will experience symptoms related to these conditions and complain about them—especially in an environment where there is little else to focus upon.

Additionally, women in jails are more likely to have recently used substances that alter the sensations associated with their bodies. Cocaine, crack, alcohol, heroin, and marijuana obviously alter levels of consciousness, thereby altering perceptions of bodily and psychological cues. The abrupt abstinence imposed by incarceration often means a sudden rush of sensations and symptoms. Although physical symptoms are often the direct result of physically demonstrable pathology, in addition to expected bodily cues, situational and psychological factors play a major role in the experiencing of symptoms, the attribution assigned to those symptoms, and how and why they are reported. Symptoms, then, are dependent upon how they are perceived, either subjectively derived through the senses or through cognitive processes that guide the attention given to, and the interpretation of, somatic information.

In previous research I have discussed how incarcerated women consistently perceived themselves as inherently pathologic, often describing how their evil natures led to the tragedies in their lives—even when those tragedies began with early childhood sexual abuse. It was easy for women to jump to the conclusion that every little conceivable symptom was further representation of that inherently "felt" pathology (Maeve, 1999).

In my search for some answers, I began with a participant I will call "Alice." Alice experienced incapacitating headaches while incarcerated, along with tingling and numbness in her legs and arms. She also frequently complained of vaginal discharges and burning. During the times we met while she was incarcerated, I found her dragging, pale, often crying. She was convinced that if the nurses or doctors would just believe in her symptoms, there was a treatment that would fix her. Within three weeks of discharge, however, I found her bright, bubbly and without any of her previous symptoms. "Freedom was my cure," she told me. Watching Alice's experience of her body in and out of jail was a lesson in contrasts.

I took Alice's experience back to jail with me, and tried to explore with a particularly difficult inmate I will call "Jill" how her complaints of illness might just be the somatic sequelae of her distress at being incarcerated. We discussed the possibilities at some length, and she seemed to be thoughtfully contemplating the issues. Ultimately, after having weighed the possibilities, Jill provided her own reality check. "You don't understand, Kathy, I *really, really* feel there's something wrong with me. Hell, I'm in here aren't I?"

Thus, I found I needed reminding of my own research findings. Women were again telling me what I already knew—they felt sick because they believed they were sick. The difference was that in my previous work, my role was only as a nurse researcher. My role now was as a care provider. I was perceiving their "sickness" through a much different lens—perhaps a narrower lens, but a lens that required a different focus to accommodate my different role and obligations.

HOW INCARCERATION UNDERMINES REASONABLE SELF-CARE

No Self-Medication Possible

As I continued to explore the split between symptoms felt while incarcerated, with symptoms experienced by the women in the free world, one message was repeated over and over again. While there are many freedoms lost because of incarceration, one of the most keenly felt by women is the inability to engage in self-care generally, and the inability to self-medicate specifically.

On an everyday basis, it is a very common experience for nurses to be bombarded with requests from women for what are termed "prn" medications (those medications that can be requested and given on an as-needed basis without a prescription). The vast majority of these are over-the-counter medications in the free world.

Without a prescription, nurses may give some medications, e.g., Tylenol, to women twice a day during "pill call," and always in the presence of a correctional officer. Prescribed medicines given on a routine basis require a visit to the medical unit through a mechanism called "sick call." A woman must send a written request to the medical unit where her reported symptoms are triaged, and appointments are scheduled in terms of the nurses' perception of their urgency. Seeing a health care provider, however, does not mean that women will be prescribed the kinds of medicines they want. Many requests are reasonable, many are not. Recently we had quite a scene in the medical unit because a nurse refused to prescribe Benadryl (an antihistamine used for allergic reactions and as a sleep aid) for itching, dry skin. Itching, dry skin is not a medical problem—at least not in jails.

Paradoxically, however, growing fingernails and toenails are approached as medical problems. To trim her nails, a woman must submit a sick call request and be seen in the medical unit—just to be handed nail clippers by the nurse. Not only does this pathologize what should be considered a routine personal hygiene matter, it also trivializes nurses and nursing practice.

So, I began a little self-experimentation. I kept a log every day for a week about the pills I took and the kinds of health care behaviors I could engage in without consulting a nurse. They included taking vitamins, Tylenol, and pills that relieve allergy and sinus symptoms. I speculated on what kinds of pills I might want to take if I stayed in a confined area 23 hours of every day, in extreme boredom with little else to think about. Given this hypothetical situation, I believed I might have needed something for sleep and something (perhaps anything) to relieve the stress of being away from those I love. Because I have eaten the food in this jail, the possibilities for indigestion relievers seemed endless. I found that I took for granted the idea that I could file my fingernails as needed. I applied hand lotion several times a day. And, I wondered how I would feel if I would have had to ask the permission of a nurse for each and every thing.

Impairment of Inmate's Sense of Themselves as Women

Increasingly, I realized many of these activities were integrally tied to understanding myself as female. All of my adult life, I have taken it as a given that I might get an easily cured headache related to the hormonal realities of my body. I believe that I feel better and function better if I take supplemental vitamins. Having clean, soft skin is important to me for numerous reasons related to my self-perception as a woman. I began to notice that the men in this jail look like men—men in different clothes, but still manly. Women look much different in jail than they do in the free world—in many ways, less womanly. Wearing baggy dark green pants and pullover shirts is usual (or at least similar to) attire for most men in the free world. However, very few women wear anything resembling the garishly bright orange pants and pullover shirts incarcerated women were required to wear. And, few women wear men's boxer briefs on a daily basis as do the women in this jail.

Women could only cut their hair with the kinds of clippers barbers use to cut men's hair. For those women who wore their hair cut very close to the scalp, this posed no problem. However, most women in this jail have much longer hair and cannot adequately cut, trim, or shape their hair with such clippers. For most women, hair is highly valued as a way to express individuality, sexuality, sensuality, beauty, and the like. Arguably, hair and breasts are the two most distinctive outward features that distinguish men from women. In this jail, breasts are obliterated in the uniform and hair is quite literally "unmanageable." "I can't do a thing with my hair" really means something here.

Women must use jail issued deodorant soap for all areas of their bodies—typically a harsh soap not well suited for women's faces or vaginal areas. Institutional underarm deodorant is equally harsh. It is very common for these soaps and deodorants to cause rashes and a kind of burning redness to the skin. Women (and men) in this jail are not allowed to have lotions in their possession, nor may they purchase their own soaps, shampoos, and the like. Ironically (at least to me), women are allowed to have makeup. So, while women's hair, skin and nails might look dull and lifeless, they can wear the latest blue eye shadow. Mostly though, the women look pretty awful.

While I would not support the idea that women have any particular obligation to look good for others, caring for our bodies is an important ritual for most women. Indeed, one of the ways we decry the tragedy of "crack whores" is to describe how dirty and unkempt they are. "Who would want to...?" we ask.

As my research progressed with women after their release, I came to expect that I probably would not immediately recognize them at our first meeting. Without exception, each woman was pleased to show me what she "really" looked like, what her personal style was like. And, it was good for me too because I began to see that the way women are forced to look while incarcerated really does impact their well being.

I began to imagine how I would feel about myself, what my state of mind would be like if I had to give up most of the outward symbols of my femininity—the very idea gave me a headache, so I took a Tylenol, put on some warm fuzzy jazz, and laid down to take a nap.

RECOMMENDATIONS

The question of what to do, how to manage the symptoms and complaints of incarcerated women, has no easy, quick-fix answer. Clearly, I am not advocating for some sort of Pollyanna approach wherein we understand "where they're coming from" and exude some sort of altruistic empathy. As others have noted, the "tyranny of niceness" that sometimes pervades nursing (and presumably other helping professions), is ultimately experienced by nurses as just another burden. It is simply not enough to try to and understand and be nice. While it matters to women that care providers be understanding and empathetic, what they want, and what is needed, are solutions we can *all* live with on an everyday basis. The following are some ideas that I believe would support women's self-care behaviors, and obviate the need for undue professional nursing oversight.

- Clear information on exactly what kind of health care is available, how it can be accessed, and what the limitations are;

- Information about the kinds of testing and screening for infectious diseases inmates can expect, and how that information will be handled;

- Access to reasonable amounts of hair, skin, and nail care products either through the "store call" mechanism (currently available for candy, sodas, etc.) or through family resources;

- Access to Tylenol, antacids, and vitamins without having to have an appointment with a health care provider or provide justification to anyone. (For example, two tablets of Tylenol can be pre-packaged and handed to women just as easily by correctional officers as by nurses. As officers typically work 12-hour shifts, one package per woman, per shift would not ultimately be any more work for officers than watching a woman take the pills handed to her by a nurse. Either way, the women will only get two Tylenol);

- Institutional clothing that is more consistent with the female physique, and that supports women's identities as women;

- Access to nail-cutting instruments without having to make an appointment with a nurse; and

- Accessible and substantive psycho-social and mental health care. (Although such care is often noted to be seriously lacking in prison settings, it is virtually nonexistent in jails.)

All of the above suggestions are easily workable, and would eliminate many of the scenarios that are foundational to the adversarial relationships between women and nurses in corrective settings. Many people would respond to the above suggestions by reminding me that women are in jail to be punished. But, of course, that is an erroneous assumption. Many women in jail have not yet been convicted; even if sentenced, we do not have license to punish women within jails—*going* to jail is the punishment.

CONCLUSIONS

After much angst and frustration, I have come to see that women's health behaviors and complaints are efforts at effecting some control in an environment that affords no other avenues towards control. Men at least can fight with each other to assert their manhood—as unfortunate as that observation is. I have come to see that women in jails also believe that "real" women complain. Therefore, their health behaviors and complaints may simply represent one way to cultivate womanliness. Complaints are perhaps a way to relate to each other and to nurses. This is not a comfortable observation to make.

I often have members of the community remind me of the adage "if you can't do the time, don't do the crime." Although I would argue that even if one could do the time, one still should not do the crime, I believe that in the case of women, what we really effectively say to women is, "if you can't do the time as a man, don't do the crime." Implicit in all this is the message that "real" women do not commit crimes—men commit crimes. Real women, however, do commit crimes, just as real men do. Gender does not preclude criminal behavior. Much as we try to change that, it is still women who are incarcerated, and they must be supported and treated as such.

Forcing women to live like men, and in many ways to look like men, is counterintuitive and ultimately destructive to the very ideas we say we want to foster in women. It is such a paradox that we ask women to behave like women (by not acting like men and committing crimes), yet when they do not and we incarcerate them, we deprive them of every opportunity to actually be female in the ways we (and they) most often associate with being female. We deny them the opportunity to look and act like females or be mothers to the children we expect them to care for once released and the freedom to care for themselves and medicate themselves as women.

I and others have noted that good physical and mental health care can actually reduce criminal behavior of women and their children, as well as improve their health status. Within this notion, I believe that just as women's health care is a specialty in the free world, so should it be in jails and prisons. Women are not men. Nurses in other health care environments have long advocated for health care delivery systems that honor the differences between men's and women's health care needs. Women in jails need our advocacy as well. Structures within jails that further disconnect women from nurses (who are also mostly women) serve neither the nurses, nor the women we purport to care for.

In telling the story of my exploration into these issues, I have disclosed my own particularity and foibles as a nurse, and perhaps as a woman. With the burden of conducting research from a critical perspective comes the burden of identifying one's own position of power, with its passions and prejudices. It is simply not enough to have critical conversations with each other about the injustices present in our communities. We must explore the role of power and control not only within society, but also within ourselves. If nothing else, this exercise has helped me work through some of those issues. In my own little way, and within my own little world, my consciousness has expanded. Tentatively, I would say that the consciousness of the nurses I work with have also been expanded. I am reminded of the idea that oppression is experienced and resisted through personal biography.

I am more convinced than ever that scholars who conduct research are inevitably changed by their immersion into, and the reality of, those situations which they critique. Perhaps it really is the only way to undermine hegemonic power and thereby avoid recreating it. Intervening for others is perhaps a way of intervening for ourselves.

Nursing, and I, have something to offer incarcerated women, with a value beyond the current actualization of our role. Nurses must resist being co-opted into practicing penal harm nursing. While the co-optation is easier than I first imagined, conceptualizing the possibility that penal harm nursing might exist is powerful in itself, if for no other reason than it creates this kind of dialogue.

About the Author

M. Katherine Maeve, RN, Ph.D., is in the Department of Community Nursing at the Medical College of Georgia, Augusta, GA.

References

Maeve, M.K., "Adjudicated Health: Incarcerated Women and the Social Construction of Health," 31 *Crime, Law & Social Change* 49-71(1999).

Vaughn, M. & Smith, L., "Practicing Penal Harm Medicine in the United States: Prisoners' Voices From Jail." 16(1) *Justice Quarterly* 175-231 (1999).

Chapter 42

The Complex Needs of Mentally Ill Women in County Jails

by Diane S. Young, Ph.D. and Liete C. Dennis, M.S.W.

INTRODUCTION

Jailed mentally ill women present numerous challenges to practitioners attempting to assess and treat them. At mid-year 2001, roughly 72,600 women were incarcerated in U.S. jails, 11.6% of all jailed adults (Beck et al., 2002). More importantly, many more than this number are booked into jails nationwide on an annual basis, given the rapid turnover within jails. A significant proportion present with mental illnesses. Based on a 1996 survey of jail inmates, 22.7% of female inmates were identified as mentally ill, so identified if they reported a current mental or emotional condition or an overnight stay in a mental hospital or treatment program (Ditton, 1999). Health problems, homelessness, and substance and alcohol abuse are often concomitant with mental illness, making it more difficult for individuals to engage in and respond to mental health treatment.

The demand on correctional systems to house and manage severely mentally ill individuals seems to be in direct relationship to the availability of community-care options (Lamb & Weinberger, 1998; Torrey, 1997). When community resources for mental health care are minimal or absent, pressure is placed upon the criminal justice system to deal with and manage individuals who, because of their illnesses, create difficulties for others. Correctional facilities are seldom equipped to understand and address the magnitude of need. Teplin et al. (1997)

This chapter originally appeared in Women, Girls & Criminal Justice, *Vol. 4, No. 3, March/April 2003.*

found that only 23.5% of the 116 female jail inmates needing mental health services in their sample received them during their jail stay.

The effective treatment of female offenders with mental illnesses is pertinent to practitioners in both correctional and community settings because these individuals are also difficult to engage and maintain in treatment within the community. They cycle in and out of jail as decompensation re-occurs. Identifying the challenges that this population presents is essential for informed program planning and targeting of resources.

STUDY SETTING AND METHOD

The findings reported here are from a study conducted in a county jail located in central New York State. The jail has a capacity of 620, with an average daily population of about 570 inmates at the time of data collection. The facility is primarily for adult pre-trial detainees, but also houses juveniles remanded to adult court, individuals charged with probation and parole violations pending their hearings, federal detainees, and inmates serving sentences who require the special medical or mental health services that this facility provides. Females comprise about 14% of the jail's population. The length of stay ranges from a few hours to two years, but the majority stay for a relatively short time. Two special housing units are designated for inmates with mental illnesses who have trouble functioning in general housing because of the symptoms related to their mental disorders. One unit houses 52 males, the other 14 females. Both operate very close to capacity.

The health and mental health records of 136 female inmates were retrospectively reviewed. These records were randomly selected from a list of all females housed in the Mental Health Unit (MHU) from March through November 1998. Information abstracted from the records includes health and mental health problems, treatment history, length of stay on the MHU, and basic demographic and criminal offense characteristics. Descriptive analyses are used to portray a picture of this group of women and provide summary information about their characteristics and treatment needs. In addition, three cases are presented to further illustrate the complexity of needs and life circumstances of female mentally ill offenders.

DEMOGRAPHIC, CRIMINAL OFFENSE, AND CLINICAL CHARACTERISTICS

Table 42.1 provides demographic and criminal characteristics for the 136 women in the sample. The women are primarily Caucasian and African-American. Mean age is 31.5 years (SD = 9.0), with a range of 16-67 years. A felony was the most serious current charge for 30.9% of the sample.

Table 42.2 presents clinical characteristics of the sample. Triage level is determined by a social worker based on a brief assessment at the time of jail intake and is used to guide housing placement decisions in the jail. Because this is a sample of individuals with mental illness, it is understandable that only a small proportion of the sample (5.2%) is considered appropriate for general housing at the time of booking. The medical concerns reported at jail intake covered a range of conditions including asthma, diabetes, and pregnancy. The vast majority of the sample had previously been in psychiatric and/or alcohol or drug treatment. Treatment was defined broadly to include inpatient and outpatient treatment in a

Table 42.1: Demographic and Criminal Characteristics for the Sample

Characteristic	Frequency (N = 136)	Percent
Race/ethnicity		
Caucasian, not Hispanic	63	46.3
African-American, not Hispanic	67	49.3
Other	6	4.4
Age		
16-17 years	13	9.6
18-20 years	6	4.4
21-30	41	30.1
31-40	52	38.2
41-50	22	16.2
Over 50 years	2	1.5
Prior arrest history (N=135)		
Yes	115	85.2
No	20	14.8
Most serious charge		
Violent felony	21	15.4
Property/other felony	14	10.3
Drug-related felony	7	5.2
Misdemeanor	66	48.5
Other[a]	28	20.6

[a] Includes federal holds; probation and parole holds; traffic or other violations that are less serious than a misdemeanor

Table 42.2: Clinical Characteristics for the Sample

Characteristic	Frequency	Percent
Triage level at booking (N=135)		
High suicide risk	25	18.5
Psychotic/fragile	47	34.8
Situational problems	56	41.5
Okay for general housing	7	5.2
Report medical concern at jail intake (N=134)	97	72.4
History of psychiatric medication (N=133)	89	66.9
On psychiatric medication at jail intake (N=130)	54	41.5
Received prior psychiatric treatment (N=135)	109	80.7
Received prior treatment for drug/alcohol use (N=133)	81	60.9

variety of settings. Two-thirds of the sample had received psychiatric medication in the past, with over 40% on psychiatric medication at jail intake.

Table 42.3 displays the DSM-IV Axis I disorders (American Psychiatric Association, 2000) that were identified in the sample. (This information is missing for 14 cases, primarily because these individuals were on the MHU such a short time that a full mental health evaluation could not be completed.) A substance-related disorder is the most prevalent type by far. Just over half (54.1%) of the women have at least two disorders. The number of individuals with both a substance-related clinical disorder and an additional major mental illness accounts for a large proportion of this comorbidity.

Table 42.4 demonstrates that length of stay on the MHU is fairly short for most women. Only 24.2% of the inmates were on the unit more than two weeks. This very brief length of stay certainly has ramifications for the provision of treatment, whether related to mental health or substance abuse. Although the mean length of stay was 13 days (SD = 22.7), the median is only five, with the number of days ranging from one to 200. The discharge reasons listed in Table 42.4 provide the reasons why inmates were discharged from the MHU; a large percentage (79%) of MHU discharges occurred because the woman was released from the jail.

Eighteen inmates (13.6%) were released to some form of treatment, including alternative to incarceration programs, drug/alcohol programs, and psychiatric facilities.

CASE ILLUSTRATIONS

Summary statistics, as presented above, provide an overall picture of the characteristics of a group. Case illustrations enrich this general description, by providing greater depth about the needs and circumstances of mentally ill females in this facility. The following cases are based on composites of women, selected to demonstrate the variety and complexity of needs without jeopardizing the confidentiality of any individual. The illustrations are designed to portray challenging, but not unusual, cases, and thus provide a picture of the multi-faceted needs of many of the mentally ill female offenders in this facility.

Case #1: "Molly"

Molly is 27, Caucasian, with a history beginning seven years ago of legal problems for misdemeanor charges such as petite larceny, prostitution, and various traffic violations. The increasing severity of her legal problems within the recent past results in less frequent but longer incarcerations as a sentenced or an unsentenced inmate. These legal charges include felonies such as aggravated harassment, child abuse, assaults, and drug possession. Molly is diagnosed with bipolar disorder and polysubstance dependence and has an extensive history of physical and sexual abuse by family members. Her social history reveals that she has three children, ages 6, 3, and 18 months, all placed in foster care. She does not maintain consistent contact with her children or with family members. She is unemployed and lives with a male friend who also has a lengthy criminal record. Because of her frequent incarcerations, refusal to comply with outpatient psychiatric treatment, and relapses into substance abuse, she does not receive social welfare benefits on a consistent basis.

Efforts to maintain Molly in the community have included intensive case management services, inpatient/outpatient psychiatric and substance abuse treatment, and emergency

Table 42.3: DSM-IV Axis I Disorders Among the Sample

DSM-IV Disorder	Frequency (N=122)	Percent[a]
Substance-related	85	69.7
Adjustment	39	32.0
Mood	34	27.9
Schizophrenia/other psychotic	14	11.5
Anxiety	7	5.7
Other Axis I disorders	4	3.3
Substance-related plus major mental disorder	55	45.1
Number of Axis I Disorders per Inmate		
One	56	45.9
Two	53	43.4
Three	13	10.7

[a] Percentages do not add to 100% because of the number of individuals with more than one Axis I disorder.

[b] Includes Axis 1 disorders noted no more than twice among the sample.

Table 42.4: Length of Stay and Discharge on the MHU

Length of Stay on MHU (N=136)	Number of Inmates	Percent
1 day	31	22.8
2-4 days	31	22.8
5-7 days	19	14.0
8-14 days	22	16.2
15-21 days	12	8.8
22-31 days	7	5.1
32-60 days	9	6.6
Over 60 days	5	3.7
Discharge Reason (N=132)		
Bailed or released on recognizance	53	40.2
Moved to general housing	28	21.2
Court release or time served	18	13.6
Moved to other correctional facility	15	11.4
Released to alternative to incarceration program	10	7.6
Sent to psychiatric facility	4	3.0
Released to drug/alcohol program	4	3.0

housing and women's shelter programs. While incarcerated, Molly is usually maintained in the MHU. She is referred to a psychiatrist for medications and achieves an appropriate level of medication compliance resulting in psychiatric stability for brief periods of time.

Case #2: "Tanya"

Tanya is also 27, African American, and single, with a history of legal problems beginning four years ago. Misdemeanor charges include prostitution, criminal mischief, criminal trespassing, and disorderly conduct. Dispositions of charges have ranged from being immediately dismissed by the courts to receiving brief sentences at the county facility or placement on probation. Tanya is diagnosed with psychotic disorder not otherwise specified and polysubstance dependence. She has a history of inpatient psychiatric and substance abuse treatment. Tanya lives at home with her mother and brother. She has no children. She has a high school diploma, but reports no employment history. She supports herself by illegal means and does not receive public assistance.

Tanya has been involuntarily hospitalized while incarcerated due to psychotic symptoms and suicide gestures and has been maintained on medications both in a forensic psychiatric facility and in the county jail. Attempts by mental health staff to link her to forensic case management services upon her discharge from the criminal justice system have consistently failed. She refuses to comply with recommendations for psychiatric and substance abuse treatment which results in her continued legal and psychiatric problems.

Case #3: "Lori"

Lori is 41, Caucasian, and divorced, with a criminal record dating back 10 years. Her legal problems are mainly aggravated harassment and contempt of court charges related to pursuing contact with family members that is prohibited by the courts. She has three children, ages 5, 11, and 12, all in the custody of her mother and mother-in-law. Lori is diagnosed with schizophrenia paranoid type and polysubstance dependence. She has a history of psychiatric and substance abuse treatment since age 18. Psychiatric treatment has included numerous hospital admissions. She receives Supplemental Security Income (SSI) and Social Security Disability (SSD) and is assigned a payee to assure her needs for clothing, housing, and food are met. She is minimally compliant with psychiatric treatment in the community, however, and easily falls prey to individuals seeking to share her housing or money.

During her incarcerations, Lori is sometimes compliant with medications, but consistently refuses forensic case management services. Because of the danger she presents to herself and others in the community, she will be referred to an outpatient treatment coordinator in an effort to connect her to community mental health services or to mandate treatment by the courts upon her release from jail.

COMPREHENSIVE RESPONSE REQUIRED TO ADEQUATELY ADDRESS MULTIPLE NEEDS

Complex needs typically require a comprehensive response for successful intervention. The vast majority of these women have experienced previous arrests and attempts at psychiatric and drug/alcohol treatment and enter jail with medical concerns. About 45% have both a major mental illness and a substance-related disorder. The case illustrations also indicate problems with family relationships (including with the women's children), unemployment and insufficient legal income, maintaining treatment and/or medication compliance, being taken advantage of by others, aggression toward self and others, and abuse. This descriptive picture of the complexity of needs demonstrates the challenges that this population presents.

Improving correctional mental health services is a common goal for many correctional administrators, practitioners, and inmate advocacy organizations. To the extent that individuals with mental illnesses who come into conflict with the law are hard to reach in the community, jails provide places of opportunity for intervention to occur. However, the window of opportunity is very small. About 60% of the females admitted to the MHU were on the unit less than eight days. Keeping individuals in jail for longer periods of time in order to provide treatment is not cost-effective. Rather, as part of the mental health services that are provided, placing more emphasis on release planning (similar to hospital discharge planning) and case management services that link inmates to community services is appropriate. The case illustrations indicate that even when services are available, individuals do not always use them or continue in treatment. This can be discouraging. Nevertheless, if services are unavailable to women when they are ready to change or if available services do not address critical areas of need, then outcomes will continue to be poor.

For release planning to be successful, partnerships will have to be formed between correctional facilities and community agencies so that a continuum of services is accessible to inmates immediately upon release from custody. These services must include mental health and drug and alcohol inpatient and outpatient services, as well as other health and social services that address the medical, psychological, and relational problems of women. In addition, programs within jails that focus on serving the mentally ill will not be effective if they ignore substance-related disorders so prevalent in this population. Creating and providing integrated services that address both mental illness and alcohol and/or drug dependence or abuse at the same time (in jails and communities) have potential to more effectively address the multifaceted problems of inmates with mental illness. At present, these types of services and linkages are not in place in most correctional facilities. Jails operate outside of the social service sector, and social and mental health service agencies are often reluctant to work with offenders. There are some notable exceptions that show promise (Conly, 1999; Project Link, 1999). These programs stand out because they include components such as jail-to-street transitional case management services with strong jail-community linkages, housing for the homeless mentally ill, and attention to treating dual diagnoses.

The fiscal and societal costs of incarceration are incredibly high. Without attention to the multifaceted needs of incarcerated women, they will continue to cycle back and forth between communities and jails. Inmates with mental illnesses require specialized services to enhance their stabilization and likelihood of success upon return to the community. In part, this means allocating resources and focusing ongoing efforts toward the development of integrated treatment approaches and community-based care planning that holistically address the complex needs of mentally ill female offenders.

About the Authors

Diane S. Young, Ph.D., is in the School of Social Work at Syracuse University. Liette C. Dennis, M.S.W., is Director of Behavioral Health Services at the Onondaga County Justice Center in Syracuse, NY.

References

American Psychiatric Association, *Diagnostic and Statistical Manual of Mental Disorders* (4th Ed., Text Revision) (Author, 2000).

Beck, A.J., Karberg, J.C., & Harrison, P.M., *Prison and Jail Inmates at Midyear 2001* (NCJ 191702, U.S. Government Printing Office, 2002).

Conly, C., *Coordinating Community Services for Mentally Ill Offenders: Maryland's Community Criminal Justice Treatment Program,* (NCJ 175046, U.S. Government Printing Office, 1999).

Ditton, P.M., *Mental Health and Treatment of Inmates and Probationers* (NCJ 174463, U.S. Government Printing Office, 1999).

Lamb, H.R., & Weinberger, L.E., "Persons with Severe Mental Illness in Jails and Prisons: A Review," 49(4) *Psychiatric Services* 483-492 (1998).

Project Link, "Prevention of Jail and Hospital Recidivism Among Persons With Severe Mental Illness," 50(11) *Psychiatric Services* 1477-1480 (1999).

Teplin, L.A., Abram, K.M., & McClelland, G.M., "Mentally Disordered Women in Jail: Who Receives Services?" 87(4) *American Journal of Public Health* 604-609 (1997).

Torrey, E.F., *Out of the Shadows: Confronting America's Mental Illness Crisis* (John Wiley & Sons, 1997).

Part 6

Programs and Practices

The concluding section of this volume focuses on perhaps those most important components of strategies for gender-specific programming, e.g., innovative program practices and programs that potentially reduce reliance on the confinement of women and girls.

Within academic criminology, criminal justice, and social work, increasingly narrow focus is given to theoretical approaches toward, and understandings of, the "female offender." While the importance of connecting theory to practice is often acknowledged, the actual implementation of the practice implications of various theoretical perspectives is less likely. In this section, 10 chapters, which include detailed descriptions of advocacy efforts as well as program operations and evaluation research, report on developments as programs attempt to bridge this gap in a number of American states (and one non-American nation):

- Patricia O'Brien, who teaches at the Jane Addams School of Social Welfare at the University of Illinois at Chicago, assesses the value of parole supervision for 18 women she interviewed after they left prison over the period 1983 to 1995.

- California-based Stephanie Covington, co-director of the Center for Gender & Justice, also examines the challenges facing women released from prison and makes a series of gender-specific recommendations that will improve individual efforts at successful reentry.

- Social worker Marilyn Montenegro describes how she helps her clients, incarcerated and newly released women, confront parole practices that affront their dignity and respect.

- Researchers Kathryn Goodwin and Gill McIvor report about the use of community service orders for women in Scotland, a rare instance of such sanctions being examined as they apply to women in the criminal justice system.

- Researchers Suzanne Gonzalez Woodburn, Linda Harrison, and Kim English report findings from a study they conducted on women under community corrections supervision (halfway house residential and non-residential services) in Colorado.

- William Barton and Cheryl Justice describe in great detail the work of an Indiana-based community residential program for women and their children.

- Mary Carol Melton, Mary Grace, Nancy Schmidtgoessling, and Walter Smitson offer insight from a community-based program for Ohio women with co-occurring substance abuse and mental illness.

- Program director Joyce Dougherty offers an overview of a day reporting program for women in Pennsylvania and examines the impact its stress reduction-oriented programming.

- A New York-based group and academic researchers and women prisoners organized by psychologist Michelle Fine provide a lengthy analysis of prison education options for women, included a detailed look at college-level educational programming at the state maximum-security prison for women.

- Researcher Heather Burns reports results of her research on a restorative justice program for women incarcerated in Minnesota.

Chapter 43

The Value of Parole Supervision for Women Leaving Prison

by Patricia O'Brien, M.S.W., Ph.D.

INTRODUCTION

"I am so grateful for her today," says Mandi, a former crack addict who has been incarcerated six times for drug charges and technical violations, about her parole officer during her final period of supervision. Mandi is a "success story." She is one of those offenders we may periodically see on talk shows, but we don't know them in the aggregate. Longitudinal studies rarely examine some of the variables that contribute to women "making it" after incarceration. This chapter describes some of the findings from an exploratory study with formerly incarcerated women that identifies some of their perceptions of how correctional or parole officers successfully facilitated their transition back into their communities.

We know that more and more women are doing criminal sentences in the custody of state or federal prison systems. An increasing number of studies of incarcerated women indicate that they are mostly poor, undereducated, underemployed, disproportionately

This chapter originally appeared in Offender Programs Report, *Vol. 2, No. 2, July/August 1998.*

African American and Latina, and mothers. Data on the offenses for which women are in prison suggest that mandatory sentences, especially for crimes associated with drug use, constitute the largest proportion of new incarcerations in recent years (Chesney-Lind, 1997). Further, with the enactment of sentencing guidelines on both the federal and state levels, family responsibilities for care of children is no longer taken into consideration in the determination of sanctions (Raeder, 1993).

Contemporary sociologists and criminologists argue that it may be time to look at other alternatives to incarceration given the types of criminal activities that are producing female inmates. As the debate continues about how women are different from men or whether they should be sanctioned differently, it is clear that we have to think about the personal and social consequences of incarceration upon the thousands of women who are currently inside the walls and who will be returning to their communities as our neighbors, friends, co-workers, and family members. In the past, federal statistics have indicated that due to the lower level of crimes that women commit, the average time they serve for all offenses is 15 months as compared to 23 months for men (Bureau of Justice Statistics, 1994).

We expect women who come into prison with a number of health, addiction, and mental health issues to have figured out how to reconstruct their lives after exiting the institution in a relatively short period of time. Although many of the "pains of imprisonment" (Sykes, 1958) that men and women have to address are similar, many of the barriers facing women when they exit prison are more detrimental due to internally derived feelings about self-identity and confidence and to externally derived social and structural conditions.

Little research has examined how women who have been incarcerated return to their communities. We may learn about the number of "failures" through news stories or recidivism statistics, but we do not have studies that tell us how many women who leave the prison gates are able to reestablish their lives once they return to their communities. Or how they do it.

STUDY OF FACTORS IN SUCCESSFUL REENTRY

Identifying Themes

Several years ago, I started exploring elements related to formerly incarcerated women "making it in the free world." The literature that framed my study indicated that economic support (Fletcher, Shaver & Moon, 1993; Jurik, 1983), the impact of threat of loss of child custody (Schulke, 1993), the need for addiction treatment (Lambert & Madden, 1976), and the usefulness of peer support in resisting criminal behaviors (Schulke, 1993) have all contributed to women's post-incarceration success.

Over a two-month period in 1996, I asked 18 formerly incarcerated women living in the Midwest how they perceived their post-incarceration experiences. These interviews enabled me to use the women's own narratives to identify themes of theoretical relevance. In addition, a focus group interview was conducted with eight of the 18 women to further discuss several themes that had emerged from the individual interviews.

Demographics of the Participants

The women in this group ranged in age from 20 to 67 years old, with a median age of 35. Of the 18, 10 were white; four African American, two Hispanic, one Korean/African American, and one identified herself as Native American. Only two of the 18 women had no children. Seven of the women were married or living with an intimate partner; 13 were employed at the time of the study in either part- or full-time jobs. In terms of education, three women had less than a twelfth grade education, another three did not graduate from high school but had earned a high school equivalency diploma while in prison, two had graduated only from high school, and more than half the sample had completed some college courses. Compared with state and national samples of incarcerated women, this group of women were whiter, older, more married, and more highly educated.

Crime Profiles

While it is possible that this voluntary cohort of women represents a more stable group of ex-offenders than usual, the range of crimes and variation in institutional history reflects more consistency with typical profiles of women in prison. The same number of women (seven) had been incarcerated for property crimes as for drug offenses. Four of the women were convicted for crimes of violence against persons. Two women had been incarcerated 10 times each. The women had served sentences that ranged from six months to eight years in four state and five federal facilities. They had been released from prison anywhere from 3 months to 12 years at the time of the interviews over a time period ranging from 1983 to late 1995.

Findings

My analysis of the interview and focus group transcripts suggested two overarching themes: (1) the need to address basic survival issues and (2) the importance of developing new internal attitudes for behavioral decision-making. The women provided many examples of these two interwoven and overlapping themes for reasserting autonomy and well-being in their post-prison lives. Analysis of the interview narratives produced 427 separate categories relating to the "external" or concrete needs themes and to the "internal" or choice-making themes. Central to the "internal" category of themes, the women described relationships with friends, intimate partners, family members, and correctional staff that influenced how they made decisions about enacting non-criminal behaviors.

POSITIVE RELATIONSHIPS WITH CORRECTIONAL STAFF PROVIDE ONE KEY TO SUCCESS

The remainder of this chapter discusses the women's reflections about how their positive, or in some cases neutral, relationships with correctional staff, either while incarcerated or during their supervision period following release, contributed to their post-incarceration success.

Some of the women described how they gained a sense of self-efficacy by earning respect from correctional officers for how they did their time. "Demi" recalls, e.g., that a correctional officer told her that "you don't belong here" and that reinforced her decision to use the opportunity she had for drug treatment while she was incarcerated. "Jeanette" discussed how she learned "discipline" from the correctional officers while incarcerated at a federal boot camp. A number of the study participants talked about particular ministers, counselors, or other prison staff members who treated them as "human beings."

Many of the women described the parole or post-release supervision process as "doing what I have to do." However, since the period of post-incarceration monitoring depends on when or where the women were sentenced, the women had some time after their release to meet certain conditions so they could become eligible for discharge from the criminal justice system. At the time of the study, 10 of the 18 women were still accountable to the system under some form of supervision by state or federal officials. Thus, some participants were interviewed after the completion of parole supervision while others were still negotiating having their day-to-day activities monitored.

Negotiating Terms of Supervision

The ways women negotiated meeting their conditions of supervision and their relationship with their supervisory officers were instrumental for success in their post-incarceration transition. For example, "Racque," who essentially married out of her life on the streets in a West Coast city and moved to a small town in the Midwest, recalls that she had an "understanding" parole officer who helped her deal with the paperwork required for moving from one state to another.

"Mandi" came out of prison for the second time after a relapse, steered clear of old associations, and settled in a larger city where she knew no one. She was faced with an overwhelming list of both parole conditions and family court expectations that she had to meet in order to regain custody of her four children who were in foster care. She recounted the difficulty of her first few months:

> I didn't have a car. I found a house within walking distance of Taco Bell. It was about a mile. Obstacles were no vehicle. Trying to meet the parole requirements. I had to report once a month by phone. However, I couldn't have a phone in my name because of an outstanding bill. . . . So, finances were a real big struggle, getting to work without a vehicle, trying to go see the parole officer without a vehicle.

Mandi met all of her conditions, but not without some personal cost, and at great risk to her freedom. She tearfully recounted how she relapsed, smoking crack on two different occasions during the first year of her release, after she had started employment and was attempting to manage her parole. With the assistance of an understanding employer, she was finally able to acquire the treatment she needed, and has since celebrated her second year of sobriety. She has successfully regained legal and physical custody of her children as well as receiving a discharge from parole supervision. She also credits her parole officer for being flexible and respectful of her individual situation.

Having Effective Parole Officer

Four of the women in this study shared the same parole officer and they all recognized a number of positive attributes that promoted feelings of individual efficacy. These positive characteristics included being "treated as a person rather than a number"; "being left alone," that is, without intense intrusion into daily life; willingness to respond to changing circumstances by modifying conditions when appropriate; providing specific information about the parole process; and in several cases, requesting an early discharge for the ex-inmate because of demonstrated efforts to achieve goals.

Other specific examples that "Mandi" discussed were the parole officer's willingness to negotiate some of the specific conditions on her parole plan and meet her at her house or on the job rather than mandating her to only meet at the parole office. "Nicole" recalled that the same parole officer treated her with respect and praised her for her progress on parole:

> I think she looked at me for the person that I was instead of where I'd been. I mean, you can pretty much talk to a person and tell what their situation might be, and . . . she just knew that it was something I had to go through... she seen that I was determined, and I was not gonna go back, and so she knew right off the bat that I was gonna to be easy to work with.

It wasn't always easy for the women to believe that their parole officers weren't out to "get" them. For instance, "Elena" recounts:

> I didn't trust her. And I just heard stories about her from other girls at the halfway house, but later on I found out that they ended up usin' and they send their ownselves back. She didn't send 'em back. They sent their ownselves back. That's one thing she don't tolerate is drug usin'. She's even told me that if I ever had a dirty UA or anything that she was sendin' me back. But like, if I have any problems or any questions, I can call her up and talk to her and she's very understanding.

Several of the women recognized that because they were able to take responsibility for their behavior, they were able to have a more productive relationship with their parole officer. "Sadie" called upon her parole officer for assistance when she got into some difficulties on her job and found that the mutually respectful relationship they had already developed influenced the parole officer to be supportive in the situation:

> I think I was probably a little different than a lot of people she had dealt with. Maybe it was kinda like a breath of air, to not have to be dealing with a lot of problems, a lot of stuff, excuses for not showing up, excuses for not sending in this, or excuses for why you moved and never said anything.

Clearly Explaining the Rules of Parole

Several study participants mentioned that a parole officer who clearly informed them of "the rules" also facilitated their ability to manage their period of supervision. "Rene" observed, however, that it is difficult to follow the rules even when you know what they are and want to behave in a consistent manner. As federal prisoners move through their levels of supervision, for example, eventually they are assigned a telephone number they are required to call on a daily basis that randomly identifies whether the caller has to report for a urine analysis. Failure to make the daily call can result in a revocation, even if, as in Rene's case, it was an inadvertent mistake. She points out:

> It could cost me my freedom, and I'm not even doing drugs or anything... that's what scares you to death, you know. It's just, you might not be doin' anything, and you can lose your freedom. There are things that you have to do . . . I usually call at 7:30, and I forgot—totally forgot. But see, they don't care. You're not allowed to be human. You're not allowed to make an error, and that error could cost me my freedom.

"Nan" described her frustration at her continuing status "under the roof" of supervision:

> Right now I'm not free, even though I left the halfway house and I felt I was free, because I was away from their jurisdiction. They had their own rules and regulations. I had to abide by them. You know, I have three years paper. So, until that three years of paper is up, I'm not actually free.

The translation of "the rules" is facilitated by the parole officer. As "Ashley" complains, an individual officer's interpretation of "the rules" can be very supportive or intrusive.

> He came by my [house] at 6:30 in the morning and he did not see my car and wanted to know where the hell I was. Well, sometimes I leave to go to work early. He responded, "you don't have to be to work until 7:00." So he really believed that I was sleeping somewhere else. And I think that's hard to ask an adult. I brought that to his attention. I said, "What if I liked some-body and wanted to spend the night at their house." He said, "you have to call me and get permission." I had to call and get permission to go spend the night at my mom's house out of fear he would violate me if he happened to pass by and didn't see my car.

Although most of the women could identify ways in which the "system"—represented by various officers during and after incarceration—had supported their post-incarceration success, they often recognized the challenge of earning respect for themselves as individuals in a system that establishes general group rules for the protection of the larger public.

IMPLICATIONS

It is a testament to individual resilience that anyone survives months or years in prison. Most women, however, exit the "the concrete womb" (Watterson, 1996). As "Sadie" artic-ulated, and other participants in the study confirmed, it is important that people in the outside community recognize that former inmates are often living and working in the same com-munity:

> . . . almost everybody who goes to prison gets out [and] they are teaching in your school or shopping in the same stores . . . they are helpin' you out and

doin' this and that and the other and in many ways are part of the community. I fix your kids' bicycles now. That's who ex-cons are, you know. They are not like these people who are holed up in these houses like waiting to explode and destroy the world.

Establishing a healthy life after prison, even with a lot of support, is very difficult. However, most of the women in this study were thriving in their post-incarceration life because they had received a bit of encouragement and access to resources that enabled them to meet specific needs. Parole or post-prison supervision officers can be helpful to women exiting prison by providing information about what the women can expect in the parole process, by assisting women to learn how to manage disclosure of their status in job interviews, and by making referrals for emotional counseling and support. For the women in this study, the respect of parole officers greatly contributed to the women's sense of personal agency and belief in their ability to leave their criminal behaviors behind them.

PAROLE OFFICERS CAN ALSO HINDER SUCCESS

Two of the study participants described treatment by their parole officers that they believed hindered their successful progress on parole. Negative characteristics mentioned by the women included arbitrary interpretation of the rules, excessive intrusion in their monitoring of the parolee, and a lack of understanding of the obstacles that women coming out had to address. "Suzy," for example, talked about her struggles with meeting her condition of "mental health" and the unwillingness of her parole officer at the time to understand the conflicting demands that she had in meeting the condition:

> She was tryin' to tell me that I needed to go to counseling for my family and for my son, and parenting classes and all this stuff. She wanted me to do this, and I didn't have any money. I had just gotten home. My husband was on a low-paying job. I told her I couldn't afford it, so she called my PO. She called my PO twice tellin' him that I couldn't do it, and I was refusin' to do it. So, he was ready to send me back.

At the same time that Suzy was struggling with these expectations from mental health, she and her husband moved across county lines where she was assigned another parole officer who was more responsive to her individual situation. She recalls that he also treated her respectfully by validating her work as a mother:

> He treated me like a person, and he treated me right. He allowed me to stay home. He asked what I wanted out of life. I told him I wanted to stay home and I wanted to be a mom. He let me stay home and be a mom. I went to mental health, and I had no problem. Anytime I needed to talk to him—he gave me his pager number, and I just picked it up and called him. He was always there for me anytime I had a problem or just wanted to talk. Most people bitch about their PO's, because they treat 'em like their just a damned convict . . . John never treated me like that. I was his only female parolee, and he was proud of me.

About the Author

Patricia O'Brien, M.S.W., Ph.D. is an assistant professor at the Jane Addams College of Social Welfare of the University of Illinois at Chicago. None of the names used in chapter article are those of the actual persons referred.

References

Bureau of Justice Statistics, National Corrections Reporting Program, (Department of Justice, Bureau of Justice Statistics, 1994).

Chesney-Lind, M., *The Female Offender: Girls, Women, and Crime* (Sage Publications, 1997).

Fletcher, B.R., Shaver, L.D., & Moon, D.G. (Eds.), *Women Prisoners: A Forgotten Population* (Praeger, 1993).

Jurik, N.C., "The Economics of Female Recidivism: A Study of TARP Women Ex-Offenders," 21(4) *Criminology* 603–622 (1983).

Lambert, L.R., & Madden, P.G., "The Adult Female Offender: The Road from Institution to Community Life," 18(4) *Canadian Journal of Criminology and Corrections* 319–331 (1976).

Raeder, M.S., "Gender and Sentencing: Single Moms, Battered Women and Other Sex-Based Anomalies in the Gender-Free World of the Federal Sentencing Guidelines," 20(3) *Pepperdine Law Review* 905–990 (1993).

Schulke, B.B., "Women and Criminal Recidivism: A Study of Social Constraints" (Doctoral Dissertation, George Washington University, 1993), 54–04A Dissertation Abstracts International 1551 (1993).

Sykes, G., *A Society of Captives* (Princeton University Press, 1958).

Watterson, K, *Women in Prison: Inside the Concrete Womb* (Northeastern University Press, 1996).

Chapter 44

Challenges Facing Women Released From Prison

by Stephanie S. Covington, Ph.D., L.C.S.W.

REENTRY PLAN NEEDED

If women are to be successfully reintegrated into the community after serving custodial sentences, there must be a continuum of care that can connect them to a community following their release. The planning process should begin as soon as the woman begins serving her sentence, rather than the current practice of planning for release only during the final 30 to 60 days of a prison term. In fact, very few inmates report receiving pre-release plan-

This chapter originally appeared in Women, Girls & Criminal Justice, *Vol. 4, No. 4, June/July 2003.*

ning of any kind in prisons and jails (Lynch & Sabol, 2001). Women reentering the community after incarceration require transitional services from the institution to help them reestablish themselves and their families. They also need transitional services from community corrections and supervision to assist them as they begin living on their own again.

Ideally, a comprehensive approach to reentry services for women would include a mechanism to allow community-based programs to enter institutional program settings. At the women's prison in Rhode Island, Warden Roberta Richman has opened the institution to the community through the increased use of volunteers and community-based programs. This allows the women to develop connections with community providers as a part of the transition process. It also creates a mutual accountability between the prison and the community through the use of community-based programs (Richman, 1999).

Another means of assisting female offenders as they prepare to reintegrate themselves into their neighborhoods and communities is the use of the restorative model of justice. The framework for restorative justice involves relationships, healing, and community, which is in keeping with female psychosocial developmental theory.

For those women already involved in lawbreaking, official intervention should emphasize restorative rather than retributive goals to reduce the likelihood of future offending. Offenders should be provided opportunities to increase their "caring capacity" through victim restitution, community service, and moral development opportunities, rather than be subject to experiences that encourage violence and egocentrism (as do most prisons and juvenile institutions in the United States) (Pollock, 1999, p. 250). In turn, this can provide another mechanism to link women with support and resources.

SYSTEM OF SUPPORT NEEDED

The Problem of Fragmented Services and Requirements

There is a critical need to develop a system of support within communities to provide assistance to women transitioning from jails and prisons back to the community. Navigation of myriad systems that often provide fragmented services can pose a barrier to successful reintegration. Following their release, women must comply with conditions of probation or parole, achieve financial stability, access health care, locate housing, and attempt to reunite with their families (Bloom & Covington, 2000). They must obtain employment (often with few skills and a sporadic work history), find safe and drug-free housing, and in many cases maintain recovery from addiction. However, many women find themselves either homeless or in environments that do not support sober living. Without strong support in the community to help them navigate the multiple systems and agencies, many offenders fall back into a life of substance abuse and criminal activity.

The majority of women in the correctional system are mothers, and a major consideration for these women is reunification with their children. The 1997 Adoption and Safe Families Act (ASFA) added what Brown, Melchior, and Huba (1999) identify as an additional level of burden, with requirements for such matters as safe housing, economic support, and medical services that include the children. Because the children have needs of their own, being the custodial parent potentially brings women returning from prison into contact with more agencies, which may have conflicting or otherwise incompatible goals and values. At present, few treatment programs exist that address the needs of women, especially those with minor children.

Effective Community-Based Service Strategies for Women Offenders

Much has been learned about community-based services for women from the work done through Center for Substance Abuse Treatment (CSAT) grants and models. Treatment programs must not only offer a continuum of services, but they must also integrate these services within the larger community. The purpose of comprehensive treatment, according to a model developed by CSAT, is to address a woman's substance use in the context of her health and her relationship with her children and other family members, the community, and society. An understanding of the interrelationships among the client, the treatment program, and the community is critical to the success of the comprehensive approach (Reed & Leavitt, 2000). Because few treatment programs can respond to all the identified needs of substance-abusing women, program providers need to develop referral mechanisms and collaborative agreements in order to assist women in their recovery process (CSAT, 1994, 1999; Covington, 1999). In addition to its use in substance abuse treatment programs, CSAT's knowledge base can be applied to the development of other programs for transitioning women.

Austin, Bloom, and Donahue (1992) identified effective strategies for working with women offenders in community correctional settings. They found that the most promising community-based programs for female offenders do not employ the medical or clinical model of correctional treatment. Instead, effective programs work with clients to broaden their range of responses to various types of behavior and needs, enhancing their coping and decision-making skills with an "empowerment" model to help women achieve self-sufficiency. In addition, effective therapeutic approaches are multidimensional and deal with specific women's issues, including chemical dependency, domestic violence, sexual abuse, pregnancy and parenting, relationships, and gender bias.

According to Austin, Bloom and Donahue, promising community programs "combined supervision and services to address the specialized needs of female offenders in highly structured, safe environments where accountability is stressed" (p. 21). Additional program aspects included a continuum of care design; clearly stated program expectations, rules, and possible sanctions; consistent supervision; ethnically diverse staff, including former offenders; coordination of community resources; and aftercare.

Wellisch, Anglin, and Prendergast (1994), in another study of community-based drug treatment programs for female offenders, concluded that success appears to be positively related to the amount of time spent in treatment, with more lengthy programs having greater success rates. The authors noted that services needed by women are more likely to be found in programs for women only than in coed programs. They also concluded that it was necessary to improve the assessment of client needs in order to develop better programs to deliver a range of appropriate services. The assessment process should provide the basis for developing individual treatment plans, establishing a baseline from which progress in treatment can be monitored; the process should also generate data for program evaluation.

When allied with probation, electronic monitoring, community service, and/or work release, community-based treatment programs could be an effective alternative to the spiraling rates of recidivism and reincarceration.

Benefits of Wraparound Services

There is clearly a need for "wraparound" services—that is, a holistic and culturally sensitive plan for each individual that draws on a coordinated continuum of services located within a community. As Jacobs notes, "[W]orking with women in the criminal justice system requires ways of working more effectively with the many other human service systems that are involved in their lives" (Jacobs, 2001, p. 47). The types of organizations that must work as partners to assist women's reentry into the community include mental health systems; alcohol and other drug programs; programs for survivors of family and sexual violence; family service agencies; emergency shelter, food, and financial assistance programs; educational, vocational, and employment services; health care; the child welfare system; transportation; child care; children's services; educational organizations; self-help groups; organizations concerned with subgroups of women; consumer advocacy groups; organizations that provide leisure options; faith-based organizations; and community service clubs.

Wraparound models and other integrated and holistic approaches can be very effective because they address multiple goals and needs in a coordinated way and facilitate access to services (Reed & Leavitt, 2000). Wraparound models stem from the idea of "wrapping necessary resources into an individualized support plan" (Malysiak, 1997, p. 12). Both client-level and system-level linkages are stressed. The need for wraparound services is highest for clients with multiple and complex needs that cannot be addressed by limited services from a few locations in the community.

Community-based wraparound services can be particularly useful for two primary reasons:

1. Women have been socialized to value relationships and connectedness and to approach life within interpersonal contexts (Covington, 1998). Approaches to service delivery that are based on ongoing relationships, that make connections among different life areas, and that work within women's existing support systems are especially congruent with female characteristics and needs.

2. A higher percentage of female than male offenders are the primary caregivers of young children. These children have needs of their own and require other caregivers if their mothers are incarcerated. Support for parenting, safe housing, and an appropriate family wage level are crucial when the welfare of children is at stake.

Summary

Programming that is responsive in terms of both gender and culture emphasizes support. Service providers need to focus on women's strengths, and they need to recognize that a woman cannot be treated successfully in isolation from her social support network (e.g., relationships with her partner, family, children, and friends). Coordinating systems that link a broad range of services will promote a continuity-of-care model. Such a comprehensive approach would provide a sustained continuity of treatment, recovery, and support services, beginning at the start of incarceration and continuing through the full transition to the community.

GENDER RESPONSIVE PROGRAM MODELS FOR A COMMUNITY APPROACH

Effective, gender-responsive models exist for programs and agencies that provide a continuity-of-care approach. The models described in this section are examples of interventions that can be used at various points within the criminal justice system and in community-based services. They respond to the needs of women transitioning back to their communities.

Helping Women Recover

This program for treating substance abuse is a gender-responsive treatment model designed especially for women in correctional settings. It is currently in use in both institutional and community-based programs. The program provides treatment for women recovering from chemical dependency and trauma by dealing with their specific issues in a safe and nurturing environment that is based on respect, mutuality, and compassion. It addresses the issues of self-esteem, parenting, relationships, sexual concerns, and spirituality that have been identified by the Center for Substance Abuse Treatment in its guidelines for comprehensive treatment (CSAT 1994, 1999).

Helping Women Recover integrates the theoretical perspectives of addiction, women's psychological development, and trauma in separate program modules of four sessions each (Covington, 1999). Using a female facilitator, its modules address the issues of self, relationships, sexuality, and spirituality through the use of guided discussions, workbook exercises, and interactive activities. According to recovering women, these are the four areas most crucial to address in order to prevent relapse (Covington, 1994).

The Sanctuary Model

The Sanctuary Model is an institutional-based and community milieu program that addresses the issues of mental health, substance abuse, and trauma. *The Sanctuary Model* uses Safety, Affect Management, Grieving, and Emancipation (SAGE) to provide a staged model for the treatment of trauma (Foderaro & Ryan, 2000). This model provides for either an inpatient or outpatient milieu in which trauma survivors are supported in a process to establish safety and individual empowerment.

Seeking Safety

Seeking Safety is a cognitive-behavioral program for women who have substance dependence and co-occurring PTSD. It is based on five key principles:

1. Safety as the priority of this "first stage" treatment;

2. Integrated treatment of PTSD and substance abuse;

3. A focus on ideals;

4. Four content areas: cognitive, behavioral, interpersonal, and case management; and

5. Attention to therapist processes (Najavits, 2002).

The ATRIUM Model

The *Addiction and Trauma Recovery Integration Model* (ATRIUM) is a psychoeducational program with expressive activities designed for a 12-week period. It is an assessment and recovery model designed to intervene on the levels of body, mind, and spirit (Miller & Giudry, 2001).

The TREM Model

The *Trauma Recovery and Empowerment Model* (TREM) is a psychoeducational group approach that includes survivor empowerment, techniques for self-soothing, secondary maintenance, and problem solving, in 33 sessions over a 9-month period (Harris & Anglin, 1998).

Agency Models

The two agency models described in this section share a similar conceptual basis. They are based on the concept of the settlement house. Social worker Jane Addams opened the first settlement house in the United States in 1886 with the aim of providing multiple services to "strangers in a new land" (Elshtain, 2001). This concept of resettlement is particularly applicable to the experiences of women who are returning to their communities with multiple challenges. "Being a stranger," "feeling alone," and feeling "overwhelmed by changes in the community" are fears that were expressed by several women who had had lengthy incarcerations and who were preparing to leave institutions (personal communication to S. Covington, 2000).

Our Place, D.C. Located in Washington, D.C., this is an example of a community-based organization that provides a continuum of services and addresses the important issue of family reunification. The organization's mission is to empower women who are or have been in the criminal justice system by providing them with the support and resources they need to resettle in the community, reunite with their families, and find decent housing and jobs. The center also supports women while they are in prison through pre-release classes, a family support program, family transportation to the prisons, and a quarterly newsletter, *Finding Our Place*. When women are released, the center assists them with housing, employment, clothing, substance-abuse treatment, mental health services, health care, HIV services, legal services, and support groups. Support is ongoing, and there are no time limits. Over 90% of the women who utilize the center have made the choice to do so themselves.

The Refugee Model. This model provides a well-coordinated, comprehensive example of a community response to the issue of prisoner reentry that could be made applicable to women. To do so would entail appropriate site and staff selection, a focus on women's specific issues, and the use of gender-responsive materials. For the past 30 years, the Catholic Church has resettled tens of thousands of refugees from all over the world. Through local parishes, this experience has been expanded to assist parolees as well. Using *the Refugee Model,* Catholic dioceses work to promote the coordination of services and supportive relationships for parolees transitioning to the community. In turn, the church believes the experience enriches the parishes. The use of this model reflects an understanding of the complexity of reentry issues and acknowledges the similarities between the needs of refugees and those of offenders. Although this model provides an excellent conceptual foundation for reentry, it has not yet been redesigned to be gender-specific.

ISSUES IN THE CURRENT SOCIAL CLIMATE

All offenders have similar categories of needs. Both women and men returning to the community from prison typically require substance-abuse treatment and vocational and educational training. Family and community reintegration issues are also shared, as are physical and mental health care. However, the research on differences between women and men suggests that the degree or intensity of these needs and the ways in which they should be addressed by the criminal justice system are quite different.

In planning for gender-responsive policies and practice, it is necessary to consider the differences that exist between women and men in terms of both behavior under correctional supervision and responses to programs and treatment.

We must also understand the current social climate, which is reflected in policies and legislation, and the differential impact of that climate on women and men. For example, the following are just some of the provisions that have a greater negative impact on women transitioning to their communities (and, subsequently, their children) than on men:

- *Drug Policy.* The War on Drugs has had a particularly devastating impact on women. As previously mentioned, drug offenses have accounted for the largest proportion of growth in the numbers of women prisoners. Women are more likely than men to be incarcerated for drug offenses. The emphasis on punishment rather than treatment has brought many low-income women and women of color into the criminal justice system (The Sentencing Project, 2001).

- *Welfare Benefits.* Section 115 of the Welfare Reform Act, "Temporary Assistance for Needy Families" (TANF), stipulates that persons convicted of using or selling drugs are subject to a lifetime ban on receiving cash assistance and food stamps. No other offenses result in a loss of benefits (Allard, 2002).

- *Drug Treatment.* Access to drug treatment is frequently impeded for women who lose welfare benefits because of drug-offense convictions. Cash assistance and food stamps are critical for the successful recovery of low-income women, for whom work obligations may prevent participation in treatment. In addition, there are limited numbers of programs that accommodate women with children (Legal Action Center, 1999).

- *Housing.* Federal housing policies permit (and, in some cases, require) public housing authorities, Section 8 providers, and other federally assisted housing programs to deny housing to individuals who have engaged in drug-related activity (Legal Action Center, 1999).

- *Education.* Although correctional institutions have increased the number of general education programs, there are still fewer for women than for men. As of 1996, only 52% of correctional facilities for women offered postsecondary education (Allard, 2002). Access to college education was further limited in 1994, when prisoners were declared ineligible for college Pell Grants (Allard, 2002).

- *Reunification With Children.* The 1997 Adoption and Safe Families Act (ASFA) allows states to file for termination of parental rights once a child has been in foster care for 15 or more of the past 22 months. It is difficult enough for single mothers with substance abuse problems to meet ASFA requirements when they live in the community, but the short deadline has particularly severe consequences for incarcerated women who serve an average of 18 months (Jacobs, 2001).

RECOMMENDATIONS

Clearly, women's inability to access various social entitlements critical to successful reentry into the community undermines their efforts to recover, care for their children, and become full, productive members of their communities. Our current policies and legislation must be reviewed and revised to prevent harmful short- and long-term consequences for both women and their children.

A gender-responsive approach includes services that are comprehensive and that relate to the reality of women's lives, both in content and in context (i.e., structure and environment). While the overarching standard for gender-responsive practice is to do no harm, the specific guidelines that follow can be used in the development of services in both institutional and community-based settings (Bloom & Covington, 1998):

- The theoretical perspectives used consider women's particular pathways into the criminal justice system, fit the psychological and social needs of women, and reflect the realities of their lives (e.g., relational theory, trauma theory);

- Treatment and services are based on women's competencies and strengths and promote self-reliance;

- Programs use a variety of interventions (e.g., behavioral, cognitive, affective/dynamic, and systems perspectives) to fully address the needs of women;

- Homogeneous groups are used, especially for primary treatment (e.g., trauma, substance abuse);

- Services/treatment address women's practical needs, such as housing, transportation, childcare, and vocational training and job placement;

- Participants receive opportunities to develop skills in a range of educational and vocational (including nontraditional) areas;

- Staff members reflect the client population in terms of gender, race/ethnicity, sexual orientation, language (bilingual), and ex-offender and recovery status;

- Female role models and mentors are provided who reflect the racial/ethnic/cultural backgrounds of the clients;

- Cultural awareness and sensitivity are promoted using the resources and strengths available in various communities;

- Gender-responsive assessment tools and individualized treatment plans are utilized, with appropriate treatment matched to the identified needs and assets of each client;

- There is an emphasis on parenting education, child development, and relationships/reunification with children (if relevant);

- The environment is child friendly, with age-appropriate activities designed for children; and

- Transitional programs are included as part of gender-responsive practices, with a particular focus on building long-term community support networks for women.

Because of the high rates of violence against women and children, it is imperative that all services become trauma informed. Trauma-informed services are services that have been created to provide assistance for problems other than trauma, but in which all practitioners have a shared knowledge base/core of understanding about the trauma that occurs as a result of violence. Knowledge about violence and the impact of trauma helps providers avoid both the triggering of reactions to trauma and retraumatization. It also allows women to manage their trauma symptoms successfully so that they are able to benefit from these services (Harris & Fallot, 2001).

CONCLUSION

In looking at the overarching themes and issues affecting women in the criminal justice system, there is no escaping the fact that "women's issues" are also society's issues: sexism, racism, poverty, domestic violence, sexual abuse, and substance abuse. While the impact of incarceration and reentry sets the stage and defines the individual experiences of women, their children and families, and their communities, what is required is a social response. Agencies and actions are not only about the individual; they are also, unavoidably, about family, institutions, and society. As Carol Gilligan (1990) suggests, we are all inextricably linked to one another and all of our actions are relational.

If we expect women to successfully return to their communities and avoid rearrest, the social response needed is a change in community conditions. The following is what Richie concluded from a series of in-depth interviews with women:

> They need families that are not divided by public policy, streets and homes that are safe from violence and abuse, and health and mental health services that are accessible. The challenges women face must be met with expanded opportunity and a more thoughtful criminal justice policy. This would require a plan for reinvestment in low-income communities in this country that centers around women's needs for safety and self-sufficiency. (Richie, 2001, p. 386)

Communities need to increase their caring capacity and create a community response to the issues that negatively impact women's lives and increase their risks of incarceration and of recidivism.

> [W]e have become a careless society.... Care is the consenting commitment of citizens to one another.... Care is the manifestation of a community. The community is the site of the relationships of citizens. And it is at this site that the primary work of a caring society must occur. (McKnight, 1995, p. x)

A series of focus groups conducted with women in the criminal justice system asked this question: How could things in your community have been different to help prevent you from being here? The respondents identified a number of factors whose absence they believed had put them at risk for criminal justice involvement. The needs the women identified were housing, physical and psychological safety, education, job training and opportunities, community-based substance-abuse treatment, economic support, positive female role models, and a community response to violence against women (Bloom, Owen, & Covington, 2002). These are the critical components of a gender-responsive prevention program.

Perhaps we can begin to learn from other nations, applying in our own communities the knowledge we gain. Poor countries around the world have found that spending money on health, education, and income-generation programs such as microcredit for women is the most efficient way to reduce poverty, because a woman's progress also helps her family: Women spend their money on their children. As women receive education and health care, and as they enter the work force and increase their power both in the family and in society, they have fewer and healthier children. Also, because women are poorer than men, each dollar spent on them means proportionally more ("Liberating the Women of Afghanistan," 2001).

In conclusion, the true experts in understanding a woman's journey home are women themselves. Galbraith (1998) interviewed women who had successfully transitioned from correctional settings to their communities. These women said that what had really helped them do this were the following:

- Relationships with people who cared and listened, and who could be trusted;

- Relationships with other women who were supportive and who were role models;

- Proper assessment/classification;

- Well-trained staff, especially female staff;

- Proper medication;

- Programs such as job training, education, substance-abuse and mental health treatment, and parenting;

- Inmate-centered programs;

- Efforts to reduce trauma and revictimization through alternatives to seclusion and restraint;

- Financial resources; and

- Safe environments.

The reasons why the majority of criminal justice programming is still based on the male experience are complex, and the primary barriers to providing gender-responsive treatment are multilayered. They are theoretical, administrative, and structural, and they involve policy and funding decisions. There are, therefore, a great number of us in a diversity of professions who play a role within the continuum of care for women in the criminal justice system.

About the Author

Stephanie S. Covington, Ph.D., L.C.S.W., is Co-director, Center for Gender & Justice in La Jolla, CA.

References

Allard, P., *Life Sentences: Denying Welfare Benefits to Women Convicted of Drug Offenses* (The Sentencing Project, February 2002).

Austin, J., Bloom, B., & Donahue, T., *Female Offenders in the Community: An Analysis of Innovative Strategies and Programs* (National Institute of Corrections, 1992).

Bloom, B., & Covington, S., "Gender-Specific Programming for Female Offenders: What it Is and Why it Is Important." Paper presented at the 50th annual meeting of the America Society of Criminology, San Francisco, CA, November 15–18, 1998.

Bloom, B., & Covington, S., *Gendered Justice: Programming for Women in Correctional Settings*, Paper presented at the 52nd Annual Meeting of the American Society of Criminology, San Francisco, CA, November 2000).

Bloom, B., Owen, B., & Covington, S., *Gender-Responsive Strategies: Research, Practice, and Guiding Principles for Women Offenders Project* (National Institute of Corrections, 2002).

Brown, V., Melchior, L., & Huba, G., "Level of Burden Among Women Diagnosed With Severe Mental Illness. 31(1) *Journal of Psychoactive Drugs* 31-40 (1999).

Center for Substance Abuse Treatment (CSAT), *Practical Approaches in the Treatment of Women Who Abuse AAlcohol and Other Drugs* (Department of Health and Human Services, Public Health Service, 1994).

Center for Substance Abuse Treatment (CSAT), *Substance Abuse Treatment for Women Offenders: Guide to Promising Practices* (U.S. Department of Health and Human Services, Public Health Service, Substance Abuse and Mental Health Services Administration, 1999).

Covington, S., *A Woman's Way Through the Twelve Steps* (Hazelden, 1994).

Covington, S., "The Relational Theory of Women's Psychological Development: Implications for the Criminal Justice System," in R. Zaplin (Ed.), *Female Offenders: Critical Perspectives and Effective Intervention* (pp. 113-131) (Aspen, 1998).

Covington, S., *Helping Women Recover: A Program for Treating Substance Abuse* (special edition for the criminal justice system) (Jossey-Bass, 1999).

Elshtain, J., *Jane Addams and the Dream of American Democracy* (Basic Books, 2001).

Foderaro, J., & Ryan, R., "SAGE: Mapping the Course of Recovery," 21(2) *Therapeutic Communities* 91-104 (2000).

Galbraith, S., *And So I Began to Listen to Their Stories. . . : Working With Women in the Criminal Justice System* (Policy Research, Inc, 1998).

Gilligan, J., Lyons, N. P. & Hammer, T. J., (Eds.), *Making Connections* (Harvard University Press, 1990).

Gilligan, J., *Violence: Our Deadly Epidemic and its Causes* (Putnam, 1996).

Harris, M., & Anglin, J., *Trauma Recovery and Empowerment: A Clinical Guide for Working With Women in Groups* (Free Press, 1998).

Jacobs, A., "Give 'em a Fighting Chance: Women Offenders Reenter Society," 45 *Criminal Justice Magazine* 44-47 (Spring 2001).

Legal Action Center, *Steps to Success: Helping Women with Alcohol and Drug Problems Move From Welfare to Work* (Author, 1999).

"Liberating the Women of Afghanistan," Editorial, *New York Times,* November 24, 2001.

Lynch, J., & Sabol, W., *Prisoner Reentry in Perspective* (Urban Institute Crime Policy Report, Vol. 3 (2001).

Malysiak, R., "Exploring the Theory and Paradigm Base for Wraparound Fidelity," 7(1) *Journal of Child and Family Studies* 11-25 (1997).

McKnight, J., *The Careless Society: Community and its Counterfeits* (Basic Books, 1995).

Miller, D., & Giudry, L., *Addictions and Trauma Recovery: Healing the Body, Mind and Spirit* (W.W. Norton, 2001).

Najavits, L., *Seeking Safety* (Guilford Press, 2002).

Pollock, J., *Criminal Women* (Anderson Publishing, 1999).

Reed, B., & Leavitt, M., "Modified Wraparound and Women Offenders in Community Corrections: Strategies, Opportunities and Tensions," in M. McMahon (Ed.), *Assessment to Assistance: Programs for Women in Community Corrections* (pp. 1-106) (American Correctional Association, 2000).

Richie, B., "Challenges Incarcerated Women Face as They Return to Their Communities: Findings From Life History Interviews," 47(3) *Crime and Delinquency* 368-389 (2001).

Richman, R., " Women in Prison: Are Anybody's Needs Being Met?" Presentation at the Association of Women in Psychology Conference, Providence, RI (March 6-9, 1999).

The Sentencing Project, *Drug Policy and the Criminal Justice System* (Author, May 2001).

Wellisch, J., Anglin, M.D., & Prendergast, M., "Treatment Strategies for Drug-Abusing Women Offenders," in J. Inciardi (Ed.), *Drug Treatment and the Criminal Justice System* (pp. 5-25) (Sage Publications, 1994).

Chapter 45

Client Advocates Use First-Hand Experience to Improve Services

by Marilyn Montenegro, Ph.D., L.C.S.W.

CASE EXAMPLE

"Alice" had two months of her prison sentence left to serve when she first arrived at a work furlough program in Southern California. She had been in the institution for three years and now she was in the community, preparing to reenter the "free world." When she went to the Department of Motor Vehicles to get a state identification, she was told that she could not get a driver's license because she owed money for child support. Alice did not know that she would be charged for the welfare her mother collected for the children while she was imprisoned.

I am a consulting social worker with a nonprofit agency that operates several programs providing transitional housing for women prisoners and former prisoners. Part of my work assignment is that I, and the student interns that I supervise, will see only women who request services. This requirement is based on the belief that clients, not the "authorities," should determine which services an individual receives. It is often difficult for women in prison to seek help from a social worker. Many know social workers as people who "steal babies" from their mothers and are unaware that a social worker's primary responsibility is to promote the well-being of her client, including clients who are prisoners. In this agency, it is incumbent upon the social worker to attract clients by providing services that the clients value. Clients are not coerced into receiving services. When they do receive social work services, confidentiality is respected (a unique experience for a prisoner).

This chapter originally appeared in Women, Girls & Criminal Justice, *Vol. 4, No. 5, August/September 2003.*

Women in prison and women leaving prison have an altered sense of reality. They have lived in a milieu in which behavioral requirements were arbitrary and constantly shifting. Hypervigilance and suspicion of others have been required to survive physically and emotionally.

Alice decided to ask for assistance from the agency social worker. As a social work consultant for the agency, I meet with those clients who specifically ask to speak with me. When I provide services for women in the work furlough program, in addition to the usual parameters, I must first determine how the problem might be solved without breaking any rules that the Department of Corrections imposes on its prisoners. In this case, my task was to try to find a solution to Alice's problem regarding the money she allegedly owed for child support. I started by explaining the situation, as I understood it. I told her that my experience has been that often the Office of Child Support will forgive the amount that accrues while a person is in prison, but only after legal motions are filed. On the other hand, the District Attorney will release the "hold" on the driver's license if a woman will agree to sign a statement indicating that she owes the full amount and will pay when she begins to receive income. It is not uncommon for women leaving prison to owe $20,000 to $30,000.

I explained both options to Alice and strongly suggested that she take the longer, more complicated path, with the hope of having her debt forgiven or significantly reduced. I told her that I would assist her if she decided to do so.

Alice wanted to start a new life free from debt and was willing to spend the time to meet with a representative of the Office of the Family Law Facilitator in the Los Angeles County Superior Court, file legal papers some 20 miles away, and participate in the hearing that would be held eventually.

THE SOCIAL WORKER'S RESPONSIBILITY

The Family Law Facilitator's Office is located in the local courthouse. Telephone contact is not possible. Clients are seen on a first come/first served basis, with the exception of individuals who are referred from the courtroom by a judge. Judge-referred individuals are seen immediately—ahead of those already in line. It is not uncommon to spend the better part of a day waiting.

I accompanied Alice to the Family Law Facilitator's office. I often accompany clients when they need to complete a transaction with a governmental entity. This can serve many purposes. On the most basic level, it means that the client can leave the waiting area to use the restroom without fearing that her name will be called while she is gone, causing her to lose her turn. Social workers who become psychotherapists are advised to experience therapy as clients to, among other things, know what it's like to be a client. Similarly, those of us who work as client advocates should know what it like to negotiate the systems that control lives of our clients.

Moreover, by sharing the visceral impact of maneuvering "social service" and "criminal justice" systems with a client, a social worker demonstrates that she (the social worker) takes seriously her responsibility for the well-being of her client. The social worker acts as a recorder and interpreter of events. Often, even those whose job is to assist the client talk in a "social service code" that clients do not fully understand. The client may become emotionally frozen with the fear that she may lose her children, be imprisoned, have her income attached in perpetuity, or lose her financial support. She is often unable to absorb the information that is hurriedly transmitted to her. The social worker can ask questions, clarify comments and advocate when necessary.

Alice and I saw the Family Law Facilitator after only a wait of one hour. She was friendly and helpful. She handed Alice a stack of forms to complete and wrote down the five steps that needed to be completed before we would return for the facilitator to complete the forms we would need to file.

We both saw Alice's eyes glaze over. The facilitator told Alice, "It took you a long time to create this mess, it's going to take a long time to fix it." Alice smiled and agreed, walked out of the office, and asked, "Can you help me do this?"

I spend too much time waiting at Dependency Court, hospitals, the Child Support Office, and the Social Security Administration. I am accused of creating dependency and being easily manipulated because I often accompany my clients when I know that they are subject to being baffled and humiliated after waiting for extended periods of time. I rarely, if ever, see another "professional" waiting with her client.

Possibly that is why every client is told to arrive at Dependency Court at 8:30 a.m., why no schedule is posted, why at least half of those who arrive at 8:30 in the morning will not have their cases heard until the afternoon, and why there are often a few people (including those who took a day off work) who are told that there is not time to hear their cases on the scheduled day and are asked to return the next morning.

REFRAMING AND BUILDING ON STRENGTHS

Long waits, which can be avoided, indicate disrespect for those who are required to wait. When the social worker shares the wait and verbalizes the disrespect it implies, she begins to assist her client to view the world through another lens in which individual outcomes are often as dependent upon systemic preconceptions as individual actions.

The client's survival after being subjected to lost freedom, individuality, and control of one's future can then be viewed from a strength-based perspective, with a reasonable possibility of building self-esteem. Social systems frequently focus on the client's weakness. They remind her that she is addicted, battered, and a felon and/or has a bad credit history, a poor employment record, and no marketable job skills. Social workers can remind clients of their strengths including surviving prison with a determination to change their lives demonstrated by activities of daily living. Characteristics such as persistence, humor, kindness, and hope are all strengths upon which self-esteem and success can be built.

For example, during the hour I spent with Alice, waiting, she began to talk about her hopes for the future. On our way back we stopped for a cup of coffee and continued to talk. I reflected on her period of captivity, her removal from the community for a period of three years, and the expectation by many that she would be able to "reenter" the free world if she just "tried." I compared it to recent news of military personnel returning from 10 months on a submarine and the sacrifice that these young people had made by being away from home. I contrasted their homecoming with that afforded prisoners upon their release.

REENTRY PROBLEMS BEGIN AT PRISON GATE

Women who are able to enter work furlough programs are luckier than most because they have a few weeks in which to obtain identification papers and acclimate themselves to the hectic pace of the "free world," but this opportunity is afforded only a few women leaving prison. At this writing, there are fewer than 50 beds for women in work furlough programs in Los Angeles County, where I am based. At any given time there are approximately 4,000 women on parole in Los Angeles County.

Women paroling from the institution are given $200 "gate money." If they have no friends or family to pick them up at the door of the institution they must use part of that $200 for a bus ticket home. The majority of women prisoners in California are at Chowchilla, in the Central Valley of California, about four hours from Los Angeles. Sixty percent of women prisoners will need return to Los Angeles County as a condition of parole. Once home, if the women have no clothes of their own that still fit, they must use part of the $200 to buy the clothes that they have been issued by the prison.

In Los Angeles, the bus station is near skid row. Women returning from prison are usually not met by friends or family, but by men who prey on the vulnerability of these returning women, some of whom want a housekeeper who will also provide sex on demand in exchange for room and board, others who offer to act as pimps if the women will prostitute, and yet others who will provide free drugs in the hope of recruiting a customer.

If there are no family or friends to provide housing and the woman has not made prior arrangements to enter a drug treatment program (not an easy thing to do), she must decide how to spend her first night of "freedom." She can use the last of her money to rent a motel room, she can go to a shelter, or she can seek housing in the parole department's facility on skid row.

Regardless, the released woman is required to report to her parole agent within 24 hours of release and can be sent back to prison if she does not appear. Unfortunately, the parole agent will not be able to provide housing or work. If she is lucky, she may get a few bus tokens.

To obtain a California identification and a duplicate social security card, she will need an address so that these documents can be mailed to her.

There will be no one to help her overcome the effects of Post-Incarceration Syndrome (PICS), to drive her to the various offices or even to discuss what to do next over a meal.

Seventy percent of women leaving prison will return within the year, mostly for "technical" violations such as failing to inform the parole agent of their current address or having a dirty urine test.

There is little sympathy for the situation of the returning former prisoner. As one supervising parole agent commented recently, "They wouldn't be homeless if they didn't want to be."

CASE EXAMPLE CONTINUED: WHAT WAS ACCOMPLISHED?

Alice has begun the process of reducing or eliminating the child support debt she now owes. Because she is in a work furlough program with case management services, there is a good probability that the necessary papers will be filed, there will be a hearing, and there will be a positive outcome.

If so, one of many obstacles to successful reentry will have been eliminated.

Has Alice internalized the awareness of her own strengths? Some of these strengths are her determination to deal with "the wreckage of her past," her desire to live life "honestly" by addressing problems rather than running from them, her willingness to risk looking inadequate by asking for help, her attentiveness in trying to understand the child support system and all that is involved in working through it. Will her self-esteem increase? Can she overcome the feeling that she acted stupidly in assuming that welfare was an entitlement she could count on to support her children while she was in prison, the idea that she is "weak" because she became addicted to drugs, and the belief that everyone will view her as a "bad," possibly "evil," person because she was imprisoned for using drugs? Does she view her own imprisonment in terms of the prison/industrial complex? Will she come to believe that her drug use was the result of the conjunction of a life filled with abuse and injustice and the availability of drugs? Will she see that abuse as the product of a patriarchal society in which women and children are property to be used and discarded at will, rather than as something she "deserved" because of individual actions? Will she question how drugs have become so available in poor communities and communities of color and why a disease has been criminalized? That I don't know.

Alice said she was glad that I had gone with her, that it had made her feel safe, and she remarked that going out for coffee made her feel like a normal person. I felt that I had met my minimal social work commitment to my client's well-being.

VALUE OF FIRST-HAND EXPERIENCE

I now had first-hand experience trying to deal with child support debt. My best guess is that had I simply referred Alice to the Family Law Facilitator she might never have found her. Having gone with Alice, I know that the office had changed location and that even once located it was difficult to understand what process should be followed to inform the facilitator that someone was waiting for her.

This means that if in the future I am not able to accompany a client I can give her (or hopefully a student intern who can accompany her) detailed information about accessing services. This also means that when I next attend a meeting with a representative of the Office of Family Law Facilitator I can discuss the problems of access with some authority.

This first-hand experience allows me to be a more effective advocate for systemic change, using my experience to refute arguments implying that a client was not able to understand, didn't really want services, or was being "manipulative."

CONCLUSION

Challenging the social injustices that impinge on our clients is difficult. In my experience most mid-level administrators actually believe that their agency or program is fair and just. They continue to believe this because they never confront the reality of the (often subtle) disrespect to which our clients are subjected. Because our clients are so universally subjected to the disrespect of long waits, inadequate explanations, referrals to distant agencies and services, and other impossible-to-meet demands, they often do not even mention these indignities to the social worker. But when we experience these humiliations first-hand we, as social workers, are able and obligated to challenge them and the ways in which they serve to perpetuate oppression.

About the Author

Marilyn Montenegro, Ph.D., L.C.S.W., is the Coordinator of the California Chapter of the NASW Women's Council Prison Project.

Chapter 46

Women and Community Service Orders: The Experience in Scotland

Kathryn Goodwin and Gill McIvor, Ph.D.

This chapter originally appeared in Women, Girls & Criminal Justice, *Vol. 1, No. 3, April/May 2000.*

INTRODUCTION

Since its introduction in Scotland in 1977, the community service order has been a popular sentencing option. It has experienced rapid growth in use over the last 20 years and its operation and impact have been assessed through research which has explored, among other things, the effectiveness of different operational practices, sentencers' views of community service, offenders' experiences of this measure, the views of the beneficiaries of unpaid work, and the impact of community service upon subsequent reconviction (McIvor, 1992). Scottish law indicates that the courts can impose a community service order only if the offender would otherwise be dealt with by a sentence of detention or imprisonment.

Community service has typically been used as a young man's option, and women have consistently been underrepresented on community service since its introduction (McIvor, 1998). Recent research suggests that women offenders are less likely to be diverted from custody by this sentencing option (McIvor, 1998). This underrepresentation of women on community service has in itself tended to preclude a separate and systematic consideration of women's experiences in previous studies of the community service order.

Barker's (1993) study of women on community service in England and Wales raises a number of issues worthy of exploration in Scotland and elsewhere. Barker found, for instance, that most women considered their experience of community service to have been reasonably rewarding and ascribed equal value to group and individual placements. There was a tendency, however, for women to be placed in individual agency placements where they could make use of their existing skills rather than in group placements where they might have an opportunity to acquire new skills. The comparatively limited use of group placements for women offenders reflected the absence of a women-only group provision and, as a consequence, attempts to ensure that group placements were used only if women could be "clustered" in mixed sex groups. A clustering policy appeared to ameliorate the effects of sexual or racial harassment (though such incidents were, fortunately, relatively rare).

Placement choices for women offenders were found constrained by geographical factors and, in the case of women with dependent children, by child care considerations. Although Barker found probation services in England and Wales had made available child care facilities for mothers undertaking community service, most women were reluctant to leave their children with strangers, preferring instead to make their own informal arrangements for the care of their children. Women's absences from placement were frequently attributed to a breakdown in child care arrangements, often arising from the woman's reluctance to leave a sick child with another person, even if that person was a family member or friend.

This chapter reports on a study that examined women offenders' experiences of and attitudes towards community service to identify factors that impact positively and negatively upon women's experiences on community service and to identify the implications for policy and practice.

STUDY METHODS

This study was conducted in two stages and employed a mixture of qualitative and quantitative research methods. The first stage of the study consisted of a fixed choice and open-ended questionnaire survey mailed to all women in 24 local authority social work departments who completed community service orders in Scotland in 1997, whether via satisfactory completion, revocation in the interests of justice, or breach. Information sought from respondents included:

- Personal characteristics (e.g., age, marital and employment status, dependent children);

- Details of sentence (e.g., number of hours, index offense) and attitude toward sentence (e.g., purpose, fairness, what it replaced);

- Details of work placement (e.g., type(s) of setting and work carried out), factors influencing choice of placement, and attitude towards placement;

- Where relevant, child care arrangements while completing order; and

- Overall attitude toward community service and factors impacting positively and negatively upon the experience of undertaking unpaid work.

Self-Reporting Surveys

The purpose of the questionnaire survey was to obtain a broad overview of women's experiences of community service, with significant issues subsequently being examined through interviews with a smaller sub-sample of women.

Self-completion questionnaires were forwarded to 326 women who had completed community service orders—successfully or otherwise—in 1997. Thirty-seven questionnaires were returned, representing a response rate of 11%. The low response rate clearly limits the generalization of the findings, though the questionnaire responses still provide useful pointers toward issues that have subsequently been explored in interviews with a sub-sample of women.

Semi-Structured Interviews

The second stage of the research consisted of semi-structured interviews. The interviews were planned to take place in the women's homes. The interview schedule was designed to explore in more depth some of the issues arising from both Barker's (1993) study and the completed self-report questionnaires. Issues covered included views about the range and choice of community service placements offered, factors believed to have influenced placement allocation, and difficulties encountered in successfully completing the work ordered by the court. It was hoped that the interview sample could contain women whose community service orders had been breached in addition to those who had completed their orders. Seven interviews have been completed.

PERSONAL CHARACTERISTICS OF QUESTIONNAIRE RESPONDENTS

The women in the study varied in age between 17 and 58 years, with an average age of 32 years. Two-thirds of the women were between 21 and 40 years old, while fewer than one in seven were aged 20 years or younger. The majority of women described themselves as unemployed (15) or housewives (11). Three others were employed full-time and four were employed on a part-time basis. Two women indicated that they were unable to work for health reasons, one described herself as a prostitute and one was unavailable for work as a result of looking after her husband who was ill. Just under half the women (17) were living with a partner and just over half were single, separated, or divorced. Sixteen women had a total of 38 dependent children living with them at the time of the survey, all but one of whom had one or more dependent children when they carried out their community service work.

SENTENCE DETAILS

The Community Service Order

Around two-thirds of the women who completed questionnaires (25) had been sentenced to a standard community service order and the remainder (12) to community service as a requirement of probation. The number of hours of community service ordered varied from 50 to 400, with an average of 162 hours. Although 13 women had received relatively short orders of 100 hours or less, 14 had been sentenced to relatively long orders of 200 or more hours. The period of probation supervision imposed upon women given community service orders as a requirement of probation varied from eight to 24 months, averaging 17 months.

Offenses of Record

The offenses for which some of the women received community service orders included fraud (8), assault (5), drugs (3), embezzlement (3), theft (3), breach of the peace (3), serious assault (2), police assault (2), drunk driving (1), attempted fraud (1), attempted theft (1), and resisting arrest (1). Twelve women were first offenders while 25 had previous convictions when they were given community service. Sixteen women had previous experience of community-based social work disposals or imprisonment, 11 had previous sentences of probation, eight had previously been given a community service order, and seven had previously served a custodial sentence. Most of the women (21) had no prior experience of high tariff sentencing options.

DETAILS OF WORK PLACEMENTS

Community Service Setting

Women were most likely to be placed individually in a voluntary or statutory agency, under the supervision of an agency staff member. Almost half, however, had completed all or some of their order in a team or workshop setting.

Type of Work

A wide range of tasks were performed by the women, although those based in agency settings were more often involved in work of a people-oriented nature. Twenty-nine women carried out all of their community service work on weekdays. Five others worked both on weekdays and on weekends and one completed her order on weekdays, on weekday evenings, and on weekends.

The women indicated that a range of factors had influenced the type of work they were required to carry out. Placement allocation was most often influenced by the woman's expressed preference for or experience of particular types of work. In seven cases, however, the accessibility of placements was thought to have been influential—reflecting the availability of transport and, in one case, the geographical remoteness of the woman's home—and in five cases the woman's child care commitments were said to have had a direct bearing on the placement chosen.

Successful Completion or Absence From Community Service

Although most of the women (33) had successfully completed their community service order, seven indicated that they had had difficulty completing the work ordered by the court. Two women had sustained absences from placement as a result of pregnancy; one woman moved to another area halfway through her order; and one had to combine her community service with a full-time job. One woman was imprisoned during her order and apparently resented the fact that she had to complete her community service when she was released, while another alluded to "other misfortunes" in her life which included her house being flooded and then being robbed of all her possessions, including her pet dog.

In total, 22 women indicated that they had failed to attend their community service placement on at least one occasion. Two of those who provided the relevant information indicated that they had one absence, eight had two absences, and a further eight had three absences or more. The reported reasons for their absences are summarized in Table 46.1.

Child Care Arrangements

The 16 women who had dependent children when they were carrying out their community service work made various arrangements for their children to be cared for in their absence. Informal arrangements—with family members, partners or, less often, friends—

Table 46.1: Reported Reasons for Absences From Placement

Reason provided	Number of women	Reason provided	Number of women
Illness	12	Work commitments	1
Family illness	6	Problems related to pregnancy	1
Child care arrangements	6	Mental health problems	1
Practical problems	3	Medical appointment	1
Lack of transport	1	CS van was full	1
Lack of money	1		

were most common, although five women also indicated that their children were looked after at school, with their community service having been arranged to fit into the school day. Two women said that they had paid for the services of a childminder and only one had made use of a childminder who was paid for by the community service scheme.

WOMEN'S EXPERIENCES AND ATTITUDES

Impact of Children

Five women felt their child care commitments had directly influenced the type of work placement to which they were allocated. The age of dependent children may also have impacted on the women's experience of community service. As noted previously, five women reported that their children were looked after at school while they were carrying out community service work. One woman explained, for example, that "they all attended school at the time, the community service met my times for my kids" while another said "my children were at school most of the time." However, women who were responsible for the care of very young children could not rely on schools and had to make alternative arrangements for them to be cared for in their absence. Some of the children were cared for by childminders (paid for by the community service scheme or the woman herself) while most were looked after by family members, partners, or friends.

Some women with young children mentioned problems associated with arranging child care and leaving their children with childminders. One woman suggested that "having to leave my smallest child with childminders" was the worst thing about community service. Concerns about leaving children in the care of *unknown* minders have similarly been expressed in completed interviews. When asked whether she had experienced problems in completing her order one woman mentioned that "getting a babysitter for my own child while I had to go was hard." One woman stated that child care for single parents was an area where community service could be improved.

Financial Support for Child Care and Travel

Although women sentenced to community service are entitled to financial support for child care, only one woman out of the 20 who provided information about child care arrangements had made use of this provision. Two others employed a childminder, which they paid for themselves. There seemed to be some confusion about this entitlement; one woman suggested that there had been a lack of clarity about which part of the agency was responsible for meeting payments. It is interesting, therefore, that only one woman said that "lack of money" had been the reason for her absence from community service. It is possible that few women exercised their right to financial entitlement because they were not provided with clear information as to what their rights were.

The way financial payments are made to women on community service created a number of difficulties and tensions for some of the women. One woman who travelled on the bus to her placement mentioned her embarrassment at having to use a conspicuous bus pass and she told us that she paid the bus fare on occasion to avoid such embarrassment. Some of the women interviewed raised the issue of having to use registered childminders to care for their children in order to qualify for financial support from the local authority. Some of the women would have liked the option of paying people they knew to look after their children, but this was not possible because they were not registered childminders.

Employment and the Transition to Working Life

Some women mentioned anxieties about going in to community service work for the first time, such as "filling the hours usefully at the beginning" and not being able to plan anything—such as holidays—until the work was completed. Two of the women disliked the early mornings; one mentioned the long days; one mentioned that she disliked the people she "had to mix with." One woman reported that "I had to work round my job, changing hours and sometimes my kids not seeing me for a day at a time." Feelings of tiredness and exhaustion were reported.

Some women noted poor organizational arrangements at their community service placement. One woman said that records of her hours were not kept properly and as a result she did more than her ordered hours. Others complained of having turned up for a team placement only to be sent home because the supervisor was absent or there were not enough supervisors to accommodate all those attending on a particular day, with the view being expressed that under these circumstances they should have been credited with the full seven hours rather than with just two hours as had been the case.

Flexibility was raised as an issue by some of the women. One woman, for instance, stated that she would have liked to have done more hours each day. Another woman said, "sometimes I would have liked to change the day I worked because of other commitments." A third women suggested that "when you're doing your community service you should have the choice of when, within a specific time, when you are going to do it…. You're still giving something back into the community."

Impact of the Actual Work

On the whole, questionnaire responses suggested that the majority of women gained something positive from the actual work they carried out. In response to a question about what they liked most about their community service, 35 women provided 47 comments, 22 of these focused on the work they had carried out: skills acquired; feelings of satisfaction from "helping." When asked what they least liked about community service, 31 women provided 33 responses and only six of these focused on the specific work they were required to complete, which included gardening, weeding, and washing pots in cold water. Some women raised questions about the suitability of the work.

There is some evidence that employment can have an impact on the level of offending (Downes, 1993). Community service may have the potential to engage women in the workforce on a longer-term basis. Some women had apparently asked that they be considered for jobs at their placements in the future and some reported that they gained experience through community service which helped them get a job elsewhere.

Some women who completed questionnaires said they carried on working in the same setting after completing their order, with one woman, for example, reporting that the thing she had liked most about community service was "learning about child care work, going on to being employed by the same association." The interviews completed to date suggest that a number of women were given the option of continuing to work at their placement, either on a paid or voluntary basis, after they had completed their order and some had done so. This is consistent with previous research that found that a high proportion of agencies offered those on community service the option of carrying on working with them after they had completed their orders (McIvor, 1992). Despite this generally positive picture, one woman commented that community service was "a waste of time" because she "could have been looking for a real paid job."

During interviews, one woman who carried out her work in a community center looking after children told us about the difficulties she experienced when she was asked to carry on working at the center. After applying for a paid post at the encouragement of the center manager, she was told by the local authority who ran the center that she would be unable to work with children because of her criminal record.

Working Relationships

On the whole, the women who completed questionnaires reported good relationships with supervisors and other workers. When asked what they liked least about community service, only three out of 33 responses concerned relationships with others. One woman said she disliked the people she had to mix with and felt that some of the team members didn't pull their weight. One woman mentioned that staff was not sympathetic when she was late because of problems with child care arrangements.

When asked what they liked most about community service, 14 from a total of 47 responses from the women focused on relationships with others. What is particularly interesting about this finding is that the women said that what they liked most was being treated as a person, not being judged by other people, meeting people who knew they had committed an offense but did not judge them for it, and being treated equally and fairly. As one woman explained, "people were prepared to take me as they found me."

The fact that their fair treatment warranted comment, suggests that the women were not expecting to be treated so well. One woman said, "*by a bit of luck* the people at the resource centre made mine a pleasure" (emphasis added). The women's responses suggest that they had considered themselves to have had an unusual experience in being fortunate with their placements and the people with whom they came into contact.

Problems Encountered During Community Service

Despite the strong gender bias in group placements, the majority of women (33) indicated that they had not been made to feel uncomfortable on account of their gender, with one woman explaining that the team supervisor had explicitly warned the other offenders in her team against the use of sexist or otherwise discriminatory behavior. One woman, however, said that she had been sexually harassed by other team members while another said that she had had to put up with "snide comments from dafties" and two others indicated that they had been made to feel uncomfortable because they were women without providing further explanation of their answers.

Most women (30) indicated that they encountered no problems at their community service placement. Problems reported by other women included: excessive demands placed by agency staff; not being fully credited with all the hours they had worked; and difficulties in making appropriate child care arrangements. One woman admitted that she had found the work she was asked to perform—care duties in a residential home for older people—

emotionally draining, while another complained of back pains having been brought about by having to carry out gardening duties while pregnant.

How Community Service Could Be Improved

Twenty-two of the 37 women who completed questionnaires offered 28 suggestions as to how community service could be improved. Nine responses focused on the limited choice and availability of different placements for women. Seven women indicated that their placement allocation was affected by the accessibility of the placement and two that felt that it was influenced by limited availability of placements. In one case this was related to a view that women should not be placed in an all-male work team, raising interesting issues about the appropriate gender composition of teams. Completed interviews support the finding that women have few options, if any, as to their work placement and the geographical location can generate additional difficulties for the women. For some this means travelling to another town, placing additional strain on the women in terms of child care and travel time. One of the nine responses about the availability of placements suggested that community service could be improved by placing people where they have skills to enhance the community since this could, in turn, enhance the woman's self-esteem. There is an unresolved question as to whether it is more beneficial to women if they are placed where they can use their existing skills or whether it is better that they are given the opportunity to learn new skills. It is not clear from the responses in this study to what extent different types of placement provided women with the opportunity to acquire new skills or to develop existing abilities.

PERCEIVED PURPOSE AND EFFECT OF COMMUNITY SERVICE

Almost four-fifths of the women in this study believed that they had been given community service as a punishment for their offending and almost two-thirds were of the view that the imposition of a community service order had helped them avoid a custodial sentence. Only about a quarter of the women considered that they had been given community service for reparative purposes—to pay something back to the community—and fewer still believed that the court's intention when imposing their order was that it might help stop them from re-offending. The women's perceptions are, therefore, broadly in accordance with the national objectives and standards for community service in Scotland, which identify community service first and foremost as a punishment that constitutes a fine upon the offender's free time and which promote community service as a direct alternative to custody (Social Work Services Group, 1996).

Some of the women felt that community service had made them reconsider their offending behavior: "It certainly made me think twice about what I'd done"; "It's a good thing for offenders because I think they won't re-offend, well I wouldn't." One woman said community service work had kept her occupied and reduced the possibilities for her to re-offend, "I liked it because it gave me something to do otherwise I would just be out shoplifting or worse." Another woman, whose social worker had helped her obtain state benefits to which she was entitled, said that this had made it unnecessary for her to offend since she now had enough money to feed and clothe her children.

One woman said community service "saved me from getting sent to prison" and another wrote "I feel prison is inappropriate for the vast majority of women offenders and therefore community service should always be considered as an alternative to a custodial sentence." It is clear that these women felt community service was preferable to a custodial sentence. When asked whether their views about offending had changed as a result of community service one woman said, "It scared me.... It's not so much having to do the community service, it was the thought of having to go back to courts. Not getting community service again because I knew I wouldn't get that a second time." The questionnaires do not contain any information as to why these women felt community service was preferable to prison but it may be that possible consequences in terms of the welfare of any children influenced their view.

Despite this apparent preference for punishment in the community, the very public nature of community service was disliked by a number of the women involved in the study. One woman stated that what she liked least about community service was "[p]eople knowing I had committed a crime." Another woman wrote, "I live in a small town, so everyone who worked in the home knew I was doing community service." It seems that in some instances community service may be operating as a public shaming. Five of the six interviewees who were in agency placements reported having told others at their placement that they were on a community service order. In each case the women had had the opportunity to withhold this information if they wished. However, in some circumstances or settings, for example, where women were working in a charity shop, they felt that there was a risk of people who knew they were on community service inadvertently letting others in the agency know. One woman, for instance, indicated that her decision to "come clean" with the other workers in the shop had at least partly been influenced by her concern that someone she knew may come into the shop and say, "Oh, you're doing community service."

IMPLICATIONS FOR POLICY AND PRACTICE

Most women appeared to have found the experience of community service positive in certain respects, with only six of the 37 failing to identify any positive features of the experience. Over 75% of responses about what women liked best about community service focused on the work they carried out and the relationships formed during their order. On the whole, these women enjoyed working. The rewards that they obtained varied from increased self-esteem to paid employment. However, the women in this study identified a number of difficulties associated with completing their orders and offered a number of suggestions that might improve community service.

Women's experiences of community service are, it appears, influenced by practical issues, which are less likely to impact directly on experiences of men. Women who are sentenced to community service have few choices as to the type of work they will complete. This results in women not being able to choose a preferred work option and it may reduce both their commitment to their work and the rewards they may gain from it. The narrow range of placements available can also mean that women may have to travel long distances to carry out their work, increasing travel costs and the time spent away from their children.

One possible option to increase the range of work placements might be to expand the use of team or workshop placements for women. However, this raises questions about the appropriateness of placing women in placements that are dominated by men. Furthermore, the relatively small numbers of women on community service militates against the possibility of women-only workshops or teams, especially in rural areas. However some basic practical changes could be made to reduce the difficulties encountered by women when completing a community service order. For example, there appears to be a need for clearer information about entitlement to financial support for child care and travel and this should be provided to all women who are sentenced to community service.

A number of women in this study raised the issue of flexible hours. Some of the women were able to choose when and for how long they worked each week but others had to work as and when instructed. Flexible working times that could take account of women's other family and work commitments could alleviate some of the difficulties that they encountered. Crèche (a children's nursery) provision was suggested as an option by some women. Most, however, expressed a preference for informal child care arrangements and regretted that they were unable to claim financial support to pay friends, neighbors, or relatives who took on this task.

A number of the women involved in this study were offered paid or unpaid employment on completion of their orders. This potential to engage women in the workforce could be harnessed more effectively and more investment made in this aspect of community service. Scope exists for community service to be developed into an order that offers women training and the possibility to develop their own skills. Such "value added" community service could provide women with a vehicle for change as well as operating as a fine upon the offender's free time and a direct alternative to custody.

About the Authors

Kathryn Goodwin is with the Central Research Unit of the Scottish Executive. Gill McIvor, Ph.D., is Director of the Social Work Research Centre, University of Stirling, Scotland.

References

Barker, M., *Community Service and Women Offenders* (Association of Chief Officers of Probation, 1993).

Downes, D., *Employment Opportunities for Offenders* (HMSO, 1993).

McIvor, G., *Sentenced to Serve: The Operation and Impact of Community Service by Offenders* (Avebury, 1992).

McIvor, G., Jobs for the Boys?: Gender Differences in Referral to Community Service, *The Howard Journal of Criminal Justice* 3, 280-90 (1998).

Chapter 47

Women in Community Corrections in Colorado

by Suzanne Gonzalez Woodburn, M.A., Linda Harrison, M.A. and Kim English

INTRODUCTION

Community corrections in Colorado refers to a system of specific halfway house facilities that provide residential and non-residential services to convicted offenders. These facilities, or programs as we sometimes call them, receive state funds but are based and operated in local communities. They provide an intermediate residential sanction at the front end of the system between probation and prison, or reintegration services at the tail end of the system between prison and parole. Community corrections placements allow offenders access to community resources, including treatment and employment opportunities, while living in a non-secure correctional setting. Offenders are expected to pay approximately $10 per day while in the facility and to start a savings account for first and last month rent.

The facilities are non-secure but each provides 24-hour staffing. Each offender must sign out and in as they leave and return to the facility, and staff monitor the location of off-site offenders by field visits and telephone calls. Several facilities use electronic monitoring and a few programs use geographic satellite surveillance to track offenders when they are away from the halfway house.

This chapter originally appeared in Women, Girls & Criminal Justice, *Vol. 3, No. 5, August/September 2002.*

Table 47.1: Comparison of ORS Studies of Community Corrections

Publication Year/Study Year	N	% Program Success	% Abscond/ Escape	% Revocation/ TVs	% Crime while in program	% Recidivism after program release: 12 mo.	ORS CH Mean Score*
1991/1989**	1796	44.4%	17.1%	27.8%	2.7%	Not measured	Not measured
1996/1991***	1348	55.1%	19.6%	22.4%	3.0%	22.5%	1.80
2002/1998****	3054	62.0%	15.8%	19.8%	2.4%	19.0%	2.35

* The ORS Criminal History Score is an index of an offender's past adjudications, convictions, placements, and revocations. Collapsed scores range from 0 to 4, with 0 representing virtually no prior involvement in crime and 4 reflecting very serious offending histories.

** In 1991, recidivism was not measured. Also program termination reasons do not total 100% in this chart because additional termination categories were included in this study's analysis. Additional categories included death (0.1%), warrant—pending case (0.7%), lateral transfer (1.4%), unknown (3.2%), and missing data (2.6%).

*** In 1996, recidivism was measured as re-arrest 12 months after release.

**** In the current study, recidivism was measured as a new felony or misdemeanor court filing at 12 and 24-month increments. The 12-month recidivism rate appears in the chart.
At 24 months after program release, offenders had an overall recidivism rate of 31.0%.

Table 47.2: Offender Characteristics, 1996 Study*

Offender Characteristics	Men (n = 1129)	Women (n = 211)
Drug problems	59.4%	74.5%
Family/relationship Problems	40.4%	51.9%
Placement is result of probation failure	28.0%	42.0%
Financial problems	21.4%	47.7%
Employed full time at termination	75.5%	66.2%

* This table contains only statistically significant findings, p<.05.

Series of Studies on Program Operations and Outcomes

The state is of course interested in knowing whether this community corrections system is working effectively. To that end, between 1985 and 2000 the Colorado Division of Criminal Justice's Office of Research and Statistics (ORS) conducted four studies of the community corrections halfway house system in Colorado. The first study (English & Kraus, 1986) was primarily a qualitative study and focused on the administration of community corrections. The next two studies (English & Mande, 1991; English, Pullen & Colling-Chadwick, 1996) analyzed offender characteristics and program outcomes for offenders who participated in the residential portion of the community corrections system. Table 47.1 contains a summary of the overall findings from these studies. Efforts of the state administrative agency, combined with statutorily mandated use of needs assessment instruments to help target offender services are the most likely reasons for the increase in success rates, particularly since offenders entering criminal justice programs in the 1990s had more serious crime records compared to those in the 1980s. As research showed gender differences in offender success rates, later studies included a focus on gender.

Focus on Gender

The 1996 research report included a special section on gender because women were doing poorly, in general, in community corrections. Table 47.2 details some important distinguishing characteristics found between men and women in community corrections. Note that women were significantly more likely to have drug and family/relationship problems than men. Women were also more likely than men to have been placed in a halfway house as a result of probation failure. Moreover, women had more financial problems and were less likely to be employed full time at program termination than men.

The most noteworthy finding from the 1996 study (Table 47.3) was that men were significantly more likely to successfully terminate from community corrections programs than women. In fact, women were significantly more likely to abscond than men. This finding may reflect the disparate gender distribution within facilities (more men than women), fewer programs focused on women, or issues with dependents. Moreover, the findings in Table 47.2 suggest programmatic areas of focus to improve women's experiences in community corrections.

In the current study, the ORS analyzed information on all Colorado offenders (n = 3,054) who terminated from 25 community corrections facilities during 1998 and explored why some clients fail community corrections and others succeed. The ORS then tracked nearly 2,000 cases that successfully terminated the programs for 24 months to obtain recidivism information about cases that were arrested and filed in district court. Researchers conducted site visits to each facility and interviewed 206 staff and offenders. Since many community corrections facilities are coed, we were particularly interested in the experiences of women sentenced to these programs.

CURRENT STUDY FINDINGS

Criminal Histories of Offenders

Community corrections facilities house both diversion and transition offenders. "Diversion" refers to offenders sentenced to community corrections at the front end of the system as an intermediate sanction intended to *divert* them from prison. "Transition" refers to those sent to community corrections at the back end of the system and is intended to reintegrate

Table 47.3: Gender Diff e rences in Program Outcome, 1996 Study

P rogram Outcome	Men (n=1129)	Women (n=211)
Successful Termination*	56.1%	47.6%
Technical Violation	23.5%	19.4%
Abscond/Escape*	17.5%	29.7%
New Crime	2.9%	3.3%
Total	100.0%	100.0%

* Indicates a statistically si**g**ificant diff e renceat p<.05.

Table 47.4: Criminal History Scores of Men and Women in Community Corrections in 1998

Criminal History Score	Men (%)	Women (%)
0	16.6	20.3
1	16.3	15.6
2	16.0	18.0
3	15.2	16.1
4	35.9	30.0

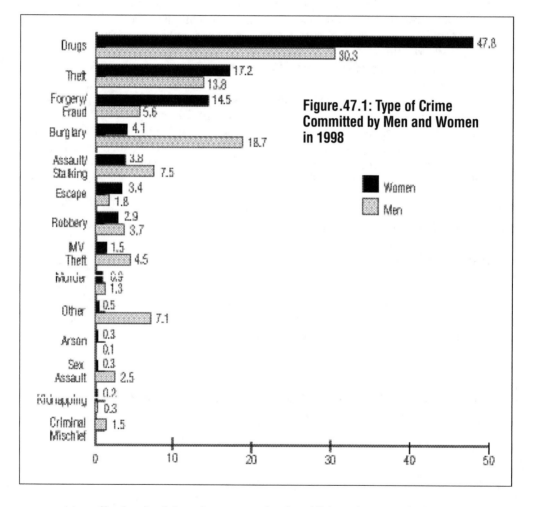

Figure.47.1: Type of Crime Committed by Men and Women in 1998

or *transition* offenders back into the community. In addition, the type of offender served is also diverse. Figure 47.1 details the types of crimes men and women committed most recently. The finding that nearly half of women and one-third of men committed drug-related offenses is particularly notable.

Table 47.5: 1998 Program Completion Rates for Single-Gendered Versus Coed Facilities

Program Completion	Coed Facility	Male Only Facility	Female Only Facility	OVERALL
Unsuccessful Program	44.3% (n=1085)	42.9% (n=411)	29.0% (n=54)	32.0%
Completion	*Men: 44.2%,* *Women: 44.8%*			
Successful Program	55.7% (n=1366)	57.1% (n=546)	71.0% (n=132)	68.0%
Completion	*Men: 55.8%,* *Women: 55.2%*			
TOTAL	100%	100%	100%	100%

The ORS Criminal History Score breakdown for men and women is detailed in Table 47.4. The Criminal History Score is a measure of past criminal involvement and by including two juvenile history variables, it taps early onset of deviant behavior. The score is an index created by weighting and collapsing the following information in an offender's criminal record: number of juvenile adjudications (x .5) + number of placements in youth corrections (x 1) + number of prior adult felony convictions (x 1) + number of prior adult violent arrests (x 1.5) + number of adult probation revocations (x .75) + number of parole revocations (x 2).

Positive Impact of Female-Only Facilities

Women in community corrections did considerably better in 1998 compared to our previous 1996 study and this improvement may be linked, in part, to the introduction of female-only facilities into the large system of halfway houses. In 1998, women in female-only facilities were significantly more likely to successfully complete the halfway house program than women housed in coed facilities.

In 1998, two halfway houses served women only and at this writing there are four women-only facilities. Women housed in the 16 coed facilities in 1998 were far outnumbered by men, usually 10 to one. Nearly every person interviewed in a coed facility discussed the difficulties associated with housing both men and women. For example, according to interview data, coed halfway houses can lead to relationships between male and female offenders and these relationships can distract offenders from the goal of successful program completion. Phrases like "the love connection" and "the dating game" were used to describe this common dynamic within coed facilities.

Both staff and offenders expressed the desire to have single-gender facilities to focus on the distinct needs of the residents. Some staff expressed significant concern when questioned about coed facilities, suggesting the complexities inherent in these halfway houses. Many women we interviewed indicated that they disliked coed facilities because the men belittled what they said during the groups and they felt intimidated by the men. For example:

> I miss being around other women who support and understand me. It's hard to be a woman in this place.... The other women are always focused on impressing the men and looking good instead of the real reason they're here.
>
> *—A female resident in a halfway house that houses about 50 males and four females*

> Right now I'm in a group that we have to go to and I'm the only woman with all these men…. Most the time I don't say nothing (sic).
> *—A female resident in a disproportionately male coed facility*

> The women now have more time to work on their therapeutic concerns and they have less personality conflicts since the men left.
> *— Director of a facility that recently converted from a coed to a female-only facility*

> Women living together create a supportive environment [emotionally]
> *—Case manager at a female facility*

> We have sparse female-specific programming because there are not enough women in the facility to warrant i
> *—Director of a coed facility housing only three females*

Safety Concerns

In addition, women in coed houses reported personal safety concerns, and these concerns coincided with the location of the bedrooms allocated for women. Some facilities located women's bedrooms near the security desk to enhance safety. However, most of the women we interviewed in coed facilities felt a lack of safety and some women mentioned harassment by male offenders. For example:

> My room is right here and I gotta go all the way over there to take a shower…. I just take my clothes with me and get dressed in there so I don't have to walk by them [the men]. They always say things when they're [security staff] not around.
> *—A woman in a coed facility whose bedroom is located on a different wing of the facility from the bathroom designated for females*

Interview data also revealed that some women participating in community corrections felt unsafe because of the location of the facility itself. At one site, the route from the bus stop to the facility was long and lacked adequate streetlights at night. Construction and warehouse workers employed in the neighborhood intimidated several women in one halfway house because they yelled and heckled them from the nearby job site:

> "I have to walk all the way around the block to get around the railroad tracks—since we're not supposed to walk across them—to get to the bus stop. It's scary at night."

> "… yeah, and those perverted men and truck drivers are always trying to pick up on us when we're outside."
> *—Two women housed in a female-only facility, speaking during a focus group session*

Lack of Female-Specific Services

Many women and staff who were interviewed in coed facilities consistently reported that services were tailored to men. Most staff and offenders indicated that sparse female-specific programming exists in coed facilities. During an interview, one woman stated that she paid for outside services rather than participating in free in-house services where she would have been the only woman in an all-male group.

Some staff in coed facilities reported that they lacked female-specific programming because the number of women served was too small to warrant special programs. Some of the programs that do exist are apparently less than adequate. For example, many women interviewed said they thought that parenting classes focused on raising babies and young children and did not adequately address topics concerning older children and teenagers.

According to interview data, women also lacked adequate job skills and opportunities to make salaries comparable to men. As a result, it was more difficult for women to pay for rent, restitution, and treatment while in the halfway house. Low wages make it financially difficult for women to move back into the community. The lack of adequate compensation for work undermines women's efforts for long-term success in any criminal justice placement. During interviews, some women indicated that obtaining a job positively impacted their mood, self-esteem, and progress in treatment. Most facility staff interviewed, however, recognized that women need vocational training and job skills in order to succeed in the community.

During interviews, staff and offenders reported a lack of female-oriented services in the following areas:

- *Medical Care:* Interview and focus group data revealed that many programs lacked access to medical care for women. Medical services mentioned included prenatal care, contraceptive and pregnancy assistance, and annual gynecological examinations.

- *Parenting Classes:* Some facilities offered parenting classes aimed primarily at caring for babies.

- *Vocational Training and Job Skills:* While some facilities offered job placement assistance and job skills training, others failed to provide these services.

- *Life Skills:* According to interviews, many women need basic life skills (i.e., completing annual tax forms, accessing community resources, completing job applications, developing a résumé, and managing a budget) training and education in order to complete these day-to-day tasks. Some staff reported that they did not assume that the women they supervised knew basic life skills, especially women who previously relied on others to complete these duties. These staff focused on life skills for all offenders.

- *Victimization Classes:* Most women and staff discussed victimization treatment for sexual, emotional, and physical abuse as a lacking but needed service in community corrections.

- *Relationship Building:* Many women told us they had a history of violent or anti-social partners and unhealthy relationships. Some women reported the link between these relationships and their criminal activity but many told us they were unsure of how to stay away from unhealthy relationships. Research indicates that women are more oriented to interpersonal relationships than men, and women's lives are experienced in large part through their relationships with others. The corrections literature shows that female inmates rely on one another for social support. (Maher, 2001; McMahon, 2001; Shaw & Hanna-Moffat, 2001; Office of Justice Programs, 1999). Relationship building was a fundamental program component of one female-only facility with high program completion rates and low recidivism rates.

- *Health and Wellness:* Some women, particularly those with drug and alcohol problems, wanted to learn more about women's health in order to take better care of themselves. These women lacked access to health awareness and education services while in the community corrections program.

- *Self-Esteem:* Staff in nearly every facility that housed females indicated that low self-esteem was a critical problem among the female offender population. However, staff and administrators in most facilities recognized that their program lacked adequate services to address low self-esteem. This was especially the case in coed facilities, where females were treated with male-oriented modalities and staff found it difficult to incorporate female-specific interventions.

- *Eating Disorders:* Staff in many sites reported eating disorders as one of the many psychological disturbances suffered by female offenders. Eating disorders are thought to be symptoms of other underlying issues, most commonly self-esteem, control, and perfectionism (Costin, 1999), so it is not surprising that these disorders pervade the female offender population. Some staff thought eating disorders were more prevalent in coed facilities, where the presence of men increased the pressure to be thin. Despite its common occurrence, most facilities lacked access to specialized treatment for eating disorders and instead attempted to combine this issue with other accessible treatments.

NEED FOR DISTINCT PROGRAMMING GEARED TO WOMEN'S RISKS AND NEEDS

The research literature is clear that women offenders require distinct programming because they have different risks and needs. The International Community Corrections Association's *Journal* published an excellent discussion of female-specific programming in its December 1998 issue. Reed and Leavitt (1998, p. 20) note that programming must address "sexual and physical abuse, substance use/abuse, mental illness and mental health issues, poor physical health, insufficient job skills, lack of safe/affordable housing, many relationship issues and complex family and care giving responsibilities." Women's mental and physical health care is often more complicated and severe than men's, and services should be "welcoming, accessible, supportive and sensitive to trauma-related issues."

Stephanie Covington (1998), in the same issue cites research regarding effective substance abuse programming for women focused on both treatment content and the environment in which service was delivered. Content topics include "self" (sources of self-esteem, effects of sexism, racism and stigma on a sense of self); "relationships" (family of origin, myths of motherhood, relationship histories including violent relationships, and building health support systems); "sexuality" (body image, connections between addiction and sexuality); and "spirituality" (introduction to the concepts of spirituality, prayer, and meditation). Covington describes a supportive environment as one characterized by:

- *Safety:* Free from physical, emotional, and sexual harassment; rules of conduct provide appropriate boundaries; group therapy is guaranteed to be a safe place to discuss and work personal issues.

- *Connection:* Exchanges among the facilitator and group members feel mutual rather than authoritarian; the facilitator wants to understand their experiences and is not overwhelmed by their stories.

- *Empowerment:* The facilitator models how a woman can use power with and for others, and encourages group members to believe and exercise their abilities (Covington, 1998, pp. 27-28).

Covington, who has developed an intervention program called *Helping Women Recover* (Covington, 1999) based on research and clinical experience, notes that it is important that a group intended to help women be composed solely of women and that the facilitator be a woman. Additionally, cultural awareness and sensitivity, resources, and strengths are key ingredients in correctional programs for women.

Assessment tools are typically designed for and tested on male offenders and do not necessarily address needs specific to women. Some researchers recommend the use of "asset assessments" to help women see the strengths and skills that they already have, whereas needs assessments focus on what is wrong with the client and these women are typically struggling with problems of poor self-esteem.

The fact that female-specific assessments are not used in the Colorado halfway house system both reflects and perpetuates the lack of program emphasis for female offenders. Consequently, many women may not receive services they need. In the current study, one facility that provides comprehensive, female-specific programming to serious offenders had a 69.0% program completion rate, and 85.0% of these women remained crime free after 24 months. These success rates are statistically significantly higher than the statewide averages for program completion and 24-month success rates for women (60.4% and 69.5%, respectively). These data suggest that women benefit from female-specific programming. However, without appropriate needs assessment tools, matching pertinent services to needs is a difficult task.

PRACTICE IMPLICATIONS

Despite the problems mentioned here, women in our study recidivated at a lower rate (24.8%) than men (32.4%) 24 months after successful program completion. These findings may be deceiving, however, because women—even women with a criminal past—are less likely than men to engage in crime. Women serving time in female-only facilities significantly increased the overall success rate of women in this study.

Both the program completion findings and the recidivism data reflect that, overall, women were doing markedly better in Colorado community corrections in 1998 than they did in the past. This could be the result of an increase in female-specific programming dealing with needs specific to women since, in earlier studies, the female-only programs were not yet available.

But success rates could be higher still. Many women in Colorado's community correction system still lack access to appropriate services and some feel unsafe in the environment inside and outside the facility. These factors can severely limit a woman's opportunity to succeed, both during and after the community corrections program. The dramatic change in outcomes for female community corrections clients over the years is promising. Facility staff have moved toward providing women the tools they need to succeed. Continued movement in this direction can only provide more opportunity for success for female offenders.

Efforts should be made to expand gender-specific facilities and programming. Facilities should minimize the use of coed facilities for female offenders. Women need very specific program content and they must feel safe to maximize the effect of interventions. These services must be tailored to meet the special needs of women.

Vocational training must focus on moving women from their economic disadvantage so that they can support themselves and their children in the community. And since women are at a higher risk to become crime victims than men and many have a history of violent partners, victimization classes and treatment would be beneficial. Women with co-dependency issues could benefit from relationship building and empowerment classes teaching them how to be self-sufficient and independent, and how to form and maintain healthy and supportive relationships.

CONCLUSION

Equality of service delivery is not simply allowing women access to services traditionally reserved for men. Equality must be defined in terms of providing opportunities that are relevant to each gender. Women housed in coed facilities should receive separate services specific to their needs. Treatment services, then, may appear very different depending on who receives the service.

Failure to implement these changes far outweighs the cost of the services themselves. Over time, improving outcomes will generate significant cost savings to the criminal justice and other social systems.

About the Authors

Suzanne Gonzalez Woodburn, M.A., is a statistical analyst for the Colorado Division of Criminal Justice (CDCJ). Linda Harrison, M.A., is a senior analyst at CDCJ, and Kim English is Director of the CDCJ Office of Research and Statistics.

References

Colorado Department of Public Safety, *Report of Findings: Comparison of Intensive Supervision Probation and Community Corrections Clientele* (Division of Criminal Justice, Office of Research and Statistics, 1996).

Costin, C., *The Eating Disorder Sourcebook: A Comprehensive Guide to the Causes, Treatments, and Prevention of Eating Disorders* (Lowell House, 1999).

Covington, S. S., "Creating Gender-Specific Treatment for Substance-Abusing Women and Girls in Community Correctional Settings," 9(1) *The ICCA Journal of Community Corrections* 24-29 (1998).

Covington, S. S., *Helping Women Recover: A Program for Treating Substance Abuse (Special Edition for Use in the Criminal Justice System)* (Jossey-Bass, 1999).

English, K. & Mande, M. J., *Community Corrections in Colorado: Why Do Some Clients Succeed and Others Fail?* (Colorado Division of Criminal Justice, 1991).

English, K., & Kraus, S., *Community Corrections in Colorado: 1986* (Colorado Division of Criminal Justice, 1986).

English, K., Pullen, S., & Colling-Chadwick, S., *Comparison of Intensive Supervision Probation and Community Corrections Clientele* (Colorado Division of Criminal Justice, 1996).

Maher, J. "The Bridge to Success Lies in Remedial Education: A Teacher's View from Prison," 2(1)*Women, Girls & Criminal Justice* 1, 7-11 (2001).

McMahon, M., "Is Assisting Female Offenders an Art or Science? Reflections on the 1998 ICCA Conference on Women and Juvenile Females in Community Corrections," 2(2)*Women, Girls & Criminal Justice* 1-2, 29-32 (2001).

Office of Justice Programs, *National Symposium on Women Offenders* (U.S. Department of Justice, 1999).

Reed, B. G. & Leavitt, M. E., "Modified Wraparound & Women Offenders: A Community Corrections Continuum," 9(1)*The ICCA Journal of Community Corrections* 18-23 (1998).

Shaw, M. & Hannah-Moffat, K., "Risk Assessment in Canadian Corrections: Some Diverse and Gendered Issues," 2(1)*Women, Girls & Criminal Justice* 1-2, 12-16 (2001).

Chapter 48

The John P. Craine House: A Community Residential Program for Indiana Women and Their Children

by William H. Barton, Ph.D., and Cheryl Justice, M.S.W.

INTRODUCTION

Special issues concerning female offenders who are also mothers receive occasional attention (Bloom, 1995; Bloom & Steinhart, 1993; Hairston, 1991; McGowan & Blumenthal, 1978; Zaplin & Dougherty, 1998), but relatively little has been developed in the way of policies or programs to deal with them. In a report for the National Institute of Corrections, Austin, Bloom and Donahue (1992) noted, "It is said that 'When a man goes to prison, he

This chapter originally appeared in Women, Girls & Criminal Justice, *Vol. 2, No. 3, April/May 2003.*

loses his freedom, but when a woman goes to prison, she loses her children'" (p. 5). The majority of incarcerated women are mothers, and the pains of imprisonment are borne by their children as well, many of whom may themselves develop problems requiring interventions. Among their recommendations, Austin et al. called for the development of community residential programs that would permit female offenders and their children to live together.

Located in Marion County, Indianapolis, the John P. Craine House is the first such program in Indiana and one of only a small number throughout the country. As a model for the development of similar programs, it merits careful study. This chapter describes the program, presents preliminary evaluation information regarding the effectiveness of the program, and discusses the potential value of such programs for community corrections.

WOMEN OFFENDERS AND THEIR CRIMES

Statistical and empirical evidence suggests that:

- Most incarcerated women are not sentenced for violent crimes, so that community corrections alternatives to incarceration may often be appropriate;

- Most incarcerated women are also mothers, and most of these have children under the age of 18;

- Children of incarcerated parents suffer adverse effects;

- There are relatively few community-based alternatives to preserve the mother-child relationship;

- There has as yet been little evaluation of such alternatives.

Although the incarceration rate for men is nearly 12 times that for women, the rate for women is increasing more rapidly. The number of females incarcerated more than doubled in the 1990s, from 44,065 in 1990 to 90,688 by the end of 1999 (Beck, 2000b). The rate of incarceration of women has increased at an average annual rate of 8.4% (Beck, 2000a).

Despite the increases in incarceration rates, relatively few women are arrested or sentenced for violent crimes. Nationally, Greenfield and Snell (1999) report that about one-fourth of the women (28%) in state prisons were committed for violent offenses, and an additional 27% for property offenses, 34% for drug offenses and 11% for public order offenses. Even these figures may overstate the offense seriousness, as they report nearly three in four violent offenses committed by females were simple assaults, compared with just over half of the violence committed by males. As would be expected, they found even fewer women held in local jails (12%) were sentenced for violent offenses.

Of the 19,874 persons held in Indiana's state prisons on July 1, 2000, 6.8% were women (Indiana DOC, 2000). Among the 1,223 women held on September 28, 1999, 18% had been sentenced for murder or Class A felonies, and 31% for Class B felonies. More than half of the Class A and Class B felonies (52%) were drug related. About one-fourth of the women (27.6%) had been sentenced for Class C felonies, of which forgery accounted for about half (49%). Finally, Class D felonies accounted for 22% of the women (Indiana DOC, 1999). Of course, these figures overestimate the seriousness of women's offending, since one-day population counts overrepresent those serving longer sentences (presumably the more serious offenders).

INCARCERATED MOTHERS

For the past 20 years, several researchers have noted that a substantial proportion of incarcerated women were single, heads-of-household with one or more young children (Bloom & Steinhart, 1993; Johnston, 1995a; McGowan & Blumenthal, 1978; Stanton, 1980). The 1997 Survey of Inmates in State and Federal Correctional Facilities (Mumola, 2000) provides more recent data concerning parents in prison. A majority of prisoners have one or more children under the age of 18. Among inmates in state prisons, 55% of the males and 65% of the females report having one or more minor children. Put differently, nearly 1.5 million minor children (2.1% of all U.S. minor children) had a parent in a state or federal prison in 1999. The number of children with a mother in prison nearly doubled from 1991 to 1999. Of the mothers in state prisons, about three fifths (58.5%) reported living with their minor children in the month prior to arrest. In the vast majority of these cases (about 80%), these were single parent households (Mumola, 2000).

EFFECTS OF PARENTS' INCARCERATION ON THEIR CHILDREN

Several studies have documented the adverse effect a parent's incarceration is likely to have upon children. The experience is certainly emotionally stressful, producing anxiety, depression, aggression, and learning disorders (Sack, Seidler, & Thomas, 1976; Sametz, 1980; Stanton, 1980; Fishman, 1982). Jose-Kampfner (1995) has suggested that children of prisoners may suffer from posttraumatic stress syndrome, especially those who witnessed their mothers' arrest.

Mumola (2000) reports that most children of incarcerated mothers are cared for by grandparents or other relatives; fewer than a third of the mothers (28%) indicated that at least one of their children was in the care of the child's father, and 10% reported that their children were in the care of a foster home, agency, or institution. Earlier studies have shown that between one-fourth and one-third of the children are placed apart from their siblings during the mother's incarceration (Koban, 1983; Stanton, 1980). Some of these children may experience changes in placement, and such changes are generally believed to have detrimental effects. Johnston (1995a) estimates that about 14% change households two or more times during their mothers' incarceration.

In a detailed summary of the literature, Johnston (1995a) suggests that effects of maternal incarceration vary according to the developmental stage of the children. For example, pregnant prisoners and their unborn infants are at high risk for morbidity and mortality; children in the first two years of life may not develop sufficient bonds with incarcerated mothers; children between three and six may experience severe emotional trauma; children in the middle years are apt to react to the trauma with antisocial and aggressive behaviors; early adolescents may react with maladaptive coping behaviors, such as theft, gang activity, and violence; and older adolescents may experience difficulties in identity formation, and the cumulative effects of their parents' incarceration may lead to their own problems with the justice system.

It is clear from the summary above that the children of offenders experience multiple problems at a higher rate than their peers. For example, in one study (Johnston, 1992), the large majority of students (78%) in an intermediate school referred to a therapeutic intervention program for serious classroom behavior or disciplinary problems were children of previously or currently incarcerated parents.

The intergenerational pattern of crime and incarceration is especially troubling. Bloom and Steinhart (1993) cite evidence that such children are five to six times more likely than other children to eventually become incarcerated themselves. Johnston (1995a) notes that nearly one-third of the 11- to 14-year-old children in her study of incarcerated offenders had parents who had been arrested and/or incarcerated.

EXAMPLES OF EXISTING PROGRAM MODELS

There are examples of programs for women that intend to preserve or strengthen the mother-child relationship (for reviews, see Austin, Bloom, & Donahue, 1992; Bloom, 1995; Chesney-Lind & Immarigeon, 1995; Johnston, 1995b; Zaplin & Dougherty, 1998). Many of these are rather limited in scope and take place within prisons, e.g., parenting programs for incarcerated women (Clement, 1993; Gwinn, 1992) and special visitation programs, such as overnight visits, nurseries, scout troops, and other activity-based programs (Allen, 1992; Jose-Kampfner, 1991; Logan, 1992; Moses, 1993; Plummer, 1991; Stumbo & Little, 1990).

Regarding community-based programs, the Austin, Bloom, and Donahue (1992) national survey of community corrections programs for women identified 111 programs; 72 of these were residential programs, but only 23 housed both women and their children. Some of these are aftercare-reentry programs while some are alternatives to incarceration. Partly because such programs are relatively new, and because they tend to serve small numbers of residents, little has been done in the way of evaluation of any of these programs (Austin et al., 1992; Johnston 1995b).

One such program, Summit House in North Carolina, provided recidivism data in its 1997-1998 Annual Report (Summit House, 1998). Of the 75 mothers served between 1990 and 1998, 25% were reconvicted within three years. Of those convictions, most (74%) were for misdemeanors.

Although few specific evaluations of community-based, residential alternatives have yet appeared, there is reason to expect that such programs have promise. They should mitigate some of the deleterious effects on children discussed previously. They may also produce more successful outcomes for the women as well. Hairston (1988) cites evidence that maintaining family ties is associated with lower recidivism and better subsequent adjustment. However, little is known about how to structure such programs effectively. Therefore, the lessons learned from the development of Craine House, Summit House, and the few similar programs are timely and necessary.

THE CRAINE HOUSE PROGRAM

Group Residential Alternative to Incarceration

With primary funding from the Indiana Department of Correction through a contract with Marion County Community Corrections, Craine House is a nonprofit organization providing a family living program to a small group of female offenders together with their preschool-aged children. Craine House has also received support from other public and private funding sources. Eligibility for placement at Craine House is limited to women with preschool-aged children who have been convicted of misdemeanors, Level C or Level

D felonies, thus excluding violent and other serious felony offenders. However, as noted above, about half of all women in prison in Indiana are Level C or D felony offenders.

As an alternative to incarceration, the program, which opened in December of 1993 in a residential neighborhood in Indianapolis, is intended to prevent problems associated with separating young children from their mothers, while providing supervision and support to the women. Craine House has been designed to serve approximately six adults and eight preschool-aged children in a group setting. Older children, although not residing at Craine House, are encouraged to participate with their mothers and younger siblings in program activities whenever possible. Craine House added a day reporting component in 1997, but this chapter focuses exclusively on the residential program.

The idea for this program was shaped by two considerations:

- Many women currently incarcerated do not appear to pose serious threats to public safety, and thus appear capable of remaining in the community provided that they receive adequate supervision and support.

- The children of incarcerated women have much higher rates of subsequent involvement with the juvenile and/or adult correctional systems.

Thus, the Craine House program has been designed both as an alternative to incarceration for the women and as a preventive intervention for their children.

In general terms, the program provides a structured residential group setting for the women and their children. Resident staff and caseworkers assess each client and provide necessary support and supervision. Specific interventions focus on parenting skills, substance abuse treatment, job seeking skills, educational and/or job placement in the community, personal budgeting, nutrition information, and advocacy as indicated by individualized assessments. The program arranges for daycare for the children at nearby locations to enable the women to work in the community. The program is staffed around the clock by counselors and family living specialists.

Program Goals and Objectives

Basic goals for the Craine House program are to provide a safe, structured environment; promote the preservation of mother-child relationships; enhance the offenders' abilities to maintain economic and emotional independence while leading responsible, law-abiding lives; and prevent the neglect, abuse, and potential delinquency of the offenders' children. The program is congruent with contemporary welfare reform policies in emphasizing family preservation and self-sufficiency.

The stated objectives of the program are:

- To establish a community corrections model for women offenders and their children, with residential and continuing care programs;

- Eighty-five percent of the residents will successfully attain the goals of their individualized Person/Family Living Plans;

- Seventy percent of the program graduates will continue to live successfully in the community (i.e., without risk to themselves or public safety) for at least 12 months after graduation from Craine House;

- The Craine House Family Living Program will establish a model of coordination of public-private services in community corrections, child welfare, education, and employment; and

- Evaluation of the Family Living Program will provide new data about cost-effectiveness and successful methods of intervention, through use of gender-specific treatment.

EVALUATION METHODOLOGY

This preliminary evaluation is modest in scope. Feasibility constraints prevented the use of an experimental or quasi-experimental design. This study can only be seen as establishing a baseline of program outcomes during its first few years of operation. The study examines the number of women and children served, their length of stay, their termination status, and recidivism (in terms of new charges filed after leaving the program). In the absence of a control group, these results can be viewed in comparison only with those found in other, similar programs elsewhere, such as Summit House, and with more general expectations for correctional program outcomes with female offenders.

Information about the women was obtained from Craine House case files, supplemented with offense data from the Marion County Justice Information System. Case file data included entry and exit dates, exit status (successful program graduation, or new violation), number of children, educational and employment status at exit, and amount of fees paid. The Justice Information System provided recidivism data. The study was based on data collected in October of 1999.

EVALUATION RESULTS

Residents Assigned

Between 1993 and 1999, Craine House served 80 women and 107 children in its residential

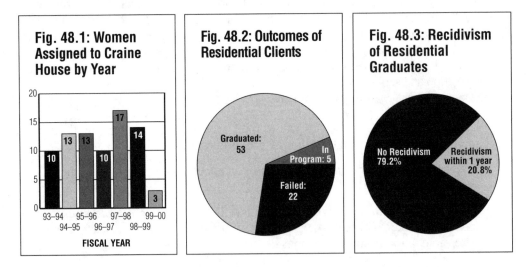

Fig. 48.1: Women Assigned to Craine House by Year

Fig. 48.2: Outcomes of Residential Clients

Fig. 48.3: Recidivism of Residential Graduates

program. Figure 48.1 shows that between 10 and 17 women arrive at Craine House each year. Most bring one or two young children with them, a few have brought three children. Length of stay ranged from two days to nearly two years, with an average of about five months (151 days). Successful program graduates averaged between six and seven months (193 days), while those who did not successfully complete the program lasted an average of less than two months (49 days).

Program Outcomes

Figure 48.2 depicts the termination status of each of the 80 women. As can be seen, 53 successfully completed the program, 22 were removed from the program for violations or new offenses, and five were still in residence at the time of the study. Considering all of the women who left the program (N = 75) the successful graduation rate was 70%.

Recidivism

Of the 80 women assigned to Craine House, 33 (41%) had reappeared in court on new charges or for program violations as of October 1, 1999. These included the 22 whose new offenses or program violations led to their removal from the program. None of the new charges were for violent offenses, most were for program violations (10), absconding (8), property offenses such as theft or forgery (8) or drug possession (5). As Figure 48.3 shows, however, only 11 of the 53 program graduates had reappeared in court within a year of termination, for a one-year recidivism rate of only 21% for graduates. Furthermore, at the time of follow-up, the 53 graduates had averaged more than two years of time in the community since leaving Craine House.

Cost

The Craine House program is not inexpensive. The per diem cost per residential client is approximately $80, considerably higher than the comparable per diem cost of incarceration in a state prison (approximately $55). However, Craine House requires that residents contribute to the cost of the program via a portion of income earned while in the program. As of October 1, 1999, residents had reimbursed a total of more than $76,000 to the program. In any event, cost effectiveness depends on the long-term trajectories of the women *and* their children, for which relevant data are not yet available.

AN ILLUSTRATIVE CASE

"Carolyn" (not her real name) was sentenced to Craine House for one year because she violated probation with a positive drug test. She arrived with two children, ages two and four, and was four months pregnant. Her mother admitted that she, herself, was addicted to crack, but stopped using drugs when Carolyn came to Craine House. Carolyn's support system was made up of her very ill mother (diagnosed with uterine cancer), an elderly grandmother, and a younger sister. None of her children's fathers gave financial or nurturing support. Carolyn wanted to take the GED test, and a tutor came to Craine House twice a week to help her study for the exam. Craine House arranged for her four-year-old daughter to attend a Head Start program and for transportation and child care for her two-year-old. Staff assisted Carolyn through her pregnancy, took her to the hospital, and were the only ones present during the delivery of her baby. While at Craine House, Carolyn learned how to open a bank account and save money. The program helped her obtain rental assistance, furniture, and other items for her very first apartment. She was encouraged to file for child support from all three of her children's fathers. She completed a 10-week parenting program, a 10-week independent living program and other classes to enhance her skills, and obtained a job at a nearby restaurant where she completed management training. She successfully graduated from the program. While still on probation, she continues to work, live independently, and provide for her family.

DISCUSSION

Since the majority of incarcerated women are mothers of young children, and since most do not appear to pose a high risk to public safety, there would appear to be a widespread need for programs like Craine House that allow women to remain in the community and to continue parenting their young children. Craine House, in its seventh year of operation at this writing, has developed an impressive record of success in preventing recidivism and promoting the successful reintegration of its residents into the community. As one of the few programs that permit female offenders and their young children to live together, Craine House deserves attention, along with its few peers around the country, as a promising model for an alternative to incarceration for mothers with young children.

Further research is obviously needed, focusing on the outcomes of both the women and their children. As many promising programs are small in size, rigorous quantitative studies are difficult to design. In addition, feasibility constraints often prevent the introduction of experimental designs involving random assignment. Finally, the time considerations for examining long-term child outcomes mean that such results cannot be known for many years. Perhaps a major research effort could be funded that simultaneously examined the outcomes of several promising programs that used a similar program model. Perhaps a quasi-experimental control group could be established from jurisdictions that lacked these alternatives. In the absence of larger scale studies, individual programs can at least attempt to track their own outcome data over time, including repeated follow-up data collection, to establish trends and allow for comparisons across programs.

About the Authors

William H. Barton, Ph.D., is Associate Professor, Indiana University School of Social Work, Indiana University-Purdue University Indianapolis; Cheryl Justice, M.S.W., former Executive Director, John P. Craine House, Indianapolis, Indiana, is currently Division Director, Mississippi Department of Education Office of Student Assessment.

References

Allen, P., "World Beyond the Walls," *San Antonio Express-News Magazine*, September 27, 1992, pp. 6, 18-21, 23.

Austin, J., Bloom, B., & Donahue, T., *Female Offenders in the Community: An Analysis of Innovative Strategies and Programs* (National Council on Crime and Delinquency, National Institute of Corrections, 1992).

Beck, A. J., *Prison and Jail Inmates at Midyear 1999* (U.S. Department of Justice Publication No. NCJ 181643, 2000a).

Beck, A. J., Prisoners in 1999 (U.S. Department of Justice Publication No. NCJ 183476, 2000b).

Bloom, B., "Imprisoned Mothers." In K. Gabel & D. Johnston, (Eds.), *Children of Incarcerated Parents* (pp. 21-30) (Lexington Books, 1995).

Bloom, B., & Steinhart, D., *Why Punish the Children? A Reappraisal of the Children of Incarcerated Mothers in America* (National Council on Crime and Delinquency, 1993).

Chesney-Lind, M., & Immarigeon, R., "Alternatives to Women's Incarceration." In K. Gabel & D. Johnston, (Eds.), *Children of Incarcerated Parents* (pp. 299-309) (Lexington Books, 1995).

Clement, M. J., "Parenting in Prison: A National Survey of Programs for Incarcerated Women," 19 *Journal of Offender Rehabilitation* 89-100 (1993).

Fishman, S. H., "The Impact of Incarceration on Children of Offenders," 15 *Journal of Children in Contemporary Society* 89-99 (1982).

Greenfield, L. A., & Snell, T. L., *Women Offenders* (U.S. Department of Justice Publication No. NCJ 175688, 1999).

Gwinn, B., "Linking Inmate Families Together: The L. I. F. T. Program at FPC Alderson," 3 *Federal Prisons Journal* 37-40 (1992).

Hairston, C. F., "Family Ties During Imprisonment: Do They Influence Future Criminal Behavior?," 52 *Federal Probation* 48-52 (March 1988),

Hairston, C. F., "Mother in Jail: Parent-Child Separation and Jail Visitation," *6(2) Affilia* 9-27 (1991).

Indiana Department of Correction, "Review of Adult Females Held in State Prisons on September 28, 1999," [Unpublished custom report].

Indiana Department of Correction, Offender population statistics [Online]. Available: *http://www.state.in.us/indcorrection/statistics/statistics.html* [October 4, 2000].

Johnston, D., Report No. 6: Children of Offenders" (Pacific Oaks College, Center for Children of Incarcerated Parents, 1992).

Johnston, D., "Effects of Parental Incarceration." In K. Gabel & D. Johnston, (Eds.), *Children of Incarcerated Parents* (pp. 59-88) (New York, 1995).

Johnston, D., "Intervention." In K. Gabel & D. Johnston, (Eds.), *Children of Incarcerated Parents* (pp. 199-236) (Lexington Books, 1995).

Jose-Kampfner, C., "Michigan Program Makes Children's Visits Meaningful," 53(5) *Corrections Today* 130, 132, 134 (1991).

Jose-Kampfner, C., "Post-Traumatic Stress Reactions in Children of Imprisoned Mothers." In K. Gabel & D. Johnston, (Eds.), *Children of Incarcerated Parents* (pp. 89-100) (Lexington Books, 1995).

Koban, L., "Parents in Prison: A Comparative Analysis of the Effects of Incarceration on the Families of Men and Women," 5 *Research in Law, Deviance & Social Control* 171-183 (1983).

Logan, G., "Family Ties Take Top Priority in Women's Visiting Program," 54(6) *Corrections Today* 160-161 (1992).

McGowan, B. G., & Blumenthal, K. L., *Why Punish the Children? A Study of Children of Women Prisoners* (National Council on Crime and Delinquency, 1978).

Moses, M. C., "New Program at Women's Prison Benefits Mothers and Children," 55(5) *Corrections Today* 132, 134-135 (1993).

Mumola, C. J., *Incarcerated Parents and Their Children* (U.S. Department of Justice Publication No. NCJ 182335, 2000).

Plummer, C. C., "Alameda County Jail Offers Parenting Education," 2(5) *Large Jail Network Bulletin* 14-15 (1991).

Sack, W. H., Seidler, J., & Thomas, S., "The Children of Imprisoned Parents: A Psychosocial Explanation," 46 *American Journal of Orthopsychiatry* 618-628 (1976).

Sametz, L., "Children of Incarcerated Women," 25 *Social Work* 298-303 (1980).

Stanton, A. M., *When Mothers Go to Jail* (Lexington Books, 1980).

Stumbo, N. J., & Little, S. L., *Camp Celebration: Incarcerated Mothers and Their Children Camping Together* (Research report. National Institute of Justice, 1990).

Summit House, *Annual report 1997-1998* (1998).

Zaplin, R. T., & Dougherty, J., "Programs That Work: Mothers." In R. T. Zaplin (Ed.), *Female Offenders: Critical Perspectives and Effective Interventions* (pp. 331-347, 1998).

Chapter 49

Alternative Interventions for Women in Ohio

**by Mary Carol Melton, Mary Grace, M.Ed., M.S.,
Nancy Schmidtgoessling, Ph.D. and Walter S. Smitson, Ph.D.**

INTRODUCTION

In March 2001, the Alternative Interventions for Women program opened its doors in Cincinnati, Ohio, as an innovative early intervention program for female offenders with co-occurring mental health and substance abuse disorders to help support criminal justice diversion and sentencing sanctions. The program, located within the Court Clinic, a community-based agency that provides mental health and forensic services for the Hamilton County Courts, was made possible through a funding partnership with The Health Foundation of Greater Cincinnati, the Hamilton County Department of Probation, the Hamilton County Department of Pretrial Services, Hamilton County TASC, and the Hamilton County Community Mental Health Board.

The Alternative Interventions for Women program came to life after a needs assessment suggested relevant parameters for its services. For three years, members of the criminal justice system and community mental health leaders in Hamilton County worked together, with the support of the National Institute of Corrections (NIC), to learn about and plan alternative sanctions and services for women offenders. One result of this intersystem collaboration, which occurred when local service providers were convening to identify and discuss specific issues and, at the same time, NIC was seeking sites to help local jurisdictions improve the level and quality of services to female offenders in the criminal justice system, was the recommendation for an in-depth assessment study.

This chapter originally appeared in Women, Girls & Criminal Justice, *Vol. 3, No. 4, June/July 2002.*

The assessment project, formally named the Women's Assessment Project, was funded by the Hamilton County Department of Probation to determine rates of psychiatric and substance abuse disorders, traumatic events, and cognitive functioning, using standardized assessment tools, in a small sample of women arraigned through the Hamilton County Municipal Court between October and December 1999. The results of that study indicated significant incidence of mental health, substance abuse, and co-occurring disorders in this group (Grace et al., 2002). The findings suggested that institutionalizing a system of early screening, assessment, and treatment would assist the courts in determining if treatment, as an alternative to incarceration, would be beneficial for this high-risk and underserved population of women offenders in Hamilton County.

As a result, the Alternative Interventions for Women program was developed to provide a continuum of assessment and treatment services for women with co-occurring mental health and substance abuse disorders including early identification, assessment and referral, treatment, and community reintegration. This initiative, led by the Court Clinic, is a collaborative effort across the criminal justice, mental health, and substance abuse systems.

EARLY IDENTIFICATION

The first step in the early identification, assessment and referral, treatment, and community reintegration continuum of the Alternative Interventions for Women program, is a brief symptom screening of women coming through the Department of Pretrial Services in order to detect those who would likely meet criteria for co-occurring disorders. Staff administers the self-report BASIS-32 to all women coming through the Department of Pretrial Services as part of the standard pretrial assessment. Results for each client are computer scored and faxed to the Court Clinic Liaison who reviews the data and makes recommendations to pretrial staff, based on the BASIS-32 score, about seeking an in-depth assessment referral from the judge.

The court then has the option of referring a woman for the in-depth clinical assessment and, if the co-occurring disorders are confirmed, a recommendation for participation in the Alternative Interventions for Women treatment program, or other appropriate treatment could be made.

IN-DEPTH ASSESSMENT

Women referred by the court receive an in-depth clinical assessment performed by Court Clinic assessment specialists and licensed clinical psychologists. The assessment includes the Structured Clinical Interview for DSM-IV (SCID), a trauma-screening inventory, an abbreviated IQ test, and a measure of cognitive functioning. The clinical assessment determines if the woman meets criteria for co-occurring disorders and is appropriate for referral to the Alternative Interventions for Women treatment program. The examining psychologist makes a final report to the judge, including treatment recommendations.

THE PROGRAM IN OPERATION

Women deemed eligible for the program are introduced to the program with a packet of information that includes the following:

- Mission and purpose of the program;

- Consent to treatment and to collaboration with probation;;

- Introduction to basic elements of the program, including group, individual, and case management; and

- Explanations of medical-somatic services, program days and times, staff, expectations for the participants, assessment of participant's practical needs such as childcare and transportation, and expected outcomes.

The Alternative Interventions for Women treatment program has three stages: the Core Program, Transition/Aftercare; and Community Reintegration.

The Core Program

The Core Program, which includes a pre-treatment group, is intensive and each woman is required to attend from 9:00 a.m. to 3:00 p.m. daily, five days/week, for at least five weeks and up to three months. Aftercare is available after completion of the program. Each woman starts by setting personal goals for the program and developing, with staff guidance, an individual treatment plan. Outcomes will be assessed at the beginning and end of the program, and at the completion of the aftercare program.

Dr. Stephanie Covington's (1999) Model, *Helping Women Recover,* is at the core of the program, along with the Dartmouth/New Hampshire model of treatment for individuals with co-occurring disorders (Becker & Drake, 2003). Additional groups that all women are expected to attend involve:

- Co-occurring disorders;

- Stages and progression of mental health and substance abuse;

- Program participation;

- Changing behavior; and

- Alcoholics/Narcotics Anonymous groups.

In addition to these core sessions, each client, in collaboration with a clinician, when developing a treatment plan will choose group sessions that are specific to her individual needs. Some options to choose from include the following:

- Anger management;

- Assertiveness;

- Anxiety management (relaxation and meditation);

- Brain functioning;

- Communication skills;

- Conflict resolution;

- Culture;

- Educational issues (GED);

- Feelings;

- Humor;

- Leisure activities;

- Medications (identifying and managing them);

- Mental Illness (bipolar, depression, panic disorder, PTSD);

- Nutrition;

- Self-esteem;

- Smoking cessation;

- Stress relief;

- Symptom management;

- Values; and

- Vocational issues.

As mentioned earlier, the women are also expected to attend community Alcoholics/Narcotics Anonymous groups as they progress through treatment. The program has an all female staff and offers a safe environment for the clients. A therapeutic lunch is provided daily, during which time women can work on socialization skills or incorporate a recent Alcoholics Anonymous meeting. Staff shares meals with the women.

Transition/Aftercare

At the end of the five weeks, each participant's schedule is re-evaluated according to her needs. A treatment-planning meeting will take place with each woman to determine whether her continued level of care indicates one of the following:

- Continued five days-a-week attendance in the program;

- Program attendance can be reduced to three days a week; or

- Completion of the program (ready for aftercare).

At the end of five weeks, a treatment-planning meeting will take place in order for each woman to evaluate her progress in meeting her goals. Her schedule will then be adjusted according to her needs.

Community Reintegration

A critical component of the program is community reintegration. Clients are at high risk for relapse as they leave the milieu of the successful treatment program where services have been delivered, connections made, and community built within one program.

To address this risk, personalized community support planning for community reintegration will begin during the Core Program. These community support services will establish connections between the client and community providers, in many cases actually enrolling clients in programs, arranging jobs and assisting women in making appropriate child care plans.

A strong collaborative partnership is key to the success of this initiative and an integral component of this collaborative is the commitment to measurable outcomes. Evaluation of each woman at each step of the program is done in measurable terms, using standardized and nationally normed measurement tools. Data is reviewed in an ongoing way as part of a continuous quality management plan and these data are used to drive program modifications and establish performance standards.

About the Authors

Mary Carol Melton is Assistant Director of Central Clinic of Cincinnati, OH. Mary Grace, M.Ed., is Outcomes and Quality Management Director of Central Clinic. Walter S. Smitson, Ph.D., is President and CEO of Central Clinic. Nancy Schmidtgoessling, Ph.D., is Director of Court Clinic, Cincinnati, OH.

References

Becker, D. R., & Drake, R. E., *A Working Life for People With Severe Mental Illness* (Oxford University Press, 2003).

Covington, S., *Helping Women Recover: A Program for Treating Substance Abuse* (special edition for the criminal justice system) (Jossey-Bass, 1999).

Grace, M., O'Donnell, J., Walters, W., Smitson, W. S., & Melton, M. C., "The Women's Assessment Project: Final Report," 3(4) *Women, Girls & Criminal Justice* 53-54, 57 (June/July 2002).

Chapter 50

Day Reporting Program for Women in Pennsylvania

by Joyce Dougherty, Ph.D.

INTRODUCTION

The PROGRAM for Women and Families in Allentown, Pennsylvania, operates a day reporting program that not only keeps women who would otherwise be incarcerated out of prison, but also teaches them the skills they need, and provides them with the support they require, to prevent them from reentering the criminal justice system. This chapter provides a brief overview of this community-based, intermediate punishment program and details the findings of a research project on *Working With Emotions*, the stress management component of the day reporting program.

This chapter originally appeared in Women, Girls & Criminal Justice, *Vol. 4, No. 2, February/March 2003.*

THE DAY REPORTING PROGRAM: AN OVERVIEW

Originally, the sole focus of the day reporting program was to help women who were preparing to leave prison and to secure employment in the community. Since its inception in 1993, however, the day reporting program has evolved into a comprehensive 12-week structured program that teaches disadvantaged women transitioning out of the criminal justice system to overcome adversity and to develop self-sufficiency.

Client Demographics

The adversity women in the day reporting program face is graphically illustrated by the demographics of typical clients. They are young—usually between 20 to 34 years of age—single mothers with an average of three children. These aging adolescent mothers are poor, typically earning anywhere from $10,000 to $18,000 a year, well below Allentown's median annual income of $34,345. (MESH, July 1996, p. 22.) They are disproportionately minority women. A recent study of the Allentown area showed that 2% of the general population is African American and 5% is Hispanic/Latino. By contrast, 27% of the program's clients are African American and 23% are Hispanic/Latino. Women in the program are undereducated and underemployed. Seventy-one percent have not graduated from high school. Their educational testing level is between sixth and eighth grades in reading and fourth and sixth grades in math. Seventy-eight percent have a sporadic work history or no work history at all. They come to the program with just over three prior convictions, most of which are for drug related, non-violent offenses.

The day reporting program serves women who struggle with the long-term effects of extreme abuse. Eighty percent report having been the victims of some form of domestic violence. Sixty-three percent report having been the victims of sexual abuse as children. Additionally, 10% to 15% of the women who have been abused *do not* report it during the intake process.

Impact of Violence/Need for Programming

These women have come to look upon violence as the norm in interpersonal relationships, and as a result they have difficulty identifying the abusiveness of the violence they have endured. Women only begin to recognize what they have experienced as abuse after working with the day reporting program's counselor. This "normalization of violence" is most apt to occur among women who have been severely abused multiple times and in varied ways over an extended period of time (Dougherty, 1998, p. 240). Kelly, Thornberry, and Smith (1997) note the long-term consequences of child abuse often encompass a wide variety of emotional and interpersonal problems including anxiety, impulsiveness, anger, aggression, inattentiveness, and withdrawal. These are the kinds of problems the women bring with them when they are referred to our program. Typically, they exhibit signs of chronic depression and anxiety. According to Goleman (1998), the capacity to learn can be crippled by this kind of continual emotional distress. He asserts, "people who cannot marshal some control over their emotional life fight inner battles that sabotage their ability for focused work and clear thought" (p. 36). They will act, as so many of the day reporting program clients do, impulsively—reacting before thinking, relying on maladaptive coping skills to survive. What this suggests is that before these women can learn to lead productive, self-sufficient lives—how to hold down a job, how to stay clean and sober, how to be responsible mothers—they need to learn healthy ways to manage the stress that has overwhelmed their lives for so long. That is why stress management and individual supportive counseling have emerged as the two key components of the program.

Client Enrollment

The Day Reporting Program has a system of open enrollment—as one woman completes the 12-week program, another woman may just be enrolling. Judges or prison treatment staff refer women directly to the county work release facility with the stipulation that they enroll in the program. Women do not enter the program voluntarily. Clients who do not reside in the work release facility while attending the program may be ordered there by county probation. Like their work release counterparts, these community-based clients do not enter the program voluntarily either.

Program Components

Classes are held every day from 9:00 a.m. to 3:00 p.m. On Thursday, classes run until 4:30 p.m. to accommodate the stress management program. In addition to individual supportive counseling and stress management components, the women have access to job readiness training, vocational and employment counseling, adult basic education including GED classes, and nutrition, HIV prevention education, and parenting instruction. As we demonstrate in the next section, graduates of the day reporting program leave with the tools they need to transition into self-sufficiency, to make healthy choices, and to access the community-based services they need to live lives free of abuse.

Program Impact

Typically the day reporting program serves an average of 50 to 60 women every year. In 2001, 85% of those receiving individual supportive counseling showed an average increase of 20 points in an inventory measuring improvement in communication skills. Of the 93% who graduated, 77% demonstrated an increase of 20 points or more in tests that measured improvement in life-skills (i.e., problem-solving, decision-making, and household budgeting). Of those participating in the GED classes, 30% passed the first time they took the test. Coming to the program with a sporadic work history or no work history at all, an impressive 69% of the women found employment upon graduation.

STRESS MANAGEMENT PROGRAMMING

Working With Emotions, which began as a grant supported pilot project in 1998, is an innovative stress management program that has been modified from a hospital-based stress management model to meet the specific emotional needs and abilities of the women enrolled in the day reporting program. Originally, the five primary objectives of the research project funded were:

1. To show a significant reduction in "global distress" (i.e., depression, anxiety, anger, and hostility) among 50% of the women who successfully complete the three month *Working With Emotions* program;

2. To find 45% to 50% of the women participating in the program follow-up leading less stressful, productive lives in the community one year after successful completion of *Working With Emotions*;

3. To determine which women benefit most from this type of treatment intervention;

4. To assess how effective *Working With Emotions* program is as an intervention that is integrated into an already established, well structured treatment program (i.e., the agency's day reporting program) versus how effective it is as a relatively independently functioning treatment intervention (i.e., as a program referral for women housed at the county work release facility but not enrolled in the day reporting program); and

5. To have all agency staff who interact with the target population on a routine basis be able to support the effort to reduce stress among the women by acquiring a basic understanding of the *Working With Emotions* program.

After the first year of the project, we determined that *Working With Emotions* was more effective if integrated into a well-established and -structured treatment program, such as the day reporting program. As a result, we stopped offering it at the end of the first year of the project as an independently functioning treatment intervention to the women at the work release facility.

Working With Emotions: Activities and Evaluation

As originally proposed, the six strategic components of the *Working With Emotions* program were:

1. The initial assessment;

2. The 12 weeks of the *Working With Emotions* instruction;

3. The peer educator training and daily practice sessions;

4. The staff in-services;

5. The final assessment; and

6. The program follow-up.

We hoped to implement all six components by the end of the project's second year. With the exception of the fourth component—the staff in-services—this was accomplished during the first year of the project with only minor modifications of the original plan.

In November 1999, we began the initial assessment of all of the women enrolled in the *Working With Emotions* program. This involved administering three reliable and valid testing instruments. First, the Symptom Check List 90-Revised (SCL-90-R) was used as a pre- and post-test because it measures the number and intensity of a variety of key symptoms including anxiety, phobic anxiety, depression, somatization, hostility, paranoid ideation, psychoticism, obsessive-compulsive, and interpersonal sensitivity. Second, the Structured Interview of Reported Symptoms (SIRS) was used to identify inconsistent reporting that would verify the reliability of the SCL-90-R findings. Finally, the Toronto Alexithymia Scale (TAS-20) was used as a baseline personality trait measure. Alexithymic individuals are unable to identify their own feelings. They do not communicate emotional distress effectively to others and, therefore, typically do not seek others out for help when they experience distress (Dunn & Brown, 1991). They also tend to release tension through impulsive, sometimes violent acts (Keltikangas-Jarvinenk, 1982). The hypothesis was that the women who measured high on the alexithymia scale would not benefit as much from the *Working With Emotions* program as the woman who measured low on the scale. If this hypothesis held up, then the TAS-20 could be used as a screening tool to determine who might benefit most from the program.

The following year, we continued the 12-week program of *Working With Emotions* in uninterrupted consecutive cycles. As was the case during the project's first year, instead of requiring homework to be completed outside of class, readings were done out loud to ensure certain materials were covered. Classroom presentations used less technical language and terminology that might otherwise be used to ensure all of the women could understand and follow the program. Due to the physical limitations of the population, no physical exercises were included. Finally, we continued to maintain a system of open enrollment.

As was also the case in the project's first year, we modified implementation of the peer educator component of the study. Originally, we planned to select three women who had completed the program and pay them as peer educators responsible for facilitating the daily practice of stress management techniques. However, the facilitator/instructor of *Working With Emotions*, in consultation with agency staff, determined it would be therapeutically more beneficial for clients to do this work voluntarily—receiving a special certificate of achievement rather than monetary compensation. Additionally, we decided that volunteers for peer educator positions should be selected from among the women currently enrolled in the program, since graduates of the program usually leave to pursue jobs.

As planned, the final assessments using the SCL-90-R as the post-test measure were done on all of the women who successfully completed the 30-hour program. During the final assessment, the follow-up component of the program was explained to each woman. All of the women were informed they would receive a monetary incentive of $20 each time they participated in the follow-up program. They were asked to leave an address and phone number where they could be reached three months after the final assessment for the first follow-up, then again six months after that assessment, and finally again nine months after the final assessment for a full year after they began the program. The follow-up work began on schedule, using information given by the women as to their whereabouts, as well as information from agency staff.

Analysis of the data collected throughout the year was completed at the end of the second year of the project.

Setbacks/Obstacles

All of the project's objectives were achieved successfully, with the exception of objective five. Once again, during the second year, the staff in-service component could not be implemented because the schedule of the *Working With Emotions* facilitator/instructor conflicted with the times when agency staff was available. Nonetheless, lack of staff training appears *not* to have had a negative impact on the effectiveness of the *Working With Emotions* program.

Other setbacks or obstacles called for minor modifications of the original plan. In the second year, the project coordinator continued to have difficulty identifying viable candidates for the control group. Given the extensive nature of the pre- and post-testing process, women not enrolled in *Working With Emotions* often challenged the legitimacy of personal, probing questions. Many simply refused to participate. Ultimately, only six women were recruited for the control group in the second year and, as the data analysis later revealed, only three of the six sets of responses were reliable. All three reliable participants in the control group re-offended prior to the end of the year.

We were not surprised that the project's follow up work was difficult. Program clients are an extremely poor, transient population. Of the total number of women that completed the *Working With Emotions* program, only 47% participated in the follow-up testing. When no direct contact could be made to continue the post-testing process, we examined official county records to learn whether or not any of the women re-entered the criminal justice system. This enabled us to accurately determine the recidivism rate of the project's participants.

Study Findings

If recidivism is measured by monitoring who returns to prison, then one of the findings of this research project is that it has established an accurate recidivism rate for this population. The recidivism rate is 39% among graduates of the day reporting program who have been out of the program one year or more. This means that 61% of the women did not end up back in prison one year after completing the program. This is a remarkable figure for a population with an average of three prior convictions.

More significant findings relate back to the following objectives:

Is There a Reduction in Stress? Results show a statistically significant decline between the pre- and post-test scores among the 43 program participants on the Global Severity Index (SCL-90-R) in the latest analysis. Of these 43 participants, 30 (70%) had at least a five-point reduction (exceeding the original objective's mark by 20%).

Does the Stress Reduction Last? Of the participants who completed the follow-up component at the time of the last analysis, 47% maintained a Global Severity Index (SCL-90-R) score similar to the score they had when they completed *Working With Emotions*. This falls within the grasp of our second objective, which predicted 45% to 50% of participants would reduce this level of stress after a full year of completing the program.

Is Distress Related to Emotional Intelligence? This remains one of the more interesting findings. The original hypothesis was that women who scored high on the alexithymia scale (TAS-20) would benefit less from the program than those who scored low. Within the current analysis, those who scored high on the alexithemia scale (indicating some difficulty identifying and discriminating emotion) had an average of 10-point reduction on their Global Severity Index whereas non-alexithymic participants had on average a five-point reduction. What this means is that high scores alone did not present an obstacle to benefiting from the program. This also means that using the TAS-20 as an intake tool for *Working With Emotions* would be ill-advised.

CONCLUSION

The day reporting program described here is a highly effective intermediate punishment program that not only serves to keep women out of prison immediately after sentencing, but also keeps the majority of women who graduate from the program—women with chronic patterns of re-offending—from returning to prison. Replicating the program is not as much of a challenge as establishing the funding to support it. While the program is clearly more cost effective than imprisoning women, providing such comprehensive programming to women who have been convicted of crimes can be difficult in politically hostile communities. Demonstrating the effectiveness of the day reporting program through grant-funded research has proven vital to the continuation of its funding and expansion of its services.

About the Author

Joyce Dougherty, Ph.D., is Executive Director, The Program for Women and Families, Inc.

References

Dougherty, J., "Female Offenders and Childhood Maltreatment: Understanding the Connections." In R.T. Zaplin, (Ed.), *Female Offenders: Critical Perspectives and Effective Interventions* (pp. 227-244) (Aspen Publishers, 1998).

Dunn, J. & Brown J., "Relationships, Talk About Feelings and the Development of Affect Regulation in Early Childhood." In J. Garber & K.A. Dodge, (Eds.), *The Development of Emotion Regulation and Dysregulation* (pp. 89-108) (Cambridge University Press, 1991).

Goleman, D., *Working With Emotional Intelligence* (Bantam Books, 1998).

Kelly, B.T., Thornberry, T.P., & Smith, C.A., "In the Wake of Childhood Maltreatment." (*Juvenile justice bulletin*, NCJ Publication No. 165257) (U.S. Department of Justice, 1997).

Keltikangas-Javinenk, L. , "Alexithymia in Violent Offenders," 46 *Journal of Personality Assessment*, 462-467 (1982).

Measurable Enhancement of the Status of Health in the Lehigh Valley (MESH), A report prepared for the Rider Pool Health Care Trust (Department of Community and Health Studies, Lehigh Valley Hospital, July, 1996).

Chapter 51

Changing Minds:
Going to College at a
Maximum-Security Prison

by Michelle Fine, Ph.D., Maria Elena Torre, M.A.,
Kathy Boudin, M.A., Iris Bowen, M.A., Judith Clark, M.A.,
Donna Hylton, M.A., Migdalia Martinez, B.A.,
"Missy (Anonymous Prisoner)," Rosemarie A. Roberts, Ph.D.,
Pamela Smart, M.A., M.S. and Debora Upegui

An earlier version of this chapter appeared in Women, Girls & Criminal Justice, *Vol. 4, Nos. 2 and 3, February/March 2003 and April/May 2003. This chapter is an extended excerpt adapted from the September 2001 Report,* Changing Minds: The Impact of College in a Maximum Security Prison *(www.changing minds.ws), and is used with permission.*

INTRODUCTION

A broad based multi-method research design was undertaken to document the impact of a college program within a maximum-security prison on incarcerated women, the prison environment, and women released from confinement. This chapter reveals the extraordinary personal, social, and fiscal costs that all Americans pay today for not educating prisoners and also offers national and local policymakers and activists a new policy direction that creates safer communities; reduces re-incarceration rates; and helps prisoners, their families, and the prison environment.

Three main conclusions organize the findings:

- *College-in-prison reduces re-incarceration rates and saves taxpayer money.* A cost/benefit analysis demonstrates that it is fiscally far more efficient to provide access to higher education for prisoners than to incur the inflated rates of re-incarceration and diminished employability likely to result from no access to higher education;

- *College-in-prison enables positive management of the prison environment.* Interviews with prison administrators, corrections officers, women in prison, and college faculty confirm that the presence of a college program alters the prison environment by rendering it safer and more manageable with fewer disciplinary incidents; and

- *College-in-prison transforms the lives of students and their children and promotes lasting transitions out of prison.* Reduced re-incarceration rates occur because involvement in college provides women in prison with skills, knowledge, and healthier social networks necessary for successful transitions out of prison.

BACKGROUND

In 1994, President Bill Clinton signed the Violent Crime Control and Law Enforcement Act, which included a provision that denied incarcerated men and women access to Pell Grants. In that year, over 350 college programs in prisons were shut down throughout the nation. This federal tuition assistance program, previously available to all low-income persons, supported most college-in-prison programs. New York State, like most other states, soon withdrew its financial support for college-in-prison programs, and effectively ended all higher education for men and women in prisons across the state. In 1997, however, a maximum-security prison for women located in Westchester County, just north of New York City, reestablished a college-in-prison program through a consortium of private colleges and universities, community members, prisoners, and the facility's superintendent.

In this chapter, we report empirically on the effects of that college program on its students and the prison environment. The analysis focuses on the impact of college on women while inside prison; the effects of college on the prison environment; the effects of college on other inmates; the effects of a mother's college experience on her children; and the long term effects of college on the economic, social, and civic engagements of women once released from prison.

Neither federal nor state governments pay for prison-based higher education programs, with the exception of recent funding for youthful offenders. A federal grant program—Workplace and Community Transition for Incarcerated Youth Offenders—provides funding to state correctional education agencies to "assist and encourage incarcerated youths to acquire functional literacy and life and job skills through the pursuit of a post-secondary education certificate, or an associate or arts or bachelor's degree while in prison." In addition, eligible correctional education programs should provide "employment counseling and other related services which start during incarceration and continue through prerelease and while on parole." State correctional education agencies applying for funding of post-secondary education programs must provide services to "youth offenders" who are 25 years of age or younger.

Given the precarious state of higher education within prison facilities, then, it is important to document the consequences of current public policy that does not support college-in-prison programs and to evaluate the costs and benefits of a college program that is broadly available to prisoners within a maximum-security facility.

The subject of this study, the College Bound program at the Bedford Hills Correctional Facility (BHCF) in Bedford Hills, New York, is a fully volunteer effort. In the midst of national conversations about prison reform, education in prison, and transitions out of prison, this report reintroduces a debate about college-in-prison programs to the public agenda.

INMATES' EDUCATIONAL NEEDS

Most women and men in our nation's jails and prisons come from economically depressed African-American and Hispanic/Latino/a communities with failing urban schools. In New York State, according to figures from the New York State Department of Correctional Services and the Correctional Association of New York, there were 73,826 people in New York State prisons in January 2001, up from 12,500 in 1973 and 28,500 in 1983. The state prison population is 84% African American and Hispanic; 65% of the total population is from New York City, almost all from poor communities of color. Approximately two-thirds of the men and women in New York State prisons have neither a high school diploma nor a GED. This figure jumps to 90% in New York City jails, where between 50% and 70% of the adult inmate population reads below the sixth grade level in English.

The women at BHCF reflect national and state trends. Fifty-one percent of the women enter BHCF with neither a high school diploma nor a GED. Most of these women lived in poor neighborhoods of New York City prior to arrest and over 80% are African American or Latina.

While our country may waffle on whether or not we believe prisoners are entitled to higher education, we are consistent with respect to who ends up in prison—men and women who have never received adequate education. It is no small irony, then, that those most often denied quality education prior to their involvement with prison are also those most likely to serve time in prisons and jails.

Understanding the link between educational inequities and incarceration, the National Prison Association, which subsequently became the American Correctional Association (ACA), endorsed a provision in 1870 for education within prison. In 1970, 100 years after this declaration was written, sections 136 and 137 of the Corrections Law in the State of New York were passed, requiring the Department of Correctional Services to assess a prisoner's "educational and vocational needs" and "provide each inmate with a program of education which seems most likely to further the process of socialization and rehabilitation, the objective being to return these inmates to society with a more wholesome attitude toward living, with a desire to conduct themselves as good citizens, and with the skills and knowledge which will give them a reasonable chance to maintain themselves and their dependents through honest labor."

Nationally, federal support for higher education in prison materialized in the form of allowing incarcerated women and men eligibility for Pell grants, the non-competitive, needs-based federal funding available to qualifying low-income students. In New York State, Pell grants were supplemented with Tuition Assistance Program (TAP) grants to subsidize college-in-prison programs. From 1970 through 1994, the federal and state governments were true to their commitments to support prison-based higher education.

In 1994, when federal support was removed for prison-based education programs, extensive research demonstrated that recidivism rates decline significantly with higher education (Clark, 1991; Lockwood, 1988; Tracy & Johnson, 1994). Despite this evidence, all but eight of the 350 college programs in prisons nationwide were swiftly closed. As public funds for college education in New York State prisons were eliminated, Mercy College closed its successful college program, which had run at BHCF from 1984 through 1994.

BEDFORD HILLS' RESPONSE TO LOSS OF ORIGINAL COLLEGE PROGRAM

Given the extraordinarily low levels of educational achievement with which most women enter prison, women and corrections officers at BHCF reported this loss was not only educationally consequential but also profound in terms of morale and discipline.

The last graduation took place in June 1995. During the following weeks, the women who had staffed the Learning Center, who had received their bachelor's and master's degrees and who had acted as role models, packed books, put computers in boxes, took posters off walls, and turned their learning center into an empty shell. A feeling of despair settled over the prison as women experienced a loss of hope about their own futures and the futures of younger women coming into the prison.

Soon, however, community members and educational leaders began to gather information as to how they could restore college-in-prison at BHCF. In March 1996, seven women in BHCF asked to meet with Superintendent Elaine Lord and the Deputy Superintendent of Programs about the possible restoration of the college program. Shortly thereafter, the Superintendent and Deputy Superintendent, the Inmate Committee, and a local community leader convened a meeting to explore the possibility of creating a new, privately funded college program. The response from citizen groups across Westchester County and New York City was immediate and positive. A strong alliance emerged between three communities: the prison community (administration, staff, and incarcerated women); the Westchester and metropolitan New York City community, including hundreds of citizens committed to the return of college and responsible for equipping the Learning Center with staff, desks, files, computers, and books; and the academic community, led by the President of Marymount Manhattan College, which served as the degree granting institution.

Over the next few months, a Task Force was established consisting of community members from the Westchester area; local government officials; local clergy and church members; professors and administrators from local colleges and universities; and officials from BHCF and inmates from the Inmate Advisory Committee. It was at this point that the concept of a "consortium of colleges" was realized. If one college would offer the degree, then many colleges could work together to donate courses. The Superintendent, the inmates, and community members generated Statements of Commitment. By the spring of 1997, a Bachelor of Arts (BA) in sociology program was underway in the facility.

DEMOGRAPHICS—GENERAL POPULATION AND BEDFORD HILLS WOMEN IN COLLEGE

The BHCF functions as the maximum-security correctional facility for women in New York State and as the reception center for all women entering the state system. Women in the general population number approximately 650 and serve an average minimum sentence of 8 1/3 years, with close to 200 women serving far more. Over 75% of the women are mothers, most with children under the age of 18. Seventy-eight percent of the women at BHCF are from New York City and its suburban areas. They range in age from 16 to 75 years, with 52% African American, 29% Latina, 16% White, and the remainder Native or Asian American. Substantial numbers of the women at BHCF report long histories of child sexual abuse (Bowen, 1998; Finkle, 1998). Seventy-five percent have histories with drug and/or alcohol abuse (Browne, Miller, & Maguin, 1999; Mancuso & Miller, 1999). Many were incarcerated as juveniles (Burnett, 1998). Twenty-five percent have previously attempted suicide, and over 50% have a history and/or carry a diagnosis of mental illness (Lord, 2000). That said, the women at BHCF mirror the men and women of the broader national prison population (Browne, 1987; Richie, 1996).

The women who have attended college at BHCF from 1997 to 2000 came to prison, for the most part, with histories of academic failure. Upon entering the facility, 43% held neither high school diploma nor GED; 21% had a GED; 22% had a high school diploma; and 14% had some college credits.

Since the rebirth of the college program, a total of 196 women at BHCF have become college students (defined as completing at least one semester of college classes). Fifteen students have earned Associate of Arts (AA) degrees as of this writing, and eight have earned Bachelor of Arts (BA) degrees.

As of Spring 2000, 55% (108) of the original cohort remained as active students. Thirty-one percent (62) interrupted their studies because they were sent to other facilities; 10% (19) were paroled. With a strikingly low drop out rate, only 4% of the students are currently inactive, which in practice means "once enrolled for at least a semester but not registered for classes within the last three semesters."

At least 16% of the women who have been part of the College Bound program started their college education in the original Mercy College program. Thirteen of the first 23 college degrees (AAs and BAs together) awarded by the College Bound program were awarded to former Mercy College students.

Interestingly, the groups of women not well served by public education on the outside (young adults of poverty, disproportionately African American and Latina) are the women, aged 17 to 58 years, who are now pursuing rigorous college education behind bars at BHCF (Bowen & Bok, 1998). African Americans represent 59% of the college students at BHCF, whites 27%, Latinas 13%, and "other" 1%.

Pre-college is an essential feature of the College Bound program, it is important to note. Women who have neither a high school diploma nor a GED upon arriving at BHCF rely heavily on pre-college preparation to gain entry into the college. At least 64% (126) of these college students, at one point or another, participated in pre-college classes to improve their math, reading and/or writing skills in English. Often women who pass the English requirement will continue to take pre-college math and college classes simultaneously, until they pass the math requirement.

STUDY PARAMETERS

Research Design

The research reported in here was designed to answer four questions:

1. *What are the fiscal costs and benefits of providing college to women in prison, and what are the fiscal costs and benefits of withholding college from women in prison?* Outcomes include financial costs of provision of college, and calculations for re-incarceration rates with and without college.

2. *What is the impact of college-in-prison on the safety and management of the prison environment?* Outcomes include prison disciplinary environment, prison climate, corrections officers' views of and experiences with college, and faculty views of the college program.

3. *What are the personal and social effects of college-in-prison on students and their children?* Outcomes include academic, social, and psychological effects including academic achievement and perseverance; sense of responsibility for past and future; personal transformation; and civic engagement in prison and beyond.

4. *What is the impact of the college experience on the transition home from prison?* Outcomes include economic well being; health; civic participation; continued pursuit of higher education; relations with family, children, and friends; and re-incarceration rates.

Methods

Conducted over the course of three years, the research design required a quantitative analysis to assess the extent to which college affected re-incarceration rates (conducted by the New York State Department of Correctional Services) and thereby affected the tax burden imposed on citizens of New York State for prisons (conducted in part by Michael Jacobson, a former Commissioner of the New York City Department of Corrections, former Commissioner of Probation and former Deputy Director of the New York City Office of Management and Budget). A qualitative analysis was undertaken to determine the psychosocial effects of college on the women, the prison environment, the children of students, and post-release transitions.

The methods include:

- *Archival analysis:* Review of the records of the college program since inception (1997), tracking rates of persistence, women drafted (transferred to other prisons mid-sentence), drop out rates, racial and ethnic distribution, percent in pre-college and college courses;

- *Inmate initiated research:* The impact of college, which consisted of one-on-one interviews of four to five women each by 15 inmates (N=65 interviews by 15 inmates);

- *Focus group interviews:* Interviews conducted with women at BHCF, selected on the basis of the women's status in the program: dropouts; ABE/GED students; pre-college students; first-time college students; adolescent children of women in college; college leaders/mentors; women in the ESL class (N=43);

- *Individual interviews with women who were in college at BHCF, now released from prison:* Each interview was conducted at the Graduate Center, City University, and lasted anywhere from one to three hours. Women were compensated $50 for participating in the interview (N=20);

- *Interviews with corrections administrators and officers:* In order to understand the impact of the college program on the prison environment, interviews were conducted with administrators and corrections officers (N=6). Each interview lasted between 20 and 40 minutes;

- *Focus group interviews:* Surveys of educators. In order to document the impact of the college program on educators and college communities, a focus group with college faculty (N=20) was conducted by the research team in 1999. A survey was distributed to faculty in the Spring 2000 semester (N=33). Two group discussions were held with the Presidents of the Consortium universities (seven Presidents or designees);

- *Quantitative tracking of women who attended college while in prison and a comparison group of women who did not attend:* Two hundred and seventy four women who participated in the Mercy College program at BHCF and a comparison group of 2,031 women who did not attend college during the same period of time were tracked statistically to document the rates of re-incarceration for women who did not attend college; women who attended some classes but received no degree; women who earned an AA degree; and women who earned a BA degree. This analysis was conducted by E. Michele Staley of the New York State Department of Correctional Services;

- *Cost/benefit analysis:* Fiscal analysis of the College Bound Program, relying on data from 2000-2001, was conducted, in part, by Michael Jacobson of the John Jay College of Criminal Justice.

IMPACT OF COLLEGE ON CRIME, TAXES, AND RE-INCARCERATION RATES

Re-Incarceration Rates for Inmates With and Without College-in-Prison

Evidence of the impact of higher education in reducing rates of re-incarceration, and therefore reducing further crime, is remarkably consistent (Harer, 1994; Anderson, Anderson, & Schumacher, 1988; Beck & Shipley, 1989; Gainous, 1992; Holloway & Moke, 1986). Indeed, a national review of 20 empirical studies reveals that higher education in prison dramatically reduces re-incarceration rates for both men and women (Johnson, 2001). Quality education prior to, during, and after prison has enormous benefits for individuals, families, and communities.

In 1991, the New York State Department of Correctional Services (NYSDOCS) conducted a recidivism study that concluded, "Inmate college program participants in 1986-1987 who had earned a degree were found to return at a significantly lower rate than participants who did not earn a degree" (NYSDOCS, 1991).

Six years later, the Center on Crime, Communities and Culture of the Open Society Institute (1997) published a comprehensive literature review on education and prison that concluded, "Programmatic efforts to reduce recidivism have ranged from boot camps and shock incarceration facilities to prison-based education efforts. The effectiveness of these programs varies, but research shows that prison-based education and literacy programs are much more effective at lowering recidivism rates than either boot camps or shock incarceration" (pp 5-6).

In order to investigate the question of re-incarceration for the BHCF College Bound program, the research team requested from the NYDOCS a replication of the 1991 longitudinal analysis to determine the extent to which women in the Mercy College program were returned to custody within 36 months. E. Michele Staley, a NYSDOCS program evaluator, undertook a longitudinal analysis of the re-incarceration rates for the BHCF women who had participated in the Mercy College program. Using the standard measure of 36 months, 21 college participants returned to custody out of the 274 women tracked longitudinally. Women who participated in college while in prison had a 7.7% return-to-custody rate. In contrast, an analysis tracking all 2,031 female offenders released between 1985 and 1995 revealed a 29.9% return-to-custody rate, within 36 months.

Women without college-in-prison programming are almost four times more likely to be returned to custody than women who participated in college while in prison. Women without college-in-prison programming are twice as likely to be rearrested for a new crime than women with any college while in prison. Further, women without college-in-prison are 18 times more likely to violate parole than women with any college. This is particularly significant given that 92% of the "with college" sample were convicted of violent felonies. In other words, college-in-prison programming reduces the amount of post-release crime and even more significantly heightens responsible compliance with parole expectations.

These data confirm earlier studies that suggest it is efficient social policy to offer inmates quality higher education within prison (Barton & Cooley, 1996). As the remainder of this text will testify, college enables women in prison to experience personal growth and refine a sense of personal and social responsibility; college has become a "positive management tool" for prison administrators and staff, and college-in-prison appears to be a significant feature of successful transitions out of prison.

As former Attorney General Janet Reno has commented on women and men who are released from prison every year, "In the year 2000, 585,000 [were] anticipated to return [from prison] to communities. They come into prison with rage, with a sense that they had been treated unfairly. They come into prison as dropouts or illiterate. They come into prison without life skills, without a job or an anticipated job. They come with so little chance of getting off on the right foot, unless we do it the right way. [I]s it any surprise that nationwide two-thirds are rearrested?"

Cost-Benefit Analysis of Providing vs. Withholding College-in-Prison

Policymakers, community activists, journalists, and citizens are beginning to challenge the cumulative financial burden imposed on taxpayers because the government denies prisoners access to college and other support services.

Fox Butterfield (2000) argued in *The New York Times* that a "revolving door parole policy" is made worse through the absence of developmental programs within prison facilities. The OSI Center for Crime, Communities and Culture reports that over the long term the expense of providing higher education to women and men in prison is minimal relative to the costs of re-arrests, additional crime, and re-imprisonment, because an estimated 97% of adult felony inmates are released back into local communities and because recidivism rates now average between 40% to 60% (Open Society Institute, 1997).

The OSI report argues,

> New York State estimates that it costs $2,500 per year per individual to provide higher education in a correctional facility. In contrast the average cost of incarcerating an adult inmate per year is $25,000. Why are correctional education programs so inexpensive? For the most part, higher education in correctional facilities is provided by community colleges and universities that offer moderately priced tuition. A combination of funding sources supports an inmate's education, including in-kind donations from universities and colleges, outside support (foundations, community-based organizations, private donations), and individual contributions from inmates themselves, garnered while working at prison-based jobs.... Even in a hypothetical situation with a comparatively expensive correctional higher education program ($2,500 per year, per inmate in New York State) and one of the highest recorded rates of recidivism upon completion of such a program (15%), the savings of providing higher education are still substantial: The cost of incarcerating 100 individuals over 4 years is approximately $10 million. For an additional 1/10th of that cost, or $1 million, those same individuals could be given a full, four-year college education while incarcerated. Assuming a recidivism rate of 15% (as opposed to the general rate of 40-60%), 85 of those initial 100 individuals will not return to prison, saving U.S. taxpayers millions of dollars each year. In addition to the millions saved by preventing an individual's return to incarceration and dependence on the criminal justice system, providing higher education to prisoners can save money in other ways. The prevention of crime helps to eliminate costs to crime victims and the courts, lost wages of the inmate while incarcerated, or costs to the inmate's family." (p.5-6).

Cost estimates of college-in-prison programs after 1995 confirm relatively low per-student instructional costs for college-in-prison. In June 2001, Michael Jacobson calculated the estimates for the Center for Redirection/College Bound and found that costs per student average approximately $1,465.45.

To estimate the costs and benefits over time of college-in-prison, consider the case of 100 men or women who cost an average of $25,000 per year to incarcerate, totaling $2.5 million dollars per year. This is a very conservative estimate, insofar as the New York State cost in 1999 was $27,006.35 per inmate per year (Camp & Camp, 2000). With college calculated to cost $1,905 a year per student, the annual cost equals $2,690,500 per 100 educated inmates. While it is true that the same number of inmates without college costs $2,500,000 annually, the differential re-incarceration rates for the two groups turn this initial savings into an increased expense.

Following release, it is estimated that 7.7% of the educated group and 29.9% of the non-educated group will be re-incarcerated, conservatively, for an estimated average of two years. The extra expenses incurred for withholding college, for 100 women and men in prison (much less the full prison population in New York State), comes to almost $300,000 for one additional year of imprisonment and over $900,000 for two. This tax saving does not calculate the fiscal and emotional costs of foster care for children of incarcerated adults or elderly care for their parents, lost wages, and tax contributions, welfare dependency, disrupted families, and communities worsened by re-incarceration. Nor does it take into account the loss of emotional, financial, and civic resources that well-educated men and women, post-release, contribute to their families and communities.

As of January 2000, New York State had 73,826 prisoners. If only one-third of these men and women in prison were to participate in a college program while in prison, over $150,000,000 in tax dollars could be saved or, better yet, allocated to quality education to prevent imprisonment.

We do not argue that women and men in prison deserve more than other citizens. To the contrary, if prisoners had access to the same support as other citizens, the tax benefits to society at large, as well as the personal/social benefits to women and men in prison, their families and their communities would be enormous. At present, our tax dollars are paying the equivalent of an elite private college education for women and men in prison to be uneducated, without adequate drug treatment, and to emerge more cynical, more hardened, more difficult to employ, and less likely to engage in productive lives than before they entered prison.

COLLEGE AS A POSITIVE MANAGEMENT TOOL IN THE PRISON

> [College] opens the door to viable alternatives to cycles of criminal behavior and further incarceration. Within the prison, it can be a positive management tool motivating women to change.
> —Elaine Lord, Superintendent, BHCF

> I cannot stress enough how powerful a factor college has been in maintaining peace and well-being in prisons.
> —George W. Webber, Professor of Urban
> Ministry and President Emeritus, New York
> Theological Seminary

We could not collect direct evidence on disciplinary incidents for this study due to the strictly confidential nature of such reports, but interviews with administrators, corrections officers, inmates, and faculty consistently confirm the observations of Superintendent Lord and theologian Webber that college creates a more "peaceful" and manageable prison environment. Indeed, nationally, 93% of prison wardens strongly support educational and vocational programming for adult inmates (Elikann, 1996, p. 151). Disciplinary incidents are less likely to occur. When tensions do arise, educated inmates are more likely to opt away from trouble, especially if participation in college courses is jeopardized (Butterfield, 2001).

One student in the program said, "When faced with a confrontation, I walk away. I don't let them bother me…. I don't react to everything they say. In the past I would have fought the girl, [but now] I don't want to lose the program. I don't want to fight because I'm in college."

A corrections officer further observed, "I mean to a point where we don't have to worry about the stabbings, the fighting within the facility. College gives them something else to occupy their time and occupy their minds. The more educated the women are, the better they can express themselves and the easier it is to manage them. The better educated women can take care of themselves better within the facility."

Corrections officers who agreed to be interviewed for this study varied with respect to whether or not they believe that college-in-prison should be publicly funded, but they were unanimous in noting the positive impact of college on the women and the prison environment.

One officer, for instance, pleased with the program although disapproving of public funding for prisoner education, observed,

> Everyone should have an education, whether they are an inmate or a teenager on the street. Education improves a person. [The prison administration is] trying to do everything they can to improve the lives of these women. The women are here because they committed a crime and they really need to be helped and this is one way of giving them help. But it is not fair for taxpayers to be footing the bill, particularly when there are people who haven't committed crimes who can't afford to send their own kids to college, but college is a great way to keep the inmates occupied and busy so that they don't get into trouble. You don't want inmates to get out of prison with the same limited opportunities they had when they came in. You have to make sure they have some new opportunities, so that they can enter the blue-collar workforce.

Another officer who participated as a student in a sign language class with some of the college students said, "We learned each other's names and a lot of [inmate students] went into detail about how they grew up and what occurred in their families, so I found that to be very interesting and it gives you a different outlook as far as your feelings toward these women. You get to know them a little better. I mean, unfortunately, it could be any of us in the same position, it definitely could be any of us, but I'm glad I chose a different route, because it is not what I wanted, but unfortunately it happens."

All of the officers agreed that when funds were withdrawn from Mercy College, the loss of college caused "a definite change in morale, the women seemed deflated." In contrast, the presence of college enriches the prison environment in terms of discipline.

Said one officer, "Maturity! Maturity! They're more mature because they are learning and they have something to occupy their time and they have less time to get into other activities."

Faculty, students, and officers commented that women's involvement in and appreciation of college seemed to take the rough edge off of potentially tense or confrontational classroom moments. One faculty member noted that students in her classroom discipline each other. "I think in my Bedford classes, these are the only places I've ever taught where other students have cooperated in disciplining somebody who gets out of hand. I've never experienced that with such wisdom."

While faculty testify about the power of teaching within a prison, perhaps most compelling are the comments from corrections officers, often hard-working men and women struggling to support their own or their children's college educations. These officers, for the most part, resonate with the words of an officer who was initially quite skeptical about college-in-prison and yet went on to say:

> Well, [education] does a few things. Predominantly, it gives the inmates self-esteem that they lack when they come in. It gives them something to strive for. I mean, there are so many miracle stories down there [in the education department]. At first I was like, you know, as a corrections officer you learn to separate yourself. Inmates are inmates, and officers are officers. But after dealing with them on a one-to-one basis and you start learning about them, you get a sense that you get where they come from, what kind of background they had. They ask for advice and you become a counselor also, besides a corrections officer. And they'll bring you their grades and if they have a problem they come over and ask me to see if I can help them. And overall, the transformation they make from coming in initially. I can't even put it into words.

COLLEGE SUPPORTS POWERFUL TRANSFORMATIONS WITHIN STUDENTS AND THEIR CHILDREN

Statistics provided by NYSDOCS and Michael Jacobson tell us that college-in-prison programming reduces re-incarceration, crime, and taxes. Corrections administrators and officers report that college diminishes the likelihood of disciplinary incidents. The interviews with women in prison and their children, correction officers, faculty, community members, and women post-release tell us why. In some ways the story is simple. College offers an opportunity for women in prison to think, grow, reflect on the past, and re-imagine responsible futures. College signals a process of personal development and transforms the devastation of prison into an opportunity to turn one's life around. College enables—for most—a safe and final transition out of prison.

The College Bound program was designed carefully and collaboratively to help women in prison develop the skills and strength necessary for successful transitions out of prison. It was structured to stimulate intellectual and personal growth for individual students; build a supportive community of learners among the women in the college; and encourage inmate participation, responsibility, and a commitment to giving back to the prison environment and communities post-release.

The College Bound program expected students to engage in serious academic work. Students must satisfy the same entrance criteria that students on the outside are required to fulfill, including passing a set of rigorous entrance exams, to gain entrance into the Mary-mount Manhattan College program. Once in, most students aim to complete a degree, to the extent possible, before they leave prison.

At the heart of the program are rules for student participation and giving back. College builds a context for transformation and responsibility that the women take with them as they leave the facility. As suggested by the Inmate Committee, all women pay a fee of $10 per semester for their education, the equivalent of one month's wages. In order to encourage student ownership of the program, the Inmate Committee and outside volunteers agreed that such payment would be psychologically and politically significant. Further, the contribution was designed to recognize the difficulty poor and working-class people who are not in prison confront as they try to pay for higher education.

Classes are offered in the evening after a full day of work. Women promise to tutor other women while in the facility, and others once they are released. The women are, many for the first time in their lives, expected to participate as engaged "citizens" in this community of learners, taking much and giving back more. Indeed, as you will read later in this chapter, many of these women find themselves surprised that they can be effective mentors, that they have something to give back, and that they are able to make an academic contribution to others.

At BHCF, the college program sits within a carefully structured matrix of educational programs, ranging from Adult Basic Education (ABE) to the GED, pre-college, vocational programs and College Bound. Once the college program developed as "a light to redirect ourselves," enrollment in prerequisite and auxiliary programs heightened as well. Passing the GED, in this context, is often a first step into the little-known world of higher education.

Debra, an inmate, described a typical, bumpy road toward the GED, "[F]inally the GED came. I took it and I didn't pass. I was so devastated. I only needed like one or two points and I was like really, really hurt, crushed. But I was like, maybe if I study a little harder next time, I could get it. So that pushed me. Whenever I had free time after that, I was always studying my books."

A month later an officer called Debra to come to the education center. Two of her teachers and several fellow students were waiting for her. She recalled, "So I got the envelope. I opened it and a copy of my diploma fell out, and I just started crying. Tears just started coming to my eyes. I was like 'Oh! I got it! I finally.' I was so happy. I made so many copies. I sent it to my grandfather, to my son, to my daughter, to everybody! To let them know, you know, that I was in school and just, you know, I may be away but I'm doing something to better myself while I'm here. My grandpa was so proud."

As women move from ABE to GED, and on to pre-college and college, they acquire new skills, points of view, networks, and expectations for themselves. They also shed old views of themselves, insecurities, some old friends, and even older habits.

A faculty member notes, "[It takes time for the women] to take away their masks. Their voices should be heard because many of these young women and older women have never had an occasion to speak and be heard. Initially there's a shyness and reticence; then they learn that their lives have been valuable and unique, and there's a dignity within themselves that they could hold onto."

The women describe the plunge into college as an immersion in books and ideas. It is important to remember that, for the most part, these are the very women for whom public education did not work the first time. Their academic biographies are heavily seasoned with failure. With college, the capacity to reflect on the past actions and plan responsible futures strengthens. A student in the program admits with irony, "I was in a much bigger prison before I got here, but I didn't know it."

Many women talk about college-in-prison as a kind of insurance on their futures. For these women, college isn't simply a credential or a promotion at work. College is an opportunity to prepare for the final transition out of prison. In the following quote, a woman who is serving a 50-year-to-life sentence speaks like many of the women. She describes an "old self" in need of change, anxiety about the rigorous nature of college work, the experience of a "whole new world" opening up, and the powerful relationship between her new found sense of personal agency and social responsibility. She continues,

> I was so young when I came here. I waited ten years to go to school. And when I started going to school, it was a whole new world. Being able to exchange ideas and learn new ways of life, and learn about the classics and learn about methodology—opened this whole new world for me. I was overwhelmed at first, but then I got to a point where inside of me it was an urge. It was, like, "You can do this." You know, I wanted to learn more. I wanted to get more. I sort of started identifying with the world, understanding the world better; understanding my crime and why I was here. I just wanted to read everything. I wanted to know more. I wanted to explore. And I found that I started surrounding myself with people of like minds. Because when I first came here I had a chip on my shoulder that I wanted somebody to knock off. I stayed in trouble. I was disrespectful. I had no self-respect, no respect for others. And it took a while for me to change gradually through the years, and when I started going to college that was like the key point for me of rehabilitation, of changing myself. And nobody did it for me. I did it for myself. I realize that, you know, I have an education and this education is going to carry me someplace. And even if I don't get a better job, I'll be a better person because of it. And that's, that's what it's all about.

Our data validate for college-in-prison what other researchers have found about higher education for "non-traditional" students in general. The core elements of education, such as self-reflection, critique, and inquiry, enable a transformed sense of self and, in turn, the women contribute to a rich college community (Germanotta, 1995; Greene, 1995; Rivera, 1995; Faith, 1993; Conway, 1998). Women see themselves and society, critically and reflexively. Said another way, college enables students to move from seeing themselves as passive objects into seeing themselves as active subjects. They become critical thinkers who actively participate in their lives and social surroundings, who take responsibility for past and future actions, and who view themselves as engaged in changing society and themselves.

A faculty member, a poet, explains how the women develop what she calls voices of the soul,

> Poetry has to come from inside. And there's always a little bit of a resistance at first, and then a little hiding, a little secretiveness. Like one person who wrote a poem about the old man, or her old man. And then we all finally learned to jump on her and say, "What is it? What does it mean? You can't hide!" And she said, "That's what I call my virus." And it was that way, through those kinds of needs, that we got to know each other. And you have to trust people. I was happy to see a kind of competition starting in that those

who were willing to divulge encountered those who had been hiding all the time. You know, the adults that I teach on the outside, they come regularly because they've paid their good money. The kids at colleges don't come regularly because it's their parents' good money they're spending. What do they care? But these women at Bedford feel that this is their good time, and so it's been just that, for me, and I really thank them for that.

College prepares women for their transition out of prison because it provokes critical perspectives. Students come to see themselves as independent thinkers who have decisions to make. Faculty members attest that students in their classrooms often start out seeing the social deck stacked against them. Most have experienced a combination of poverty, racial discrimination, poor schools, and often-violent homes.

Women new to BHCF typically see life as a "set up." They argue that little can be done to improve their circumstances. Such an attitude disables women in prison from seeing that they do have options, can make choices, and can embark on actions to alter the course of their lives and participate in social change projects. Through education, many of the women take the opportunity to critically re-assess social conditions, their pasts, presents and futures, and the opportunities available (and denied) to others in their home communities. The women develop a language and ethic of personal and social responsibility.

STRENGTHENED SENSE OF RESPONSIBILITY

A woman who graduated from the BHCF college program recalls:

"I can think and talk about my victim now. It's not just 'the bitch cut me and I cut her back.' Even that idea comes out differently now, 'the girl cut me and I chose to strike back.' Those words weren't in me before, but now, just having the words to articulate things, puts them into perspective differently."

Women at BHCF often describe a connection between their college experiences and a growing sense of responsibility—for their crime; to their victims and victims' families; to their children, families, and communities from whom they are separated; to friends and fellow students; and to social change. One of the more difficult aspects of this process occurs when the women reflect, deliberately and critically, on their crimes and the consequences to the victims and the victims' families. In the college program, they join a community through which they are able to make sense of sometimes horrifying pasts, terrible mistakes, and possible futures.

Another woman talks about how college affected her feelings about her crime:

At first I was incapable of feeling anything but a fretful kind of regret. After having time to reevaluate how many people were hurt and the ridiculous choices I made, I had a chance to feel sorry. I know what role I would like to play now.... I think the process of going to college and all these other things, my remorse turned into wanting to make amends. Wanting to make things better. Helping others not make the same mistakes.... [College creates] a lot of self-reflection. [I recognize] the pain of being separated from my family, of knowing that I hurt others from my actions. [I] definitely thank God.

Mentoring and "giving back" have been embroidered into the fabric of the college program. In a culture of peer support, tutoring, and mentoring, the women come to understand themselves as being connected to a larger social context, one that is affected by their actions and one to which they are accountable.

A college official provides an image of how the women, once educated, commit to educating others even after they leave BHCF: "One woman told me last June about a former Bedford student who was so appreciative about having the college program because now at Albion [another prison] she and other students were the leaders there, working to educate other women. They're tutors and mentors to other students and they feel that just having that college program at Bedford Hills has really allowed them to begin to help other people."

A faculty member in the College Program notes that this commitment to "giving back" becomes contagious: "The women are like shooting stars that move from one world to another [but so too are the faculty]. We have a teacher who taught a class and met some students who were involved in the parenting program [at Bedford] and working with the teens, the teenage children of inmates. As a result of his coming to the teen meeting last Saturday, he's going to help get some kids into camp this summer [and work with] the Beacon School programs in New York City. So there's just a myriad of ways that the impact of the college program connects with other programs within and beyond the facility."

Our research was designed, in part, to investigate the extent to which involvement in college facilitates women's sense of responsibility and civic participation while in prison and post-release. The research team learned from interviews with faculty, corrections officers, women in prison, and women on post-release, that college graduates go on to develop, facilitate, and evaluate many prison and community-based programs. These programs address far-ranging issues such as anger management, substance abuse, HIV and AIDS, domestic violence, sexual abuse, parenting skills and support, and prenatal care. Each of these programs has to be written up as a proposal and formally submitted to the Superintendent for approval. Developing and running programs within the facility is one way college students and graduates "give back" to their peers.

INFLUENCE OF MOTHERS' EDUCATIONAL PURSUITS ON CHILDREN'S ACADEMIC MOTIVATION

With bitter acknowledgement, many of the BHCF women speak as mothers, daughters, and sisters about the impact college has had on their sense of debt to their families in terms of helping children with homework, being a role model for their children and grandchildren, and fulfilling broken promises.

There is a strong developmental literature that confirms the impact of a mother's education on her children's academic aspirations and achievement. The children of educated mothers not only do better in school but also stay longer, are held back less often, have higher educational aspirations, and are more likely to decide to go to college. (Pallas, 1989; Hersh, 1988; Tuttle, 1981). It has been found across social classes, races, and ethnicities that the best predictor of a child's educational success is the educational attainment of his or her mother.

This relationship has not been tested across the telephone lines or the geography that separate children from their mothers in prison. It is nevertheless important to note that our research team heard from both children and mothers about the strong influence that maternal commitment to college held on the academic ambitions of their adolescent children. In interviews with early adolescent children who visit the prison for a Teen Group, youth indicated an ironic pride in their mother's college experiences. For some of these youth, their mothers—although in prison—are role models pioneering new educational frontiers.

Said a 15-year-old daughter. "My mother is the only person I know who went to college. As far as anybody else, like any other grown-up I ask, they said they never went to college."

Young sons and daughters told us about the lessons they learned from their mothers' experience in college—lessons of perseverance, possibility, and hard work. Despite the stigma and shame through which many spoke, their mothers' involvement in college enabled a new story that could honestly be told to friends and teachers. A 12-year-old explains: "My teacher is always asking me how's your mother...[and I say] 'She's okay, she's at college.' I brag about her to all my teachers."

While proud of their mothers' accomplishments, the youth also described concrete ways in which they, and their mothers, worked through homework, academic problems, and tough times. A 16-year-old boy reports: "[When I] spend time with her it's like, we seem to like working together. 'Cause she'll have questions to ask, and we'll have questions to ask her, so forth and so on. And it's like I know she's happy about it. I know [for a fact]... she's not happy with what the situation is, but she has an opportunity to get an education, I know she's extremely pleased about that. 'Cause beforehand she never had that opportunity. I guess now she's taking advantage of it."

The pride, reciprocity, and delight at their mothers' educational persistence is tinged with a recognition, by some, that their mothers might not have succeeded academically had they not gone to prison. It was sobering to hear youth tell one of the bitter ironies of this study. Prison has become a place for intellectual, emotional, and social growth for some women. A space free of male violence, drugs, and overwhelming responsibilities, college-in-prison carves out a space that nurtures a kind of growth and maturity that might not have been realized on the outside. The experience of watching their mothers succeed in school opens up complicated feelings for some of the children. They ask themselves what might have been, if their mothers had not gone to prison. Some children felt strongly that their mothers would eventually have continued their education.

Others were not so sure. A 12-year-old boy explains, "I don't think she would have. I don't know, because this really, when she came here it really turned her around. I don't even know if she would have stopped doing what she was doing, or whatever. But when she came up here she, she could really [steer herself right]... for the rest of her life, she probably said, 'Well, I need a change.'"

A 13-year-old girl adds, "Well, I don't think, personally I don't think that my mother would have gone back to school if she was out there, because she would be too interested in being with her friends and fighting ... and, you know, taking [up] ... from me, 'cause I'm very violent, too, when it comes to somebody bothering me. So, I don't think she would be in school."

Through the conflicted emotions of abandonment, disappointment, pride, and inspiration, these youth have learned many tough lessons from their mothers, and from their mothers' imprisonments.

LASTING TRANSITIONS OUT OF PRISON

Life after prison is difficult, even with the skills and strengths developed through college. The world that awaits former inmates, especially those with few resources, can feel insurmountable. (Close, 2000; Gonnerman, 2000a, 2000b). Women—now with a criminal record—typically return to lives of poverty, many unable to vote, with few opportunities, and damaged, if not shattered, social networks.

The research team interviewed 20 graduates of the Mercy College program post-release. These women had been out of prison for an average of 8.6 years, ranging from one to 23 years. Of the 20, 18 were employed, one on disability, and another retired. The majority (88%) of the employed women worked in social service organizations. Thirteen (65%) were pursing graduate degrees, most commonly in social work. All but four of the women had stable housing at the time of the interview. Six women (30%) reported serious health problems.

The women spoke with us about their rocky transitions out of prison. Issues facing women as they reintegrate into society range from the details of everyday living to large structural barriers. These women must relearn how to negotiate overcrowded subways, cellphones, and ATM machines, as well as the job market and the health care system. They face challenges in housing (many women fear shelters for themselves and their children); employment (employers are not eager to hire women with felony convictions); parenting and family (long absence makes reuniting with children and family and resuming leadership roles in children's lives unexpectedly difficult); health care (inadequate health care in prison often results in cumulative problems upon release); and a lack of support networks (relationships with formerly incarcerated peers are forbidden by parole), while transitional programs for women are few and underresourced.

A woman in the program says college gave her the skills to withstand these unexpected difficulties of reentry:

> I'm a thinker now. Before I was a reactor. So that's what's changed…. If you're educated and you are well informed about a lot of things, you have a tendency to look at life through a whole different perspective. And I know people might [ask] how can just a degree add so much internally? But that's all it's about, because once you learn that you are capable, you know what I mean? It's like knowing that you're not stuck in the substance abuse world, that you do have a brain, and that brain tells you, "Oh, you do have choices," or, "You are capable of having a job." Because now you have the skills, you have the education. It makes you qualified. So, education is the biggest piece. I can't stress it enough. Without that I don't know where I would be. I'd probably be back doing another [prison term]…. Probably. I'm being perfectly honest. Because [education] was the thing that turned my whole life around. It really did.

Employers we met as we interviewed women on the outside attest to the sense of responsibility practiced by these women. Indeed, men and women who have attended college while incarcerated have a significantly higher rate of employment (60%-70%) upon release than those who do not (40%). (Taylor, 1993). The owner of a carpet business in New York City explains, "I have employed women with criminal records for years now and I have found them to be careful, hard working employees. In fact I think they are some of the best employees I have had. They take the job very seriously and because of their experiences they don't take anything for granted. We work with the public so it is important for my workers to be respectful and troubleshoot customer's needs. I have no complaints and I think my customers would say the same."

In addition to paid work, many women return to college soon after release. Governor George Pataki granted clemency to one of the authors of this article at the end of the year 2000. She went to college the day of her release, eager to learn how she could re-enroll "on the outside." Another woman, while incarcerated, received educational counseling from a former participant of the College Bound program at BHCF. Shortly after release, she enrolled in a transitional program designed to support women who are returning to higher education post-release and at this writing she was nearing completion of her Bachelor's Degree.

As women carve out new lives post-incarceration, many feel a personal and professional need to continue their education. College is viewed as a sustaining lifeline, a way to keep the mind, sense of personal growth, and social support networks alive. Another graduate, now home from BHCF, describes this draw to return to college: "[O]nce you get open for school, you know that there's another level that you can go to…. I know I probably won't be satisfied 'til I get my Master's Degree. I know that. But I'm saying, it's not that I won't feel complete. But I know, that the level that I want to be on requires that, you know what I mean? And I'll eventually get it, 'cause I really want that. I want that title, you know? CSW, you know? An MBA, or something! … [laughs]… It could be anything…. My main concern is keeping the ties [to education], you know, keeping the link open."

A problem arises, however, for the men and women who have been incarcerated in New York State under drug-related sentences. The recently added Question 28 (approved by Congress in 1998 and put into effect in 2000) on the Free Application for Federal Student Aid (FAFSA) asks, "Have you ever been convicted of possessing or selling illegal drugs?" Answering yes to Question 28 renders an individual with one drug conviction ineligible for financial aid for one year. Individuals with two convictions are ineligible for two years. Those with three or more convictions are ineligible for financial aid indefinitely (Burd, 2001). For many women interested in returning to college or pursuing graduate work, as 58% of those interviewed were, Question 28 may pose a very real threat to post-release transitions.

PRISON VS. EDUCATION DEBATE

> Educating the incarcerated is not an exercise in futility, nor is it a gift to the undeserving. It is a practical and necessary safeguard to insure that those who have found themselves without the proper resources to succeed have these needs met before they are released. It is a gift to ourselves and to our children, a gift of both compassion and peace of mind. We are not turning the other cheek to those who have hurt us. We are taking their hands and filling them with learning so that they can't strike us again."
>
> —Janice Grieshaber, Executive Director, The
> Jenna Foundation for Non-Violence

With a generosity born of tragedy that is hard to imagine, just three years after her daughter's murder, Janice Griesbacher articulates a concern voiced by many victims' families. She actively supports higher education for men and women in prison and she is concerned that the current policy of locking up criminals and offering them little support is dangerous for us all.

The qualitative and quantitative evidence in this report reaches the same conclusion: college-in-prison programs accelerate a process of personal growth and transformation, enhance a sense of social responsibility, facilitate positive prison management, reduce crime and rein-carceration rates, and reduce the burden prisons impose on taxpayers.

In recent years, young adults have moved in unprecedented numbers from poor communities, particularly communities of color, into prisons with few or no programs. In parallel fashion, public dollars have moved from education to corrections.

Nationally, from 1977 to 1995, the average state increased correctional funding by two times more than funding for public colleges. In 1988, New York's public university funding was double that of the prison system. Over the past decade, New York reduced public higher education spending by 29%, while state corrections enjoyed a 76% budget increase. During that same time period, SUNY and CUNY tuition rates were raised and remediation programs were withdrawn from the senior CUNY campuses. Tuition rates rose to account for 25% of white families' incomes and a full 42% of black or Latino families' incomes. (Gangi, et al., 1998). As public education moves out of reach for poor and working-class families, the long arm of prison moves closer in.

Prison construction has become a big business in the United States, supporting a number of rural and deindustrialized communities, restoring an economic base, for instance, to a series of towns in upstate New York. It is often said, in New York, that "Downstate's crime is Upstate's industry." Yet questions of public accountability loom large. Has the public been informed about the shift in dollars from higher education to prison? Has the public approved the mass proliferation of prisons and the dramatic increase in imprisonment, particularly within African American and Latino communities? Has the public been fully educated to understand the consequences of shifting public dollars from education into prison construction and then withdrawing public dollars for education within prison?

Quality education is needed to prevent young people from entering prisons. For those who do find themselves within prisons and jails, quality education within and after prison makes an enormous difference to inmates, the prison environment and successful post-release transitions. Quality education, from pre-kindergarten through twelfth grade and higher education, may be the most promising investment and industry that New York State can offer its citizens.

POLICY ISSUES

There are a series of policy issues that deserve further attention—for the nation, for prisons and for colleges or universities considering collaborations with prisons. National and state policy issues concern, at minimum, the restoration of Pell and Tap grants, or otherwise available public grants to support higher education within prison. The BHCF model is unique, vibrant, and built on the energy of volunteer individuals and institutions. Citizens and community members from New York's Westchester County and New York City area mobilized when Congress and the state withdrew funding. The community understood the significance of college-in-prison. However, a fully volunteer program, no matter how vibrant, is fragile. At present, federal and state governments—by refusing to subsidize college-in-prison—enforce a policy that insures heightened reincarceration rates, unsafe communities, and prolonged ignorance. This state of affairs is worsened by a provision in the 1994 Violent Crime Bill which specifies that persons convicted of a drug-related felony may be ineligible for federal financial aid even after release from prison. Former inmates affected by this provision, while eager to turn their lives around post-release, are systematically denied access to federal financial aid for college because of a crime for which they have already served time.

As former New York City Mayor Ed Koch testified at New York State Senate Hearings on Criminal Justice Reform, "When is the punishment over?" (Montgomery, et al., 2001).

In contrast to current policy, by supporting federal and state aid for college-in-prison—as in the 2001 Workplace and Community Transition for Incarcerated Youth Offenders Grant—governments would be advocating and implementing policies which reduce reincarceration rates, reduce crime, cut the tax burden of prison construction and maintenance, render prisons more "peaceful" and manageable, build stronger communities, and support healthier transitions back into society. One might deduce: To be tough on crime, we must educate prisoners.

College-in-prison must be part of the broader national conversation about prison reform, alternatives to incarceration and transitions out of prison. Likewise, the inequities of public education within impoverished communities must be redressed, for it is those schools that are, unfortunately, often the pipelines to prison.

Many issues are worth considering before and after establishing a college program within a prison. Some of the more acute issues that deserve serious deliberation include:

Addressing the Questions of Community and Student Participation in Shaping, Sustaining, and Governing the College Program

In the early conceptual stages of the college program at BHCF, the model reflected high levels of leadership and participation from among the prison administration, universities and colleges, the local community, volunteers, inmate leaders, students, and faculty. Such collaboration was crucial to the design, stability, and success of the program. Over time, however, the contradictions of a participatory college program in prison grew more apparent.

BHCF is a maximum-security facility. The prison administration maintains a strong hold on who enters, with what frequency, and how closely outsiders work with insiders. At the same time, college learning, particularly in the absence of state funding, requires extraordinary reliance upon volunteers and participatory commitment and engagement by all relevant parties. Initial and ongoing conversations about the structure and processes for participation are crucial for sustaining a college program within a prison. In the absence of regular communication and checking-in, tensions and misunderstandings are inevitable. To lose student or community participation is to sacrifice an element crucial to the success of this model.

Pre-College and English for Speakers of Other Languages

Both pre-college and ESOL programs facilitate women's entry into higher education through the provision of skills and a community of support. Given the low levels of academic achievement with which women enter the facility, a quality pre-college program is essential. Further, with respect to ESOL, the population of Latinas at BHCF has doubled in the last three decades. Many Latinas at BHCF are monolingual Spanish-speakers and many are undocumented. The particular needs of Latina students for ESOL classes and bilingual education must be addressed if they are to enjoy equal access to the college program.

Graduation Matters

The evidence presented here suggests it is not the mere taking of courses that facilitates dramatic change in the women, but the experience of earning a degree, of walking down the aisle, of completion. As one graduate beamed, "When I walked for graduation, I was walking more for the young ones behind me, than for me. They must see that the diploma is valuable and that they can achieve it." For women whose lives have been characterized by incompletes and interruptions, earning a degree is a significant accomplishment. Courses produce growth; graduation transforms.

Inmates With Mental Health Problems

At present, prisons and jails are sites in which disproportionate numbers of men and women with mental heath problems can be found. (Open Society Institute, 1996, Steadman, et al., 1976). Within BHCF, approximately 50% of the women are on mental health rolls. Seventy-five percent of these women are on psychotropic medication. An analysis conducted in June 1998 determined that 80% of the Unusual Incident reports involved women who were diagnosed as having mental health problems. The day-to-day life within prisons supervised by staff who are not trained to deal with mental health problems is precarious for all. While a college-in-prison—like any college—must be equipped to deal with issues of mental health and counseling, it is even truer that in the absence of college and other support programs, mental health problems are likely to worsen, as depression deepens and despair spreads.

Disruption of Moving Women Between Institutions

The "drafting" or moving of women from one facility to another, mid-semester, causes major disruptions for students and faculty. In the course of this three-year study, over 30% of the students were drafted during their involvement in the college program. A number of teachers commented on the problems provoked when "one of my best students has to leave the class because she is being drafted somewhere up North, eight hours from her kids in the Bronx!" The negative impact of disrupted education is magnified in the prison context, creating adverse consequences for students and faculty.

Parole Matters

Nationally, as well as in New York State, parole boards are now less likely to grant parole than under prior administrations. (Butterfield, 2000; Palacios, 1994; Citizens Budget Committee, 2000). In New York State, most inmates are denied parole at their first board hearing. In this context, women are rightfully worried, and some officers concur, that "having a college degree doesn't mean anything to the parole board."

A community lawyer who fought hard for the restoration of college explains, "At parole, these women and men are being retried on their original crime. The law is clear. The parole board is supposed evaluate inmates on the basis of what they have accomplished while in prison, not retry them on their crime."

As one woman put it, "My parole board is more likely to give me credit for my Certification in Money Addiction—because I dealt drugs—than my Master's in Forensic Psychology."

Another echoed, "The parole board—they see me as a crack addict or a murderer. I've been here 12 years, can't help my daughter from in here. I'm working for a college degree, but their personal biases take precedence over what we've accomplished. They throw cold water on your face and then you find yourself in a rut. You take courses, you try to complete your degree. If you don't go for college, they hold it against you. If you do go for college, they hold it against you. It feels like you're damned if you do, and damned if you don't."

A critical, historic analysis of parole decisions in general and as they relate to higher education would be timely and could serve as a significant opportunity for public debate about alternatives to prison, length of prison sentences, parole and clemency. Many throughout New York State and the nation are beginning to ask, "When is the punishment over?" or "When is justice served?"

A recent proliferation of critical writings by political and religious leaders about the criminal justice system and parole raises questions about the impact of mass incarceration on poor communities of color, the importance of restorative justice and reconciliation, and the significance of an ethic of redemption (see Shriver, 1997).

College Education Works for Women Prisoners

Does college work particularly well for women? Put another way, "Does college have the same benefits for male inmates?" There is substantial evidence documenting the positive impact of education, ranging from GED programs through vocational programs and college, on men and in male facilities. Indeed, most research on prison-based education has been conducted within male facilities. Evidence from social scientists, testimony from educators who have worked in male and female facilities, and interviews with corrections officers who have moved between systems, confirm that education in prison is a gender neutral intervention. While college programs must always take into account the particular circumstances of the student body (gender, language, academic biography, strengths, needs, length of sentence, age, etc.), there is nothing to suggest that college is any more effective for women than for men in prison.

Role of Corrections Officers

The relation between corrections officers and the college program needs to be explicitly addressed. When the College Bound program was first designed, there was much appropriate concern that corrections officers would be offended by the program. Community members worried that corrections officers might resent men and women in prison going to college for "free." With these concerns in mind, a number of programmatic features were instituted. First, as noted above, the college program is not free for inmates. Every student pays an average of one month's salary toward her tuition. Second, the Center for Redirection in Education awards an annual college scholarship to the child of a college student, the child of a corrections officer, and the child of a victim. Third, there have been embryonic discussions about providing higher educational opportunities to corrections officers through similar consortium arrangements. While a few courses (e.g., the Sign Language course) have successfully been offered jointly to inmates and officers, the hope is that over time officers in this and other facilities will have access to an array of courses for their own personal and professional development. It should be noted, however, that counter to early concerns, the administrators and officers who were interviewed and those who work with the college program, have supported the program.

Need for State Funding

Do college programs in prisons need state funding? This chapter presents the results of a study of a very particular kind of college-in-prison program. This is the first post-1995 empirical documentation of college-in-prison. The focus of the study is on College Bound, a thoughtfully constructed model that is heavily reliant upon the good will of private colleges and universities and the generous donations of individuals and foundations from across the country. The program is strong and sustainable. Nevertheless, an all-volunteer program is always fragile. It seems clear from the BHCF program, and certainly from comparable programs now shut down or struggling across the nation, that some steady stream of state funding is necessary in order to create and sustain a viable college program. This is particularly so in communities which are less affluent or enjoy less access to multiple colleges and universities than New York's Westchester County. Some state legislators from across the country are considering giving grants to colleges interested in prison education or to prisons interested in recruiting college partners.

It seems unlikely, in the near future, that individual Pell grants (or the equivalent) will be available to individuals in prison. However, recent federal support for youthful offenders' pursuit of higher education suggests that the strict no-support-for-higher-education-in-prison policy of the recent past is taking a turn. To educate inmates across age and geography, government-funded institutional grants offered at the equivalent of $2,500 per student would likely be sufficient to maintain a high quality college program in prison. To answer the question, then, college programs in prison do need state funding. The costs, however, given dramatic reductions in reincarceration rates, are relatively low.

Fairness; Effectiveness

Is it fair to educate prisoners? As researchers, we have been asked this question often, particularly by working-class men and women who struggle to pay for their own, or their children's higher education. The present research can only assess whether our current policies insure and enable public safety, social justice, and personal transformation.

The data presented here suggest that our present national policy of not providing higher education to men and women in prison is costly and dangerous. The decision to not educate produces negative consequences for women and men in prison, persons who work in prisons, the children of inmates, and our communities. In addition, the evidence presented here demonstrates that a national policy which supports higher education for men and women in prison is cost effective; creates safer communities and prisons; and transforms the lives of prisoners, their children, and, in all likelihood, the generation after that. Funding college-in-prison programs does not take money away from individual citizens, nor does it weaken any one person's chance of receiving federal support for college. Restoring prisoner access to Pell Grants would only allow prisoners an equal opportunity to apply for federal support.

It has been most sobering for the research team to hear responses to our work from the parents of murdered children. These men and women offered eloquent endorsements of this research. To diverse audiences, including these victim advocates, the evidence for higher education in prison is indeed compelling. Providing college education in prison is smart and effective social policy.

A NATIONAL MODEL?

BHCF is recognized nationally as a women's prison that is rich in inmate-focused and inmate-initiated programs, including the Children's Center in the 1970s, the Family Violence Program in the 1980s, and the AIDS Counseling and Education Program in 1998. The Superintendent, also well recognized within the field of corrections, practices a commitment to inmate and staff participation and leadership. In this context, two policy questions emerge: What elements of this model of college-in-prison are generalizable? And, can this model be replicated in other prisons and with other colleges?

Three data sources can be applied to the question of generalizability. First, our qualitative and quantitative databases triangulate to confirm the positive effects of college on the women, the prison environment, post-release outcomes, and re-incarceration rates. The findings reported here replicate and extend the existing literature on the positive effects of higher education for poor and working-class women and men, and the literature on prison-based education (Gittel, et al., 1996).

Second, our design explicitly sought evidence that could disconfirm positive impact. The research team interviewed women who dropped out of the college program and women dissatisfied with the college program; corrections officers who work at a distance from the college program and those who work closely were interviewed. A focus group was conducted with the teen children who have witnessed much and paid an enormous price for their mothers' incarcerations. The impact of college was subjected to a quantitative analysis of reincarceration despite overwhelming evidence of prison as a revolving door.

Third, when our research team has spoken with researchers, policymakers, corrections officers, and prison activists from San Quentin, and from women's prisons in New Zealand; and inmates/officers/superintendents from other facilities and departments of corrections across the United States, there has been a strong positive response across these very diverse contexts. Ultimately, people from these other communities understand that the key to the success of the model lies in the active involvement and support of prison administrators, community members, and college officials; a powerful inmate-centered community of programs; and a rigorous and creative inventory of community assets in all forms. The replicable and necessary elements for college-in-prison include active collaboration among prison administration, the external community, and local universities; strong student participation in shaping and sustaining the program; and serious documentation and recruitment of local community resources that can be brought to bear on the college-in-prison program.

We hope this chapter opens up conversations about prison reform, college-in-prison, and college post-prison in state legislatures; in colleges and universities; in state and federal departments of education and corrections; and, most importantly, in churches, beauty parlors, dentist offices, schools, mosques, synagogues, nail salons, bowling alleys, and community-based organizations throughout our nation.

While a dramatic shift in public dollars from education to prisons has occurred in the "war on crime," the public has been neither well educated nor informed. The results presented here suggest that this shift has been costly in fiscal and human terms. The consequences have been most devastating in low income communities of color. Public investments in higher education before, during and after prison are powerfully effective in terms of economic, social, psychological, and civic outcomes for us all.

About the Authors

Michelle Fine, Ph.D., is professor of psychology at the City University of New York. Rosemarie Roberts, Ph.D. is a post-doc fellow at Barnard College, and Marie Elena Torre is associate director of educational studies at Eugene Lang College. Their coauthors on this are either currently or formerly incarcerated women at the Bedford Hills Correctional Facility in upstate New York.

References

Anderson, D. B., Anderson S. L. & Schumacker R. E., *Correctional Education A Way to Stay Out: Recommendations for Illinois and a Report of the Anderson Study* (Illinois Council on Vocational Education, 1988).

Barton, P.E., & Cooley, R.J., *Captive Students: Education and Training in America's Prisons* (Educational Testing Service, Policy Information Center, 1996).

Beck, A. J., & Shipley, B. E., *Recidivism of Prisoners Released in 1983* (pp. 1-13) (Bureau of Justice Statistics, U.S. Department of Justice, 1989).

Bowen I., *The Impact of a College Education on Women in Prison Who Have Suffered From Domestic Violence* (unpublished manuscript, 1998).

Bowen, W., & Bok,D., *The Shape of the River* (Princeton University Press, 1998).

Browne, A., *When Battered Women Kill* (Free Press, 1987).

Browne, A., Miller, B.A., & Maguin, E., "Prevalence and Severity of Lifetime Physical and Sexual Victimization Among Incarcerated Women," 22 *International Journal of Law and Psychiatry*, 301-322 (1999).

Burd, S., "Aid Applicants to Be Required to Answer Question on Drug Convictions," *The Chronicle of Higher Education*, April 20, 2001, p. A43.

Burnett, C., *Education as a Crime Prevention for Young Women in Prison, Their Families and Communities* (unpublished manuscript, 1998).

Butterfield, F., "Often, Parole Is One Stop on the Way Back to Prison," *The New York Times,* November 29, 2000, p. A1.

Butterfield, F., "Inmate Rehabilitation Returns as Prison Goal," *The New York Times*, May 20, 2001, p. A1.

Camp, C.G., & Camp, G.M., *The Corrections Yearbook 2000* (Criminal Justice Institute, 2000).

Citizens Budget Committee, *Making More Effective Use of New York State's Prisons* (Author, 2000).

Clark, D., *Analysis of Return Rates of the Inmate College Program Participants* (New York State Department of Correctional Services, 1991).

Close, E., "The Prison Paradox," *Newsweek*, November 13, 2000.

Conway, K., *The Impact of Attending College While Incarcerated on Women's Self-Esteem* (Unpublished manuscript, 1998).

Department of Defense, Profile of American Youth (Author, 1982).

Elikann, P.T., *The Tough-on-Crime Myth: Real Solutions to Cut Crime* (Insight Books, 1996).

Faith, K., *Unruly Women: The Politics of Confinement and Resistance* (Press Gang Publishers, 1993).

Finkle, L., *The Impact of College on the Self-Image of Incarcerated Women Whose Histories Included Physical and or Sexual Abuse* (unpublished manuscript, 1998).

Gainous, F. J., *Alabama: Correctional Education Research* (Montgomery, Alabama, Department of Postsecondary Education, 1992).

Gangi, R., et al., *New York State of Mind?: Higher Education vs. Prison Funding in the Empire State, 1988-1998* (Correctional Association of New York and the Justice Policy Institute, 1998).

Germanotta, D., "Prison Education: A Contextual Analysis." In H.S. Davidson (Ed.), *Schooling in a "Total Institution:" Critical Perspectives on Prison Education* (pp. 103-121) (Bergin & Garvey, 1995).

Gittell, M., Vandersall, K., Holdaway, J., & Newman, K., *Creating Social Capital at CUNY: A Comparison of Higher Education Programs for AFDC Recipients* (Howard Samuels State Management and Policy Center, 1996).

Gonnerman, J., "Life on the Outside," *Village Voice*, December 20-26, 2000(b). [Available online: www.villagevoice.com/news/0051, gonnerman8,20849,1.html]

Gonnerman, J., "Roaming Rikers," *Village Voice*, December 13-19, 2000(a). [Available online: www.villagevoice.com/news/0050,gonnerman4,20622,1.html]

Greene, M., *Releasing the Imagination: Essays on Education, the Arts, and Social Change* (Jossey-Bass, 1995).

Harer, M. D., *Recidivism Among Federal Prison Releasees in 1987: A Preliminary Report* (Federal Bureau of Prisons, Office of Research and Evaluation, p. 2, 1994).

Hersh, L. R., *Correlates of Elementary School Retention: A Case Study* (Report #537) Horseheads (NY) Central School District. (ERIC Clearinghouse of Urban Education, Document Reproduction Service, No. ED294679, 1988).

Holloway, J., & Moke, P., *Post Secondary Correctional Education: An Evaluation of Parolee Performance* (Wilmington College, 1986).

Jacobson, M., *Changing Minds*, June 2000 [Available online: www.changingminds.ws/03_researchdesign/02html]

Johnson, A., *A Selected Bibliography on Post-Secondary Education and Reduction in Recidivism* (The League of Women Voters of New York State: Balancing Justice Task Force on Correctional Education, 2001).

Lockwood, D., *Prison Higher Education, Recidivism, and Employment After Release* (Unpublished manuscript, Utica College of Syracuse University, 1988).

Lord, Elaine, personal communication, September 21, 2000.

Mancuso, R., & Miller, B., "Crime and Punishment in the Lives of Women Alcohol and Other Drug Users: Exploring the Gender, Lifestyle and Legal Issues." In C. Renzetti & L. Goodstein, (Eds.), *Women, Crime and Criminal Justice: Original Feminist Readings* (pp. 93-110) (Roxbury, 2001).

Montgomery, V., Duane, T. K., Oppenheimer, S. & Stavisky, T. A., *Criminal Justice Reform: A Time that's Come* (A report of the New York State: Senate Democratic Task Force on Criminal Justice Reform, 2001).

New York State Department of Correctional Services, *Analyses of Return Rate Study*, Executive Summary (Author, 1991).

Open Society Institute, *Education as Crime Prevention: Providing Education to Prisoners. Research Brief* (Occasional Paper Series No. 2) (OSI Center on Crime Communities & Culture, September, 1997).

Open Society Institute, "Mental Illness in U.S. Jails: Diverting the Nonviolent, Lower-Level Offender," *(Research Brief, Occasional Paper Series No. 1)* (Center on Crime Communities & Culture, 1996).

Palacios, V. J., "Go and Sin No More: Rationality and Release Decisions by Parole Boards," 45 *South Carolina Law Review* 567-615 (1994).

Pallas, A. M., *Making Schools More Responsive to At-Risk Students* (ERIC Clearinghouse of Urban Education, Document Reproduction Service, No. ED316617, 1989)

Richie, B., *Compelled to Crime: The Gender Entrapment of Battered Black Women* (Routledge, 1996).

Rivera, J.A., "A Nontraditional Approach to Social and Criminal Justice." In H.S. Davidson (Ed.), *Schooling in a "Total Institution": Critical Perspectives on Prison Education* (pp. 159-171) (Bergin & Garvey, 1995).

Steadman, H. J., et al., "A Survey of Mental Disability Among State Prison Inmates," 38 *Hospital and Community Psychiatry*, 1086 (1987).

Taylor, J.M., "Pell Grants for Prisoners," *The Nation*, January 25, 1993, p. 88.

Tracy, C. & Johnson, C., *Review of Various Outcome Studies Relating Prison Education to Reduced Recidivism* (Windham School System, 1994).

Tuttle, R., *A Path Analytic Model of the College Going Decision* (Appalachian State University) (ERIC Clearinghouse of Urban Education, Document Reproduction Service, No. ED224434, 1981).

Chapter 52

The Citizens, Victims, and Offenders Restoring Justice Project

by Heather Burns, M.S.W.

INTRODUCTION

The Minnesota Correctional Facility (MCF) in Shakopee, Minnesota is the only correctional facility in the state designed to house adult women felons. Long considered an innovative leader in prison programming, MCF-Shakopee was selected as the site for the Citizens, Victims and Offenders Restoring Justice Project (CVORJ), a pilot project that was designed to bring crime victims, offenders and community members together to address the causes and consequences of crime in a very personal way. For nine weeks, victim and

---

This chapter originally appeared under the title "Restorative Justice in Action: A Work in Progress," in Women, Girls & Criminal Justice, *Vol. 4, No. 1, December/January 2003.*

offender participants told their stories and shared the anger, pain, and grief that resulted from criminal acts in their lives. Victim participants impressed on inmates that healing from violent crime is a long and painful process, complicated by involvement with the criminal justice system, and that their healing may never be complete. They advocated for truth-in-sentencing and victims' rights. Offenders, in turn, expressed their deep remorse for harm done to victims and a resolve to do whatever possible to right the wrongs committed. Facilitators employed a circle process in conducting the sessions. Their role was to provide a flexible structure for each meeting, to ensure that each participant had the opportunity to tell their story, and to help group members make sense of their experience. The emphasis was on creating a safe supportive environment in which to address the painful issues that would arise. Participants completed surveys before and after joining the project. These, along with observer notes and recorded quotes, provided insight into the impact the project had on participants. Significant observations included:

- Signs of increased group integration;
- Creation of a safe, supportive environment;
- Offender accountability;
- Positive changes in participants' feelings toward one another; and
- A greater willingness to consider and engage in restorative responses to crime.

The overwhelming response to the project was a positive one from the perspective of victims and offenders alike. Meetings ended with high hopes for future restorative justice projects at the Shakopee facility.

THE PILOT PROJECT

Program Structure and Participants

The MCF-Shakopee CVORJ program was based on the work of Jacqueline Helfgott and her colleagues at the Seattle University Department of Sociology and Criminal Justice (Helfgott et al., 1998). Surveys completed by participants of the Shakopee project were condensed from those used in Seattle, and a similar process of group facilitation employed. Over a period of nine weeks, participants in the Shakopee project met weekly for three hours. Meetings were held in a circle format with two facilitators present to guide discussions. Those present included four crime victims, a community member (a woman who had been a victim of violent crime in her youth), six female inmates, two facilitators, a neutral advocate, and an observer. The advocate was available for anyone who needed support, and the observer took notes on the process.

Victim and inmate participants were asked to sign up for the nights they wanted to tell their stories. Meetings consisted of an initial check-in with input from each participant, a review of the previous week with questions or comments, and time for one or two participants to tell their stories, with a brief closing exercise at the end. In addition, facilitators would incorporate exercises as needed to aid participants in making sense of their experience. This might mean leading a discussion on concepts of justice or a guided visualization to explore emotions around harm and healing.

Program Goals

Victim and inmate participants were also asked to complete surveys composed of 44 statements and six open-ended questions. Survey items were selected to measure desired outcomes as described in the Shakopee project goals. These goals were summarized into eight points:

- Provide offenders an opportunity to express empathy and remorse;

- Give offenders tools to become accountable and accept responsibility for their crime;

- Facilitate constructive communication;

- Create safe, supportive environment;

- Learn causes and results of crime;

- Enhance understanding of restorative justice principles and the centrality of harm to persons;

- Foster hope for a balanced criminal justice response; and

- Healing from harm caused by crime.

SURVEY METHODS AND RESPONSES

Two versions of the survey were used, one for victim participants and one for inmates. Responses to the statements were recorded on a four-point Likert Scale that offered the following optional responses: strongly disagree; somewhat disagree, somewhat agree, and strongly agree.

In addition, each survey included open-ended questions that allowed the participants to express themselves in their own words. These questions addressed issues such as concepts of justice, expectations for the project, hopes and fears, and safety. Surveys were administered prior to and just after completion of participation in the project.

Five victim participants and six inmates completed the surveys. For the purposes of this study, the one community member was included in the "victim" category and received surveys designed to measure victim attitudes. While this simplified the process of drawing conclusions from the data, it was recognized that community members were underrepresented in this study and future projects would do well to improve on these numbers.

Initial Pre-Program Responses

Victims' open-ended responses on pre-project surveys reflect their priorities of truth-in-sentencing, victim rights, the importance of offering support for other victims, and the hope that their stories might have a positive impact on offenders. Asked what could be done to make justice more meaningful, one victim wrote, "Make a life sentence mean life in prison. Spend as much time, money, and effort to help and heal victims as is spent on criminals." Another victim, asked about his hopes and fears for the project, responded, "I have apprehensions regarding the outcome of the meetings, but if there is a chance to turn someone in the right direction, and my participation helped, I would feel more than justified in the meetings." Also noteworthy is the unanimous "No" given in response to the question "Do you think it will be possible for you to resolve any of the conflicts/issues you have with the offender in your case by speaking with offenders unrelated to your case?" This expectation is born out in the post-project survey results, as well.

Offenders' responses to the pre-project survey reflect concern for the needs of victims, willingness to hear their stories and offer support, openness to learning from the experience, and hope for healing. Some were concerned about feeling judged, expressed remorse for their actions, and hoped for an opportunity to show how their lives had changed since their incarceration. Asked about her hopes and fears, one inmate wrote, "My fear is that I'll be judged for who I was, not whom I've become." Another offered this response, "My hopes in this program are to be able to get a better understanding of just how much of an impact our behaviors have had on others, to possibly give back to the community an understanding of the consequences of my behaviors and alcohol [use]. I would [like to] let them know all I've done to better myself."

Pre- and Post-Project Surveys Compared

Tables 52.1 - 52.8 show the results of pre- and post-program survey responses. As discussed below, overall results were positive for both victims and offenders.

Positive Changes in Attitude. Victim survey responses indicate a notable change of

Table 52.1: Offenders Just Want to Look Good for Parole Hearing

Victims (N=4)	Agree	Disagree
Before Project	75%	25%
After Project	0%	100%

Table 52.2: Offenders Should Receive Training for Living in the Community

Victims (N=4)	Agree	Disagree
Before Project	50%	50%
After Project	100%	0%

Table 52.3: The Wounds and Healing of Offenders Is Important

Victims (N=5)	Agree	Disagree
Before Project	20%	80%
After Project	100%	0%

attitude in a number of areas. Pre-project surveys show that victims suspected most offenders' participation was motivated by a desire to look good for their parole hearings. After meeting with the offenders for nine weeks, however, not one victim held this belief about the offenders involved in this project.

Prior to the project, victims were split on the question of whether incarceration should focus on training and equipping offenders for living in the community. Post-project surveys indicate a change of heart; victim responses showed unanimous support for transition services.

Similarly, before this project, most victims disagreed with the statement that the wounds and healing of offenders should be seen as important in the justice process. Afterwards, the same statement received a positive response, indicating a greater willingness to consider restorative alternatives to crime.

Statements designed to measure perceptions of offender remorse and accountability were compared. Pre-project survey results show that, in the victims' experience, most offenders do not show remorse and are not held accountable for their actions. In post-project surveys, however, victims agree unanimously that these offender participants did indeed show remorse and accept responsibility for their crimes.

Positive Expectations Confirmed—Offenders. Although offender surveys show little change in attitude, their responses indicate a confirmation or strengthening of those views that were initially consistent with project goals. This was likely due to the fact that offend-

Table 52.4: Offenders Seem to Feel Sorry for What They Did

Victims (N=5)	Agree	Disagree
Before Project	20%	80%
After Project	100%	0%

Table 52.5: Conversations With Victims Won't Accomplish Much

Victims (N=6)	Agree	Disagree
Before Project	0%	0%
After Project	100%	100%

Table 52.6: Offenders Don't Want to Do Anything for Their Victims

Victims (N=6)	Agree	Disagree
Before Project	0%	100%
After Project	0%	100%

Table 52.7: Offenders Need to Learn More About the Aftermath of Crime

Victims (N=6)	Agree	Disagree
Before Project	83%	17%
After Project	100%	0%

Table 52.8: Victims Want to Educate Offenders About Victim Needs and Interests

Victims (N=6)	Agree	Disagree
Before Project	100%	0%
After Project	100%	0%

er participants were selected from those who had successfully completed a facility class called "Making Things Right," which emphasizes offender accountability and helps prepare inmates for a face-to-face meeting with crime victims.

A brief description of the selection process for the "Making Things Right" group highlights the importance of preparation in any restorative justice work. "Making Things Right" is the name of the cognitively based curriculum developed by the EXCEL Program, Workforce Development Group of the Amherst H. Wilder Foundation in St. Paul, MN (2000). The application process for the group was fairly rigorous. Inmates first submitted an essay describing why they wished to participate in the group, what they felt they had to offer, what things they needed to make right, and their understanding of restorative justice. Applications were reviewed by group facilitators and interviews scheduled with those who successfully completed this step. Participants were chosen based on the content of their letters and their responses in the interviews. Once accepted into the program, offenders were asked to commit to attending the full 10 weeks of the course. Ten participants were selected for the group. Only those who completed the program were eligible to participate in the CVORJ project.

Before participating in the restorative justice project, all offenders disagreed with the statement "I do not expect much to come out of conversations with victims." Post-project surveys confirm their expectations were justified. All six offenders strongly disagreed with the statement "I did not get much out of the conversations with the victims in the seminar."

In the same way, offenders were unanimous in their response to the statement "I have no interest in doing anything to help the victim(s) of my crime or his/her family." Both pre- and post-project surveys register offenders' strong disagreement with this statement.

With one exception, every offender participated in the project with the hope of gaining a better understanding of what victims experience in the aftermath of crime. After the project, every offender agreed that the seminar helped her to do this.

Additionally, offenders indicated that doubts about positive outcomes for victim offender dialogues were lessened. They agreed that the project helped them to better understand how to take responsibility for their behavior. Offenders also noted that this experience helped them deal with their loss and the feelings they had regarding their crime.

Victim Expectations Met. Victim participants entered into the project motivated by a desire to educate offenders about the needs and interests of victims. Post-project surveys show this expectation was met for each respondent.

Similarly, results indicate that victims were interested in playing a greater role in the justice process and that the project made this possible. Whereas attitudes toward offenders involved in victims' own cases did not change, all agreed that the wounds and healing of victims should be considered important in the justice process. And although no one stated that this process had significantly affected their own healing, all agreed that this project was a positive experience.

A few selections from victim responses to open-ended questions on the post-project surveys provide insights that speak for themselves. One wrote, "I did not expect to develop the rapport that evolved from these meetings. I care that they got something good and positive out of this and I think they all did." To the question, what concrete things might be done to further the principle of restorative justice, one wrote, "Helping other victims receive justice and healing." In response to a question about repairing harms resulting from serious violent crimes, another victim wrote this, "They can never bring the loved one back from the grave. They can never repair this."

DISCUSSION

It became apparent early on that a large measure of the success of the project was due to prior preparation of the participants. The victims had spent several years involved in the support group Parents of Murdered Children and had shared their stories before. As noted, the offenders had participated in a group called "Making Things Right" that emphasized taking responsibility for choices and actions leading to their incarceration. Both groups had done a great deal of work coming to terms with their own very painful experiences before joining a project that brought them together.

Trends observed over the course of the project include:

- Increased integration of group members as shown in seating arrangements and socialization patterns during breaks;

- Creation of a safe, supportive environment as personal stories were shared;

- From offenders, signs of deep remorse and acceptance of responsibility for harm done; and

- For all participants, a growing appreciation for the process, the positive changes made, and hope for continued healing.

Integration

At the initial meetings, the voluntary seating arrangements were characterized by a clear segregation of victims and offenders, typically with facilitators seated between them. During breaks, victims chatted with facilitators or each other, and offenders talked among themselves. By the fifth meeting, victims were choosing seats next to offenders and during breaks informal clusters of victims and inmates engaged in friendly conversation. There was even some good-natured ribbing between group members. One victim participant stated, "The beauty of this group is having these kinds of interplays. I think this is a great group." At times, informal conversations led to an open discussion of subjects like victims' rights—for instance, the right to give an impact statement during trials. While this temporarily diverted the group from scheduled topics, it also revealed the growing ease in communication between participants. Facilitators wisely allowed room for these kinds of productive tangents.

Supportive Environment

When telling their stories, victims spoke of their convictions regarding truth-in-sentencing. "Life should be life," as one victim put it. Afterwards, inmates admitted that this was hard for them to hear because of their own hopes for a reprieve, but at no time did inmates challenge this, or respond with anything but support for victims' feelings on the subject. Offenders volunteered to write letters to key officials in support of victims' rights to offer impact statements at trial. Victims in turn offered support to inmates as they related their stories of painful abuse, praising their courage for surviving and deciding to make a positive change in their lives. Overall, participants developed a strong rapport. Near the end, victims and inmates alike said they looked forward to the meetings and were sorry they would soon be over. One victim gave his opinion that, "This has become a support group."

Accountability

A number of inmate comments indicate that they are coming to terms with the terrible cost of their crimes and accepting responsibility for their actions. "When you commit a crime," said one inmate, "your family does time with you." Another, when telling her story of the abusive, violent environment she was raised in, blamed only herself for her part in a homicide. "I hold myself wholly responsible," she said. Many offenders had difficulty telling their stories without pausing to cry, overwhelmed with painful emotion. Victims were visibly moved by offenders' genuine expression of remorse. "You're a very strong person to have come through all that," one victim said to an inmate after hearing her tale of abuse. "It's terrible that this is the safest place you've ever lived."

Changed Lives

Offenders made it clear that incarceration had given them a second chance and they were determined to use the opportunity to help others. This was something they had in common with the victims who, as part of their healing process, decided they would not let the terrible loss ruin their lives. The prospect of helping others motivated both victims and offenders to be part of the project. "I hope that in the process of us being here that your healing journey continues," said one victim to the offenders present. Another victim offered this comment, "I believe we have seen changes in the group, in all of us. I think we are all having an impact on one another. It's important to hear one another's stories, and if that's all we do, that's huge. I really think this works well." Looking back on his decision to join the project, one victim recalled he was "not exactly thrilled at the prospect. I was real apprehensive. On the first day, I saw fear and anger ... but I see the anger and fear is dissipating. I see smiles, laughter. People are growing out of their hurt. I've grown quite a bit. It's working for me, and I think for the rest of you. Makes me feel good about it."

CONCLUSION

Offenders, victims, and facilitators agreed to a follow-up meeting. Good-byes were tearful and the prospect of another, final gathering helped ease the pain of ending. Hopes were high at the prospect of on-going work in restorative justice. A few of the inmates look forward to mentoring the next group of women going through the "Making Things Right" course and sending graduates on to the next restorative justice project. Victim participants expressed their wish that inmates would continue the good work they had begun.

As is so often the case with this type of project or experience, it can be difficult to convey in words the many things that transpired, the feelings, the impressions, the general felt sense of progress and goodwill that developed out of these meetings. By all accounts, it was a success. A number of elements can be identified that made this so. Experienced and flexible facilitators, a group of victims and offenders who were well along the road in their healing process and came prepared to share their experience with others, supportive facility staff and administrators, all contributed to a positive outcome in this case.

Although it is difficult to remain neutral in a setting where intense emotion is expressed, every effort was made to draw up a summary that faithfully reflected what took place throughout the nine weeks of the project, utilizing surveys, observer notes, and participant input. In a period of severe budget cuts for corrections in Minnesota and elsewhere, it seems clear that this kind of pilot program, which offers tangible benefits for victims, offenders, and the community, deserves a second look.

About the Author

Heather Burns, MSW, is Research Assistant at the Center for Restorative Justice & Peacemaking at the School of Social Work, University of Minnesota, St. Paul, MN.

References

Helfgott, J. B., Lovell, M. L., Lawrence, C. F., *Citizens, Victims and Offenders Restoring Justice: Final Project Report* (Department of Sociology & Criminal Justice, Seattle University, 1998).

Amherst H. Wilder Foundation, *Making Things Right* (Author, 2000).

Index

[References are to page numbers.]